HELPING MISSIONARIES GROW

HELPING MISSIONARIES GROW

Readings in Mental Health and Missions

Editors

Kelly S. O'Donnell, PsyD
Michèle Lewis O'Donnell, PsyD

William Carey Library

PASADENA, CALIFORNIA

Published by
William Carey Library
P.O. Box 40129
Pasadena, California 91114

Contributing Editors:

James W. Reapsome, MTh
  Editor, Evangelical Missions Quarterly
William F. Hunter, PhD
  Editor, Journal of Psychology and Theology
J. Harold Ellens, PhD
  Editor, Journal of Psychology and Christianity

ISBN 0-87808-217-4
Library of Congress CIP# 88-071334

Cover design by Katy A. Green
Cover typesetting by Chris Krause and David Gaunt

Printed in the United States of America

5 4 3 2
95 94 93 92

CONTENTS

Missionary Couples

Missionary Children

Educating Missionary Children

PART THREE: MISSIONARY ADJUSTMENT

Entering the New Culture

Women in Missions

Repatriation

Cross-Cultural Counseling

APPENDIX

Foreword

Finally! With over sixty thousand North American missionaries serving Christ around the world, it is certainly time that we give thoughtful and thorough attention to the emotional needs of missionaries and their families. For decades concerned mission leaders have struggled to find ways of helping missionaries cope with the practical problems of personal, social, and family living that they encounter on the field. Psychologists and psychiatrists have been asked to assist in developing candidate screening procedures that will lower the missionary dropout rate and identify potential problems that can be addressed before they become debilitating. Orientation and candidate training programs have been developed to help prospective missionaries prepare for the cross-cultural stresses they will face. And long hours have been devoted to critical and heart-rending questions about the welfare of missionary children.

These concerns reflect a broadening and deepening of our Christian world view and a desire to see the whole gospel presented by whole persons. They also reflect an awareness that the greatest impact of the gospel witness often comes through the attitudes missionaries display toward nationals or in their relationship with family members and colleagues. No longer are we willing to spend scores of thousands of dollars to train and prepare a missionary couple for service only to see them leave the field after the first term. No longer are we willing to assume that the needs of missionary children will automatically be taken care of just because their parents are in full-time Christian work. And no longer are we willing to attribute interpersonal conflicts among missionaries or cross-cultural misunderstandings solely to a lack of spirituality. Important social, cultural, and psychological factors are rightly being included in our understanding of the missionary's life and ministry.

To our knowledge, *Helping Missionaries Grow: Readings in Mental Health and Missions* is the first scholarly book devoted entirely to the contributions which a psychological understanding can make to the selection, training, and effectiveness of missionary personnel in both their ministries and their personal and family lives. And who is better qualified to select, edit, and organize these materials than two missionary psychologists, Kelly and Michèle O'Donnell?

It has been our pleasure to know and work and share with Kelly and Michele as their heart for missions and missionary personnel has crystallized during the past several years. We have seen them prepare for missionary service at the same time they were bringing their resources as psychologists to bear on many crucial questions which mission leaders, boards, and educators were asking about the mental health of missionaries and their families. And now that they are on the mission field full-time, they have the firsthand experience that enables them to bring a wealth of wisdom to this vital area.

We believe this is a ground-breaking work and commend it to all who are seriously interested in the single most important link in the Church's missionary outreach--our missionary personnel.

Bruce Narramore, PhD
Professor of Psychology
Rosemead School of Psychology
Biola University

Kathy Narramore, BA
Missions Pastor
Whittier Area Baptist Fellowship
Whittier, California

Preface

This book is being published at a time when there is a recognized need among Christians working in mental health and missions to organize the literature in this field. The fact that such a compendium of readings can now be compiled is heartening commentary on the extent to which the disciplines of mental health and missions have thus far interfaced. It is also indicative of the many potential areas of collaboration which can further be explored.

It is our desire that this volume serve as a practical tool to stimulate the growing dialogue and involvement between mental health professionals and mission specialists. To this end we envision its usefulness as a textbook for courses in missiology, behavioral science, and intercultural studies; as a practical reference for workers in both fields; and as an impetus for needed research. It is with these intentions, then, that we earnestly offer this compendium of readings to you for careful study and as a resource for your personal and professional growth.

We want to thank our families and numerous colleagues who have encouraged us in our vision and development of this volume. In particular we want to acknowledge Jim Reapsome, editor of *Evangelical Missions Quarterly*, Bill Hunter, editor of the *Journal of Psychology and Theology*, and Hal Ellens, editor of the *Journal of Psychology and Christianity*, whom we have listed as contributing editors due to the quantity of articles from their journals which we have utilized. We are also indebted to our parents, Hollis and Jane Lewis, and Richard and Edna O'Donnell, who believe in and have supported our work as psychologists in missions.

A special thanks goes to Gregg Schumann, our longtime friend and missionary companion, who diligently helped in the preparation of this manuscript. We must also express our sincere appreciation to Floyd McClung, Jr. and Janet and Dudley Weiner for the use of their computers, to John Hanneman for his timely instruction on word processing, and to Jeff and Cindy Schubert for their help in proof-reading the manuscript.

Lastly, this book would not be going to press at this time were it not for the commitment of our supporters. To all of them we are deeply grateful and with them stand as fellow laborers in Christ.

Michèle Lewis O'Donnell
Kelly S. O'Donnell
Amsterdam, The Netherlands
May, 1988

LIST OF CONTRIBUTORS

Frank Allen is Minister of Missions for SEND International. Previously he served with this mission in the Philippines for 30 years. He is a graduate of the Chicago Graduate School of Theology and the University of Michigan.

Clyde Austin is Professor, Department of Psychology, at Abilene Christian University. He is a licensed psychologist and specializes in reentry counseling and programs. He has also worked as a vocational missionary in Argentina. His doctorate is from the University of Houston.

Alexander H. Bolyanatz serves with Wycliffe Bible Translators in Papua New Guinea. He is a graduate of Lawrence University and the University of Texas.

Joyce M. Bowers is Associate Director for Personnel, Division for Global Missions, for the Evangelical Lutheran Church of America. Her masters degree is in social work. She and her husband spent 11 years as educational missionaries in Liberia.

Elizabeth S. Brewster holds a PhD from the University of Texas. She has consulted in more than 70 countries in the area of language learning and cultural adjustment for missionaries. She is Professor of Language Acquisition and Applied Linguistics at Fuller Theological Seminary's School of World Missions.

E. Thomas Brewster, together with his wife Elizabeth, has specialized in helping missionaries develop effective techniques for learning a new language and adapting to the new cultural setting. He taught linguistics at the School of World Mission, Fuller Theological Seminary, until his recent death. His PhD was from the University of Arizona.

William Gordon Britt, III is a licensed psychologist with a doctorate in clinical psychology from Rosemead School of Psychology, Biola University. He has worked on staff for Campus Crusade for Christ and consults in the area of candidate selection and testing.

Raymond M. Chester is a psychologist for Unevangelized Fields Ministry and has served with this group in Mexico. His PhD is from the International Institute for Advanced Studies, Saint Louis, Missouri. He is a consultant for a number of organizations working with missionaries and is also a marriage and family therapist.

Charles B. Cureton, Professor of Psychology at Malone College, received his EdD degree from the University of Tennessee. Family therapy, along with church and industrial consultation, are areas of specialty.

Susan B. De Vries is a missionary with Overseas Crusades in Kenya. She holds a master's degree from Wheaton College Graduate School.

Sally Folger Dye has worked with Wycliffe Bible Translators translating Scripture for the Bahinemo people and planting an indigenous church among them. She has a B.S. in nursing and has studied counseling and cross-cultural adaptation at the School of World Missions, Fuller Theological Seminary.

Wayne T. Dye received his PhD from Fuller Theological Seminary in the School of World Missions. Together with his wife Sally, he has worked with Wycliffe Bible Translators among the Bahinemo people.

Kevin Dyer is the Director and Founder of International teams. He was born in Australia and received his PhD at New York University.

Robert L. Eagle serves in the Theological Education by Extension program and in church planting with the Missionary Church Department of Overseas Missions in Santo Domingo, Dominican Republic. He is a graduate of Bethel College and was a pastor in Michigan for 11 years.

Phil Elkins spent five years as a member of a missionary team among the Tonga tribe in Zambia. Now the President of the Mission Training and Resource Center, he has also directed the Cross-Cultural Studies program at Fuller Theological Seminary's School of World Mission.

Larry N. Ferguson specializes in gerontology and cross-cultural preparation. His doctorate is from the Graduate School of Psychology at Fuller Theological Seminary and he holds an MDiv from the Conservative Baptist Seminary. He has worked as the clinical director for Link Care Center and is presently serving in the Philippines.

J. Roland Fleck is a licensed psychologist in private practice. His EdD is from the University of Georgia. Specializations include developmental and counseling psychology.

Marjory Foyle, DPM, FRC Psych, a London psychiatrist, is a member of Bible and Medical Missionary Fellowship International. She has done extensive work in missionary medicine and psychiatric counseling and is a Fellow of the Royal College of Psychiatrists, London.

Laura Mae Gardner is the Director of Counseling Ministries and Personnel for Wycliffe Bible Translators. She received her DMin from the Conservative Baptist Theological Seminary.

Terri A. Gibbs is a graduate of the San Jose State University, California. She has worked as a missionary in Mexico, Colombia, Ecuador and Brazil, serving with Wycliffe Bible Translators and the Assemblies of God.

Dorothy Gish is Assistant Dean and Professor of Early Childhood and Family Life Education at Messiah College in Pennsylvania. Her PhD is from Pennsylvania State University.

Thomas Graham, PhD is a management consultant specializing in human resource development, cross-cultural training and church growth. His current position as Director of Synergy International was preceded by positions in higher education, business and industry, government and missions.

Robert P. Heinrich is Vice President of the Christian National Evangelism Committee. His B.A. is from North Central College.

David J. Hesselgrave, Professor of World Mission at Trinity Evangelical Divinity School in Illinois, served for 12 years as an Evangelical Free Church missionary in Japan. He received his PhD from the University of Minnesota.

Brian V. Hill is Professor and Dean of the School of Education within Murdoch University, Western Australia. At different times he has been president of the Australian Fellowship of Evangelical Students and the Australian Teachers' Christian Fellowship. He is the editor of the *Journal of Christian Education.*

John A. Holzmann is the associate editor for *Mission Frontiers*, and a publication specialist at the U.S. Center for World Mission. He received his MDiv from Westminster Theological Seminary.

William F. Hunter is an Associate Professor of Psychology at Rosemead School of Psychology, Biola University. He received his PhD from the United States International University and his MTh from Golden State Baptist Theological Seminary. Besides specializing in marriage and family therapy and the application of psychology to missions, he serves as the editor for the *Journal of Psychology and Theology.* He and his wife worked as missionaries in the Belgian Congo.

Cedric B. Johnson is a licensed clinical psychologist in private practice. Besides having taught psychology at Fuller's Graduate School of Psychology and at the Western Conservative Baptist Seminary, he has worked as a missionary and consultant in missions.

LeRoy N. Johnston, Jr. received his doctorate from Florida State and is a licensed psychologist. He is the Director for Missionary Candidates for Christian and Missionary Alliance and is currently working in Thailand.

Dean Kliewer is Director of Research Ministries at Link Care Center. In addition to his missions involvement, he specializes in clinical and physiological psychology. His PhD is from the University of Oregon.

Joyce Kruckeberg received her doctorate from Texas Woman's University, specializing in child development and family life. She has worked for Wycliffe Bible Translators and the Summer Institute of Linguistics.

Brent Lindquist is the Executive Vice President of Link Care Center. He is a licensed psychologist specializing in clinical psychology and missionary mental health. He received his doctorate from the California School of Professional Psychology.

Stanley L. Lindquist is the President and Founder of Link Care Center. He is Professor of Psychology at California State University, Fresno, with specialties in clinical and physiological psychology. He received his PhD from the University of Chicago.

Diane Marshall is a marriage and family therapist at the Institute of Family Living in Toronto, Canada. She is a member of the Anglican Church's Task Force on Women.

Marvin K. Mayers is Dean and Professor at the School of Intercultural Studies, Biola University. He holds an MDiv from Fuller Theological Seminary and a PhD from the University of Chicago. Some of his specializations include cross-cultural communication and social anthropology. Previously he served in Guatemala with Wycliffe Bible Translators.

Elaine Nesbit is a candidate in the graduate clinical psychology program at Wheaton College. Her specialty is family therapy. She served as a short-term worker in Mexico.

Kelly S. O'Donnell received his doctorate from Rosemead School of Psychology, Biola University. He worked as a missionary and an outreach coordinator in Mexico with Youth With A Mission. Currently he works as a clinical psychologist with Youth With A Mission Amsterdam, specializing in missionary adjustment and psychotherapy.

Michèle Lewis O'Donnell is a clinical psychologist on staff with Youth With A Mission in Amsterdam. She specializes in child/adolescent psychotherapy and psychological assessment. Her doctoral degree is from Rosemead School of Psychology, Biola University.

Phil Parshall is Director of the Asian Research Center in Manila. He has served in Bangladesh and the Philippines with the International Christian Fellowship for the past 24 years.

David R. Penner is a graduate of the doctoral program in clinical psychology at Western Conservative Baptist Seminary.

David C. Pollock is Director of Interaction, Inc., a ministry to missionary children and their families. He served in Kenya with Africa Inland Mission and provides consultation and seminars overseas on missionary family life. He served as co-chairman of the first and second International Conference on Missionary Kids.

Larry W. Sharp is a member of Unevangelized Fields Mission and Principal of Amazon Valley Academy, Belem, Brazil.

Anita Stafford is an Associate Professor at Texas Women's University. Her specialty is in child development and family living. She holds the EdD degree from Oklahoma State University.

Margaret Hooper Taylor has served as Professor of Developmental Psychology and Cultural Anthropology in the Social Department of Shikoku Christian College in Japan. She is a missionary of the Presbyterian Church in the United States.

Timothy M. Warner is Director of the School of World Mission and Evangelism at Trinity Evangelical Divinity School. Following his missionary career in Sierra Leone, he taught missions and was President of Fort Wayne Bible College. He is a graduate of Indiana University, where he received his EdD, and of New York Theological Seminary.

Frances J. White is Professor of Psychological Studies at Wheaton College Graduate School and is a marriage and family therapist. She served as a missionary for 13 years with African Inland Missions in Zaire and is still actively involved in missions as a consultant at home and on the field. Her doctoral degree is from the University of Maryland.

David Lee Wickstrom is a clinical psychologist in private practice. His doctoral degree is from Rosemead School of Psychology, Biola University. In addition to specializing in individual and family psychotherapy, he serves as a coordinator for the annual Mental Health and Missions Conference held at Angola, Indiana.

Donald E. Williams received his doctorate and MDiv from the Graduate School of Psychology, Fuller Theological Seminary. He is a clinical psychologist in private practice and consultant to Link Care Center.

Kenneth L. Williams is a counseling psychologist for Wycliffe Bible Translators. Together with his wife, he has lived and worked for 12 years among the Chuj Indians of Guatemala. He has served as the International Director of Counseling for this organization and has done extensive consultation overseas. His PhD is from the United States International University.

INTRODUCTION

Being a missionary is seldom easy. It takes a good measure of perseverance, prayer and encouragement to participate in such a demanding lifestyle. Moreover, there simply is no short-cut around the growth that must transpire in order to work effectively overseas--growth which comes through leaving the security of the familiar to embrace the challenges of a different culture. Perhaps the common denominator across all successful missionary service is an ongoing commitment to growth in response to the many adjustments one must make.

Supporting missionaries in their growth can be equally challenging, especially for the mental health professional who works in missions. Few mission agencies, for example, have a recognized mental health structure in place which can accommodate the smooth entrance of mental health professionals into the mission system. Taking time to establish rapport and credibility with missionary personnel thus becomes essential. Few mission agencies as well are able to provide on-field mental health services to missionary personnel and their families. The issue in this case is not so much the presence of financial limitations or a lack of openness to such interventions, but rather finding professionals who have the background, burden, and time required to provide consistent overseas services.

Fortunately, however, the last decade has seen an increasing interest in making mental health resources available to missionaries and mission agencies. Professionals from such fields as clinical psychology, industrial/organizational psychology, social work and psychiatry have made valuable contributions.

Furthermore, there are now many workshops, conferences, books, articles and dissertations which specifically address mental health-related issues in missions. Additional research, nonetheless, is still very much needed to build upon the insightful work which has thus far been done.

The present compendium of readings was developed in response to the need to organize and make available a representative assortment of important articles in mental health and missions. It is intended to serve as a resource for those who desire a greater understanding of how mental health concepts and tools can be applied to different mission situations. Included here would be mental health practitioners working in missions, professors and students of mental health interested in such work, mission leaders and personnel directors, mission professors and their students, missionaries and missionary candidates. For those with a background in mental health, these readings offer an opportunity to develop more of a parlance with terms and concepts used in missions. In turn, those involved in missions will become familiar with terms and concepts used in mental health work.

We have selected 50 articles from the past 15 years which are good examples of the work that has been done in this field. Some of the readings are research oriented; others involve practical helps for the missionary; and still others are more theoretical in nature. Although all the articles do not deal directly with psychological issues per se, the ramifications of the subject matter addressed are relevant to the mental health needs of missionaries, hence their inclusion in this volume. Whatever their emphases, we have judged all to be conceptually sound and have chosen them for their potential contribution to missionary adjustment, effectiveness and growth.

Nineteen of the articles are taken from the *Evangelical Missions Quarterly,* eight are from the *Journal of Psychology and Theology,* seven are from the annual Conference on Mental Health and Missions, and seven are from the *Journal of Psychology and Christianity.* The remainder are from such sources as *Missiology* and the *International Bulletin of Missionary Research.*

The articles in this compendium are grouped into four main parts, with each part further subdivided into four sections (thus 16 sections). Each section focuses on a current issue of import for mental health and missions. Organizing the articles into these sections reflects the numerous topics that can be found in the literature, yet is not indicative of the more extensive interdisciplinary parameters which define the scope of this field.

A brief outline of the book is now presented, followed by an overview of the content of the main parts.

Introduction
Part One: Missionary Preparation
A. Candidate Selection
B. Psychological Assessment
C. Missionary Effectiveness
D. Training Considerations
Part Two: Missionary Families
A. Family Life
B. Missionary Couples
C. Missionary Children
D. Educating Missionary Children
Part Three: Missionary Adjustment
A. Entering the New Culture
B. Cross-Cultural Stress
C. Interpersonal Relationships
D. Attrition
Part Four: Special Issues
A. Mission Agencies
B. Women in Missions
C. Repatriation
D. Cross-Cultural Counseling
Appendix

The introductory article by Hunter and Mayers focuses on the process of relating psychology and other behavioral sciences to missions. It also provides both an overview and historical perspective on the relatively new and developing field of mental health and missions

Part One, *Missionary Preparation,* considers pre-field assessment and training of missionaries. Section A looks at the procedures and criteria used in selecting candidates. Section B discusses the rationale for using psychological tests and assessment with missionaries and provides information on the testing process. Missionary effectiveness is explored in Section C. Specific variables are identified which are predictive of missionary success overseas. The articles in Section D offer suggestions for training missionaries, missionary teams and mental health workers in missions.

Missionary family life is the topic of the second part. All four sections of this part look at the variety of stresses and challenges faced by the missionary family: by the missionary family itself

(Section A), the missionary couple (Section B) and missionary children (Section C). A special section is devoted to the issues surrounding the education of missionary children (Section D).

Part Three, dealing with *missionary adjustment*, starts out with a discussion of the challenges which are frequently experienced by missionaries as they enter the new culture (Section A). Some suggestions are made for making it through this decisive transitional period. Section B scans the typical stressors which affect missionaries throughout all phases of their work. Section C looks at the role of interpersonal relationships in adjustment, highlighting such factors as frequent separations and singleness. Some reasons for missionary drop-out and ways to prevent this from happening are presented in Section D.

Four *special issues* are examined in Part Four. First, the use of mental health sevices by mission agencies is considered (Section A). Subjects such as the felt needs of mission personnel and ethical principles for providing mental health services are treated. Next, Section B targets the roles and deployment of missionary women. Women's issues in general, as well as the importance of their contributions to missions, are emphasized. Section C addresses the reentry experiences of missionaries and missionary children (MKs) returning to their homeland. Finally, Section D considers some important issues involved in counseling others from different cultures.

The *Appendix* consists of a bibliography of readings in mental health and missions. It provides an extensive listing of over 175 articles and dissertations that have been written during the last 25 years in this field.

In summary, the articles found in this book may be considered a sampler of the literature dealing with the broad range of mental health concerns which are part of missions today. Hopefully it will be followed by additional compendiums which can organize previous and future research and writings in this field. Throughout this work we have endeavored to maintain a unifying theme by the emphasis on growth--*missionary* growth--which promotes fulfillment through a fuller participation in the cause of Christ for all peoples.

1

William F. Hunter
Marvin K. Mayers

Psychology and Missions:
Reflections on Status and Need

This article proposes some reasons for the uneasy acceptance by conservatives of an adjunctive or supportive role in missions by psychology and the other behavioral sciences. The extant literature on Psychology and Missions is unified by an underlying assumption that missionary endeavor and its personnel are important issues for psychology and other behavioral sciences. Contributions to the developing literature in psychology and missions suggest that the area is still very broad in its approach and focus. A concerted and coordinated direction of research is required in future studies.

There may be few aspects of integration of greater practical value than that of psychology and missions. In both endeavors the human person is at the forefront of thinking and action. The very essence of Christianity and missions is proclaiming the Good News of the Gospel of Jesus Christ to the peoples of all nations (Matt. 28:19-20), an obligation that remains in force today and shall remain until the return of Christ. There is nothing to suggest that Christian psychologists and other professional helpers are exempt from cross-cultural responsibility in missions to persons for whom Christ died.

This article is a slightly revised version by the authors of their introduction to the second special issue of the *Journal of Psychology and Theology* on "Psychology and Missions" (1987, *15*, 269-273). Copyright 1987 by the Rosemead School of Psychology, Biola University. Reprinted by permission.

The history of missions throughout the centuries suggests that each era has determined how learning and scholarship would serve adjunctive and supportive functions in Gospel proclamation. For example, both medicine and education have played important roles in mission strategy and practice for many decades. It is as natural as life and breath for the bearers of the Good News to disply the compassion of Christ through medicine and to open to believers the world of knowledge through teaching.

Psychology and the Behavioral Sciences

The relatively new discipline of psychology has struggled to find acceptance and opportunity in the overall strategy of missions. The suspicion that the assumptions of psychology are inimical to the truth of the Word of God, based usually on only a vague idea of what psychology is, has caused many evangelicals in general and missions in particular to shy away from attempting to integrate the strategy and practice of missions with applicable content from the behavioral sciences, of which psychology is one. Others of the behavioral sciences, notably the disciplines of anthropology and sociology, have been viewed with similar suspicion. For many years the behavioral sciences, not least of which is psychology, have been conceived of in conservative theological circles as leading an assault on the integrity and authority of the Word of God. Popular anti-psychology works even today are marketing this idea within the evangelical community with much success (e.g., Hunt & McMahon, 1985).

The behavioral sciences are scientifically based disciplines that probe the various individual and corporate parameters of human behavior. In that they deal with human subjects the research results in the behavioral sciences have neither the validity nor the potential for predictability of the findings of the physical sciences, which deal with inanimate matter and the physical laws of the universe. They further fail to deal with so-called "truth," logical certainties, or philosophical constructs. Since they do deal with actual human behavior, however, the findings of the behavioral sciences are beginning to have a significant impact on missions development and practice.

It should be no surprise that a number of misconceptions and unfortunate practices have caused the Christian public (even more specifically, its more conservative element) to question the value of the contributions of Christian behavioral scientists. As in any discipline, behavioral scientists utilize specific language and thought forms characteristic of their specific disciplines. These are quite distinct from the language and thought forms of theology and philosophy. Christian professionals in the behavioral sciences have often been brought up in local churchs and in an ecclesiastical culture whose language and thought processes have been dominated by pastors or teachers trained in the humanities at seminaries and Bible schools where theology and philosophy are seen as the accepted disciplines relevant to the dissemination of the Gospel. Thus, in spite of the fact that they use the language and concepts of their specific disciplines in everyday life, Christian professionals revert to kind when they enter a church or church-related institution; their language and thought forms are reframed so that their "message" or teaching does not sound unlike that of humanities-trained leaders of the church. There is therefore little distinctiveness, and where there is, it is suspect, since it doesn't fit what the people have been taught. That is, it doesn't have the ring of the more familiar language and thought forms of theology and philosophy, however popularized they have become for the "person in the pew." Unfamiliar language and thought forms are thought of as incursions upon the greater truthfulness of theological language and thought forms.

Further, liberal theologians were more receptive to new ideas and consequently more open in embracing the behavioral sciences and exploiting their language and thought forms in biblical and theological studies. This made the behavioral sciences highly suspect in conservative and evangelical circles since the use of the language of the behavioral sciences triggered, and continues to trigger even in our time, fear of the theological and spiritual errors of the liberals. Evangelical Christians are much more likely to be consumers of psychology if it is sufficiently couched in the language and thought forms of theology to sound to the hearer as though it is biblically derived and not from secular psychology. Psychologists may be the first of the behavioral scientists to break through this wall of ignorance, largely due to the fact that they have in so many instances helped people come to terms with their own personal problems. Adams (1978) has been a leader of the anti-psychology movement among evangelicals, going so far as to suggest that counseling is a function reserved exclusively for the professional minister but usurped by mental health professionals. In spite of the difficulties many evangelical believers, agencies and institutions have had in accepting the efforts of the behavioral sciences, and especially of the discipline of psychology, their integration in missions is a recognizable and growing phenomenon.

Psychology in the Service of Missions

The involvement of psychology in missions is not altogether new. Daring and creative pioneers in the late 1920s began to use psychological and psychiatric services in the process of selecting missionaries for overseas service (Hunter, 1965). Those initial ventures were harbingers of what has been a slow but growing use of psychological services by missionary agencies (Johnson & Penner, 1981) and continuing efforts to create effective working relationships between mental health professionals and mission agencies (Johnston, 1983). It has become increasingly common for mission agencies, even those once totally opposed to the idea, to involve psychologists and other helping professionals in either candidate selection and/or the ongoing care of career personnel both on the field and during periodic home assignment. Most of the involvement has been at the clinical and consultational level either through contracted services or through referral arrangements. As the working relationship develops between them, mission agencies are much more alert to new approaches using mental health professionals.

A movement is now underway to make psychological services available for missionary children (popularly referred to as MKs) in overseas mission schools. The issue of culture shock and reentry is also taking on new dimensions as a result of the growing research interests of Christian psychologists and the involvement of such organizations as Link Care and the Narramore Christian Foundation.

Psychologists and other helping professionals are becoming increasingly involved with mission agencies in various clinical and consultative roles. It may be predicted that the greater the use of psychological services the more creative and innovative their use will become. While once confined almost entirely to work with personnel on home assignment in the sending countries, now it is not at all unusual to hear that psychologists and other professional helpers have undertaken a short-term consultative role with missionary personnel in the receiving countries themselves.

Most helpers working actively on overseas fields are master's level counselors; for example, such Wycliffe counselors as Harry and Patricia Miersma who have been stationed at Ukurumpa, Papua, New Guinea for the past two years. While doctoral level professionals have on a number of occasions assisted missionaries in on-site consultation throughout the world, it is only now that agencies are beginning to appoint them as career missionaries. For example, psychologists Kelly and Michèle O'Donnell have recently been appointed by Youth with a Mission (YWAM) for full-time ministry as clinical psychologists in Amsterdam and Europe.

A forum for the integration of psychology and missions developed only 8 years ago is the informal Conference on Mental Health and Missions held annually at Pokagon State Park near Angola, Indiana. The convenors of this Conference, Dr. John R. Powell of Michigan State University, and Dr. David Wickstrom, a psychologist in private practice in Maryland who was raised by missionary parents in Africa, have effectively gathered both helping professionals and mission administrators for mutual consultation on the use of psychological services in many aspects of mission endeavor.

Another effort has been that of the two conferences on Missionary Children (MKs), the first held in Manila in November, 1984, and the most recent held in Quito in January, 1986.

Journal Publication Efforts

The *Journal of Psychology and Theology* published its first special issue on "Psychology and Missions" in 1983 (Volume 11, Number 3). The topics of article submissions for the issue varied widely. There was no unique theme on which each contribution focused attention, rather the issue was a potpourri showing how wide in fact are the interests of professional helpers. However, the lodestar for the issue was the underlying assumption that mission endeavor and its related personnel are important issues for the behavioral sciences.

Shortly thereafter, the *Journal of Psychology and Christianity*, a publication of the Christian Association for Psychological Studies, published a theme issue on "Missionary Candidate Assessment" in 1983 (Volume 2, Number 4). This special issue, together with that of the *Journal of Psychology and Theology*, represent the initial attempts to publish a collection of research and articles in psychology and missions.

A second special issue of the *Journal of Psychology and Theology* on "Psychology and Missions" followed in 1987 (Volume 15, Number 4). In planning the issue, its editors had hoped to receive submissions which would develop in greater depth some specific piece of the psychological discipline. That was not to be. The reader again found a potpourri of topics. While these topics varied from those of the first special issue, its major value lay in its underscoring of the various areas in which psychological theory and practice have relevance for psychology and missions. However, it again demonstrated quite clearly the scattered and unfocused interests of researchers and authors. It is our conviction that articles in both special issues generally reflected the inchoate nature of the interface of psychology in the service of missions and the struggle for this developing area to find a major focus of effort.

Aside from the special or theme issues, both journals have published single artcles from time to time relevant to psychology and missions. What seems most evident, however, is that those who are interested in psychology and missions have yet to develop and pursue a concerted and coordinated direction of research. Various investigators tend to work alone, each working in his or her own area with little or no consultation with others holding similar interests. The focus in the research on the topics of reentry and missionary children appears to be an exception to the rule. It seems to us that those most heavily invested in the integration of psychology and missions are usually themselves clinicians whose interests, skills or available time do not easily embrace a research orientation. There is simply not a great deal of research and writing being done in the integration of psychology and missions.

Conclusion

With rising interest in the relevance of psychology to the mission enterprise, it is our hope that what has been published thus far will (a) inspire a larger volume of research and writing interfacing psychology and missions and (b) point to areas where Christian behavioral scientists need to commit themselves and the resources of their disciplines, institutions, and clinical practices in a more aggressive and focused research effort. The effort itself could be expected to make an early and giant leap forwad were missions or other Christian organizations and foundations to see the value of such research and assist by providing the funding for it.

We would also encourage strategic thinking about the need or even the potential for Christian psychological services for nationals in third world countries. Along with it is the need for considering the mutual part that mission organizations and Christian professionals with cross-cultural training and sensitivity could play in helping encourage the establishment of such services. It would appear that similar creative strategies for employing psychology and the other behavioral sciences in missions are beginning to develop and will likely have an important part in the changing face of missions in the years ahead.

Note

The term *missions* is used throughout this article, though a distinction is generally made in missiological literature between *mission* and *missions* (Peters, 1972). According to Grunlan and Mayers (1978), "mission" is used to describe "the total biblical mandate of the church of Jesus Christ" while "missions" denotes "local assemblies or groups of assemblies sending authorized persons to other cultures to evangelize and plant indigenous assemblies" (p. 23). The authors here view missions as one aspect of mission, namely, the church in one culture sending workers to another culture to evangelize and disciple.

References

Adams, J.E. (1978). *Lectures on counseling.* Grand Rapids: Baker.

Grunlan, S.A., & Mayers, M.K. (1978). *Cultural anthropology: A Christian perspective.* Grand Rapids: Zondervan.

Hunt, D., & McMahon, T.A. (1985). *The seduction of Christianity: Spiritual discernment in the last days.* Eugene, OR: Harvest House.

Hunter, W.F. (1965). *A survey of psychological evaluation programs in the selection of overseas missionary candidates.* Unpublished master's thesis, Golden Gate Baptist Theological Seminary, Mill Valley, CA.

Johnson, C.B., & Penner, D.R. (1981). The current status of the provision of psychological services in missionary agencies in North America. *The Bulletin of the Christian Association for Psychological Studies, 7* (4), 25-27.

Johnston, L.N., Jr. (1983, November). *Building relationships between mental health specialists and mission agencies.* Paper presented at the fourth annual Conference on Mental Health and Missions, Pokagon State Park, Angola, IN.

Peters, G.W. (1972). *A biblical theology of missions.* Chicago: Moody.

PART ONE
MISSIONARY PREPARATION

PART ONE

MISSIONARY PREPARATION

Missionaries are not just trained, they are grown. That is to say, personal growth is an essential, ongoing process for the missionary candidate, occurring throughout the pre-field orientation program and beyond. In this section we focus on some of the mental health issues involved in this first stage of missionary growth, candidate preparation. The basic thrust is twofold: to identify candidate characteristics which are related to overseas performance and to identify ways to train missionaries prior to departure overseas. Both of these areas, as will be seen, are rich in possibilities for integrating clinical, organizational and personnel psychology with missions.

Candidate Selection, the first section, begins with a helpful article by Johnston on conducting interviews with potential candidates. This author encourages a frank discussion of the motivation for missions, the person's competencies and his or her preparation plans for overseas work. The next two articles, by Ferguson, et al. and Foyle, address the selection process itself, and key in on the factors which influence selection decisions. Ferguson et al. list some of the selection criteria identified from their survey of 78 missionary-sending agencies: Christian commitment, Bible knowledge, successful church work and emotional stability. Foyle suggests a thorough investigation of the candidate, including family history, sexuality, marital relationship and personality characteristics, such as flexibility and humility. Both of these articles place a high value on psychological assessment for understanding the candidate. The next article by Graham points out the value of "task specific measures" of performance which complement the data uncovered through interview and application material. He encourages the use of simulation experiences and assessment centers to evaluate and train missionaries and missionary teams.

Most North American mission agencies utilize some form of psychological assessment for screening missionary candidates. Several reasons for *assessing missionaries and missionary candidates,* the subject of the next section, are outlined in the first article by Stanley Lindquist. One of the primary reasons discussed is the need to identify potential emotional patterns that may contribute to problems during cross-cultural adjustment. Intervention through therapy can then be done to prevent or minimize significant struggles abroad. Some of the psychological tests which are used in assessment, as well as the theory behind their use, are discussed by Ferguson et al. Although a wide variety of tests are employed, some of the more frequently used ones include the Minnesota Multiphasic Personality Inventory (MMPI), the California Personality Inventory (CPI), the Sixteen Personality Factor Test (16PF) and the Strong-Campbell Vocational Interest Inventory (SCII). Brent Lindquist, although strongly advocating the practice of psychological assessment, closes this part by discussing some of the possible misuses of assessment.

Evaluating prospective missionary effectiveness (the third section) is of great importance in light of the emotional and financial cost to both missionaries and mission boards as a result of attrition. Two problems are of interest here. The first one is agreeing upon the criteria for missionary "success" and then finding or developing a way that accurately measures this construct. Second, the relationship between missionary characteristics and successful performance overseas must be established. Another aspect of missionary effectiveness, the periodic evaluation of job performance, is not addressed in this section.

The first article, by Parshall, introduces us to the idea of assessing the quality or effectiveness of missionary spirituality. Based on his survey of 390 missionaries, significant struggles were reported in such areas as having personal devotions and dealing with discouragement. Similar findings reported by Johnston (1981) point to the significant felt needs of missionaries with respect to their spirituality (see his article in Part Four). Being a missionary can thus be marked with difficulties in maintaining one's spiritual life. The next two articles in this section are good examples of the research that has been done on missionary performance overseas. Cureton, for example, identifies characteristics of the successful missionary from the perspective of mission leaders and mental health professionals. Britt, on the other hand, focuses his research on one mission agency, and statistically derives 12 variables which are correlated with successful service. Some of the variables with greatest predictive value were measures of being "undisciplined versus controlled" (16PF), moodiness and birth order.

Important *considerations for training* are probed in the final section of Part One. The first article by Elkins emphasizes training which is commensurate with the type and duration of the work to be pursued. He begins his article by placing missionary service in the context of servanthood. He goes on to develop a helpful model which links the type of missionary preparation needed with the type of missionary service desired. How should psychologists and other mental health professionals be trained to work in mission settings? This is the subject of the second article by O'Donnell which surveys psychologists in missions to determine their backgrounds, present work in missions and recommendations for preparation. Team preparation is the topic of the next article. Here Dyer outlines some general factors which, from his experience, lead to successful team functioning. Some of these are godly leadership, commitment, good communication and prayer. The final article by Warner argues for more training in spiritual warfare and describes a course useful for missionaries which he teaches in this area.

Collectively, the 14 articles in this section point out the serious nature of missionary evaluation and development. Coming up with an appropriate job-person-organization match is difficult at times. Nevertheless, it is essential if high levels of employee satisfaction, motivation, performance and longevity are to be maintained.

2

LeRoy N. Johnston, Jr.

Should I Be a Missionary?

There are many reasons why a person would wish to become a candidate for overseas missionary service. In the process of realistically clarifying those reasons, numerous questions need to be asked in order to come to grip with issues that are often hidden, but which are very important. This paper deals with three basic questions that any person seeking missionary service needs to ask, with the information reviewed in depth before decisions are made. These questions are: 1. Why do you want to go overseas? 2. Can you execute the responsibilities which are expected of you when you are in an overseas position? 3. How will you prepare yourself in order to accomplish the ministry to which God has called you? Each of these questions is subdivided into four parts which help expand and answer the original questions. Needless to say, the decision to become a missionary is very personal, and cannot be based on any particular formula.

Recently I spent two hours presenting one missionary candidate to the Christian and Missionary Alliance Review Board, an experience that underscores the need of this discussion. With some candidates, there are very few questions, but with others there seem to be a host of contingencies which make it hard to reach a decision concerning appointment to missionary service. This presentation to the Board illustrated many aspects of the life and

---

ministry of this individual. At the conclusion of the discussion, the chairman of the committee looked at me and asked one question: "Do you think this person will be an effective missionary?"

This is the basic question that must be answered. One can review the candidate's spiritual growth, educational background, social skills, psychological stability, physical health, family constellation, but in the midst of all the domains under consideration, the bottom line still reads, "Can this person not only fulfill the biblical and mission organization's requirements, but is he/she the person to go?"

Recently I estimated the number of people I have interviewed during the past 10 years. These individuals believed God wanted them to seriously investigate the possibility of missions service. They needed counsel and direction related to what next steps needed to be taken. Some questioned whether missions would be a viable life vocation for them.

I was surprised to realize that I had counseled at least 10,000 individuals regarding their possible commitment to missionary service. The following questions evolved from these sessions as I learned to help them with their decisions related to missionary service. It became evident that most inquirers do not know the correct questions to ask of themselves. Certain questions seemed to separate out from the mass of information that could help to clarify the individual's personal perspective and motivation for missionary service. These factors we will now consider.

Three basic questions need to be investigated. Each of these inquiries has been separated into subquestions which help the individual to examine his responses. These are the questions I would like to share with you.

Question I: "Why do you want to go overseas?"
The first question sounds trite, but it must be pursued in depth. The answer may seem obvious, as in the case of a personal response to a missionary presentation. I soon became sensitively aware that there are many reasons, some good and some not so good, as to why people want to go overseas. One of the adages developed regarding this question states, "Good reasons as well as bad reasons can generate high motivation." In order to help a person focus on this initial consideration, four subquestions can be discussed.

First, we talk about a personal inner-fixed persuasion which should accompany a decision to follow God in full-time Christian ministry. This persuasion is not necessarily associated with a location, although it may be. God may be calling the individual overseas, but at this point the "call" is into ministry and the matter of specific direction will follow. At other times persons know God wants them overseas in a specific country doing a specific work. Nevertheless I look for that inner-fixed persuasion that missions is God's call for that individual, and he/she can do nothing other than heed that call.

Needless to say, it is important to explore this "persuasion" factor. I believe this particular assurance must be more than a personal feeling or the satisfaction of a personal interest. This conviction must be the work of the Holy Spirit, where one's spirit joins in unison with the Holy Spirit in response to the voice of God for service in His Name.

The *second* part to be discussed is more external in terms of verification of the "call." There needs to be some form of affirmation by responsible leadership concerning the individual. I encourage the individual to talk with five spiritual leaders who know him/her well. These leaders should be asked to point out the strengths and weaknesses which they have observed. These lay leaders as well as professional ministers should also give some statement as to their belief concerning this person's ability to satisfy the Scriptural requirements, such as the manner, skills, and gifts associated with the particular ministry under consideration.

It is interesting to note in the New Testament when the deacons were selected, an important criterion was that they should be recognized by others as people characterized by wisdom and being filled by the Holy Spirit (Acts 6:3). Leadership of the early Church recognized future leaders and identified them for special ministry.

A *third* aspect centers around Scriptural support. I personally believe God gives particular passages or portions of Scripture to substantiate the work He is presently doing in the life of the believer. It is common to hear veteran missionaries refer to a time when God called and refer to a particular Scripture verse supporting that calling. The Holy Spirit takes the Word and uses it to instruct, guide, and provide affirmation.

The *fourth* dimension of this first basic questions of "Why do I want to go?" centers around the practical life experiences of the individual. It is necessary to explore the experiences this individual has had in Christian ministry. Does he/she enjoy going to church, working on a committee, or being involved in personal evangelism? If so, review what he/she is presently doing. It is not unusual to find many inconsistencies in present-life practices of people. Potential candidates who want to be involved in church planting are often found to have no church home affiliation or regular church attendance. Some persons who want to do evangelism and overseas outreach ministries, have no ongoing ministry in their local church. Thus one of the important areas to consider centers in the question, "What are you doing now and how do these present experiences suggest the possible effectiveness of an overseas ministry?"

Being direct about the "why missions" questions cuts through much verbiage. One girl, in response to the query of why she wanted to be a missionary, stated, "I can't be a pastor and I don't like the field of education so I guess the only choice is to go into missions."

Question II: *"Can you execute the responsibilities which are expected of you when you are in an overseas position?"*

This second issue is related to helping persons understand what a call to overseas work has to do with being able to accomplish the tasks that need to be done. This is not a query about availability as was first considered, but rather is a question of *ability*. It is the other side of the coin which says willingness is important but there must be a realistic appraisal of one's capabilities.

I never will forget the first time I asked a potential candidate, "If pastors preach and teachers teach, how does a missionary mish?" Needless to say, the student looked at me, totally perplexed, and had absolutely no response. The silence was broken with a feeble attempt to talk about some of the principles and practices learned in Missions 102. In order to understand this particular question of executing ministry, there are again a subset of four issues to be discussed.

First, one must begin with a basic understanding of what missions is all about. What are the tasks or assignments to be carried out by the missionary? It is important to help the inquirer understand the philosophy of ministry developed by the particular mission under consideration.

The *second* area to be discussed is job skills and possible approaches to mission work. This is often referred to as methodology or application of missiology. The individual must see if he/she personally has developed skills or potential for evangelism, discipleship, preaching, teaching, administration, etc. Now is the time to look at the requirements for functioning overseas. The more technical support ministries, such as aviation, linguistics, etc., must be carefully reviewed.

Many personnel men make the potential mistake of listing all requirements and telling a prospective candidate, "These are the things you must be able to do in order to gain an appointment." I have found it much more beneficial to begin with a "functioning-in-ministry" approach, an attempt to describe the missionary at work. Once the inquirer understands the tasks to be done, it is possible to develop an appreciation and motivation for preparation. The need for graduate school and study in biblical theology, missiology, and anthropology, plus other training for necessary skills, make sense in light of future ministry expectations.

The *third* issue has to do with the qualities of personhood. Within this domain we talk about the dimensions of personality. Spiritual qualities and those Biblical characteristics given by the Apostle Paul in his writings to Timothy and Titus need to be discussed.

Research has validated that 75 percent of the problems faced by missionaries on the field have to do with interpersonal conflicts with colleagues. A person may have fine job qualifications and personal talents but be unable to accomplish ministry due to inadequacies in the area of social skills.

The *fourth dimension* relates to a meaningful evaluation of present abilities associated with overseas responsibility. There needs to be a review of accountability in ministry experiences. Ministry experiences can be divided into three specific categories: (a) informal experiences, (b) internship, and (c) a licensed staff position.

Many candidates do not realize the benefits derived from teaching Sunday School or leading a Bible study, during their college years. These experiences and exposures are fundamental in forming attitudes about church ministry, and helping to maintain motivation in Christian work.

Internship, especially for those who were not reared in local Christian churches, has a specific place in candidate preparation. It provides opportunity for formal learning but without heavy staff responsibility, and in which there is limited accountability. This experience provides a learning encounter under specified conditions, with a supervisor.

My position is that every person preparing for overseas missionary service should have a minimum of 2 years fulltime work experience in a Christian ministry. This particular activity should be similar to that which will be done overseas. It should be licensed by a recognized group with periodic evaluations and reports to the candidate and the mission board.

About a year and a half ago, I met the personnel director associated with a major ministry. Under his responsibility, he recruited international directors for overseas business as well as executives for North America. He stated that one of his basic beliefs in terms of evaluating people was "Past performance is the best predictor of future performance." He did not imply the negating of the work of the Holy Spirit in the life of Christians or the possibility of human change. However, generally speaking, he emphasized that what an individual has been doing for the past 18-24 months would be a good predictor of what he will be in terms of attitude, accountability, and workload in the next 24 months.

Question III: "How will you prepare, in order to accomplish the ministry to which God has called you?"
This final basic question to individuals seeking to understand God's work and will in their lives, has to do with goal setting, which involves planning and organizing. This preparation is made in order to meet the expectations that the mission board has, as well as expectations that the individual should have for himself/herself.

The *first* issue to settle is, "Do you have a life plan?" For example, in terms of the next 5 years, "What do you need to accomplish in order to be what you believe God wants you to be?" I specifically limit the plan to 5 years, as much information has now come into focus. There needs to be a clarification of goals as well as a rationale for what is required in order to reach those goals. The logical steps should be developed on paper.

It is necessary to be flexible while being very specific. Various options, alternatives, and routes need to be explored. There probably is no one best way to prepare people for cross-cultural ministries. God has as many ways as He has people with whom to work. But there seems to be a certain level of preparation that can be accomplished in specific domains before proceeding overseas. A plan is required to reach these levels of preparation.

The *second* area has to do with accountability. One reason academic programs have some semblance of success is their accountability factor, including tests. Needless to say, it is best to have an intrinsic accountability where the individual wants to learn for himself regardless of whether or not there is a test or other evaluation. However, if the teacher never gave tests on required reading assignments, the reading may not be done.

The candidate may have a plan of action but he also needs to have someone to whom he is accountable on a regular schedule. He needs an advisor or supervisor, to whom he can go with questions. He needs to have his ministries amplified and his vision broadened. This requires contact with leaders who want to assist in the preparation of this person. Helping the prospective missionary establish this type of relationship is critical.

The *third* dimension of preparation is related to the "now." Individuals often will develop a "game plan" and then put it on the "back burner." If this happens, it could be seen as positive and part of a screening process. Maybe their motivation or concern for overseas work wasn't very serious. But many individuals need to be moved into that first or second step, as something can be done now. Regardless of their present condition, there is always something that will be of service to the Lord and be preparation for possible overseas work. The individuals need to realize that they are in ministry "now." The ministry to which God has called them, does not begin when they have crossed a certain body of water and learned a new language. Ministry must be "now," as well as preparation for the future. One must never lose sight of immediate ministry opportunities.

The *fourth* dimension has to do with a patient attitude. The day of the "instant" continues to plague this generation, especially as it has to do with preparation. There are no shortcuts in training for overseas ministry. The following illustration helps to highlight the need for time in preparation. A patient came to the doctor because of pain. The doctor stated that the reason for the pain in the lower abdomen had to do with appendicitis. The doctor suggested that the patient go immediately to the hospital for an appendectomy. The patient concurred. As they were going out of the door, the doctor stated, "You should realize that, after 6 years of school, I became tired and broke. So I cut short my medical practice by 2 years. I have not studied surgery in medical school or had that experience in my training. I have read two books on the subject. I am sure this will not make any difference to you.!" Such a statement would bring a halt to your surgery! It underscores the fact that there are no shortcuts in preparation when dealing with physical life. Even more do we need to be thorough in our preparation for spiritual ministries which deal with eternal life and death issues, as compared to physical aspects of life.

I believe it is necessary to establish some form of working plan with built-in accountability. It seems that people will do what is inspected, not what is expected. This is not a matter of playing watchdog over the daily routines of the person in preparation. But it is a guided attempt to enable the individual to develop self-discipline in the process of acquiring the characteristics, skills, and the described Biblical qualities necessary to function as a missionary.

Conclusion

Most leaders, in looking for associates, would prefer to have "wild stallions" rather than tired nags. In some cases this may not be true. But most mission organizations desire candidates who possess energy, life, enthusiasm, desire, and interest. To assume that their life energy is properly channeled or that the ramifications of their work are understood by them would be an error. In most cases, they have not had the opportunity to clarify their thinking about missions. They do not understand the type of work or ministries in which they may be involved once in an overseas position. The directing of this process becomes the work of the personnel director. These three questions seem to get at the heart of the issues and should aid the candidate in planning for his/her future vocation.

3

Marjory Foyle

How to Choose the Right Missionary

Missionaries are not superpeople; they are flesh and blood like everyone else. But there is one thing that sets them apart from other people: God has called them to missionary service. I am convinced that God does call people, and that a call should be carefully respected, examined, and nurtured.

Missions usually have a selection procedure, and they will commonly examine a candidate's call. But the selection process itself introduces potential areas of stress and it is important that we examine these. Stress may first of all be related to the screening process. Missions that do little screening--believing God's call to be sufficient of itself--sometimes find that problem areas that were neither revealed nor addressed in the selection process create later difficulty for both the new missionary and the overseas administration.

A candidate's acceptance or rejection by the mission is another stressful area. To many candidates, acceptance indicates that they are "okay": that they have correctly interpreted and carried out God's will is confirmed. On the other hand, rejection communicates to a candidate that he or she is not "okay": something has gone wrong. This can cause great stress unless the candidate has clearly understood the true situation from the earliest stages of the selection procedure.

But rejection by a mission board can be a positive experience. It may be, for example, that though the reality of God's call is not in doubt, the place of service has not been made clear. It is a tragedy that a rejected candidate rarely understands this experience positively and instead is angry, resentful, bitter, or totally confused.

As I have talked with 121 missionaries and many mission leaders over a three-year period, I have become convinced of the importance of good selection--and of the dangers of inadequacy in the process. Fifty-four percent of the missionaries I saw complained of problems that were present long before they entered the selection process. Either they were not asked about these problems during their selection, or the problems were minimized or overspiritualized. Only about one-quarter of those who had problems prior to their selection received any help--and that was usually minimal.

The goal of the selection process is to obtain a total profile of candidates, one that includes many facets of their lives. We will confine our discussion here to observations of some of the psychological and social factors that are important in selection procedures. W. Gordon Britt of Loma Linda University has made the following observation: "The history of one's behavior, past responses, and experience tends to be the best predictor of the future. God's call and motivation are important, but in the ambiguity and stress of another culture, past experience and events tend to shape how the individual will respond. Consequently, a combination of God's call, motivation, and past experiences must be used in selection" (*Journal of Psychology and Theology*, Fall, 1983). To learn about these things, we must obtain information about the candidate. Three means of obtaining information are commonly used: forms, references, and interviews.

1. *Forms.* One mission recently discovered that its forms had totally omitted any reference to candidates' children! This points up the importance of reviewing all forms regularly. Questions should be designed to produce maximum information, even if the relevancy of the question to the application is not immediately apparent. The object is to understand events that were formative in the candidate's life.

One important area that is often poorly documented is family history: the physical and mental health of grandparents, parents, uncles, aunts, cousins, brothers and sisters, spouse and children. While few candidates are likely to be rejected solely on grounds of their family history, some have histories so loaded that it would be a disservice to them to send them overseas.

Direct questions about the candidate's previous mental health also are often poorly handled. However, if no questions are asked, a candidate may believe that a history of mental health problems is not relevant--especially if the problem occurred prior to conversion. But all life events should form part of a candidate's total profile. This inquiry can be described in terms of "emotional and mental health," and it often can be fitted into the routine health questionnaire.

I know I am treading on delicate ground, for I believe spiritual problems exist. But I must say that as a psychiatrist, I am concerned about the amount of stress missionaries have that is due to an overload of old emotional problems.

2. *References.* This word makes mission executives groan--for helpful references are difficult to obtain. For example, church references may be contaminated by the "halo effect": the difficulty church leaders have in detaching themselves from their candidate--of whom they are proud--in order to give a totally objective report. This is not a matter of dishonesty: it is simply the way the human mind works.

Bible or missionary training college reports can be very useful if the college was residential, and if it had a staff trained to observe problems.

Secular references are often the most valuable. Employers are usually very well informed about their employees, though they may not always be willing to put opinions in writing. Usually, however, they provide a phone number, and it's always worthwhile checking.

3. *Personal interviews.* In my opinion, these are the core of the selection process. Three types are important: general, physical, and psychological-mental health.

The *general interview* should include spiritual life, past education and work, the candidate's call, interests, and so on. Most missions do this very adequately.

The *physical interview* is done by a doctor or nurse and includes a history and physical report for every member of the family.

Let me make a personal observation in light of the fact that it is not always easy to get doctors to do this kind of work. Their reluctance is not always understood, and it needs to be addressed. Doctors, like everyone else, have to eat, and they have enormous overhead expenses. Screening physicals on potential or active missionaries takes a great deal of time when done properly, and the task is poorly paid. An overabundance of such patients can create serious financial problems for a doctor--but if he tries to cut down the number he sees, he may be accused of backsliding (poor doctor)!

Some large boards are able to employ a doctor full-time and pay him a reasonable salary. I have long urged smaller missions to join together to employ a doctor to do this work; some doctors would view that occupation as a full-time call to missionary service. But they must be adequately paid.

The *psychological-mental health examination* conducted by many mission groups now employs psychological tests as part of the screening procedure. The usual pattern is a combination of formal testing and personal interview. (I am personally uneasy about the use of formal testing without an interview.) The aim of this screening is to add to the candidate's total profile, and it is useful in identifying areas of strength and weakness, as well as possible abnormalities.

Four conclusions may result from psychological testing. (1) The candidate is unsuitable for overseas service and should not be selected. (It is, of course, disastrous simply to drop unsuitable candidates. They need to know the reason why they were rejected and, if necessary, guided along the pathway to obtaining help.) (2) Identifiable problems exist that should delay final acceptance until help is obtained and the candidacy reassessed, with advice from the helping agency. (3) A straightforward problem that can be dealt with immediately is identified, and no delay in acceptance is necessary. (4) No problems are discerned.

Specially Sensitive Areas

At some point in the selection process, areas of special sensitivity need to be discussed. These areas are often culturally related: matters that are sensitive in one country may be commonly discussed in another. It is therefore important for examiners to be familiar with the cultural background of each applicant.

Interviewers need to decide who is to discuss sensitive issues with candidates, and avoid either neglect of certain topics or overquestioning. I have been told sometimes that one should not explore delicate issues, and interviewers may fear a candidate will become angry. A display of anger, however, makes it even more important to discuss sensitive topics. In my own experience, rather than resent it, candidates as well as missionaries welcome the chance to talk over sensitive personal matters.

1. *Sexual life.* Three areas cause particular stress: homosexuality, extramarital heterosexual relationships, and heterosexual relationships among singles.

Homosexuality is currently a live issue. It is important that every mission board makes its own policy decision--one that must, of course, include the views of the countries to which they send missionaries. In a recent survey of bishops in a large church group, overseas bishops were 100 percent against homosexuals as missionaries.

It is important to consider several aspects of this matter. A candidate may have engaged in homosexual practice before conversion, and it may or may not have been discontinued; an individual may have had one steady partner, or multiple partners; for someone else, homosexuality may have been a regular sexual pattern, or a stress-induced symptom.

The matter of persons who are homosexually oriented, with little or no heterosexual potential, demands very sensitive handling. Some are devout Christians who determine to live as celibates for Christ's sake. Each mission must determine its policy in this situation, and be supportive and helpful to the candidate.

Extramarital heterosexual relationships may be either stress-induced, or a regular pattern of behavior. This matter needs careful sorting out, and a candidate's acceptance should be delayed until the situation is clarified. The culture of the country of destination must also be carefully considered, for it is unwise to send as missionaries those who, by their own patterns of behavior, may cause confusion to the local Christians.

Heterosexual relationships in single persons are common in our present social climate. And while conversion frequently results in a change of sexual behavior, with chastity becoming the norm, this does not always happen, and a candidate's views must be ascertained. Many Christians in host countries do not appreciate the sexual freedom of some Western travelers--and they certainly do not expect to see it in missionaries.

Candidates often welcome discussion in these areas, and they may be greatly helped in learning alternative methods of handling stress.

2. *Singleness.* Some candidates have no problem with being single. For others, singleness is a problem tinged with hope. The degree of adjustment necessary for singleness should be determined, and methods suggested to cope with it. A suggestion was made recently in Scotland that a preselection singleness seminar ought to be held for the purposes of fuller discussion and to orient people to a possible future as a single. Neither are the

problems of single parents today the same as in the past, and they should be carefully discussed.

3. *Marital Problems.* Sometimes churches or missionary college staff know a couple is having problems but do not tell the mission examiners. In other cases, couples know they have problems but conceal them. These situations are dangerous. Working overseas creates added stress in a marriage, which makes the quality of the basic relationship profoundly important. No one is looking for perfection, but couples should at least know how to resolve their differences and how to communicate.

Problems such as frequent quarreling (with or without violence), poor communication, childlessness and its impact on the couple, role problems, sexual and contraception problems, and the care of children are all areas where advice and guidance may be needed before a couple's acceptance. Some missions now hold preselection marriage seminars in order to assess current problems and teach marital enrichment techniques. Most missions have a rule about how soon a couple can go abroad after marriage; perhaps six months to one year.

4. *Occult experiences.* Occultism is a comparatively new area of concern to selecting personnel. Much depends on the mission, but I believe it is important to know the degree to which a person has been involved. Candidates must have a well-balanced Christian faith with plenty of sound doctrine, and a living, personal experience of Jesus Christ. Otherwise, people who have had heavy previous occult experience may experience stress that can lead to an unhealthy overpreoccupation with demons and their influence.

5. *Previous drug involvement.* A person previously involved with drugs needs careful professional assessment. For example, we still see a few cases of people once heavily involved with LSD who suffer from flashbacks for some time after coming off the drug. It is important to know past history and present situation.

6. *A recent broken love affair, or recent bereavement.* Selection procedures should not be finalized until at least six months after such an event has occurred, and evidence that mourning processes are more or less completed ought to be obtained.

Selection: The Positive Side

This article has commented on some of the negative factors to be explored in the selection process. There are, of course, many positive factors that can be identified, and current research is attempting to quantify factors that will make a successful missionary.

One area of great importance is the type and degree of maturity of the candidate's personality. Though this area is notoriously difficult to assess, a judicious combination of psychological testing, references, and interviews may give a reasonably good picture.

People with certain personality traits appear to be specially at risk, excluding those who can be psychologically diagnosed as having a personality disorder.

1. *Overrigidity.* Missionaries must be rigid in the sense of being determined to follow up their calling. But determination is not the same as rigidity, which implies inability to seek and use other people's opinions, to make healthy adult compromises, and to work as a member of a team. Such people can drive other team members to distraction--especially if they are in leadership positions.

2. *Immaturity.* I have referred to this in a previous article and only wish to comment here on the dangers of hysterical overdramatization and constant demands for attention. Maturity takes a lifetime to achieve, with many failures along the way, but candidates should at least show some evidence of understanding their own personalities and ways to continue maturing.

3. *Overaggressiveness.* A capacity for aggression harnessed to the will and grace of God is a valuable thing, otherwise it may be merely destructive and divisive. Such destructive aggression may be based on subconscious negative dynamite, or on assertiveness training gone wrong. Constructive Christian aggression is in a different category: it is mature, peaceable, and valuable.

4. *Overmysticism.* The Protestant church needs a few "holy hermits" whose primary task is prayer, but the exercise of their ministry should be done "decently and in order." There have been missionaries who announced suddenly that they would no more daily work, since God had called them to prayer. He probably had--but such a calling should be combined with the grace and patience to make necessary arrangements so that already overburdened colleagues do not have to take over another person's work with no prior warning.

What type of personality, then, is required for missionary service? Though God values no one type over any other, certain factors ought to underlie each personality type:

(1) *Insight capacity.* People without problems are either dead, or possess an abnormally vegetable-like passivity! The really valuable people are those who have accepted the reality of their problems, begun to understand their origins, and know how to handle them. This is known as insight capacity, and it is most valuable.

(2) *Reasonable adaptability.* I recently talked to a very angry candidate who had just been oriented into the correct behavior for women in the country to which she was going. She said, "If I adapt myself to behave like that, how will those women ever learn anything?" She had a good point. But she needed to learn that there are degrees of adjustment necessary to gain local confidence. The best candidates are those who understand the weaknesses of their host country, but who are able to make reasonable changes in their own behavior where the job demands it.

(3) *Some knowledge of personal strengths and weaknesses.* Insight usually concentrates on weaknesses, but an equally valuable insight recognizes personal strengths. In considering weakness, the great pitfall to avoid is wallowing in guilt. This is a useless occupation unless it leads to true repentance when that is indicated, followed by an experience of God's forgiveness and a new entry into his healing power. Unfortunately, too many missionaries and candidates seem to enjoy wallowing, and call it humility. But it is a false humility which may be based on a false guilt.

It is not common for individuals to understand personal strengths. Christians seem to view this as pride. In reality, however, we can get just as much enjoyment from that aspect of God's creation as we do from a flower garden. There is nothing within us that God has not created; therefore, it is right that we enjoy and appreciate all that he has done for us.

There was once a missionary who began every prayer, "I know, Lord, that I am a worm and no man." This gradually drove one of his colleagues nuts--until one morning, after the usual worn statement, the colleague could stand it no longer. He got up and said in a loud voice, "Thank you, Lord, that I am not a worm. I am a man created in your image, and proud of it!" He had understood the need to balance our understanding of our own emptiness with the good things God had created within him.

(4) *A humble learning attitude.* A few months ago I was in an Indian church listening to a well-meaning foreign preacher. He apologized at great length for preaching, saying he felt embarrassed being in the pulpit because he had everything in his own country and the church possessed so little. But his apology came across as a profound insult. His congregation included members of some of the most prestigious academic and government organizations, and some of them had world achievements. It did not seem to enter the preacher's head that people in other countries, as well as in his own, had done things they were proud of, and that they had a valuable culture.

Missionary candidates must be prepared to be humble. While they may have something to offer in terms of professional skills, they, too, have much to learn and receive. On arrival they are illiterate, unable to speak, read, or write the local language. They are culturally ignorant. They must, therefore, be ready to kill stone dead any remnants of a know-all, have-all attitude. They must go with a concept of servanthood that says, "Thank God, I can help a little with the skill God has given me. But there is a lot I do not know and cannot do. Please teach me, please help me."

4

Larry N. Ferguson, Dean Kliewer,
Stanley E. Lindquist,
Donald E. Williams, and Robert P. Heinrich

Candidate Selection Criteria: A Survey

A 1980 survey of 78 missionary sending agencies was designed to gather information about candidate selection and other personnel procedures. The questionnaire explored the selection process, the selection experience, the importance of selection factors, candidate rejection issues, and service discontinuation. 280 primary findings indicate that psychological assessment comprises from one fourth to one third of the average selection interview time; no specific psychological test was used universally; and most mission agency personnel declared a desire to improve their ability to select missionaries. Four important candidate selection factors were found to be depth of Christian commitment, knowledge of the Bible, past performance in church work, and overall emotional stability.

In the fall of 1979 the authors were asked to organize a convention workshop on "the place of psychological assessment in missionary candidate selection and rehabilitation" for the Evangelical Foreign Missions Association (EFMA). Growing concern was expressed regarding the significant number of missionary personnel who were leaving the field after one term or less. Mission agency personnel wanted to improve their selection procedures and wanted to examine the use of psychological

Copyright 1983 by the Rosemead School of Psychology, Biola University. Reprinted by permission from the *Journal of Psychology and Theology,* 1983, *11,* 243-250.

35

assessment in the candidate selection process. An arrangement was made to survey the affiliated mission agencies of the Evangelical Foreign Missions Association. The results of the survey were presented at the EFMA convention in March 1980. This article is a summary of the significant findings derived from the survey response.

Methodology

The 78 member organizations of the Evangelical Foreign Mission Association (EFMA) represents a broad base of evangelical mission sending agencies, all of whom subscribe to an evangelical statement of faith and participate regularly in the various EFMA programs. This group was chosen when the program chairman for the 1980 EFMA convention requested a presentation on "The Place of Psychological Assessment in Missionary Candidate Selection and Rehabilitation." It was felt that a survey of the member agencies would provide information directly related to candidate selection and assessment.

A survey instrument was developed and mailed to the 78 EFMA member organizations. Cover letters were submitted to authenticate the request for completion. Thirty-nine mission agencies responded by returning the questionnaires. This 50% return-rate was considered exceptional considering the amount of work and time that the survey required. The letters and survey form were sent to the personnel secretary of the mission agency. In most cases, the staff of the agency compiled the data and pulled it together for the administration who then approved the content and returned it to Link Care Center.

The candidate selection survey included three sections. First was a series of questions on the selection process. Information was collected on who does the candidate interviews and the procedures used for assessing candidates. Second was a selection experience summary, requesting information on the number of applications received and the number accepted. For those individuals who were not accepted as candidates, reasons for discontinuance were requested. Also, the average length of time a candidate worked with the agency before being discontinued was explored. The third section explored the importance of selection factors. Training experience, personal resources, validation, and background/status items were ranked in terms of importance to the selection decision.

The remainder of the questionnaire requested information on service discontinuation. Categories of discontinuation included non-acceptance in the candidate process, and termination from foreign service.

Results

Selection Process

The first question asked who is involved in the pre-selection interviews, how much time was devoted to interviewing, and when the interviews were conducted. Table I summarizes the response.

As can be seen, as many as 20 hours may be spent in interviewing the missionary candidate before acceptance. A large number of individuals may also be involved in the interview process: Agency staff members, board members, other missionaries, and outside professionals who are called in for specific situations.

Table 1
The Use of Interviews in Candidate Selection

Person Conducting Interview	Average Hours per Candidate	Stage when Interview Occurs or Reason
Mission Agency Staff	5.6	Pre-application
Mission Board Members	3	After acceptance
Other Missionaries	2.8	Informally as available
Psychiatrist (MD)	3	Referral if special problems are noted
Psychologist (PhD)	3.6	For test interpretation and evaluation
Other (Physician, pastor, screening committee, etc.)	2	When needed

The second component of the selection process examined candidate assessment procedures. Most mission agencies used at least three primary procedures: Preliminary questionnaires, formal application forms, and letters of reference. In addition, several mission agencies include psychological tests. Pre-field simulated stress situations similar to missionary internship, were mentioned several times. While some mission agencies required several years of practical experience before appointment, on-the-job assessments typically were not required. The use of psychological tests, pre-field simulated stress situations, and on the job assessments were being reconsidered by several agencies. A final procedure mentioned was the use of specific orientation sessions by the mission agency after selection.

One clear finding was that many agencies did not seem to maintain adequate records. Information was requested in 5-year increments, beginning with 1960. During the last 5-year period, 1975-1979, considerably more mission agencies responded with information. But even then some mission agencies did not seem to have their records in retrievable form. As many as 30 agencies responded to some items while as few as 12 agencies responded to other items. Because a percentage of the number responding is often presented, not always will the percentages total 100%. Over the period of time 1960-1964, as few as 5 agencies responded to the questions and as many as 18. Record keeping was certainly not standard among the responding agencies. From the following information some conclusions may be drawn about the selection experience for long term missionary personnel.

Selection Experience

Information was requested from records regarding the number of applications received, accepted, and refused. When an individual was not sent to the field, or left the field, the survey asked for reasons for the action.

Figure 1 displays the average number of applications received each of the five years questioned in the survey. The average for long term workers was compiled by taking the total number of individuals indicated by the agency and dividing by the number of responding agencies. One interesting point is apparent. It can be seen that the average number of long term applications remained fairly consistent during the twenty years.

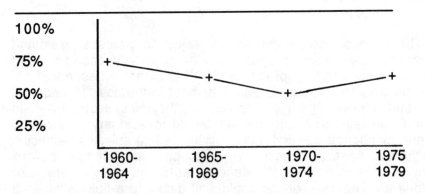

Figure 1: Average Number of Applications Received per Agency

Figure 2 represents the ratio of the total number of accepted applications with those refused. This ratio is represented as a percentage of individuals accepted divided by the number of individuals refused. From 1960-1964, for example, the ratio is 5 to 1, meaning that five candidates were accepted for each candidate rejected. It should be noted that the ratio took a significant drop during the last five years. Mission agencies either were becoming more selective or were using more adequate selection processes.

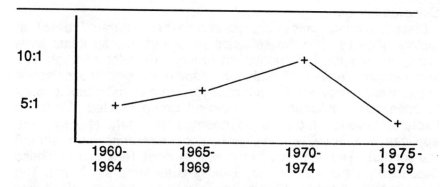

Figure 2: Average Ratio of Accepted
Applications to Rejected per Agency

An average of 70 written applications for long term service were received by each agency during each five year period. An average of 51 of those applications were accepted by the agency and 48 of these were actually sent to the field. The average number of persons on the field at the time of the study was 116 per agency.

The data on the discontinuation of service among long term missionaries indicated an average of 32 persons discontinued missionary service for each agency during each 5 year period. Of the numerous reasons for discontinuation, four were explored. During each five year period physical health reasons accounted for an average of 4 terminations, emotional adjustment for 2, marital adjustment for 2, and retirement for 4.5.

This inquiry focused particularly on the psychological aspects of discontinuation. It is interesting to note that 25% of the average discontinuances are due to physical and emotional difficulties. Most mission boards have fairly accurate information on discontinuation. They know when, where, and why, usually in great detail. However, the "real reason" and the "given reason" may not match. The motive often may be to help protect the missionary and family. In addition, the reasons for discontinuation most often may be multiple rather than singular. It would appear significant that an average of 8 out of 32 actually discontinued for emotional or health reasons.

For the long term workers, the average length of service for reported discontinuation was 9 years. This places the typical discontinuation near the end of the second term. A term is frequently considered 5 years, and the person may be on the field four years with a 1-year furlough.

Selection Factors

Discussion with mission representatives generated a list of factors often used in the selection procedure. These items were clustered into four categories according to similar content. The first category entitled Training Factors dealt with those issues which were considered significant for educational training prior to candidate application. The second group labeled Validation Factors, included those items deemed important to verify the applicant's credibility (i.e., letters of reference and school transcripts). The third cluster was Personal Resources. These described personal skills and qualities considered significant. The fourth was Background Status. These rating scale items dealt with previous experiences in church work, family, and marital factors.

Table 2 indicates the importance of candidate selection factors as reported by the fifty-eight agencies responding to this part of the survey. The four clusters of factors are listed in rank order from those rated most important to those rated least important. The most important Training Factor was knowledge of the Bible, while psychology training was ranked in the seventh or least important position.

For each of the items under each cluster the agency personnel were asked to rate the importance of that item using a scale from 1 ("least important") to 7 ("most important"). By summing the rating each agency gave to that item and dividing by the number of agencies making a rating, an average rating for each item was obtained. The average rating can then be compared with all of the other items.

Table 3 indicates the ten most important candidate selection factors from the thirty-two possible factors. The average rating and the factors receiving those ratings are listed. Since each item was independently judged on a scale of one to seven, the 32 items may be compared and the highest ratings can be seen as important.

Table 2. Importance of Candidate Selection Factors

Rank Order	Average Rating	Factors Rated
		Background Status Factors
1	6.0	Past Performance in Church Work
2	5.6	Marriage Status (Divorced/Remarried)
3	5.3	Previous Vocation Success
4	5.0	Study of Life History Process and Events
5	4.7	Family of Origin (Physical Health)
6	4.0	Marriage Status (Married/Not Married)
7	3.8	Size of Family (Children?)
8	3.7	Length of Marriage
		Training Factors
1	6.1	Knowledge of the Bible
2	5.7	General Educational Level
3	5.1	Theology Training
4	4.6	Missions Training
5	4.3	Language/Linguistics
6	3.7	Anthropology Training
7	2.7	Psychology Training
		Personal Resources
1	6.7	Depth of Christian Commitment
2	6.0	Overall Emotional Stability
3	5.8	Motivation for Choice of Foreign Missions
4	5.8	Flexibility/Adaptability
5	5.2	Interpersonal/Communication Skills
6	4.7	Intelligence/Intellectual Ability
7	4.6	Creativity
8	3.8	Administrative Skills
9	3.6	Ability to do Deputation Work
10	2.7	Construction Skills
		Validation Factors
1	5.8	Ability to Relate to Persons of Other Cultures
2	5.4	Letters of Reference
3	5.3	Matching of Unique Needs with Candidate Gifts
4	5.2	Ability to Adapt to Novel Environment
5	5.1	Reaction Under Stress
6	4.2	School Transcripts
7	3.9	Qualifying Examinations

A combination of factors from each of the four clusters (Table 3) may be viewed as those considered most significant for candidate selection. Having the items clustered into four groups may bias the arbitrary ranking of the top ten. Were all thirty-two items ranked as a unit rather than in four clusters it is possible that the rankings would differ. However, it is interesting to note those items generally considered significant by mission agencies in their selection process. A combination of Christian commitment, biblical knowledge, previous experience, and general emotional stability combine as the four most significant issues in candidate selection.

Table 3
Ten Most Important Candidate Selection Factors

Average Rating	Factors Rated Most Important
6.7	Depth of Christian Commitment
6.1	Knowledge of the Bible
6.0	Past Performance in Church Work
6.0	Overall Emotional Stability
5.8	Ability to Relate to Persons in Other Cultures
5.8	Flexibility/Adaptability
5.8	Motivation for Choice of Foreign Missions
5.7	General Educational Level
5.6	Marriage Status (Divorced/Remarried)
5.4	Letters of Reference

Rejection Issues
Mission agencies were asked to write a brief narrative describing the sort of counsel or guidance provided to those who are not accepted by the agency after the formal written application has been completed. While there was considerable variance in the process of candidate rejection, of those responding it appeared that the rejection process could occur at any time during the application procedure. In some cases the individuals excluded themselves. In other cases the individual was informed of the rejection and the process of application was terminated. Most agencies stated that when a candidate was rejected someone sat down with the candidate and explained the reasons fairly thoroughly. In cases of rejection because of an emotional or

personal difficulty the agencies indicated that they would make referrals to psychiatrists or psychologists as needed.

Discontinuation Issues

Agencies were asked to describe the provision made for those who after an assignment in foreign service terminated for various reasons.

For those discontinued from service due to retirement, some respondents provided complete care. Some based their level of support on length of service, some provided only a small pension, or gave a maximum of six months salary. Some agencies provided pre-retirement seminars for missionaries age 50 or above. For a few agencies there were reports of a current policy review and attempts to meet needs effectively. For individuals discontinuing for physical health reasons, policies included continuance of salary until the end of the committed term or a set number months of salary. Some provided assistance in job research, attempts to provide rehabilitation (which sometimes included financial support or other assistance), and reassignment from the field to work in the home country. Most agencies appear to handle each case individually although many cite a policy of salary continuance or job retraining.

For those individuals who discontinue for emotional or mental health reasons, most of those responding indicated that they provide an extended furlough with pay and appropriate psychological services. Generally before termination all possible resources for counseling and rehabilitation are attempted by the agencies. In some cases their health insurance policies provide for psychological or psychiatric care.

When discontinuation occurs because of marital problems, most agencies indicated that they will provide counseling if the individuals are willing, and may permit extended furloughs. Some agencies reported they had not yet faced such needs. The other extreme was for an agency to summarily dismiss the individual from service.

For those individuals discontinuing because of administrative decisions, reference might be made to mission board policy changes or other circumstances causing the service of the individual to be unnecessary. Respondents indicated that they often sought to re-deploy the persons to other areas, or provide some notice and severance pay with assistance in finding other jobs.

Financial assistance and psychological support as well as rehabilitation and restoration is provided depending upon specific family needs.

Discussion

Several conclusions and implications can be drawn from the survey response. First, psychological assessment as represented by interviews with psychologists, psychiatrists, or counselors occupies approximately one-fourth to one-third of the average selection interview time. Some form of consultation from a mental health professional is a fairly common practice. Still, a majority of those responding to the survey used psychological assessment consultation only when special personnel problems emerged. While no standard psychological testing process was identified and most responding mission personnel seemed reasonably well satisfied with their screening procedures, it was noted that the majority of the agencies indicated they would like to improve their ability to select missionaries and to develop an adequate psychological screening program.

Second, it was apparent from the response that records and information on discontinuation of missionaries were rather scattered. Consequently, the reliability of our data on the extent of emotional, marital, and family difficulties may be low. From conversations with numerous mission agencies and missionaries themselves, it is apparent that there is a higher degree of emotional or family difficulty contributing to the termination of missionaries than often is recorded by the mission agency. This suggests that missionaries and agencies do have difficulty in handling termination due to mental health, interpersonal, and emotional problems.

Third, many respondents indicate a desire to learn how to select candidates to avoid first-term failures. They wanted to develop more uniform personnel policies and improve their records and information retrieval capabilities. Many agencies expressed a concern that some workers continue beyond their period of effectiveness. These problems suggest that competent program development and program evaluation consultation services to missionary agencies are needed. Such consultation efforts might fruitfully impact mission programs at levels beyond only personnel assessment technology.

Fourth, ratings of selection factors suggest the potential for developing assessment tools based on those factors, tools specifically designed to assist in the selection process. Currently available psychological assessment strategies could be applied more systematically to the candidate selection process. A standardized approach to measuring the particular qualities necessary for cross-cultural living would appear desireable as an obvious next step. It is apparent that better personnel assessment strategies need to be developed specifically for the benefit of missionary-sending agencies. While those responding to the survey did not call for such development directly, the survey response clearly seems to express the need for more effort being focused upon personnel performance prediction. Such strategies may well enhance efforts to improve the candidate selection process, the pre-field orientation process, and the definition of an effective cross-cultural worker.

Fifth, it is apparent that the level of responsibility assumed by a mission agency for those who discontinue service is highly variable. It is heartening to note the number of preretirement seminars that are now being offered to missionaries. The retirement benefit packages, the insurance programs and other needs for those who leave service for health or emotional reasons might well be improved.

It is clear that much research and careful planning is necessary to improve the level of psychological services available to mission agencies. The task of selecting those candidates most likely to serve effectively in the calling which God gives is a complicated one. The task of developing more adequate applicant selection criteria and more appropriate personnel strategies is desirable to support the work of spreading the Gospel of Christ.

5

Thomas Graham

How to Select the Best Church Planters

One of the dominant trends in missions is cross-cultural church planting. The team approach uses members with a variety of complementary gift mixes and skills.

Multiple demands are often made on these missionaries. On occasions, they will be called upon to exert a leadership role, perhaps developing indigenous leadership; at other times, they must assume the role of follower as they work with the team per se. Few team members have had much training or experience in leadership and/or team building.

While it is culturally conceded that the success of a cross-cultural church planting team is greatly influenced by the leadership/followership skills, gifts, and abilities of the team members, the selection procedures used by missions organizations have often not been designed to assess leadership and teamwork qualifications among their candidates.

Traditionally, there have been four sources of data regarding the qualifications of missionary candidates: (1) application materials, including doctrinal statements; (2) letters of reference; (3) interviews, and (4) psychological tests. Application materials are often collected without a firm notion of what information is needed, or how the information will be used to predict success. This lack of clarity leads to unsystematic or imprecise evaluation of candidates.

Much of the problem is attributable to the complexity of the tasks involved. For example, it is difficult to precisely define the job of a missionary church planter. The situational, demographic, cultural, and organizational demands may fluctuate and strongly influence the nature of the church-planting task. Furthermore, the criteria for "success" in one situation may not be the same as the criteria in a quite different setting.

Personal interviews and letters of reference are generally conceded to be the *least* reliable procedures for personnel selection. Evidence for their predictive validity in the selection process is usually non-existent. Notwithstanding, they are also the most commonly used. Of course, both of these techniques *can* be improved upon, but in general they are of questionable merit. The clinical interview is sometimes an exception, but this is more often used to disqualify a candidate than to predict success.

Psychological tests are also commonly used. However, these are "derived" measures, and, while they can be useful in assessing certain general adjustment factors, it is not usually clear how these relate to *task specific* measures of success. That is, a person can be well adjusted and not necessarily have the qualifications or spiritual gifts for successfully performing a particular ministry.

Psychological tests measure the "traits" of an applicant. Traits are really *propensities*, statistical probabilities, that the person will respond in a particular way. Whether, in fact, the individual *does* act that way will be influenced by many situational factors. The dilemma arises when you try to predict what behavior will occur in settings in which unknown and/or highly variable cultural events interact with an individual's propensities. Put another way, psychological tests can often be used to tell us who clearly is *not* qualified, but are not so well suited for telling us who will be effective in a given task.

Recently, many missions organizations have begun to look more closely at their selection procedures. There is a growing concern about the more traditional methods of selecting personnel. Missions boards are reporting attrition during the first term of between 10 and 40 percent, and the cost of sending a missionary family now runs between $35,000 and $50,000 per year. This does not include the one-time costs of getting a missionary family to the field. Clearly, the consequences of poor selection are severe. The result is often an acute sense of failure in the individual missionary, fields are not developed, and lost persons are not reached.

In order to improve selection procedures, three steps must be undertaken. First, the missions organization must be able to clearly state its philosophy and mission. This should be as specific as possible. Second, and arising out of the mission statement, the organization must define the tasks/ministries that they wish to fill. Ideally, the description of the tasks should include performance criteria, whereby we can determine when a task has been successfully accomplished. Determining the criteria for success is usually the most difficult aspect of this task. The third step is determining the characteristics and qualifications that an individual must have in order to successfully perform the tasks described in step two. Missionary task descriptions often do not make clear distinctions between the task description and the characteristics required to do the task. Occasionally, we are also prone to over-spiritualize when it comes to a candidate's ability to perform a task.

Only after an organization has carefully defined each of these three components can it design an effective, valid selection procedure. It should be pointed out that this is not a process that can be undertaken once and forgotten thereafter. Regular review of these three steps must be undertaken to ensure that the organization remains responsive to the people it serves.

What are the alternatives, then, in selecting candidates? Clearly, the very best evidence of an individual's capability of performing a task is to observe him or her doing it. Obviously, since that is not always practical or possible, other methods must be devised. The assessment center is one such possibility. In assessment centers, multiple techniques are used which provide *behavioral* data from which a candidate's ability to perform the task can be evaluated. The strength of this approach lies in the fact that *actual* behavior in task-related activities is observed rather than relying on presumptive evidence from test scores, application materials, references, and/or interviews. It should be noted that application materials, recommendations by references, and/or test data will continue to be used along with assessment center data in most instances.

What is an Assessment Center?

The pioneering efforts in the establishment of assessment centers occurred in World War II with the development of the British War Office Selection Boards. The British officer corps had sustained heavy losses and in order to rapidly fill the ranks with new officers, paper and pencil tests (basically intelligence) were initially used. These "ninety day wonders" did not prove to be effective leaders in battle, and so the British army began to use situational exercises to observe some actual leadership potential before selecting an officer.

After WWII interest waned, to be revived by the Office of Strategic Services, the forerunner to the CIA. Beginning in 1956, under the direction of Douglas Bray, American Telephone and Telegraph began using assessment centers for selecting middle and upper management personnel. Bray also carefully collected follow-up data on individuals who went through assessment centers and found that the method was highly successful. Some of the organizations now using assessment centers are: IBM, Sears, SOHIO, General Electric, and government agencies such as the Peace Corps. To meet professional standards, assessment centers must have the following characteristics:

(1) Multiple assessment techniques are used. (2) Assessment simulations are selected or tailored to relevant aspects of the task for which candidates are to be selected. (3) Multiple *trained* observers are used. (4) The data from all assessment exercises and instruments and from all observers is pooled and evaluated. (5) A single, final overall evaluation is arrived at by the assessment staff for each candidate.

Compared to other selection procedures, the reliability of composite ratings from assessment centers is quite good, at least for relatively short intervals. Further, the validity of assessment ratings (the extent to which they successfully predict success) is better than most other approaches. Specifically, ratings from an assessment center at their worst are generally as good or better than any other predictive approach.

The Mission to the World Assessment Center

In 1983 Mission to North America (Presbyterian Church in America) began experimenting with assessment centers as a means of improving procedures for selecting church planters for the United States and Canada. After observing their sister organization's success, Mission to the World (also Presbyterian Church in America) developed their own assessment centers. Prior to that time, Mission to the World (MTW) was using a selection process that consisted of evaluating information collected from application materials, letters of reference, psychological tests, and interviews. Candidates who were recommended were then interviewed by the MTW Committee.

Characteristics of a Successful Church Planter

Before conducting their first assessment center, the MTW staff conducted a careful analysis of the activities performed by a missionary church planting team. A profile was developed describing the gifts, skills, abilities, and traits that are desirable in a church planter. The following factors were identified:

A sense of call; spiritual maturity; submissive leadership; goal/performance orientation; discipling/nurturance skills; psychological maturity; functional intelligence; creativity; communication skills; cross-cultural adaptability; physical vitality; a godly family life.

The Objectives of the MTW Assessment Center

Briefly, there are four objectives of MTW assessment centers:

1. Through the use of experiential exercises, simulations and other instrumented activities, selected and constructed on the basis of tasks expected of missionary church planters, assessors observe and evaluate the task related behaviors of MTW candidates.

2. Candidates observe and evaluate the behavior of themselves and others as they participate in experiential exercises, simulations, and various other instrumented activities.

3. Candidates will acquire new skills and knowledge through the exercises, discussions, lectures, etc. in which they participate. While assessment centers are not primarily for learning, significant new skills are acquired.

4. Assessment and training activities will focus on (1) the specific activities in which an MTW church planter will be involved in order to build God's Kingdom, and (2) the qualifications, gifts, etc., desirable in an individual who will successfully carry out those activities.

At the conclusion of the assessment center all of the data collected by the assessors as they observed each of the candidates in the various exercises, is discussed and evaluated. Consensus is reached for each candidate, and an overall rating is applied. Each candidate then has an interview with one or more assessors in which careful feedback is given about his or her status and the next steps the candidate should take.

The Format of the MTW Assessment Center

The following will provide the reader with a rather brief overview of the activities that are included in a typical MTW assessment center.

Orientation Session. This session brings candidates and assessors together for the first time and the stage is set for the ensuing days. Candidates are told what to expect--that they will be expected to actively participate in a series of exercises which are designed to evaluate their performance in tasks that are related to those in which an organizing pastor would be involved. They are not in competition with one another, nor is there any quota for how many can be selected. MTW can use all of the church-planting missionaries that it can get.

Personal Profile/LEAD Administration. The Personal Profile is an instrument that is very useful in identifying an individual's work behavioral style. Candidates usually become quite enthusiastic during the scoring and interpretation of the Personal Profile and it also serves as an ice breaker. The Leadership Effectiveness and Adaptability Description (LEAD) Instrument provides candidates with information about their flexibility and adaptability in applying leadership techniques. The interpretation of the LEAD follows the Oikomenia Role Play Exercise where its impact is greatest.

Orientation to Cross-Cultural Church Planting. This session provides an opportunity for the MTW staff to explain MTW's philosophy and goals for church planting in urban centers throughout the world.

Call Presentation. Each husband/wife team (or single) is required to make a 30-minute presentation in which they describe their respective calls to cross-cultural ministry and particularly to church planting. They are encouraged to be specific about how, when, where, key influences, etc. They are asked to describe their concept of family ministry, their gift mixes, etc., and to discuss the directions of their spiritual growth. These 30-minute sessions are interspersed throughout the assessment center to keep them fresh and interesting. After each presentation prayer is offered for the person(s) making the presentation.

Prayer/praise. Volunteers from among the candidates conduct prayer and praise sessions each evening, in which both candidates and assessors participate.

Oikomenia Role Play Exercise. Candidates are assigned to small groups of six to eight. This is a case study of an actual missionary church-planting team. This team is having some success in meeting its objectives, but is also having considerable inter-team friction. Since the actual Personal Profiles are known of the original team members, candidates are assigned to play roles *based upon the similarity of their own style.* The group's task is to deal with team tensions, as well as meet objectives. A leaderless group case analysis follows the role play. The assessors observe the group process to determine leadership patterns, group dynamics, etc., that emerge. The case study is followed by a lecture and handout on the subject of team effectiveness.

Analysis of LEAD Scores. The LEAD Instrument provides information about candidates' leadership styles, their ability to adapt their leadership style to people, and their ability to develop leadership skills in their followers. This will be related to the problems of the Oikomenia Role Play Exercise.

Cross-Cultural Evangelism Exercise. This session begins with a short lecture and discussion of the difficulties encountered in entering a new culture, culture shock, and exploring ways of understanding the new from what we know about our own culture and our individual methods of coping. The group is divided into two teams, playing either the alpha or beta culture in the BAFA/BAFA game. In this game the two cultures initially send representatives to the other culture to attempt to discover basic cultural rules and values and to adapt to the other culture. They are then asked to develop a plan of evangelism that will be most effective within the opposite cultural context. This is followed by a general discussion between candidates and assessors regarding cross-cultural issues, evangelism, contextualization, etc. References and handouts are provided. Candidates evaluate team members for their effectiveness on their various approaches to contextualization.

Team Strategy Development Exercise. This is an analysis problem. This is a macro-church planting exercise in which demographic data is provided about an urban area in the world that is a prime target for church planting. The task for candidates is to study the background information and to develop some strategies for planting churches in the area. They are then asked to prepare a written plan, a phased approach through which five new churches and a presbytery can be established within 10 years. Candidates are required to form teams in any fashion they wish for this exercise with only two restrictions: husbands and wives must be together and the groups should be as equal in size as possible. Teams will spend four to five hours on this exercise.

Strategy Presentation. Based upon the plan developed in the previous Strategy Development Exercise, each team will make a presentation to the assessment staff. It is expected that this presentation will be well organized and show a high degree of professionalism. The plans, as well as the presentations, will be evaluated by both candidates and assessment staff.

Individual Interviews. Individual interviews with candidates are scheduled by the assessment staff during the Strategy Development Exercise. During these interviews the assessors follow up on issues that are more appropriately discussed individually, and/or to respond to questions that have arisen during the exercises. It will also be an opportunity for candidates to discuss matters of their own choosing.

Feedback Interviews. After the final assessment staff meeting has been conducted and a final composite rating has been determined for each candidate, feedback interviews are scheduled. Each candidate is given information about the strengths and weaknesses perceived by the assessment staff. Finally, each candidate is advised of the recommendation that the staff will make regarding their candidacy. Candidates are asked to complete a written evaluation of the assessment center after the close of all activities.

Thus far, 102 MTW church-planting candidates have attended assessment centers. In addition, almost 150 candidates have attended assessment centers for Mission to North America. The selection ratio has been about 66 percent. While one might expect that there would be considerable stress associated with this process, there is almost always an atmosphere of warmth and togetherness among candidates and between candidates and assessors. To a great extent, this is due to the air of openness that is fostered as well as the importance attached to providing candidates complete, accurate, and constructive feedback at the end of the assessment center.

Those candidates who have not been selected are shown the greatest concern. Some candidates who are not selected are *potentially* qualifiable with further experience, maturity, and/or training. Candidates often begin to prayerfully examine their call and their gift mix for church planting more closely and, as a result, are sometimes led into a ministry more suited to their gifts. In a significant number of cases, candidates have an opportunity to explore aspects of their personality, marriage, and/or spiritual walk, and this produces constructive changes as well as generating new vigor and enthusiasm in their ministry. In other instances, individuals become aware of areas in which they need to acquire additional training, (e.g., leadership).

How successful these missionary church planters will be is yet to be determined. The data regarding the success of U.S. church planters selected in Mission to North America assessment centers is very encouraging. The correlation between final assessment ratings and measures of growth in newly organized works is strong. Since the process of getting a missionary church planter to the field requires a number of steps (e.g., building the team, deputation, etc.) data regarding the success of MTW church planters is slower in coming. The reaction of MTW and MNA Committees, presbyteries, seminary and Bible college students, and administrators to this experience with assessment centers has been extremely positive and great interest is being expressed in developing other generic types of assessment centers.

The use of assessment centers is not a panacea that will eliminate all of the problems in selecting missionary candidates. Further, they require considerable effort to perform a careful task analysis and to define candidate characteristics. It takes still more time to develop exercises that accurately simulate aspects of the cross-cultural church planter's task. Obviously, the expense of the development work as well as costs associated with bringing candidates and assessors together for a four-day period will seem high compared to other selection procedures. To put the matter into proper perspective, however, one must balance the costs of attrition against the cost of an assessment center.

PSYCHOLOGICAL ASSESSMENT

6

Stanley E. Lindquist

A Rationale for Psychological Assessment of Missionary Candidates

Psychologists and others in the behavioral sciences must become involved in the process of developing and validating assessment and pre-field orientation strategies. The formulation of research plans leading to the reduction of the personal heartache due to early return, and the saving of funds, are compelling reasons to use the very best of our skills and efforts. We need to be ready to serve in the most effective way possible to be faithful stewards in the Kingdom of God. We are asked to be involved; there are demanding needs to be met; we care; the size of the missionary program itself is so significant; stewardship and prevention of loss force us to consider using all our strengths and capabilities to that end.

Missionaries, people in business, diplomats, or tourists--no group is immune to cross-cultural adjustment difficulties. Too many return to the United States after an overseas assignment broken in body, spirit, and emotions. These people are victims of what some call "culture-shock," which implies an inability to adjust to a strange culture and perceived hostile environment. A lack of preparation for the new and different style of life may result in conditions which reduce the ability of the body to fight off infections, or which create an atmosphere of carelessness, allowing accidents to happen. Such factors may force an early return for what appears to be physical reasons rather than the actual underlying adjustment-related cause. Or the result may be an emotional breakdown which renders the person ineffective. In some cases others associated with the person may develop an intolerance for adjustment-related idiosyncracies or impaired abilities. Sometimes associates create conditions which lead the disturbed person to leave the cross-cultural setting.

Most often the underlying factor in cross-cultural adjustment is an emotional reaction which sets up the person for other problems. This pattern was brought to my attention by a nurse who said in effect that she wouldn't have succumbed to malaria and other tropical diseases had she been stronger emotionally. She implied that greater emotional reserves would have permitted her body's immune system to eliminate the germs which caused the disease. It is interesting that she made her statement long before results from the recent research on stress were discovered. These findings show that culture shock can cause bodily reactions similar to those the nurse felt had been weakening her and making her susceptible to disease.

Is this state of affairs inevitable? Can something be done about adjustment failure? It would seem that to accomplish anything in such a complex arena, it is necessary to start with basic causes. For missionaries this appears associated with the assessment and preparation of candidates before they go overseas.

The overriding questions we need to ask ourselves, before getting into the discussion of the big program of prediction, assessment, training, and prevention, are, "Why should psychologists be involved in the selection and training process of missionary candidates? Further, what right do we have to be so involved, assuming we can justify being involved at all? How can the expenditure of personnel time and financial resources be justified for such a project?" These are basic questions to be considered, and to which we will address ourselves in these papers. Therefore, let us ask ourselves:

Why Should We Be Involved with Missionary Assessment?
1. Because we have been asked to become involved. The Link Care Center's Division of Missionary Services and Research Ministries has received direct requests for help. As well requests for services come to every professional, either for direct services or financial support. Requests come from such organizations as the Evangelical Foreign Missions and Interdenominational Foreign Missions Associations, and from several individual denominations and independent missions, all of whom supervise over 50% of all

the theologically conservative missionaries sent overseas from the United States and Canada. Members of these groups are becoming increasingly aware of the necessity for the involvement of psychologists and other professionals in order to help candidates become more effective and to reduce the early return of those who go overseas. The primary need expressed is to help board's become better able to predict potential effectiveness, and once such a capability is developed, to assist in the preparation of those workers to meet exigencies of cross-cultural work.

Problems encountered in overseas service, many of which create conditions that can result in early return of missionaries or reduce their effectiveness on the field, can be traced to the lack of information about personal strengths and weaknesses at the time of candidacy. Had such information been available to mission boards prior to overseas assignment, perhaps remedial preparation or change of assignment could have alleviated the difficulty. This diagnostic and training function is an arena where the tools and skills of the psychologist are badly needed. Psychologists and other professionals should be ready to provide the most effective and reliable service available. The need for assessment services for missionaries is not only a choice on our part, it is a demand, even a requirement, to permit the work of the Kingdom of God on earth to go forward with fewer hindrances.

2. We are involved because we care. When faced with the tragedies in lives of missionary workers who have had to leave service prematurely, one's priorities for expenditure of time and effort are reordered. The general need becomes personalized through contact with the worker. When confronted with the detrimental effects of inadequately applied diagnostic procedures, one feels considerable distress. Adequate training prior to going to the field might reduce remedial problems. Breakdowns and interruptions of service might be avoided. Not to do something about a problem of this magnitude and compelling need would truly demonstrate a lack of caring.

3. The sheer size of the missionary ventures requires our special attention. Almost $500,000,000.00 per year are expended for overseas missionary ministries. The number of persons involved, depending on the way statistics are analyzed, conservatively is estimated to be over 35,000 persons overseas from Evangelical groups alone. A considerable number of support staff involved in home operations are not included in the above figure. The number of persons involved in this cross-cultural enterprise requires those of us familiar with psychological assessment technology to make available our service in this

increasingly important arena. To ignore this significant opportunity is to abrogate our personal responsibility.

4. Special needs of candidates and missionaries underscore the need for help. Symptoms of the underlying problems become clearly evident as we examine missionaries who have dropped out or have been pushed out, and who are thus in need of restoration. We become more aware of the need as we increasingly interact with those who get into adjustment difficulty. Each person demonstrates symptoms of underlying problems that often could have been anticipated prior to leaving for an overseas assignment. The number of persons forced to drop out, or who are pushed out, variously estimated at from 10 to 50% of those entering service, gives clear evidence of the relevance of this concern. Tucker (1982) pointed out that 33% of all overseas employees (non-missionary) return within the first year, which confirms estimates of missionary early return rates. Those who have had to return early reveal to us a keen sense of frustration and failure.

5. A special need for criterion measures of effectiveness in cross-cultural work exists. Unfortunately, such criteria, demonstrated through validation by prediction and follow-up evaluation over a period of years, are not available for any field (Tucker 1982). While it is true that every mission board executive, missionary, and national worker evaluates performance and effectiveness, there is no systematic, comprehensive measure of worker performance capability. What tells us that the missionary task is actually going forward? What signs mark effective mission work? Can a measure of mission goal attainment be developed? While statistics of overall progress can be accumulated, much-needed personal effectiveness measures are lacking, and much research is required. Superior performance by one person, averaged out with others not performing as well, may give an impression of overall progress. As a result the worker not performing adequately may not receive any remedial help.

The most difficult task in development of any measurement tool is specification of a criterion which can validate the meaning of the measurement. Thus, before a predictive screening measure of applicant characteristics can be developed, the target of the prediction, a criterion of effective service must be identified. When one realizes that a different success criterion may exist for every mission agency, every field, and perhaps even for each missionary, one becomes aware that the task is truly monumental. However, with the analysis and statistical capabilities currently available, the task becomes comprehensible.

Worker performance can be teased out of the mass of information and made applicable to the job at hand. Procedures have been developed which are capable of giving information to compare levels of success in varying objectives for different people (e.g., see the work of T.J. Kiresuk et al., 1968). Such technologies are now available to become part of this effort to establish criteria of cross-cultural effectiveness in communicating the Gospel and in helping missionaries deal with cross-cultural adjustment stresses.

Selection profiles which describe missionary applicant characteristics are a significant tool for those agency personnel who determine which candidates should go to the field. Since profile information which is not predictive of "on-the-job" performance is invalid and unreliable, the credibility of any selection profile must be established through validation by on-field performance, with the relationship to be demonstrated between predictor and target measures.

Few studies predict and verify criteria of cross-cultural adjustment. The methodology and study findings presented in this series of CAPS journal articles hopefully will provide some information about the current progress in assessment service development.

6. Another reason for this focus includes the necessity for conservation of resources. In every organization, funds for God's work are limited. No longer can a mission organization raise funds easily. The competition for limited funds is keen. Further, personnel are also less available because of the higher standards required for highly specialized tasks. All of this points to a reality that has been important from the first, namely, the need to care for and preserve all kinds of resources. The goal is to maximize the use of both personnel and financial resources, which God has entrusted to the care of the Church.

Assignment of the wrong person to a significant task compromises the missionary effort. Such selection errors sap the strength of the program and often demoralize the spirit of mission workers and families. Early return of a missionary has a ripple effect involving the person who appears to be the reason for the departure, the family who has to return along with the identified person, other missionaries, the extended family, the church, the mission board, and perhaps most important with respect to the long—range effects, the nationals who are being abandoned.

Stewardship of finances, specifically, provides a powerful justification for the use of enlightened assessment procedures. The foreign mission worker who leaves his post prematurely costs the sending agency from $35,000 to $60,000 according to the reports from mission organizations. Figures from the business field indicate similar loss, approximately two and a half times the base salary. Assuming that these figures are reasonably accurate, and using a conservative 10% early return rate, the return of 370 first-time missionaries costs about 13 million dollars each year (Lindquist, 1983). This means that if selection screening improvements were to lead to only a one percentage point decrease (10% of the total early return rate), the annual savings would be approximately 1 million 300 thousand dollars. Good stewardship requires each of us to do what we can to meet these needs in the most expeditious way possible.

We are called to be stewards of both human and financial resources, and this call provides compelling motivation to be involved in our important task.

7. Another reason to be engaged in this activity is prevention of future problems. In mission, mental health, and physical health, it is clear that disease prevention strategies are profoundly superior to remedial treatment strategies. One example from medicine illustrates this concept. If one is seeking to reduce the effects of polio virus infection in a population, a vaccine is much more powerful than an iron lung.

The important factor in research and application is discovery of competencies required for effective service. Following this, instruments capable of measuring these competencies must be validated. When this endeavor is accomplished, diagnostic predictions can be made indicating the need for additional preparation before going overseas, or the immediate capability of that person for such service. When all the above is accomplished, adjustment-related breakdowns can be prevented to a greater degree than is possible at the present.

Adequate preparation is the key for future effective service. The development of training procedures in personal adjustment and problem solving techniques could become the key to a realistic prevention program. Training based on the competencies required for effective service in each of the many countries, also must be coordinated with diagnostic evaluation. There is much prevention-oriented work to be done.

In the missionary personnel arena, the prevention issue deserves more attention than it is now receiving. This problem will require the best and most dedicated service from friends of missions in psychological and behavioral sciences professions.

Personnel concerns begin with the selection process. Obviously, the key prevention strategy is to improve selection and assignment procedures to avoid dropouts and assignment mismatches.

References

Arndt, J. R. & Lindquist, S. E. (1978). Twenty to fifty percent fail to make it--why? *Evangelical Missions Quarterly, 14,* 40-46.

Ferguson, L., Kliewer, D., Lindquist, B., & Lindquist, S. (1981). *The use of psychological assessment in the evaluation of missionary candidates:* A handbook. Paper presented at IFMA/EFMA Personnel Committee Workshop, Detroit.

Goleman, (1981). The new competency tests: Matching the right people to the right jobs. *Psychology Today,* January, 80-83.

Hawes, F. & Kelley, J. (1979). *An empirical study of adaptation and effectiveness on overseas assignment.* Toronto: Communication Branch Briefing Centre, Government of Canada.

Kiresuk, T. J. & Sherman, R. (1968). Goal attainment scaling. *Journal of Community Mental Health, 4,* 443-453.

Kliewer, D., Heinrich, B., Lindquist, S., & Williams, D. (1980). *Evangelical foreign missions missionary candidate survey.* Fresno, Link Care Press.

Lindquist, S.E. (1982). *Hardiness as a factor in cross-cultural adjustment.* Paper presented to the Christian Association for Psychological Studies West. Portland, Oregon.

Lindquist, S. E. (1982). Prediction of success in overseas adjustment. *Journal of Psychology and Christianity, 1,* 43-48.

Lindquist, S.E. (1983). Use of psychological tests in missionary candidate assessment. *Evangelical Missions Quarterly, 19,* 78-83.

Lindquist, S.E. (1979). The missing link. *Evangelical Missions Quarterly, 15,* 24-30.

Tucker, M. (1981). *Factors influencing cross-cultural adjustment.* Paper presented at the Society for Intercultural Education and Research, Long Beach, California.

7

Larry N. Ferguson, Dean Kliewer
Brent Lindquist, and Stanley E. Lindquist

Essentials and Tools
of Psychological Assessment

Psychological assessment developed earlier this century out of the need to determine which children were appropriate for schooling. Later the ideas were applied to selection of military personnel and grew rapidly after World War II. Today psychological assessment is applied to numerous facets of life: in selection, evaluation, diagnosis, and treatment planning. As testing became an accepted technique, concerns were voiced about application, usefulness, and interpretation. This brief overview will orient you to the major concepts of psychological testing.

What is a Test?

A psychological test is a standardized procedure for observing the behavior that a person exhibits in a specific situation and the description of it with the aid of numerical or category-like systems. In *standardized testing* all the material and instruments are identical so that different administrations of a specific test will be the same for all people. Psychological tests may measure emotional or intellectual aspects of a person, including emotional adjustment, interpersonal relationships, motivation, interests, and attitudes.

It is understood in psychological assessment that there are similarities in all people. These similarities enable the.psychologist to compare individual differences to determine

---

Based on a paper presented at the IFMA/EFMA Personnel Committee Workshop held at Farmington, Michigan in December, 1981. Used by permission of the authors.

strengths, weaknesses, or problems. A test does not measure the entire experience of a person. It only tests specific areas and it is therefore, up to the psychologist to determine which tests to employ to gather the information needed. A psychologist will choose a particular test based on its reliability, validity and relevance, and its norms.

Reliability

Reliability refers to the consistency of test scores obtained by the same people when re-tested with the same test on different occasions. A test is considered reliable when a person is re-tested, at a later date, using the same test, and receives a similar score. This, of course, assumes that the person undergoes no major personality or environmental changes that would affect the results. If a test were not demonstrated to be reliable, then one could not be certain that the test was measuring the same material at the later date. A reliable test allows us to hypothesize about the person and determine what strengths or weaknesses there are. A lower score on a second test would indicate some change that could be significant in working with the person.

Validity

Validity concerns what the test measures. When the test includes a representative sample of the particular area that it claims to measure, it is said to have *content validity*. In simpler terms, does the test measure what it says it measures? An example of a test with content validity would be a test of depression that has questions accurately dealing with depression, rather than with questions dealing with anxiety or another variable.

When a test looks or sounds like it measures what it says it does, it is said to have *face validity*. A test dealing with vocational decisions must be called a vocational test, and must refer to vocational options. A test may also be said to have face validity if its appearance is professional looking. A test that is handwritten on dirty paper does not appear to the person taking the test to be a valid test. Without face validity the test taking attitude of the person may be seriously affected and the results would be questionable.

If a test is used to predict an individual's behavior, it is said to have *criterion-related validity*. When the test has criterion-related validity, the results of the test will accurately describe how the person will behave in a future situation. The test compares a person's scores with a criterion, usually scores from a representative sample of persons. For example, we could assess a group of missionaries on language acquisition abilities. We might predict that a candidate with a high score on our test will succeed in learning a language. Those who score low, we predict, would have considerable difficulty learning the language. These predictions would be based on the criterion established in our sample where we noted that high scorers did, indeed, learn the language better than those with low scores.

Norms

Once a test meets the criteria concerning reliability and validity, it must offer comparisons with the subjects' peers on relevant variables. This refers to the concept of *norms*. Norms are established on a group of people who have already been tested, from which results have already been obtained and summarized. The tester evaluates the particular subject's score against this group to determine the degree of fit or dissimilarity. It is crucial to have accurate norms against which to compare a persons' score. Imagine using children's norms to judge an adult score; the results would be rediculous!

Summary

Psychological assessment is carried on while taking into account the important concepts of reliability, validity, and norms. The following three questions guide test construction, selection and use:

1. Is the test consistent over time? (reliable)

2. Does the test measure important aspects desired, and is it relevant? (valid)

3. Does the test allow comparisons with the subject's peers on relevant variables? (norms)

Assessment Categories

Psychological assessment is generally divided into two categories: Intellectual and Emotional. Tests from each of these categories will be chosen dependent upon the needed information.

Intellectual Assessment

Intellectual assessment measures a person's intellectual functioning for the purpose of determining that person's strengths and weaknesses. Intellectual assessment taps information that people consistently learn in school, including word knowledge, general information, abstract reasoning, visual and motor tasks, and sequential thought. This part of a test battery compares the individual with the "average" intellectual capacity. It will help assess whether a person can think clearly, remember information, learn new material easily or perform tasks that we expect an "average" person to perform. While many people expect this to give an "IQ" score, a number tells little. It is more important to talk about abilities and strengths or weaknesses than to simply give a number.

Emotional Assessment

Emotional assessment endeavors to measure a person's personality or emotional functioning. There is an attempt to state what the current level of functioning is, as well as indicate the "normal" personality or emotional functioning. These tests may be objective or projective.

Objective assessment tests are strictly standardized tests which give much structure to the person taking the test and allow limited response patterns. A person is asked to answer a question or statement with either a true-false response, an agree-disagree response, or by circling a number between 1 and 5. Objective instruments are carefully normed on similar groups and are researched in terms of reliability and validity.

Projective assessments are tests that are unstructured and allow the individual to "project" his or her personality into the problem or task. The assumption underlying this procedure is that the person will project their characteristic way of relating to the world onto a vague, incomplete task where little structure is given. A person could, with no further instruction, be asked to draw a picture or tell a story. While interpretation of such tests is more subjective, there is enough research to allow practical use of such information. When used together, objective and projective techniques provide a broad sampling of a specified person's personality structure.

Vocational Assessment

In some cases, it is appropriate to measure a person's vocational interests and abilities. There are a number of ways to measure vocational areas, the most common being to have the person respond as to his/her degree of "interest" in a particular occupation. The person's responses are then compared to responses of people actually in those occupations. This theory of vocational adjustment assumes that the person will find greater satisfaction in a job that interests him or her.

Another way of measuring the vocational area is to have the person complete a self-guided task of discovering what his/her talents might be. The assumption here is that unless a person has a degree of talent in a particular area, he or she will be unable to attain job satisfaction, or perform well. The best approach is to use both assumptions which would result in information as to both talents and interests.

Ethical Considerations

Psychological assessment has come under increasing challenge in recent years. It has been accused of making predictions or statements that are not accurate, are misleading, or are culturally biased. The information is then shared, creating stigmas and discriminations because of the connotations of words or numbers. It is important in any type of testing that ethical considerations and protections be maintained. The American Psychological Association has published ethical guidelines for the use and dissemination of testing information. These restrictions protect the givers and takers of tests, assuring high quality and appropriate reporting.

Confidentiality
Of paramount importance is the issue of privacy of the person who takes the tests. The person should have the right and the understanding that none of his/her test data will be shared outside of the group of people who actually need to know that information. Any sharing of information outside of those evaluators is an invasion of that person's privacy. Consequently, no information should be disseminated in any way that would allow another person to associate the name of a participant in a test with his or her individual test scores. A person who is tested may sign a written release form allowing a report to be written, for example, to the personnel committee.

Training
The second important area is the training of the evaluators. Many tests are referred to as "restricted" psychological tests. That is to say, their use is restricted only to people who have training in psychological assessment. At no time should an inexperienced person be in any position to administer or evaluate a test. With some of the tests a person would need to be trained in order to provide the proper environment for the testing to take place. Needed training may be obtained from an expert, including the essentials of psychological assessment and ethical considerations. The trained person could then provide the proper environment for testing and insure ethical standards.

It is also important to note that most all tests used with missionaries are normed on standard American populations. Therefore, their predictability about cross-cultural performance is severely restricted. An evaluator who has a good working knowledge of cross-cultural issues can help to make the test more valid for this use, but care should still be taken.

Instrument Description and Analysis

In this section a brief description of several psychological tests will be given. These tests were chosen from the hundreds available because of their regular use, applicability, and general acceptance. The reason for including each test will be stated, and a statement about information obtainable will be presented. This in no way is an exhaustive description. It is only a sample overview to acquaint you with specific tests.

In general, the assessment of missionary candidates and appointees should include information on developmental background, family relationships, and a personal appraisal of problem areas. There should be an objective measure of personality characteristics. If the individual is married, an objective measure of the current marital and family relationship should be included. It is helpful to include a projective component to elicit the more vague, personal approaches to handling important areas of concern.

Test Descriptions

The *California Psychological Inventory, (CPI),* is a personality inventory developed for non-psychiatrically disturbed, or normal populations of people. It deals with personality characteristics important for social living and interaction. It is widely researched and has specific norms developed for a wide range of occupations or ethnic groups.

The *FIRO-B* assesses three fundamental interpersonal dimensions of behavior. The first is *inclusion* and is defined as the need to be involved and to interact with people in a satisfactory manner. The second is *control* and is defined as the need to establish a relationship with people in terms of control and power. The third is *affection* and is seen to be the maintenance of love in relationships with other people. Each dimension is measured in terms of what the individual expresses towards others and what the individual wants others to express toward him/herself. The test results provide a quick, yet rich index of a person's overall relationship to others.

The *Millon Clinical Multiaxial Inventory, (MCMI)* assesses behavioral dysfunctions and disorders in terms of both longstanding personality or character patterns and of more transient disorders. Eight basic personality scales reflect a person's relatively lifelong traits that existed prior to behavioral dysfunctioning. Three pathological personality syndrome scales describe chronic or severe abnormalities. Nine symptom disorder scales describe episodes or states in which an active pathological process is clearly evidenced. This test would be used primarily for rehabilitative purposes, as it is designed to describe problem areas. (Information on this test is taken from descriptive material published by the NCS Interpretive Scoring Systems.)

The *Minnesota Multiphasic Personality Inventory, (MMPI),* is a well researched instrument which identifies major personality characteristics that affect personal and social adjustment. The 550 items form numerous clusters which, when compared to various norm groups, indicate levels of functioning that are adequate or pathological. The MMPI has three validity scales which allow the interpreter to see how accurate the test is. In addition, there are special scales which are useful in looking at specific problem or strength areas. The MMPI has been used in cross-cultural contexts, thus developing norms for a number of other cultural settings. As a widely used test, the MMPI has been helpful in initial screening procedures.

The *Mooney Problem Checklist* asks an individual to indicate problems related to health, economic issues, security, self-improvement, personality, home and family, courtship, sex, religion, and occupation. The adult form lists 320 problems an adult would experience. The individual reads the list and marks those areas which currently bother him or her. Scores are given to each cluster of problems. Discussion with the individual about designated problem areas is thus facilitated.

The *Projective Figure Drawings* provide an unstructured component to testing. An individual is asked to draw several figures, one at a time. These tests are not used to check artistic ability, but to determine how the individual responds to directions in drawing objects in his/her environment. The unstructured nature provides clues about the person's ability to handle vague situations. Responses can be used to support or discount various hypotheses developed from other tests.

The *Sentence Completion Test* requires the person to respond to incomplete sentences on work-related subjects, personal issues, friendship, family, the future, and other areas. By looking at these responses, clues be found as to problem areas, one's general approach to life, and levels of dealing with conflict issues.

The *Shipley Institute of Living Scale,* sometimes referred to as the *Shipley-Hartford Scale,* is a widely used measure of intellectual ability and impairment. It consists of a vocabulary test and an abstract thinking test. Impairment is measured by the extent to which abstract thinking falls short of vocabulary. Its primary use is as an aid in detecting mild degrees of intellectual impairment in individuals of normal intelligence. It allows a fairly reliable test of intelligence as well as impairment.

The *Sixteen Personality Factor Test (16 PF),* was developed as a test of adult personality. It measures levels of assertiveness, emotional maturity, shrewdness, self-sufficiency, tension, and eleven other primary traits. This test can be used to aid in the selection, placement, and promotion of personnel or for advising individuals in treatment. It is one of the most widely used tests of normal adult personality. The test basically emphasizes individual strengths.

The *Strong-Campbell Interest Inventory (SCII)*, is a vocational interest survey recommended for people desiring to see how their interests coincide with the interests of other people in diverse occupations. Scores are provided on general occupational themes, basic interest scales, and occupational scales. The test describes a person's orientation to work, measures the strength or weakness of specific areas, and compares these results with specific occupations. SCII is useful in helping a person see where his/her interests are in comparison with the vocational interests of other people.

The *Taylor-Johnson Temperament Analysis (TJTA)*, is a well known personality inventory giving insight into nine bipolar personality traits which influence personal, social, scholastic and vocational functioning and adjustment. An individual responds to 180 items. Norms are based on general populations, college populations and other groups. One primary value of the TJTA is the "criss-cross" where one person completes the test on another person. This is particularly valuable in assessing marital relationships as spouse's responses can be compared.

Test Analysis and Report

A test battery is a group of tests chosen to evaluate several areas of a person's functioning. Test batteries usually include both objective and projective tests and measure intellectual, emotional, personality, and vocational functioning.

When a battery of tests is chosen to answer a particular series of questions, an analysis and report will provide an integrated comprehensive evaluation of the individuals current personality functioning. The report would include background information, observations made during testing, results and analysis of testing, and recommendations pertinent to the questions asked. It would describe the individual in more general personality terms as well as focus on specific strengths and weaknesses.

Some test reports may be brief, while others are lengthy. The number of tests administered and questions asked would determine the length. Attempting to tie together several sources of information requires considerable effort. A thorough report, therefore, will provide general observations, specific responses, and inferences based on the results. It is often the inferences drawn from the data that leads to specific recommendations.

8

Brent Lindquist

Misuses of Psychological Assessment with Missionaries

Psychological assessment services for missionary selection and training presents a number of exciting opportunities for service to world missions. Along with the opportunities, there is the potential for misuse, possible unethical application of psychological services. Examples of the misuse of psychological assessment, the different assumptions involved in selection versus assessment, and the "confounding" cross-cultural interaction effects are discussed. A tongue-in-cheek cookbook approach to misusing psychological assessment is presented as well.

Psychological assessment applied to missionary selection and training has gained increasing importance with mission boards over the past few years. While data is somewhat difficult to gather, a 1980 survey of EFMA Member Organizations revealed that 20% of the mission boards respondents felt psychological testing was a useful part of their candidacy assessment and evaluation process. That number probably will increase as more psychologists become aware of the opportunity for service to mission boards and missionaries and make their services available. This indeed is momentous because it allows psychologists to use their skills in an intimate and important way for the furthering of world missions. However, in the headlong rush to be of service, psychologists face a number of ethical dilemmas.

Link Care Center has provided psychological assessment services for missionaries and mission boards in various programs for over 10 years. As such, Link Care staff have tried to follow appropriate ethical requirements and has consulted with other psychologists for confirmation of procedures. Conversations with various mission board personnel have led to the discovery of a number of abuses in the psychological assessment of mission workers. This paper provides a brief discussion of these abuses.

The American Psychological Association manual, *Ethical Principles of Psychologists,* Principle 8, deals with assessment techniques:

In the development, publication, and utilization of psychological assessment techniques, psychologists make every effort to promote the welfare and best interests of the client. They guard against the misuse of assessment results. They respect the client's right to know the results, the interpretations made and the bases for their conclusions and recommendations. Psychologists make every effort to maintain the security of tests and other assessment techniques within limits of legal mandate. They strive to assure the appropriate use of assessment techniques by others.

The ethical violations observed probably are related to a lack of information on both sides, not due to a willful violation of the principle. Obviously, mission board members have a limited understanding of principles involved in the ethical practice of psychology. This lack of information is even more apparent concerning the issue of psychological assessment. Unfortunately, many people assume that a psychological test is much like a blood test. Few assessment tools, however, provide succinct information that can be taken at face value and interpreted literally with limited considerations of validity and reliability. Naive approaches to psychological assessment are detrimental because of the implications that result from this process.

Occasionally, mission board members report that they have employed a psychologist in the past but discontinued the service because they were dissatisfied with the results. The complaint might be that the psychologists had told them nothing new. They saw the method as a waste of money.

We need to evaluate our procedures to see if the assessment information is redundant or irrelevant.

A central issue contributing to misunderstanding or even ethical violation in psychological assessment is the issue of selection versus assessment. Using a psychological test as a selection instrument designed to discern whether a person should be a missionary or not illustrates potential abuse. This viewpoint disregards the importance of the call, letters of recommendation, and many cross-cultural considerations, all of which are necessary to make an appropriate determination.

A greater concern ethically is the use of "blind diagnosis." Psychologists who make recommendations based on detailed reports concerning missionary candidates whom they have never seen are violating APA Principle 8. As an example, a mission board sent overseas a person with multiple physical and emotional problems. Eventually this single selection error cost the mission board over $100,000 when salary, support costs, and planning time were considered. The mission executive asked why the psychologist did not discover problems prior to assignment. In talking with the executive about this missionary, it became apparent that a number of danger signals noted by the psychologist had been ignored, based on the limited testing that was done. Also, the person who had administered the tests in question had evaluated the tests without interviewing the candidate. Damaging results can come from such a procedure. Not only is this potentially damaging to the board and for the person, but it is also unethical. The client, in this case the missionary candidate, has the right to a full explanation of the nature and purpose of the assessment process. How those results might affect the person being evaluated also needs to be considered.

Link Care personnel frequently conduct assessments with candidates from its mission institute programs. Some come with a negative attitude toward psychology and psychological assessment because of previous experiences. Too often mission boards or psychological consultants have previously sent a test to the person who was evaluated without giving personal feedback. For example, one couple had been assessed three times yet had never heard any explanation of the results. They approached assessment, which potentially provides helpful information for them, with much ambivalence and suspicion. Their attitude changed after feedback. When they saw what the tests were, how they were used, the results, and how these would apply to their own daily living, this couple was much more open to understand the importance of psychological assessment. In providing such service to mission boards, our goal is that each person become aware of its benefits. Missionary personnel can learn to see the psychologist or counselor in a supportive rather than an adversary role and in case future problems cause them to need help, they will be aware of the place to get that help.

Doing "blind diagnosis" also is problematic because of the danger of false negatives and false positives. Without time spent personally with the missionary candidate, the psychologist will be unaware of the potential for alternative explanations or differing interpretations of the results. Psychologists typically find that interviews with candidates cause some of their original impressions to be moderated to some extent. The results must not be seen as cast in concrete. There must be dialogue with people. Their explanations must be heard.

This process adds a richness to the report that is generated. Such breadth of understanding would not be available without meeting the client. The "blind diagnosis" approach reduces the overall effectiveness of psychological assessment.

Finally, the importance of appropriate norms may be underplayed. Any testing of missionaries or missionary candidate populations must take into account the possible "confounding" effects of cross-cultural ministry. The psychologist must be careful that the norms used in interpreting the tests match the assessment subject. With the current tests in use, this may be impossible, unless specific norms are developed for missionaries. As an example, many healthy missionaries have elevated (70+) Sc scores on the MMPI. What is the proper interpretation? A rigid and simplistic interpretation would indicate that all are schizophrenic. A more reasonable alternative explanation is that they show an unusual level of creativity and enhanced abstraction.

A limited number of abuses or potential abuses of psychological assessment with missionaries have been considered. Behavioral scientists and assessment specialists are encouraged to examine their methods, and bring them in harmony with established ethical practice and the needs of the missions program.

Summary

A tongue-in-cheek expression of the way to violate principles when applying psychological assessment processes with missionary populations would be:

1. See psychological assessment as providing clear-cut criteria for deciding who will and who will not do well in a missionary assignment.

2. Teach mission board personnel cookbook procedures for administering and interpreting psychological tests.

3. Do not be concerned about reliability, validity or the appropriateness of normative samples for the missionary populations.

4. Conduct blind assessments of missionaries and missionary candidates: Do not let your objectivity be compromised by any contacts with those being assessed.

5. Avoid any feedback to the missionaries being assessed about the results of the assessment process. Keep the missionaries in the dark about how their test data is used.

6. Do not conduct any research to evaluate the long-term predictions implied by your assessment reports.

7. Carefully cultivate your image as an expert by not indicating the difficulties in prediction across cultural boundaries.

8. Be very open to any who ask, especially church mission committees or friends, about information regarding the candidates being assessed. After all, if we are all in the family of God, release of information forms are irrelevant.

9. Stick to the basic tests, regardless of their uselessness. If they are good enough for the good old USA, then they are good enough for anywhere.

10. Don't bother with follow-up. Who wants to find out if they were wrong?

References

Ethical principles of psychologists. (1981). *American Psychologist, 36*, 633-638.

MISSIONARY EFFECTIVENESS

9

Phil Parshall

How Spiritual Are Missionaries?

Spirituality is an abstraction subject to many definitions. Can one ever be declared to be a spiritual person? Is spirituality being, or doing, or both? What mix of the active and passive is most pleasing to God?

It would seem impossible to construct a generally accepted "Spirituality Scale." Yet, while interacting with many missionaries, I have found that they share trials, struggles, and spiritual aspirations.

To test my theory on a wider scale, I sent a questionnaire to 800 missionaries. Undoubtedly, the range and depth of issues covered will not satisfy everyone. But I do hope to pry open a veil of secrecy and allow a fresh wind of frank openness to blow among us. As one respondent observed, "A study of missionary spirituality is in order and overdue."

From 32 countries, 390 missionaries serving with 37 different mission societies returned the completed questionnaire--a 49 percent response, unusually high for a survey. The great majority of the respondents are affiliated with member missions of the Evangelical Foreign Missions Association and the Interdenominational Foreign Missions Association.

Prayer and Bible Reading

Two hundred and fifty-seven missionaries cited mind wandering during prayer as a frequent occurrence (1). Only one respondent stated this never happened to him.

How much time do missionaries actually spend in prayer (25)? Eleven percent pray less than an average of five minutes a day, while 60 percent pray between 11 and 30 minutes daily.

The reading of the Word of God is a "joy" to 92 percent (2). The majority are New Testament oriented in their reading (3). Only 19 percent use a commentary with any regularity (4).

Seventy percent spend between 11 and 30 minutes daily in reading the Bible (27). Twelve percent exceed the 30-minute mark.

Seventy-six percent of the married missionaries have family devotions on a sustained basis (5). Yet, 24 percent infrequently or never pray together as a family.

One hundred and eighteen respondents identified the problem of maintaining a systematic devotional time as their greatest spiritual struggle (30). No other problem in the Christian life even came close to this one.

Present and Future

Some missionaries grapple deeply with the question, "How can an all-powerful God who is good and just allow people to suffer?" Yet other missionaries can, with apparent ease, shrug off any discussion of the subject with a statement like, "It's all a mystery. There is no sense trying to comprehend the complexities of life."

In the survey, 30 percent stated they never questioned God regarding evil and suffering (6). This, however, leaves 70 percent who do engage in some measure of introspection on the subject. It may seem contradictory that over 90 percent of the respondents have absolute assurance of eternal life (7), while 42 percent stated that at times, they are "afraid to die" (8). Probably, this group is commenting on the process of dying rather than the fact of death. Married women under 40 have the highest degree (97 percent) of assurance of eternal life and at the same time the top level (58 percent) of the fear of dying. However, this anxiety is not obsessive, as most of these respondents marked "infrequent" as their response rather than "always."

A rather surprising eschatological insight relates to 22 percent who indicate that the return of Christ is less than a dynamic reality to them (9).

Mission Relationships

"Do you ever feel you would like to be something other than a missionary?" (10). It seems this sentiment affects, to some degree, 64 percent of the missionaries. This statistic reinforces the professional ambivalence I often find in confidential talks with my peers.

An overwhelming 97 percent stated they are pleased with the policies of their mission board (11). This is a high commendation.

Many boards make it possible for their missionaries to study while on furlough. Seventy percent indicated that they have some interest in doing so (12).

Among missionaries, deputation is frequently criticized. Thousands of miles to drive, messages to repeat ad nauseum, hands to shake ad infinitum, and support raising nightmares all combine to make "hitting the circuit" one of the least liked parts of missionary life. Thus, it was no surprise to note that 85 percent of the respondents had some reservation about deputation (13). Unexpectedly, 14 percent said they always enjoyed it.

Reading

Magazines most read are (31):	Number of respondents:
Time	84
Moody Monthly	78
Christianity Today	72
Reader's Digest	56
Newsweek	53
Evangelical Missions Quarterly	52

Fifty-three percent do not read any secular books in a one-month period of time (32) In regard to Christian books, the picture is somewhat brighter. Forty-four percent read one book a month (33). However, 21 percent read none.

Theological Fidelity

Is there such a thing as a "closet agnostic" evangelical missionary? Possibly not, but there certainly are a significant number of missionaries who are troubled by doubts about their mission's doctrinal statement. I have talked to missionaries who have questioned the basic tenets of the Christian faith. They are sincerely perplexed about the dividing line between hypocrisy and integrity. When do doubts become convictions? How can one suddenly give up all one has lived for in regard to mission, supporters, and life's work? Most will never even broach the subject with their mission leadership for fear of becoming the object of critical scrutiny.

My questionnaire provided an opportunity for some missionaries to respond to this issue in an anonymous forum. Thirty-nine percent of all respondents indicated some problem with "intellectual doubts about Christianity" (14). Another parallel question was, "Do you ever feel you are preaching a message you don't fully believe?" (15). Thirty-one percent answered "infrequently," and 4 percent indicated "frequently."

Biblical inerrancy is a controversial issue in some circles. Three questions (34-36) probe this matter. The first question was, "Do you understand the doctrine of inerrancy?" Ninety-seven percent answered in the affirmative. Some of the responses were fiesty. "You've got to be kidding!"; "What is inerrancy?"; and "Mostly fruitless babble."

"Do you fully subscribe to inerrancy?" This question was affirmed by 358 and denied by 15.

The most provocative response came from the following question: "If you subscribe to inerrancy and came to doubt it, would you inform your mission leadership and colleagues?" Thirty-five did not answer the question. Fifteen said no. Then a fairly large group of 70 expressed some reservation about whether they would share this doubt with their fellow missionaries. Comments included, "Not unless asked, I suppose"; "I would reveal it only to thinking colleagues"; "Yes, but not immediately"; "I should"; and "If I were to doubt it, what point would there be in living?"

Their answers must be seen in light of the fact that almost all of them are members of missions which require a clear and strong commitment to inerrancy. Therefore, it would seem appropriate for missions to encourage non-threatening discussions on doctrinal issues like inerrancy.

Depression

Emotional breakdowns have been the cause of many missionaries leaving the field. In the survey, a very large majority of 276 missionaries indicated they experience discouragement (16).

"Is frustration a part of your life?" (17). The affirmative response to this question soared to 99 percent. It is therefore not surprising to find 124 missionaries who are very often emotionally tense and another 248 who experience tension on an occasional basis (18). This represents 97 percent of the respondents who are forced to deal with tension as an integral part of their lives.

Seventy-seven missionaries (20 percent) have taken tranquilizers at some time since becoming a missionary (37). Alcohol may or may not be utilized as a relaxant. Twenty-six percent stated that they drink occasionally (35). Fifty-four percent of the unmarried women under 40 drink alcoholic beverages.

Holiness

It is no easy task to define a holy life. I have chosen only a few areas for investigation, while acknowledging that there are many other important facets of spirituality.

Anger is an occasional problem to 71 percent of the respondents, while 17 percent placed it in the frequent category (19). This comes to a rather unexpected total of 88 percent. I wonder if the high tension level experienced by missionaries does not help explain their anger.

Forty-four percent stated that pride is a "significant spiritual battle" (20). Another 53 percent indicated "infrequently" in the response. One can only speculate about whether these responses tell us more about missionary pride or about missionary humility.

Missionaries apparently get along well. Eighteen percent stated that they always "love their missionary colleagues," while 79 percent indicated "frequently" (21). Ninety-seven percent find it easy to forgive missionaries who have offended them (22). In recent years, I have visited a number of Third World countries and often I have found serious church-mission tensions. Therefore, I was particularly interested in obtaining the missionary perspective on relationships with nationals. One hundred and one respondents "always" are able to love national Christians (23). Another 276 find no problem in this area. This represents 97 percent of all who responded.

Sexual temptation is an ongoing battle for a large number of the respondents. Five questions were asked which directly related to this subject (24-27, 39).

Women and men were about even in answering "infrequently" to the question about lust, as well as attending R-rated movies. More women occasionally read sexually stimulating literature than do men. The 10 missionaries who have not remained sexually moral since becoming missionaries are equally divided between men and women. The question was asked, "What is the greatest spiritual struggle in your life?" (30). "Lust" came in third after (1) maintaining a successful devotional time, and (2) having spiritual victory.

	Frequently	Infrequently	Never
Do you have sexual fantasies of lust?	57	215	112
Do you read sexually stimulating literature?	4	127	268
Do you attend R rated movies?	1	61	322
Do you attend X rated movies?	0	12	375
Have you remained sexually moral since becoming a missionary?		YES: 372	NO: 10

Sex is seldom dealt with in pre-field orientation. This is a mistake. We live in a promiscuous society that flaunts pre- and extra-marital sex as an easily available and desirable experience. Awareness is the first step toward deterrence. Missions should alert their missionaries to the danger signs of deviant sexual behavior. Support and accountability should be a normal function of fellow believers.

The Charismatic Experience
How sad to see divisions among Christians emerge out of controversies over sanctification. The very thing that is purported to make us more humble, gracious, sensitive, and godly has ended up splitting Christians into "haves" and "have nots."

Twenty-four percent of the respondents stated that they have had a charismatic type experience (40). In looking through the breakdown of the survey, I was surprised to find the 24 percent ratio holds almost constant for each group: age, sex, etc. This fact undercuts some of the stereotypes about who is more prone to be a charismatic.

A more specific question asked was, "Have you ever spoken in tongues?" (41). Only 17 percent said yes, thus indicating that 7 percent of those who stated that they have had a charismatic-type experience have not actually spoken in tongues. This bears out the general confusion about the meaning of "charismatic."

Another related question was, "Do you feel post-salvation sanctification experiences can be biblically valid?" (42). A large majority of 86 percent answered in the affirmative. At least this forms some basis for common ground among missionaries. If we can calmly accept a pluralistic view on this subject, and refrain from offensive propagation of any one particular view, I'm sure the body of believers will be spiritually strengthened.

Reflections

Are missionaries spiritual? The question should cause not a small amount of probing and introspection. Perhaps it is time to have field seminars on the subject. Often a close frind or colleague can be a catalyst between us and the Lord. Group dynamics can be a sensitive method for team interaction.

Missionaries are sensing needs in their times of prayer and Bible study. Annual spiritual life retreats should be scheduled that are not encumbered with business agendas. Missions may want to consider the appointment of a field chaplain, whose only task is to minister to missionaries. Such a person could be shared among several smaller missions.

Tension and depression continue to be major problems. Mission leaders should seek to alleviate continuous pressure points. Regular vacations and changes in routine are vital.

This survey indicates intellectual stagnation on the part of many. Reading programs, team seminars, and furlough study should all be incorporated into the normal flow of missionary life. Busyness should never be allowed to become an excuse for the neglect of one's personal growth.

In the Evangelical Dictionary of Theology, spirituality is defined as "the state of a deep relationship with God." This must be our goal, if we are to make our ministries fruitful and abiding.

Questionnaire on Missionary Spirituality

[The first 27 questions were answered in terms of four categories: *Always Frequently, Infrequently Never* --The editors.]

1. Does your mind wander when you pray?
2. Is Bible reading a joy?
3. Is your Bible reading New Testament oriented?
4. Do you use a commentary as you read the Bible?
5. If married, do you have family devotions together?
6. Do you question God regarding evil and suffering?
7. Do you have absolute assurance of eternal life with Christ?
8. Are you afraid to die?
9. Is Christ's return a dynamic reality to you?
10. Do you ever feel you would like to be something other than a missionary?
11. Are you happy with the policies of your mission board?
12. Do you ever wish you had more academic degrees?
13. Do you enjoy deputation?
14. Do you have intellectual doubts about Christianity?

15. Do you ever feel you are preaching a message you don't fully believe?

16. Are you ever discouraged about life?

17. Is frustration a part of your life?

18. Are you ever emotionally tense?

19. Is anger a problem to you?

20. Is pride a problem to you?

21. Do you love your missionary colleagues?

22. Can you forgive missionaries who have hurt you?

23. Do you love national Christians on the mission field?

24. Do you have sexual fantasies of lust?

25. Do you read sexually stimulating literature?

26. Do you attend R-rated movies?

27. Do you attend X-rated movies?

28. On an average, how much time do you spend in prayer each day?

29. On an average, how much time do you spend reading the Bible each day?

30. What is your greatest spiritual struggle in life?

31. What magazines do you read regularly?

32. How many secular books do you read each month?

33. How many Christian-type books do you read each month?

34. Do you understand the doctrine of inerrancy?

35. Do you fully subscribe to inerrancy?

36. If you subscribed to inerrancy and came to doubt it, would you inform your mission leadership and colleagues?

37. Have you taken tranquilizers since becoming a missionary?

38. Do you drink alcoholic beverages?

39. Have you remained sexually moral since becoming a missionary?

40. Have you had a charismatic-type experience?

41. Have you ever spoken in tongues?

42. Do you feel post-salvation sanctification experiences can be biblically valid?

10

Charles B. Cureton

Missionary Fit: A Criterion-Related Model

Missionary-sending agencies are becoming concerned about missionary attrition. Thus, there is an urgent need to develop a strategy for identifying the antecedents to successful missionary service. Forty-four participants, attending the National Conference on Mental Health and Missions, formed three groups for the present study. Mental health professionals, missionary leaders, and professionals with missionary personnel experience were measured on three criteria for the task of identifying a successful missionary: A job-function analysis, a value-orientation scale, and a personality checklist. The three groups were significantly alike in their perceptions, thereby permitting the development of a statistical model representative of all participants. Slight statistical variances which did exist among and within the three groups suggest that missionary organizations should seriously consider developing their own statistical model for identifying and selecting successful missionaries.

The antecedents to success in overseas missionary service seem to vary in accordance with the particular researcher and the nature of the research being conducted. Recent literature on this subject reveals considerable agreement that is gaining acknowledgement by researchers in cross-cultural studies. For example, among the many psychological tests and projective techniques presently being used there is a marked deficit in criterion-selected assessment for the selection of successful missionaries (Williams & Kliewer, 1979). Norm-referenced evaluations based on clinical instruments seldom represent the uniqueness of a sending-agency and what is required for success on a given missionary field. Thus, it would seem that an effort should be made to fit the missionary personality and make-up with the ethos of a specific country and thereby reduce the socio-cultural antecedents that generate psychopathology (Rommen, Note 3). Antecedents to cross-cultural and missionary effectiveness have been studied through criterion research, but these studies are few (Williams, 1973); Tucker, Benson & Blanchard, 1978; Hawes & Kealy, 1979; Britt, 1980). Thus, clearly identifiable relationships between missionary selection profiles and later on-the-job performance have yet to be satisfactorily established.

Criterion-related validity refers to the effectiveness of a test in predicting an individual's behavior in specified situations (Anastasi, 1982). This is done by comparing performance on the test with an independent measure of validity, that is a criterion. For several years the prevalent opinion in personnel psychology was that selection tests should undergo full scale validation against local criteria of on-the-job performance. Specific procedures for such criterion-related validation would include (a) conducting a job analysis for identifying the major job elements and specifying the corresponding skills, knowledge, values, perceptions, and personality required by the job; (b) selecting or constructing a test to assess these characteristics; (c) correlating the test with appropriate criteria of job performance; and (d) formulating a strategy for personnel decisions (Anastasi, 1982).

This approach is contrasted to the clinical approach of missionary assessment which is typically a norm-referenced evaluation. McClellan (cited in Goleman, 1981) concludes that our goal should be to match the right people to the right jobs. Competencies are defined not only as aspects of a given job but as specific characteristics of people who actually do the job. For example, if one wants to find out who will be an effective missionary, it is necessary to first determine what it is an "effective" missionary does. This implies the need for criterion-related research in any organization to assure more consistent hiring practice. The "fit" between the configuration of the mission board administrators' values, perceptions, and personality characteristics is essential. According to Tucker et al. (1978) and Hawes and Kealy (1979) criterion-related research seems to be the only reasonable approach to identifying the success levels of overseas personnel in cross-cultural adjustment.

Selection practices have become sophisticated managerial tools which attempt to discover potential personnel capable of entering an organization and successfully accomplish a given task. Regardless of the entry level, the potential missionary should be screened concerning three major areas: (a) *Skills Competence*. Can the missionary do the job? Does the missionary have the several kinds of knowledge required, the cognitive skills? Does the missionary have the necessary physical abilities, psychomotor skills? Does the missionary have the necessary background, the experiential skills? (b) *Personality Characteristics*. Does the missionary have the type of personality characteristics desired by the sending agency? Regarding attitude, are the missionary's perceptions similar to those of the sending agency? Regarding behavior, does the missionary act as expected? (c) *Interpersonal Skills*. Will the missionary fit into the organizational environment at home and on the field? In terms of horizontal relationships, will the missionary interact as expected with other missionaries on a given field? In terms of vertical relationships, will the missionary interact effectively with higher and lower level personnel within the organization on a given field?

At every level and for every position, emphases upon these areas are adjusted. Within every level, requirements within these areas are adjusted. Typically, a mission agency determines the suitability or accuracy of its selection practices through an examination of the reasons for attrition of its missionaries. Whatever the reasons for a missionary's departure, a termination may be an indication of inadequacies in the organization's selection procedures. Concern for attrition is reflected in some mission organizations by a probationary period for every new missionary.

Missionary early return, push-out, and rehabilitation needs are becoming more evident (Lindquist & Lindquist, Note 2). North American Protestant overseas missionary personnel in 1980 numbered approximately 35,000, and an estimated 3,500 new missionaries begin overseas assignments each year. Even though the estimated early return rate among missionary organizations is not published, Tucker et al. (1978) found that of all overseas employees (non-missionaries) 33% returned within the first year. If only 15% of long-term missionaries fail to complete a first term or less, the financial cost to the cooperative sending agencies and the damage being experienced by early returning missionaries, their families, supporting constituents, and nationals being served is overwhelming (Lindquist, 1982).

Mental health professionals and missionary-sending agencies cooperatively are attempting to identify the antecedents to successful missionary service. These two professional groups are commissioned to the task of identifying a "fit" between mission board administrators and missionary candidates. The primary concern in identifying successful missionaries is how to use effectively the knowledge and insights of both groups. Yet because of their professional orientations, they could have incompatible notions of what constitutes an appropriate model of success.

Rare indeed is the opportunity to unite a group of mental health professionals who are uniquely interested in identifying the antecedents to successful missionary service with a group of missionary leaders from major evangelical sending agencies throughout the United States. Such an aggregate, though, attended a national conference in Angola, Indiana, on a theme of "Mental Health and Missions." They consented to participate in a workshop on identifying criteria for missionary success abroad. The purpose of the workshop was to determine if a fit could be identified by way of a statistical model utilizing the perceptions of both mental health professionals and missionary leaders. The workshop, thus, emphasized model development, not model validity. Three specific questions were proposed: (a) Do mental health professionals and missionary leaders agree on some particulars concerning successful missionary service? (b) Is the extent of agreement among the groups sufficient for one statistical model to represent perceptions of all groups? (c) What are the implications of these areas of agreement, if they exist?

The Workshop

Forty-four subjects took part in the workshop. A three-group design was used in an ex post facto quasi-experimental manner to analyze the information gleaned from their participation. Participants were not randomly selected; thus, the project could not be strictly considered a laboratory experiment. The three groups consisted of mental health professionals ($n=16$), missionary personnel ($n=18$), and mental health professionals with missionary personnel experience ($n=10$).

Three instruments were used to describe the skills competence, personality characteristics, and interpersonal skills of hypothetical successful missionaries. The Scales of Worker Functions (Fine, 1973) was used to provide a comparison of the three groups' descriptions of minimal job performance in the following areas: "People," "data," "things," "mathematics," "language," and "reasoning." These scales are an adaption of The Functional Job Analysis Scales (Fine, 1973) which were originally developed for the US Employment Service from 1950-1955.

The Successful Employment Profile (SEP; Cureton & Hoskins, Note 1) was used to compare the three groups' rankings of 27 personal and demographic traits necessary for successful missionary service. This instrument requires a rating of the relative importance of each trait on a five-point Likert-type scale from "very little" to "very much" importance. It also allows for subjects to order the traits from 1, "most important for successful employment," to 27, "least important."

The Osgood Semantic Differential (Osgood, Suci & Tannebaum, 1957) was used to compare the groups' perceptions of 20 paired, polar adjectives with respect to their usefulness in differentiating successful and unsuccessful missionaries' interpersonal characteristics. Each adjective pair was rated by subjects on a seven-point scale. The 20 pairs were completed once regarding a hypothetical successful missionary and then again regarding a hypothetical unsuccessful missionary.

The Participants' Responses

The three groups' descriptions on the Scales of Worker Functions were identical. This suggests that mental health workers, missionary workers, and mental health workers with missionary personnel experience agree about the kind of competence skills essential for a successful missionary.

The correlations of the groups' rankings of the 27 SEP traits were all .90 or higher and were significant ($p < .01$). The groups' rankings of the traits are shown in Table 1. The level of correlation in the groups' rankings implies a high degree of congruence as to the perceived importance of the traits. All three groups independently said that the ability to display behavior usual and expected for one's own chronological age as well as a serenity of mind and stability of feelings in problem-solving are most important criteria for missionary success. They agreed that a missionary, in order to be successful, must desire to understand and be understood by others, be sensitive to the needs of others, must be willing to conform to the changing patterns of a society, and even move to another geographical area. Even though 80% of the variance in each of the groups' scores on the SEP may be accounted for by the intergroup correlations, there was a significant difference in the groups' ratings of certain factors, such as a liberal arts orientation including studies in language, philosophy, history, literature, and the abstract sciences, as well as their ratings of community involvement preceding overseas services.

Table 1
Successful Employment Profile Rankings

Factor Traits	Ordered Rankings		
	Group 1	Group 2	Group 3
Physical Stamina	6	6	7
Extra-Curricular Activity	17	13	17
Academic Accomplishment	12	11	12
Emotional Maturity	1	1	1
Hand-Eye Coordination Skills	21	17	20
Physical Appearance	18	15	22
Letters of Recommendation	8	9	8
Rating Scales	10	8	10
Punctuality	15	20	16
Related Work Experience	5	7	6
Non-Related Experience	16	12	18
Willingness to Relate to Others	2	2	2
Flexibility	3	3	3
Marital Status	20	25	23
Chronological Age	23	23	21
Associate in Arts Degree	26	22	25
Bachelor Degree or Higher	19	14	11
Physical Dimensions	27	26	26
Written Communication Skills	9	10	9
Spoken Communication Skills	4	5	5
Expressed Interest in Job	7	4	4
Standardized Test Scores	13	18	13
Liberal Arts Orientation	22	19	14
Double Academic Concentration	25	24	24
Community Involvement	11	21	15
Family Background	14	16	19
Athletic Skills	24	27	27

Utilizing a series of *t*-tests, it was found that all three groups identified 18 of the 20 paired adjectives on the semantic differential as significantly ($p < .05$) differentiating between hypothetical successful and unsuccessful missionaries. These 18 pairs were "active-passive," "approach-avoid," "fresh-stale," "interesting-boring," "open-closed," "progressive-traditional," "genuine-false," "pleasurable-painful," "original-stereotyped," "understandable-mysterious," "graceful-awkward," "free-constrained," "complete-incomplete," "deep-shallow," "flexible-rigid," "accepting-rejecting," "predictable-unpredictable," and "systematic-unsystematic." All three groups were also in agreement that the "tough-tender" and "structured-unstructured" pairs were not significant in this regard.

The Model

The similarity of the three groups in their responses to the SEP and the semantic-differential permitted the creation of a statistical model to represent the perceptions of all three groups. The model represents a standardization of both the SEP and semantic differential scores for the groups, thus providing a matrix for defining the hypothetical relationship between a potential missionary's qualifications/characteristics and a missions organization's expectations. Interpretation of such a model may give direction to the selection task so that individual and group strengths and needs may be identified and matched efficiently. This 3x3 contingency model appears in Figure 1.

Agreement Regarding Personal Characteristics
and Demographics (SEP)

		High		*Low*
Agreement Regarding	*High*	cell 1	cell 2	cell 3
Interpersonal Characteristics		cell 4	cell 5	cell 6
(Semantic Differential)	*Low*	cell 7	cell 8	cell 9

Figure 1. A contingency model defining the hypothetical relationship between a potential missionary's qualifications/characteristics and a mission agency's expectations.

In the model, Cell 1 may be interpreted to represent that missionary candidate population whose conception of personal and demographic traits necessary for missionary service is most consistent with that of the mission agency, and whose evaluation of interpersonal characteristics necessary for successful missionary service is likewise consistent with the mission agency's. Cell 2 includes those candidates who agree marginally with the sending agency regarding personal factors but agree highly with respect to interpersonal factors. Cell 3 includes candidates who agree the least with the agency's conception of personal factors but the most with their perspective on interpersonal factors. Cell 4 represents candidate-agency agreement that is high regarding personal factors and marginal regarding interpersonal factors, while Cell 5 represents marginal agreement in both domains. Cell 6 indicates a candidate population agreeing minimally on interpersonal factors. Cell 7 indicates minimal candidate-agency agreement regarding the interpersonal dimension but high agreement on the personal dimension. Cell 8 represents low agreement in the interpersonal realm and marginal agreement in the personal, and Cell 9 represents low agreement in both personal and interpersonal realms.

Summary

The research results suggest significant agreement among all three groups as to what constitutes a "successful" missionary. They independently were able to agree on the minimal job performance skills required for the target person. A typical successful missionary is able to minimally perform the following functions: (a) To influence others in favor of a point of view by verbal communications and by demonstrations; (b) to gather, collate, and classify information about data, people, and things; (c) to start, stop, control, and adjust various machines and equipment designed to help them accomplish their task (this would involve setting up and adjusting the machine as work progresses as well as controlling the equipment which involves monitoring gauges, dials, and turning of valves); (d) to make arithmetic calculations involving fractions, decimals, and percentages; (e) to use language effectively in writing routine business correspondence, understanding technical manuals and verbal instructions, interviewing applicants to determine the work best suited for their abilities and experiences, and conducting some opinion research surveys involving stratified samples of a population; and (f) to devise a system of interrelated procedures applicable to solving practical everyday problems and dealing with a variety of concrete variables and situations where only limited standardization exists.

The participants were independently similar in suggesting the personal and demographic traits that a missionary must have in order to be successful, and they were able to statistically agree on the interpersonal factors that are most important and those that are the least important in assisting the missionary to adjust and function effectively within an overseas culture.

Since the profiles for the three groups were very similar when being compared on the job functional analysis, SEP, and semantic differential, a model representing all three groups was developed. A major function of criterion research has been achieved. The criteria for a missionary "fit" have been identified. But, on the other hand, when calculating the perceptions of the participants within the three groups there was some noticeable variance. Thus, if a model were developed for each of the three groups the models woud differ somewhat in identifying the successful missionary. In such a case, "fit" between the new missionary and the specific group would be even more precise than has been achieved in the present situation.

In conclusion, the implications of this workshop are clear: (a) Mental health professionals and missionary leaders can function well in cooperatively identifying the antecedents of potentially successful missionary service. (b) Three statistical models should be developed based upon the data collected in this study and validated concurrently using missionaries who are already experiencing varying levels of success on the mission field. (c) The more specific and unique a particular missionary organization, the greater the need for this organization to identify its own successful missionaries through this procedure or a similar one and validate the "fit" with new missionaries. (d) The more unique a mission agency is, the less dependent it should become upon general notions of success which so seldom represent its unique and individualized missionary program.

Notes

1. Cureton, C., & Hoskins, D. *Successful Employment Profile, Form A: A rating scale of factors-traits for potential salaried employees*, 1976. (Available from Charles B. Cureton, EdD, Malone College, 515-25th Street, Northwest, Canton, Ohio 44709.)

2. Lindquist, S., & Lindquist, B. *Missionary family restoration for early returnees.* Paper presented at the Mental Health and Missions Conference, Pokagan State Park, Indiana, 1982.

3. Rommen, E. *Cultural stress as a source of psychological distress among missionaries.* A paper based upon *Familial and socio-cultural antecedents of psychopathology* by Victor Sinua, 1981.

References

Anastasi, A. (1982). *Psychological testing.* New York: Collier.

Britt, W.G. (1980). The prediction of missionary success overseas using pretraining variables (Doctoral dissertation, Rosemead Graduate School of Professional Psychology). *Dissertation Abstracts International*, 1981, *42*, 1162B-1163B. (University Microfilms No. 8118192)

Fine, S.A. (1973). *Functional job analysis scales.* Washington, DC: Upjohn Institute.

Goleman, D. (1981). The new competency tests: Matching the right people to the right jobs. *Psychology Today*, January.

Hawes, F., & Kealy, D.J. (1979). *Canadians in development: An empirical study of adaptation and effectiveness on overseas assignment.* Communications Branch Briefing Centre, Government of Canada.

Lindquist, S.E. (1982). Prediction of success in overseas adjustment. *Journal of Psychology and Christianity, 1,* 22-25.

Osgood, C.E., Suci, G.J., & Tannebaum, P.H. (1957). *The measurement of meaning.* Urbana, IL: University of Illinois.

Tucker, M.F., Benson, P.G., & Blanchard, F. (1978). *The development and longitudinal validation of the Navy Overseas Assignment Inventory.* Task Order 77/95/D, U.S. Navy Contract #N00600-73-0780.

Williams, D., & Kliewer, D. (1979). *Perspectives on psychological assessment of candidates for cross-cultural Christian missions.* Fresno, CA: Link Care Center.

Williams, K.L. (1973). Characteristics of the more successful and less successful missionaries (Doctoral dissertation, United States International University). *Dissertation Abstracts International*, 1973, *34*, 1786B-1787B. (University Microfilms No. 73-22, 697)

11

William Gordon Britt, III

Pretraining Variables in the Prediction of Missionary Success Overseas

A set of twelve variables was obtained in order to predict missionary success from a combination of pretraining data which included elements of personality, interpersonal skill, attitudes, and biographical information. This data was gathered from structured interviews, open-ended references, and psychological tests available from each subject's application file. A screening sample of 111 vocational missionaries who had served overseas a minimum of one year was used to derive the predictors, and a calibration sample of 42 missionaries with the same qualifications was used for cross-validation purposes. The twelve significant variables selected accounted for 56 percent of the variance of the criterion (success). Cross-validation yielded mixed results.

Over the years a number of problems have surfaced for organizations which select individuals to serve in an overseas capacity. A major difficulty has been the lack of knowledge as to exactly what areas to focus on in the person's background and personality which might give clues to future successful performance. Tucker (1974), after surveying the literature from 1960 to 1972, concluded that problems Americans have in adjusting overseas are of such a magnitude as to warrant strong efforts to improve selection procedures.

Missionary adjustment overseas has been plagued with these

difficulties also. Williams (1973) identified (a) mental health and (b) failure to adjust, as accounting for over 30 percent of the missionary resignations by one large mission board. The cost in terms of inferior work, relationship with nationals, and the missionaries' own sense of failure is enormous.

A renewed interest in missions suggested by attendance in recent years at the Urbana Conference at the University of Illinois suggests a large number of young Christians are seriously considering becoming missionaries and will be making application to mission agencies in the next few years. These mission agencies could be faced with more applicants than they can process by present methods. The need is for a method of predicting success overseas before the applicant is accepted for training.

The question addressed in the present study was "Are there pretraining variables which will differentiate between those judged most successful and least successful among overseas field staff?"

In dealing with the development of selection procedures, it was important to find the best tools for gathering the needed data. Gordon (1967) found that psychometric assessment predicted as well as or better than clinical interviews. In fact, Duhl (1964) and Fisher, Epstein and Harris (1967) found that psychiatric interviews had very little predictive value. According to Gunderson and Kapfer (1966) however, when both psychologists and psychiatrists were given biological information on the subject and a rating scale of personality traits, clinical prediction did become significant.

Wright (1969) discovered that structured interviews are more reliable than unstructured ones, while Browning (1968) found open-ended questionnaire-type references had better predictive validity. The most recent findings have revealed that a combination of tools, including biographical information, psychological assessment, letters of reference, and interviews provide the best set of predictors, and that pretraining assessment using these tools is as valid as any other method examined (Doll, Gunderson, & Ryman, 1969; Dicken, 1969).

The problem of developing a criterion of success has been discussed by Peter and Henry (1962), who also suggest a combination of tools be used, including supervisor ratings, the individual's self-appraisal, and objective measures of performance. Horowitz, Inouye, and Siegelman (1979) found that using multiple judges and averaging the ratings yielded higher reliabilities.

A major task has been to determine what data should be used as predictor variables. Williams (1973) found age and family size at entrance, college grade point average, self-reports of mood swings, anxiety, and depression significantly differentiated success groups. Birth order and father absence have been found to be significant predictors in Peace Corps studies by Suedfeld (1967), Dohrenwend (1966), and Exner and Sutton-Smith (1970). Guynes (1975), Hare (1966), Uhes and Shybut (1971), Wright, Sisler and Chylinksi (1963), Harris (1973), and Guthrie and Zektick (1967) all discovered that psychological tests and other rating measures positively correlated with success. Kennedy and Dreger (1974) even discovered that they could develop a measure for a specific culture using nationals as raters, and then determine significant predictor variables.

The consensus of the literature seems to justify the use of a combination of data from which to derive a set of predictor variables.

Method

Subjects

The study utilized both a screening sample of 111 subjects from which the predictors were derived and a calibration sample of 42 for cross-validation purposes. The subjects consisted of male and female overseas field staff of the Agape Movement of Campus Crusade for Christ. These subjects were engaged in both vocational service and Christian ministry service consisting primarily of evangelism and discipleship. The screening sample comprised the whole population of the Agape Movement who had served a minimum of one year overseas. The calibration sample served their year overseas during the course of the study and were rated at the completion of that requirement. All pretraining data used in the study was gathered from the application files of these subjects.

Design and Procedure

The design of the study was correlational in nature since the relationship between predictor variables and success was being measured. Stepwise Linear Multiple Regression Analysis was used to determine how much of the variance of the criterion (success) was accounted for by the best linear combination of independent variables.

The dependent variable was the criterion measure, and was identified via a success inventory which was adapted from a rating system used by the Agape Movement. Success was divided into personal, emotional, social and spiritual maturity. Seven raters were used for the screening sample, consisting of four continental Directors of Affairs, who only rated the subjects reporting to them on their respective continents, and three raters from the headquarters of the Agape Movement. They consisted of the International Director, the Personnel Director, and a File Rater. The first two raters rated the subjects based on their firsthand knowledge of them, while the File Rater systematically read the monthly self-reports from each subject and rated them using the Success Inventory. The ratings were then averaged to yield a single score for each subject, whether Most Successful -- Group 4, Moderately Successful -- Group 3, Less Successful -- Group 2, or Least Successful -- Group 1. Interrater reliability was estimated by correlations.

The same procedure was followed for the calibration sample, with the exception that the Directors of Affairs were not included as raters because of organizational changes in the Agape Movement.

Independent variables were taken from the information in the subject's application and included biographical data, psychological test data, reference data, and interview data. Psychological tests used included the FIRO-B (Schutz, 1977), Sixteen Personality Factors (16PF, Institute for Personality and Ability Testing, 1972), Holland Vocational Preference Inventory (Holland, 1978), and the Modern Language Aptitude Test (Carroll & Sapon, 1955-1965).

Certain variables were selected from the Reference Questionnaire, the Field Interview Questionnaire, and the Agape Entrance Interview, all of which are used by the Agape Movement in their current selection procedure.

Results

An examination of the interrater reliability of the screening sample (see Table 1) revealed significant correlations for all raters. The highest correlation was found between the File Rater and the Personnel Director ($r= .80$), and correlations were lowest with the Directors of Affairs (ranging from $r= .48$ to $r= .59$).

Most of the subjects in the screening sample were placed in the Most Successful and Moderately Successful groups, with only 15.3 percent in the two lowest success groups, a common occurrence in overseas predictive studies.

Table 1
Correlations Between Raters of Screening Groups (*n* = 7)

	Inter. Director	Personnel Director	Director of Affairs	File Rater
International Director (1)	1.00	.73*	.48*	.73*
Personnel Director (2)		1.00	.53*	.80*
Director of Affairs (3)			1.00	.59*
File Rater (4)			1.00	

*p <.001

The results of Stepwise Multiple Regression Analysis yielded 17 significant variables. A determination was then made of the significant contribution of each variable to the equation and only 12 variables were retained, accounting for 56 percent of the criterion variance (see Table 2). Of the 12, the variable "Family Size" was found to be a suppressor variable because of its high correlation with "Age," the fifth predictor in the equation. The prediction formula with regression coefficients is as follows: Y = 4.277 - .1683 (Var. 1) - .5297 (Var. 2) - .3687 (Var. 3) + .1143 (Var. 4) - .0318 (Var. 5) + .1869 (Var. 6) - .3476 (Var. 7) + .2322 (Var. 8) + .4252 (Var. 9) - .3276 (Var. 10) + .1918 (Var. 11) + .5228 (Var. 12).

In order for Stepwise Linear Multiple Regression Analysis to be effective, it is important that the independent variables be relatively uncorrelated among themselves. Although 13 significant intercorrelations were found, all were low except "Age" with "Family Size," which has been identified as a suppressor effect.

Pearson correlations between predictors and the criterion (see Table 3) revealed the highest correlations were negative for "Undisciplined versus Controlled," "Age," "Moodiness," "Birth Order," "Perseverance-Discipline" and "Relates to Others," corresponding to the negative regression coefficients in the regression analysis.

Table 2
Stepwise Multiple Regression Results for 12 Selected Variables

Multiple R	0.75	Anal. of Var.	*DF*	*SS*	*MS*	*F*
R Square	0.56	Regression	12	45.86	3.82	9.94(p<.01)
Adj. R Square	0.50	Residual	95	36.53	0.38	
Standard Error	0.62					

Table 2 (continued)

Source	Variables	Regress. Coeff.	Std. Error	F	Mult. R	R^2	R^2 Change
16PF	Undisciplined vs Controlled	-0.1683	0.04	20.66**	0.29	0.09	0.09
Ref.	Moodiness	-0.5297	0.12	18.33**	0.40	0.16	0.00
Biograph.	Birth Order	-0.3687	0.08	22.15**	0.45	0.21	0.05
16PF	Forthright vs. Astute	0.1143	0.03	13.97**	0.49	0.25	0.04
Biograph.	Age	-0.0318	0.008	15.67**	0.55	0.30	0.05
Biograph.	Fam.Size	0.1869	0.06	10.25**	0.61	0.37	0.07
Field Interview	Relates w Others	-0.3476	0.09	13.84**	0.64	0.41	0.04
Ref. (Question)	Response Author	0.2322	0.10	5.51*	0.67	0.45	0.04
References (Traits)	Social Poise	0.4252	0.13	11.49**	0.69	0.48	0.03
Ref. (Traits)	Perseverence Discipline	-0.3276	0.12	7.75**	0.71	0.51	0.03
Field Interview	Flexibility	0.1918	0.08	6.84*	0.73	0.54	0.03
Biograph.	Father Absence	0.5228	0.26	4.10*	0.75	0.56	0.02

* $p < .05$ ** $p < .01$

Analysis of Variance was utilized to help explain the meaning of each variable by examining group mean differences (see Table 4). "Undisciplined versus Controlled" accounted for most of the variance, and there was a significant difference ($p < .02$) indicating that more successful subjects were rated as experiencing "Moodiness" less frequently than less successful subjects. The third variable was "Birth Order," and the significant group difference ($p<.02$) seemed to be primarily explained by later borns being placed in the Least Successful group most frequently.

Table 3 Correlations Between Predictors and Performance
Criterion (Success) (n =111)

Predictors	Criterion
Age	-.28**
Family Size	-.04
Birth Order	-.21**
Father Absence	.16
Forthright vs. Astute	.16
Undisciplined vs. Controlled	-.29**
Moodiness	-.25**
Perseverance—Discipline	-.21**
Social Poise	.08
Response to Authority	.07
Flexibility	.11
Relates to Others	-.19

Note: df=109; *p <.05 = .195; **p <.01=.254

"Forthright versus Astute" was the fourth variable, with a significance level of p <.30. Although this level is too low for strict research, mission agencies might accept the mean difference for their purposes. The trend indicated more successful subjects tended to score in the somewhat more "Astute" range.

There was a significant group difference in the fifth variable, "Age" (p <.03), indicating that those who were older at application tended to be rated less successful on the field. "Family Size," the suppressor variable highly correlated with "Age," indicates primarily that older subjects have larger families.

Although the next three variables in the regression equation show no group mean significance, some trends can be observed. "Relates to Others" was the seventh variable which indicated that those who answered in the positive direction on the Field Interview Questionnaire tended to be rated as more successful. The eighth variable, "Response to Authority," revealed that those who were rated by referents as "outstanding" in their responses tended to be rated Less Successful on the field. "Social Poise," the ninth variable, had a similar trend.

A significant group difference (p <.05) was found on the tenth variable, "Perseverance-Discipline," indicating in this case that those subjects rated Most Successful were rated on the Reference Questionnaire as Above Average on this combination trait.

Table 4 Means and Analysis of Variance:
Criterion Variable with Predictors

| | Analysis of Variance | | | |
Variable	SS	MS	F	Sig.
.1. Undiscip. vs. Controlled	43.51	14.50	5.47	.002
2. Moodiness	2.50	0.84	3.3	.02
3. Birth Order	7.36	2.45	3.44	.02
4. Forthright vs. Astute	15.74	5.25	1.23	.30NS
5. Age	978.28	326.09	3.23	.03
6. Family Size	1.15	0.38	0.17	.90NS
7. Relates to Others	2.18	0.73	1.54	.20NS
8. Response to Authority	0.37	0.12	0.31	.80NS
9. Social Poise	0.54	0.18	0.62	.60NS
10. Perseverance-Discipline	2.41	0.80	2.75	.05
11. Flexibility	1.03	0.34	0.49	.89NS
12. Father Absence	0.28	0.09	1.56	.20NS

	Groups									
	1		2		3		4			
	Least Success		Less Success		Moderate Success		Most Success		Total Pop.	
	Mean	SD	Mean	SD	Mean	SD	Mean	SD	Mean	SD
1. Undiscip.	8.90	1.20	8.14	2.04	6.86	1.65	6.97	1.61	7.16	1.72
2. Mood.	1.70	0.82	1.29	.49	1.20	.45	1.15	0.49	1.23	.52
3. Birth O.	2.30	.67	1.57	.79	2.0	.94	1.59	.75	1.89	.87
4. Forth.	4.80	1.87	4.43	2.07	5.09	2.12	5.6	2.03	5.23	2.07
5. Age	35.6	15.63	0.1	14.0	26.7	10.6	24.9	6.0	27.1	10.30
6. Fam. S.	1.90	1.66	1.7	1.89	1.55	1.54	1.62	.29	1.61	1.48
7. Relates	2.00	.67	2.14	.69	1.80	.70	1.64	.67	1.78	.69
8.Authority	1.70	.67	1.71	.49	1.87	.70	1.85	.54	1.84	.63
9. Poise	1.40	.52	1.29	.49	.55	.54	1.51	.56	1.50	.54
10. Persev.	1.60	.52	1.71	.76	1.60	.56	1.31	.47	1.51	.55
11. Flex.	1.70	.95	.71	. 76	1.93	.81	2.00	.86	1.92	.83
12. Fath. A.	1.80	.42	.00	.00	1.93	.26	1.97	.16	1.94	.24

The final two variables did not have a significant group difference, but a trend was observed. "Flexibility" was the eleventh variable, and subjects in the More Successful groups tended to score average or below on this variable. "Father Absence" was last, revealing Least Successful subjects tended to have a higher frequency of absent fathers than the other subjects.

It should be pointed out that all of these variables were significant at least at the $p < .05$ level in the regression analysis, but some of them did not have significant group means, indicating only a trend. Nonsignificant group means certainly do not invalidate these variables as predictors, however.

Discussion

Interrater reliability for the screening sample was high enough to indicate that averaging the ratings was a valid measure of success. An interesting finding was the high correlation of the File Rater's ratings with those of the other raters, since she based her ratings on the subjects' monthly self-reports. This finding would indicate that subjects are honest in their self-evaluations and tend to be congruent in self-perception with their supervisors.

The coefficient of determination ($R2$) of .56 was significant at $p < .01$, and the 12 variables significantly added to the prediction at $p < .05$ level or better. Peter and Henry (1962) stated that accounting for one-third of the variance would be a significant achievement, yet this equation accounts for over half, 56 percent of the variance of the criterion.

Predictor Variables
The variable accounting for most of the variance was "Undisciplined versus Controlled" from the 16PF, which measures the ability to bind anxiety (Karson & O'Dell, 1976). The more successful groups scored moderately high on the "Controlled" end, indicating they possess good work habits and keep their emotions somewhat controlled. They are dependable in organizing things and getting the job done. The less successful groups obtained extreme scores on this variable, which indicates their anxiety was too tightly bound, causing them to be overly controlled and rigid, resulting in loss of creativity and flexibility. The ability to cope with ambiguity and disorder is thus severely diminished.

"Moodiness" was taken from the Reference Questionnaire; thus, for it to be registered on the questionnaire it would have to be observed by the referent enough to make an impression. This variable is found more frequently in past studies than any others (Guynes, 1975; Thayer, 1973; Wright et al., 1963; Williams, 1973). Group 1 had the biggest difference in group means, indicating the least successful were more likely to experience "Moodiness" more frequently.

"Birth Order" was a complex variable with evidence of inconsistency in the more successful groups, but a tendency for them to represent more firstborns. The significant difference appears to be in the Least Successful group, who have more later borns. A similar finding was reported by Suedfeld (1967) who discovered firstborns remained overseas longer than later borns.

Another variable from the 16PF, "Forthright versus astute," revealed that the more successful subjects tended to be somewhat more polished and socially aware. According to Karson and O'Dell (1976), subjects scoring on the more "Astute" side of average tend to be somewhat more insightful concerning themselves and others, and tend to promote group cohesion rather than stating their opinions. Being slightly more emotionally detached, they are able to be more effective in getting a group of people to remain on a task or goal. Those on the "Forthright" side of average were rated less successful in this study, being genuine but somewhat blunt with others. They have less self-insight and become more emotionally involved.

These interpretations suggest that astute subjects may be more attuned to subtle cultural cues and have better self-perception, while the more forthright ones may offend the nationals with their openness.

"Age" at the time of application was the next variable, clearly showing younger subjects were rated more successful and older ones least successful. This finding replicates that of Williams (1973) on Wycliffe missionaries. Younger subjects are generally more flexible and adaptable and are generally single without family worries. Older subjects generally have a patterned lifestyle more susceptible to disruption by entering a new culture, especially with the stress of a family. This study reveals the optimal age for beginning overseas service is 22 to 30.

"Family Size" was correlated with "Age" ($r=.65$) and serves as a suppressor variable. Basically, it reflects the fact that older subjects usually have larger families, and is similar to the finding by Williams (1973) on Wycliffe subjects.

"Relates to Others" was taken from the Field Interview Questionnaire in which the subjects were rated on how they related to other people according to their reports to the interviewers. Subjects answering that they relate well tended to be rated more successful overseas, which is expected. The requirements of a missionary to be able to establish relationships and initiate activities with people would certainly require such ability.

"Response to Authority" was taken from the Reference Questionnaire and a surprising result was found. Those subjects whom the referents reported as "outstanding" or "responds with a servant's heart" tended to be rated less successful overseas, whereas those who questioned authority or struggled with directives somewhat tend to be rated more successful. This suggests that subjects rated highly on this question might be somewhat too accommodating and easily led to be the leaders needed overseas. There is no indication that more successful subjects rebelled or refused to obey, but they appeared more able to be assertive with their superiors.

"Social Poise" came from the Reference Questionnaire, and the trend was for those rated above average by referents to be less successful. This trait perhaps distinguishes subjects who are very acculturated to American social mores and have a difficult time accepting those of other cultures. Their feeling is that there is a "right and proper" way to do things and are either offended or stressed when they come in contact with conflicting views.

"Perseverance-Discipline" primarily differentiated the Most Successful group from the others. This variable, taken from the Reference Questionnaire, indicates that referents believe these subjects showed a prior history of ability to persevere through difficulties more than most people. Harris (1973) also found that perseverance was the most effective item in discriminating the High Success Peace Corps volunteers from Early Terminators.

Another unexpected finding came from the variable "Flexibility." This variable reflects the question on the Field Interview Questionnaire concerning how the subjects respond when things do not go as they planned. Those who have to struggle somewhat and "pray about it" tend to be rated more successful than those who answered "great" or "trust God." Either this variable is tapping a tendency to deny problems and difficulties, or untruthfulness in responding in an interview. Subjects who give an above average answer appear to be very flexible, but apparently at a cost of suppressed anger which surfaces in some other way.

"Father Absence" was the final variable which significantly contributed to the regression. The trend was for Least Successful subjects to have more father absence, defined as physical absence for any five-year period prior to the 15th birthday of the subject. This finding is a replication of the Peace Corps study by Suedfeld (1967) who found on two separate samples that this variable clearly differentiated successful subjects from early terminators. Fathers have historically been responsible for modeling more instrumental behaviors and for providing the child with contact with the outside world. An absence of this would apparently make it more difficult for subjects to meet the demands of a new culture.

Cross-validation

An examination of these 12 predictor variables reveals that most of them are replications of other studies, which is strong evidence for their validity. Cross-validation on a calibration sample is the best way to establish validity and was attempted in this study. However, two major problems arose. One was an organizational change which resulted in a reduction of raters for this sample and consequent lower reliability. The other problem was the skewedness of the calibration sample, in that only 3 out of 42 were placed in the Less Successful group, thus eliminating a test of the power of the power of the prediction equation to predict unsuccessful subjects. The result of these difficulties was low correlation between the prediction equation and the criterion.

In examining the accuracy of predictions, the equation was accurate in assigning most of the subjects to the more successful groups and none to the Least Successful group. It was less accurate in making fine discriminations between adjacent groups. Until further cross-validation is completed, it can be concluded that the prediction equation does serve as an accurate rough screen between high success subjects and low success subjects, but is less effective in serving as a fine screen.

Conclusions

One of the conclusions of this study is that because missionary samples tend to be skewed toward success, fine discrimination between success groups will continue to pose problems. The accuracy of a laboratory study must be sacrificed for the more realistic results of the field study. However, it was possible to utilize a combination of pretraining variables to yield a set of predictors which provide selection committees with some objective criteria to focus on, in combination with their subjective experience, in the selection of missionary personnel.

The predictors were basically the same for missionary samples as for secular samples, which indicates that they are generalizable to any person from the American culture going to live and work in another culture. The traits and skills needed to succeed tend to be the same for everyone. A very important conclusion of this study is that the history of one's behavior, past responses, and experiences tends to be the best predictor of the future. God's call and motivation are important, but in the ambiguity and stress of another culture, past experience and events tends to shape how an individual will respond. Consequently, a combination of God's call, motivation, and past experience must be used in selection.

The importance of interpersonal relationships and adaptability has been indicated upon examining the group of predictor variables. In preparing individuals for overseas work, attention must be given to helping them recognize stressful situations and respond to them appropriately. Persons who are rigid and inflexible will need special help in this regard. Interpersonally, successful overseas workers must not be so enculturated as to be unable to tolerate differences in other cultures, and must be able to understand subtle cultural cues in the new culture and incorporate these cues into their own system of responding. In addition, the present study indicates that supervisors should be willing to tolerate disagreement among their workers and not expect unquestioned obedience. Accommodating, more passive persons who would respond to more authoritarian supervisors tend to be less successful overseas. However, further research is needed in this area.

A history of moodiness and depression has surfaced in this study as an important sign of difficulty overseas, as has this variable in most of the major studies. It is thus important in preparing persons for overseas service to deal with the emotional aspects of their lives, helping them to learn proper expression of anger and fear. This predictor variable clearly shows that overseas service is not the place for someone to deal with inner turmoil. Timing and maturity must be considered.

A final conclusion reached from the results of this study is that the use of pretraining data for the purpose of prediction has merit. Mission agencies can thus be encouraged to make use of such data to screen applicants prior to the training period with a greater level of confidence.

Note

The author wishes to thank Nancy S. Duvall, PhD, for her guidance in preparation of this article and for her service as Dissertation Committee Chairperson for the dissertation on which it is based.

References

Browning, R. C. (1968). Validity of reference ratings from previous employers. *Personnel Psychology, 21*, 389-393.

106 Missionary Preparation

Carroll, J. B., & Sapon, I. M. (1955-1965). *Modern Language Aptitude Test.* New York: The Psychological Corp.

Dicken, C. R. (1969). Predicting the success of Peace Corps community development workers. *Journal of Consulting and Clinical Psychology, 33,* 597-606.

Dohrenwend, B., & Dohrenwend, B. P. (1966). Stress situations, birth order, and psychological symptoms. *Journal of Abnormal Psychology, 71,* 215-223.

Doll, R. E., Gunderson, E. K., & Ryman, D. K. (1969). Relative predictability of occupational groups and performance criteria in an extreme environment. *Journal of Clinical Psychology, 25,* 299-402.

Duhl, L. J., Leopold, R. L., & English, J. T. (1964). A mental health program for the Peace Corps. *Human Organization, 23,* 131-136.

Exner, J. E., & Sutton-Smith, B. (1970). Birth order and hierarchical versus innovative role requirements. *Journal of Personality, 38,* 581-587.

Fisher, J., Epstein, L. J., & Harris, M. R. (1967). Validity of the psychiatric interview: Predicting the effectiveness of first Peace Corps volunteers in Ghana. *Archives of General Psychiatry, 17,* 744-750.

Gordon, V. (1967). Clinical, psychometric, and work-sample approaches in the prediction of success in Peace Corps training. *Journal of Applied Psychology, 51,* 111-119.

Gunderson, E. K., & Kapfer, E. L. (1966). The predictive validity of clinical ratings for an extreme environment. *British Journal of Psychiatry, 112,* 405-412.

Guthrie, G. M., & Zektick, I. N. (1967). Predicting performance in the Peace Corps. *Journal of Social Psychology, 71,* 11-21.

Guynes, R. (1975). A study of relationships between selected personality factors and personal adjustment of overseas personnel (Doctoral dissertation, North Texas State University). *Dissertation Abstracts International,* 1975, *36,* 2629A-2630A. (University Microfilms No. 75-24, 169).

Hare, A. J. (1966). Factors associated with Peace Corps volunteer success in the Philippines. *Human Organization, 25*, 150-153.

Harris, J. G. (1973). A science of the South Pacific Analysis of the character structure of the Peace Corps volunteer. *American Psychologist, 28*, 232-247.

Holland, J. G. (1978). *Holland Vocational Preference Inventory.* Palo Alto: Consulting Psychologists Press.

Horowitz, L. M., Inouye, D., & Siegelman, E. Y. (1979). On averaging judges ratings to increase their correlation with an external criterion. *Journal of Consulting and Clinical Psychology, 47*, 453-458.

Karson, S., & O'Dell, W. (1976). *Clinical use of the 16PF.* Champaign, IL: Institute for Personality and Ability Testing.

Kennedy, P. W., & Dreger, R. M. (1974). Development of criterion measures of overseas missionary performance. *Journal of Applied Psychology, 59*, 69-73.

Peter, H. W., & Henry, E. R. (1962). Steps to better selection and training for overseas jobs. *Personnel, 39*, 18-25.

Schutz, W. L. (1977). *FIRO-B.* Palo Alto, CA: Consulting Psychologists Press.

Sixteen Personality Factors (1972). Champaign, IL: Institute for Personality and Ability Testing.

Suedfeld, P. (1967). Paternal absence and overseas success of Peace Corps volunteers. *Journal of Consulting Psychology, 31*, 424-425.

Thayer, L. R. (1973). Relationship between clinical judgments of missionary fitness and subsequent ratings of actual field adjustment. *Review of Religious Research, 14*, 112-116.

Tucker, M. F. (1974). *Screening and selection for overseas assignment: Assessment and recommendations to the U.S. Navy.* Denver: Center for Research and Education.

Uhes, M. J., & Shybut, J. (1974). Personal Orientation Inventory as a predictor of success in Peace Corps training. *Journal of Applied Psychology, 55*, 498-499.

Williams, K. (1973). Characteristics of the more successful and less successful missionaries (Doctoral dissertation, United States International University). *Dissertation Abstracts International, 1973, 34,* 1786B-1787B. (University Microfilms No. 73-22, 697).

Wright, M. W., Sisler, G. L., & Chylinski, J. (1963). Personality factors in the selection of civilians for isolated northern stations. *Journal of Applied Psychology, 47,* 24-29.

Wright, O. R. (1969). Summary of research on the selection interview since 1964. *Personnel Psychology, 22,* 391-413.

TRAINING CONSIDERATIONS

12

Phil Elkins

Preparation: Pay the Price!

I am frequently asked by Americans, "What kind of training do I need to be an effective missionary?" My response is, "What kind of missionary do you want to be?" If you want to follow the Apostle Paul and be a church planter in differing cultural environments, the requirements are pretty stiff. If you want an evangelistic ministry among American servicemen stationed in Japan, the requirements are much less. This latter task for the committed American Christian is no less holy, but one's life experience in America puts one in a much better position to do that job than it does to plant a church among an isolated tribe in Southeast Asia.

Servants and Master Builders
First, read with me some passages from I Cor. 3:5-13: "Who is Apollos? And who is Paul? We are simply *servants*, by whom you were led to believe. Each one of us does the work the Lord gave him to do: I planted the seed, Apollos watered the plant....There is no difference between the person who *plants* and the person who *waters;* ...Using the gift that God gave me, I did the work the work of an *expert builder* and laid the foundation, and another person is building on it. But everyone must be careful how they build...the quality of each person's work will be seen when the Day of Christ exposes it. For the real Day's fire will reveal everyone's work; the fire will test it and show its real quality."

There are several observations I want to draw from this passage. The first is that regardless of one's role or task, that person is a *servant*. Second, there are distinct roles and jobs that different people are called to do. Third, Paul's gift and role in church planting was that of an *expert builder* (some translations say *master builder*). Fourth, God is concerned with the quality of the work we do and commits Himself to judge the quality of our efforts.

Let me try to illustrate this and some additional comments with the following grid.

WHAT KIND OF SERVANT?

Servant	Piece Work Job Assigned Single Responsibility Limited Training and Experience	Apprentice	Teacher	Orderly Aide
Servant and Steward	More Responsible More Authority Greater Experience and Training Greater Investment	Foreman	Principal	Physician's Assistant
Servant and Master Builder	Added Experience and Training Faces More Alternatives Decisions Affect Many Major Responsibility	Architect	Superintendent	Medical Doctor

Regardless of one's life work and position, we are all servants. In the above listing of nine professions, none can be considered better or more noble or holy. But, as one moves from the three positions on the top squares to those at the bottom, the experience and training required to fulfill the task and position increases. The authority and responsibilities of a principal are greater than a teacher, but no more sacred or honorable. The school superintendent has to deal with options, alternatives, and decisions which in turn affect the lives of principals and teachers, the facilities they use, and students they teach. The architect carries the responsibility to provide guidance and directions for the foreman, who in turn is responsible for delegating tasks to apprentices.

A doctor is expected to know how to do what an orderly or physician's assistant does. But, for a physician's assistant to be a doctor, he or she must have more training and experience to be able to handle competently the additional responsibility. We would object strenuously to a physician's assistant, who without paying the price to quality as a physician began to call himself "Doctor" and tell us, "I think I can do the job, let me practice on you!"

Defining the Missionary Role

Missionary roles can be defined in terms of cultural distance. Ralph Winter has suggested the terms E-0, E-1. E-2, and E-3 to describe the distance of the missionary from the target people. The categories on the left describe servant roles, and how they are influenced by experience, training, and the ability to handle responsibility. As one contemplates a shift from E-0 Servant to E-1, E-2, or E-3, the task becomes increasingly difficult and would require an increased amount of training to do an effective job. Similarly, as one moves from E-0 Servant to E-0 Steward or Master Builder, more experience and training are necessary. The difference between aptitude, training and experience is greatest as one contrasts E-0 Servant and the square representing E-3 Master Builder. To function within the latter category, one must be prepared to pay the price of years of preparation (including internship).

Let me briefly describe each of the three church planting categories (below). The *E-1 Master Builder* is a friend of mine. He served one church as a pastor for over a decade. Later, he entered a radio-preaching ministry. As time went on, he decided to plant new churches in areas where he had a large radio response. He would then be in a position to help people like the "Yankee Pastor" with 20 years of preaching and nurturing experience to plant a new church in Guilford, Connecticut. An inexperienced but committed resident of Guilford could assist both of the above people through his knowledge of the town and through his personal witness. This inexperienced person could, in time, get the necessary training and experience to serve as a *steward* or eventually in a *master builder* role. But, he would need to seek a balance between his personal knowledge of the community and the kind of theological training necessary for those performing this kind of ministry.

DEFINING THE MISSIONARY ROLE

	E-0 SPIRITUAL NURTURE NOT CONVERSION GROWTH	E-1 CHURCH PLANTING WITHIN YOUR CULTURE	E-2 CHURCH PLANTING IN SIMILAR CULTURE	E-3 CHURCH PLANTING IN A CULTURE RADICALLY DIFFERENT
SERVANT	Sunday School teacher in a Community Church	Inexperienced but committed Christian excited about planting a new church in his town --Guilford, Conn.	25 year-old WASP witnessing to University students in Columbia	23 year-old WASP witnessing to Amazon Indian tribe in Columbia
SERVANT/ STEWARD	Sunday School Director--same church	Yankee pastor-- 20 years experience, assisting in planting a new church	WASP Bible translator starting one church in Ladino town	WASP Bible translator starting a church in a single Amazon village
SERVANT/ MASTER BUILDER	Senior pastor	A successful church planter in many parts of the United States	WASP 10 year veteran church planter among Ladinos in Colombia	WASP 10 year veteran church planter among Indian tribes in Colombia

E = Evangelism

1, 2, 3 = The higher the number, the greater the cultural distance from the sending community

WASP = White Anglo-Saxon Protestant

The same could be said for the 23-year-old "WASP." Before she entered a drastically different culture in an E-3 situation, she should have some experience witnessing in her own culture. She should have enough training to be able to learn the language and adjust her lifestyle radically. She might not have a good perception of how to plant churches, but should seek guidance form those already doing effective work. Her role, at first, would be that of an apprentice and learner. She might never want to move beyond the role of apprentice and learner, but rather to return to her own country to serve world evangelism in a different way. However, if her aspiration is to be an effective church planter among Indian tribes in Colombia, she must anticipate years of academic training and internship.

The Price of Preparation

It is my strong personal conviction that pioneer church planting is at least as complicated as learning to be a surgeon. Everyone desiring to become a surgeon knows he must receive much classroom training, read widely, pass standardized examinations, and then do extensive internship. Aspiring physicians who want to perform heart transplants, or enter some other specialty, know they must pay the price of added study and internship. Physicians wanting to practice as psychiatrists must complete years of additional preparation to meet that goal.

A friend of mine, an outstanding pastor, decided to become a lawyer. His goal was to represent people before the Supreme Court of the United States. His goal was high and he calculated the price. He knew he had at least three years of law school, stiff bar examinations, and additional years of specialized practice before he could represent a client before the Supreme Court. He found many attorneys who could counsel him on the minimum educational and experiential requirements to be effective in his anticipated job.

When it comes to preparing to become an effective missionary, the task of getting good counsel is much more difficult than it was for my attorney friend. It is difficult because of the practice of labeling all who function in overseas ministries with the one term, *missionary.* Frequently the career missionaries themselves do not communicate the broader and more complex picture because they are under severe pressure to raise funds and recruit for their particular ministry, project and field. The result is that one finds little clarity and definition is provided for the extremely complex number of tasks and roles which missionaries are called upon to perform.

A great deal of energy has been expended recently in focusing attention on the unreached and hidden peoples of the world. For Western Christians, these people are a radically different culture (E-3). The complexities of reaching them would, at least from a human perspective, probably exceed those faced by the Apostle Paul and his team companions. Yet, notice the extraordinary efforts God took to prepare Paul, a Jew, to go to the Gentiles. He was a mature man when he accepted Christ. At that time he had already received extraordinary training under Gamaliel, a well respected doctor of the Jewish Law.

Paul had already developed a reputation for his religious zeal and leadership. In spite of this, God worked in preparing Paul for at least 13 more years, including a time of tutorship under Barnabas (an outstanding Christian leader and missionary). The necessity of this extensive time of preparation becomes clear as we read of his missionary church planting efforts in the book of. Acts. His spiritual fiber had to be strong. His theological perspective had to be mature and more flexible than the apostles and church leaders back home (in Jerusalem). He had to have the personal confidence to withstand attacks from outside and within the Christian faith. He even had to withstand and confront Peter publicly. Today, the task that Paul faced is complicated by nearly 2,000 years of history, innumerable divisions between Christendom, and a population at least ten times as large.

Specialization

Another dimension is illustrated by the following chart, used by C. Peter Wagner in one of his courses at Fuller Theological Seminary.

Missionaries? Yes--But What Kind?

This expands the previous model I used. There I spoke only of the nine categories relating to missions as evangelism and church planting (E-1, E-2, E-3). Here N-1, N-2, N-3 could be expanded into those same nine categories. It is not the intention of the above model to isolate church planting from Christian nurture and social service. I believe in a holistic approach to the task. But aspects of the training needed for effective social service and church planting differ significantly. One should not lump the training as all being the same, though both need the same basics.

Sometimes physicians are teamed with people who are involved in church planting and evangelism; most frequently they are not. Sometimes their perspective is, "I am a Christian and a specialist in medicine [or nutrition, engineering, education, etc.]. I don't know anything about church planting, cross-cultural evangelism or how missions operate, but I want to help. Is there a place for me?" Someone says "yes" too quickly and they go straight to the field. Their response should be, "Yes, you are needed, but you need some additional specialty training to prepare you to use your vocational skills in a cross-cultural context. Before you go, learn the basics involved in being an effective witness, church planter and discipler in a radical new environment. It is an extremely complex task to apply your skills toward the development of a strong national church."

Primary Vocational Responsibility		*Cultural Distance from Sending Community*			
		0	1	2	3
Evangelism & Church Planting	**E:**	E-0	E-1	E-2	E-3
Christian Nurture	**N:**	N-0	N-1	N-2	N-3
Social Service	**S:**	S-0	S-1	S-2	S-3
		Cx Com.	Non-Xh Com.	Similar Culture	Distinct Culture
		MONOCULTURAL MINISTRY		CROSS-CULTURAL MINISTRY	
		Stained-glass Barrier		Cultural Barrier	

- -

Getting the Basics

What are these basics that everyone needs prior to entering the field? A person needs a solid introductory course in missions taught by one or more experienced missionaries who are professionally trained in the discipline of missiology. Many undergraduate colleges and seminaries offer such a course. If the course includes experiential dimensions of learning, so much the better. Preceding, or during this training, should be solid college level biblical training. This should be followed by three to twelve months of field experience under the tutorship of a competent, effective missionary or national church leader.

A Model for Missionary Training

TRAINING AND EXPERIENCE LEVELS	TYPE OF PREPARATION		EXPERIENCE
	CLASSROOM	FIELD TRAINING	
LEVEL I - *Pre-Mission*: Four to five years of undergraduate work.	College Undergraduate: Bible, sociology, anthropology & theory of language, French or Spanish.	One year formal education in another culture and language.	Four summers or interterms with two different agencies and fields
LEVEL II - *Mission Training*: Three to four years of graduate work.	University graduate study: theology, biblical studies, Greek, missionary anthropology and sociology, communication theory and practice.	One to two years of field work in area near expected service.	Field work done in cooperation with and under supervision of selected mission agency.
LEVEL III - *Intern*: Two years of language acquisition and people study.	None	Coaching by senior missionary and former professors via correspondence. Language study.	Assignment to specific people group. Language study among group.
LEVEL IV - *Associate Missionary*: Two to six years of work on field.	Nine months of field work at School of World Mission at *end* of field work. Review, evaluate.	Supervision *by* senior missionary	Work with mission team attempting to evangelize assigned group
LEVEL V - *Missionary*: Two to six years of work on field.	None	Supervision *of* associate missionaries.	Decision on assignment to new field or continuance in present field
LEVEL VI - *Senior Missionary*: Four to eight years of field work and teaching.	Two years of graduate study leading to PhD or equivalent.	Teaching of trainees and interns. Field evaluation assignments.	Decision to return to a people or to a *field* teaching situation.

This experience should be followed by further biblical studies which speak to the issues of contextualizing the Gospel. They should separate biblical and church customs from the universal messages. Additional time should be spent in learning the skills of language acquisition (how to learn a language *outside* the classroom). Other basics at this stage include missionary anthropology (cultural anthropology is helpful but needs applications), cross-cultural communication, and extensive studies of what causes churches to grow and what retards growth on the mission field.

By the time you have done the above, you will not need further guidance from this article. You will have your data base for selecting an agency or experienced missionary or national church to apprentice yourself with. You will know what additional training you need for the area of specialization God is calling you to.

If you desire to serve as a missionary in another culture, I hope you have *not* been discouraged by the above comments. They are *not* intended to frustrate, but to challenge you to give the best you have to offer. Those of us who have been used by God as church planters in other cultures are conscious we are made of clay, prone to sin, frequently break God's heart, and are "average" humans. But God's love challenges us to think His great thoughts, respond to His great acts, attempt great things for His glory.

I would encourage you to read closely the comments of two of my most respected colleagues, Edward R. Dayton and David Fraser, in their book, *Planning Strategies for World Evangelism,* 1980, pp. 243-251. They suggest different levels of training and experience. Where the one term, *missionary,* has been used, they recommend six terms according to the level of service. Let me encourage you to be challenged by this model.

Finally, they quote in their book from an outstanding missionary educator, J. Herbert Kane. This shall serve as my concluding thought:

There's still a prevailing notion that one can major in any subject in college or seminary and be a good missionary. No special courses are necessary! Most leading missions have a minimum requirement--one year of Bible--nothing is said of missions! I think this is a great mistake. To go overseas without missionary anthropology, cross-cultural communication, area studies, missionary life at work--to say nothing of the history of missions and non-Christian religions, is an act of consummate folly!

13

Kelly S. O'Donnell

A Preliminary Study on Psychologists in Missions

This study is an initial attempt to identify important factors which are needed to effectively work in missions as a psychologist. Ten psychologists working for various mission agencies responded to a questionnaire which assessed (a) their current missions involvement, (b) their preparation for missions, and (c) their recommendations for training. Results indicated that most of the psychologists provided counseling, screening, and training services to missionaries. Important preparation experiences included working on the mission field, receiving formal study in psychology, and having background counseling experience. Overall, the five most useful components suggested for training were overseas mission involvement, an academic background in psychology, training in missiology and anthropology, general cross-cultural experience, and supervision and/or an internship experience in mental health and missions. Some recommendations for training psychologists and other mental health workers are discussed in light of the results.

What kinds of training experiences do psychologists believe are most helpful for their work in mission settings? This study explores this question through the responses of ten psychologists involved in mental health and missions. A review of the literature on psychology and missions revealed no research which looked at

Based on a paper presented during a poster session at the Eighth Annual Conference on Mental Health and Missions, held at Angola, Indiana in November, 1987. Reprinted by permission of the author.

the specific background preparation of professionals who work in this specialized field.

Method

A ten-item questionnaire was developed for use in this study. Most of the items involved open-ended questions which covered three basic areas: the current types of services being provided, the significant academic and cross-cultural experiences which helped prepare the individual for "mission psychology", and suggestions for training mental health professionals in this field. Most questions also required the respondent to rank order his or her responses. An overall rank ordering for each item was then computed, based on the summation of all the respondents' answers to the item. Table 1 provides a paraphrased version of the questionnaire items.

Table 1
Items from the Questionnaire on Psychologists in Missions
1. Which services do you provide to missionaries and mission agencies? How long have you been working in this area?
2. Outline your formal academic training.
3. What general aspects of your academic program helped prepare you to work as a psychologist in missions? List up to five and rank order their importance.
4. Which specific psychology courses have been most valuable for your work in mental health and missions? List up to five and rank order their importance.
5. Which specific non-psychology courses have been most useful for your work in missions as a psychologist? List up to five and rank order their importance.
6. List up to five ways that you continue to develop your skills in this area and rank order their importance. How many hours each month do you average developing these skills?
7. List and rank order the significant cross-cultural experiences which helped prepare you for work as a psychologist in missions. How much total time have you spent overseas?
8. In general, what are the most significant factors which have prepared you for this field? List up to five and rank order their significance. What do you think influences Christian mental health professionals to work in this area?
9. List and rank order the most important ways to train psychologists for mental health and missions involvement.
10. Additional comments.

The psychologists in this study provided either full- or part-time services, each to a different mission agency or school in the United States. Four were clinical psychologists, four were counseling psychologists, one was a professor, and one was a "pastoral" psychologist. One of the respondents was a woman.

Results

Services Provided

Nine psychologists provided counseling services to missionaries, most of which were done prior to departure for the field or else during furlough. The full-time psychologists spent an average of 45 hours each month doing counseling.

Eight psychologists were involved in some kind of candidate screening through psychological testing and assessment. Those who worked full-time averaged about 15 hours per month providing this service.

Eight psychologists spent time training missionaries. Training included pre-field and on-field instruction in such areas as counseling skills, self-understanding, cross-cultural adaptation, marriage, stress management, and interpersonal relationships.

Four psychologists had been involved in research related to mental health and missions. Only one psychologist was currently involved in work as a missionary (about five hours a month).

The average time for having worked in missions as a psychologist was eight years, with the range being from half a year to 20 years.

Educational Background

The third questionnaire item assessed the general aspects of one's educational background which helped prepare him or her to work in missions as a psychologist. The five most important areas, in order, were reported as (a) having gone through seminary; (b) having studied anthropology; (c) having received basic training as a psychologist; (d) involvement in a campus ministry organization while attending school; and (e) having attended a Christian school. Also mentioned, though less frequently, were the influence of professors, being able to spend time with missionaries, interacting with foreign students, writing a dissertation on a missions topic, and doing an internship which involved working with missionaries.

The most important psychology courses for working in missions as a psychologist were also explored. Testing and assessment were rated highest, followed by general counseling courses, personality theory, marriage and family, and, finally, courses dealing with cross-cultural issues.

Non-psychology courses, in order of importance, were anthropology, missiology, biblical studies, theology, and courses on organizational behavior and analysis.

Ongoing Training

The psychologists in this study spent an average of about eleven hours per month developing their expertise in mental health and missions, with the range being from two to 23 hours. Methods for improving their skills, in order of emphasis, included (a) personal study in the area of missions and psychology; (b) attending conferences; (c) consulting with other professionals in this field; (d) interacting with church leaders, missionaries, and mission agencies; and (e) attending seminars and workshops. Bible study, research, writing, and involvement on a church missions committee were also listed.

Cross-Cultural Experience

Question 7 asked for a description of the foreign and/or domestic experiences which helped prepare the individual for work as a psychologist in missions. Extended travel, missionary work, and significant ethnic experience in the United States were the most relevant experiences. Reported less frequently were overseas secular work, military service, and taking a sabbatical to another country.

The average amount of time spent overseas was about four and one-half years, with the range from one month to 16 years. All ten psychologists reported having spent time overseas.

Personal Preparation for Mental Health and Missions

The eighth item probed for the most significant factors, in general, which the psychologists felt helped prepare them for work in mission settings. In order, the most important factors were (a) working on the mission field; (b) formal training in psychology; (c) background experience in counseling; (d) general overseas experience; and (e) personal interest in this area. Several other factors were also mentioned and included working in a personnel department, local church involvement, training others for missions work, experience with different ethnic groups, attending a Christian university, working in a campus missions organization, taking anthropology courses, conducting dissertation research, involvement with others who work in this field, pastoral experience, seminary training, undergoing personal therapy, and being a parent/spouse.

Which factors seem to influence the decision of mental health workers to become involved in this area? Being aware of and having a burden for the mental health needs of missionaries was reported to be very influential, as were having had previous missions experience and having made a commitment to missions.

Training Suggestions

The final question asked each psychologist to describe the most important components needed for training in mission psychology. The psychologists made several suggestions. The five most important ones, in order, were (a) missions involvement overseas for at least a short-term period; (b) a thorough academic background in psychology; (c) training in missiology and anthropology; (d) general cross-cultural experience; and (e) supervised experience and/or an internship at an agency specializing in this field. Some of the other less emphasized training suggestions were having a well-informed mentor in this area, having a solid and practical background in the integration of psychology and theology, being involved in a local missions committee, having opportunities for doing overseas counseling, training in biblical studies, participating with missionaries in aspects of their training program, having contact with missionaries, reading widely in related disciplines, going through management training, and receiving personal therapy.

Summary and Conclusions

This study has focused on the responses of psychologists. It would also be useful to include other types of mental health professionals in a future study rather than only psychologists. Psychologists who work in missions and mental health are apparently still few in number. Having a larger and more diverse sample would also lend itself to statistical analysis and increase the generalizability of the results.

The psychologists in this study were primarily involved in counseling missionaries, screening candidates, training missionaries, and conducting research. These areas correspond with the typical services which mental health professionals in general have been reported to provide mission agencies--namely, consultation involving counseling, assessment, teaching, and research (Johnson and Penner, 1981; Johnston, 1983).

None of the psychologists reported having been raised overseas. Perhaps this implies that few psychologists in this field are themselves missionary children and/or that few missionary children end up working in the area of missions and mental health. Also, only one of the respondents was a woman. This may indicate that there is an under-representation of women working in this field. More research, of course, is needed to explore these possibilities.

Psychologists spend a considerable amount of time improving their skills and staying updated on topics related to mental health and missions. This was true of both full-time workers and part-time workers (average =11 hours/month). Continuing one's education in this field may require a more extensive effort due to the interdisciplinary nature of the work.

The most significant academic and cross-cultural factors which helped prepare the psychologists in this study were having worked on the mission field, receiving formal training in psychology, and having a counseling background. These factors suggest that it is the unique combination of one's training and experience in psychology, especially counseling, plus his or her understanding of missionary life through actual involvement therein, which enable the professional to work in mission settings.

The psychologists in this study felt that cross-cultural experiences played a major preparatory role for their work in missions. The general sense seemed to be that the more time one could spend overseas, the better equipped he or she would be for work in mental health and missions.

Perhaps the most important part of this study is the overall "blueprint" for training suggested by the psychologists. First, an individual should spend time overseas doing missionary work. This needs to involve at least a short-term experience and hopefully more. In this way the professional will be able to better understand and empathize with missionary clients as well as increase one's credibility and hence acceptability with them.

Second, there needs to be a thorough academic background in psychology. The most useful psychology courses were reported to be testing and assessment first, followed by general counseling, personality theory, marriage and family, and cross-cultural issues.

Next, there is the need to study missiology and anthropology. Looking back at their training, many psychologists apparently wished they had a more thorough background in these areas. Few reported having studied cultural anthropology and missiology at the graduate level. Study in both of these fields was apparently done on one's own rather than in graduate school. These subjects were the weakest point of their academic training as it related to work in mission settings.

Fourth, general cross-cultural experience was recommended. Exposure to and interaction with different cultures was suggested, such as extended travel and interaction with various ethnic groups. Having a lifestyle which naturally gravitates toward such experiences seemed to be indicated.

Finally, undergoing an internship experience or at least some supervised experience in mission psychology was encouraged. As this is a specialized area of psychology with a multidisciplinary emphasis, such supervisory and/or internship experience was viewed as highly desirable. The thought here seemed to be that competency in one's typical psychological setting did not necessarily imply competence in the mission setting. This is in line with the second principle of the American Psychological Association's "Ethical Principles of Psychologists" (1981), which asserts that psychologists "only provide services and only use techniques for which they are qualified by training and experience"(p. 634).

Currently there are no academic programs which are specifically designed to prepare mental health workers in this field. There are, however, a few internship or post-doctoral internship positions available. One example is the two year internship program developed by Wycliffe Bible Translators to prepare counselors to work with its missionary personnel. Much of the practical experience in this area, though, still seems to be based on a careful and informal "learn by doing" approach.

Increasing the number of mental health personnel on the field is still needed, yet this must be accompanied by adequate training. Especially needed would be some graduate programs which could offer a few courses in mission psychology (such as the one at Gordon Conwell Theological Seminary) along with supervised experience and possible short-term mission experience overseas. These courses could be an optional area of specialization and could be taken as electives within the regular course load. Given the availability of this option, interested graduate students would be better equipped to provide important services to missionaries and mission agencies.

Another training possibility, which is increasingly being implemented, would be to develop a series of intensive workshops where basic principles of mental health and missions, case studies, and ethical issues could be addressed. Such workshops could be offered through mental health agencies working in missions and at various professional conferences.

Ultimately, some type of certification or special recognition in this area, based on an established criteria for training and experience, would be useful. One suggestion for certification criteria would be having a license in one's respective mental health discipline, plus undergoing 1,000 hours of supervised experience in a mission setting. Certification might be done at either the organizational level, such as through an individual mission agency, and/or at the interorganizational level through a recognized affiliation of mission agencies. An example of the latter would be the Evangelical Foreign Missions Association, an organization which has been actively involved in the area of missions and mental health (Ferguson, Kliewer, Lindquist, Williams, and Heinrich, 1983; Johnson and Penner, 1981).

Cooperation between mission agencies, Christian graduate schools, and mental health professionals experienced in missions will be necessary to develop the ongoing training opportunities needed for effective service in mental health and missions.

References

American Psychological Association (1981). Ethical principles of psychologists, *American Psychologist, 6,* 633-638.

Johnson, C. & Penner, D., (1981). The current status of the provision of psychological services in missionary agencies in North America. *Bulletin of the Christian Association for Psychological Studies, 7,* (4), 25-27.

Johnston, L. (1983). *Building relationships between mental health specialists and mission agencies.* Proceedings of the Fourth Conference on Mental Health and Missions, Angola, Indiana.

Ferguson, L., Kliewer, D., Lindquist, S., Williams, D., & Heinrich, R. (1983). Candidate selection criteria: A survey. *Journal of Psychology and Theology, 11,* 243-250.

14

Kevin Dyer

Crucial Factors in Building Good Teams

John and Jean Wilson were new recruits joining a team of North Americans and British missionaries in Europe. The team's objective was to plant a church in a city where there was no evangelical witness. After language study, they arrived at the location and participated in the ministry. They soon found frustration and difference of opinion to be a common occurrence. The emotional strain of new workers clashing with older, more experienced missionaries took its toll. Cultural differences, health problems, difficult interpersonal relations, lack of results and disunity among the team members tore them apart. John and Jean lasted two years; they returned home disillusioned and defeated.

In vivid contrast, Jack and Rene Austin were members of a team to Brazil. The eight missionaries were determined to impact their particular area for Christ. Although all were from different church backgrounds with a variety of opinions on methodology and doctrine, they were enormously successful in their ministry. Today all of them are continuing in vibrant service for the Lord.

What made the difference?

For the past 25 years I have been involved with International Teams in sending groups of missionaries to Asia, Africa, Europe and Latin America. During that time we have sent well over 100 teams to more than 55 countries. We are thoroughly convinced of the value of the team effort. What can be accomplished together is so much greater than what can be accomplished by individuals working on their own.

When we began back in the early 60s, we just went to the field and began the work. It wasn't long before we realized that if teams were going to be effective, they needed to be trained together before going to the field. Merely bringing people together and sending them to the field wasn't enough. They needed time for indepth preparation and interpersonal bonding. They came from all kinds of sub-cultures and religious backgrounds and minor differences in personal taste became magnified when living and working in the team situation.

Training, the Key

So training became the indispensable key to success for building and developing our teams. Since we began a six-month intensive training program, our casualty rate on the field has plummeted to four percent. Many missionary groups have suggested that if we would reduce the preparation time they would avail themselves of the opportunity of training with us. But we have found that six months is about the optimum time. Most prospective missionaries can put on a spiritual front for about six weeks, but after that the cracks begin to appear under intense pressure. At about the four month stage, another crucial time is faced. The reality of what is ahead has clearly been faced and the team has or has not jelled.

At the International Teams Missions Center each team lives in a large, eight-bedroom, bi-level home. They live, work, study, cook, tea, play, pray, cry, disagree and share together. The intensity of this daily personal interaction is something that cannot be duplicated in a dormitory or in locations where living together is impossible. The family style process results in uniting and bonding a team in a way that produces tremendous results once they arrive on a field. Although we don't continue this close living situation on the field, in the training process it is a vital part of unifying a team for service. It is also invaluable in helping those who can't make it on the team to opt out gracefully. About 10 percent do.

The training revolves around six areas of preparation: (1) language; (2) cross-cultural communication; (3) interpersonal relations and team building; (4) evangelism and church planting; (5) missions; (6) special studies for specific fields; e.g., relief and development, ministering to Christians in communist countries, etc.

The primary focus of this article is related to the crucial area of interpersonal relations and team building. During the six months of preparation a major focus is placed on seven important areas of team building.

1. *Godly leadership.* The team leader must see himself primarily as an enabler to the team. His major focus is the team members. He oils the machinery of team life. He encourages the spiritual life of the group. He helps them reach their goals. When a team leader is primarily concerned with what he personally is going to do, the team often is less successful. If the leader commits himself to helping each member of the team become successful, great things begin to happen.

Phil was the leader of the team going to Zambia. He and his wife had long-term goals of their own. They went into the program for what they could get out of it themselves. They weren't interested and weren't capable of handling a group of missionaries. Once we changed leaders the tone of the team greatly improved. Unity and cooperation developed, and the team planted a church with great success.

2. *Commitment to one another.* This takes time. But as team members learn to trust one another they begin to share and open their hearts to each other. This commitment process helps bring about a crucial change of attitudes. Independent spirits are replaced with interdependence. The missionaries begin to develop a servant attitude. Team members see themselves in the role of a servant, and the biblical injunctions of submitting to one another and serving one another shines through.

On one team a national from another country was a part of the group. His financial support was very low but other team members picked up the responsibility and he went overseas with full provision.

3. *Communication.*   A key element in the training process is to learn how to communicate openly with each other. The great majority of new missionaries in our program have never learned to do this. Our evangelical churches and parachurch organizations seem to have given many people a good biblical background but communication skills are desperately lacking.

Most don't really know how to resolve conflicts. Few have learned to say, "I was wrong, please forgive me." Many have never learned to compromise where they can so that the whole team can benefit.

Two men on one team in the Caribbean had great difficulty confronting each other over differences. Both eventually returned home because they could not communicate effectively. Unless each team member is willing to subject his own personal desires to the needs of the team, there will be many difficulties.

Obviously, we want them to stick to their guns if they are right as far as God and his Word are concerned. But often minor issues gnaw at the life of a team and selfishness destroys effectiveness. Only time spent together in training can reveal whether there will be problems in this area.

4. *Agreed objectives.* One interesting facet of training revolves around setting goals and strategies for the project ahead. In-depth discussion and united approval of the plan are vital to developing a common, unified focus. Each team spends hours preparing a strategy and finding where each person fits the plan.

5. *Recognition of gifts.* Learning to accept each other is crucial in developing unity. Not everybody has the same gifts. Some are excellent Bible teachers, others terrific evangelists, some work well with children, and some are good small group leaders. This diversity strengthens the total input of the team. Yet each one contributes to the whole. It is very rewarding to understand that no one is inferior or superior because they have certain gifts. Administrators, nurses, nutrition teachers, evangelists, Bible teachers, and builders all combine their efforts and a church is established. Just having the team accept you for who you are is very important.

6. *United prayer.* We have said it many times, but it is still true: the missionary family that prays together stays together. Praying and ministering to each other help to bind the team together. There is tremendous power in a unified group of 10 missionaries with a common goal crying out to God to work mightily among them. Six months of praying, combined with six months of language study, and six months of deep interpersonal involvement is a powerful program that can lead to successful team ministries.

7. *Accountability.* The team leader is accountable to the field director, and the team is accountable to the leader. Both set personal goals which are reviewed by their supervisors. Monitoring progress on a monthly or quarterly basis is very important. New missionaries can then regularly evaluate how they are doing. And the peer pressure of other team members who urge you on to meet your goals can be extremely beneficial in developing personal maturity and an effective ministry.

In our experience, six months of training in interpersonal relations prior to going to the field has been the key to building and developing successful teams.

Team life is not for everyone, but a powerful work for the Lord can be accomplished by well-trained missionaries with a united goal and a commitment to each other to share their life and work for the glory of God.

15

Timothy Warner

Teaching Power Encounter

"His eyes were glassy, his clothes ragged, his hair matted, and he was desperate. 'I'm going to kill this animal,' he repeated three times." A demon in a man trapped in spiritism was challenging the crowd of people around him including an evangelical missionary.

I remembered the words of Jesus, "Behold, I give you power over all the power of the enemy, and nothing by any means shall hurt you." I felt I should rebuke the demon in the name of Jesus, but what if nothing happened? All the people gathered would ridicule me. I slipped behind another man and watched as the man finally got up and started down the street being held by two men. Abruptly he threw them off and started running...

There I was--a defeated missionary in the interior of Brazil, ready to pack up and go home. When face to face with the enemy I was afraid. Who had told me how to deal with demons? (Paul Lewis in *Attack From the Spirit World*. Wheaton: Tyndale Press, 1973, pp. 203-4).

Unfortunately, this story could be repeated over and over from various parts of the world because missionaries have been sent to the field with no preparation for power encounter with the demonic forces at work in the world.

One of the most glaring gaps in our missionary curriculums is in our failure to help missionaries understand the reality of demons from a position of spiritual authority. An increasing number of writers are indicating an awareness of this problem, however. Alan Tippett has pointed it out frequently in his writings. In his perceptive article, "Probing Missionary Inadequacies at the Popular Level," he says,

A missionary geared to a metaphysical level of evangelism in his generator cannot drive a motor of shamanistic voltage. It is a tragic experience to find oneself with the right kind of power but the wrong kind of voltage.

There may be theological or missionary training institutions which provide for this but they are few and far between (Alan R. Tippett, "Probing Missionary Inadequacies at the Popular Level." *International Review of Missions, 49*, October, 1960, p. 413).

In the same article Tippett points out that if this subject were to be offered, the professor would be hard pressed to find good textbooks or other resource material. Most of what has been written on the subject of demons and spiritual power encounter has not been in a missionary context.

The fact is, however, that most of the people in the unreached areas of the world practice a religion at the folk level which is dominated by concepts of spirit power. Donald Jacobs, the Mennonite anthropologist, contends that "most people in the non-Western world convert to another faith because of seeking more power" (In John P. Newport, "Satan and Demons: A Theological Perspective." In John W. Montgomery, *Demon Possession*. Minneapolis: Bethany House Publishers, 1976, p. 334).

Alan Tippett reinforces this when he says, "Western missions might do well to face up to the statistical evidence that animists are being won today by a Bible of power encounter, not a demythologized edition" (Alan R. Tippett, *Solomon Islands Christianity*. Pasadena: William Carey Library, 1967, p. 100).

Tippett supports this by citing the contention of the secular anthropologist Melville Herskovitz that "it is no accident that the type of Protestantism most successful in Haiti is the form most hostile to *voodoo,* because it comes into *encounter* with it on a meaningful level..." (Alan R. Tippett, "Spirit Possession as It Relates to Culture and Religion." In John W. Montgomery, *Demon Possession*. Minneapolis: Bethany House Publishers, 1976, p. 156).

I look back on my own missionary experience in a tribal village in West Africa with a combination of regret and incredulity that I attempted ministry there with almost no understanding of either the biblical teaching on demons nor of the reality of the demonic world to the people with whom I lived and worked.

While I have spoken on the issue in the years since my days in Africa and have continued to study the subject, it was only this year that I ventured to teach a whole course on the subject. The response from the missionaries in the classes has been overwhelmingly positive. Many have expressed thoughts like, "If only I had had this course before I went to the field!"

I should perhaps add that a stimulus to venture into teaching has come in the form of personal experience in dealing with demonized people in the area in which we live. Being able to use illustrations from personal experience rather than just from the experience of others makes the instruction more credible.

I always begin the course with a brief discussion of my philosophy of balance as expressed in the statement, "The Christian life is the exciting process of trying to keep your balance." This stems from the more basic consideration that evil is always the perversion of a good which God has written into his order for man. Satan is on all sides of an issue and doesn't care whether we are on one side or the other--just so we are not at the balance point where God intends for us to be. This subject is no exception. There are those who find demons everywhere, and there are those who find them nowhere. Both extremes are unbiblical, but most of us have sought a place of safety in simply avoiding the subject. Unfortunately, there is no place of safety in this conflict--only places of ineffectiveness.

In connection with the idea of balance, it is important to make clear at the beginning that this is not a panacea for missionary ills nor a strategy or methodology which can or should dominate missionary ministry. It is simply one approach which is essential in many areas of the world to effective communication and effective ministry, because without the confidence to confront demonic powers, we will forfeit the opportunity to minister to many people.

To deal with the subject of power encounter, it is essential to deal with the concept of worldview, especially the difference between the animist view, the Western view, and the biblical view. We often encounter syncretism in the Third World churches, but we fail to understand that we as missionaries are also syncretistic but from the opposite end of the continuum. Our worldview has been influenced by the secularism and materialism around us more than we want to recognize, and we end up as victims of Hiebert's "flaw of the excluded middle" (Paul Hiebert,

"The Flaw of the Excluded Middle." *Missiology, 10,* January, 1982, pp. 35-47).

The aim is to develop a biblical worldview which includes angels and demons as functioning elements in everyday life, not just for animists or people in other cultures, but for everyone. Without such a worldview, the subject will never have the reality it must have if it is to become a vital factor in our ministries.

This discussion leads very naturally into an examination of the biblical teaching on Satan and demons. It is important, I believe, to see the "big picture," that is, to understand the key issue in the conflict between God and Satan. That issue will be clearly demonstrated in the antichrist as the personification of Satan who "even sets himself up in God's temple, proclaiming himself to be God" (2 Thess. 2:4). The issue is the glory of God. Satan is gripped with envy desiring to have the glory which God has. He realizes that he will never have it; so he is now out to gain all the satisfaction he can by depriving God of all the glory he can. From an eternal perspective that is impossible, but in the present order of things, he can achieve his objective partially and gain some satisfaction by causing men to live at a level below their privileges as God's children--children by creation or children by redemption.

This article is not the place to develop that concept; but it is very helpful, if not imperative, to see this perspective on the conflict in which we are all engaged whether we want to be or not. It is important that the role of angels be clarified in the treatment of this topic so that we do not get an unbalanced view of the spirit world.

As part of this section I also review and clarify the position of victory and authority of the Christian based on being "in Christ." The fear of the demonic world evident in so many Christians is essentially an expression of unbelief. Early in the course the absolute victory of Christ over Satan and all of his hosts and our participation in that victory must be made crystal clear. Without it there will be no victory in a spiritual power encounter on the mission field.

So, it is always wise to deal with the positive side of the question early in the course, but just as we need to know the authority on the basis of which we wage spiritual warfare and the resources available to us in that warfare, we also need to know our enemy. Paul said that he was not "unaware of [Satan's] schemes" (2 Cor. 2:11). Those "schemes" are studied as a basis for our resisting him "standing firm in the faith" (1 Pet. 5:9).

I prefer the term "demonization" to "demon possession" for the generic term denoting the various relationships between men and demons. I see these relationships falling along a continuum of influence ranging from temptation and harassment to actual control in the more classical concept of demon possession. A study of the Greek words used in passages dealing with demonized people is helpful.

Having laid the biblical foundation, I next move to the application of this specifically to the missionary. This is done first in terms of possible areas of attack on the missionary. One of the primary aims of Satan for Christians is to render them ineffective in Christian life and ministry. This can be accomplished in many ways; and when the source is not recognized as being demonic, it is very effective. It is always important, however, to make clear that the normal old nature-new nature conflicts cannot be avoided or solved by casting out demons. We can, however, prevent demons from taking advantage of such conflicts to bring us into deeper bondage.

The second area of missionary application is ways in which missionaries take the initiative in claiming territory held by Satan. This begins with evangelism (bringing people "from the power of Satan to God", but it also includes the destruction of occult objects or paraphernalia, healing, confrontation of practitioners of the black arts, and the casting out of demons. I do not suggest that missionaries go on a "lion" hunt trying to set up a series of dramatic power encounters. But neither do I suggest that we back off in fear when the power and glory of God are being challenged by men under the power of demons.

The course is concluded with a presentation of the practical methodology used in confronting demons. It is essential that we do not see our effectiveness in such a ministry as residing in saying the right words or phrases. This becomes magic. It is the flow of Christ's power and authority through us which produces the desired results. But it is helpful to be able to learn from the experience of others.

Audio tapes of actual confrontations are helpful in bringing an air of reality to what is too often just more theory. Nothing can substitute for experience in learning about this subject, but it is seldom possible to bring such experience into the classroom. Tapes for this purpose are available from Faith and Life Publications, 632 N. Prosperity Lane, Andover, KS 67002.

Some will question the absence of any historical perspectives on this subject. They have been omitted in the course I teach only because of time constraints. I think it is more important to deal with the current situation than to trace the historical positions on the subject.

There are other related areas which could be included in such a course, but the important thing is to equip missionaries to engage in power encounter when that is required.

PART TWO

MISSIONARY FAMILIES

PART TWO

MISSIONARY FAMILIES

The quality of life for missionary families has drawn a lot of attention during the last few years. Many important and often controversial areas have been discussed and debated, not the least of which has been the education of missionary children (MKs). Part Two enters the world of the missionary family by presenting 14 articles which examine characteristics of family life, missionary couples, and missionary children. A special section is also included which overviews the issues surrounding the education of missionary children.

In the first section, *Family Life*, White incorporates a "family systems" perspective to describe both the healthy and pathological functioning of missionary families and, by extension, mission organizations. Insights from the systems model are discussed in terms of family structure, boundaries, communication, intimacy, and patterns of change. The next article by O'Donnell brings together three dimensions which affect missionary life: the family life cycle, the stages of individual psychosocial development, and the different stages of missionary involvement. Emphasis is placed on understanding and anticipating family developmental tasks in light of the interaction of these three dimensions. Chester's article explores the various stresses experienced by missionary families. His conclusion that "missionaries appear to be under no more stress than other helping professionals" is surprising, and equally surprising is his finding that few missionaries take advantage of outside help for dealing with the stresses of missionary life. Kruckeberg and Stafford, specialists in child development, encourage pre-field and in-service training for strengthening family relationships. Particular emphasis is placed on healthy child-rearing practices. The final article by Stanley and Brent Lindquist discusses the important role which psychotherapy and counseling can have for missionary families who return early from the field. These psychologists present some representative cases of families needing help, followed by a description of the restoration approaches used by Link Care Center, a mental health agency specializing in missionary care.

The next section, entitled *Missionary Couples*, draws from the experiences of a psychiatrist, a church planter, and a psychologist in treating the area of missionary marriages. Marital expectations, spousal roles, and sexuality are just a few of the topics addressed in the first article by Foyle. This author generally feels positive about the overall quality of marital relationships among missionaries. Mid-life transitions are dealt with in the second article. Eagle's comments on the issues which couples go through at this time, such as adjusting to the aging process and maintaining a sense of productivity, will be especially appreciated by those who are going through this period. In "Resolving Conflicts in Christian Marriage," Williams gives some useful steps for working through marital conflict. Both spiritual and psychological principles are insightfully woven together to help missionary couples improve their communication and problem solving skills.

How does missionary life affect *children*? This is the perplexing question of many missionary parents and the subject of the next section. Sharp's review of the research on MKs points towards the generally healthy adjustment of MKs. While exceptions do occur, the bi-cultural lifestyle of MKs is held to positively impact such areas as academic performance and social relationships. The next article by Taylor applies Erik Erickson's psychosocial developmental theory to the growth of missionary children. Helpful comments are made for understanding the experiences of MKs at different developmental stages. Wickstrom and Fleck, clinical psychologists, report on their research on MK self-esteem and dependency for boarding school and nonboarding school students. Their data suggest "a significant positive correlation between number of years boarding and self-esteem." This study serves as an excellent example of the valuable information which can be obtained from well-designed research.

Missionary children have some unique educational needs. These needs must be addressed in light of the mission family's ministry, location, finances, and developmental stage. Such issues are touched upon in this final section which focuses on the *education of MKs*. Chester begins this section with a discussion of three general educational options for MKs: attending boarding school, undergoing correspondence courses, and attending local missionary-sponsored and national schools. Holzmann, reporting on the 1986 MK Education Symposium held at the U.S. Center for World Mission, lists 12 specific options for schooling, ranging from home schooling opportunities to attending an international school. Both of these articles address the pros and cons of the various educational possibilities. This section concludes with research by Hill which surveys the educational needs of MKs at over 70 locations. Based on this needs assessment and his own observations, Hill proposes a curriculum philosophy and plan to provide a balanced and quality education for MKs.

Perhaps the underlying issue for most families on the field is the need to balance family cohesiveness and growth with the need to participate in the tasks of cross-cultural living and ministry. The healthy family, in our view, is one which can use cross-cultural challenges to stimulate family solidarity, as well as draw upon family strengths to increase the effectiveness of its ministry and adjustment. Adequate preparation, a family system which fosters spiritual and emotional health, and an organizational structure sensitive to the developmental needs of the family, are necessary to encourage the growth and unique contribution of each family member.

FAMILY LIFE

FAMILY LIFE

16

Frances J. White

Characteristics of a Healthy Mission System

This presentation has a two-fold thrust. The first is to suggest some criteria, drawn from family systems concepts, for evaluating the degree of health of a missionary family. Secondly, these criteria are applied to examine the health of a mission's system.

The realization of the need to look at these criteria has grown out of the increasing request of candidate departments for help in evaluating the entire family in its selection process. This stems from the awareness that every individual missionary is affected by the family system in which he/she functions. The extension of the application of these characteristics of healthy family dynamics to evaluate the health of a mission system emanates from the correlation missionaries themselves have recognized between the two when I have done seminars on the family with mission groups. This is not surprising to those who have experienced the membership in the extended family provided by a mission system.

The characteristics of healthy functioning will be presented under the rubric of five areas around which every family forms patterns. "Families" is being used to speak of both nuclear as well as broader mission families.

The areas are presented on a spectrum starting with the ideal as the center point and contrasting qualities as end points. The following is an example:

Based on a paper presented at the Fourth Annual Conference on Mental Health and Missions held at Angola, Indiana in November, 1983. Reprinted by permission of the author.

INTIMACY

dependency	interdependency	independency

Although the entire range could be within the scope of normal functioning, several considerations condition the point along the spectrum that indicate maximum health at a given point in time. The first is that members of a family/mission necessarily fluctuate along the continuum according to their need to adjust to the changing developmental and situational circumstances of life. For example, between the polarities on the intimacy spectrum, younger children would require a more dependent type of relationship with parents, whereas the presence of adolescents calls for greater independency with parents. In times of emergency, families tend to move toward more dependent behavior. Likewise, new missionaries are generally more dependent upon their more experienced co-workers until they have become more acculturated. Also, in times of crises there is a needed pulling together.

A second consideration is the importance of recognizing the uniqueness of each family's/mission's endowment as part of its contribution to the total body of Christ. The very differences among family groups that would place them at different points between the polarities demonstrate the broad range of health that provides the complementarity of functioning through which needs are met.

A third factor is that, at either extreme, there is a precariously fine line between health and pathology. Again taking the area of intimacy as an example, the extensive sharing that might be anxiety-reducing on the dependency end can result in a crippled individual incapable of acting independently if carried too far. This leads to the fourth consideration of the need for a degree of balance between the polarities. This vital equilibrium, which should be the rule rather than the exception, permits individuals within the family/mission to be more flexible in accepting and meeting their needs as well as contributing to those of other members.

The following five pattern areas suggest some insights about healthy and unhealthy systems. Under each heading the health that results from an integration of polarities (middle characteristics) is described. Unhealthy manifestations are then delineated. They are possible rather than inevitable outcomes of functioning at a particular polarity. Implications for mission structure will be the focus of discussion at the end.

1. PATTERNS OF INTIMACY

dependency	interdependency	independency
(enmeshed)	(true intimacy)	(disengaged)

Healthy intimacy fosters a harmonious balance between these two polarities in a way that permits its members to develop and maintain their individual uniqueness and yet experience a sense of unity with others. When dependency is overly cullied, enmeshed relationships form that deprive participants of growth in their uniqueness. Differences become disloyalty. Guilt messages are often communicated to anyone, either expressing something new or questioning aspects of the old. An exclusive attitude tends to produce isolation from others. The boundary around the group is so solid that new ideas, people, etc. cannot easily enter the inner ring. The boundaries between those already in the circle, however, are too permeable, eliminating privacy and individuality. Every incident has a ripple effect, affecting every other individual in the system.

Functioning too strongly at the other extreme (independency) leads to a disengaged stance. There is too much individuality to the detriment of commitment and mutual support. There is, therefore, little protective function. The boundary is too loose around the group and too tight within it. Each one becomes more or less an island in him/herself. "I-ness" is the norm. Often people who form a disengaged pattern may not even be aware of their loneliness.

Mission organizations that are more enmeshed tend to have too much togetherness with a suspicion of people who are different. There is a sameness that prevents change. The enmeshment could be reproduced by the mission in the local church with a greater inclination to operate as parents attempting to keep the national under its jurisdiction. Cooperation with other organizations is minimal. This is particularly difficult in cases where the government sets up agencies as channels for handling mission/government logistics. Outdated methods, thinking and ways of relating are slow to change. The organization often fails to differentiate between Biblical absolutes and cultural relatives.

The more disengaged structure would have the opposite effect. Competition serving self-interests may be rife. Autonomy tends to be ignored with each person doing his/her own thing. The model to the local church is confusing. Accountability, warmth, and commitment, so important in a ministry, are minimal. Changes are embarqued upon without considering the effects of the separation and loss involved upon others.

2. PATTERNS OF STRUCTURE

over-structured   flexibly structured   under-structured

|—————————————————————————————————|

(rigid)   (chaotic)

The more flexibly structured a system is, the more adaptable it is. Principles, rather than specific injunctions, determine the limits and maintain the control. More freedom of action is left up to members. Feedback channels exist. Negotiation is possible within the parameters of valid problem-solving methods. A sufficient number of clearly defined rules exist to prevent problems and give a sense of security. They are amenable to adjustment as situations change.

The greater the number of specific rules, the more rigid the system tends to be. There is a higher level of control generally imposed externally rather than developed internally with opportunity for input from all the members. It is harder to adjust rules to changing conditions.

On the other hand, too few rules, unexecuted rules, or unclear rules lead to a chaotic situation. Core values that serve as guidelines are unidentified. A sense of disorganization, lack of responsibility, and unpredictability offer too little sense of security.

3. PATTERNS OF BOUNDARIES

tight   clear   confused

|—————————————————————————————————|

(overly defined)   (flexible)   (underly defined)

Boundaries refer to the invisible lines drawn in a family/mission group around given members (e.g., the marital/executive coalition and the siblings/missionaries at large). The members within the parameters or boundaries can be called sub-groups or sub-systems. Each subsystem is an organized unit within the overall system.

A healthy family/mission group forms clearly defined subsystems. Each subsystem is a unit responsible for carrying out distinct functions within the overall system. Its tasks, privileges, and limitations are well understood.

Members often belong to several subsystems simultaneously. For example, a man can be a husband in the spouse subsystem and a father in the parental subsystem. On the mission level he can be a business manager in the executive subsystem and a member of a team in a particular project subsystem. His role in each group is unambiguous. Yet, there is access to and communication among subsystems (e.g., a mission school director having input into policy formulated by field leaders). Also, within subsystems there is complementarity of function (e.g., an executive in charge of business functioning hand-in-hand with an executive in charge of personnel.

When the boundaries of subsystems are too closed, the necessary movement from one to another as roles fluctuate becomes difficult. Communication breaks down. Reasons for actions are possibly misunderstood. Suspicion results. Authoritarianism, legalism, constriction of affect, cognitions, and behaviors develop.

On the other hand, boundaries that are too loose or open can produce insecurity with confusion about roles, responsibility for decisions, respect, etc. Members feel leaderless and powerless.

4. PATTERNS OF COMMUNICATION

dogmatic   clear   mystifying

├──┤

(closed)   (open or unambiguous)   (obscure)

For any family/mission to function effectively, it must maintain open communication channels in all directions. Messages must be clearly understood. There is opportunity for feedback in the form of seeking or giving clarification, expressing favorable reactions or disagreements, making suggestions, and offering alternatives. This means active listening whereby one nears the content and feelings being expressed. Defensiveness and attacking are minimal. Statements are neither critical nor patronizingly nurturing.

A fixed dogmatic pattern forces the object of the message into a one-down role. This, in turn, leads to the development of dependent accommodating or rebellious, angry underlings. The former stifles positive growth. The latter leads to open or covert conflict.

Obscure communication leaves family/mission members confused about intent and expectations. It generally leads to behavior whereby the recipients of such communication try to create some sense for themselves. This, in turn, might well result in everyone doing his own thing

5. PATTERNS OF CHANGE

status quo   stability   flux

├──┤

Healthy families/missions develop balance between the amount of constancy they maintain and the change they promote. Enough status quo is present to permit an adequate period to accommodate new elements to existing patterns in order to assimilate them with the least amount of trauma. The more static periods also provide a period of respite from the ambiguities, risks, and anxieties that often accompany change.

However, functioning too extremely at the status quo polarity prevents the essential adaptations to a changing society. A family/mission would thereby fail to have an influence on the directions and consequences of new developments. A certain amount of seclusion would have to be present to prevent new elements from entering the system. Therefore, the adequate stimulation for creativity and progress is lacking and an apathetic and/or suspicious attitude easily develops.

Constant flux, however, can result in hyperactivity, confusion, agitation, and anxiety. Members experience a decreasing sense of belonging. The familiar moorings that provide predictability are undermined. Sufficient time for an in-depth evaluation of what to keep, modify or thoroughly change is lacking. Continuing change can lead to a diminishing realization of the immutability of Scriptural truths.

In today's world, periods of rapid change are unavoidable. To the degree that the stability that comes from an equilibrium between change and flux exists, the family/mission is more prepared to handle the new developments.

17

Kelly S. O'Donnell

Developmental Tasks in the Life Cycle of Mission Families

This study focuses on some of the developmental tasks common to mission families. These tasks are discussed in terms of McGoldrick and Carter's (1982) six stages of the family life cycle. A tripartite developmental model of the mission family is also presented which takes into account the interaction of the family life cycle, individual psychosocial development, and the stages of mission involvement. Considering family developmental tasks in light of this model serves to organize and clarify the various adjustment challenges of mission families.

Missionary families face several unique challenges due to the nature of their cross-cultural location and lifestyle. Several studies have focused on the adjustment issues for various members of the mission family, such as the missionary child (Wickstrom and Fleck, 1983), the missionary wife (Bowers, 1984), and the missionary couple (Foyle, 1987), as well as on the overall adjustment of the mission family itself (Kenny, 1983). Both individual and family systems perspectives have been used as a means to better understand the cross-cultural and developmental experiences of mission families.

One important way to further explore the mission family would be through the construct known as the *family life cycle* (FLC).

Copyright 1987 by the Rosemead School of Psychology, Biola University. Reprinted by permission from the *Journal of Psychology and Theology*, 1987, *15*, 281-290.

This approach provides a framework from which family development can be studied by identifying major transition points in the family's history from its formation to its dissolution. Examples would be the transitions which result from marriage, childbearing, and widowhood. Research on the family life cycle has been occurring since the 1930s and continues to be an important area of study for family theorists (Norton, 1983).

Similar to the individual developmental stages of Erikson (1963), FLC assumes a progression of stages in the family experience with specific developmental crises and tasks occurring at each particular stage. Further, transitions between stages usually bring about a shift in the internal dynamics of families and are typically experienced by the family as stressful (Nock, 1981). As in family systems theory, both the ongoing changes in the marital couple and those occurring for the children are examined in light of their impact on the overall family. Perhaps the greatest value of FLC theory for missions is found in its emphasis on organizing and understanding the important developmental sequences and tasks of families.

Several classifications of FLC have been discussed in the literature (e.g., Duvall, 1971; Glick, 1977; Loomis, 1936; Rodgers, 1973). One basic classification of relevance to the mission family is that of McGoldrick and Carter (1982). These researchers organize the family life cycle into six distinct stages: (a) the unattached young adult, (b) the newly married couple, (c) the family with young children, (d) the family with adolescents, (e) launching children and moving on, and (f) the family in later life. Noteworthy in this FLC classification is the inclusion of the "unattached young adult" stage, primarily because of its significance in influencing the characteristics of the new nuclear family which the individual will establish.

Each of the six FLC stages identified by McGoldrick and Carter can be discussed in terms of two ongoing family processes: *the realignment of generational boundaries* and *the renegotiation of roles*. These two processes provide a further structure in which many of the developmental tasks of mission families can be categorized. Generational realignment involves the changing boundaries and relationships between nuclear and extended families as well as between differing subsystems within the nuclear family. An example of this would be the need for the newly married missionary couple to function as an autonomous unit by establishing clear boundaries between itself and each spouse's original nuclear family. Role renegotiation, the second process, also occurs at each stage and pertains to issues of interdependency and differentiation as a result of the changing roles of family members. With the assumption of childbearing roles, for example, missionary couples enter into new areas of interdependency as they seek to educate, discipline, and care for their children.

In addition to FLC stages, two other types of developmental stages must be considered. When related together, these three types of stages can form a tripartite model which more fully addresses the complex developmental challenges of the mission family. These stages are: (a) FLC per se; (b) the individual psychosocial stages of development for each family member (infancy, toddlerhood, early school age, middle school age, early adolescence, later adolescence, early adulthood, middle adulthood, later adulthood, and very old age--Newman and Newman, 1987); and (c) the typical missionary stages experienced by most long-term missionaries (recruitment, preparation, cultural entrance, ongoing ministry, reentry for furlough, return to the field, and retirement).

Each of the previous three types of stages are diagrammed in Figure 1, with the horizontal dimension representing FLC stages, the diagonal dimension representing individual stages of psychosocial development, and the vertical dimension representing mission stages.

The essential feature of this model is its consideration of the interaction effects of all three dimensions as a means to understand and anticipate the developmental tasks of mission families.

Two of the three dimensions in Figure 1, the FLC and mission stages, can be maneuvered to reflect a variety of interaction patterns during mission family life. An example of this is seen in Figure 2, which relates the various developmental stages for a nuclear mission family of four members, with the parents in their middle forties, and the children ages 14 and 18. As can be seen in the diagram, the family has recently returned to the field for a second term and is at the FLC stage of "the family with adolescents". In addition, each family member can be plotted along the diagonal dimension to correspond with his or her present stage of psychosocial development.

Figure 2 illustrates how the various developmental tasks for this mission family (and other mission families) can be concisely represented.

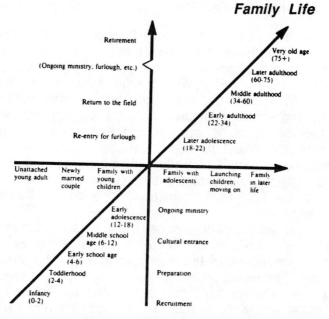

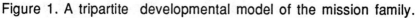

Figure 1. A tripartite developmental model of the mission family.

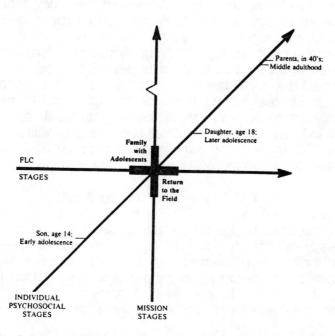

Figure 2. A representation of the *current developmental status* of a four member mission family in its second term of service.

Note that the point on Figure 2 where the FLC and mission dimensions intersect (the darkest part of the lines), along with those stages marked on the individual psychosocial dimension, represent the *current developmental status* of the family. This family would thus be expected to be experiencing several developmental tasks stemming from the ongoing FLC stage (e.g., transitioning towards greater independence for adolescent members), the actual developmental challenges of each respective member (e.g., transitioning through middle adulthood issues for the parents, such as managing a career and a household), and the return to the field (e.g., transitioning back to a different culture and lifestyle).

Additional factors, of course, beyond these three dimensions need to be considered. Included would be such areas as the overall psychological health of the marital couple and the family system, the type of missionary setting, the social support network for the family, and whether the family is an intact nuclear, single parent, or blended family. As is true of their contemporaries back home, mission families show a great deal of diversity, and thus many variables must be assessed when seeking to understand them.

With these background concepts in mind, this study endeavors to outline some of the developmental tasks experienced by the mission family. Most of the tasks discussed are also applicable to military and business families living abroad on a long-term basis. The framework for this analysis is provided by the FLC stages presented by McGoldrick and Carter, and the concepts of generational realignment and role renegotiation. Some of the possible interaction effects of family, individual, and mission stages will also be addressed. Each section begins with an overview of the FLC stage being examined, followed by a discussion of important stage-related tasks for the mission family.

The Unattached Young Adult

This first stage begins during later adolescence and can last well into early adulthood. Some of the developmental tasks of this period include experimenting with adult work roles, making adult friendships, and becoming intimate with another person (Erikson, 1963). In general, it is a time of emotionally and physically leaving home as well as a time of establishing a clearer sense of identity.

The developmental processes of physical separation and psychological differentiation from one's family of origin can be facilitated at this time through missions involvement.

Participation in cross-cultural service necessitates a change in geographic and cultural environments, which then provides a context for engaging in the separation-differentiation process. Family boundaries, though, must be flexible enough to allow its members to make such a cross-cultural venture into adulthood. A sense of bonding and belonging to a new family can also occur as the young missionary makes adult friendships with members of the missionary team.

The centrality of the task of role experimentation during this period suggests that this is a prime time for the young adult to become acquainted with cross-cultural lifestyles. Exposure to the missionary role now is thus crucial for the individual to be able to evaluate and later possibly choose missions as a career. Short-term involvement can thus be seen as both a participation in and a preparation for missions work. A greater appreciation for cultural diversity as well as a greater sense of life purpose and identity can also result through mission service at this time.

Another developmental task for the young adult which can be influenced by mission involvement is that of becoming intimate with a potential spouse. In fact, many who take on missionary roles during this stage may actually seek out a spouse who has also prioritized mission work. The significance of mission involvement for the unattached young adult is ultimately seen in its lasting effect on the life direction for his or her future marriage and family.

The Newly Married Couple

The second FLC stage begins at the time of marriage and lasts until the birth of the first child. In the United States, the average age at marriage is 22 for women and 24 for men (Glick, 1984). The prevailing trend is to defer childbearing until later, often due to the desire to have fewer children as well as to pursue career goals. In spite of the many adjustments that take place at this time, the first few years of marriage are usually reported to be the most satisfying (Glenn and McLanahan, 1982). Over 90% of all individuals in the United States will eventually marry (Glick, 1984).

The boundaries between the young couple beginning missionary work and their families of origin can be readily established due to geographic location. Although differentiation of the couple is usually viewed as a healthy occurrence, decreased contact with one's family implies less access to their emotional support.

Decreased contact may also result in increased concern for members of the extended family (Gish, 1983).

Taking on spousal roles and trying to bond to a new culture as missionaries may be two competing developmental tasks for the newly married couple. The stresses associated with each of these challenges are difficult to simultaneously negotiate, and can detract from both the couple's relationship and their mission focus. Add to this the need to steer a course between the host culture's expectations for husband and wife roles and those from the missionaries' homeland and an even more difficult adjustment challenge can ensue. It would probably be better, therefore, for a couple to first establish themselves firmly in their marriage in their own country before attempting to begin missionary work, or else to marry during a later stage of mission involvement.

The Family with Young Children

Transition into this next stage requires that a couple shift into a new generational category by becoming parents. Some significant sources of stress for new parents during this period include loss of sleep, financial strain, and more restrictions on what the couple can do together. Most studies thus indicate a decrease in marital satisfaction following the birth of the first child (Glenn and McLanahan, 1982). As with other FLC stages, this stage can involve a time of marital evaluation for both partners as they reassess what they want in their marriage and in life.

One of the important developmental tasks for the young mission family at the cultural entrance stage is finding a *family niche* or place where it can fit into the new culture. Family members can facilitate this process through becoming actively involved with the host culture by making friends and learning the new language and social customs (Brewster and Brewster, 1981). *Affiliated families* (Kempler, 1976) usually develop, whereby nationals who become close to the mission family function as if they were part of the extended family. Fitting in as a family with the parents' original home culture can also be a significant challenge during the reentry stage of missions (Austin, 1983).

Different family boundary expectations are often present for the mission family, members of the host culture, and fellow expatriates. The adjustment task is to balance the family's need for some privacy and time together with the need to make good family contact with nationals. Dealing with these different expectations can be particularly challenging for the missionary couple that is rearing children as well as the missionary family entering the new culture for a first term of service.

For the missionary couple, childbearing may be delayed by the decision to first pursue full-time missionary work. On the one hand, the presence of children brings added responsibilities which may interfere with more fully attending to mission tasks. On the other hand, children may also serve as "cross-cultural links" to nationals by means of the friendships which they are able to form. In this way, through children, members of the host culture and the mission family may become initially acquainted. Secondly, having children may influence the nationals' perception that the "foreigners are like us"--that is, a family with children. The presence of missionary children can thus provide a common bond between families, helping to transcend cultural differences by pointing to areas of similarity.

The socialization of children is yet another developmental challenge for the mission family. One of the major concerns centers on the extent to which children should differentiate from their parents' culture by adopting the language and customs of the host culture (Sharp, 1985). The choice of school setting, for example, can be one of the most influential factors affecting the enculturation process of missionary children. Missionary parents must, therefore, carefully assess both the academic and social ramifications of various educational options for their children, such as home schooling, national schools, or boarding schools.

Missionary wives at this time face added adjustment pressure from the multiplicity of roles that they assume (Jackson, 1980). It should be noted that missionary wives, during all stages of the family life cycle, report experiencing more stress than their husbands (Chester, 1983). Much of this difference is attributable to the added responsibility of childbearing which the wives primarily bear in addition to their regular mission-related work and domestic duties.

The Family with Adolescents

The fourth FLC stage starts when one or two children reach early adolescence, somewhere around age 12. Qualitative changes in relationships between the parents and the adolescents are now required, reflecting the greater need for the youth to become more independent. Peer affiliation, along with the search for identity and autonomy, are key developmental tasks for adolescent family members (Erikson, 1963). Most American families experience some increased conflict as a result of the transitions at this time, but this tends to be more mild than severe (Montemayor, 1982; Steinberg, 1981).

The decision of whether or not to send adolescents to a boarding school is a special developmental task for the mission family. Separation from the family for the sake of education is seldom easy, even if such a move is not permanent. Choosing to utilize a boarding school may require the adolescent to experience an early, modified form of *launching* and the parents to experience an early, modified form of *empty nest.*

Another developmental task of this period involves the missionary adolescent's relationship with a peer group. Certain adolescents transitioning through the mission stages of cultural entrance and reentry may have special difficulty identifying with a group of peers. This is especially true during the middle and later part of adolescence where peer groups are already formed and the adolescent may feel that they can neither relate to nor gain entrance into the peer group. Peer group involvement may be easier during the initial part of adolescence as peer groups are just beginning to be formed and thus may be more accessible to the younger missionary adolescent.

A third challenge of this stage for the missionary family may involve the resolution of midlife career issues for the husband and/or wife. For the missionary husband, this can be a time of questioning one's identity, occupation, and overall sense of purpose (Levinson, 1978). For the missionary wife, this adjustment challenge may take the form of wanting to develop herself further as a person beyond the roles of childbearing and homemaking. Most of the research to date tends to indicate that midlife career issues, if they are even present, are best seen as transition times rather than times of personal crisis (Schaie and Willis, 1986). Those missionaries who do leave the field during this or other stages, however, may be especially vulnerable to feelings of frustration and failure (Lindquist, 1983). Obviously the entire family will be affected by the outcome of a career change by either husband or wife.

Launching Children and Moving On

During this stage, a major restructuring of the family system is required as the family sends some of its members into the adult world. Separation can range from being a gradual to an abrupt process and may involve several *rebounds* or returns to the family system (Moore and Hotch, 1981). The central process of *launching out* during this period usually occurs during later adolescence and anywhere from age 40 to 65 for the parents. Parents thus generally launch their children about 20 years before their retirement. Clemens and Axelson (1985) report that approximately five percent of all American families continue to have one or more children living at home who are age 25 or older.

One important developmental task of this stage for the mission family is the particular country into which the grown child will launch. For the *third culture kid* who feels part of two different cultures, this event can be as perplexing as it is stressful. One possible solution is for the young adult to have a *trial launch* into the proximity of extended family members who live in their parents' original country. Educational and/or career goals are then typically pursued. While launching does not solve the third culture dilemma, extended family relationships can help support grown missionary children as they seek to clarify their cultural and vocational identity.

The new change in family structure necessitates the added task of role adjustments within the marital system. This is true for missionary couples as well as their counterparts back home. Reinvestment in the marriage usually begins along with a concommitant increase in marital satisfaction (Glenn and McLanahan, 1982). Parents may also have more time to devote to mission work as a result of the departure of some or all of their children. Depending on the couple's past experiences, mission work now may involve any of the mission stages, ranging from recruitment to returning to the field. Furthermore, as middle adulthood often brings with it the desire to contribute to the quality of life for future generations, couples may be even more motivated to increase their mission involvement.

The Family in Later Life

This is the final stage for the initial two members of the nuclear family. Grandparenthood, retirement, and widowhood are important experiences which effect both the couple and the entire family. This period continues to be characterized by the older parents' investment in the lives of their children and grandchildren. A process of *life review* also occurs, in which one's past life is examined, integrated, and placed in perspective (Butler, 1963). Research generally supports the idea that the healthiest adjustment during old age occurs for those elderly individuals who continue their involvement with others and maintain diverse interests and pastimes (Butler and Lewis, 1977).

Three developmental experiences of later adulthood can affect mission involvement during this stage. First, retirement abroad as a missionary is a possibility (Siemans, 1981). This may be considered by the missionary or missionary couple who were once involved in missions, as well as by those individuals who have never served on the mission field. Such involvement can engage the older family members in life and therefore help continue their level of adjustment.

A second developmental challenge of this time is dealing with the declining health of older adults. This fact must be recognized for its effect on the types of roles and involvements which the older missionary can assume. Realistic adjustments in job expectations, for example, or possible retirement will thus have to be considered as a result of the physical changes accompanying the stages of later adulthood and very old age.

Finally, the desire to care for an aged parent--either by a grown member of the mission family or by someone who desires to go to the mission field--can postpone missionary service. The aged parent may seek to live with or close to one of the children, as seen in the fact that about 80% of parents in the United States over age 65 live within one hour's distance from at least one of their children (Walsh, 1980). Mission families might consider having an older family member live with them on the field, though this might not be the most practical arrangement.

Conclusions and Suggestions

This article has focused on the unique developmental tasks of mission families. Some of the more significant tasks are summarized in Table 1, and are presented in terms of the processes of generational realignment and role renegotiation for each FLC stage.

The developmental tasks for the mission family suggested in this article are, of course, both general and representative, and not meant to be exhaustive. The relevance of their actual application will depend upon the characteristics of the particular mission family and mission setting in question. Mission agencies may, therefore, want to develop their own individualized list of developmental tasks for its families, similar to those in Table 1, especially as an aid to on-field and reentry adjustment. The thought here is that an increased awareness of individual, family, and cross-cultural issues will promote the current and future health of the mission family.

Table 1
Developmental Tasks of Mission Families at Different FLC Stages

	Realignment of Generations	Renegotiation of Roles
Unattached Young Adult	1. Geographic and cultural distance furthers differentiation from family. 2. Individual becomes a member of a new family --the missionary team.	1. Experimentation with adult roles and identity as a missionary. 2. Choice of spouse and direction of future family influenced by missions.
Newly Married Couple	1. Boundaries for newly married affected by geographic distance from families. 2. Geographic distance limits emotional support from families of origin.	1. Assuming spousal and missionary roles simultaneously is difficult. 2. Different expectations for husband and wife roles in the host culture.
Family With Young Children	1. Need to find a "family niche" and "affiliated family" in the host culture. 2. Different boundary expectations; time together as a family and privacy issues. 3. Presence of children can create "intercultural links" with nationals.	1. Childbearing and childrearing may be deferred for the sake of missions. 2. Different socialization experiences; language, customs, and schooling. 3. Multiple roles and role confusion for missionary wives creates stress.
Family With Adolescents	1. Separation via boarding school: early launching and empty nest experiences. 2. Extended family relationships continue to be limited by geographical distance.	1. Peer group identification difficulty in cultural entrance and re-entry stages. 2. Mid-life issues for husbands and wives: identity, marriage, career.

Launching Children; Moving On	1. Grown child must choose a country and culture into which to launch. 2. Young adult may "trial launch" in the proximity of extended family members who live in the parents' homeland.	1. New non-parental roles may free the couple for missions. 2. Desire to contribute to future generations in middle-aged may increase mission involvement.
Family In Later Life	1. Desire to care for aged parent may postpone going overseas. 2. Retired missionary may seek to live closer to or with family.	1. Retirement abroad as a missionary is a possibility. 2. Missionary role affected by health of the older adult.

The emphasis in FLC theory on the stresses surrounding transition times can be incorporated into the pre-field selection and training of mission families. Mission boards, for instance, would do well to assess past coping strategies which the entire family has used during transitions between FLC stages. Two important areas to explore would be the typical responses of each family member as well as the levels of family cohesiveness and satisfaction during these transition times.

Mission agencies may also want to periodically assess the *current developmental status* of each of the families serving in their organization. This type of assessment could be easily integrated into the ongoing evaluation process of the agency. Extra support and care may be required for mission families experiencing multiple developmental challenges at the individual, familial, and mission stages. An example would be the mission family that has recently returned home for a one-year furlough (reentry adjustment), launched its first adolescent into a university (empty nest syndrome), and where the father is questioning his career choice (midlife career issues).

Additional research is needed which can provide a greater empirical foundation for the stage-related developmental tasks of the mission family. Multivariate research which compares FLC experiences and stages for different types of mission families (e.g., marriages without children, blended families) and different mission settings would be especially valuable. Still other research might contrast FLC statistics for American families with those for missionary and other expatriate families. One example would be comparing the average age of retirement for career missionaries with that of their contemporaries back home. Dividing the FLC stage of "the family with young children" into two stages would also be useful, as it would help specify the different developmental tasks for mission families with young versus very young children.

References

Austin, C. (1983). Reentry stress: The pain of coming home. *Evangelical Missions Quarterly, 19,* 278-287.

Bowers, J. M. (1984). Roles of married women missionaries: A case study. *International Bulletin of Missionary Research, 8,* 4-7.

Brewster, E. T., & Brewster, E. S., (1981). Bonding and the missionary task. In R. Winter and S. Hawthorne (Eds.),*Perspectives on the world Christian movement: A reader* (pp.452-464). Pasadena, CA: William Carey Library.

Butler, R. N. (1963). The life review: An interpretation of reminiscence in the aged. *Psychiatry, 26,* 65-76.

Butler, R. N., & Lewis, M. I. (1977). *Aging and mental health* (2nd ed.). St. Louis: Mosby.

Chester, R. M. (1983). Stress on mission families living in "other culture" situations. *Journall of Psychology and Christianity, 2,* 30-37.

Clemens, A., & Axelson, L. (1985). The not-so-empty-nest: The return of the fledgling adult. *Family Relations, 34,* 259-264.

Duvall, E. M. (1971). *Family development.* Philadelphia: Lippincott.

Erikson, E. (1963). *Childhood and society* (2nd edition). New York: Norton.

Foyle, M. (1987). Stress factors in missionary marriages. *Evangelical Missions Quarterly, 23,* 20-28.

Gish, D. (1983). Sources of missionary stress, *Journal of Psychology and Theology, 11,* 236-242.

Glenn, N., & McLanahan, S. (1982). Children and marital happiness: A further specification of the relationship. *Journal of Marriage and the Family, 43,* 63-72.

Glick, P. (1977). Updating the life cycle of the family. *Journal of Marriage and the Family, 39*, 5-13.

Glick, P. (1984). Marriage, divorce, and living arrangements: Prospective changes. *Journal of Family Issues, 5*, 7-26.

Jackson, E. (1980). Women's role in missions. *Evangelical Missions Quarterly, 16*, 197-205.

Kempler, H. (1976, April). Extended kinship ties and some modern alternatives. *Family Coordinator*, 143-149.

Kenny, B. J. (1983). *The missionary family.* Pasadena, CA: William Carey Library.

Levinson, D. (1978). *The season of a man's life.* New York: Knopf.

Lindquist, S. (1983). A rational for psychological assessment of missionary candidates. *Journal of Psychology and Christianity, 2*, 10-14.

Loomis, C. P. (1936). The study of the life cycle of families. *Rural Sociology, 1*, 180-199.

McGoldrick, M., & Carter, E. (1982). The stages of the family life cycle. In F. Walsh (Ed.), *Normal family processes.* New York: Guilford Press.

Moore, D., & Hotch, D. (1981). Late adolescents' conceptualizations of home-leaving. *Journal of Youth and Adolescence, 10*, 1-10.

Montemayor, R. (1982). The relationship between parent- adolescent conflict and the amount of time adolescents spend alone and with parents and peers. *Child Development, 53*, 1512-1519.

Newman, B., & Newman, P. (1987). *Development through life: A psychosocial approach* (4th ed.). Homewood, IL: Dorsey Press.

Nock, S. L. (1981). Family life cycle transitions: Longitudinal effects on family members. *Journal of Marriage and the Family, 43*, 703-713.

Norton, A. J. (1983). Family life cycle: 1980. *Journal of Marriage and the Family, 45*, 267-275.

Rodgers, R. H. (1973). *Family interaction and transaction: The developmental approach.* Englewood Cliffs, NJ: Prentice-Hall.

Schaie, K., & Willis, S. (1986). *Adult development and aging.* Boston: Little, Brown.

Sharp, L. W. (1985). Toward a greater understanding of the real MK: A review of recent research.*Journal of Psychology and Christianity, 4,* 73-78.

Siemans, R. (1981). Secular options for missionary work. In R. Winter & S. Hawthorne (Eds.), *Perspectives on the world Christian movement: A reader* (pp. 770-774). Pasadena, CA: William Carey Library.

Steinberg, L. D. (1981). Transformations in family relations at puberty. *Developmental Psychology, 17,* 833-840.

Walsh, F. (1980). The family in later life. In E. Carter & M. McGoldrick (Eds.), *The family life cycle: A framework for family therapy.* New York: Gardner Press.

Wickstrom, D., & Fleck, J. (1983). Missionary children: Correlates of self-esteem and dependency. *Journal of Psychology and Theology, 11,* 226-235.

18

Raymond M. Chester

Stress on Missionary Families Living in *Other Culture* Situations

Stress and burnout on missionary families living in "other culture" situations is examined. A questionnaire containing 14 questions was formulated and sent to 100 married men and 100 married women working as missionaries in 11 countries. Included in the questionnaire was the Pines and Aronson Tedium/Burnout Self-Diagnosis instrument. Stress levels obtained from the missionary population, when compared with other professions, show that missionaries appear to be under no more stress than other helping professionals. Yet missionaries in the population surveyed do not seem to recognize the actual amount of stress under which they are actually living. They are under a significant amount of stress but have no way to turn to find relief.

The idea that someone in the "ministry has a problem" is a new concept. People still like to hold up the pastor, and especially the missionary, as a *Super Saint* who is impervious to both pain and problem. The ministry is a "vocation where a person must be all things to all people" (Daniel, 1981). The minister is never free from his duties, which are usually not clearly defined. "The criteria for knowing when they have done their duty are often ambiguous" (p. 244).

My personal counseling load has changed in the past 5 years to include, almost exclusively, pastors, missionaries, and those preparing for the ministry. If stress and burnout are reaching them, just how widespread is the problem? "Marital stress and family conflicts were another reason often cited for leaving the vocation...Marital problems and feelings of failure and inadequacy are highly correlated with burnout" (Daniel, 1981, p. 144).

Pines and Aronson explain tedium and burnout in this way:

Tedium and burnout are similar in terms of symptomatology but are different in origin. Both are clusters of exhaustion reactions. Tedium can be the result of any prolonged chronic pressures (mental, physical, or emotional); burnout is the result of constant or repeated emotional pressure associated with an intense involvement with people over long periods of time. (Pines & Aronson, 1981, p. 15)

They go on to say that the key elements of burnout are the feelings of helplessness, hopelessness, and entrapment. In their research they have found that the "people who start out with the highest ideals (unless they managed to develop effective coping strategies on their own) are likely to experience the most severe burnout" (p. 34). If the responsibility for another's well-being is a primary source of strain leading to burnout, then "how much greater is the strain when one 'feels' responsible for an entire church" (Daniel, 1981, p. 245).

Daniel (1981) points out that:

The cost of burn-out is high, both in terms of loss of service to clients, who feel depersonalized and are made to feel like a burden to the burned-out worker, and in terms of professional job turnover. The average length of stay in many people-helping professions such as social workers, poverty lawyers, child care workers, pastors, et cetera, is two years or less. The problems for pastors are only beginning to be recognized as part of the same burnout syndrome that has plagued other human service professions. Researchers in the field of burn-out have almost universally echoed the same cry; it is the social, interpersonal pressures of the job, and not a basic personality fault within the worker that is responsible for burn-out. (p. 233)

The cost of stress and burnout seems to be high in missions. "Experts in this field report that up to 50 percent of the first termers return early, or do not return after the first term" (Lindquist, 1982, p. 22). If missionaries are under stress, just how much stress are they under and compared to whom?

Survey

Method. A self-administered questionnaire survey was used to study stress on missionary families living in other cultures.

Subjects. All of the participants come from an evangelical theological perspective. They all ministered in cultures other than their culture of origin. One hundred married men and 100 married women (100 married couples) were chosen by random selection.

Apparatus. A questionnaire was formulated requesting basic demographic information in 14 questions. For question #13, the Pines and Aronson Tedium/Burn-out Self-Diagnosis instrument was used. It consists of 21 short, concise questions to be rated from 1 (never) to 7 (always). Pines and Aronson (1981) have concluded that a score of 0.0 to 1.9 would indicate that the person is in a state of euphoria. A score from 2.0 to 2.9 means that one is doing well. A score in the range of 3.0 to 3.9 would mean that it would be wise to reexamine one's work, evaluate priorities, and then consider possible changes. A score of 4.0 or higher would indicate that a person is experiencing burnout to the extent that it is mandatory that something be done immediately.

Procedure. A cover letter with brief instructions was attached to each questionnaire sent.

Results

General population. A question regarding age identification was used so the missionary would feel less identifiable. The mean age grouping was 41-45 with husbands and wives married for 16-20 years. The mean years on the field was 11-15 for husbands and wives. The mean number of children was 2.53.

The missionaries were asked if they felt that missionary life is stressful. Thirty percent of the husbands (24 percent of the wives) reported that they felt it was very stressful while 67 percent of the husbands (62 percent of the wives) felt it was only somewhat stressful. Three percent of the husbands (14 percent of the wives) said it was less stressful than life before missionary service. When asked if they felt that they "personally" were under more stress as a missionary, 59 percent of the husbands (62 percent of the wives) reported: "yes," while 29 percent of the husbands (29 percent of the wives) said they were under the same amount of stress. Twelve percent of the husbands (9 percent of the wives) reported being personally under less stress as a missionary.

The mean tedium/burnout level for the husbands was 2.95 and the mean level for the wives was 3.06. Age group scores are presented in Figure 1.

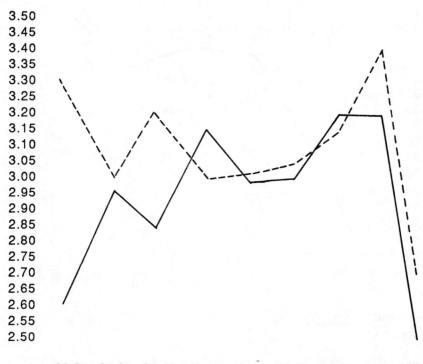

Husbands _____

Wives - - - - - - - - - - - - -

Figure 1
Tedium/Burnout Scores vs. Age Groupings--General Population

In question 14, the missionaries were asked what method they personally used within their family to cope with stress. Thirty-three percent of the husbands (31 percent of the wives) said they used prayer and/or devotions. Exercise and/or games were used by 15 percent of the husbands (14 percent of the wives). Family talks were used by 22 percent of the husbands (25 percent of the wives). Thirteen percent of the husbands (11 percent of the wives) used various other methods to "handle" stress.

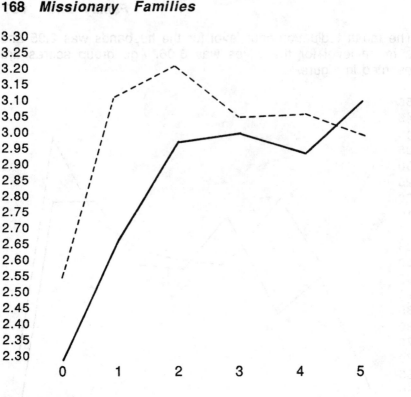

Husbands_____
Wives----------

Figure 2
Tedium/Burnout Scores vs. No. of Children --General Population

The Tedium/Burnout scores, when compared with the number of children, resulted in the scores as seen as Figure 2.

A comparison of Tedium/Burnout scores and years married is shown in Figure 3.

Figure 4 compares the Tedium/Burnout scores with the number of years a missionary has lived in "another culture."

The mean Tedium/Burnout score for husbands in this study was 2.95 (n=56) and 3.06 (n=58) for wives. Pines and Aronson (1981) show a mean for males of 3.20 (n=1,188) and for females of 3.30 (n=2,529), while Fowler (Note 1), in his study of married college students, found a mean of 3.08 (n=30) for husbands and 2.93 (n=30) for wives. The overall mean for missionaries in this study was 3.00 (n=114).

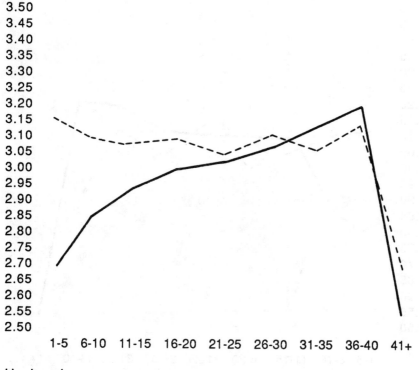

Husbands_____
Wives- - - - - - - - - -

Figure 3
Tedium/Burnout Scores vs. Years Married--General Population

Discussion

The original hypothesis of the author was that missionaries would be found to be living under more stress in other cultures than in their culture of origin. This study does not support that opinion as will be seen.

Pines and Aronson provide a list of 45 professional groups studied using their instrument. The mean tedium/burnout for those professions ranges from 2.80 to 3.80. The 3.80 scores included professions such as social work, nursing and education while the 2.80 scores were managers in Israel. Counseling scored 3.70, with therapy at 3.60. The 3.00 scores included science, technical and clerical, professional homemaking, and nursing aide.

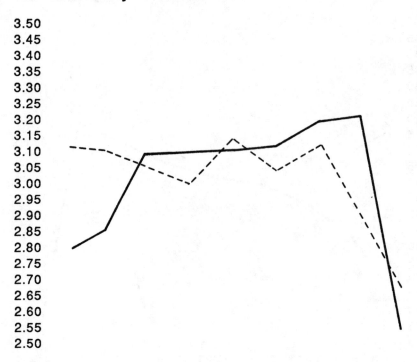

Figure 4
Tedium/Burnout Scores vs. Years on Field--General Population

Pines and Aronson say that:

Of the thousand who responded to this self-diagnosis instrument, none scored either 1 or 7. The reason is obvious. It is unlikely for one to be in a state of eternal euphoria implied by the score 1, and it is unlikely that a person who scores 7 will be able to cope with the world well enough to participate in a...research project. (p. 38)

In our study one male missionary did score 1.80. The responses of five couples who participated in the experiment from the same field (the field with the lowest tedium/burnout score) indicated that all felt that they were under a "tremendous" amount of stress. That score along with the responses from the couples may indicate that these missionaries do not comprehend the true stress under which they live or that they do not feel that they should show so much stress and so try to ignore it.

Coupled with this was the response to two of the questions concerning stress. It will be remembered that only 30 percent of the husbands and 24 percent of the wives felt that missionary life was stressful. However, the very next question showed that 59 percent of the husbands and 62 percent of the wives felt that they were "personally" under more stress as a missionary. What we have here is a situation where the majority of the missionaries believe the other missionaries are not facing much stress, and yet this same majority see themselves as being personally under a lot of stress. In other words, the missionary is saying, "Though I'm under a lot of stress I cannot let the other know. I don't understand why they look so calm and seem to not be under much stress. I must keep up my front of calmness." I believe this shows that we are still facing the problem mentioned in the first paragraph of this paper. The missionary must keep up the image of the *Super Saint* who is impervious to pain and problem alike.

Even if we accept the score of $\bar{x}=3.00$ for this group of people, we may be looking at an even more difficult problem: the denial of the existence of stress. Daniel (1981) says that members of the same staff, or what we would call "team members" in missions, are unaware that the "others are also experiencing the emotional exhaustion and physical symptoms of burn-out (p. 235). He feels that this ignorance is even greater among ministers than it is among other helping professionals. He goes on to say:

One factor is the physical isolation of many pastors, but even greater factors are: (a) the competitive atmosphere of pastoral meetings which inhibit sharing of problems, (b) the identification with deity and pedestal on which one must live, and (c) the increased defensiveness found in ministers....(p.245)

If the observations of Daniel and this author are correct, then we in the counseling profession have a much more difficult task when dealing with these people. To bring someone from denial to acceptance and then to change can be a long process.

Missionaries seemed to be expressing feelings of isolation and loneliness. Remember that Pines and Aronson (1981) say that the key elements of burnout are feelings of helplessness, hopelessness, and entrapment. I hear more and more of these feelings expressed in counseling sessions, especially from the wives. Adler (1982) says that the whole area of married women going overseas has been neglected. Lindquist (1979) noted some of the attitudes of men concerning overseas service for women:

The responsibility seems too often to be limited to rearing children and serving cookies at staff meetings. Jealousy between married and single women regarding differing job roles, is also a factor. Wives are often the determining factor for families staying or leaving the field. (p. 22)

Because the wives' tedium/burnout score was higher than the husbands' score in most countries, along with what I am seeing in the counseling room and the observations from Adler and Lindquist, I believe we must take a long, hard look at missionary wives serving in other cultures. Mace and Mace (1981) gave five major areas in which clergymen's wives felt they needed help in adjusting to their husbands' ministry. These areas were: (a) the need for the time alone with each other, (b) understanding the role of the pastor's wife, (c) the wife's role in her husband's counseling activity, (d) the need for friends outside the church, and (e) the wife's status in the church.

I could find no correlation between tedium/burnout and time married or time on the field for the wives (cf. Figures 3 and 4). Wives did score over the 3.00 mark, indicating that they are experiencing stress. It would seem that this study, coupled with the interviews with missionaries, would indicate that missionary wives are experiencing stress because of the "role" into which they feel they must fit along with the confinement (both cultural and social) that they experience in the home. Many of the wives had been involved in expanding their education (25 percent of the wives had a four-year Bible College degree and 22 percent had a degree from a university) and were socially active in their churches and communities prior to leaving for the field. Then, upon reaching this new culture (including the missionary subculture) they found that their role was completely changed. We must find ways of tapping the many resources of the missionary wife.

Husbands, on the other hand, show a direct correlation between tedium/burnout and years on the field along with the number of years married (cf. Figures 3 and 4). What this study shows is that missionary husbands, as they become more involved in the "ministry" over the years, also show a tendency to develop classical signs of stress and burnout. Few professionals are more caught up in the success syndrome than the ministry (Mace and Mace 1981). Time pressures create major stress in clergy marriages, though these stresses are largely self-generated. As a class, clergymen tend to be workaholics. The minister generally sees his work as a particular vocation or calling from God, which is allowed to take priority over family needs. Mace continues by saying that when faced with a conflict between the two, the minister must determine which is the more important in a given situation, a choice not always easy for him to make. Freudenberger (1980) complicates the picture when he says that "where burn-out exists, the sufferer unwittingly selects a cure which intensifies the burn-out, spreading it faster and further" (p. 104). He adds later that "By keeping ourselves perpetually busy, we get to avoid closeness in what, to all appearance, are legitimate ways" (p. 127). Yet, "just as other-directedness and distance are the allies of burn-out, so closeness and inner-directedness are its foes" (p. 123).

Some of the husbands reach a point of over-involvement with people. This leads to a dehumanization of the people they have gone to work with. Pines and Aronson (1981) define humanization "as a decreased awareness of the human attributes of others and a loss of humanity in interpersonal interactions" (p. 19). Another problem pointed out by Freudenberger (1980) is that "as people grow older and see more of their dreams fade, they become increasingly susceptible to burn-out" (p. 111). He adds that "they are what I refer to as the Interface Generation, those who like Janus, the Roman god of beginnings and endings, look ever forward and back...The segment of the population I am likening to him are those who straddle two cultures" (p. 112). This straddle could be true of the older missionary as well. With computers being introduced into almost every phase of missionary work now, the older missionary is faced with a new culture brought on by advanced technology. He is faced with a *new* language brought into his culture by the new missionaries. After 20 or 30 years of doing it *his way* he is faced with doing it *our way*. All of this adds up to what Freudenberger says is an "increasingly susceptible" atmosphere for burnout. We must find ways to communicate the possibility of burnout to missionary husbands or we will continue to see the increase in dehumanization of people.

The correlation between tedium/burnout and number of children was a surprise (cf. Figure 2). I did not expect to find that wives with five children would have the second lowest stress level. Husbands, on the other hand, show a marked increase in stress with five children. Without proper guidance and help, we have a great potential for missionary loss just from the need to school their children (this is the predominate theme in family counseling with missionaries). We can conclude then, that as children are introduced into missionary family life, stress increases, especially for the husband. We want to help missionary families understand and learn to cope in this area of their lives.

How missionaries coped with stress was interesting. One would think that people functioning in a *spiritual job* would turn to spiritual resources for help. However, 67 percent of the missionary husbands (69 percent of the wives) reported not seeking help of any kind for the pressures of stress in this area. This may be another indication that the *Super Saint* may not be quite as super or saintly as others have thought. He or she just may be human after all. Also interesting was the fact that 85 percent of the husbands (86 percent of the wives) did not use exercise or play to help cope with stress. Daniel (1981), speaking of pastors' families, says that "he or she...needs to find a decompression routine that fits his or her personal style, becoming involved in some outside activities to meet physical, emotional, and interpersonal needs" (p. 246). A "decompression routine" is something that will "help with the separation between home life and work life" (p. 240). It would seem that missionaries need to be taught how to play.

In summary, we would have to say that statistically, missionaries, are under no more stress than the other helping professions. Also, there are indications that this group of "helping professionals" may be denying or simply unable or unwilling to recognize the existence of the actual stress under which they live.

This study is only a beginning. The purpose is to get a feel for where the missionary family *is*. Further study is needed. I believe that now we must look at the area of providing a program to help the missionaries understand the stress they are under and how it affects them and their families.

References

Adler, N. J. (1982). *Women as expatriots: Assignment to ambiguity.* Paper at SIETAR Convention, Long Beach.

Daniel, S., & Rogers, M. L. (1981). Burn-out and the pastorate: A critical review with implications for pastors. *Journal of Psychology and Theology, 9,* 232-249.

Freudenberger, H. J. (1980). *Burn out: How to beat the high cost of success.* New York: Bantom Books.

Fowler, R. (1982). *An analysis of the stress and burn-out level of married students at LeTourneau* College. Longview, TX, Letourneau College. Spring.

Lindquist, S. E. (1979). *Women on the mission field.* Paper presented to the Evangelical Foreign Missions Association, Los Angeles.

Mace, D., & Mace, V. (1981). *What's happening to clergy marriages?* Nashville: Abingdon.

Malony, H. N. (1980). Ministerial burn out. *Leadership, 1,* 71-74.

Maslach, C. (1978). Job burn-out.: How people cope. *Public Welfare, 56,* 76-85.

Pines, A. M., & Aronson, E. (1981). *Burnout: From tedium to personal growth.* New York: The Free Press.

19

Joyce Kruckeberg
Anita Stafford

The Missionary's Need
of Family Life Training

Childrearing in any culture is a challenge to the patience, endurance, and ingenuity of parents. Missionaries taking their children with them to a foreign country will experience unique demands on their coping ability. Skill will be needed, to survey the options available to supplement their own resources, for child training and family living (Smith, 1974).

Even in their own home countries many couples are unprepared for the experience of rearing children and may encounter some anxiety as they assume the parental role. One obvious reason some couples assume their childbearing responsibilities with more anxiety and less practice in child care methods and discipline techniques is due to a limited exposure to young children. The small nuclear family that many parents were reared in did not provide them with the opportunity to care for brothers and sisters (Rossi, 1968).

Furlough periods, separation of family members for school or work reasons, frequent moves, heavy demands on the parents' time and energy, and the unfamiliar culture are often distressing factors to family life on the mission field (Gibson, 1978). The constant demands of childrearing coupled with the vocational stress of mission service may influence some families to return to their home country or to actually retire prematurely from mission work (O'Donovan, 1975).

In order to reduce the loss of valuable talent and assist family life, specialists can work with mission boards to provide information and training that will reinforce personal capacities in these potentially stressful situations. Competence in decision making and time management complements training in communication skills, child development and guidance, and early childhood education. Parents need practice in setting goals for themselves and their children in addition to evaluating available options in order to meet the long-range needs of each family (Dinkmeyer & McKay, 1973).

The Research

The investigation of parents' satisfaction with childrearing on the mission field was instituted by the authors in January, 1979. Three hundred *Missionary Parents' Attitude Questionnaires* were mailed to active missionaries in eleven countries. The parents represented three groups: families serving on a mission field outside the United States, families on assignment in the United States, and families on furlough. Names and addresses were obtained from mission boards and from denominations.

A profile of parental satisfaction and skills for childrearing on the foreign mission field resulted from the responses of the 191 parents. The parents revealed a high level of enjoyment in their experiences as parents and an appreciation of the mission field as an environment for children. Sixty-four percent believed they were doing a good job of preparing their children for life outside the nuclear family when the child leaves home for boarding school or college. A majority of the parents stated that more childrearing problems were anticipated than had actually been experienced.

Family Life Education

A definition of family life education was presented in the *Missionary Parents' Attitude Questionnaire* as follows: "Family life education includes a broad range of information designed to increase skills of family living; for example: needs of children of all ages, communication between family members, discipline techniques, nutrition and health, optimum use of time, energy, money, and community resources." Based on this definition the missionary parents were asked to respond to the following:

"Counselors and family life education materials are easily available to help missionary families on the foreign field." More than half (58 percent) of the respondents disagreed with this statement. Thus it was implied that such help was either not available to them, or if available, the families were not aware of the resources. Seventy-two percent agreed that "Family life education would be helpful if given before the field assignment." There was also positive agreement by 82 percent of the parents with this statement: "Family life education would be helpful if available as workshops on the mission field." Nearly 50 percent of the parents indicated they had taken a course or study program, not directly related to parenting, that they believed had increased their skills for family living. Courses mentioned were diverse; e.g., nurses training, Seminar in Basic Youth Conflicts, or a Bible school course on marriage and family.

Topics pertaining to family living were presented to the parents. Analysis of their responses indicated that 79 percent desired help in one or more of the subjects listed on the chart below.

PARENTS' DESIRE FOR TRAINING IN FAMILY LIFE SKILLS

TOPICS		NUMBER	PERCENT
Preschool children's	Yes	55	28.8
needs and behavior	No	136	71.2
Communication skills	Yes	88	46.1
among family members	No	103	53.9
Setting behavior	Yes	65	34.1
standards for children	No	126	65.9
Time management and	Yes	77	40.3
other resources	No	114	59.7
Budgeting limited	Yes	51	26.7
income	No	140	73.3
Helping children	Yes	77	40.3
adjust to the new situations	No	114	59.7
Coping with furloughs	Yes	85	44.5
and travel	No	106	55.5

(Family Life Survey, continued)		Number	Percent
Enriching family life	Yes	71	37.2
through leisure	No	120	62.8
activities			
Expressed other	Yes	33	17.3
interests	No	158	82.7
Overall composite	Yes	152	79.2
score to parents	No	3	20.4
desiring help with			
one or more above			
suggested topics			

Seventeen percent of the participating parents suggested additional subjects that they believed would be appropriate for family enrichment. Needs were expressed and help solicited in guiding devotions for children of various ages and providing Christian education for preschool children. Handling sibling rivalry and understanding the teen-age years were needs of some parents, while others desired help with nutrition or in establishing and maintaining the priorities of work and family time.

Parents wanted help in developing their child's positive self-concept and in preparing older children for life in the home country. Coping with the child's diagnosed learning disability was a problem for certain parents. Others were challenged in teaching their children with correspondence materials.

Many parents mentioned titles of books that had been especially helpful to their family at some particular time. As expected, the Bible was the most popular resource for counsel on child guidance.

Needs of Parents

Before initiating any program designed to increase family living skills and coping abilities of missionary parents, professionals should be aware of the unique stresses faced by couples with children at a mission location. At any one time a mission community can benefit from a variety of subjects. Education for family life is a life-long process as parents reorganize their time and priorities to accommodate each new addition to the family and then learn new behaviors appropriate to the needs of each child (Rapport, Rapport, & Strelitz, 1977).

A mission community's empathy and support is critical to the new parents' adjustment. Mothers are especially prone to lowered self-esteem and depression because of the nearly constant exposure to their child's needs (Rossi, 1968). Although well trained to perform mission service, a young mother may have little opportunity to practice infant care. A few lessons on the care of the newborn child, given by a mission's nurse, can help at this time.

Childrearing is an emotional investment. The young parents' attitude toward their child is affected by their feeling of adequacy and their adjustment to the new role (Hermann, 1977). Young couples working in isolated locations are particularly vulnerable, as they guide their children's development, without supportive services of a mission center. With increased self-confidence in their ability to nurture and control their children, parents often gain greater satisfaction from interaction with their children and more appreciation of their own contribution to each child's development.

With children under five years in the home, a great deal of time is spent in preparing each child for school (Moock, 1974). This critical period of the child's development is already filled with other demands on the parents' time as they train for missionary service, speak at churches, learn languages, select gear for field use, travel, and then make adjustment to life and service at the chosen location. In many cases there will be no nursery services to supplement the parents' child care, so that any mission duties undertaken by the mother will be done with preschool children nearby and requiring attention (Taylor, 1976). With or without child care services, the parents can experience exhaustion and frustration in coping with the needs of their preschool children while performing mission duties.

Appreciation of the early childhood years and the parents' contribution to the child's development is increased by a greater understanding of the developmental stages and the behaviors that are typical of those stages. Every parent faces the challenge of providing four basic emotional needs for his child: love and security, praise and encouragement, new experiences, and training for responsible living. The unique personality of each child complicates the task as parents must assess the physical and emotional strengths and liabilities of each child (Pringle, 1975).

Effective childrearing requires long-range goals be set for the child's training and preparation for life away from home. In missionary families this becomes critical since the child may leave home for boarding school at an early age. The parents' composure will be sustained if they have encouraged independence and responsibility through a series of planned experiences designed to equip the child for effective living (Beck, 1968). A child that has household chores, cares for his own possessions, and speaks for his own needs will usually be well prepared for school life. A positive family atmosphere is a strong foundation for developing the child's self-esteem and a sense of security (Pringle, 1975).

When faced with making a decision for the child's education, parents may be uneasy with the nontraditional alternatives available to the missionary family. They often have several choices depending on the location of the mission assignment. Time is required to consider national schools, correspondence courses, boarding schools, but finding the best solution for each child will result in the parents' peace of mind (Smith, 1974). Some families decide to use a combination of these alternatives because of the child's individual needs and emotional maturity (Narramore, 1966).

Consideration of the national culture forces each family to adjust their children's social activities and contacts with national children. By participating in the local community life and making friends there, the child develops self-confidence and is better able to adjust to the parents' culture when returning to the home country. However, there may be aspects of the national culture that influence parents to remove the child at a particular development stage (Rosenau, 1974; Larson, 1971).

Little has been printed about the parents' role as primary educator of the missionary child. Parents equip the child with fundamental attitudes and a sense of security through membership in a congenial group. Their encouragement provides direction in the child's endeavors and promotes a sense of personal worth (Pringle, 1975). Although parents may not have the time and energy, teaching ability, or interest necessary to teach their child during the early elementary years, the foundational experiences of the first six years must be recognized as pivotal to the child's adjustment to formal education and community life (Schaefer, 1972).

School entrance dilutes the family's influence as the peer group becomes more important to the child's life. As children mature, parents are forced to accept the child's increasing desire for independence (Walters & Stinnett, 1971). Communication skills, that have been practiced between parent and child through the years, will smooth the way for maintaining relationships between childhood and maturity (Rapport et al, 1977).

Discussion of sexual development with the child was difficult for more than seventy percent of the parents that answered the questionnaire. This is congruent with the challenge faced by parents in all modern societies, but in the United States there are secular and religious oriented books and courses to aid or substitute for the parents' instruction. Sex education is not only for the adolescent, but is a life-long learning task as individuals strive to understand their own sexuality and assume behaviors and attitudes appropriate to their changing role in society (Duvall, 1970).

Development of character in a child demands a commitment of time and interest, which the child equates with love and concern (Herrmann, 1977). There is a danger that the desire to serve humanity can be so intense that mission projects assume a higher priority than the child's need for the parents' time and energy. Without television and other distractions there can be more time for family sharing of books, hobbies, games, family projects, worship, and community service. How much time the family actually spends together depends on the priorities and time management of the parents (O'Donovan, 1975).

Young parents often encounter difficulty in coordinating leisure time with child care needs, homemaking duties, and available finances. Parents have needs for privacy and experiences apart from their children's lives. They must balance their devotion to their children with concern for their own growth and recreation (Rapport et al., 1977). The missionary parents of this survey indicated a desire for information that could enrich family life through leisure activities.

Furlough periods can be a distressing experience for missionary children (Narramore, 1966). More than half the respondents revealed that their children were anxious to return to their home on the mission field, while traveling with their parents doing furloughs. Less than one-third of the parents believed their children enjoyed visiting churches and associates in the home country. Workshops on furlough planning should acknowledge the possibility of family stress during times of increased mobility.

Mission Boards

Most parents viewed their respective mission board as supportive of special needs of their children. However, many believed their mission board could better prepare the family for possible stress resulting from separation of parent and child for education.

In order to reduce the loss of valuable talent and to assist families, professionals must encourage families to seek creative alternatives that meet individual needs and encourage parents to evaluate the goals of family members. Mission boards that have initiated some preparation for the demands of family life on the mission field have had a reduction in premature retirement by their field personnel (O'Donovan, 1975).

Planning Family Life Education

A survey of the needs and interests of the mission's families should precede any attempt at family life enrichment, since the objective is to improve family functioning in weak areas as well as to enhance family strengths. Before inviting professionals to present seminars on certain subjects, a mission board might look within its own membership for knowledgeable people. Too often the popular seminar approach merely provides prescriptions for success rather than encouraging creative coping styles that meet individual needs and consider family personalities.

A mission couple trained in the basics of family processes and committed to personal growth of mission families could provide long-term interaction with families. Experienced adults contributing to small group discussions will encourage young parents to synthesize coping techniques that will suit their particular values. If serious adjustment problems surface, referral can be made to competent professional counselors.

In presenting family life education, principles and guidelines will often be sufficient to initiate a group discussion of the topic. Assimilation of such emotionally charged subjects as sex education or discipline techniques is best accomplished through repeated exposure to various media presentations, exploration of the concepts in light of biblical principles, and then application of appropriate ideas in a practical situation.

Evaluation should be part of all family life programs. Objective review of the original goals and actual accomplishments or deficiencies will enable parents and planners to maintain quality and interest in future presentations.

Summary

The 191 missionary parents of the survey indicated an interest in family life education that would better equip them for parental responsibilities on the mission field. Mission boards can respond to this interest during training programs before field assignment and by providing current information to families on the foreign field. Selected members of the mission community can make valuable contributions to family life as they share their interests and skills or lead discussions of selected books or films.

Missionary family life is subject to the pressures of intercultural living, limited resources of time and energy for mission duties and childrearing, family mobility, and nontraditional options for the children's education. Recognition by the mission community of the effect of these stresses is the first step toward strengthening family life.

Programs designed to encourage parental growth and family strengths reflect a faith in the ability of families to remain autonomous and vigorous even during transitions and in multicultural sitations. The life-long process of education for family life can strengthen personal and collective resources for coping with stress and subsequently promote the welfare and significance of the mission community.

References

Beck, J. (1968). *Parental preparation of missionary children for boarding school.* Teipei, Taiwan: Mei Ya Publications.

Dinkmeyer, D., & McKay, G. (1973). *Raising a responsible child: Practical steps to successful family relationships.* New York: Simon and Schuster.

Duvall, E. (1970). *Faith in families.* Nashville: Abingdon.

Gibson, D. (1978). *The mission family: Advantages, problems, and solutions.* Unpublished research, Liberia, West Africa.

Hermann, C. (1977). *Foundational factors of trust and autonomy influencing the identity formation of the multicultural lifestyle MK.* Unpublished doctoral dissertation, Northwestern University.

Larson, L. (1971). *A Program of guidance in the missionary boarding school based on the self-concept system.* Unpublished Master's thesis, Kansas State University.

Moock, P. (1974). Economic aspects of the family as educator, in H. Leichter (ed.), *The Family as educator.* New York: Teachers College Press.

Narramore, C. (1966). *Child of the missionary.* Rosemead, CA: Narramore Christian Foundation.

O'Donovan, W. (1975). *The problem of priorities between the missionary's and his family.* Unpublished research, Columbia Graduate School of Bible and Missions.

Pringle, M. (1975). *The Needs of children.* New York: Schocken Books.

Rapport, R., Rapport, R. N., & Strelitz, Z. (1977). *Fathers, mothers and society: Towards new alliances.* New York: Basic Books.

Rosenau, D. (1974). Growing up on the mission *field.* Unpublished Master's thesis, Dallas Theological Seminary.

Rossi, A. (1968). Transition to Parenthood. *Journal of Marriage and the Family, 30,* 26-39.

Schaefer, E. (1972). The Family and the educational process. In Iowa State University (ed.), *Families of the Future,* Ames, Iowa: The Iowa State University Press.

Smith, W. (1974). *Planning Your MK's Education.* Unpublished Master's thesis, Dallas Theological Seminary.

Taylor, M. (1976). Personality development in the children of missionary parents. *The Japan Christian Quarterly, 42,* 72-78.

Walters, J., & Stinnett, N. (1971). "Parent-child relationships: A decade review of research. In C. Broderick (ed.), *A Decade of family research and action,* Minneapolis, Minn: National Council on Family Relations.

20

Stanley E. Lindquist
Brent Lindquist

Missionary Family Restoration for Early Returnees

"I have failed my calling. I have short-circuited 10 years of preparation. I have lost my reason for living."

Words like that are often expressed by missionaries who are forced to return early because of emotional problems within the family. What can a psychologist do to help meet this need?

The percentage of early returnees is not known. Estimates from mission boards and experts in the field vary from 1 to 50% first-term missionaries. A reasonable figure could be in the 15% range. As there are approximately 3,500 new missionaries that go out each year, this means that about 525 return early. Add to that figure a growing percentage of those who return after 10 to 15 years of service, primarily due to family adjustment problems, and one is confronted with a sizeable number of candidates for restoration and vocational re-direction.

When one becomes aware of the keen anguish and dislocation of each person, the importance of valid programs for help is amplified. The ripple effect of the early return touches the immediate family, the home church, the mission home office, the supporters, the national church and the missionaries remaining on the field. One can estimate that for each casualty at least 300 persons are affected. Using a figure of 800 early returnees (525

Based on a paper presented at the Third Annual Conference on Mental Health and Missions held at Angola, Indiana in November, 1983. Reprinted by permission of the authors.

first term, 275 third or fourth term), some 240,000 persons are affected each year, and they may wonder what happened and why it happened. The long-range effect of these dislocations can only be imagined.

In addition, the added cost to the church is measured in millions of dollars each year. As the cost of one family's early return has been estimated between $35,000 and $60,000 by mission executives who have studied these figures, the problem is one of increasing financial significance.

Obviously, prevention is the best solution, and this aspect will be discussed later. However, the problem is here, staring us professionals in the face, and the question has to be: "What are we going to do about it?"

Typical Case Histories
from Link Care Center's Experience

The following brief examples sampling the variety of problems that we have met, are disguised and are for illustrative purposes only.

1. *Mid-first term.* A man who had had some severe problems in the field with respect to cross-cultural adjustment, attempted suicide. He was found, resuscitated, and sent home, with hospitalization indicated. We settled the family in one of our apartments set aside for missionaries, provided close supervision, medications, and intensive psychotherapy for four months. He returned to his mission and is functioning unusually well after several years.

2. *One-term missionary.* This missionary was involved in a position of responsibility. He was unable to function well, causing problems in the mission community. He was sent home with his family to Link Care for treatment. He resented the therapy, although his wife was cooperative. After one month, he left against our advice. He was seen by a psychiatrist in his hometown, who had no cross-cultural experience and who pronounced him prepared for return to the field after one interview. He went overseas, and in three months he was again sent home by the field executives with instructions not to return. It is interesting to note that he was sent home the second time for the same reasons as the first time.

3. *14-year missionary.* This lady was one of the best equipped and effective missionaries we have ever dealt with at our center. She became delusional on the field, primarily with sexual overtones, and was forced to return. She was given intensive

individual and group psychotherapy for one month, after which she had to return home due to family constraints. She continued working on her problems by herself and six months later returned to the field.

4. *18-year veteran.* This family demonstrated severe problems, and was returned home with instructions not to go back to the field. Intensive psychotherapy for depression, coupled with some medication, seemed ineffective for the husband, although the wife responded well. After a few months, the husband overdosed on his medication, necessitating heroic measures for saving his life. After a four-week hospitalization, he was discharged in our care, as the supervising psychiatrist said, "You get much more therapy at Link Care than you do here."

As the family could not return to the field, vocational training was instituted, along with decreasing frequency of therapy. The husband completed the program after 18 months and has been gainfully employed since treatment.

5. *25-year veteran.* The mother in the family suffered from severe depressive episodes over many years. Finally, they were returned to the United States. First contacts indicated rather complete dissociation and inability to orient herself. A careful course of psychotherapy, with some medication, was instituted. As with other cases, involvement in our wholistic program of aiding our day-to-day operations, in addition to the therapy, seemed effective. She did not return to the field and is maintaining a somewhat precarious balance at the present time.

6. *Adolescent Female.* The oldest daughter of three girls had been rebellious throughout most of her lifetime and her rebellion had increased during her adolescent years. It finally reached the point that when the family returned for furlough, when she was in middle adolescence, she announced that she would not be going back with them and would do just about anything in order to stay and go to school in the U.S.

There were a number of family-related issues in addition to her own personal concerns. The family saw the girl as someone who had made little attempt to identify with the missionary call and felt that staying at home to take care of the girl would abrogate their ministry overseas. When they were on the mission field, the family was concerned that the girl had over-identified with the national people and had dated some of the national kids her age without their consent. The parents were concerned that she was losing her faith. The family spent a total of three months with Link Care, with the husband and wife engaged in marital therapy and the family participating in training programs and mission institutes.

The girl was allowed to ventilate her feelings and talk about her frustration with "not feeling called" to the field, but having to do that because her parents had been called. Once a therapeutic alliance was established, conjoint sessions with her parents were scheduled, where numerous issues were worked out regarding authority conflicts, discipline strategies and family activities. At this point in treatment, the school year began and the girl needed to return to school and was referred to another center in order to continue treatment.

7. *Twenty-five-year-old missionary "kid"*. The eldest daughter of a career missionary family was in college and experiencing significant difficulty through transient-depressive episodes. These were compounded by a very low self-concept and poor self-esteem. Relationships with others were difficult to establish and/or maintain and she had the feeling that she was very different from other people. A four-month treatment strategy was followed using the cognitive treatment for depression, as well as going back over the experiences when she was growing up. At the end of treatment, she returned to college with little problem of the same nature.

8. *Latency age missionary child*. This young man was the adopted multi-racial eldest son of a young missionary couple. He was adopted at age one and, at that time, was already exhibiting a number of hyperactive symptoms. The family, shortly after his adoption, left for the field and the behavior became increasingly more difficult, with the problem being compounded by the hyperactive syndrome. Medical treatment was established with a national psychiatrist. The mother, who was a nurse, became increasingly alarmed at the treatment regimen. Knowing something about the treatment of hyperactivity in the United States, she was very concerned because the treatment in the foreign country was very different and involved much stronger medication in much larger amounts. The son was taken off the medication and seemed to improve somewhat. However, the behavior problem returned a few months later, shortly before furlough. While the family was receiving additional education, they contacted Link Care and brought their son in for evaluation. Play therapy and behavior management skills were among the things used for the treatment. A referral to a psychiatrist was necessary for managing the hyperactivity and the young man improved to the point of being discharged to his parents' control. Follow-up contact with the parents indicated that the son was progressing and that he was reducing medication and that his behavior was improving.

Procedural Considerations

Case History

Too often psychologists and boards neglect case histories in the treatment process attempting to deal only with the "here and now". In working with returned missionaries, complete histories are especially important for information that give clues in understanding how the past experiences are affecting present perceptions and attempts at adjustment.

For example, in one of the cases previously discussed, there had been a previous suicide attempt noted in the physical examination that had not been noticed by the mission board prior to the overseas assignment.

Previous test information gives information about longitudinal development that aids in meeting specific problem areas. Information about any previous therapy and reports from psychotherapists need to be integrated with the total treatment process and often speeds up the healing.

History-taking relative to cross-cultural experiences is also very important. A family was having difficulty overseas and returned to spend some time with Link Care for some restorative counseling. The couple initially presented as a well-adjusted couple with very few difficulties. The major problem was that the husband was very non-communicative. Upon closer questioning, the history came out that the husband had been very frustrated with the national people, feeling that they were all liars, that the only reason they were interested in talking to Americans was to get visas to get out of the country, and that they would just as soon stab you in the back. He was having great difficulty placing his patriotism underneath that of love for his adopted country. While the treatment was successful in getting the couple to open up more in terms of their relationship, the family is felt to continue to have difficulty overseas because of the interaction of the allegiance to the United States versus the acceptance of the new culture.

Focus of Treatment

Ideally, psychotherapeutic intervention should be done on the field. We have, in our overseas seminars, been made keenly aware of this need. Short-term therapy of this kind may help temporarily, but often long-term treatment is necessary. Making on-field psychotherapy available seems impractical at this time, but could become a goal for future plans.

To hospitalize or not is the question for severe emotional disorders. Following the usually accepted procedure, we generally try to avoid hospitalization if possible. We have excellent in-patient facilities available in the community where we can continue our treatment program personally if it is necessary. Time complications and client dependencies become problems that have to be dealt with realistically.

Out-patient clinics are readily available around the country. The limitation of most of them is that they have little or no experience in dealing with cross-cultural problems. The biggest problem is the lack of close supervision between therapy sessions.

Out-patient residential on—campus care seems to be a very promising avenue for wholistic restoration. This procedure combines some of the advantages of hospital care with the flexibility of clinic treatment. Having 107 apartments available on our 8-1/2 acre site makes this method our choice at the Link Care Center whenever it is possible to do so.

Between therapy sessions, clients are involved in a program including video and audiotaped courses. They may work on the grounds aiding the gardener and the custodian, according to their abilities and desire. Some work in the office with our staff. All are involved with other missionaries, retirees who live on our grounds, in formal workshops we provide for the community, local churches, and other activities. This wholistic approach often disarms, defuses, and allows for the training to be comprehensive.

Complete Diagnostic Testing As a Basis for Setting Out a Program of Treatment (discussion during conference presentation)

Psychotherapeutic Procedures Applied to Missionary Restoration

The general philosophy of psychotherapeutic intervention we follow is to teach problem-solving techniques that can be transferred to new situations. The presenting problem or problems then become the subject for learning how to attack problems in general, as much as can be done. Thus, when a course of treatment is completed, the missionary or others may not need to return for later help, as they hopefully have developed an armamentarium to deal with new problems as they come up. Even so, each one must also be aware of his own limitations as to the method which is built into the procedure. Warning signs are noted, which may signal the need for additional help.

Brief psychotherapy involving prescriptive assessment procedures is usually the norm. Often clients come with only a week or two to spare. In some cases, recognition of need lengthens the stay, but in any case, careful assessment which pinpoints areas of concern, followed by procedures to alleviate the problem, have to be quickly utilized.

Our group of seven psychologists and seven other counselors, plus support staff, allow this flexibility. Overburdened clinics would find it difficult to be suddenly faced with a family requiring five to ten hours of therapy a week, as seems to be standard operating procedure for us. We believe God has provided us with facilities and staff to meet these unusual needs, although our caseload is rapidly increasing, and we may have to modify our procedures.

We use an eclectic approach to therapy, ordinarily starting with client-centered approaches to develop rapport, often followed by more confrontive behavioral treatment. In each case, we tailor the method to suit the client, the time available and the goals of the person. We feel that the Spirit of God uses psychological tools to achieve the necessary healing and, therefore, we must be flexible in our procedures. Weekly meetings with him assure that the missionaries in treatment have a special opportunity to work on *pastoral issues.*

Long-term emotive therapies are a luxury we seldom are allowed. Usually our treatment has to be brief in order to fit into the missionaries' schedules. An additional, integral part of the program is the work of our pastoral counselor. Specific phobias are especially helped by desensitization procedures. One woman was afraid of dogs, which limited her usefulness in church planting, as she had to do door-to-door visitation. A four-week desensitization process cured her of this fear, and a subsequent visit to the field by a staff member confirmed her ability to perform well in those situations.

A case of fear of water severely limited the mobility of a missionary, as the area where she was to work required frequent crossings of rivers by canoe. She progressed rapidly so that, by the time she left, she was swimming in our pool, and was able to go in a boat.

Prevention Measures

As was mentioned earlier, the crux of the total problem is prevention. As noted in a previous article (Lindquist, 1982), adequate assessment, followed by prescriptive directions, should begin to reduce the need for restoration. This preventive program is essential. We are now working on a long-range research program aimed at trying to meet that need. Psychologists and others can combine our resources to achieve the needed end result.

Summary

Missionary restoration is a multi-faceted program, requiring careful application of psychological tools by Christian psychotherapists intimately led by the Spirit of God. The task is one which requires the help of every qualified person to meet the need.

The church constituency likewise needs to be informed in order that adequate support can be correlated with the treatment program. A specialized method utilized at the Link Care Center model holds promise for more widespread use. Above all, preventive measures need to be harmonized with existing training and preparation.

References

Kliewer, D., Heinrick, R., Lindquist, S., Williams, D. (1980). *EFMA missionary candidate selection survey.* Paper presented at the EFMA Conference on March 4, 1980. Fresno, CA: Link Care Center.

Lindquist, S., 1982. Prediction of success in overseas adjustment. *Journal of Psychology and Christianity, 1,* 43-48.

Lindquist, S., et al. (1979). *Women on the mission field.* Paper presented to the Evangelical Foreign Mission Association, 1979.

Link Care Staff (1981). *Use of psychological assessment with missionaries. A handbook.* Paper presented at EFMA and IFMA Personnel Directors' meeting, Detroit, Michigan, December 5, 1981.

Tucker, M. (1982). *Cross-cultural adjustment and effectiveness.* Paper presented at the Society for International Education, Training and Research, Long Beach, CA.

Williams, D. & Kliewer, D. (1980). *Perspectives on psychological assessment of candidates for cross-cultural Christian missions.* Fresno, CA: Link Care Center.

Williams, K. (1973). *Characteristics of the more successful and less successful missionaries.* Doctoral dissertation, U.S. International University (Univ. microfilms no. 73-22,697).

21

Marjory Foyle

Stress Factors in Missionary Marriages

The overall quality of missionary marriages is impressive. Exceptions do occur, but generally speaking there is a high standard of caring and sharing.

Missionary marriages have to survive two major stress areas. One is the stress common to all marriages in the present social climate. The extent of such stress is revealed in the high divorce rate and rising incidence of battered families.

The other area is related to the Christian concept of marriage. God has chosen human relationships to describe some of the most profound spiritual truths. Widows and orphans, virgins, husbands and wives, parents, brothers and sisters are all repeated biblical themes. Many Christians feel that part of their ministry is to demonstrate the truth of what God has been teaching through their relationships.

Married missionaries, as well as single ones, regard this aspect of their calling as very important. They believe their marriage should show the people around them what God has been saying in the Scripture. Hence, any marital problem involves not only the difficulty itself but also guilt at the failure of Christian witness.

This witnessing aspect of missionary marriage can get out of proportion due to the "goldfish bowl" experience. Many couples are scrutinized constantly by loving but curious national neighbors. Everything they do is noted and discussed. The major source of information may be the cook, and he can misinterpret what is going on.

For example, husbands and wives have the right to an occasional bad mood. Indians, with their habitual courtesy, call this an "off mood," and handle it with tolerance. The cook, however, may misunderstand the "off mood." "He didn't speak to her much this morning," he reports to the neighbors. "Perhaps he is tired of her and going to take a second wife." So the gossip goes around.

Missionary couples need to come to terms with this sort of thing. There is no point wallowing in guilt over a local misinterpretation of a trivial marital misunderstanding. In the end it is the daily quality of the marriage that counts, not the rumor-mongering bulletin from the cook!

Changed Marital Expectations

In considering stressful features of missionary marriages, certain factors are important. The first is changed marital expectations. As Jack Dominian points out in his helpful book, *Marital Breakdown*, earlier expectations were of security through a hierarchy. The husband was at the top, usually with God over him. Then came the wife, children, and servants, in that order. Nowadays, however, the major expectation is the degree of personal fulfillment and growth experienced by both partners.

In common with many Christians, missionaries have an added expectation--spiritual enrichment through the marriage. Believing it to be a part of God's will for them, they expect it to be a good experience. If the marriage does not work out, they become confused and feel they must somehow have messed up God's plans for them. One missionary wife told me, "When we married we had high expectations of our future together. When the marriage began to go wrong I felt as if God had slapped me in the face."

If serious marital problems emerge, field leaders must take prompt action. Inaction can lead to disaster. Of course, it is much easier to handle such a delicate matter if there has been a regular pattern of pastoral interviews. Local counseling can be arranged, or, if necessary, repatriation for professional help.

God's Call to the Couple

The second potential stress point concerns God's call to the couple. Both husband and wife should be called. Sometimes the husband may be pushed into missionary service because of his wife's call, and vice-versa. Married couples are a unit, and although the timing may be different, if God calls the one he also calls the other. Some wives have told me that they had no sense of calling at all. They resented being taken along like a piece of baggage.

Husbands and wives should be interviewed separately as well as together. The importance of this came home to me a few years ago when I was seeing a couple with a view to missionary selection. Noting that the man did all the talking, I asked him to leave us. As soon as he had gone the wife began to talk, and it was like a dam bursting. No one had ever heard what she had to say, and there were important issues involved. This, and subsequent experience, taught me that couples are two people, as well as a family unit.

Marital and Working Roles

The third stress is marital and working roles. Missionary appointments are usually made on the basis of the husband's role, although I have known two couples where the reverse was true. In these two cases, the husbands accepted their position as a challenge, and found roles for themselves as soon as the conditions of the overseas location were assessed.

Usually, however, it is the husband's role that is discussed, and wives to begin to wonder what their role will be. This is not always taken up as a separate issue, and this leads to role-related stress. Certain locations are noted for their high stress levels, some creating more stress for women than men.

The best example is Islamic countries, where women's position is a sensitive, tension-filled issue. Single women working in schools or hospitals are an anomaly in strictly Islamic countries, and their position is therefore easier. They remain social enigmas and simply get on with their work. Married women, however, are a part of the Islamic social structure, and herein lies the problem. They are expected to behave as Muslim wives, not coming out of the home to be seen in public, and restricting their social lives according to local views and customs.

The Preliminary "Look-See"

Perhaps one of the things that helps couples most is a preliminary "look-see" visit to the proposed host country. At a recent conference in London on expatriate stress, the personnel director of a large company said this was their practice before any overseas assignment was made. They got tired of sending people to high stress areas without making sure they "had the necessary personal equipment to cope." They had not only lost money, they had also wasted people's lives through an unwise overseas posting. Finally, the company arranged to send the couple for a look at the place, and if either of them felt that honestly they could not cope with it, they were not sent and they did not lose their promotion prospects.

Mission sending agencies may find it hard to implement this idea, first, because of the cost and second, because it may seem unspiritual. The financial need could be resolved by asking candidates to raise the funds. This makes application a serious affair, and heightens the sense of realism needed for coping strategies. The second objection is difficult, since we think missionaries ought to be able to handle anything through God's power. It's true that God does give us unusual power and strength, but in deploying missionaries to difficult places God also asks us to use common sense.

All of us are different, with different personalities and physiques. Generally, because of our different gifts, we can serve God in a wide variety of ways. God usually puts "square pegs in square holes." Sometimes square pegs have their corners rubbed off on the job, so they fit more comfortably, but this is not always God's way. Therefore, an advance "look-see" visit to the field can be a distinct advantage.

The purpose is not so much to assess a couple's ability to cope as it is to provide an overall impression of the work and personal suitability for it. Seeing the stress factors and the entire setup firsthand enables a couple to say yes or no to the potential assignment. Once they've made a commitment to it, this dedication to the task ahead will hold them firm when the going gets tough.

If such a plan is used, it's important that the couple does not feel guilty for deciding against the location. They should understand that the aim is to find out just where God wants them to serve. In this process, a negative response after a *look-see* visit is just as important as a positive one. If such a *look-see* trip isn't possible, couples should pray carefully about what they're headed into and seek the best counsel they can from veteran missionaries and local believers.

The Fear of Mental Stagnation

During my recent travels throughout Asia I found that although missionary wives are finding their role satisfaction in being wives, mothers, and in some cases teachers of their children, some still worry about their personal gifts and abilities. They usually have good minds, and fear mental stagnation. "I sometimes think I will scream at having to talk on a four-year-old level all day. I never have the chance of stretching my brain," some of them tell me.

There are two ways to handle this. The first is to remember that God is a great economist who wastes nothing. If missionary wives are not using all of their gifts now, God keeps them safely in store. When he needs them they will be taken out in prime condition. The second way is to take steps to stimulate the mind. Some wives take credit-earning correspondence courses during field service. Others join local book clubs or community affairs organizations. One missionary I knew made a study of local history and became quite an authority on it. By training she was a scientist, but the local study helped her to retain her intellectual sharpness during the years she was at home with her children.

Another problem is the hazard of changing roles because of travel. In her husband's absence the wife has to do everything. She is homemaker, home administrator, emergency plumber and electrician, and general mopper-up of problems. When the husband comes home, there is an immediate role switch. Both revert to their usual roles, and problems can arise almost at once. "It's marvelous when he comes home," said a wife, "but we begin to quarrel about where we put the toothpaste." Occasionally, the husband is too exhausted to want any role at all, and the wife resents having to go on as before.

Neither one gets the message the other is trying to communicate. The husband calls his wife demanding and she calls him uncooperative. Such situations can be resolved by patience, humor, and increasing mutual understanding. In such times the quality of previous husband-wife communication is revealed. If the quality was high, then good communication can be reestablished quickly after separation.

Both husbands and wives can experience role frustration, which in turn often arouses anger. They need to learn how to handle anger safely. One special way is relevant here. Suppose the husband has had a bad day. He's fuming by the time he gets home and lashes out at his wife for nothing. She in turn may scold the children. This is called *displacement*, or letting off anger on a substitute rather than handling the real cause.

Releasing Anger Safely

Actually, it's difficult to deal with the real cause while you are angry. The anger should first be safely released so that the basic problem can be carefully examined. There are healthy ways to do this, rather than using your spouse. In many Asian countries, for example, there are tea shops where people gather to drink tea, read the paper, and often argue politics. The angry husband should stop there, and whether or not he takes sugar, he should add a spoonful and stir it hard. The sugar raises his depleted blood sugar (in itself a good thing to do when you're angry) and the act of stirring vigorously is a physical way to displace anger. Then he should read the paper and discuss the news with others, if suitable. By so doing he can displace his anger harmlessly and go home in a calmer frame of mind. He can greet his wife, not with anger, but with, "Darling, I've had an awful day and will be so glad to talk with you about it." The result: loving sympathy and a wide open hearing ear.

This is a little more difficult for wives who may not be free to go out to a tea shop. The solution for a friend of mine was to take a bath before her husband came home, scrubbing herself hard. This displaced the irritations of the day. Other women bake bread when annoyed, the physical activity of kneading it helping to remove anger. Whatever the pattern, a healthy way of displacing anger is essential for a good marriage. After getting rid of it, the problems behind it can be discussed more reasonably, and the facts and issues understood more clearly.

Sexual Stress

Sexual fulfillment is a major part of marital expectations. Missionaries may not understand the possible changes in sexual patterns during early adjustment to their host country. On arrival, there is a lot to do. A home has to be established, often under cramped conditions near language school. New colleagues have to be met, and work assignments discussed.

The end result may be a rather anxious husband, and an exhausted wife. He turns to sex relations as a means of handling his insecurities, whereas all she wants is a hug, "Darling, I love you," and a long sleep. This difference in reaction may cause quarrels, one partner thinking "she doesn't love me," and the other grumbling to herself that "he never thinks of my needs." Neither indicates the true state of the marriage; it is only a temporary condition caused by settling into a new country. Extra sensitivity to each other's needs is the key to surmounting the problem.

Privacy is a rare commodity for all missionaries, and is of special importance in the sexual areas of the marital relationship. During language school the couple may only have room which they share with the baby. This is destruction both to the language study and to sexual relationships.

When they reach their final location, it may be even worse. Walls are thin, neighbors are in and out of the house the whole time, and doors often do not lock. Neither partner can relax and enjoy intercourse.

Several things can help. Door locks can be purchased and used in a way that will not cause local offense. One couple told me that they lock the door on the outside once a week, coming into the house by the back door. In other words, they pretend they are out. They do not put the light on, but spend some hours together in privacy. Their marital relationship gained enormously.

Marital stress is also created by local rules. In some Asian countries, touching each other in public is taboo. Any display of affection, even at home if the servant is present, is considered socially unacceptable. Husband and wife may not be able to walk side by side, and to make it worse for the wife, the husband has to go first! Missionary couples may therefore feel deprived of the oil of daily affection. The demands on them for an unfamiliar pattern of restraint are enormously stressful.

Husbands and wives must find alternative ways of showing affection. Some of these may seem positively childish, but are nonetheless important. Some couples write notes to each other expressing affection and respect. Extra hugging and kissing in the few private areas of the home keep the fires of love burning. One husband I knew used to pick local flowers and stick a label on them, "Red roses for love." Wives can make similar gestures with a favorite cake.

Stress in Separation

Sexual temptations should never be underestimated. Missionary husbands and wives may be separated for unusually long periods of time. They experience loneliness and sexual frustration, and in this situation become very vulnerable. Additional stress just at this time can lead to sexual infidelity if everything becomes overwhelming.

Couples need to be very wise during separation. Men who work with attractive girls should be careful not to invite them to the home when their wives are away. Even having other guests at the same time may not be enough to handle the attraction. Similarly, wives need to behave discreetly. They are lonely and under pressure, and local people can be very attractive sexually. The couple needs to be secure enough to discuss the problems they experience during separation. There are some cultures where chastity is not understood, and especially during periods of marital separation the husband is expected to have another woman. Should this arise, the husband needs to state his position clearly to those who want to find him a temporary woman. If the explanation is given in religious terms, it is usually accepted, although it may not be understood.

Relieving sexual pressures at these times is a difficult matter. It is this type of stress that often makes the power of God a more personal reality.

Differing Personalities

Certain personality characteristics are known to promote marital harmony, thus reducing stress. Reasonable emotional stability, consideration for others, ability to yield and make adult compromises, a certain degree of maturity and personal confidence, and mature patterns of dependency are important. Few of us have all of these to an adequate degree, but understanding them may help us to progress.

Stress can arise when personality needs create undue expectations of what marriage can achieve. If one of the partners had a deprived childhood, especially in affectional terms, the other partner is often expected to make this up. Add on the expectations of the person as spouse, and this all becomes too much.

Where personalities are so immature that over-dependency on parents has never been resolved, any additional stress can magnify the problem. The immature partner begins to behave as a child, constantly seeking reassurance from the other. Or else the extra reassurance needs are met by someone outside the marriage, creating an unhealthy situation. Single missionaries need to be aware of this, for they may become the third person in the triangle, from the best of motives.

Another aspect of such immaturity is an intolerance of disapproval. All mature marriages have a healthy disapproval content. Wives who do not like their husband's sermons are free to say so in a well established marriage, and the husband can also express his disapproval of things as well. If the basic link is secure, loving, and mature, this is all a part of normal daily life. Where this is not so, constant care has to be exercised. One man told me, "I have to pussyfoot around her all the time in case I hurt her feelings. It is very wearing."

Handling personality immaturity has been discussed in previous articles in this series. If this becomes a very severe problem, skilled help may be required. Severity can be judged roughly by the degree of disruption caused to personal and family life. The first step is recognition of the need to mature. There is no reason why this cannot be accomplished by your own determination, God's help, professional help, and the support of your loving spouse.

Knowledge that the marital partner is genuinely seeking to mature often makes the relationship richer as time goes on.

22

Robert L. Eagle

Positive Possibilities
of Mid-life Transitions

"Yes, dad, but..." I stopped. What was the use? We had been over this ground a half dozen times in the last week alone. My stepmother had died, and I felt my elderly father needed adult foster care. He felt he did not. We were at an impasse. In a few days my family and I would leave for our mission's furlough orientation meetings, and it was obvious that we would have to take my father along.

Already this furlough had been difficult. My older sister had died, my children were not sure they wanted to return to the field, and there had been a tempting job offer for a ministry at home. I found myself thinking soberly about the past and uncertainly about the future.

My wife and I were 45. Six years before, we had left the security of a district administration job to embark on a career in missions. Now, on our first furlough, we looked forward to returning to the field to which we were certain God had called us. And yet, bewildering obstacles loomed like mountains before us, and knotty problems defied untangling. We were in *transition,* and it was not a comfortable place to be.

Often thought to be the exclusive property of the adolescent, transition is actually found in three stages of a person's life. Daniel Levinson, in his book, *The Seasons of a Man's Life,* identifies the stages as (1) an early adult transition between the ages of 17 and 22; (2) a mid-life transition from 40 to 45 years of age, and (3) a late adult transition at 60 to 65 years of age.

Although the problems that surface in each of the three transitions may be somewhat different, they have in common an identification with both the past and the future. "In all transitions," Levinson says, "a man must come to terms with the past and prepare for the future."

We either cope during the time of transition and use it as a stepping-stone to another more fruitful era of our lives, or it becomes a stumbling block to future development.

It is interesting to note that Martin Luther's steps of faith were taken in the years just prior to and during his mid-life transition. He was 34 when he posted his ninety-five theses on the church door, and he was 42 when he was married. During those important transitional years, he experienced mind-boggling changes--and the church along with him.

Although few of us will experience those kinds of changes during our mid-life transition years, that period is for most people a time of turbulence and upheaval. It is a time when it seems that all of the balances in a person's life shift--when the familiar becomes strange; when it is no longer possible to anticipate either events or one's own reactions to events. Life, it seems, turns upside down.

Mid-life Tasks

Although the circumstances of people in mid-life transition may vary considerably, their tasks--or the underlying issues they must resolve--are quite similar. Levinson identifies five tasks, or polarities, "whose resolution is the principle task of mid-life individuation."

Young/old. Every person has in him both the child and the aging adult--the promise, vision, and excitement of the young, and the stability and thoughtfulness of the old. "In every transitional period throughout the life cycle, the internal figures of young and old are modified and placed in a new balance," Levinson says. "The task of every transition is to create a new young/old integration appropriate to that time of life."

Mortality/immortality. It is at mid-life that a person begins to understand that he is not immortal. It has been brought home to me recently more forcefully than ever that my body is not what it used to be. I have always enjoyed softball, but recent games have shown me that my reactions and abilities no longer measure up to my expectations. Such reminders of my mortality point to the fact that more of my life may be past than is ahead.

At such a time, a man begins to desire to create a legacy made up of family, work, or other valued contributions that will ensure his immortaility. This desire, says Levinson, enriches a man's life in middle adulthood. "He has major contributions to offer as a father, grandfather, son, brother, husband, lover, friend, mentor, healer, leader, mediator, authority, author, creator, and appreciator of the human heritage."

Destruction/creation. The destructive and creative properties of nature--and of mankind--are delicately balanced. During mid-life transition, a person becomes more acutely aware of these forces as the balance shifts and a new destructive/creative integration forms.

During transition, there is an "acute sense of his own ultimate destruction" which "intensifies a man's desire for creation. His growing wish to be creative is accompanied by a greater awareness of the destructive forces in nature, in human life generally, and in himself."

Masculine/feminine. "Every male selectively draws upon and adopts the gender images of his culture," says Levinson. "He develops attitudes, wishes, and fantasies about the masculine and feminine in himself and about his relationships with other men and women. Feelings about masculinity and femininity enter into a man's gender identity--his sense of who he is as a man, who he wants to be, and who he is terrified of being." The transitional period offers a "developmental opportunity to reintegrate the masculine/feminine polarity."

Attachment/separation. An intense desire to win, to be right, to achieve the noble dream is a characteristic of the adolescent and young adult. He desires to be highly regarded by those who matter, or actually by everyone. "With further development in middle adulthood, some of those desires fade away," says Levinson. "Those that remain have a less urgent quality. They can also be realized more fully. He can be more loving, sensual, authoritative, intimate, solitary--more attached and more separate."

Although the resolution of these five polarities is at the heart of mid-life transition, they are worked out by individuals in the context of daily life experiences, both good and bad. Each person brings unique circumstances to his experience of mid-life transition, but those who are missionaries additionally face a special set of potentially stress-producing factors.

Often, by the time missionaries are entering mid-life transition, their children are becoming old enough to express their feelings about missionary life. Many parents must make difficult, "no-win" decisions when their children are determined to remain in the United States at the end of a furlough.

Others watch their children growing up with "identity problems," feeling truly "at home" neither in the host culture nor in the United States.

The emotional stress of sending a child to a boarding school many miles away is balanced by the pressures of home teaching with its potentially straining effect on family life.

Not only do missionaries in mid-life transition confront various crises involving their children--some of whom may be going through their own adolescent transition--but they face the dilemma of dealing with aging parents. What do you do when you are half a world away from a parent who has just had a stroke? Or how does a missionary who has primary responsibility for his parents carry out that responsibility from 6,000 miles away?

There are the cultural pressures of serving in a foreign country among a sometimes bewildering people. And there is the equally stressful experience of reentering the homeland after a long absence.

Once at home, missionaries often experience a period of nearly rootless wandering as they reestablish contacts with churches, friends, relatives, and the mission organization.

If the missionary decides to stay at home for a period of time, perhaps while the children are in high school, he faces a significant vocational change during what are some very vulnerable years. There are the usual frustrations of a job search by a man in his middle life, but the missionary has the additional disadvantage of having to admit his intention to resign in two to five years. Under those circumstances, it may be difficult to get a really challenging and worthwhile job.

Meanwhile, there is the memory of a fulfilling and productive work on the field. By this time, he has facility with the language, knows the customs, understands the culture, has credibility with the national, and has established goals and a strategy to reach them. At a time when he may be able to make his most valuable contribution on the field, he is "sitting at home" in the United States, waiting for his children to graduate from high school.

Missionaries who return to the field without their children, once they are old enough to be on their own, find they must deal with loneliness and a helpless concern for offspring who are now thousands of miles away.

Without the children in the home, the husband-wife relationship undergoes significant changes. And, perhaps for the first time, the wife is able to become deeply involved in service and ministry outside of her home. It can be not only an exciting time, but a period of real trauma and adjustment for both husband and wife.

Mid-life transition--it can sound like a fatal disease. Yet, for those who weather the storms of those vulnerable years and make the necessary adjustments, that period can be a launching pad into the most creative and productive years of a person's life.

Support Groups

One of a person's most valuable resources during the time of transition are those who make up the "support group network." Although a person needs friends throughout his lifetime to whom he can turn when he is hurting, during mid-life transition (or any other transitional period) those friends become critically important.

Who are these friends? They are people in whom you have total confidence, and with whom you can share the depths of your heart.

Jess Lair, in his book, *I Ain't Well, But I Sure Am Better,* identifies the personal support system as (1) a wife who loves you; (2) a job that challenges you; and (3) the five friends whose faces light up when they meet you.

Most of us have a support group in the homeland--people who have promised to pray for us; those to whom we know we can turn when we need help or counsel. Such relationships should be carefully nurtured so that time and distance do not diminish their significance in our lives.

Every missionary, however, needs to build a support group not only at home, but right on the field. Some of those in the support group may be fellow missionaries from your mission--perhaps a "grandpa" or "grandma" who has experienced what you are going through now, or someone else who has befriended you and helped you to feel loved or wanted.

There are the nationals--the men and women to whom and with whom you have been sent to minister. If God has helped to build a strong relationship, don't be afraid to use it. The confidence you show in baring your heart should strengthen the relationship and help to build a valuable friendship.

Another source of solid friendships may be found in the missionaries from other misisons in your area. Sometimes, we may be able to talk more freely simply because they are not members of our own mission, and yet they understand the problems and crises unique to missionary life.

"Look for one or more support groups," Ray Ragsdale urges in his book, *The Mid-life Crises of a Minister.* "It will help you greatly to understand and deal with your particular situation if you can share with others of like mind and state."

Handling Stress

Because stress is one of the major characteristics of the mid-life transition, a person who learns how to deal constructively with stress can reduce the trauma of the transitional period. Much of the stress we experience can be reduced through the application of common sense and prayer. There are, however, some helpful principles for reducing stress.

1. Read one or more good books that give practical suggestions for coping with mid-life transition.

2. Work out a program of regular physical exercise to offset the effects of an increasingly sedentary lifestyle. An active, trim body not only promotes good physical health, but contributes to good mental health as well.

3. Undergo regular physical examinations, including the "stress test." A physician can identify potential problems and give good advice designed to lengthen your life and improve its quality.

4. Attend a stress management seminar like the one offered by Missionary Internship in Farmington, Mich., February 13-17, 1984. The practical suggestions, printed materials, and testing within a framework of positive interaction are helpful. If possible, husband and wife should attend the seminar together, in order to derive the greatest benefit from the experience.

5. Maintain a healthy spiritual life, being careful not to neglect the disciplines of regular prayer, and Bible study. Take all problems into the Scripture, bathing them with prayer, and examining them in the light of God's Word.

6. Learn how to praise God in every circumstance. Practice offering praise to God and cultivate a quiet confidence that rests in the omniscience and omnipotence of a loving and faithful God.

7. Practice making right choices. We really do have a choice in all relationships and in all circumstances. We can choose to react, to love, to become involved, to cooperate, or to retreat.

8. One important choice to be made is in the area of sex. It is during these vulnerable transition years that many have fallen. James Sparks, in his book, *Friendship After Forty,* writes: "We do have choices. To have sexual intercourse within the context of a friendship is one choice, but it's not the only one. A person can also choose not to. The capacity to make a different choice in friendship, or in other areas of life, is one of the God-given gifts of being human."

9. Focus on the power of God. God is greater than our mid-life transition and all the crises it may precipitate. Bring your problems to him in prayer, but don't focus on those problems. I find when I am deeply hurt or oppressed by a situation or experience that I tend to focus my attention on the problem, examining it from every angle as I pray about it. And the longer I pray, the bigger it grows. Instead, we need to focus on the power of God and his ability and resources to supply our needs, asking him for wisdom to see the creative alternatives.

Help from the Mission

Because the mid-life transition is a critical time of vulnerability for the missionary, the mission organization and its administrators should be aware of those who are struggling and be ready to offer appropriate help.

Often, the missionary will be unable to share openly and in-depth with the person(s) to whom he is responsible through the chain of command. However, the field chairman and other supervisory personnel on the field can give caring attention to missionaries who are experiencing a period of transition and point the way to help. They can search out appropriate books, tapes, and other helps, and direct the missionary to appropriate counseling help.

The mission organization can also help people who are experiencing the crisis of mid-life transition while on furlough. The furlough period is a significant time for the missionary family. Many who come home on furlough during mid-life transition experience indecision about their return to the field and their future involvement with the mission.

It is in the best interest of the mission organization to provide as much help as possible during this difficult period. Many mission organizations have furlough orientation meetings that reorient missionaries not only to life in the United States, but to the mission and its personnel. On such occasions, the mission could make available to its missionaries the services of a psychologist, pastor, or layman who is skilled in listening and counseling.

Mission organizations could require an informal introductory counseling session for each returning couple, where they would meet and talk with the counselor and begin to develop a relationship that would be expected to continue throughout the length of the furlough.

Final Thought

One morning near the end of our furlough, as I bounded out of the door for my daily jog, I was awed to see that my familiar neighborhood had been transformed by a heavy fog into a shadowy stage with shifting images. The effect was beautiful--and bizarre. I could see less than 50 yards ahead, and as I jogged down the street, my eyes probed the trees, houses, fences, and cars. As I approached one landmark after another, the shadows turned to outlines, and then the familar substance of the reality I knew to exist.

Most of mid-life transition seems like that morning run in the fog. The familiar is shrouded in a shifting cloud, and only one issue at a time may be focused on and dealt with, while shadows clothe the rest of the surroundings, and the whole is never quite clear until finally the "Son" shines through the haze and our blanket of fog is lifted.

Bibliography

Levinson, D. (1978). *The seasons of a man's life*. New York: Knopf.

Ragsdale, R. (1978). *The mid-life crisis of a minister*. Waco, Texas: Word Books.

Sparks, J. (1980). *Friendship after forty*. Nashville, Tenn: Abingdon.

23

Kenneth L. Williams

Resolving Conflicts in Christian Marriage

Marriage provides you the most intimate possible relationship. It can also give you the most possible trouble! Especially if you aren't able to handle your disagreements well. Let's look at handling conflicts in marriage and see if these principles can help make your marriage all that you and God want it to be.

Three Helpful Concepts

1. *Conflict in marriage is inevitable.* Accepting conflict as a fact of life can help you deal with it. You have different backgrounds, tastes, needs and opinions. If you *didn't*, your marriage would be extremely dull! And being Christians does *not* keep you from having disagreements. But it can surely help the way you deal with them.

2. *Conflict can be a sign of a good marriage.* Conflicts are not harmful or destructive in themselves. The manner in which you handle them determines whether they are damaging or not. In fact, when you handle your conflicts well you draw *closer* to one another; your love and appreciation is re-kindled in the process. Couples who have few or no conflicts risk losing their intimacy as time goes by.

3. *Unresolved conflicts can destroy your marriage.* Conflict is like temptation. It isn't harmful in itself, but it is nothing to fool around with! Couples who consistently use disagreements to hurt

---

Based on a paper presented at the Sixth Annual Conference on Mental Health and Missions held at Angola, Indiana in November 1985. Reprinted by permission of the author.

each other eventually see cords of love fray and snap one by one until nothing is left but two broken and bitter hearts. Few issues need greater care and skill than handling conflicts!

Five Vital Commitments

1. *Commitment to Jesus as Lord.* In 1 Peter 3:1-7 God gave husbands and wives several helpful commands. Shortly afterward he says, "...in your hearts reverence Christ as Lord" (3:15). A deep commitment to Jesus as Lord by both partners is the first essential element of a good Christian marriage. Your devotion to Christ provides you with a common purpose beyond your marriage. This helps focus your hearts away from self to Him, so that when you disagree, your focus won't be "me against you" but "we together finding a solution which glorifies Christ."

2. *Commitment to one another in a life-long relationship.* When Christ is Lord in your hearts your commitment to one another is for life, knowing that this is His perfect will for you. This double commitment provides solid rock upon which to build your marriage, even when you have earth-shaking differences which might otherwise crumble your relationship.

3. *Commitment to love one another with Christ-like love.* Apply I Cor. 13:1-7 to how you react during your disagreements. This kind of love is more than tender emotion; it is a tough love that is clearly seen in your attitudes, words and actions. This love goes far beyond a 50-50 arrangement. It says, "I'm willing to consistently give *more* than my half, whether my partner responds or not." In fact, it doesn't even think about who is giving the most. Ask Christ to fill you with more and more of His love, so that you may grow toward the 100% mark.

4. *Commitment to honesty in love.* God's command to utter honesty in Eph. 4:25 certainly applies to marriage. This means being transparent with your feelings to the point of utter vulnerability, even if you might be misjudged and misunderstood when you reveal your true feelings. Eph. 4:15 balances honesty with love. This kind of loving transparency holds out a golden promise for true intimacy; of sharing in the deepest level of one another's feelings. It isn't easy to accept your partner's feelings, especially when they reveal your failures!

5. *Commitment to "let's win together."* This rejects the goal of coming to an "I win--you lose" solution. Since you are one in Christ, you *both* lose or win. When your mutual purpose is to find a solution which satisfies *both* of you, you move from a "me vs. you" approach to a "we vs. the problem" approach. Then you can

both seek a solution that brings you closer without being forced to sacrifice your unique feelings and ideas to the other's pressure.

Ten Ground Rules

Discuss these ground rules together and decide which you want to try to follow when you're discussing a conflict. Applying these biblical principles will increase your chances of coming to a win-win solution.

1. Deal with conflicts quickly. Eph. 4:26 provides a healthy principle for handling anger: resolve it the same day it comes up. Feelings are like cement. They begin to harden quickly. You can't always handle a situation immediately, but agree together to bring things up the same day if possible. Jumping into an issue the instant it comes up, without thinking through and praying first, is dangerous, too. Balance is needed.

2. *Keep to one issue.* Prov. 20:3 says, "It is to a man's honor to avoid strife, but every fool is quick to quarrel." To avoid quarreling, make sure you know exactly what is bothering you, and keep to that one issue. Don't bring up other problems, especially from the past. If your partner brings up a conflict, avoid bringing up one or two of your own in self-defense. When more than one issue is thrown in, the whole process breaks down into a hopeless quarrel. When another issue legitimately comes up as part of the first, stop and decide whether it must be resolved before handling the original issue. Avoid using "always" and "never" to describe your partner's behavior.

3. *Use "I" messages.* "Put away from you crooked speech, and put devious talk far from you." (Prov. 4:24) See Prov. 16:21, 23 and 24. In expressing feelings, avoid "crooked" and "devious" talk by stating clearly how you feel, rather than attacking or blaming your partner. For example, say "I really feel hurt and disappointed that our dinner together didn't work out as I had planned," rather than "Why do you have to come home so late without telling me?" Beware of hiding an attack inside an "I" statement, e.g., "I feel that you are a no-good inconsiderate klutz for not telling me you were going to be late!" See David's use of "I" statements in Psalm 38, and Paul's in 2 Corinthians.

4. *Avoid attacks on your partner's character.* Prov. 11:12 says, "A man who lacks judgment derides (belittles) his neighbor, but a man of understanding holds his tongue." Talk about behavior rather than personality. "I feel frustrated trying to keep the house clean when papers and clothes are left lying around" is better than

"Why did I have to marry the town slob?" Attacks on character easily degenerate into mutual character assassination.

5. *Avoid mind reading.* Don't try to analyze your partner's motives and thoughts. It's easy to think you understand the "why" behind your partner's behavior, but we don't have the right to tell another person what his or her motives are, and then to condemn the person for those motives. See Prov. 20:5.

6. *Avoid prophesying.* "...the fool multiplies words. No one knows what is coming--who can tell him what will happen...?" (Ecc. 10:14) Very few people can fortell the future. So be careful about predicting how your partner will react in actions, thoughts or feelings. To assume that your partner will always continue to react as in the past denies God's power to change us. If he or she has reacted negatively in the past, pray for God's working to change either their reaction or your approach. You may be surprised at the outcome!

7. *Keep emotional expression appropriate.* It's important to let your partner know how you feel during a conflict. But the unrestrained venting of anger is usually destructive. Don't use a sledge hammer to swat a fly! If you are given to exploding with your partner, try venting it alone to the Lord first. This can be a good way to let off steam, and He is big enough to take your temper without being hurt. See Prov. 29:11; 15:18; 29:22.

8. *Do not counter-attack.* When your partner brings up a problem, be willing to talk about it without reference to his or her failures and weaknesses. To say something like, "Well, you're no better than me. Look what you did when..." guarantees that even a little conflict will escalate into a full-blown war. If your partner is hurting by something you're doing, allow him or her to share their feelings and then work together to find a solution. This means setting aside your desire to avoid blame by laying it on him or her. See 1 Peter 21:22,23; 3:8-11.

9. *Don't try to win.* In Eph. 5:29-33 God says that man and wife are "one flesh" and that the marriage relationship compares to that of Christ and His church. Any attempt to win at the expense of your partner destroys that unity. A desire to win usually means getting the best of the other person--of getting your way at his or her expense. When one of you loses, both lose in reality, because the conflict is not really resolved. Mutually satisfactory solutions *are* possible with God's help, if both of you can give up the idea of winning over your partner.

10. *Establish and observe belt-lines.* Be careful that your words do not crush your partner's spirit. (Prov. 18:14; 13:10) Each of you should make clear what kinds of remarks "hit below the belt,"

i.e., comments that are designed to hurt. If you catch yourself hitting below the belt, stop and ask forgiveness immediately. Accept the responsibility for what you say when you're angry. If your partner beings to hit below the belt, call him or her on it immediately. Don't let it pass by, because it is too damaging to your relationship to ignore.

You may want to seal your commitment to these ground rules by signing below.

I hereby express my desire and commitment to follow these ground rules with God's help, and to confess to my partner any failure to do so.

_____

Signature   Date

Three Pre-confrontation Principles

1. *Pray first.* Pray before you jump into battle! Whenever possible, take your problem to the Lord first. He wants to be involved. Ask Him to show you what you might be doing to aggravate the problem. If the problem is a one-time event rather than a continuing source of irritation, you may be able to resolve it alone with the Lord. The solution may come through forbearing and forgiving. See Prov. 19:11 and Col. 3:13. But beware of putting a band-aid on a festering problem. Ask God for wisdom to know whether to "overlook the offense" or to bring it up with your partner.

2. *Give up all desire for revenge.* Prov. 24:29 says, "Do not say, 'I'll do to him as he has done to me; I'll pay that man back for what he did.'" Revenge has no place in Christian marriage, and yet it seems so natural. When you feel vengeful, admit it to the Lord and decide to give it up to Him. See Rom. 12:17-21.

3. *Avoid dumping your problem on other people.* Prov. 20:19 says, "A gossip betrays a confidence; so avoid a man who talks too much." Secretly telling a friend or relative not only betrays your partner; it may make you more resentful. On the other hand, with your partner's permission, it may help to talk to a counselor or a close friend who will be honest with you. Watch your motives! Are you looking for help to solve the issue or for sympathy?

Eight Steps to Resolve Conflict

No one procedure is ideal for everyone, but this procedure gives key biblical guidelines helpful in resolving conflict. You may find these steps cumbersome and artificial at first, but learning them will be worth the effort. Then you can modify them to fit your relationship.

Step 1. You have a problem and take it to God
When you are bothered about something your partner has been doing, tell God how you feel and confess any desire for retribution. Don't hesitate to freely express your feelings to Him using "I" messages, preferably aloud. This usually helps calm your feelings. (Ps. 142:2).

Then ask yourself: 1) Is this problem a one-time event which I can forgive and forget without bringing it up? 2) Is this a real issue or is my complaint a trivial one which hides a deeper grievance? 3) Am I willing to be honest and loving? 4) Am I ready to present a specific request for change?

Before going to your partner, ask God for a "spirit of gentleness" (Gal. 6:1), and ask Him to prepare your partner's heart. See Prov. 14:17,29; 15:18.

Step 2. Bring up the issue with your partner
Open the issue with a statement like, "I've got a problem I need to talk over. When is a good time?" Timing is crucial. (Ecc. 3:7,8) It may or may not be best to state what the problem is at this point. Agree on a time together; the sooner the better.

Step 3. Explain your problem
Share 1) what the problem is, and 2) how you feel about it, keeping your statements short and simple so you don't overload the communication channels. State exactly what your partner does (or doesn't do) and how you feel about it, without attacking.

Your partner listens carefully and gives feedback at frequent intervals, i.e., restating in his/her own words his/her understanding of what is wrong and how you feel about it. Neither spouse should become defensive or counterattack. James 1:19 and Prov. 15:1 fit perfectly here.

As he/she listens and shows understanding, feelings will probably lessen, especially if the other spouse can accept them with a loving attitude. This in no way implies being in agreement; only that he/she acknowledges your feelings as real and valid, without judging you. See Prov. 18:2; 15:28; 17:27; 24:26.

Step 4. Propose a tentative solution
Now say what you would like done in order to correct the problem, realizing that this is a tentative attempt to find a mutually satisfactory solution. Also say what it would mean to you and how it might benefit both of you. Prov. 16:21,23 indicate the effective way to persuade someone.

Again, your partner gives frequent feedback to show that he understands you. It isn't enough to say, "I understand." He should be able to accurately describe in his own words what you want and what it would mean to both of you. When you are sure that he/she understands, you may go on to Step 5.

Step 5. Your partner responds
This is your partner's opportunity to tell how he/she feels about the issue and your proposal for solving it. Statements are best kept short and simple, so you can restate in your own words to see if you understand what he is saying. Your spouse needs the same acceptance and understanding as you received earlier.

Your partner has three alternatives at this point: 1) He/she may agree with your request; 2) he/she may disagree completely; or 3) he/she may suggest an alternate solution--a totally new proposal or some modification of your proposal. Your spouse might be willing to go along with you if you concede to counter requests. But beware of the barter trap! Application of Phil. 2:3,4 by both of you makes this process not only possible, but a joyful experience.

If you come to an agreement, a contract for change is negotiated. this is an agreement clearly stating what each of you will try to do so that the problem will hopefully be taken care of. When agreement is made, you may go on to Step 7. But if you can't agree on a solution in a short time, you should go on to Step 6.

Step 6. Take an intermission
If a solution isn't reached quickly, it usually helps to agree to let the matter rest without further discussion for a day or two. It will probably be much easier to reach a solution after a time to allow God to reveal creative alternatives, and to bring healing for hurt feelings. In Prov. 14:17 discretion and patience go together. Decide on a time for coming back to the issue, and commit your feelings to God for the time being. Pray that He will give each of you the wisdom and willingness needed to find a solution which will bring joy to both of you.

Step 7. Ask for and grant forgiveness

Christian marriage has no room for unresolved anger or resentment. Apply Col. 3:13 and I Cor. 13:5 to your relationship. Before a conflict can be totally resolved, these feelings must be dealt with. In this step both of you ask for forgiveness. This doesn't necessarily imply that you were wrong or that you intentionally hurt your partner. It means that you acknowledge that your partner is hurting, and you want him or her to be free from any resentment that may have come up, so that your relationship may be restored.

Then each of you makes a decision to forgive the other in the power of Christ, and states this decision. This act of love allows God to neutralize the feelings. After some experience, you may find that you can better work through this step alone before the Lord rather than together. Then you must demonstrate your forgiveness by your actions and expressions of renewed love for each other.

Step 8. Review the situation

Take time to rethink the conflict alone and see what God would have you learn from it. Ask yourself: 1) What have I learned from it? 2) Did I abide by the ground rules? 3) Have all hurts been forgiven? 4) How can I do better next time?

Also, review the situation together after a time to see if the solution is actually working out as planned, and both of you are happy about it. If not, reexamine it and seek alternative solutions.

Conclusion

Yes, this approach does seem cumbersome. However, this very fact can help you to concentrate on the process of resolving your disagreements. It slows down the process to enable you to work at it step by step. Yes, it does take a lot of effort to master. But if you do, you will dramatically improve your ability to really resolve your conflicts. Try it and see!

MISSIONARY CHILDREN

24

Larry W. Sharp

Toward A Greater Understanding of the Real MK: A Review of Recent Research

It is becoming increasingly apparent that the missionary child as part of the third culture has a unique potential in his generation. The latest research on MKs should interest missionary parents and personnel working with the missionary family. Such literature serves to debunk many of the common myths about MKs and shows that MKs are not disadvantaged but are an intelligent, normal, well-adjusted and privileged group of young people. With a proper understanding of their needs, unique problems and potential we can help develop a very important resource for world understanding and missions.

The first International Conference on Missionary Kids (ICMK) was held in Manila, Philippines, November 5-9, 1984. Over three hundred delegates representing a cross section of evangelical missions from all continents convened to address issues relative to the welfare of the missionary family and especially the MKs. Based on several "New Realities in Mission," various attempts were made to examine strategies for developing a truly transnational education, to evaluate a variety of models which may be used to meet educational needs in a multicultural community and to explore potential networks for intermission cooperation in developing and implementing pre-field, on-field and post-field (reentry) programs for MKs.

Among the concerns relative to MKs was the desire to understand the results of research in recent years. My own experience in working with MKs for the past twelve years, coupled with a literature review on the subject, has convinced me that a host of myths exists in North America about MKs.

Missionary children are part of a unique culture sometimes called the third culture, hence the term *third culture kids* (TCKs). TCKs live in the middle between the overseas national culture and the parents' culture. They may grow up in Brazil but are not totally Brazilian, neither are they fully aware of or integrated into their parents' home country. They have a sense of belonging to two cultures while not having a sense of total ownership in either. Useem and Downie (1976) say that:

Where they feel most like themselves is in that interstitial culture, the third culture, which is created, shared, and carried by persons who are relating societies or sections thereof, to each other. (p. 103)

MKs as members of the third culture, are in many ways advantaged, having been exposed to an extended world perspective, developed cross-cultural skills, acquired other languages and the ability to relate comfortably to other nationals as peers. At a time when North America finds itself active in international affairs yet with a dearth of interculturally competent persons, we might anticipate a future for MKs as "link-people" who can play a role as mediators on the world human relations scene.

The following is an attempt to bring together much of the recent research and at the same time expose a popular mythology regarding MKs. The research demonstrates a very different typology than that perpetuated in the evangelical church community. My own experience also has convinced me that MKs are an intelligent, normal, well adjusted and privileged group of young people and a very important, yet often latent, resource for world understanding and missions.

Myth 1: There is a Certain Amount of Deprivation and Personality Underdevelopment resulting from the Missionary Overseas Upbringing.

Nothing could be further from the truth. Edward Danielson, in a 1981 PhD study, gave the Sixteen Personality Factor Test and the Tennessee Self-Concept Scale Personality Test to MKs in Ecuador, East Africa and the Philippines and compared them to a control group of preachers' kids in the U.S. His conclusion was that MKs develop slightly different profiles but they develop traits which are generally more favorable; the strongest and most predominant trait being emotional stability (Danielson, 1982).

Danielson indicated no need for concern with regard to foreign residence. Typical MKs are highly intelligent, emotionally stable, conscientious, conservative, relaxed, submissive, honest and slightly group dependent (Danielson, 1981). They do tend to be more reserved and have slight problems with regard to their self-concept. Ruth Useem of Michigan State University, probably the foremost authority on TCKs in general, declares that some have emotional problems, but the rate is not greater than among the general American population. TCKs in general, however, according to Downs, have fewer psychological problems than youth from similar backgrounds in the USA (Downs, 1976).

My own experience is that MKs have a tendency to withdraw somewhat in new situations, but there is not a significant deprivation factor built into the overseas experience per se. The cross-cultural international exposure provides for a personality depth beyond the level of the average American teenager.

Myth 2: MKs Suffer Academically.

There is simply no evidence for a generalization such as this, though of course individuals may have specific problems. Each missionary family must evaluate the educational options and decide what is best for their children: national schools, structured home program, MK school or return to the homeland. The average IQ score of MKs runs between 15 and 20 points above the general public in the USA (Danielson, 1982) and, in general, MKs produce better test scores than the overall USA population. In a 1969 study, Krajewski determined MKs to be the highest academic achievers among all TCK groupings, maintaining a "sterling" record of academic achievement (Krajewski, 1969).

MKs take their academic work seriously and are frequently over-achievers. They do a great deal of reading and are more likely to enjoy writing than their peers in the USA. Downs reports that TCKs, in general, are gaining in measured intellectual performance at the same time that general test scores in the USA are going down (Downs, 1976). The Amazon Valley Academy, a UFM International school in Belem, Brazil, tests its students regularly using the well known test of student progress, the Stanford Achievement Test. In 1982 AVA students ranked 14.5 months above the USA national average. On college board exams, the average AVA graduate ranks 24 percentile points above the national average. I have every reason to believe that such is typical of MK schools.

Myth 3: MKs are Rebellious Towards their Parents and the Christian Faith.

Some TCK research indicates that when asked to identify their best friend, ninety per cent of the TCK respondents listed their parents (Downs, 1976). Judith Campbell reported at ICMK in Manila that in a 1984 survey at Wheaton College, MKs were asked what they missed the most. The majority response was, their parents. Albrecht reported from his sample that 77% said "No, I do not resent my parents being missionaries." Generally, the research indicates that MKs are more intimately related to and dependent on the family than would be true in the USA. Parents play a more potent role in the socialization of their children.

Many high school age MKs are involved with parents' work in ministries such as evangelism and preaching, tribal identification, and in technical areas like computer word processing. They are more apt to be leaders in local church groups or teach a children's class than their North American counterparts. Incredibly, Sprinkle discovered in a 1976 survey of MKs that 95% answered "yes" to the question, "If you could 'do it again," would you choose to be an MK?"

Nevertheless, probably empirical evidence for the denial of this myth is the weakest due to the difficulty in measuring in an operational way just what Christian commitment is and what it really means to be "rebellious towards their parents." The author's studies will attempt to develop a multi-dimensional scale of MK commitment in order to measure MKs and then identify variables which contribute to MKs' maintenance of the commitment dimension.

Myth 4: Boarding Homes are Basically Detrimental to a Child's Development and Serve to Lower Self-Concept.

This subject stimulates many heated debates with considerable variances of ideas since a large percentage of Mks spend at least some time overseas in a boarding home. As of this date, I know of no study which presents any proof that the boarding experience itself damages an MK's development. In fact, the opposite has been substantiated.

David Schipper at Rosemead Graduate School of Psychology hypothesized that a boarding student would suffer from lower self-concept and that the longer he boarded, the lower his self-control would get. His statistical study of over 500 children in the Orient not only failed to support the hypothesis, but indicated the opposite:

In fact, the significant results obtained for the sense of belongingness suggest that post-puberty separation from the nuclear family and affiliations with one's peer group in the controlled setting of a boarding school may enhance the adolescent missionary student's self-concept. (Schipper, 1977, p. 86)

Wickstrom, in a similar study, was not able to support the hypothesis that a boarding school experience is detrimental to a child's development, but concluded by saying, "...if any implication is present it would be the earlier the children are sent to boarding school the better" (Wickstrom, 1978). Danielson did extensive research in the area of MK personality development and concludes:

The facts document that MKs in boarding schools develop personalities very much like those of non-boarders. Out of thirty-two personality traits, MK boarders differed from day   students only on one trait. The difference was not great, but the MK boarders are on the average very slightly restrained while the non-boarder is very slightly adventurous. Both boarders and non-boarders develop wholesome and emotionally stable personalities (Danielson, 1982, p. 9).

To be sure, there are no easy solutions. I have observed good and bad boarding situations on the mission field. One of the key factors is the attitude of the parents. It is primarily the parents who determine the child's reaction to expatriate life in general since the child will reflect the parents' feeling about school, the boarding homes, furlough, and the like. It is also mandatory that houseparents be carefully selected to represent the values and principles most closely linked to the parents. Even with all precautions, the boarding experience is not for everyone, but one thing is sure: the boarding home concept itself does not inherently produce detrimental effects; problems are attributed to parents' attitudes, houseparent conflicts or problems within the child himself.

Myth 5: Because the MK Parents are "Busy Serving the Lord Full-Time," the Lord Makes Up the Gaps in the Children's Upbringing.
This myth has overtaken missionary parents more than church members in the homelands. The barrage of books, articles, film series and seminars of the past decade has made us all aware of the importance of traditional family values even among missionary families. Yet it is still true that some missionary families put the

"work" ahead of their other God-given priorities. Without making "family theology" an idol, as Ray Chester warns (Chester, 1984), missionary parents still need to remember their responsibilities to their children. I have seen too many parents reaping the results of their deliberate refusal to accept God's total mandate because "God called me first to the heathen of the Amazon."

Carole Herrmann, in a scientific study in 1977 of over 200 MKs, discovered that the biggest single factor in successful MK adjustment later in life was the quality of trust and autonomy formation at an early age (Herrmann, 1977). Parent-child relationship is the key to MK adjustment. The essential elements are a consistent acceptance and respect for the child as a person and the freedom to test his/her independence within the carefully defined limits of the family. It is important that missionaries do not expect their spirituality and call to "rub off" on the children. Relationships and communication are mandatory as each child is brought up to become his unique self.

Herrmann concludes:

Consequently, in the family where the communication network of relationships between members of the family has not played an essential part in the life of the MK, foundational factors in trust and autonomy are negatively correlated with identity formation. As a result, these MKs are currently finding it more difficult to adapt to new situations (Herrmann, 1979, p. 6).

Clearly, the Lord does not make up for gaps in parental responsibility.

Myth 6: MKs Really Don't Have Any Problems to Worry About.

All of this is not to say that MKs do not have needs and problems. MKs are kids...like all the kids we know. The temptations and transition to adulthood and also between first and second culture residence often bring heartache, discouragement and failure. There are problems and pressures which may frustrate and retard the realization of the MK potential.

Probably most of the needs and potential problems for MKs are in the area of social adjustment when they return to North America after years in another culture. They tend to become socially marginal and, according to Useem and Downie:

...they cope rather than adjust, and as one student of multicultural persons describes them, they become both "a part of" and "apart from" whatever situation they are in (p. 105).

Krajewski reported that MKs enjoy least what is traditionally known as "social life" at college. They are often shocked in North America by what seems to be the prevalence of immoral and/or frivolous behavior among their classmates (Downs, 1976). This may lead to disillusionment with the entire college experience, if not with society at large. They exhibit a slightly higher than average drop-out rate in the freshman year of college, though most return later to complete their degrees.

MK friendship patterns are different. MKs may be relatively inexperienced and insecure in peer group relations, particularly with members of the opposite sex (Downs). Most grow up in close living situations with extended family relationships. MKs, while overseas, depend on one or two close friends, referred to by one MK as "total friendship," and find it difficult to make and break relationships.

If MKs suffer psychologically, it is most likely at the hands of insensitive ethnocentric North Americans who simply do not understand multiculturalism and appear to have little understanding of all that is involved in cross-cultural transition. There is more damage to self-concept from comments like, "What, you mean you don't like Big Macs?" or "Hey, you've been in the jungle too long if you don't know who J.R. is!" than from a whole term on the mission field. What kid in this country is expected to know the status of church planting efforts in Togo or to repeat John 3:16 in a strange language to his peers week after week? No wonder that only 34% of Sprinkle's sample indicated "yes" to the question, "Has the U.S. become home for you?" (Sprinkle, 1976).

Of the 234 MKs who responded to Viser's survey, over 50% reported problems in the adjustment stages. The three most common difficulties were a longing for foreign roots, culture shock and no sense of loyalty or commitment to a local church. This concurs with a review of other studies and should help to focus attempts in North America to help MKs accommodate to their changing lifestyle. North American Christians could help MKs in the transition period if they would put out the effort to learn more about their MK friends (Sharp, 1983). The socialization process is not easy, but friendliness, sensitivity and positive understanding can go a long way toward helping MKs who find a rootlessness in North America, do not know family relatives, have no home church and need time to learn to drive, catch the lingo and learn the proper customs.

One of the exciting frontiers relative to MKs is the beginning of a networking of resources for MK care in the pre-field, on-field and reentry stages of the MK's experience. The negative impact of the pressures faced by MKs can be minimized by appropriate actions at various points of intervention. These frontiers involve the preparation and training of "care givers": parents, teachers and house parents; orientation and cross-cultural training, spiritual emphasis ministries, guidance programs for MKs on the field, family life conferences, reentry seminars, care networks of counselors and legal/medical advisors, open homes in North America, hot-line networks, communiques for MKs and MK outreach involvement programs in North America.

Some of the organizations in the forefront of MK care are Link Care Foundation, Interaction Inc., CHED division of Wycliffe Bible Translators, Assemblies of God and the Southern Baptist Foreign Mission Board. The Overseas Division of Interaction, Inc., for example, is committed to the task of being a catalyst and resource for the Christian community to respond to the needs of the TCK-MK. Let us join them as individuals, churches and para-church organizations to develop the potential of thousands of MKs around the world.

Let us put our myths to rest and try to understand where MKs are coming from, inasmuch as we have every reason to be confident that MKs benefit from the experience of life overseas. MKs are not just a costly appendage to their parents' ministry, but they are an important present and future resource for missions and world understanding at home and abroad. We would not be excessively optimistic in suggesting that perhaps MKs hold potential answers to some of the cross-cultural problems of international misunderstanding in our day.

References

Allbrecht, J. (1971). *Adjustments of missionaries' children on the mission field and upon return to America.* Unpublished manuscript, Association of Baptists for World Evangelism.

Chester, R. M. (1984). To send or not to send? Missionary parents ask. *Evangelical Missions Quarterly, 20,* 252-259.

Danielson, E. E. (1981). *The effects of foreign residence in personality development of the children of American evangelical ministers.* Unpublished doctoral dissertation, University of Santo Tomas, Philippines.

Downs, R. F. (1976, Spring). A look at the third culture child. *The Japan Christian Quarterly*, 68-71.

Herrmann, C. B. (1977). *Foundational factors of trust and autonomy influencing the identity formation of multi-cultural life-styled missionaries' children.* Unpublished doctoral dissertation, Northwestern University. Ann Arbor, Mich.: University Microfilms, No. 7800710.

Herrmann, C. B. (1979, October). MKs and their parents. *Emissary, 10.*

Krajewski, F. R. (1969). A study of the relationship of an overseas-experienced population based on sponsorship of parent and subsequent academic adjustment to college in the United States. Unpublished doctoral dissertation, Michigan State University. Ann Arbor, Mich.: University Microfilms, No. 70-15,068.

Schipper, D. J. (1977). *Self-concept differences between early, late, and non—boarding missionary children.* Unpublished doctoral dissertation, Rosemead Graduate School of Professional Psychology. Ann Arbor, Mich.: University Microfilms, No. 77-21,536.

Sharp, L. W. (1983). How to minister to MKs in North America. *Lifeline, . 45*, No. 2:5.

Sprinkle, L. (1976). *Survey: Missionary kids share their feelings about being MKs.* Unpublished manuscript, Carson-Newman College.

Useem, R. (1978). Third culture kids. T*he Window*, January 22.

Useem, R. and Downie, R. D. (1976). Third culture kids. *Today's Education* 65, 103-105.

Viser, W. C. (1978). *A psychological profile of missionary children in college and the relationship of intense group therapy in the treatment of personality problems as reflected by the Minnesota Multiphasic Personality Inventory.* Unpublished doctoral dissertation, Southwestern Baptist Theological Seminary.

Wickstrom, D. L. (1978). *Self-esteem and dependence in early, late and non-boarding missionary children.* Unpublished doctoral dissertation, Rosemead Graduate School of Professional Psychology, La Mirada, CA.

Wickstrom, D. L. and Fleck, J. R. (1983). Missionary children: correlates of self-esteem and dependency. *Journal of Psychology and Theology, 11,* 226-235.

25

Margaret Hopper Taylor

Personality Development in the Children of Missionary Parents

Personality development and concurrent individual identity formation are issues of major concern in all the social sciences from anthropology to theology. In recent years attention has been focused on personality development of young people who have been reared in a land whose culture is different from that of their parents. Because they are the products of two cultural streams, such young people are sometimes referred to as "third culture people." Scholars hope that studies of this small, clearly defined group will throw light on the development process in whole cultures and even of all people. Hopefully, new insights will help both children and parents understand one another more clearly and grow in appreciation of the problems and challenges of generations not their own.

Leading psychologists and psychiatrists like Erik Erikson of Harvard University have emphasized the importance of adolescence as a crisis period in the establishment of individual identity. Identity, in this usage, can be defined simply as understanding who one is and where one belongs. It is obvious that identity formation for third culture youth will have different aspects from that of persons who spend nearly all their lives in one area among people of similar presuppositions. Identity formation and re-formation begin as soon as there is consciousness, perhaps prenatally, and continue until death. The

---

adolescent period with its various crises coincides in the lives of many or most missionary children with the time when they leave home for boarding school and then leave the country where they were reared to enter college in the country where their parents were reared. To Erikson "crisis" is not a cataclysm but a turning point, as in an illness, with each of the development stages having crises resolved by moving in one direction or another.

Because the major impact upon missionary children of being bi-cultural comes when they return to their parents' native land more or less on their own, I have used in this paper the opinions and experiences of children of missionaries to Japan who have been away from home at college. With the help of Joy Norton, Senior Fellow, East-West Center, Honolulu, a survey was made of twenty-six young people in this category. Professors Abram H. Koop and George F. Samuel of the Canadian Academy in Kobe also generously shared the results of a survey they made in 1971 of 103 alumni of that institution. In addition, long conversations with young people themselves as well as discussions with parents and other interested persons have aided in the development of the ideas expressed here.

Even after limiting the subject of our study to missionary youth, reared in Japan, who have been away to North America to college, there is so much diversity of experience and reactions to experience that broad generalizations can rarely be made. Young people reared in small towns and whose primary schooling was at home have little in common with those who grew up in a metropolitan area where both church and school were conducted in English by persons with the same general cultural background as their parents. Youth who attended Japanese school know a different Japan from those whose Japanese contacts were primarily with maids, tradespeople, and their parents' friends. Added to the mix are the variety of methods of child care and discipline used by parents, parental ways of regarding spouse and marriage relationships as well as their attitudes toward children, war, drugs, racial differences, and--crucial for missionary families--articles of faith and their expression. Number of brothers and sisters, if any, and position among siblings affect personality development. Having called attention to the infinite variety of strands in our study, like a coat of many colors, the "coat" in this study obviously will not fit all persons in all situations. It may, nevertheless, have a pattern and quality which will add warmth, brightness, and comfort to those who try it on, or it may scratch and irritate.

Basic Trust and Distrust

From earliest consciousness an infant begins to develop either an attitude of basic trust toward caretakers and toward himself or herself, or one of fundamental distrust. A part of trust is a feeling on the part of the child of being trustworthy in the eyes of others, or its opposite, untrustworthy. If the infant finds the environment and his or her body responsive to needs, physical and psychological, basic trust can begin to grow, forming the basis for a healthy personality.

How can parents, in addition to supplying the necessary physical needs promptly in a loving manner, contribute to the building of the all-important basic trust in their child? Erikson believes that one essential is that parents themselves have a deep confidence, almost somatic in nature, in the lifestyle, mores, and philosophy of their own culture. He concentrates on the importance of the attitude of the mothering person toward her role as mother, position in the family and community, as well as a feeling of oneness with women everywhere throughout history in the importance of her role. I believe the fathering person in attitude and behavior toward the child and its mother provides equally essential elements in the development of trust, and that subsequent studies of this function will demonstrate its vitality in personality development for all members of the family.

Religion is the social institution which corresponds to trust in the individual. Christians with a clear understanding of what they believe have a good opportunity, inherent even in their physical behavior and bearing, to help a child develop trust, the cornerstone for successful interpersonal living. Missionary parents from the nature and conviction of their calling should be well prepared to start their children on the road to successful living.

Autonomy and Initiative

Given the ground plan for personality growth believed by psychologists to be essentially the same in all persons, before reaching school age a child goes through a period when he develops preponderantly autonomy or shame and doubt, followed by a period during which initiative or guilt is a major characteristic. Thus, by age six fundamental personality patterns are well set, and according to some, the child knows two-thirds of all he or she will learn in a lifetime. Certainly basic speech patterns are set by this period, as are early social organization; and in the opinion of Harris in *I'm OK; You're OK*, all the parents basic moods, attitudes, prejudices, beliefs, and opinions have been communicated to the child many times. It is rare, I think, for parents to understand the crucial nature of this early period and particularly the elements of basic trust, autonomy, and initiative which have peak developmental periods within the pre-school years. One cringes at the psychological damage done by a father spanking a three-year-old because the little boy could not sit still during a long church service (see July, 1975) or a mother speaking to a four-year-old who is screaming hysterically with fatigue and fear as they climb up a long flight of steps, "I don't like you either, and I'll spank you again if you are rude to me" (August. 1975). Basic trust? Autonomy? Initiative?

The child care practiced by some missionaries virtually guarantees later behavior problems. Before guilt feelings become too heavy for parents to bear, however, it is necessary to say that not all behavior problems are the result of parental errors. Prenatal or birth injuries, inability to assimilate essential vitamins and minerals, and no doubt many others yet to be pinpointed causes such as pollution, heredity, and social unrest, also play a part. The evidence indicates, nonetheless, that the pre-school years are more crucial than most parents are aware of. Unfortunately, many missionaries are pulled by demands of supporting churches, language learning, professional development and service, household tasks, and overseas family needs into neglecting to study this period of child care and to organize time to do a successful job of rearing the pre-schooler.

Many of us may have had more children than we were able to care for properly. Given the larger number of demands upon missionary parents, it would seem the first step to successful parenting might well be to decide how many can be capably reared. Poor parent practice is, of course, not limited to missionaries, but few professions devour the time, energy, and psychic resources of persons as does the missionary life. Wise persons will take this fact into account when deciding whether to have children, how many, who is to provide what kinds of care, and what study to do in preparation for the events. For persons who marry, nothing is more crucial for happiness than affirmative marriage and parental relations, yet both relationships are sometimes entered into with scarcely a book read or class attended to help participants understand the human dynamics at work. Long, hard self-analysis should be a prerequisite to the decision to become parents and especially before having more than two children. Few individuals have the physical, emotional, and psychological resources to carry on effective missionary service and rear a family.

Assuming the correctness of psychological theory (Freud, Erikson, Piaget) that lifetime attitudes are firmly set in the pre-school period, how do missionaries go about assisting a child to develop trust, autonomy, and initiative? Every effort of the child to feed, dress, and wash self, hang up clothes, and put away possessions should be patiently encouraged, not prevented by anxious parents who think such efforts should be done "properly" or not at all. As early as possible the child should be encouraged to take short trips alone to see friends. As a teenager the same person will likely travel alone thousands of miles from home to college. Let the child, male or female, buy the train tickets, make reservations, pay for the restaurant meal, go to the bank to learn withdrawing (and, hopefully, depositing) procedures, shop for food and clothes, change a tire, mail packages overseas--in fact, as early as possible, do all the daily business necessary to life in our complex modern age.

Basic speech patterns are firmly set before age six, perhaps before age three. This is the age to become bilingual. Japanese playmates and kindergarten, maids (now almost extinct in Japan), TV, and most important of all, parental attitudes are crucial factors. Parents afflicted with colonial attitudes of the superiority of their native tongue and unwilling to exercise the self-discipline to learn Japanese themselves can hardly be surprised if their children do not display a lively curiosity about and a desire to acquire facility in an "inferior" language. Like all learning, language learning can be less arduous if it becomes a family project or is turned into a game (a fun game, not a parent-forced exercise) graded for age. "How many signs can you read in a thirty-minute ride?" or "How many animals can you name in Japanese?" The variety of intellectual stimulation is set only by the limits of the imagination and endurance of parents and the intelligence level of the child.

Of the twenty-six missionary children completing our survey, six had attended Japanese school (not all respondents were clear in answering). Of the remaining twenty replying to the question "What parts would you change if you could repeat your life?", five replied that they would like to have attended a Japanese school. An additional eight wished they had learned more Japanese language, customs, history, art, and crafts. This desire to know more than they do about Japan is the only major regret voiced by respondents. This positive attitude toward Japan is a credit, I believe, to the teaching, both conscious and unconscious, of parents and to Japanese society in general. At the same time, it is a challenge to missionary parents to enrich and deepen the contacts of their children with Japan. In addition to simultaneous Japanese school and English language education at home, almost unlimited options are open to residents of Japan, where education appears to be almost a religion. Missionary children have received lessons in soroban (abacus), Japanese art and ballet, flower-arranging, music, language and kanji writing, martial arts, and pottery-making, to name only a few of the many areas of study available in most communities. Some, since the flourishing of the economy, have had side jobs delivering newspapers or milk, assisting carpenters or gardeners. Teaching English and fashion-modeling are lucrative and may develop responsible work habits, but are less likely to contribute to a foreigner's understanding of Japanese culture.

Industry vs. Inferiority
Having moved by way of language learning to school and work, we are ready for Erikson's fourth stage of personality development, one which he calls *Industry vs. Inferiority.* The period to which the major development of this characteristic, either in its positive or negative form, roughly corresponds is elementary school age, seven to eleven. Of course all personality characteristics continue to develop and change throughout life, but there appear to be certain ages when the emergence of particular characteristics are in their ascendancy. Parents are frequently unaware of the variety and importance of childhood activities that in an adult we would call study or work. A two-year-old may open and close a hinged box seventy-six times in succession. This is not aimless waste of time. It is a way of learning about shadow and light, elementary mechanics, how this particular material feels, looks and smells as it is held in one's hand. The child is developing the small muscles in the fingers that are prerequisite to learning to write, draw, type, play the piano, or drive an automobile. During school age, learning to do required tasks well becomes a cornerstone to the self-confidence necessary to assume adult responsibilities. At the same time out-of-school achievements-- making and flying a kite, climbing a fence, tree or mountain, playing a musical instrument, writing verse, learning to swim or sail, painting a picture or fence, mowing a lawn, knitting a sock-- are not unimportant sidelines of "play" but vital personality bricks in building a "can do" person who in adolescence will need the memory of many accomplishments to provide the psychic

energy and courage to enter and relate to a strange college full of parochial North Americans, who know little about Japan, and perhaps care less.

Given the language consciousness of missionaries, it may not be necessary to dwell on the pervasive effect of vocabulary on reading, writing, and thinking. A few children who have attended Japanese school have been considered poorly prepared for secondary education in English. Such a lack is not necessary. Missionary parents can prevent such a condition if they listen carefully to young children, avoid baby talk, bowlderized words, grammatical mistakes, and engage their children in conversation on as advanced a level as rapidly developing minds can accept. Playing word games, table games, and charades with children, subscribing to appropriately graded magazines and records, answering every question with respect and courtesy will bridge gaps and increase a child's self-esteem, always in short supply in a world of bigger, stronger, and more knowledgeable adults and perhaps siblings. With their double culture, race, and language systems to sort out, missionary children need all the help they can get.

It is easy for a missionary couple devoting themselves to service in a land not their own to lose touch with changes in the homeland. Mission boards, supporting churches, friends, family, and the missionary need to be alert to this problem and to exert considerable effort to updating missionary information on events and interpretation of events in the home country. Consistent communication of news from national elections to new ice cream flavors is important for the child who will one day suddenly arrive in his parents' homeland more or less an independent entity at a time in life when major decisions such as career choice and marriage partner may be made. It is sad and unnecessary for the young person to appear at Yale or Carlton not knowing the vocabulary, wearing weird clothing, looking and feeling like the proverbial Martian. Visits to several college campuses on a furlough during the high school period, subscribing to a few college newspapers, corresponding with a friend who has gone a year or two ahead to college, talking with home-visiting collegians in the foreign community in Japan may help. Parents can discuss freely what they think college classmates may be like and how they may differ from missionary youth. Parents often prefer small, regional, church-related colleges for their children. Some young people have found the parochialism of small campuses oppressive and have quickly transferred to a campus with more international students and perhaps a broader world view. Parents and youth need to discuss frankly the advantages of the several kinds of education, of postponing college, or of choosing careers not requiring advanced education.

Mission work itself involves so many problems that missionaries may prefer to avoid confronting the moral choices posed by their own nation's foreign and domestic policies--for the past generation of Americans, Vietnam, the draft, Watergate. It is dangerous in our fast-moving age for a missionary to remain uninformed and uninvolved in his own nation's actions, but to send a child back to college without having discussed political issues of the day, the alcohol-drug problem, crime, sexual mores, and the changing roles of women and men is a form of child neglect. Fortunately in Japan excellent news services in both English and Japanese make it easy to get national information about North America. Missionaries from other countries may have more difficulty.

Identity and Identity Confusion

Just as each age pushes against the succeeding one, discussion of each ascendant set of personality characteristics pushes against the next. Practical discussion of vocabulary building and development of work habits moves inexorably toward the age of adolescence with its special challenges of identity formation. The circumstances surrounding a child reared in a land whose culture is foreign to that of his or her parents give an added dimension to identity formation.

Unfortunately, in the opinion of some psychologists, identity is most often ascribed to a person in terms of her or his occupation. Who is he? He is a lawyer, or dentist, or bus driver; not he is a Christian, a champion golfer, or an expert flower-arranger. In the past, married women have generally had only a shadow identity reflecting that of someone else, such as she is Joe's mother or the doctor's wife. Changes in the roles of women are altering identity building, as some women, though married, retain their maiden names, consider their careers co-equal with those of their husbands, and make conscious choices as to whether or not to become mothers. We are living in a fundamental social revolution in this regard. Arriving at opinions about social change based on broad information will assist missionaries in understanding and maintaining communication with children who, after all, belong to a very different generation.

Anna Freud stressed the dramatic hormonal, emotional, and social upheavals going on in adolescents and concluded that behavior that might be viewed as neurotic or psychotic at another age may very well be merely a normal, temporary phase for the adolescent still in the throes of identity confusion. Making a meaningful, appropriate career choice in an age of almost unlimited varieties of occupations but widespread unemployment would tax a mature person. Yet, arriving at a clear decision, acquiring needed training and securing a job one can do well seem to be the sine qua non of successful identity formation. Whatever help a youth can get from vocational counseling, aptitude tests, and exposure to actual job situations through summer work or observation would seem to be a plus. Nevertheless, many young people must change colleges or drop out a while, move from job to job or country to country, test themselves against the job market, and develop their own ideals and family expectations before arriving at a plateau of job and identity formation--which even then may not be permanent. This transitional period, called a moratorium by some psychologists, may continue a number of years. It is often a trying time for parents. One Harvard professor said that adolescence is the period from age twelve to thirty!

How do parents help departed adolescents? Efforts by mission boards, supporting churches, or wealthy friends to assist young collegians in returning home occasionally are helpful; but for most missionaries most of the time the major means of communicating during this important period of separation is by letter. How do you set up an environment in which the child wants to write home and share innermost feelings? First, in the child's early years, how often did he or she see the missionaries write to their parents? To use the imagery of I'm OK; You're OK, parental behavior records on the tape recorder of the child's brain innumerable, indelible impressions that are always a part of the child. A person may consciously draw to the fore and "replay" parental recordings and choose to re-record them in his own adult computer or decide to omit them from his personality, but the original recording is always on file, never totally erased. When the child was small, did the parent listen with attention, respond courteously, and respect the little person's individuality? When the child learned to write, what part did writing thank you letters to grandparents play? A child who hears parents speak often and mournfully of the onerous duty of writing letters records in the permanent computer, "Writing letters is an onerous duty." The receipt of letters from family members, joyfully shared and discussed, is recorded, "Letters are warm, happy things that erase distance and unite families."

Letter-writing as a responsibility and accomplishment can be communicated. Effective self-expression and verbal sharing can be praised, becoming a source of pleasure to both sharer and recipient. Regular weekly letters from parents full of news of interest to the child, make letter-receiving pleasant for the child. Teenagers may scoff at parents who save all their letters but secretly appreciate the high value placed on their writing at a period in their lives when self-confidence may be hard to maintain. Not writing regularly to a child to "punish" the child for not writing damages fragile adolescent self-trust and may permanently scar family relationships. Parents need to act like parents, not petulant children, if they hope to aid an unfolding personality to find the necessary nourishment for maturation in its environment.

An essential part of normal adolescent maturation is separating oneself psychologically from identification with parents and establishing an identity of one's own. For some children this transition seems to happen so gradually and painlessly as to be almost unnoticeable. For others the achieving of wholeness of self may mean a dramatic, sharp cutting oneself off from parental values and lifestyle. When a healthy youth feels an urgent need to be different from missionary parents, what is the most obvious point at which to decide to be different? The missionaries' religion, of course. Rejection of Christianity by one's son or daughter is about as painful a rejection as a missionary can experience, but at this time of life an adolescent is so fully preoccupied with testing, developing, and understanding his or her own feelings that the pain caused is dimly perceived and rated unimportant compared with the vital task ahead of building a coherent self. In discussing this issue, one young person said that missionary parents' making it clear "the work" is more important than the children may underlie a child's rejection of the faith which for years may have seemed like a competitor for parental attention.

It can be helpful at this point for the missionary, who may quake at this threat to life commitment and work, to recall that many of our foremothers and forefathers went from Europe to America precisely in search of religious freedom, which they enshrined in a constitution and which has also been incorporated in the constitution of Japan. It is senseless (and ineffective) to force our descendants to fight old wars won long ago by our ancestors. Catherine Marshall says, "God has no grandchildren." To have a religion of value, an individual man must make his commitment independently. It is comforting to recall the prayers, Bible readings, and hymns faithfully recorded in the child's permanent file, ready for use when the young adult feels safely "identical" and thus able to open self to faith and the establishment of a permanent set of values.

The final question on our survey gave me the most satisfaction. The question was, "Would you like your own children to have a similar dual-cultural experience?" Of the twenty-six respondents, one wrote a flat "No."--written very small with a period after it. Several replied they did not intend to have children. More than twenty replied in the affirmative, many writing a large "Yes" with an exclamation mark after it. I suspect that children reared in few communities in the United States would reply in such large numbers in the affirmative about their rearing.

While not minimizing the problems and difficulties, Japan-reared Caucasians again and again express their appreciation for the advantages of their bi-cultural backgrounds in enlarging their world view ("I think I see the world rotating on its axis, not around some small town") and in helping them understand diversity and relate to it. Alvin Toffler in *Future Shock* thinks the elite of the future will jet from country to country, easily adjusting to language and cultural differences. If he is correct, missionary youth are better prepared than most to supply leadership to our world in the future. An extremely important personal ingredient for our bi-cultural children is a strong personal identity built from birth through successive stages of basic trust, autonomy, initiative, and industry, all passing through ascendant stages at an age when still at home with parents. In articulating his feeling of the importance of self-assurance in the bi-cultural individual, one respondent wrote, "The meek may inherit the earth, but they had better do it one culture at a time."

26

David Lee Wickstrom
J. Roland Fleck

Missionary Children: Correlates of Self-Esteem and Dependency

The purpose of the research was to study the correlates of self-esteem, negative attention-seeking dependency, and passive-approval-seeking dependency in missionary boarding school and nonboarding school students. Self-esteem was positively correlated with perceived approval of others, parental and houseparental acceptance, and identification with parents. Negative attention-seeking dependency for males was correlated positively with paternal acceptance and identification with father. For females there were significant positive correlations between passive approval-seeking dependency and the variables of father acceptance, father psychological control, and identification with mother. Consensual religious orientation was negatively correlated with self-esteem, and committed religiosity was negatively correlated with negative attention-seeking dependency. There were no significant differences between the specific groups of early, late, and nonboarders on any of the relevant variables, although, for those who boarded, there was a significant positive correlation between number of years boarding and self-esteem.

The study of the self has generated an enormous amount of literature during the past 100 years. The evaluative component of the self has received special attention during the past two decades.

This evaluative component, the self-concept, is seen to be vital in the development of the personality. The level of one's self-esteem, especially, is seen to be associated with psychological adjustment.

The process by which one develops a healthy self-evaluation has many facets. James (1890) postulated that self-concept develops either positively or negatively depending on the fortune or misfortune experienced during one's early years. Other theorists centered their attention on the effects of family upbringing and the evaluations of others. And researchers (Gergen, 1971; Miyamoto & Dornbusch, 1956) confirm that the evaluations of us by others strongly affect our evaluations of ourselves. Theorists have also hypothesized that identification with parents is related to self-esteem (Freud, 1917/1943; Mowrer, 1950), a hypothesis which researchers have substantiated (Becker & McArdle, 1967; Heilbrun, 1965; Heilbrun & Fromme, 1965).

Another family dynamic which has received theoretical and research study is the effects of parental acceptance on a child's self-esteem. Rogers (1961) and others theorized that parental acceptance and positive regard are significantly related to the development of self-esteem. These theories have received substantial research support (Coopersmith, 1967; Sears, 1970; Grow, 1980; Graybill, 1978).

Obvious in the discussion so far is the belief that parents are important factors in the development of a child's self-esteem. But what of the child who is separated from his parents? The group of subjects under consideration in this study were missionary children, many of whom were sent to boarding school for their education. The literature reveals that for many children separated from their parents, there are devastating effects on personality adjustment (Bowlby, 1951; Hetherington, 1972; Lynn & Sawrey, 1959; Rutter, 1972). Part of the purpose of the current study was to research the correlates of self-esteem for missionary children raised both at home and at boarding school and to see if there would be any differences between early boarders (those who went to boarding school before 10 years of age), late boarders (those who went to boarding school after the age of 10) and nonboarders.

Inherent in the discussion so far on the correlates of self-esteem is the dependency of the child on the evaluations and input of others. The growing child is constantly seeking approval, evaluation, and attention from others. How those evaluations are obtained and how the child seeks to be noticed is a set of behaviors which can be generally subsumed under the heading "dependency."

It is difficult to define the concept of dependency behaviorally. For the purposes of this study, two specific sets or clusters of behavior were researched. These behaviors as defined by Sears, Rau, and Alpert (1965) are negative attention-seeking dependency, which includes behavior such as disruption, defiance, oppositional behavior and aggressive activity with minimal provocation; and passive approval-seeking behavior or the need to have reassurance, praise of one's actions and seeking help from others.

The research indicates different correlates for the two types of dependency. In several studies (McCord, McCord, & Verden, 1962; Sears, Rau, & Alpert, 1965; Winder & Rau, 1962; Bloom-Feschbach, & Gaughran, 1980) negative attention-seeking has been related to a general permissiveness and lack of standards or demands for mature behavior from the child. A combination of mother neglect-permissiveness and father acceptance-control appeared to be related to negative attention-seeking for girls, while a combination of father neglect-permissiveness and mother acceptance-control appeared to be related to negative attention-seeking in boys.

The more passive approval-seeking type of dependency has different correlates. In a number of studies (Baumrind & Black, 1967; Cairns, 1961; Finney, 1961; Sears, Maccoby, & Levin, 1957; Bloom-Feschbach, Bloom-Feschbach, & Gaughran, 1980) there was a strong relationship between parental restrictiveness-control and passive dependency for both males and females. In addition, there was little warmth from the parents, accompanied by very high demands for achievement.

Based on the theoretical and research literature, the following was expected: (a) Self-esteem would be positively correlated with parental and house-parental acceptance of the child, perceived approval of others, and degree of identification with a child's parent. (b) Negative attention-seeking dependency would be negatively correlated for males who experienced high paternal control and acceptance; at the same time, there would be a positive correlation with maternal acceptance and control. Also, for females there would be a negative correlation with the dimensions of maternal control and acceptance and positive correlations with paternal acceptance and control. (c) Passive approval-seeking dependency would positively correlate with parental control and parental psychological control. (d) There would be significant differences in self-esteem among early, late, and nonboarders, with nonboarders having the highest self-esteem and early boarders the lowest.

Method

Subjects

A sample of 130 college students from 12 Christian colleges in four states was inventoried. There were 77 females and 53 males, ranging in age from 17 to 24. They were divided into three boarding-group classifications: (a) Early boarders, of which there were 48, (b) late boarders, of which there were 24, and (c) nonboarders, of which there were 58. All of the above subjects were children of missionaries and had at some time in their lives lived overseas.

Instruments

Six research instruments were used in this study. The Coopersmith Self Esteem Inventory (shortened form) was used to measure self-esteem. Five subscales of the Personality Research Form (Form E) were used to give an objective measure of the two different types of dependency. The Autonomy and Aggression scales were combined to measure the variety of dependency known as negative attention-seeking dependency; while the Abasement, Affiliation and Succorance subscales were combined to measure passive approval-seeking dependency.

The Gough-Heilbrun-Adjective Check List was used to objectively measure identification with parents. The method used was to ask the subject to check the adjectives perceived to be self-descriptive; then on separate answer sheets the subject was to check the adjectives which were descriptive, first of the subject's mother, then the father, then the houseparent the subject favored the most while in boarding school. Adjectives on the "parent" lists which were identical to the adjectives on the subjects' lists were counted as a measure of identification with the parents.

The Parent-Child Relations Inventory was used to measure three dimensions of parent-child relationship for the father, mother, and houseparents in general. The three dimensions of interest were acceptance, punitive control (also called firm control), and psychological control (a type of control which incorporates guilt and rejection).

A questionnaire developed, though not validated, by the researcher was used to measure the perceived evaluations of others from the subject's viewpoint, reflecting back upon his boarding school experience. This questionnaire had items which dealt with peer relationships, houseparent relationships, and faculty and staff relationships.

A Religious Attitudes Inventory was included in the total questionnaire given to each subject. This inventory measured two dimensions of religiosity, a dimension reflecting a committed religious orientation in which religion was strongly integrated into the subject's life and actions, and a dimension reflecting an orientation in which the religious beliefs were not integrated into the subject's life. This latter orientation was labeled a consensual orientation.

Procedure

The six instruments and a demographic questionnaire were mailed to members of psychology and missions faculty at the various schools or to students who had volunteered to help with the study. These assistants then administered the questionnaires to students at the college who had been identified as missionary children. After the questionnaires were filled out, they were mailed back to the researcher for scoring and statistical analysis.

A note should be made here regarding the retrospective nature of the data presented. It is difficult for a person reflecting back on past experiences to give an accurate accounting of the actual experience. It would be interesting to complete a study of this nature with subjects currently undergoing the experience. The results--because of the methodological differences--might reveal different trends.

Statistical Analyses

Basic zero-order Pearson correlations were computed giving an overview of the relationships among the independent and dependent variables. Following this procedure, a stepwise multiple regression analysis on selected variables was computed, using self-esteem, negative attention-seeking dependency, and passive approval-seeking dependency as dependent variables using male and female scores separately. Following the stepwise multiple discriminant analysis was used to investigate and characterize the differences among the three boarding groups on 13 discriminating variables.

Results

Self-Esteem

The matrix of correlations between self-esteem and three parent-child and houseparent-child variables is presented in Table 1. Examination of the variables indicates that the relationship between acceptance and self-esteem is positive for all three "parents." However, the relationship appears to be strongest for the mother acceptance variable ($r = .44$, $p < .001$).

Table 1
Correlations Between Self-Esteem and
Parent and Houseparent Variables

	Self-Esteem
Mother Acceptance	.44**
Mother Control	.19*
Mother Psychological Control	-.36**
Father Acceptance	.17*
Father Control	-.11
Father Psychological Control	-.10
Houseparent Acceptance	.25*
Houseparent Control	-.07
Houseparent Psychological Control	-.11

* $p < .05$
** $p < .001$

The matrix also reveals correlations between self-esteem and the variables of control and psychological control. These variables are significantly and negatively related for the mother ($r = -.19$, $p < .05$; $r = -.36$, $p < .001$), but are nonsignificant for the father and houseparent, although a negative correlational trend is present. It appears that parental acceptance of the child is positively associated with high self-esteem, while psychological control and firm punitive control are negatively related to the development of self-esteem.

The correlations between self-esteem and the perceived evaluations of others and identification with a parent are consistent with the hypothesis. The data--some of which is not presented in table form--indicate that the child's perception of positive evaluations by others is significantly associated with self-esteem ($r = -.42$, $p < .001$). The data regarding identification with parents showed that although the correlations were positive for all three "parents," the strongest relationship--taking all subjects together--was between self-esteem and identification with the father ($r = .27$, $p < .002$). However, separate correlations were computed for males and females to see if there were different correlates on the identification variable. The computations yielded results which indicated that for males, identification with mother ($r = .35, p < .005$) and with father ($r = .30, p < .01$) was significantly correlated with self-esteem, with the correlations being stronger for identification with mother. For females, there were no significant correlations between self-esteem and identification.

A stepwise multiple regression was used to correlate a composite of 16 variables with self-esteem the dependent variable. The results are presented in Table 2. It is clear that the first variable (mother acceptance) makes the major contribution to the multiple correlation. Identification with father, sex of the subject, and consensual religious orientation also make significant contributions to the overall multiple correlation. These data substantiate the results of the Pearson correlations which indicate that mother acceptance is a critical variable related to self-esteem.

Table 2
Summary of Stepwise Multiple Regression of Self-Esteem

Step Variable Entered	Simple r	Multiple R	R^2	Incrml R^2	F Test Incrmt	Sig Lvl
1 Mother Acceptance	0.438	0.438	0.192	0.192	30.406	.01
2 ID with Father	0.245	0.473	0.223	0.031	5.126	.05
3 Sex	-0.180	0.497	0.247	0.024	4.014	.05
4 Consensual Religion	-0.156	0.521	0.272	0.024	4.172	.05
5 Early v Late Board	-0.169	0.536	0.287	0.016	2.769	NS
6 Committed Religion	0.196	0.550	0.302	0.015	2.584	NS
7 Mother Psy. Cont.	-0.356	0.564	0.318	0.016	2.899	NS
8 Board vs Nonboard	-0.007	0.569	0.323	0.005	.873	NS
9 Eval. by Others	0.080	0.594	0.353	0.030	5.578	.05
10 Father Control	-0.114	0.598	0.358	0.004	.813	NS
11 Father Accep.	0.173	0.604	0.365	0.007	1.323	NS
12 ID w/ Housepar.	0.108	0.606	0.367	0.003	.653	NS
13 Mother Control	-0.185	0.608	0.370	0.002	.436	NS
14 Years Boarding	0.085	0.610	0.372	0.002	.390	NS
15 Houseparent Accep	0.094	0.610	0.373	0.001	.167	NS
16 ID with Mother	0.181	0.611	0.373	0.000	.07	NS

The stepwise multiple discriminant analysis of the self-esteem variable indicated no significant differences among the three boarding groups on self-esteem. This suggests that other variables than separation from the parents are the salient variables related to self-esteem.

Negative Attention-Seeking Dependency
The correlations for males regarding parent-child variables and their relationship to negative attention-seeking dependency revealed only one significant relationship. There was a significant positive relationship between father psychological control and male negative attention-seeking.

The stepwise multiple regression analysis for males, on the other hand, reveals two factors as contributing significantly to the multiple correlation. Committed religious orientation is negatively related to negative attention-seeking dependency, while father psychological control is again positively related to negative attention-seeking.

The correlations for females indicate that only two correlations are significantly related to negative attention-seeking dependency, a negative correlation with father acceptance and a positive relationship with houseparent control. The stepwise multiple regression for females indicates that only one variable, identification with father, contributes significantly to the multiple correlation, and this is a negative correlation.

A correlation matrix was also computed for all subjects taken together on the variable of negative attention-seeking dependency and its relationship with parent variables. The results are presented in Table 3. It appears that negative attention-seeking is associated with houseparents and fathers who are not accepting of the child and who exert their authority by using punitive and guilt-inducing controls.

Passive Approval-Seeking Dependency
The matrix of correlations for all subjects between passive approval-seeking dependency and parent and houseparent variables is presented in Table 4. The data suggest that a combination of a guilt-inducing controlling mother, an accepting father, and an accepting permissive houseparent are associated with the development of passive approval-seeking dependency. A multiple regression analysis was computed, however, which indicated that sex of subject was a major contributor to the correlation equation. Therefore, separate correlation matrices were computed for males and females, as well as separate stepwise multiple regression analyses. When the data for males, which indicated no significant correlations between parent variables and passive approval-seeking dependency were removed, the data for

females (see Tables 5 & 6) indicated that father acceptance and father psychological control are significantly positively related to the development of passive approval-seeking in females. The data indicate that the father possibly is giving conflicting messages-- accepting on the one hand, but guilt-inducing and perhaps rejecting in his control methods. Further discussion will be made regarding these data later.

Table 3
Correlations Between Negative Attention-Seeking Dependency
and Parent andHouseparent Variables for All Subjects

	Negative Attention-Seeking Dependency
Mother Acceptance	-.05
Mother Control	.11
Mother Psychological Control	.09
Father Acceptance	-.18*
Father Control	.18*
Father Psychological Control	.20**
Houseparent Acceptance	-.24**
Houseparent Control	.23*
Houseparent Psychological Control	.29**

* $p < .05$ ** $p < .01$

Table 4
Correlations Between Passive Approval-Seeking Dependency
and Parent andHouseparent Variables for All Subjects

	Passive Approval-Seeking Dependency
Mother Acceptance	.08
Mother Control	.10
Mother Psychological Control	.15*
Father Acceptance	.16*
Father Control	.05
Father Psychological Control	.06
Houseparent Acceptance	.23*
Houseparent Control	.18
Houseparent Psychological Control	-.20*

* $p < .05$

Table 5
Correlations Between Female Passive Approval-Seeking
Dependency and Parentand Houseparent Variables

	Passive Approval- Seeking Dependency
Mother Acceptance	.20
Mother Control	.14
Mother Psychological Control	.11
Father Acceptance	.37*
Father Control	.08
Father Psychological Control	.04
Houseparent Acceptance	.03
Houseparent Control	-.24
Houseparent Psychological Control	-.22

* $p < .01$

Table 6
Summary of Stepwise Multiple Regression of Passive
Approval-Seeking Dependency for Females

Step Variable Entered	Simple r	Mltple. R	R^2	Incrml. R^2	F Test Incrmnt.	Sig Lvl
1 Father Acceptance	.369	.369	.136	.136	11.819	.01
2 Father Psych. Cont.	.037	.454	.206	.070	6.554	.05
3 Committed Religion	.337	.495	.245	.039	3.726	NS
4 Houseparent Control	-.239	.520	.270	.025	2.501	NS
5 Houseparent Accep.	.025	.575	.331	.060	6.391	.05
6 Evaluation by Others	-.186	.597	.357	.026	2.931	NS
7 Mother Psych. Cont.	.112	.607	.369	.012	1.271	NS
8 Mother Acceptance	.195	.621	.386	.017	1.929	NS
9 Father Control	.075	.628	.394	.009	.973	NS
10 ID with Father	.222	.631	.398	.004	.398	NS
11 Missionary Plans	.183	.634	.402	.004	.470	NS
12 ID with Mother	.254	.638	.407	.004	.450	NS
13 Mother Control	.140	.639	.409	.002	.228	NS
14 Hspar. Psy. Cntrl	-.221	.640	.410	.001	.145	NS
15 Board vs Nonboard	.154	.643	.413	.003	.290	NS

Discussion

Regarding self-esteem, the data indicate that for the sample under consideration, self-esteem is related to family relationships in which the parents are seen to be warm and accepting and use a low level of punitive or guilt-inducing control. This appears to be consistent with Baumrind's (1967) data. It is also a family which encourages the child--and especially the male--to identify with the parents. Should the child be sent to boarding school, the indications are that a warm, accepting houseparent with whom the child can identify is associated with self-esteem. During the boarding school experience, the child who perceives the evaluations of houseparents, staff, and peers as being positive will likely have higher self-esteem than students who perceive evaluations as being negative.

The data concerning group differences indicate that separation from parents is not necessarily negatively associated with self-esteem. In fact, contrary to the hypothesized direction, there is evidence that among those who boarded, those who boarded the longest had the highest self-esteem (correlation between years boarding and self-esteem, $r = .32$, $p < .003$). In addition, the means on self-esteem indicated that self-esteem was higher, though not significantly, for early boarders than for nonboarders, who were higher than late boarders. The possible explanation for these data is that with numerous and consistent evaluations by many peers, the child can better develop a sense of his strengths and weaknesses. Also, there are more people with whom the child can form accepting relationships than if he were to stay at home with only a few peers and the child's parents. These data are supported by Rutter's review of the literature and personal research (1978) which indicates that the quality of the boarding school experience could mitigate detrimental factors associated with separation experiences. In fact Rutter indicates that attending a high quality school could protect a child from developing problems, particularly children from disruptive or discordant homes. Field's (1979) research indicates that adjustment, especially in peer contacts, may actually be facilitated in the absence of a mother by continuing exposure to the same peers, a condition commonly present in boarding schools.

The data regarding identification with a parent raise some questions. The data indicated a stronger relationship between self-esteem and identification with mother for males than the relationship between self-esteem and identification with father. This is contrary to the research of Becker and McArdle, (1967)

Heilbrun, (1965) which indicate that identification with father is usually more strongly associated with adjustment in males than is identification with mother. Several hypotheses and research data can be advanced to account for this finding. Besides the methodological considerations, further data reveal trends which can provide clues. First, the correlation matrix and the stepwise multiple regression analysis on self-esteem indicate that mother acceptance is more strongly associated with self-esteem than is father acceptance. From a social-learning viewpoint it could be argued that the more accepting (rewarding?) parent would be the model whom the child would imitate. Second, a demographic variable regarding involvement of the mother in the work of the missionary enterprise indicates that her invovement is not usually as great as that of the father. Therefore, she would likely be the one spending the most time with the children and would thus provide a more available model with whom to identify. This could then be related to the literature concerning father absence (Hetheringtom, 1972; Lynn & Sawrey, 1959) which indicates poorer adjustment and less identification with a father who is absent. It would also be substantiated by a study by Elrod and Crase (1980) which indicated that mothers do interact more with sons than do fathers and thus would have the greatest effect. Finally, it may be that the more accepting parent is perceived by males to be the healthier, better-adjusted parent. If this is the case, it will substantiate studies by George (1970) and Bloom-Feschbach, Bloom-Feschbach, & Gaughran (1980) which indicate that a child will identify with or be more affected by the better adjusted parent. These hypotheses could account for the observation that the highest male self-esteem was associated with identification with the mother rather than with the father as some literature would suggest.

The data regarding negative attention-seeking dependency indicate that a combination of paternal and houseparental rejection, control, and psychological control are significantly associated with negative attention-seeking dependency. These data do not support the hypotheses regarding negative attention-seeking dependency, unless this style of behavior is viewed as having hostile and aggressive components. The frustration-aggression hypothesis is well-known and substantiated in the literature. There is also literature which notes a relationship between such situations as parental neglect and mother-busy situations and their relationship to negative attention-seeking (Sears, Rau, & Alpert, 1965). Cameron (1978) found that parental intolerance and inconsistency were also related to "negative temperament changes" in the children, and Simonds and Simonds (1981) found that mothers of children grouped in the "difficult" or "slow-to-warmup" clusters were more likely to use the "guilt-inducing" parenting style. The "difficult" child was described as easily angered, hard to handle, and aggressive. Feschbach's (1970) review of the literature regarding aggression, and research by Bloom-Feschbach, Bloom-Feschbach and Gaughran (1980) and Baumrind (1967) further indicate that there is a relationship between the absence of warmth and nurturance in a home and child aggressiveness. It is suggested that the child in the sample under scrutiny in the present study develops a negative attention-seeking type of dependency in response to a father and houseparent who are cold and rejecting (as evidenced by the negative relationship between acceptance and negative attention-seeking) and who further are perceived as rejecting by their restrictive, punitive, and guilt-inducing control. This fits well with Rogers' theory (1961) which suggests that negative emotions and pathology result from a child perceiving rejection and conditions of worth. The child needs warmth and acceptance but when frustrated reacts by becoming aggressive.

The data regarding passive approval-seeking dependency revealed no significant correlations for males. Further research is needed to ascertain the reasons for this. For females, the three variables most significantly associated with this type of dependency appear to be the variables of identification with mother, father acceptance, and psychological control by the father. Baumrind's (1967) research on child-rearing patterns and Bloom-Feschbach et al.'s (1980) extension of Baumrind's research seem to substantiate the present research. Those researchers state that a combination of varying parenting styles will often produce a passive, withdrawn child--especially at separation--a child who will express needs indirectly and often in a style consistent with the passive approval-seeking type of dependency. The girl will also have a model after which to pattern herself (high identification with mother) and since in our culture the role of the mother is usually less aggressive than the role of the father and aggression in females is not accepted well, the girl is left with the choice of a passive approval-seeking style if she is to feel acceptance.

Finally, the data regarding religious orientation are consistent with the published literature on committed and consensual religiosity. The literature indicates that consensually-oriented people have negative self-esteem, feelings of powerlessness, and feel a lack of control over their lives (Spilka & Mullin, 1974). This is consistent with the data obtained in the present study.

The second variable, committed religious orientation, is the most significant variable in the multiple regression of negative attention-seeking for all subjects, and in the multiple regression of negative attention-seeking for males. The correlation is also a negative one, again consistent with the literature which states that consensual people have feelings of greater interpersonal distance, move away from people (Spilka & Mullin, 1974), perceive others as less trustworthy (Maddock & Kenny, 1971), and evaluate others on the basis of social position and other materialistic concerns (Spilka & Minton, 1975). If the subject perceives rejection and guilt-inducing control coming from significant others, the likely result will be an associated negative relationship with commitment to a religion.

The implication of the present study for the missionary family could--with further research substantiation--be significant. First, the data indicate that it is not necessarily the boarding school experience which is associated with lowered self-esteem. If any implication is present, it would be that the earlier the children are sent to boarding school the better, if that is the only option. Late boarding is associated with lowered self-esteem. Second, the variable of parental acceptance of the child is crucial, since the data indicate that this variable has the strongest association with self-esteem. There are also implications for missionary fathers. There appears to be an especially strong relationship between father variables and negative attention-seeking dependency. The suggestions are that the father needs to be an involved parent, especially in the supportive warmth and firm control he can give. It is also important that the parents maintain fairly close styles of parenting. Finally, there are implications for houseparents in missionary boarding schools. Since houseparental acceptance is significantly associated with self-esteem, it would seem that the houseparent-child relationship needs to be a fairly good one in terms of warmth and acceptance and nurturance. It would appear that the likelihood of negative attention-seeking would decrease if houseparents would practice firm, accepting controls without harshness and guilt inducement. Implications for mission-board placement of personnel in the positions of houseparents would include the need for careful screening and perhaps training of the personnel--if the data in this study do indeed hold true and can be substantiated by other studies of the same nature.

It is hoped that this study will provide an impetus for further research, and that together the studies would provide some guidelines for missionary families and missionary boarding schools in the rearing of their children.

References

Baumrind, D. (1967). Child-care practices anteceding three patterns of pre-school behavior. *Genetic Psychology Monographs, 75*, 43-48.

Baumrind, D., & Black, A. E. (1967). Socialization practices associated with dimensions of competence in pre-school boys and girls. *Child Development, 38*, 291-328.

Becker, J., & McArdle, J. (1967). Nonlexical speech similarities as an index of intrafamilial identifications. *Journal of Abnormal Psychology, 72*, 408-414.

Bloom-Feschbach, S., Bloom-Feschbach, J., & Gaughran, J. (1980). The child's tie to both parents: Separation patterns and nursery school adjustment. *American Journal of Orthopsychiatry, 50*, 505-521.

Bowlby, J. (1951). *Maternal care and mental health*. Paper presented to the World Health Organization, Geneva.

Cairns, R. B. (1961). The influence of dependency inhibition on the effectiveness of social reinforcement. *Journal of Personality, 29*, 461-488.

Cameron, J. R. (1978). Parental treatment, children's temperament, and the risk of childhood behavioral problems: I. Relationships between parental characteristics and changes in children's temperament over time. *Annual Progress in Child Psychiatry & Child Development*, 233-244.

Coopersmith, S. (1967). *The antecedents of self esteem*. San Francisco: W. H. Freeman.

Elrod, M. M., & Crase, S. J. (1980). Sex differences in self-esteem and parental behavior. *Psychological Reports, 46*, 719-727.

Feschbach, S. (1975). Aggression. In P. H. Mussen (Ed.), *Carmichael's manual of child psychology* (Vol. 2). New York: John Wiley & Sons.

Field, T. M. (1979). Infant behaviors directed toward peers and adults in the presence and absence of the mother. *Infant Behavior and Development, 2,* 47-54.

Finney, J. C. (1961). Some maternal influences on children's personality and character. *Genetic Psychology Monographs, 63,* 199-278.

Freud, S. (1943). *A general introduction to psychoanalysis.* Garden City, NJ: Garden City Publishing. (Originally published, 1917).

George, F. H. (1970). The relationship of the self concept, ideal self concept, values and parental self concept to the vocational aspiration of adolescent Negro males. *Dissertation Abstracts International.* (University Microfilms No. 70-9130)

Gergen, K. J., (1971). *The concept of self.* New York: Holt, Rinehart & Winston.

Graybill, D. (1978). Relationship of maternal child-rearing behaviors to children's self esteem. *Journal of Psychology, 100,* 45-47.

Growe, G. A. (1980). Parental behavior and self-esteem in children. *Psychological Reports, 47,* 499-502.

Heilbrun, A. B., Jr. (1965). Parental identification of late adolescents and level of adjustment: The importance of parent-model attributes, ordinal position and sex of the child. *Journal of Genetic Psychology, 107,* 49-59.

Hetherington, E. M. (1972). Effects of father absence on personality development in adolescent daughters. *Developmental Psychology, 7,* 313-326.

Lynn, D. B., & Sawrey, W. L. (1959). The effects of father-absence on Norwegian boys and girls. *Journal of Abnormal and Social Psychology, 59,* 258-262.

Maddock, R., & Kenny, C. (1972). Philosophies of human nature and personal religious orientation. *Journal for the Scientific Study of Religion, 11,* 271-277.

McCord, W., McCord, J., & Verden, P. (1962). Familial and behavioral correlates of dependency in male children. *Child Development, 33*, 313-326.

Miyamoto, S. F., & Dornbusch, S. M. (1956). A test of interactionist hypotheses of self-conception. American Journal of Sociology, 41, 399-403.

Mowrer, O. H., (1950). *Learning theory and personality dynamics.* New York: Ronald.

Rogers, C. R. (1961). *On becoming a person.* Boston: Houghton-Mifflin.

Rutter, M. (1972). *Maternal deprivation reassessed.* Harmondsworth, Middlesex, England: Penguin Books.

Rutter, M. (1979). Maternal deprivation, 1972-1978: New findings, new concepts, new approaches. *Child Development, 50*, 283-305.

Sears, R. R. (1970). Relation of early socialization experiences to self-concepts and gender role in middle childhood. *Child Development, 41*, 267-289.

Sears, R. R., Maccoby, E. E., & Levin, H. (1957). *Patterns of child rearing.* Evanston, IL: Row, Peterson.

Sears, R. R., Rau, L., & Alpert, R. (1965). *Identification and child rearing.* Evanston, IL: Row, Peterson.

Simonds, M. P., & Simonds, J. F. (1981). Relationship of maternal parenting behaviors to preschool children's temperament. *Child Psychiatry and Human Developmemt, 12*, 19-31.

Spilka, B., & Minton, B. (1975). *Defining personal religion: Psychometric, cognitive and instrumental dimensions.* Paper presented at the 1975 convention of the Society for the Scientific Study of Religion, Washington, D.C., October, 1975.

Spilka, B., & Mullin, M. (1974). *Personal religion and psychosocial schemata: A research approach to a theological psychology of religion.* Paper presented at the 1974 convention of the Society for the Scientific Study of Religion, Washington, D.C., October, 1974.

Winder, C. L., & Rau, L. (1962). Parental attitudes associated with social deviance in preadolescent boys. *Journal of Abnormal and Social Psychology*, *64*, 418-424.

27

Raymond M. Chester

To Send or Not to Send? Missionary Parents Ask

"We believe that God has called us to tribal work, but we will not send our children away to one of those missionary schools. It's wrong to give our children to some stranger to rear." An increasing number of prospective missionaries and field missionaries are making statements like this. Is it really wrong or sin, as some have said, to send MKs away to be educated by strangers in a mission school?

The education of missionary children is a growing cause of friction between mission agencies, missionaries, and even sending churches. Should mission agencies regulate MK education, or should the decision of how and when be left up to the parents? The problem is further complicated by some popular family life teaching, which says that "the family is the most important thing." I have never been able to get a satisfactory definition of "thing." Some churches have even dropped their support of MK teachers. No wonder there is both confusion and fear over MK education.

I am not advocating a return to sacrificing the family at all cost for the ministry. Many of us have seen or experienced the destruction of a family when the ministry or anything was exalted out of its proper scriptural position. However, as a reaction to the pendulum swing in the direction of sacrificing the family for the ministry, it seems that the pendulum has now swung (in its natural human motion) to the other extreme, that is, to sacrificing the ministry for the family. The swinging motion of the pendulum will not stop. Church history indicates that the pendulum (what I call reactionary Christianity) will not cease its motion here, but will proceed to yet another extreme.

Before going on to discuss some pros and cons of MK education, we need to consider the impact of this teaching about the priority of the family, which seems to put the family at the center of God's total program.

The family is not more important or less important than other relationships. It is just as important as the church, the job, and your other relationships....Some will no doubt plead for the priority of the family because it started way back in Genesis, long before the church and human government. Doesn't that make the family more important? No. Chronology does not necessarily imply superiority. The world and work came before the family in Genesis. That doesn't make them more important. Heaven comes last on God's timetable. That doesn't make it less important (Howard, 1983).

It is as if some believe that Ephesians 6:10 reads: "Finally, be strong in the family and the security of togetherness." However, after a rather long discourse on family and interpersonal relationships, Paul concludes by saying: "Finally, be strong in the Lord and in the strength of his might."

Missionary parents have been flooded with books, sermons, and lectures about how they must keep their families close together. They listen to it and consequently they produce SKs (smothered kids).

Missionary children, more than might be expected of them, know the demands made of a career missionary. Many desire to get out of the protective environment and lead a life like their missionary parents. Confusion results when missionary parents try every means to separate the children from everything and everyone that is native (Hsieh, 1976).

This pseudo-togetherness (or smothering) produces tremendous fear in the family.

Reserved commitment results in overprotection...extreme forms of overprotection, caused by certain reservations which parents have, seem to be interpreted by children as rejection or disapproval. Since

Mother and Dad do everything for them, they come to believe that they are incapable of doing anything on their own. In adulthood these MKs may continue a life of overdependence, and may choose a life partner on the basis of how much that spouse is willing to do for them. They may look upon any relationship as a means of receiving rather than giving (Danielson, 1982).

The increasingly common motivation for family togetherness that I see today is fear. The logic is, "I spend time with you because if I don't, something terrible will happen to you." Fear has displaced love and nurturing. Since fear always distorts reality (Matt. 14:26), the perception surrounding circumstances is distorted. Non-family becomes the enemy, even if *they* are fellow missionaries whose ministry is MK school teacher.

The greatest tragedy of all is that smothering seems also to block what God wants to do directly with the child. Remember, Ephesians 6:1-3 was written for children to respond to, not parents. Children are responsible directly to God and his Word.

Many young parents went forward in a church service to dedicate themselves to the Lord, with the promise to raise their children to the best of their ability, with his help. Why is it that when their children reach school age, they make a futile attempt to snatch them out of God's hands? Our security does not come from family members, or family closeness, but from God himself: "...for thou, Lord, alone makest me dwell in safety" (Ps. 4:8).

Missionaries are told that they can love their children only if they spend a lot of time talking with and touching them. If that is true--and current *family theology* seems to indicate that it is-- then I am in a bind. Suppose our country is overthrown by a foreign power and all Christian families are divided up and put into separate prisons. (This has happened more than once in the past.) Since I can no longer talk to or touch my child, does that mean I no longer love him or her also? Or, is family unity based on something deeper than geographical location? I believe it is.

Our Lord said that he was "one" with his Father, even though at that time he was walking among men. His prayer was that we would have that same oneness, even in separation (Jn. 17:21). Obviously, we all want to have our children close by, but to "obey is better than sacrifice..." (I Sam. 15:22). If God truly wants us in a missionary situation where we must send our children away to school, then we can send and trust.

No one method is correct or incorrect for all children. It is critical to look at all your options and then choose the best way (method) available for each individual child. As a counselor to missionaries I am primarily concerned with the motivation behind how they educate their children and, secondly, what options really are available today to accomplish the how of MK education.

I know of no studies that would support the idea that sending a child away to school is, by that act alone, detrimental to a child. In fact, a study on MKs and self-esteem reported this year stated that:

...it is not necessarily the boarding school experience which is associated with lowered self-esteem. If any implication is present, it would be that the earlier the children are sent to boarding school the better, if that is the only option (Wickstrom and Fleck, 1983).

They stated earlier that:

...separation from parent is not necessarily associated with self-esteem. In fact, contrary to the hypothesized direction, there is evidence that among those who boarded, those who boarded the longest had the highest self-esteem..."

In another study, it was reported that:

MKs concurred that the element basic to early trust within their family included the security of knowing their father loved their mother. Their parents were able to display open affection for one another (Herrmann, 1979).

If the parents are not getting along, there is a direct affect on their children. In such a situation another study:

...indicates that attending a high quality school could protect a child from developing problems, particularly children from disruptive or discordant homes (Wickstrom and Fleck, 1983).

It would appear, therefore, that if missionary families are not healthy, it will not matter how the children are educated. If the parents are having troubles, to send away or not to send away is not the primary question.

With those factors in mind, let us look at the current state of the art in MK education. There are three basic options, with a number of variations of each. (1) They can send their children to an MK school. I would include here sending their children back to the States for education. The key word here is *send*. (2) They can teach at home using correspondence courses. (3) They can live and work near an MK or national school, where they hope their children will receive the desired education.

Send

First, let us look at some considerations in the sending option. Mandatory sending of children at specific ages or grades is an unwise policy, though it is held by some organizations. Each individual child is unique. Even within a family, each child is different. They mature at different ages, adapt to change differently, and have different needs. Every child must be looked at individually as to when would be the best time to send, if at all. This decision is best left up to the individual family, if they have sufficient information.

Some children with specialized learning situations need the continued involvement of the parents. When they went to the field, the parents may not have known the problem existed. Rare though this situation is, it still happens. The two possible solutions are: (1) The parents move so as to be near their child, to provide the needed support, e.g., changing to an urban ministry; (2) Return home, or to a place where help can be obtained.

"Surveys of many missions indicate that a leading reason missionaries leave their field of ministry is to meet the educational needs of their children" (Lewis, 1983). In either situation, counseling may be needed to sort through the many issues. One further possibility would be to send a specialized teacher to work with the child.

One final thought on sending. Mission organizations could make one immediate change in their MK schools. I have interviewed many MKs concerning their experience away at school. I have found one consistent theme: "Do not put missionaries in as houseparents who are simply waiting for something better to do, or have nowhere else to go at present."

Finally, there are implications for houseparents in missionary boarding schools. Since houseparental acceptance is significantly associated with self-esteem, it would seem that the houseparents-child relationship needs to be a fairly good one in terms of warmth and acceptance and nurturance (Wickstrom and Fleck, 1983).

MKs want houseparents who are older (having raised their own children) and who are dedicated to the ministry of raising children. Mission organizations must be looking and screening for this type of couple.

One other new trend affecting MK education is what I call the *first-term teen-ager.* This issue must be addressed by sending churches, missionary organizations, and the receiving missionary community. More and more families are going to the field with teen-agers. One problem faced by these teens is that they have not grown up with the existing MK community. Often they have left educational systems in their homeland that were vastly different.

Within a boarding school context they are often not seen as Mks by their peers. Great care must be taken by the mission and parents to help these new MKs adjust to their new culture. There are some boarding schools with large non-MK population where these *first-term teen-agers* seem to blend in with fewer transitional problems (crises). However, if you are considering a boarding school for your *first-term teen,* it would be wise to give your teen time to become acquainted with the new culture before considering a boarding school.

Correspondence

The second option available to missionary parents is teaching with correspondence school courses.

The disadvantages (with correspondence courses) include the lack of classroom interaction and competition. Correspondence courses seem especially weak in the areas of physical education, laboratory sciences, music and foreign languages. Perhaps the greatest drawback in correspondence courses is the study habits which they seem to produce. Students tend to spend the most time on subjects they like. Furthermore, since there are almost no deadlines, they may procrastinate. After all, if they don't feel ready to take a test today, they can do so tomorrow. In the everyday world we are not always blessed with such options (Danielson, 1982).

There are additional problems with this method. First, as time progresses and the demands of the ministry increase, something must give. What usually gives is the time parents spend helping their children. The child is put on his own to complete the material. This usually happens when one or both of the parents are married to their work.

Second is the lack of peer socialization. We have the same problem in the United States at some Christian schools that do not allow for social interaction among students.

Coupled with this is the lack of listening skills. I have observed that children coming from self-taught correspondence programs, or any program where they are not required to listen to someone for extended lengths of time, are educationally handicapped. This is especially pronounced when the student reaches college and is flooded with lecture after lecture. There is only one way to develop listening skills and that is by listening to something and then being required to be accountable for that information (testing).

The matter of the missionary's accountability to supporters for time spent teachng at home should also be mentioned. A growing help to parents who use the correspondence approach has been the tutor who will go to the missionary's location and design a program for the parents and children.

Living Near a School

More and more missionaries are taking the third option. As our world continues to centralize into urban settings, they have the opportunity to live near MK or national schools. However, along with the advantages comes the problem of increased financial pressure. It simply costs more to live in the city. It also costs more for the education. Therefore, higher support levels are needed. However, my main concern here is motivation, and this has already been discussed.

Are these the only options available? At present, they seem to be for most missionaries. However, what about the future? That's where we must look. Therefore, on November 5-9, 1984, an International Conference on Missionary Kids will be held in Manila, Philippines, to discuss such topics as:

1. The causes and effects of changing attitudes toward boarding schools for missionaries' children,

2. Recruitment and preparation of boarding home parents,

3. The Third Culture Syndrome and its impact on MKs,

4. The effective use of itinerant teachers on the mission field,

5. The implications of future mission strategies for educating MKs.

It is therefore, time to examine what motivates us as missionary parents. Before we make a decision about MK education, we must ask God to search our hearts.

Remember, you are not in this alone. There are many resources and resource people available today to assist in these often difficult decisions. Though we have focused here on educational needs, this is only one facet of the MK. The ICMK will explore the MK of the '80s and how best to meet their needs and the needs of the MK family.

Finally, instead of drawing up battle lines, let us draw together and examine where we are and what we must do in the future about the education of our MKs.

Bibliography

Danielson, E. (1982). *Missionary kid--MK*. Faith Academy, Philippines, pp 24-25, 54.

Herrmann, C. B. (1979). *Emissary,10*, (3).

Howard, J. G. (1983). *Balancing life's demands.* Portland, Oregon: Multnomah Press, p. 89.

Hsieh, T. (1976). Missionary family behavior, dissonance, and children's career decision. *Journal of Psychology and Theology, 4*, 221-226.

Lewis, K. (1983). Creative concerns for important kids. *In Other Words*, 9, (8), 2.

Wickstrom, D. L., & Fleck, J. R. (1983). Missionary children: Correlates of self-esteem and dependency. *Journal of Psychology and Theology, 11*, 226-235.

28

John A. Holzmann

What About the Kids?
MK Education Symposium

"One of the most burning questions in the hearts and minds of virtually every couple who has ever considered missionary service is what they will do in the way of educating their children," said Elsie Purnell, a staff counselor with the U.S. Center for World Mission and OMF missionary who served in Thailand. She was discussing the need for the "MK (Missionary Kid) Education Symposium" held at the U.S. Center for World Mission November 15, 1985.

"Many couples think there are no educational options--boarding school is all there is. So they have decided they will never go to the mission field.

"Others say, 'Maybe after the kids are out of the house, then we can go, but not now....'

"Most of these people don't know what choices are available to them. The fact is, *there are options, good options!* Boarding school may be an excellent option. We aren't interested in arguing for boarding school over other choices. We just want people to know all the things that may be available to them and their families."

The MK Education Symposium described at least 12 options. Panelists included Jim Smotherman, former principal of Wycliffe's school in Peru, and currently assistant superintendent of children's education in Wycliffe Bible Translators' Personnel Department; Dr. Ed Danielson, clinical psychologist, chairman of the Counseling Department, Christian Heritage College, San Diego, and author of *MK: Missionary Kid*; Carol Richardson, member of the on-going Steering Committee of the International Conference on MKs; and Dr. Virgil Olson, then president, William Carey University and former general director of the Baptist General Conference Board of Missions.

A couple of speakers prefaced their remarks with general comments that provide a good overview of the kinds of attitudes and perspectives one should bring to any discussion of MK education.

Dr. Danielson made a comment about a change he has seen within mission agencies. "In years past," he said, "it was not uncommon for boards to send people into a situation and get something started and *then* think about children.

"Today, almost across the board, mission agencies are not only looking at the opportunities God gives them to work in different parts of the world, but, before they go in, they are saying, 'If we go, what about kids?' I'm excited about that change."

Mr. Smotherman stressed the importance of parents being flexible and open to discerning the will of God in specific circumstances. "Those engaged in missions, by the very nature of the task, must be flexible in lifestyle and also in the matter of caring for and educating their children. For the missionary and mission board, it is safe to say that there is no one way that is best to care for and educate children."

Besides a general overview of each of the 12 options listed below, the Symposium included a lengthy and practical question-and-answer period. In addition to the panelists themselves, several missionaries and MKs were able to share their down-to-earth insights into such questions as, "What part do singles have in the lives of missionary families?" "How do you handle the situation when the dorm parents' standards or forms of discipline are different from the parents?" "How did you educate your children at home?" "What about furloughs?"

A brief report of some of the key items brought out by the panelists follows.

Home Schooling Options

1. *"Pure" Home Schooling.*

Where missions have allowed freedom for parents to take care of their children's education, many missionaries have taught their children in their own homes. There is a whole generation who grew up under the Calvert Correspondence Course. Home schooling, in that context, is not new. The Calvert course was developed early this century.

But home schooling, as defined by many today, is more than merely teaching one's children at home. It is a total philosophy of education. That is different from what has occurred in the past on the mission field where parents taught their children at home because there were no other options.

There are advantages to home schooling:

a. Parents have an intense interest and concern for the success of their children; they have a partiality toward their children that encourages their children to succeed.

b. Children tend to learn better with fewer children.

c. There are more adult-child interactions in an ordinary day: perhaps 200 or more, versus an average classroom experience of maybe 10.

d. The child is freer to explore and think.

e. Because self-directed, the child is free of some of the pressures of competition.

Yet home schooling--especially a rigid interpretation of that philosophy--is not a perfect solution in all cases, and it can have serious difficulties when imported to the mission field.

a. If one really believes, totally, that home schooling is God's will for everyone, then it may be very difficult to live with others who are doing "less than God's best," and it can become a point of conflict and disharmony.

b. Not all mission settings lend themselves well toward home schooling. For instance, many missionaries in isolated contexts become the sole links between the group in which they are working and the outside world. That in itself is an immense task; add to it the responsibility of teaching one's own children without outside assistance can be overwhelming.

c. The wife is frequently limited in her involvement in ministry when she is responsible for teaching children. What happens when children come along and both mother and father have been trained to do mission work? Must it be assumed that the mother has to leave the work?

d. Not all mothers or children can separate the role of teacher from the role of mother. Major family conflicts can result.

e. Not all mothers and children can cope with the intense relationship of daily, one-on-one teaching.

f. Those with a rigid home school philosophy often neglect the opportunity to use other educational resources available to them, resulting in a lower-quality education than might otherwise be had.

A missionary mother wrote a poem:

> Teaching kindergarten was fun all right.
> Teaching the first grade was still a cinch.
> Teaching second grade and kindergarten--I felt the pinch.
> Teaching first grade and third grade, my schedule was tight.
> And next year: grades K, 2, and 4 are in sight.
> If I'm not mistaken, there's trouble ahead.
> Oh Lord! Please give me strength--or send a teacher instead.

Maintaining many of the strengths of the home school philosophy, yet providing some of the help and support that many parents find they need, the following two alternatives have been recently developed.

2. *The Traveling Teacher.*

Wycliffe has families scattered all over Ghana. The parents in each of these cases are totally responsible for teaching their own children. Yet to help them, Wycliffe has established a classroom-sized resource center filled with textbooks, reference materials, artwork, paper, etc. This center is staffed with three teachers, each of whom has classroom and curriculum experience, and is gifted in working one-on-one and in diagnostics.

Parents around Ghana can call on these teachers and ask for their assistance. The teachers are available even to go to live with a family for a month if they want it. The teachers will teach the children, if that's required, or will teach the parents how to teach. Whatever the need, the teachers are available to provide assistance.

This "Traveling Teacher" plan has all the advantages of home schooling, yet takes away some of the lonesome, overwhelming feelings parents may have while attempting to teach their own children in an isolated context.

3. *The Field Education System.*

The Field Education System (FES) is being developed right now in Guatemala. The concept is similar to the Traveling Teacher except for one major point. Whereas in the Traveling Teacher plan the parents develop the curriculum and lesson plans and take on primary responsibility for educating their children, in the FES the teacher takes primary responsibility.

In the FES, a teacher in a centrally-located curriculum center builds a theme-based curriculum that integrates science, math, cultural studies, language skills, etc. The parents and children then come to the teacher, the teacher maps out a nine-week strategy for the parents to pursue with their children out in their field locations, and the parents and children carry out the plan. After nine weeks, the parents and children come back to the central location where the teacher will go over the nine-weeks' work, do diagnostic teaching, help the parents understand their children's learning needs, and then send the parents and children back out with a new plan and strategy.

This pattern is repeated three times each academic year.

Advantages:

a. The program allows children to stay at home with their parents and friends.

b. It is flexible, giving children who have difficulties with textbook and correspondence work a program that meets their needs.

c. It uses the local environment as an educational "laboratory."

d. It is an independent, personnally-, and professionally-designed program.

Disadvantages: it can mean tremendous travel expenses for the missionaries. This can be alleviated, at least partially, by having the teacher go to the family. But either way, there is a significant cost involved.

In Guatemala, those who are participating in the program love it.

Another twist on the home schooling idea is:

4. *The Local Co-op School.*

In this plan, the parents get together and team-teach using correspondence courses. This plan has many of the same advantages and disadvantages as "pure" home schooling, except it alleviates some of the pressure upon parents.

Boarding Schools

As suggested by the comments of many potential missionary candidates, boarding school is an option they seem to want to avoid at all costs. Yet several studies have been done that show no adverse effects upon children in a boarding school environment.

"In fact," said Dr. Danielson, "in one study, the assumption going in was that the earlier a child is sent to boarding school, the poorer his self-concept will be. When it was all over, the psychiatrist who was doing the study said, 'I am sorry that my statistics don't prove what I set out to prove!'"

"Another study was done. This one used the idea of self-esteem rather than self-concept. The same basic hypothesis was used going into the study: that self-esteem would be lower the earlier a child went to boarding school. At the end of the study, the researcher said, 'My statistics don't prove what I set out to prove. In fact, if anything, they prove that the *earlier* the child boards, the greater his self-esteem!'"

Danielson said no studies have been done to try to determine *why* these results were obtained, but he hypothesized that one major factor has to do with the quality of time spent when the parents and children are together.

"When children go to boarding schools," he said, "they have many positive inputs. The parents give all the input they can to a child thy know is going to go to boarding school. They give quality time. They schedule their time and spend it with their children very carefully. There's no thought of, 'Well, we'll spend the time *next* week.'

"So the parents are doing this, the staff at the schools are doing this, and the boarding parents (in the dorms) are usually well-chosen and provide more positive input. There is a great sensitivity and concern for these children."

5. *The Boarding School in One's Home Country.*

Missionaries in the late 1800s and early 1900s frequently left their children in their home countries. Up until the 1940s and '50s, many missions had policies that they would never establish a high school on foreign soil. This meant that parents had to look for other options. And so the boarding school "back home" was common.

Today, this option is less common than it was at one time, yet several schools are still around. These are not second-rate schools, by any means. Stony Brook is a school like this.

The advantage: students are enculturated in their "home" culture.

Disadvantage: it is very hard on family relations, especially during the teenage years.

Another option that has been used by some missionaries is to have:

6. *The Children Stay with Friends or Relatives.*
a. In the Home Country.

This option is not too common, but may be chosen when a couple is on the move a lot and their children would be better served by a more stable environment. Another factor contributing to this choice is parents' wishes to have their children enculturated in the "home" culture.

Advantages and disadvantages are similar to those of the boarding school in one's home country. One additional factor: the personal involvement of relatives can often lead to extreme care--either extreme harshness ("trying to set the child straight") or extreme laxness ("the poor thing is being so mistreated...").

b. On the Field.

Circumstances under which the parents labor, either long- or short-term, may make this a good option in order to enable the children to attend a local mission or international school. This is not an uncommon arrangement. Parents see their children quite often and the track record is good.

An option that some parents choose is to send their children to :

7. *Mission Hostel in One's Home Country.*

As with other "back home" kinds of options, this is less common than it once was. None of the panelists knew of a hostel program available today in the United States. OMF's last hostel in the U.S. closed just two years ago. In the United Kingdom, however, several missions still have hostels.

Under this plan, children go to public school but stay at a mission-sponsored home. The advantages and disadvantages of this system were not distinguished from other "back home" options during the Symposium, yet afterward, one missionary said, "Unlike the boarding schools, in the hostels there is a definite home atmosphere, and this is important!"

Nowadays, the boarding school option most commonly chosen is the:

8. *Mission-Run School "On the Field."*

Most of these schools were raised up as better alternatives to the boarding schools and mission hostels back in the home countries. There are two types of mission-run schools.

a. *The Single-Mission School.*

A single-mission school is what the name implies: it is owned and operated by a single mission organization.

One of the advantages of these schools is that the staff and dorm parents are usually well-acquainted with the parents. This gives these schools a real family flavor.

Then, too, every mission has its own sub-culture. If children are in their "own" school, they know they will fit, they know what to expect.

On the negative side, if the school is small, it can have such a mono-cultural flavor that children who are brought up in it can have a difficult time adjusting when, later, they go somewhere else (back to their "home" countries or to multi-mission schools).

At the same time, if there is room, most of these schools allow children from other missions. Some of these schools have over half their students from "outside." In these cases, other missions will sometimes run their own hostels that "their" children can have a smaller, family—type atmosphere. But when they all get together at school, there may be very little sense of being on the "inside" or "outside." The children may hardly know which mission they are from, but just know they are all MKs.

b. *The Cooperative or Multi-Mission School.*

Multi-mission schools are very similar to single-mission schools. The main difference is that they are owned and operated by a number of boards, and their policies are set up as cooperative efforts between a number of agencies.

Though teachers and administrators may come from a diversity of doctrinal positions, their teaching philosophies, more often than not, will be amazingly compatible. Curriculum is usually U.S.-based, though some schools integrate curriculum from Australia, Britain, or other countries from which the MKs come.

Though most of these schools began as boarding institutions, many are opening up to day-school students. Faith Academy in Manila, for instance, has over 50 perent non-boarding students. These children commute to school each day. The students who board at Morrison Academy in Taiwan are mostly high schoolers. The younger children now attend Morrison "satellite" schools around Taiwan. They live at home with their parents, but attend schools that are supervised by Morrison.

Most multi-mission schools also serve the international community--children from military bases, United Nations, and the lcoal peoples.

Other Options

9. *The National Public School.*

Since World War II many missionaries have found that sending their children to national schools is a viable and good option. Overall, however, this is a very small percentage of the total.

In general, the reason one would want to send one's children to a national school is because one wants to say to the nationals, "We want to integrate and identify with you people."

This can be a very good option, especially for children with above-average intelligence. Yet there are problems.

a. For older children going out for the first time, there is, of course, a language barrier.

b. Customs are different. As with any meeting between cultures, clashes can result. It requires sensitivity.

c. Discipline is often very rigid--certainly more rigid than we are used to in our culture. Sometimes this is a form of persecution.

d. The teaching aids and facilities in many schools are very poor.

10. *The National School Run by Missionaries.*

This has generally been a more attractive option to missionaries than sending their children to national public schools.

The problems associated with national public schools are usually not so evident in schools run by missionaries. The language barrier alone is lower since English is a drawing card for nationals, and at least some of the lessons are likely to be in English.

11. *The "Third Language" School.*

Some missionaries have found good third-language schools in the countries where they are located. For example, some English-speaking Canadian missionaries in Indonesia are sending their children to a French school. This was the best option available to them.

12. *The International School--Including American and Military Schools.*

As the international community began to expand--particularly the American international community, the diplomatic corp, and multinational corporations--there was a need to educate these people's children. As a result, in most leading cities and on American military bases around the world, you will find international schools.

Missionaries usually choose international schools when other schools are not available and, considering the needs of the parents and the children, it seems wise that the children should stay with their parents and be bused back and forth to school. In other words, the international school plays much the same role as the public school "back home."

These schools are usually well-run and have good educational programs.

On the other hand :

Most of these schools are self-funded. Tuition, therefore, is quite high.

Many of those who have taken this option have found themselves falling prey to the temptation to become part of the "international ghetto community," and failing to participate as fully as they would have liked with the nationals to whom they had intended to preach the Gospel.

Yet while there is a temptation to join the international community, there is also a great deal of anti-Americanism in the non-Western world and this often comes through in the schools. American MKs may have to contend with this.

Conclusion

Overall, the Symposium panelists and missionaries and MKs in the audience gave a clear message. The problem of finding quality education for their children should not hinder parents who are considering missionary service. There are a number of good educational options available. If you are willing to pursue and use them, the resources are there.

29

Brian V. Hill

The Educational Needs
of the Children of Expatriates

As a preliminary to theorizing about meeting the needs of missionary children, a questionnaire was distributed to parents in over seventy missionary locations. Their responses exhibited a contradiction in their thought between the benefits they perceived the multicultural experience conferred on their children and the readiness with which they embraced quite different values when deciding on their children's further formal education. A more consistent rationale is developed in the second part of the study, arguing for four elements in a balanced education for such children. From these are derived a charter of specific curriculum expectations.

Parental Perceptions

This article arose from an invitation to lecture at the International Conference on Missionary Kids convened by Wycliffe Bible Translators in Manila, in November 1984. As part of the data-gathering phase of my preparation, I asked Wycliffe if they would be willing to distribute a questionnaire polling parental opinion and practice in the field.

In the event, 75 busy families from over a dozen national backgrounds and in as many different national placements spared the time to respond. They did so with care, often writing additional notes which drew me closer to their situation and raised further issues. I feel a responsibility to speak for them, and will report as well as I can on what they revealed. Following this, I will address the issues at a more philosophical level, hoping to develop a rationale for the education of the children of missionaries (and other expatriates) which takes realistic account of the information supplied, while suggesting ways ahead for mission boards in this matter.

The Questionnaire

Time did not permit a preliminary testing of the questionnaire, and a few questions proved ambiguous or difficult to translate onto computer (see note 1). The sample was large but not, strictly speaking, statistically random, so that questions of statistical significance cannot be confidently addressed, especially where subgroup correlations (for example, by country of origin) have been pulled out. Nevertheless, the patterns that emerged (and some did) are reported for what they are worth, and may suggest hypotheses for more reliable studies by others.

Respondents were asked to indicate what educational options had been available to their children at primary, junior secondary, senior secondary, and post-school levels, and what, in ideal circumstances, they would have preferred, stating their reasons if they wished. These data were correlated with respondents' countries of origin and placement, length of field service, and own educational levels. Respondents were also asked to identify the advantages and disadvantages they perceived their children to have derived from being the children of missionaries. Finally, they were invited to indicate the relative importance they attached to various suggested aims for formal schooling. I will comment first on a number of issues raised in response to the more open-ended questions.

Arrangements for Furlough

Asked what arrangements they made for their children's education while on furlough, a sixth of the respondents said that they sought out Christian schools in their country of origin. A smaller number utilized correspondence school materials, or arranged to take their leave during their children's school vacations.

Over two-thirds, however, indicated that they placed their children in state schools near their place of temporary residence. Their reasons were various. Some cited reasons of convenience and economy. Others spoke of their desire to keep the family together during this time. Many, however, also made reference to what they saw to be positive educational gains from public schools in the country of parental origin (note 2). They welcomed such things as a realistic exposure to the home culture, wider choices for study, and a tough-minded encounter with the Western curriculum and peers.

Choices in the Primary Years

Discussing available and preferred schooling in the primary years, 25 respondents emphasized the first importance of home influence during infancy and early childhood, and expressed the belief that it should continue through the years of primary school. It is therefore not surprising that the great majority of parents were in favor (41 first preference, 4 second, 5 third) of local schooling, provided that it was in English and taught by expatriates. A small but interesting minority of parents expressed preferences for indigenous local schooling in the vernacular (5,3,3), but in lieu of a local expatriate school being available, most parents (8,16,9) turned to the expatriate boarding school elsewhere in the country of service. Most, that is, preferred to send their children away rather than have them taught in an indigenous vernacular context. Alternatively, 10 parents utilized correspondence materials for home teaching. There was virtually no support (0,1,1) for boarding children of this age in the country of parental origin.

If we may regard a correspondence between the form of primary schooling available and that preferred as an evidence of satisfaction, then it appeared that 52 respondents were satisfied, 23 were not. Australians (+26,-6) were more generally satisfied than North Americans (+18,-15). Other nationalities were represented by too few to warrant comparisons of this kind.

Respondents were asked to say whether at this level they preferred a Christian school or a secular one, or would be happy either way. Overall, the preferences were 45, 10, 20, but when the North American preferences (27,1,5) are taken out, the result (18,9,15) swings the other way. That is, a majority of the non-Americans don't consider Christian schooling essential.

Reasons advanced for the preferences outlined above are a perceived need for primary children to be educated in the language and culture of the country of parental origin (11), low educational standards in the indigenous schools (6), and the opportunity (presumably in expatriate schools) to gain valuable cross-cultural experiences (3). Once again, an interestingly divergent small group of respondents expressed a desire to have their children learn about the local indigenous culture (4), but most comments ran the other way. One respondent noted that the indigenous culture in his country was very difficult for girls after the age of nine; another said that villages were very dull.

Choices in the Junior Secondary Years

Parental choices for the junior secondary years showed some interesting changes from their attitudes in regard to primary schooling. While some continued to highlight family interaction (4) and 6 nominated correspondence lessons, others commented that interaction with Western curriculum and Western peers was important (9) and that children at this age could cope without their parents (2). A clear majority (35,4,2) continued to prefer the local expatriate school, but the fall in this preference was balanced by increases in preference for boarding schools in the country of placement (14,16,6) or parental origin (2,7,13).

The level of satisfaction with what was available (+46,-29) was lower than it had been in reference to primary schooling (+52,-23) but not markedly so, and preferences for Christian and secular alternatives were almost the same as before.

Choices in the Senior Secondary Years

Statistically, the picture for parental choice did not change much between junior and senior high school. Nor did the reasons given. There was an increasing awareness that, in most missionary fields, expatriates "have no continuing city," and neither citizenship nor work permits were likely to be available to missionary youth in the country of placement. The option of a boarding school placement in the country of origin had been slightly increasing in favor through the levels, but even at this level attracted only 4 primary votes (4,9,12). Some families were intending to return home at this point for the children's sake, notwithstanding the possibility that their mission boards might be less sympathetic with their reasons.

The level of satisfaction with what was available, and the preferences in regard to Christian or secular alternatives, were virtually the same as at junior secondary level. There were, in fact, few signs that any respondents regarded the issues of senior secondary schooling as in any way different from the junior school. For developmental reasons, I would suggest this assumption warrants further investigation.

Choices for Post-School Experience

As 7 parents pointed out, the question of post-school choices was basically one for the individuals themselves. Nevertheless there was a strong desire to be protective. Three respondents indicated that they would be returning home for this phase of their children's education. The majority (37,6,1) wanted the benefit of a university in the country of parental origin, remarking that indigenous universities were either not academically adequate or not open to expatriates. Another group (9,8,5; note 3) nominated teachers' or technical colleges in the country of origin.

Another sizable group (10,10,5) said that they wanted their children to have Bible college training in the country of origin. Several added that they thought this appropriate only *after* either other tertiary training or work experience. These respondents were predominantly (10,7,1) North American.

Apart from such local deterrents as unavailability of citizenship, study places or work permits, the reasons given emphasized the perceived need for the children of missionaries to become acculturated to Western society (18). Others referred to the availability of financial aid in the tertiary system (an Australian), wider curriculum options (6), training in critical thinking (1), adjustment to the job market in the country of parental origin (14), and the chance to prepare for one's lifework, with an option of either of two cultures (5). One parent wanted the children to find marriage partners of their own race.

Again there was a minority group which regarded post-school experiences in the indigenous culture as valuable for their children, whether in local universities (4,7,3), technical or teachers' colleges (11,2,2), Bible colleges (3,2,2), or job placements (8,1,3). One parent shrewdly observed that "education can become a fetish. Let's remember it was the Pharisees who were the educated elite and Jesus the technical college tradesman."

The level of satisfaction with what was available increased again at this level (+54,-21), but for reasons opposite to the similar figure recorded for primary. At post-school level, country-of-origin preferences predominated, and that is what the majority had obtained. Choice of Christian institutions was desired by 24, of whom 15 were North American, while 12 (non-North Americans) expressed a preference for secular institutions and 28 were content to go for the best of either.

Aims of Formal Schooling

The questionnaire set out nine aims for respondents to rank, with space to add other suggestions. Only 13 offered additions. Despite emphasis on the fact that the aims were only to be evaluated with respect to their appropriateness to formal schooling, many respondents nominated inappropriate aims and then wrote notes next to them indicating that they were more correctly regarded as objectives of family and church! Others declined to rank strictly and created many tied choices. Both reactions indicated a defective test item. But some findings can be salvaged from the resulting statistics, as shown in Diagram 1.

The unambiguous favorite was the aim of achieving academic levels adequate to gain admission to the institutions for which parents had expressed preferences. These, as we have seen, were predominantly universities in the country of parental origin. The second, on first preferences, was Bible knowledge and understanding of the Christian faith, but at the same time a significant number of parents wrote against this entry that it was primarily a home responsibility. The aim of relating to, and communicating with, other people including non-Christians rated high, but must be interpreted as applying mainly to the exercise of these skills in Western culture.

Lowest priorities were given to studies of the indigenous culture and its faith communities, and studies aiming at a transcultural perspective. Later in this article I will argue for a realignment of these priorities.

Other aims suggested for schooling included the encouragement of self-reliance, independence, confidence in the presence of others, capacity to reach out to others, and self-acceptance regardless of academic achievement. Some wanted the school to provide opportunities for exercising responsibility, good adult Christian models, arts and crafts, a biblical perspective on adult life, and frequent reinforcement of effort and hard work. Mention was made of problems experienced by children from British Commonwealth countries in schools with an all-pervasive American ethos.

Other Educational Variables

As several parents remarked in relation to the educational aims presented for their comment, many of them belonged more properly to teaching agencies beyond the school; in particular, the home. It was good to see this qualifying remark coming through so often, for, as I have frequently maintained in other places (e.g., 1982, 1985), Western society is far too addicting to viewing the school as the heart of the educational process, the universal solvent for all society's problems. Diagram 1 shows the priorities accorded to the nine suggested aims.

Diagram 1: Aims of Formal Schooling

Suggested Aim	Priority				Composite Weighting	Reser-vation
	1	2	3	4		
1. Academic levels adequate to gain admission to preferred institutions	32	11	5	4	175	-
2. Ability to relate to, and communicate with others, including non-Christians	18	16	18	9	165	2
3. Comprehensive under-standing of the Bible and Christian faith	26	11	7	4	155	8
4. Employment and job skills needed by school leavers	10	10	12	3	97	-
5. Understanding of, and respect for, culture of parental country of origin	6	7	7	11	70	3
6. Experiences of Christian fellowship and services through voluntary activities	9	5	5	8	69	4
7. Understanding of, and respect for, culture of country of placement	5	8	7	3	61	4
8. Transcultural awareness of the conditioning features of any culture	5	5	6	6	53	3
9. Understanding of other major faiths, especially those in indigenous culture	3	2	3	3	27	2

Notes on Diagram 1:

1. *Composite Weightings*: Only first four priorities used; Priorities 1,2,3,4 weighted respectively 4,3,2,1 and added.
2. *Reservation*: Number of respondents who expressed the reservation that this was primarily the responsibility of family and community interaction.

In the attempt, therefore, to detect the influence of other factors on the education of the children of missionaries, I asked two open-ended questions about what were perceived to be the main advantages and disadvantages of being the children of missionaries (note 4). The yield was very rich indeed, far exceeding the bounds of formal education. Twice as many advantages as disadvantages were mentioned, with at least 10 respondents insisting that there were no special *dis* advantages at all. It had not occurred to me, unfortunately, to ask which parents were themselves children of missionaries, but 6 respondents drew attention to the fact that they themselvers were "M.K.'s," and their comments were at least as positive as the rest.

Forty-seven parents rejoiced in the broader cultural experience their children had been able to share. Twenty-three commented on their wider general knowledge and understanding of life, their access to travel in many places (17), earlier independence and maturity (9), their sociability and wide range of friendships across cultures (6), and their emancipation from ethnocentrism and racist attitudes (11). Several rejoiced in the simpler lifestyle and less materialistic environment of their countries of placement (9), offering a better value-system than the parent's home cultures, characterized as they were by consumerism, rampant sexuality, crime and irresponsible mass media (8). One parent exclaimed, "No TV--our kids read books!" Several others noted the same benefit. Fourteen parents made particular reference also to the benefits of bilingualism.

Many specifically Christian benefits were also cited. A strong emphasis was placed on the value of Christian family life and home training (10), often assisted by a generally Christian community environment (15). Only 3 parents mentioned gaining a more realistic knowledge of the two thirds world, but the sentiment was implicit in many other comments. Several parents rejoiced in their children's opportunity to see people living by faith (5) and encountering God's miraculous hand in people's lives (5). They were delighted to have their children participate in missionary ministry (5) and catch the vision (4). One parent welcomed the contacts her children had with visitors in the home, and another noted that the children of missionaries may well be prayed for by a wider group of people than other children are supported by.

Most of the comments majored on education *inputs*, but some references were also made to the kind of person resulting. It was believed that individuals were more self-reliant, adaptable, creative, and capable of developing their own interests. They had deeper peer group relationships and had learned to reach out to others and care for them. And, as I mentioned earlier, at least 6 respondents were "missionary kids" who had themselves returned to serve on the mission field. Another respondent said: "Unlike some other missionaries, we feel that our children are privileged to be in this situation. The advantages far outweigh the disadvantages." He added that the term "missionary kids" was misleading because it implied peculiarity and even disadvantage, and we should stop using it.

Nevertheless, it is clear that most parents were conscious also of a debit side. A few mentioned hazards to health and safety, but the major deficits were seen to be reduced time with parents (16), little contact with blood relations back home (18), frequent moves and lack of a permanent home (10)--indeed, of psychological roots in any one place (9). Friends were likely to be dispersed to faraway places (9), and parents were often unavailable in crises (3).

Another set of tensions was created by return to the country of parental origin. Psychological adjustment could be stressful (10) and the individual was at risk from naivete, inadequate acculturation to Western values (16), and competitive materialism (9). Such comments might be taken to suggest that expatriate boarding schools in the country of placement were falling down on the job, except that there were indications that some American schools in this category were felt to be already too mono-cultural. There is probably no way of becoming effectually re-acculturated short of actually returning home. The important thing is to provide support structures for the individual when the transition is made.

In summary, while a number of disadvantages were identified, the balance of comments were clearly positive, especially where expatriate schools were available within the country of placement. But one category of comments pointed to an adjustment problem which should be of great concern to mission boards, expatriate schools and churches in the countries of missionary origin.

The "Loner"

One parent, a former child of missionaries herself, identified the problem as "hyper-independence." As she put it:

The many separations cause us to "get tough" but when we really need to reach out and "cry" for help, we don't know how. We're reluctant to lose our protective masks. I find a truly close relationship, i.e., with my husband--can almost be scary when it's feeling totally wonderful because I feel God will take him away too.

In remarks which ran strikingly parallel to these, another respondent--a second-generation M.K.--said:

The thing that concerns me the most is not the academic needs of missionary kids, but the long-term effects of these multiple separations on later relationships with parents, siblings, their own mates and children, friends and so on. There is a particular syndrome I have seen in missionary families. The kids get a certain Mr. or Miss Independent Tough-guy feeling about themselves. We get proud that everyone says we seem "so much older." We've learned to cope with many things most other kids need their parents for. Our parents are proud of our independence and cite how "well-adjusted" we are--how we love boarding schools, etc. What I would like to propose is that in fact that very toughness is the only protection an M.K. can make for the intense pain of separation. It becomes impossible to let others get too close. Even on vacation we can't let ourselves or our parents know our deepest needs because once you go back to a close, dependent relationship, the pain of the next separation will only intensify...To not bring this wall into marriage has been difficult. As missionary parents get older, they long to be part of their children's lives--but there is a barrier. Perhaps the child is going through a divorce, or other deep crises, and the parents don't know how to help for their child refuses to ask for or accept help.

So it appears that there is another side to the earlier independence and maturity attributed to the children of missionaries. Several other respondents suggested that they may become spiritually too independent, failing to fit in to church communities and to find roots in caring fellowship. In some senses, this is what makes M.K.'s such good missionaries themselves! But it is hard to counsel such people in crises. It is a difficult balancing trick for any Christian--both to develop a mature reliance on God alone *and* to cherish the interdependence of members in the "body of Christ"--but it is made more difficult for many children of missionaries by the need to be separated from their parents at important stages in their growth. I will return to such questions as these a bit later.

Miscellaneous Correlations

The questionnaire sought to identify additional variables which might influence parents' tendencies to prefer local school alternatives to alternatives involving boarding away from home. Thus the attempt was made to detect whether there was any variation in preferences as a result of some parents having been in the field, *as parents*, longer than others. No significant difference emerged. Nor did variations in the age of parents at the time of having their first child affect the outcome in any way.

An attempt to see if patterns of responding varied according to the country of placement failed to yield significant findings because the actual numbers in each case were too small. The biggest subgroup of placements was in Papua New Guinea, where 13 preferred local school alternatives and 8 preferred boarding. At post-school level these figures were exactly reversed. Second biggest was Australia, where nonlocal placements were preferred (9:3). In both cases, one suspects that the relative closeness of facilities in Australian cities mattered more than theoretical preferences. The hope that this correlation might reveal something about the effects of different indigenous religions (e.g, Islam) on parental choice was defeated by the smallness of the sample, but could be an issue worth taking up in a larger inquiry. Finally, the attempt was made to correlate the levels of education attained by parents with their preferences for local, as opposed to nonlocal, school alternatives. This factor made no discernible difference at all.

Discussion

By way of comment on what the needs survey did, in general, reveal, I want to take up two issues. The first is the apparent discrepancy between the values attributed to the experience of being a missionary kid, and the kinds of formal education desired for them.

One was left in no doubt that notwithstanding some real risk involved in bringing children to a new, and usually underdeveloped, country, parents saw great value for them in the experience. It broadened cultural horizons, awakened sympathy, speeded personal maturity, and so on. It would therefore seem reasonable to expect that one's children might well develop an attachment to, and career interest in, the country of placement. Certainly, few could be better placed, if responsive to the call of Christ, to become missionaries themselves in such a situation. But this was seldom mentioned. Instead, the emphasis was on guaranteeing them an education which would enable them to get back into the career structures of the country of parental origin, despite frequent criticisms of the individualistic, materialistic, and licentious aspects of society in that country.

Conversely, little was said about the value of learning about the indigenous culture in one's schooling. Those who welcomed their children's access to bilingualism were not, it seemed, suggesting that indigenous languages be studied in the expatriate school.

It was as if parents were correctly assessing the educational value of life for their children in the missionary situation because they were close to it themselves and could see its value, but then tamely surrendering to the Western mythology surrounding schooling when asked to foreshadow the best educational future for their children. For example, few raised questions about the curriculum actually followed in expatriate or home country boarding schools, though that may have been a fault of my questionnaire. The important thing seemed to be the "reentry ticket."

One wonders if there may be an element of expiation in this attitude. Some parents may have feelings of guilt about having involved their children in the risks and financial privations of missionary service. As compensation, they seek to make it up to them by insuring that they will have favored access to the lifestyle of the parent culture, if they want it. Admittedly, a few parents spoke of their children having viable futures in either culture, but the school curriculum they sought for their children, even at primary level, was decisively Western.

The second issue concerns the small number of respondents expressing a preference for sending children to the country of parental origin for their schooling. General knowledge had led me to expect more, but it has been pointed out to me that few mission societies have been as vigorous as S.I.L. in providing expatriate boarding schools in the countries of placement. Many missionaries do in fact send their children to their home countries, or alternatively, board them in other Western countries.

One is then moved to ask whether, in either case, the missionaries concerned are basing their choices on biblical ideas of nurture or yielding to their own cultural conditioning. Western education is still excessively beholden to ancient Greek ideas of professionalized cultural transmission. I will suggest in the second portion of this article that some of the reactions of parents responding to the questionnaire were probably sub-Christian, because of this factor.

A Suggested Rationale

Conducting a needs survey will not of itself tell us what policies need to be adopted. The facts don't all point in the same direction, and the respondents do not all have the same aspirations for their children. We would be foolish to ignore the facts, but we must also draw on ideas and values at a wider social level. In the present case, we need to draw on modern educational theory and practice on the one hand, and biblical principles on the other. Without such resources, we may be tempted to settle for a very pragmatic solution, dominated perhaps by the bogey of university entry requirements in the country of parental origin.

A second introductory comment concerns the relevance of the Bible to this search for a rationale. We need to bear in mind that the Bible does not refer in either Testament to what we now understand by the terms "schools" or "education." Whatever rationale we develop specifically for schooling will need to be *compatible* with broad biblical principles, but that leaves us with a great deal of elbow room for responses to modern educational theory. Several approaches, different from each other, may each, nevertheless, be compatible with the responsibilities the Bible places on those who nurture the young. Thus, Dr. W. E. Andersen (1983) has identified three alternative frameworks for action which Christians might reasonably support, amongst which the "Christian school," for example, is only one possibility.

I want, therefore, to begin this inquiry by identifying some broad educational issues involved in determining what is best for the children of missionaries. After this, I will try to develop a curriculum model for the education of the children of expatriates. I will then discuss first the implications of this model for mission boarding schools, then other possibilities for its implementation in a more locally based way. Finally, I will look at other ways in which churches and mission bodies can provide effective support structures for these young people.

Some Broad Educational Issues

In raising children, parents have the difficult task of keeping a balance between *protection and exposure.* If they expose their children too quickly to the complexities and dangers of the wider world, they may blight the development of a healthy self-concept and self-esteem, producing timid neurotics. Alternatively, the child may weather the storm of new experiences, but at the cost of developing a hard exterior which repels intimacy.

If, on the other hand, parents keep their children too tightly wrapped in Christian swaddling clothes, they may be unable to adjust to the demands of study, work, and citizenship in the larger culture. Alternatively, they may cope by keeping apart as much as possible from non-Christians, thereby insulating themselves from Christ's commission to be salt in the world and to disciple all nations. They are also unfit for relationships.

A second important balance to be maintained in the education of a child is between *reason and relationship*. The domination of Greek ideas of learning in our educational institutions has led us to overemphasize intellectual development and academic achievement. We forget--though the Bible could have reminded us--that many of the most important things to be learned have to do with relationships. More than this, mastery of subject matter itself is often best promoted not by class teaching but by being subject to a master, as the apprentice to the craftsman or the disciple to the guru. That is, much head knowledge is transmitted through relationships.

This is often forgotten in schools, where the demands of public exams turn teachers into slave drivers, pushing students on in head knowledge, and damaging self-esteem by multiplying some students' experiences of failure through the interpretation of test results by application of the normal curve. The teacher-pupil relationship is soured by the tyranny of an external syllabus. Self-confidence is sapped by scolding disciplinarians.

The two balancing acts I have spoken of are related. Learning comes through progressive *exposure* to new knowledge and new experiences, but it should not occur at so fast a rate as to threaten the learner's self-concept. Secure and accepting *relationships* afford the best *protection* to the learning self, and are themselves a source of learning. *Reason* explains, while relationship sustains.

A third important balance to be maintained is that between *institutionalized and informal learning environments*. I have said enough to indicate that formal schooling has distinct limitations as a learning environment. It is most comfortable with academic development, least effective in the areas of relationship and moral commitment. We Westerners have been effectively brainwashed into thinking that the school is the pivot of education, and all else is peripheral. But such thinking has only been common in the past 150 years. Schooling was a minor strategy of education before that time and, as I mentioned earlier, is not referred to in the Bible.

What the Bible *does* give considerable attention to in the Old Testament is the family, and in the New, that voluntary group described as the "body of Christ," i.e., the local church. The family is irreplaceable as the primary matrix of relationships, the cradle of the healthy self. Studies show that the influence of the average stable home continues to be stronger than potentially competing influences such as the school and the peer group, even into the mid-teens. For this reason, policies which separate children from their parents for long periods of time during these years, for the sake of their academic advancement, are probably out of balance.

But there is an element of institutionalization and compulsory learning even in the home, and a balanced educational theory will give important status to other, more informal learning environments. Interactions in the culture at large are influential, especially with adult models who command respect and affection for the quality of their lives (whatever their skin-color!). And voluntary groups have a special part to play in personal development, for they are the most effective breeding grounds for independent personal commitment. A peer group is a voluntary association, but it may not prompt an enduring commitment because its members know that they are all transients. By contrast, a voluntary youth group led by credible adults is marvelously well placed to invite and nurture commitment. So also, for the same reason, is the local church at its best.

What a range of learning environments, then, is necessary to the balanced development of young people. If a boarding school is inevitable because of difficulties in the place to which the parents have been posted, then careful attention must be given to providing alternative support structures for the boarders, to reduce the domination in their lives of a living pattern sociologists refer to as a "total institution." I will come back to this point later.

A Curriculum Model

I come now to the development of a curriculum model. What elements belong in a balanced curriculum? Let us for a moment forget the situation of expatriate children and consider the more typical situation of a public school in a Western society. I suggest that a reasonable expectation of such schools is that they will provide a controlled exposure to the cultural heritage of that society, with a view to enabling the student to:

1. maintain a stable and positive self-image while learning new things;

2. acquire survival skills appropriate to one's culture;
3. identify and develop one's personal creative gifts;
4. gain access to the major fields of human thought and experience;
5. become aware of the dominant worldviews and value stances influencing one's social world;
6. develop capacities to think critically and choose responsibly;
7. develop empathy, respect, and a capacity for dialogue with other persons, including those whose primary beliefs differ from one's own.

This is first of all a charter for the public school, but it may also be regarded as a set of minima for any kind of school. Negatively, it judges any curriculum inadequate which fails to give students a critical understanding of their culture, coccooning them instead within one tightly monitored view of the world. That is indoctrination, not education.

Positively, it has the potential to produce individuals who are well equipped and motivated to seek the truth and make informed choices. Clearly it would be inadmissable for the public school, as servant of a pluralistic society, to go beyond this point by attempting to command allegiance to one particular faith. But I believe there are ethical grounds for drawing back from such an attempt even within the formal curriculum of the Christian school. Evangelism properly belongs in voluntary contexts.

Now let us see what amendments are necessary to adapt and expand this charter to make it applicable to a Christian curriculum for the children of expatriates. In doing so, I am not necessarily endorsing the Christian school as the best solution to the needs of missionary children. I am simply assuming for the purpose of this theoretical part of the exercise that we are able to put whatever we deem desirable into our curriculum brief. I will deal later with various ways of implementing this ideal.

I suggest that the phrases in the charter most in need of adjustment will be the references in (2) to "one's culture" and in (5) to "one's social world." We will also probably want to ensure that the Christian faith receives more comprehensive study in relation to (5) (note 6).

If one is the child of expatriates, what is "one's culture?" Such children are caught between two worlds. Their parents are neither natives nor migrants, but ultimately visitors. Hence the culture of *parental origin* (PC) is, on the face of it, the child's home culture also. But the visit is long-term, and if missionary service is to be modeled on the example of Christ, then it involves identification on many levels with the local people and their culture. It is hard to see how such identification could be genuine in a case where parents could say, as in one questionnaire: "When nationals were in the home we adapted to them and spoke their language; otherwise, we kept a very American home." But then, this attitude is not all that different from an expatriate boarding school situated in a missionary area, yet maintaining a totally Western enclave without reference to the *indigenous culture* (IC).

It may be argued that the children of missionaries absorb the indigenous culture by informal contact and don't need to have it reinforced by the school curriculum, but we don't talk that way about curriculum in our home countries. There we expect the schools to help students to come to terms with their home culture. It is an encouragement to schizophrenia to educate missionary children in a way which ignores the society which surrounds them. In some countries, such as Indonesia, it is compulsory for expatriate schools to include some IC studies, notably in the national language. This, I suggest, is to be welcomed rather than merely endured.

Of course, there is the view which says that the children's contact with the IC should be minimized so that the Western curriculum can "take" properly, like a vaccination! Accordingly, the children are placed in boarding schools, where they rarely leave the school premises, and find all their out-of-class social life and friendships within the compound. This has all the hallmarks of a "total institution," i.e., an institution which regulates all aspects of the inmates' living and minimizes contact with the larger society. Sociologists apply the term to a variety of health, welfare, and educational institutions--and prisons-- which have these features. They can also have a number of undesirable psychological effects on the inmates (Goffman, 1961).

My argument to this point, is that the curriculum must include studies related to both the PC and the IC. Curriculum areas which are particularly affected are language, literature, religion, and social studies. Is this asking too much of the school, bearing in mind the sophistication demanded by PC curricula? One objection is the sheer time factor, a point to which I will return later. It is interesting to note, however, that Western curricula are becoming themselves increasingly committed to *multiculturalism* (MC). North America, the United Kingdom, and Australia--to name only the major three represented in our sample--must all come to terms with the fact that they are multicultural societies in which bilingualism and comparative studies have positive value.

Admittedly, their concern is with the rights and gifts of ethnic minorities permanently resident within the borders, but it does not strain the analogy to think of missionaries living in non-Western countries as ethnic minorities in a similar sense. In short, even within present curriculum limits, multiculturalism is both possible and desirable. Our thinking is dated if we think we have to be doggedly mono-cultural to be credible.

But there is a fourth layer in this analysis of the meanings of "culture" for the missionary child. Neither entirely at home in the IC nor the PC, the individual needs to be given a more overarching frame of reference, through what I shall call *transcultural studies* (TC). This term is meant to apply to the development of a critical-evaluative competency, an ability to see how cultural values take shape, how individuals are socialized, and in what ways *my* culture is conditioning my responses.

In the general world of scholarship, aspects of transcultural studies are picked up in disciplines such as sociology of knowledge, cultural anthropology, and comparative religion, but I am not about to suggest that these disciplines be imported directly into the secondary school curriculum. Nevertheless, our approach to subjects such as language, literature, religion, and social studies should be modified to take more account of such analytical dimensions.

There is, however, something very special which a *Christian* curriculum can do in this regard. It can make the students aware of the transcultural dimensions of the gospel of Christ. Christianity has some claim to be regarded as the most multicultural faith of all time. Early in its development it burst out of national and racial definitions, and today it has a multitude of indigenous expressions in countries of the East and West, first world, and two third worlds (Malcolm, 1982).

The heart of Christianity's transculturalism is the universal message of Jesus and the transplantable lifestyle associated with teachings about the kingdom of God. There are two ways in which these can help us to develop a transcultural awareness in our students. First, they provide an antidote against the moral corruption and materialistic values of the two (or more) cultures our students are trying to cope with. Second, by encouraging our students to inspect and apply Christian apologetics in various cultural contexts, we will be helping them to see that Christianity is true not just "because I say so," but because its truth claims can stand up to challenge and comparison.

A part of this development of a transcultural awareness will be to introduce our students to some of the other major faiths, religious and secularist, which are contending with Christianity for the hearts of men and women. If we avoid this responsibility, we will be failing our students out of a misguided desire to protect them from the world. If such challenges are not faced in the controlled learning environment of the school, then they will be met without armor in the open society.

This is the point at which to untangle some contradictory messages coming through the questionnaires. Some suggested that an understanding of the Bible and of Christian faith are matters for the home and the church. This is undoubtedly true, but the good school will to see to it that, independent of what happens in faith communities, students are made aware of these aspects of their cultural heritage, in a reasoned and reflective way.

Conversely, the questionnaires revealed a low level of interest in giving students either a transcultural awareness, or an understanding of the indigenous culture and of major faiths significant in the two cultures of the student's life setting (PC and IC). But I have been arguing that these are precisely the elements needed to help expatriate children toward healthy adjustment and development.

In summary, curriculum throughout the school years should include bilingual and multicultural experiences, together with an objective grounding in biblical knowledge and Christian belief. As students move into the middle and later years of adolescence, they should also be introduced to issues of cross-cultural comparison and analysis, studies of other relevant major faiths, and studies of Christian apologetics in relation to contemporary cultures and other faiths.

If, now, I may take you back to the charter of curriculum expectations I began with, it will be seen that we have arrived at a model compatible with Christian values and adapted to the special needs of expatriate children (note 7). It will now read:

The educator should aim to provide a controlled exposure to the cultural backgrounds (PC and IC) of the students, with a view to enabling them to:

1. maintain a stable and positive self-image while learning new things;
2. acquire survival skills appropriate to both cultures (PC and IC);
3. identify and develop one's personal creative gifts;
4. gain access to the major fields of human thought and experience;
5. become aware of the dominant worldviews and value stances influencing one's social world, with special attention to biblical Christianity (MC and TC);

6. develop capacities to think critically and transculturally, and to choose responsibly (TC); and

7. develop empathy, respect, and a capacity for dialogue and Christian apologetic with other persons, including those whose primary beliefs differ from one's own (MC).

It will be seen that the original charter is in no way impaired or superseded, but rather enhanced. Several of its clauses acquire deeper meaning. We may go further. Given the special situation of the expatriate child, here is an opportunity to produce a world citizen (and, please God, a citizen of heaven--Phil. 3:20). uniquely equipped to communicate and relate across some of the most intimidating barriers in modern society.

The Time Factor

So much for the ideal. The crunch comes when this charter is compared with what is involved in one part of this task, namely, becoming adequately acquainted with the parent culture. Some will object that it already takes twelve solid years to prepare Western children on their home ground for entry to tertiary education. How can the education we provide for expatriate children do all this *and* satisfy the other requirements of the charter as well? I believe several answers can be given to this objection.

(1) We should not forget that those twelve years are not devoted exclusively to cumulative academic learning. Much of the time in school is absorbed by social and socializing activities, administrative exercises, elective studies to widen interests, and--let's be frank--baby-sitting to keep youngsters off the streets. The hard-core academic disciplines can be, and often are, grasped in a shorter time by people doing make-up studies in the later years of life.

(2) Even if the acquisition of PC studies *did* take the equivalent of twelve solid years, would it be good stewardship to sacrifice all the other objectives named in the charter for the sake of this alone? Do we really admire our PCs so much that we would most prefer to see our children locked in to all their values and vices? Why don't we question the Western curriculum more than we do?

(3) But the fact is that some of the other objectives in the charter can be met *during* our studies of the PC, provided that we modify the perspective from which they are usually taught. Teachers need to reduce their nationalistic fervor and develop their own transcultural skills and insights, especially in the teaching of language, literature, religion, and social studies. Often

they are more mono-cultural in their own personal backgrounds than their students are.

(4) Even so, there will need to be additional subject areas in the curriculum, drawing on the IC, on studies of other religions, and on Christian apologetics. Have we the time? A part answer is that many of these concerns can be packaged in that part of the typical Western curriculum which is left open for "electives." It should also be possible to negotiate with home institutions to gain recognition and accreditation of linguistic and multicultural options in *our* curriculum, rather than feeling that we have to mimic faithfully even the elective options of the home country.

(5) It may still prove to be the case that we cannot fit all these requirements into a typical twelve-year lock-step curriculum. So what? If one thing is becoming apparent in industrialized Western countries, it is that time is no longer of the essence in a person's education. Jobs won't automatically be available for persons who finish their formal education in minimum time. There is nothing sacrosanct or especially meritorious about young persons entering university in their nineteenth year. An increasing practice in my own and other universities is to allow students to defer entry for one or two years after they have finished their schooling so that they can move around as adults in the open society, perhaps working, before resuming formal study. If we feel that at certain points in their educational pilgrimage, perhaps because of a field relocation, children of missionaries need an extra year of adjustment, there is no shame in this. We have not let them down. All living is educational! This is exactly analogous to exchange students spending a year in another country. Similarly, if we feel that a TC curriculum is going to limit concentration on the matriculation requirements of particular countries, then let us designate a year end-on to their general schooling in which this specific objective is achieved by intensive study. In my own country, technical colleges provide precisely this service for early school leavers and mature-age applicants who now want to gain access to tertiary studies. Even the sacred English A levels can be tackled in this way!

An Example: The Mission Boarding School

Let us now take the specific case of a Christian boarding school which is trying to provide this kind of curriculum for the children of expatriates. What administrative support structures would be required? One would be that the *staff* be appropriately multicultural in race and background. It is possible to be one in faith and many in ethnic origin!

Second, the *timetable* should accommodate electives meeting particular needs, as well as core studies for all. This has resource implications, but such needs can sometimes be met by allowing students to include some courses by correspondence or external study from other institutions in their personal program package. All study does not have to be in the same mode. There is also a case, in most schools, for reducing the amount of direct class teaching time in each subject to allow more opportunity for independent study and research, provided sufficient library resources are within reach. Finally, more flexibility can be secured through developing subject modules of 9-10 weeks' duration, in place of yearlong units.

Third, the *balance* of compulsory and voluntary activities under the aegis of the school should be carefully monitored, to reduce some of the "total institution" effect. It is especially important to put activities which call for the expression of moral and religious commitments in the voluntary mode. Thus it is never inappropriate for a so-called Christian school to encourage a voluntary student Christian group to operate alongside its formal curriculum.

Again, one respondent to the questionnaire, himself a former "M.K.," uttered the following caution:

Seeing that most schools are home, school and church all in one, a child is under extreme peer pressure. Should a child not find acceptance...there is no [other] place to go for affirmation and a sense of worth.

This points up a further need to build *extended family and community relationships* into the daily life of students. The staff must be encouraged to exercise pastoral care toward students, as well as being in roles of authority such as teacher and supervisor. But this is nevertheless not sufficient to meet the need I am identifying. Students need opportunities to relate to nondirective adults on school premises as well, and also to have friends and activities "off limits," i.e., in the wider community. Local churches, for example, may be able to provide host families and youth programs, not confined to expatriates and Westerners.

Fifth, *parental involvement* should be welcomed in whatever ways possible. The bottom line is regular communication by the school to parents, detailing its activities, curriculum directions, needs, and achievements. Next is consultation, by correspondence where necessary, when major questions of policy and curriculum change are being considered. Involvement of local adults (other than staff) is another desirable thing, helping to extend the sense of family concern. Minimal restraint should be placed on access by parents to their children: better too much access than too little. Correspondence, phone calls, and visits should always be encouraged, whatever minor inconveniences they may create. The fact that most respondents were disinclined to board their children in the country of parental origin, in contrast to some of the policies of past generations, is to be regarded as a healthy sign.

Sixth, it may be timely to suggest that there are enough expatriate boarding schools now being run by evangelical missionary societies in the field to warrant the operation of a *Curriculum Clearing House* as a joint venture. Given that it is fairly uncommon for schools to pursue multicultural and transcultural objectives, the pooling of ideas to foster such developments could multiply the relevance and resources of such schools.

Other Possible Support Structures

In the previous section I commented on the implications of our curriculum model for the Christian boarding school in the country of placement. But that is not the only way one might provide such a curriculum for our children. It may not even be the best way in all circumstances. For example, it might be the case that local schooling could provide basic skills and studies in the IC, leaving some shortfall in regard to PC and TC studies. In such a case it could be feasible with older children to make this up by a judicious combination of correspondence lessons and vacation school-camp experiences.

Alternatively, a good *non*-Christian school for expatriate children could implement most of the curriculum rationale I have sketched, leaving it again to Christian parents and missions to top up with additional studies in the Bible and Christian faith, and skills in Christian apologetic. This might be done, for example, by sending mission teachers on tour through a number of local centers, giving short courses as a service not only to older secondary students, but also to their parents and interested members of local churches.

Some parents, commendably anxious to maintain close family relationships for as long as possible, have been strongly drawn to correspondence lessons. Even if considerable improvement could be made of facilities in this regard, it is not necessarily the ideal answer. Much depends on the amount of time parents can spare and their aptitudes for teaching in this mode. A valuable discussion paper prepared for World-wide Evangelization Crusade by Tony

Goodman and based on a questionnaire to WEC parents identified some potential problems in home instruction, such as a possible deficit in social education; a tendency to be too helpful to the learner, thereby inhibiting the development of skills in independent study; and a possible deterioration in family relationships when parents don the authority role of teacher and have to nag their children to learn. Against these points, however, are to be weighed the educational values of warm relationships in home, local church, and community.

In the end, the decision about what is best for the child--remembering that each child is different, even in the same family--must rest with the parents. One thing is certain: it is no crime for missionaries to have children and to be vitally concerned for their welfare. It is up to mission boards to provide, not chastisement, but counsel and support structures, both on the field and on furlough. Changes of plan due to the special needs of children should not be viewed as lapses in dedication to the work of Christ, as they sometimes have been, but as a temporary realignment of priorities in his service. Extended furloughs where necessary should be approved not grudgingly but with gratitude that the question of termination of service has not been raised.

Mission boards need appropriately to be concerned for the support structures available for the children of missionaries when they go home on furlough. It cannot be assumed that the home church will automatically be sensitive to their needs. Local churches may have to be alerted and advised on things they can do to provide extended family support. Usually, everyone is too polite and too diffident to ask what the situation is really like, and missionaries are reluctant to impose on others. The board, acting through local representatives, may need to act as a go-between.

One facility on furlough which can sometimes be organized through home churches is extra coaching in the hard-core academic disciplines, and even some guidance by correspondence when children are back on the field. Team supporters like to feel that they are able to give some tangible help like this, as well as praying for their missionaries. Unfortunately, that very independence of spirit which has been referred to before in this article, and which can be both a bane and blessing, often prompts missionaries to hold back from seeking help, especially for their children's education.

Conclusion

May I conclude on a note of hope. In seeking to educate myself about the needs of expatriate children, I have been impressed by the strong, positive feelings parents have expressed about their situation. Clearly there are often times of stress and hardship, but along with these go opportunities to become well-informed multicultural servants of the most high God. This is not a time to bow to the cultural imperialism and schooled mentalities of our diseased Western societies. Nor ought we, on the other hand, to ignore their gifts of learning and technology. The important point is to keep things in balance and to help our children become well-adjusted citizens of the world--that world which, in its entirety, Christ came to redeem.

Notes

1. I am grateful for the services of Tony Mitchell, who as research assistant, coded and analyzed the data for me, using the Statistical Package for the Social Sciences (SPSS). I valued also the opportunity to discuss some of my ideas with Bob Callaghan, general director of Asia Pacific Christian Mission, and John and Moyra Prince, missionaries at large.

2. I am using this phrase in reference to "home country," or even simply "country of origin," in order to highlight the fact that it does *not* necessarily relate to the child's own place of birth or early upbringing.

3. Sometimes these were the same respondents as in the previous case, as they weighed up the perceived needs of different children in the family.

4. Since the questions were open-ended and not all respondents made entries, the numbers in brackets hereafter indicate those who volunteered similar remarks to others.

5. My attention was drawn to a well-written short article by Barbara Eldridge supporting this positive picture in respect of children in a missionary boarding school in Indonesia.

6. Though some respondents remitted that task to home influence, I would want to argue for the more dispassionate study of the Christian evidences and truth claims at school as well, if only to show that they can stand up to the sort of critical examination to which we subject other studies in the timetable. But there are also deeper reasons, which I will advance later.

7. Technically, all that I am saying applies to the children of any expatriates, be they missionaries or other persons in government or commercial enterprise.

References

Andersen, W. (1983). Models of Christian involvement in contemporary schools. *Journal of Christian Education Papers, 78*, 8-20.

Eldridge, B. (1984). Are missionaries' children deprived? *Light and Life*, June, 4-5.

Goffman, E. (1961). *Asylums*. Harmondsworth: Penguin Books.

Hill, B. (1982). *Faith at the blackboard*. Grand Rapids: William B. Eerdmans.

Hill, B. (1985). *The greening of Christian education*. Sydney: Lancer Books.

Malcolm, I. (1982). The Christian teacher in the multicultural classroom. *Journal of Christian Education Papers, 74*, 48-60.

PART THREE
MISSIONARY ADJUSTMENT

PART THREE
MISSIONARY ADJUSTMENT

Success in overseas living and work involves more than merely adjusting to new cross-cultural challenges. It also involves developing personal competencies for successfully engaging in the new situations one encounters. This next section continues the discussion on missionary mental health by focusing on an assortment of stressors typically encountered on the field. Twelve articles have been chosen to explore the nature of these stressors. Topics include the ways for the neophyte missionary to fit into the new culture, relationships with other missionaries, and factors leading to premature departure from the mission field. Many of the articles contain useful suggestions for dealing with various stresses while also building individual competencies in the process.

Entering the New Culture, the first section, starts with an article by the Brewsters which identifies techniques for becoming a member of the host culture. Active involvement is encouraged, as is learning to get one's needs met from those in the host culture. Gibbs offers advice on setting up house overseas. A key component of adjustment includes the "personalization" of one's environment which leads to a greater sense of inner security. Next, two important strategies for reducing misunderstandings in cross-cultural interactions and for maintaining a sense of control over one's life are presented in the Bolyanatz article. These strategies require understanding basic value orientations, such as the differing concepts of time and acknowledging the underlying meanings of particular behavioral practices.

Helping missionaries to anticipate and competently deal with stress is central to the work of mental health professionals in missions. The second section explores the multifaceted nature of *missionary stress.* Wayne Dye, for example, breaks down culture shock into the components of culture confusion and culture stress. He then goes on to describe in the remainder of the article ways in which stress can be increased or decreased on the field. Sally Dye takes a more psychodynamic approach in her treatment of stress by highlighting the unconscious mechanisms that influence missionary adjustment. Some of the possible unhealthy results from overusing psychological defenses are explored, along with strategies for building psychological resources for coping with stress. This article is then followed by Gish's research, identifying general sources of missionary stress. The different types of stressors are discussed in terms of such variables as age, marital status, and length of service. The reader may want to compare this study with Chester's similar results on missionary family stress (Part Two) and the findings of both Johnson and Penner and Johnston (Part Four). The final article by Williams is actually a worksheet for balancing job and family responsibilities. It was developed specifically for Wycliffe workers, but can be easily applied to most mission settings.

Struggles with relating to other missionaries is often cited as the leading problem among missionaries. The third section takes a closer look at the many sides of *missionary relationships.* The first article by Foyle introduces the types of difficulties which can arise between personnel and administrators, and between different expatriate sub-cultures. White and Nesbit look at the phenomenon of separation, which frequently occurs for missionaries. This article expands their premise that "change is separation from the past, loss occurs as a result of separation." Suggestions for dealing with the incurring sense of loss are presented. The final article, by Foyle, explores the experiences of the single person in missions. Helpful suggestions are given for relating to married missionaries and feeling comfortable in one's singleness.

The last section, entitled *Attrition,* studies why missionaries leave the field. In the first article Allen outlines reasons for missionary dropout, disputing the notion that poor interpersonal relationships are the primary cause of its occurrence. The article continues with comments from four mission leaders who reflect on missionary attrition within their respective agencies. Next, Gardner discusses her research on missionary termination within Wycliffe. Her straightforward recommendations for prevention and organizational change will be of much interest to mission administrators.

Missionary adjustment, therefore, as the 13 articles in this section collectively indicate, involves many dimensions-- psychological, interpersonal, familial, and organizational. It also involves the knowledge and application of relevant principles from missiology, as well as from anthropology, psychology, and linguistics. The need to realistically face the demands of cross- cultural living, in all of its realms, is inevitable if personal growth and the development of personal competencies are to ensue.

ENTERING THE NEW CULTURE

30

E. Thomas Brewster
Elizabeth S. Brewster

Bonding and the Missionary Task: Establishing a Sense of Belonging

And the Word became flesh and dwelt among us. John 1:14

We have a new little boy who was born into our home just a few months ago. In preparing for his natural childbirth at home we were introduced to the concept of bonding.

In the animal world it is called imprinting. Most of us remember the picture in our college psychology books of the psychologist Konrad Lorenz being followed by ducklings. At the critical time, right after hatching, Lorenz and the ducklings were alone together and, from then on, they responded to him as though he were their parent. The imprinted duck experiences a sense of belonging to the man.

More recent studies supporting the concept of bonding have been carried out with a variety of animals, including goats, calves and monkeys. In each case, the infant and mother have an early period of sensitivity right after birth. If mother and infant are together at that time, a close bond results which can withstand subsequent separations.

But, if infant and mother are separated immediately after birth, the infant can become attached to a surrogate--a cloth doll, a different adult animal or even a human. If infant and mother are later reunited, one or both may reject the other or at least not respond to the other with normal attachment.

Studies of human infants and mothers show the importance of bonding. Apparently, just after birth, divinely-designed psychological and physiological factors in the newborn uniquely prepare him to become bonded with his parents. Certainly the excitement and adrenalin levels of both the child and his parents are at a peak. The senses of the infant are being stimulated by a multitude of new sensations. The birth is essentially an entrance into a new culture with new sights, new sounds, new smells, new positions, new environment and new ways of being held. Yet, at that particular time, he is equipped with an extraordinary ability to respond to these unusual circumstances.

People who support home birth are concerned about the bonding process between parents and the infant. An important collection of research studies published in *Maternal Infant Bonding* by Klaus and Kennell (Mosby Co., St. Louis, 1976) is widely read. It is pointed out that the non-drugged newborn is more alert during the first day than at any time during the next week or two. This was our experience as our son was full of interest and curiosity for his first six hours, then, after sleeping, he continued very alert for a few more hours.

These alert hours are the critical time for bonding to occur-- for a sense of belonging to be established.

Typical American hospital birth is not conducive to normal bonding for two reasons. Hospital-born babies are usually drugged--groggy from a variety of medications typically given to the laboring mother. Neither the baby nor mother, then, has an opportunity to experience the period of acute alertness immediately after birth.

The other reason normal bonding does not occur within the hospital establishment is that the baby is typically snatched away from his family and straightway placed in the isolation of the nursery.

When normal bonding does not occur, rejection can result. It has been demonstrated, for example, that child abuse occurs far more frequently with children who were born prematurely and then isolated from the mother for even a few days while being kept in incubators (Klaus and Kennell, pp. 2-10).

Our desire to be intimately together as a family and away from institutional commotion in order to maximize the bonding opportunity for all three of us (father included) was a major reason for choosing home birth.

The Missionary Analogy

There are some important parallels between the infant's entrance into his new culture and an adult's entrance into a new, foreign culture. In this situation the adult's senses, too, are bombarded by a multitude of new sensations, sights, sounds, and smells--but he, too, is able to respond to these new experiences and even enjoy them. Just as the participants in the birth experience, his adrenalin is up and his excitement level is at a peak. Upon arrival, he is in a state of unique readiness, both physiologically and emotionally, to become a belonger in his new environment. But then...

Just as the infant is snatched away by the hospital establishment and put into the isolation of the nursery, so the newly-arrived missionary is typically snatched away by the expatriate missionary contingency and, thus, isolated from his new language community.

He is ready to bond--to become a belonger with those to whom he is called to be good news. The timing is critical. Ducklings do not become imprinted at any old time. Imprinting occurs at the critical time. Bonding best occurs when the participants are uniquely ready for the experience.

The way the new missionary spends his first couple of weeks in his new country is of critical importance if he is to establish a sense of belonging with the local people.

It is not uncommon for a baby to become bonded with hospital personnel instead of with his own parents. The baby then cries when with the mother, and is comforted by the nurse. New missionaries, too, tend to become bonded to the other expatriates rather than to the people of the new society. It happens subtly, maybe while the newcomer is subject to the hospitality of an orientation time.

When his sense of belonging is established with the other foreigners, it is then predictable that the missionary will carry out his ministry by the "foray" method--he will live isolated from the local people, as the other foreigners do, but make a few forays out into the community each week, returning always to the security of the missionary community. Without bonding he does not have a sense of feeling at home within the local cultural context. Thus, he does not pursue, as a way of life, significant relationships in the community. When normal bonding is not established, rejection of the people, or even abuse, can occur--it is often reflected in the attitude behind statements like "Oh, these people! Why do they always do things *this* way?" or "Somebody ought to teach them how to live!" or "Won't these people ever learn?"

Implications of Bonding for the Missionary Task

A missionary is one who goes into the world to give people an opportunity to belong to God's family. He goes because he, himself, is a belonger in this most meaningful of relationships. His life should proclaim: "I belong to Jesus Who has given me a new kind of life. By my becoming a belonger here with you, God is inviting you through me to belong to Him."

The missionary's task thus parallels the model established by Jesus Who left heaven, where He belonged, and became a belonger with humankind in order to draw people into a belonging relationship with God.

We are convinced that the normal missionary newcomer is ready physiologically, emotionally and spiritually to become bonded with the people of his new community. Fulfillment of this unique readiness must be initiated at the time of arrival.

The timing is critical.

During his first couple of weeks, the newcomer is uniquely able to cope with and even enjoy the newness of a foreign country and its language. There have been months or even years of planning, and his anticipation, excitement and adrenalin are now at a peak.

The newcomer who is immediately immersed in the local community has many advantages. If he lives with a local family, he can learn how the insiders organize their lives, how they get their food and do their shopping and how they get around with public transportation. During the first couple of months, he can learn much about the insiders' attitudes and how they feel about the ways typical foreigners live. As he experiences an alternative lifestyle, he can evaluate the value of adopting it for himself and his own family. On the other hand, the missionary whose first priority is to get settled can only settle in his familiar Western way, and once this is done he is virtually locked into a pattern that is foreign to the local people.

Culture shock is predictable for the missionary who has not bonded with the local people of his new community, but is much less likely for the bonded person. The one who feels at home does not experience culture shock.

In our first culture it comes naturally for us to do things in a way that works. We know which way to look for traffic as we step off the curb, how to get a bus to stop for us, how to pay a fair price for goods or services, how to get needed information, etc., etc.

But, in a new culture, the way to do things seems to be unpredictable. As a result, newcomers experience a disorientation which can lead to culture shock.

The new missionary who establishes his sense of belonging with other missionary expatriates has his entry cushioned by these foreigners. It is generally thought that this cushioning is helpful for the adjustment of the newcomer, whose arrival is often planned to coincide with a field council pow-wow.

We would like to suggest, however, that this cushioning is an unfortunate disservice, because during the first two or three weeks the newcomer would have been especially able to cope with the unpredictable situations encountered in the new culture. Indeed, he might even revel in all the variety. But the critical first few days are the only time such a response is likely. The way these days are spent is, therefore, of crucial importance--and cushioning is the *last* thing he needs.

The first prayer letter the cushioned missionary sends from the field will typically describe his airport meeting with the local missionaries, the accommodations provided by them, and the subsequent orientation by these expatriates. After writing about how he has been accepted by the other missionaries (one of his high priorities) he will invariably close with something like: "Our prayer request at this time is that we will be accepted by the local people." A noble desire, but a concern that is being expressed about three weeks too late!--and now without a viable strategy to achieve the goal. The initial blush of life in the new environment is now gone.

The individual who hopes to enter another culture in a gradual way will probably fail to do so, and he may never enjoy the experience of belonging to the people or having them care for him.

Better to plunge right in and experience life from the insiders' perspective. Live with the people, worship with them, go shopping with them and use their public transportation. From the very first day it is important to develop many meaningful relationships with local people. The newcomer should early communicate his needs and his desire to be a learner. People help people who are in need! Then, when potentially stressful situations come up he can, as learner, secure help, answers, or insight from these insiders. (The one who is being cushioned gets outsiders' answers to insiders' situations and his foreignness and alienation are thereby perpetuated.)

A couple who has chosen to be isolated from Western people during their first months in a Muslim context wrote us about the victories they have experienced:

My husband and I knew before we left that we would have different types of adjustments. I knew the hardest time for me would be at first and he felt that his hard times would occur after he had been there a while. So it has been. I really had a hard time leaving our family. But after I started getting out with the people here, my homesickness faded. The local community has so warmly received us. At Christmas, 125 of these friends came to our Christmas celebration. And during that season, the closeness of our interpersonal relationships amazed us.

I'm not exactly sure why my husband just recently went through a depression. Christmas for us was different than it has been. Plus he was laid up for a week with the flu. During that time, he yearned for familiar things. And he says he was tired of always trying to be sensitive as to how he is coming across. The Lord has blessed our work here, and two Muslim converts that he is discipling are what is helping him get over this. We really have been alone in many ways. We supported each other but at times the burdens seemed so big and we didn't have anyone else to talk to or look to for advice. But I suppose that is why we have such good national friends.

Bonding is the factor that makes it possible for the newcomer to belong to "such good national friends." Of course there will be stressful situations, but the bonded newcomer, experiencing the wonder of close relationships, is able to derive support from the network of the local friendships he has developed. This, in turn, facilitates the acquisition of the insiders' ways and gives a sense of feeling of home. The one who feels at home may feel discouraged or even melancholy for a time and some cultural stress is to be expected, but it may not be necessary to experience culture shock. Culture shock, like severe post-partum blues, may be a problem of the structure more than a problem of individuals.

It is significant to note that the new Muslim converts mentioned in the letter above are the result of the ministry of relative newcomers. At a time when other missionaries might typically be experiencing the cushioning and isolation of a language school, those who are bonded and carrying out their language learning in the context of relationships in the new community also have the opportunity to pursue the development of their new ministry from the earliest days of language learning. A few years ago the authors supervised the initial language learning for a team of eleven newcomers in Bolivia. We published an article describing that project, in the April, 1978, *Evangelical Missions Quarterly*:

Over 30 people came to know Christ as a result of the involvement ministry that these new language learners were able to develop during those (first) three months. Many of these were either members of families with whom we were living, or were on a route of regular listeners. In both cases, as a result of the personal relationships that they had developed, they were able to follow up and disciple the new believers. Little wonder that this was a fulfilling experience for these new language learners. (pg. 103)

Insights gained through relationships can help to ensure, right from the beginning, that the wheels of ministry are not only turning but that they are on the ground and moving in a direction that makes sense to the local people.

Bonding and effective interpersonal ministry are realistic even for short-termers, and should be encouraged and facilitated. (The rapid international expansion of Mormonism is virtually all being carried out by short-termers, most of whom immediately move in with a local family and become belongers in the community. We were recently told by a Cantonese man from Hong Kong that the missionaries there who have learned the language best are Mormons!)

Only a minimum of the target language is needed to initiate bonding relationships. For example, we recently received a letter with the following comment: "The best thing that happened to me was on the first day when you challenged us to take the little we knew how to say and go talk with fifty people. I didn't talk with fifty, I only talked with forty-four. But I *did* talk with forty-four." (The "text" she was able to say that first day was limited to a greeting and an expression of her desire to learn the language; then she could tell people that she didn't know how to say any more but she would see them again. She then closed with a thank you and a leave-taking.) The ice was broken on her very first day and, from then on, she was able to begin to feel at home in her new community.

Having local friendships is essential for feeling at home. A report developed by a mission for whom we recently consulted on a language learning project compared the 18 maximumly-involved learners with a control group of missionaries who had been through language school. The report revealed that the individuals of the control group (the resident missionaries) each had an average of one close national friend, while each of the learners-- after only eleven weeks--had a minimum of 15 close local friendships. Since each learner had had contacts with dozens of local people there were at least 1,000 nationals who had had positive experiences with the learners during the weeks of the project. The report continued: "Who knows how all of this low-level public relations will ultimately benefit (the mission); it is highly improbable that it will be detrimental. 'Maximum involvement' language learning is where it's at."

Language acquisition is essentially a social activity, not an academic one. As a result, gaining proficiency in the language is normal for the person who is deeply contexted and has his sense of belonging in the new society. But language study will often be a burden and frustration for the one who is bonded to other foreign missionaries.

It is therefore important to facilitate an opportunity for new missionaries to become bonded with (and hence belongers in) their new community. New missionaries should be challenged with the bonding objective and prepared to respond to the opportunity to become a belonger.

Preparation should include an orientation to the importance of bonding, with a commitment to do so. A few sentences of the new language that will be helpful for entry purposes could be learned. Also, skills should be developed in how to carry on language training in the context of community relationships. [A recent study by Stephen M. Echerd (an in-house mission report, p. 3) included a comparison between learners that had been trained in advance and others who developed skills after arriving in the country: "Those in the group who had previous exposure to *LAMP* (*Language Acquisition Made Practical*) made 11.78 time units of progress compared to 5.82 time units of those who had no previous exposure--more than double!"]

Then, most important, from his first day he should be encouraged to totally immerse himself in the life of the new community. He should be permitted to choose to remain in isolation from other missionaries for his first few months. He should seek to worship with the people, away from churches where missionaries lead or congregate. (Our observation is that experienced but non-bonded missionaries can be a primary obstacle to the new missionary who wishes to pursue the bonding goals. We have therefore occasionally recommended that a new missionary arrive about three weeks before the other missionaries expect him.)

If a newcomer is going to successfully establish himself as a belonger, live with a local family and learn from relationships on the streets, a prior decision and commitment to do so is essential. Without such a prior commitment it doesn't happen.

When we have accompanied missionary learners at the time of their entry into other countries we have found that a prior preparation of perspectives and expectations is helpful. We therefore expect all participants in projects we supervise to meet four conditions:

1. Be willing to live with a local family,
2. Limit personal belongings to 20 kilos,
3. Use only local public transportation, and
4. Expect to carry out language learning in the context of relationships that the learner himself is responsible to develop and maintain.

A willingness to accept these conditions tells a lot about an individual's attitude and flexibility.

With a prepared mentality, a newcomer is freed to creatively respond to the bonding and learning opportunities that surround him. We have seen that with a prior decision to do so, it is almost always possible to live with a local family (though non-bonded senior missionaries are typically pessimistic). Our experience is that the new missionary--whether single, married, or even with children--can successfully live with a local family immediately upon arrival. (Live-in options may be multiplied with sleeping bags.) We have seen newcomers find their own families by learning to say something like: "We want to learn your language. We hope to find a family to live with for about three months, and we will pay our expenses. Do yo know of a possible family?" It would be unusual to say this "text" to fifty people without getting at least some positive response--a mediator to help you or a family to live with.

We do not intend to imply that immediate and total immersion in a new culture is without risk. There is no other time with so much stress and danger as birth; and entry into a new culture has its own accompanying stress and risk factors. It is likely, however, that the stress and risk components themselves are essential to the formation of the unique chemistry that makes imprinting and bonding possible.

And there is another side to the risk question. If one doesn't take the initial risk and seek to establish himself comfortably with the new society, then he is opting for a long-term risk. It seems that one or the other cannot be avoided. The problem of missionary casualties suggests that there is a heavy price to be paid by those who fail to become belongers--probably half do not return for a second term, and some who stay despite ineffectiveness may be greater casualties than those who go back home.

Indeed it is not easy to live with a family, make friends with numerous strangers and learn the language, but neither is it easy to continue as a stranger without close friendships and without knowing cultural cues, living a foreign lifestyle with all the time, effort, and alienation that that entails.

Once the new learner is securely established as a belonger he need not relate exclusively with the local people--he has not rejected either America nor Americans. (The bi-cultural apostle Paul ministered primarily to the Gentiles, but when he was back among the believing Jews in Jerusalem (Acts 21) he did not reject them, but readily shaved his head, took a vow, and purified himself in readiness for a sacrifice.) The bonded missionary will probably continue to live and minister with the local people, but after the first few weeks it might not be detrimental from the bonding perspective for him to participate in occasional activities with other expatriates. It might even be helpful for him to spend Saturday evenings with other learners or a supervisor (and, of course, he may seek to listen to the Super Bowl with other Americans).

[The question has been raised: "What about missionaries who go to the field as a team?" A team is a team because its members share certain commitments. As a group they can decide that each will become bonded in the local culture, and they can encourage each other in the pursuit of that goal. For the initial months, a sharing time each week or so should be sufficient to maintain their commitments to each other.]

The concept of bonding implies a bi-cultural individual with a healthy self-image. Bonding and "going native" are not the same thing. "Going native" generally implies the rejection of one's first culture--a reaction which is seldom seen and which may not be possible for normal, emotionally stable indiviuals. Nor is being bi-cultural the same as being schizophrenic. The schizophrenic is a broken, fragmented self. But the bi-cultural person is developing a new self--a new personality.

The development of this new personality, adapted to the new culture, can be facilitated and symbolized by taking on a new, insider's name. (The Scriptures give various examples of individuals whose names were changed to symbolize changed roles and relationships.) The new personality, with its new name, does not have an established self-image to protect, and it can therefore be free to behave in uninhibited, creative, and child-like ways; it can make mistakes and try, try again. The newly developing personality enables the individual to feel at home in a second culture.

For the Christian missionary, the process of becoming bi-cultural can begin with the recognition that God in His sovereignty does not make mistakes in creating us with our first ethnicity. Yet in His sovereignty He may step in and touch us on the shoulder, as it were, and call us to go and be good news to a people of a different ethnicity.

To become a belonger in a legal sense, through formal immigration, might also be considered by some serious missionaries. Immigration need not imply a rejection of one's first country, but rather acceptance of a new one. Throughout history, people have immigrated for political, economic, religious and marriage reasons. The challenge of reaching a people for Christ should have the potential to similarly motivate some of Christ's bond-servants. The missionary's heavenly citizenship should lift him above the provincialism and ethnocentrism of a continuing allegiance to a country where, in obedience to Christ, he no longer lives. This "recovered pilgrim spirit" was the challenge presented by Joseph F. Conley in a recent *Regions Beyond* editorial (December 1979):

For most North American missionaries, North America is *home*. That is where he goes when he's sick, and when the going gets too rough he can always return to blend in with the scenery. Tomorrow the quick retreat may be cut off. We may be forced to relive those days when missionaries went abroad, never expecting to return. Many governments which refuse entry to missionary expatriates, hold the door open to naturalized citizens of colonizing communities. The Moravians led the way in this as they set up Christian colonies around the world.

Surrender of treasured U.S. or Canadian citizenship admittedly calls for a rare variety of commitment. But is that unthinkable? To such our Lord's words will find new and glowing exegesis, "he that hath forsaken lands...for My sake...shall receive an hundredfold and shall inherit everlasting life."

Belated Bonding

Can a missionary who has lived overseas for a time without becoming a belonger and without learning the language very well change his course? Is bonding possible after the first critical months have passed? In the past decade our work has carried us to almost seventy countries, giving us opportunity to observe missionary activity in many places. Only a small percentage of these missionaries manifest the kinds of relationships with local people that would demonstrate that bonding had occurred. It is not too difficult to tell the difference--the bonded missionaries are typically the ones who feel that even their social needs are fulfilled in their relationships with local people.

"Happiness is belonging, not belongings." Yet the lifestyle of the majority of Western missionaries is a major deterrent to bonding. It is hard to devote time to pursuing the meaningful relationships with local people when concerned about getting barrels of stuff through customs and unpacked and settled. This sense of belonging to one's belongings is a bonding of the worst kind--bondage. Unfortunately, it is a subtle bondage that is difficult to throw off. "When the farmer has got his house, he may not be the richer but the poorer for it, and it be the house that got him...a man is rich in proportion to the number of things which he can afford to let alone." (Thoreau, *Walden*)

Is it possible for an established non-bonded missionary to experience a belated bonding so that his life and ministry are then characterized by a sense of belonging with local people? The answer must be yes because it is a normal human process to establish belonging relationships. But we must confess that we have seldom seen overseas Americans shift their sense of belonging for their expatriate community to the people of the local culture.

Yet we believe that potential missionary effectiveness is so greatly affected by the bonding factor and by being truly bilingual and bicultural that the issue must be pursued. Again we seek an analogy with another divinely ordained relationship of intimacy-- the marriage relationship. This model may be helpful, for in it adult participants achieve a belonging relationship with each other. In our culture, readiness for bonding is established during courtship; with the honeymoon, the bonding is culminated.

The analogy would suggest that an established but non-bonded missionary might release the potential of his ministry with steps paralleling the marriage model; acknowledge the potential and desirability of a belonging relationship with the local people; implement a decision to make such a commitment to the people; then set a date and inform the missionary community of the scope and implications of the potential change in his relationships. In all cultures, times of major life transition, like puberty, graduation, marriage and death can be facilitated through festivities at the peak of emotion. The festival itself can serve to intensify the emotion which in turn can help facilitate the transition.

The commitment to belatedly join a new community might successfully be initiated by a festive transition celebration. When the date arrives, the honeymoon analogy suggests the necessity of becoming established with the local people (maybe in another community and adopting a Learner role).

The mutual ownership of assets by a married couple might suggest the need to heed Jesus' instructions to the rich young ruler. The minimum would seem to be a need for a means of reciprocity with the people. Bonding, like marriage, implies a radical adjustment of lifestyle.

The Dilemma of the Bonded Missionary

It must be pointed out that the new missionary who pursues the bonding objective may find himself in a dilemma: his non-bonded colleagues and superiors may be threatened by the initiative he takes in pursuing his ministry through a lifestyle of relationships with the local people. His total involvement lifestyle of ministry may contrast all too sharply with the foray ventures of other missionaries.

A few years ago we became friends with an African while he was in North America. We later had the opportunity to visit him on the mission station where he worked in Kenya. In the course of our conversation he related a dilemma he was experiencing. A new missionary had arrived a few months earlier who loved the Kenyans and demonstrated it by his lifestyle. Our friend liked the new missionary and wanted to encourage him in his identification with Kenyans, but he was afraid to do so. Over the years he had observed that the missionaries who had not learned Swahili or the tribal language--and hence did not relate to the Africans--were the ones who were then advanced to administrative positions on the station and in the mission. It was his experience that new missionaries who loved Kenyans became an unacceptable threat to these administrators and did not last; and he did not want to hasten the termination of a man whose missionary approach he valued.

The bonded missionary is invariably viewed with suspicion by non-bonded colleagues. At best they may think him to be a maverick, at worst a traitor. We know those who have even been accused of losing their faith because of their efforts to make sense to the local people.

Time and again we have received feedback from new missionaries describing the resistance they experience in their efforts toward a total lifestyle approach to language learning and ministry. This resistance is expressed by other missionaries in at least four ways: rejection, jealousy, guilt and fear.

Rejection may result if the bonding behavior and motives of the newcomer are misunderstood or misinterpreted. The missionary community may feel that the newcomer has rejected them. But what he has rejected is the foray approach.

Jealousy can arise if an established missionary observes that the newcomer has many close friendships with local people while he doesn't.

Guilt may occur if an established missionary recognizes that the newcomer's bonding approach may have more potential for effectiveness, particularly if he feels that he, too, should become a belonger, yet remains unable to make such a commitment.

Fear may surface if it appears that familiar, secure ways are going to be complicated by this new mentality. Change from traditional ways in which missionaries relate to nationals can be viewed as a movement into slippery, uncharted areas. Change implies risk and potential failure. Missionaries may also fear the newcomer's well-being, fearing that his involvement with the people could cause him to lose the theological distinctives of their group, his own orthodoxy, or even his faith. There may be fear that he will go too far or lose his cultural identity.

Some of their fears may become true. The bonded newcomer could cause raised eyebrows in mission circles through his nonconformity. But it should be pointed out that through his bonding, and even his nonconformity, this bi-cultural missionary has the potential of an added dimension of cultural sensitivity. It could be the very thing that might enable him to discover a redemptive analogy within the culture and pursue its implications (see Don Richardson's *Peace Child*). His ability to gain an insider's perspective might also be a means of reducing the likelihood of syncretism among new believers.

Pioneer missionaries on most fields may have established belonging relationships with the people, but too often those who came after them have not followed their example and now there are few models for young missionaries to follow. If the concept of bonding has validity for the present-day missionary task, then it seems that established missions must find ways to affirm and encourage newcomers who choose to become bonded with the local people.

The quality of relationships between new missionaries and their senior colleagues is, of course, a primary concern for all parties involved. Open lines of communication are needed. Maybe discussion about the bonding issue could give potential missionaries information that would be helpful in developing these relationships, or even in selecting a missionary agency.

Prospective missionaries might initiate this interaction with both the home and field leadership of missions they consider joining. The new missionary must communicate his concerns in an attitude of love, and refrain from condemning or being judgmental of his predecessors who have ministered faithfully according to insights available to them. The fact is that he would have probably done things in much the same way. But new options are now open due to fresh insights available to them. A possible approach might be for him to request permission to personally experiment with a bonding strategy.

It could be that individuals who desire to become belongers within a new community might best be able to maximize their missionary potential by volunteering for service among an unreached, or hidden, people group rather than where missions have already established traditions of non-involvement. Indeed, the present practice of many established missions in regard to bonding could be the stimulus that might propel a significant number of young North Americans into the thousands of remaining groups of unreached people.

Conclusion

In summary, we have observed that the newcomer goes through a critical time for establishing his sense of identity and belonging during his first few weeks in a new country. If he becomes a belonger with expatriates he may always remain a foreigner and outsider. But at this crucial time he has the unique opportunity to establish himself as a belonger with insiders, in order to live and learn and minister within their social context.

The bonded missionary, because he is a belonger, has the opportunity to gain an empathetic understanding of insiders' ways, their feelings, desires, attitudes and fears. He can listen with sensitivity to their otherwise hidden values, concerns and motives. Thus he can acquire insights and adopt habits of lifestyle and ministry that will enable him to be good news from the perspective of local people in order to draw them into a belonging relationship with God.

Bonding is therefore a perspective many missionaries may choose to value and a goal they may choose to pursue. Making this kind of significant cultural adjustment is not easy but it is possible, especially if initiated at the critical time for bonding.

31

Terri A. Gibbs

Finding a Sense of Belonging In Your New Place

Since the days of Abraham, God has been calling men to leave their familiar surroundings, their place of belonging, to move out into the unknown, to a new place. Abraham was called to leave his home in the beautiful land of Ur to become a sojourner. Moses was called to leave his comfortable life in Midian to share the hardships of wilderness wandering with the children of Israel.

Jesus, who left his home at the age of thirty, traveled throughout the land making himself available to the needy. He called upon his disciples to do the same. Simon and Andrew left their fishing nets beside the sea. Matthew left his tax collection booth. God calls *us* to go into all the unfamiliar world.

Embarking upon a new life in a new place, missionaries leave their familiar place of belonging. This involves more than just leaving a home country. It means leaving behind the familiar world of childhood, the world of family and friends, the familiar environment, culture, and traditions. This detachment is not easy.

In his book, *A Place For You*, Dr. Paul Tournier, writes with keen insight about the effects of being "uprooted," of losing the place where we have belonged. He explains that man was created to need a "place." Adam was given the Garden of Eden. But "place" is more than an acre of land. Adam was also given Eve. Place includes all that affects man's being, that gives him a sense of belonging. It is the comfort of familiarity, family, friends, health, religion, etc. Man is attached to the place where he feels he belongs. It becomes an important support for his life. Anything that affects his place affects his person (Tournier, 1966).

When taken from his place, man experiences pain. Numerous passages in the Psalms and Prophets express the nostalgic woe and grief of the Israelites at leaving their homeland, at living in the land of the Babylonians. They long for Jerusalem. They long for the temple. Dreaming of the happiness of the past they wonder if God has forsaken them. They are not content in their new environment.

The pain of separation from our customary place affects our reaction to a new place. Moving from the familiar environment means losing a support we had leaned upon, perhaps even more strongly than suspected. With the loss of this support there is bound to be a sense of panic. A struggling to cope with change.

The new missionary, adjusting to life in a new culture and environment, finds himself confronted with this struggle. He feels inundated with a strange discontentment. His reactions seem biased and overly judgmental. The houses and villages, which at first seemed quaint and interesting, are soon seen more realistically to be dirty and strange. He feels ill at ease with his obvious separateness from the people. The differences seem to multiply daily, becoming increasingly important.

Sadly, he finds himself habitually critical of local habits and customs. He feels guilty and battles with depression. Eventually, nothing in the culture so shocks him as his own attitudes. Confused, he is afraid and wants to go "home," back to the familiar environment. Like a tender plant repotted, he is suffering, not so much from the shock of the new soil as from the whole process of being uprooted and transplanted.

It is a time of transition. He is experiencing grief at leaving the familiar place, uneasiness at being without a "place," and anxiety over finding a new "place of belonging." He needs to feel that this new environment is his place also. That it can be a meaningful place of belonging for him.

The new missionary will most quickly and adequately feel a part of the new place as he endeavors to personalize the new environment in both private and public realms. The new environment seems strange and foreign. He can make it seem like "home." New places and faces are different and seem threatening. He can reach out to leave his warm personal touch on lives and lands.

Detachment is painful and attachment can be even more so. Carlyle Marney, in *Structures of Prejudice*, explains that men tend to withdraw to the safety of the known when they are baffled by the new, especially in situations of stress and frustration in the presence of the unfamiliar (Marney, 1961). However, the process of attachment, of personalizing the new environment, can be simplified by working within the framework of a defined procedure. Listed below is a brief guideline for personalizing the new environment. It will help you achieve a sense of belonging in the new place.

Personalizing the Private Environment

To the Zuni Indians in New Mexico their mud huts are "koowi," the center of the earth (Marney, 1961). Wherever we may find ourselves, home is the center of that world. This is where we begin personalizing the environment, drawing from the resources of familiar things. Don't leave everything back "home." Be sure to take that old junk along. Without it you create an unnecessary handicap. You'll be setting out to win the Henry Royal Regatta without an oar.

1. *You can take a little bit of "home" with you wherever you go.* Grandma's picture, Aunt Sally's old lace doily. Just a few treasured belongings from the familiar place can quickly make the new environment seem yor own. Pictures, paintings, books, bedspreads, tennis rackets. I know one couple who are so crazy about peanut butter that the first thing into the moving van is without fail their "Super Duper Peanut-Butter Maker." My mother never closes her suitcase until her favorite little throw rug has been included. "So I can feel home beneath my toes first thing every morning."

2. *Make yourself at home.* Any nook, cranny, mud hut or bamboo bungalow. Paint the walls, arrange your favorite books on the table. Buy a bird. Plant a flower, or a tree. Add your personal touches and you will feel this new place is your own.

3. *Take personal customs and traditions with you.* The continued observance of these practices will make you feel less estranged. Edith Schaeffer suggests, "Choose one or two things to become a family tradition and whatever else is done, always do that special thing as well, year after year" (Schaeffer, 1975).

Traditions are important in binding families together. They give a sense of unity and continuity. Children love traditions and private family customs, on special holidays or any day of the week. For them especially, in the new environment, these customary observances can be a strong factor in feeling secure and welcome. Our children look forward to pancakes and peaches for Saturday breakfast. It's our lazy morning ritual. When we move I make it top priority to hunt down the necessary ingredients so that Saturday will still be our "lazy pancake day."

Whether a family or a single individual, you will have favorite habits, hobbies or activities that can be a big help in personalizing your new environment. Doing the things that you especially like to do is good therapy any time, any place, but particularly when you are feeling a stranger in a strange place.

Personalizing the Public Environment

The new missionary can take advantage of many unique opportunities in the public environment to make himself feel "at home." He can broaden the scope of his life, incorporating indigenous customs and habits from the new culture. He can find new friends, enjoyable in their distinctiveness. He can give the beneficial contribution of himself and his time, finding that in giving he has received a new sense of belonging.

1. *It is important to be able to speak the language well if you want to feel you belong.* Whether it be discourse or dialogue, in order for communication to be effective, the language used must be mutually comprehensible to both listener and speaker. This includes verbal and nonverbal communication. When you can communicate successfully in the speech patterns of the new environment, you will feel at ease and will be prepared to contribute to the community. Remember, you can get *by* with the weekly shopping list and local street names, but you will always feel a visitor. You will never feel you belong. And how can you tell them God is love?

2. *Maintain a movable circumference; develop a growing circle of friends.* You can choose to retire in dull seclusion from the people in your new environment or you can make the initial deposit on enjoyable current friendships. Requiring the use of a second language, this may call for extra effort, but be assured it is worth every drop of frustration. You gain new friends and improved language ability. To be at home in a new environment is to be at home with the people. To be accepted and welcomed by them, be their friend.

"But we have nothing in common," you may say. Develop areas of mutual interest. I cherish fond memories of happy hours spent with Mariza, a young Tzeltal girl in Chiapas, Mexico. She patiently taught me how to make tortillas and I, in exchange, taught her how to embroider.

In *The Friendship Factor* McGinnis distinguishes four requirements for friendship which are particularly appropriate for inter-cultural relationships: (1) Employ the language of acceptance. (2) Encourage your friends to be unique. (3) Be liberal with praise. (4) Take time to talk (McGinnis, 1975). The Bible reminds us that "A friend loveth at all times"(Prov. 17:17). This is the essence of THE CROSS-cultural communication.

3. *Participate in community events.* Wherever Christ went, he walked among the people. He was involved in their everyday lives. As you take an interest in what is going on in the new community, be it a village, district, hamlet or city, you will feel a vital part of the new environment. Active participation within the environment will give your relationship with the people depth and validity. Not only will *you* feel you belong in this place, but *they* will feel you belong; that you are not such an unusual stranger after all.

My dad didn't have to work long to gain acceptance among the Juma Indians of Brazil. Soon after moving to live among them, he agreed to spend a dark, solitary night standing guard at one of their hunting stations deep in the jungle. They were content that he was willing to participate in tribal activities, sheerly gleeful when his vigil proved fruitful. He bagged a monstrous tapir.

4. *Customs and traditions from the new culture that you can comfortably adopt as your "own" will help you to feel you belong.* Learning new traits, new foods, new habits of dress and incorporating them into your personal life style can be an exciting challenge. Depending upon your spirit of adventure, this may be a matter of adaptation rather than adoption out right, but even with the smallest act of acceptance, you will feel less a stranger.

Doing things "their way" will wonderfully uncomplicate your life, helping you to feel more at ease in the new environment. At first, things will seem odd and impractical, but give them a try. You may just find that a hammock really is more comfortable. And you can hang it anywhere.

5. *Maintain a clear sense of direction; have a definite system of long-range and short-range goals.* If you are responsible to a higher authority, ask for a well-defined job assignment. Having a specific task to perform in the new environment will help you feel necessary to the environment. This will lessen the strain of uncertainty. Having definite goals to accomplish will define your purpose for being in the new place. Given the opportunity to make a valuable contribution in the completion of these goals, you will feel a vital part of God's work in the new place. You will feel it is your place, that you belong.

In Retrospect

Moving to an unfamiliar environment, the new missionary understandably experiences strain and frustration, feeling "out of place." More accurately, he is in-between places--gone from the familiar place and not yet "at home" in the new place. The temptation is to sit in quiet stagnation, longing miserably for the lost place of belonging. To overcome his sense of loss, the new missionary needs to step out boldly in an effort to personalize the new environment, to make it, in part, his own. He will find that he does indeed come to feel "at home."

God has a unique purpose for our lives. It is important to have a "place of belonging," but more important to have the place God has willed for us. When God moves us from our familiar place to a new place, he will help us to let go of the past and accept the new. This process in life is like a trapeze artist's act. "We must always be letting go what we have acquired, and acquiring what we did not possess, leaving one place in order to find another, abandoning one support in order to reach another, turning our backs on the past in order to thrust wholeheartedly towards the future (Tournier, 1968).

References

Marney, C. (1961). *Structures of prejudice*. Nashville: Abingdon.

McGinnis, A. (1979). *The friendship factor*. Minneapolis: Augsburg.

Schaeffer, E. (1975). *What is a family?* (p. 192). Old Tappan, NJ: Fleming H. Revell.

Tournier, P. (1968). *A place for you*. New York: Harper and Row.

32

Alexander H. Bolyanatz

How We Reduced
Those Early Cultural Surprises

It was our third morning in Marakum village. In our bush house, my wife Pam and I were breakfasting on hot rice and milk, a favorite of mine. Our banter was lighthearted as we reviewed our first impressions of life among the Siroi on Papua New Guinea's Rai Coast. Then he walked up the ladder, through the doorway, and sat down. Our moods changed completely. Although he smiled, we were afraid; although he required nothing from us, we were anxious; and although he asked nothing, we felt ignorant. Should we offer him something to eat? If we offer him some, should we invite his whole family as well? Will we then be obligated to have each household in the village as breakfast guests? What is the proper behavior for us in this situation?

Predictability and Culture Confusion
Culture shock has been described as "an occupational disease of people who have been suddenly transplanted abroad" (Oberg, 1960:177). Since then, other authors (Smalley, 1963; S. F. Dye, 1974; T. W. Dye, 1974; Mayers, 1974:185-191; and Coots, 1976) have investigated the mechanisms of culture shock, and the implications for the missionary, and other cross-cultural workers.

The treatment of the subject by T. W. Dye distinguishes between culture confusion and culture stress (1974:62). Dye focuses on culture stress in his article, since confusion usually lasts for only a relatively short time, and culture stress is the problem most often encountered. However, in this article we are concerned only with that fundamental problem of the first few weeks in the new culture: culture confusion.

As a result of self-monitoring in Marakum, our ability (or inability) to predict events around us was identified as the factor that determined whether or not we experienced anxiety due to culture confusion. If we are able to predict the behavior of others (as well as their expectations of us) in a given situation, our confusion and its resultant anxiety was slight.

Predictability is serious stuff. On it, scientific hypotheses rise and fall: "Basically, science is concerned with defining, describing, and predicting...However, definition and description are not the end of science but the process; predictability is the end" (Grunlan and Mayers 1979:37).

As predictability determines the quality of a scientific hypothesis, that is, understanding the physical world around us, so is it the key to understanding people around us. A lack of such understanding results in confusion. Human beings want and need to avoid confusion by attempting to predict events and the behavior of others around them (Pike, 1976:51-53).

There are basically two ways to be able to predict the outcome of an event and/or human behavior. The first is to control it. For example, if you are chairing a committee, you will be able to make more accurate predictions about the agenda, who will dominate discussion, and the time of cessation of activities than if you are not the chairperson.

As aliens in a cross-cultural situation, however, most people are not in controlling situations. Even if one enjoys high ascribed status, the mechanisms used to exercise control are (at least initially) largely unknown. Therefore, another means of predicting must be used.

This other method is based on past experience. Because of what we have seen in the past, we can make an educated guess about the future. We can plan in advance the route we will take while we shop in a familiar supermarket or mall. We anticipate that the driver in front of us will turn left because the little light on the left rear part of his car is blinking. We know what kind of day it will be in the work place because of that all-too-familiar expression on the boss' face.

This kind of prediction is subject to certain constraints, however. Since the same event never repeats itself in exactly the same way, especially in human behavior, the use of this predictive strategy is limited. What is needed is a method of generalizing predictions so that large areas of human behavior can all be predicted with equal accuracy. To do this we need a framework (often called a "model" in academic jargon).

Anthropologist George M. Foster has written, "A good model is heuristic and explanatory, not descriptive, and it has predictive value...*a sound model should predict how people are going to behave when faced with certain alternatives*" (Foster, 1965:294; emphasis mine).

Having laid this foundation, this article will present examples of how two such frameworks of strategies were used in one initial cultural adjustment situation.

As noted at the outset of this paper, the unanswered questions that arise in a culture confusion situation can cause stress. During those first few weeks in Marakum, these questions (and others) were constantly on our minds:

Will we have guests at mealtimes?
Will someone come at an inappropriate time?
How long will they stay?
When will we be able to relax?
Will they get us water like they said they would?
When will we be able to go to bed?
Will we be able to communicate?
How will they perceive it if I do X?
How can I tell if they like me?
How can I tell if they don't like me?

Two Strategies

By the end of our first month in Marakum, we had adequate, albeit incomplete, answers. Two strategies helped us to be able to get answers: *functional equivalents* (Cf. Kraft, 1979:323-327, and Nida, 1960:47-61) and the *basic values* (Mayers, 1974:149-170, 1978).

One aspect of the basic values is the notion of time orientation vs. event orientation. An example from the Siroi will illustrate how differences in this area result in behavior that is not seen as reasonable by persons with an orientation which differs.

The day came when we were to leave the Siroi for an indefinite period of time. We sat underneath a huge mango tree waiting for the vehicle to arrive, not knowing how swollen the rivers were and thus having no idea of what time it would arrive. We all talked about the sadness we all felt at having to say farewell. Then one of the village leaders suggested that Pam and I stand up and all the village walk by and shake our hands, much like a reception line at a North American wedding.

At first I declined, thinking that since we had no idea of when the vehicle was coming, it would be an anti-climax to go through that formality and then have to wait for perhaps three more hours. I suggested that it would be better to wait until the vehicle actually arrived so that the shaking of hands--a formal good-bye--would be the last event that we shared together. My idea was rejected, on the basis that it would not be good to rush the farewell ceremony.

As a North American, I have a stronger time orientation than the Siroi, whose event orientation causes them to see timing as secondary to the event. My time orientation caused me to see the event as something that must take place within time constraints. I felt that it was important to have handshaking ceremony at a certain point in time, a very specific place within the progression of events that morning. The Siroi, however, with their event orientation, felt that the event itself should be given priority. Timing was not important; what was important was the fullness of the experience found in the completion of the event.

A functional equivalent can be quickly defined as action that can have different meanings. For example, during a Siroi village meeting, a man feels no qualms about poking his neighbor, making quiet jokes, or just generally "fooling around." To North American eyes, such behavior indicates irresponsibility and immaturity. However, in this part of Papua New Guinea, such behavior is normal meeting behavior. Irresponsibility and immaturity are demonstrated in other ways.

Another kind of a functional equivalent involves a concept that is communicated in different ways. An example of this type of functional equivalent is friendliness. In North America, friendliness is a smile and a word of greeting. In Papua New Guinea, friendliness involves a small gift of food, tobacco, or betel nut.

Application

Awareness of the time/event difference helped us to be able to predict with some accuracy an answer to the question, "When will we be able to retire for the evening?" (As Pam was six months pregnant at the time, this was somewhat important to us.)

In Marakum, the usual evening activity is conversation which begins at about 7 p.m. and lasts until whatever time people feel like breaking up. At first, we had no idea when conversation would cease and we would be able to go to bed. But, as time went on, we realized that they were more event-oriented than we were. Therefore, the idea of a bedtime by the clock was an alien concept to them. Rather, the quality and content of the conversation (the event) itself determined how long conversation would last.

Armed with this information, we could fairly well predict whether it was going to be a late evening, an early evening, or something in-between. We saw the importance of looking at those things that affect the event itself, such as the number of people present, prestige of those present, topic of presentation, place of conversation, and whether many people had worked in their gardens that day and were tired. These were the indicators by which we would know what the evening held for us. We then began to look at these kinds of indicators instead of our watches. Of course, we still preferred not to stay up late when we were tired, but it was much less stressful if we knew in advance what was coming.

In a culture confusion situation, an awareness of functional equivalents assisted us by making the unknown, or not easily understandable, become known and/or understandable. Eventually we recognized that the drop-in visit was the Siroi functional equivalent to a telephone call. In North America, when you phone someone, you take the chance that they're not busy and that they can chat with you. This was the same rationale used by our neighbors in Marakum. As with phone calls, their drop-in visits were of basically two kinds: just to chat, or to voice a request. Knowing these reasons made us feel much more relaxed and able to feel comfortable with their visits.

Conclusion

While we are not able to produce statistical data, we certainly were aware that as predictability increased, stress decreased. After a few weeks, the level of predictability in the behavior of the Siroi around us was low enough that it could be more easily handled. However, the value of these two (and other) strategies did not lessen as our culture confusion lessened; rather, they continued to help us in the ongoing struggle against culture stress.

In describing our use of these two methods of understanding others, it should not be understood that the basic values and functional equivalents models must be used, or even that the basic values and functional equivalents are inherently better than other strategies. I have used these to show that some sort of framework is needed and I have given examples of how I have used the concepts that I feel the most comfortable with. I see pattern in the world around me when I view them through the windows (Pike, 1967:30) of these strategies. Others may find it useful to view through different portals.

References

Coots D. (1976). What to do about those new missionary frustrations. *Evangelical Missions Quarterly, 12,* 205-209.

Dye, S. (1974). Decreasing fatigue and illness in field work. *Missiology, 2,* 79-109.

Dye, T. (1974). Stress-producing factors in cultural adjustment. *Missiology, 2,* 61-77.

Foster, G. (1965). Peasant society and the image of limited good. *American Anthropologist 67,* 293-315.

Grunlan, S., & Mayers, M. K. (1979). *Cultural athropology.* Grand Rapids, Michigan: The Zondervan Corporation.

Kraft, C. (1979). *Christianity in culture.* Maryknoll, New York: Orbis Books.

Mayers, M. (1974). *Christianity confronts culture.* Grand Rapids, Michigan: The Zondervan Corporation.

Mayers, M. (1978). *The basic values.* Unpublished manuscript. Dallas, Texas.

Nida, E. (1960). *Message and mission.* New York: Harper & Row.

Oberg, K. (1960). Cultural shock: Adjustment to new cultural environments. *Practical Anthropology, 7,* 177-182.

Pike, K. (1967). *Language in relation to a unified theory of the structure of human behavior.* The Hague: Mouton & Company.

Smalley, W. (1963). "Culture Shock, language shock, and the shock of self-discovery." *Practical Anthropology, 10,* 49-56.

CROSS-CULTURAL STRESS

33

T. Wayne Dye

Stress-Producing Factors
in Cultural Adjustment

I did not expect to be experiencing culture shock still after several years of living among the Bahinemo, but I was. Furthermore, I was not alone. In anthropology seminars it became apparent that quite a number of field workers continue to experience stress after many years of living in a village. From reading the early literature, we consultants had expected that the shock would be over in a couple of years; the very term "shock" implies something that is severe but brief. According to Oberg's original description (1960:177), culture shock is caused by "...the anxiety that results from losing all our familiar signs and symbols of social intercourse." These field workers, however, already knew a variety of cultural cues and used them in communication with the villagers. Yet they were still under strain. Even field workers with considerable education and preparation experienced these problems.

When Does Cultural Adjustment Occur?
In an effort to understand the source of the problem, I re-examined Oberg's article. He postulated four stages of culture shock and described the fourth as follows:

In the fourth stage your adjustment is about as complete as it can be. The visitor now accepts the customs of the country as just another way of living. You operate within the new milieu without a feeling of anxiety, although there are moments of strain. Only with the complete grasp of all the cues of social intercourse will this strain disappear. For a long time the individual will understand what the national is saying, but he is not always sure what the national means. With complete adjustment you not only accept the foods, drinks, habits and customs, but you begin to enjoy them. When you go home on leave you may even take things back with you, and if you leave for good, you generally miss the country and the people to whom you have become accustomed (Oberg, 1960:177).

This paragraph gave us the clue that we needed to understand what was happening to us and our colleagues. Though we understood the Papua New Guinean's cultures fairly well, we could never reach the place of accepting their customs for ourselves or enjoying them.

This helped me to see that two distinct kinds of stress were involved in culture shock. One was the confusion and helplessness that arose from "complete loss of cultural cues." The other was the stress which came from change to a new way of living. I prefer to call the first *culture confusion* and the second *culture stress*. Culture confusion is soon over but culture stress can continue for many years. Let us take a close look at the causes of culture stress:

Formula for Culture Stress
Several factors seem to affect directly the degree of culture stress one will experience. These factors are expressed in the following formula.

$$\frac{\text{Involvement} \times \text{Value Difference} \times \text{Frustration} \times \text{Temperament Difference} \times \text{Unknown Factors}}{\text{Acceptance} \times \text{Communication} \times \text{Emotional Security} \times \text{Inner Spiritual Resources}} = \text{Amount of Culture Stress}$$

Increasing the value of a factor above the line will increase the stress. Increasing a factor below the line will reduce the stress. No numerical values can be assigned, however, so the "formula" should not be interpreted in a true mathematical sense. The relative importance of these factors varies with the individual.

Factors Which Increase Stress

1. *Involvement*

Involvement is here defined as psychological presence in a cross-cultural situation. It can mean any interpersonal relationship, whether learning a language or teaching by discussion or trying to help materially, or working with nationals in business or research. Not only anthropologists, linguists and missionaries, but expatriates public health workers, agricultural extension agents, school teachers, magistrates trying to apply national law in a local culture, and businessmen employing many local workers, can all be extensively involved with nationals. Such involvement with one's hosts in their own cultural environment leads to a proportional amount of culture stress.

Because involvement with a foreign community increases stress, people instinctively avoid it. A person beginning work in a foreign culture may recognize the importance of involvement in bringing beneficial change and may have every intention of interacting with his hosts as much as possible. But as stress builds up, he feels forced to withdraw enough to be able to function. Usually his unconscious defense mechanisms provide good "reasons" for limiting his interaction with nationals. I believe this is the principal cause for "missionary ghettoes" (Taber, 1971:193), and for the rationalizations which keep ethnic groups separate from each other all over the world.

But for the field worker, involvement is absolutely necessary for effective communication and for constructively influencing change. It cannot simply be avoided without serious loss of effectiveness. When one is already living in an alien environment and committed to learning or teaching, or helping in some way, then keeping away from people can be worse than mixing with them. In spite of the relationship between involvement and stress, the best advice for this situation is to "get involved," to get out and get to know people. Purposeful interaction with people can minimize one's frustration by helping one meet goals; it can aid communication and acceptance. As a consequence, such involvement actually operates to decrease the net stress.

2. *Value Difference*

The greater the *difference* in *values* between one's home culture and the host culture, the greater the stress. For missionaries it is not the central Christian values which cause the most difficulty, but cultural values such as cleanliness, sense of responsibility, and use of time. For example, the Bahinemo viewpoint on caring for dogs was a source of resentment to me for years. They will not kill any dogs because of their belief in a dog's afterlife. As a result, the dogs multiply until there are more than can be fed in their subsistence economy. Only puppies and good hunting dogs are fed. The others are kept away from the family's food by frequent kicking and clubbing. Some dogs slowly starve. I hold an opposite value: a dog should either be fed and cared for or put out of its misery.

Other values that are often in conflict between Westerners and Papua New Guineans include disciplining of children, patterns of giving, when to ask for things, clan centeredness, and how much to do for the sick. These value conflicts seem to be particular aspects of cultural differences which keep us from ever completely accepting "...the customs of the country as just another way of living" (Oberg, 1960:179).

Frequently, cultures which are similar in outward form have very different values. Individuals will plunge into the outwardly similar culture expecting the values also to be the same, but they are not. I believe this may explain Guthrie's observations (as cited by Brewster, 1972:41), that Americans suffer more culture stress in the Philippines than in Thailand. I propose that the crucial factors here are value difference and involvement, not the superficial similarity. Noticing cultural similarities because of Westernization in the Philippines, Americans are likely to interact much more with the local people than would Americans in Thailand, who naturally expect to stay in separate housing, eat different foods, and use go-betweens. A more detailed look at the actual conflicting values in the Philippine cross-cultural situation would clarify the reasons for this unexpected stress.

In Papua New Guinea, Westerners from many countries work together in a common effort. In their way of life they seem to be alike; but different values, particularly in use of money, child rearing, housekeeping, and hospitality, cause unexpected stress. For instance, most Australians highly value carefulness with money. Good use of resources requires that time be taken to find and use the least expensive way in each situation. Convenience foods, ready-made women's clothing, and automatic transmissions on cars are examples of items which are considered "wasteful" and do not sell well, even to people who "can afford" them. Because purchases on credit waste interest money and encourage spending beyond one's means, they are voided, even when the consequent delay in purchasing results in more time spent maintaining wornout equipment or doing without.

In comparison, Americans generally are extremely casual about money. If one "can afford" a comfort or convenience, he should have it. To them the commodity to be guarded is time. Good use of resources requires spending money whenever needed to save "valuable time." It seems petty to use time to keep track of small expenditures and shortsighted not to "invest" in extra equipment to save time.

The difference is a matter of degree and neither group seems consciously aware of the value differences. As a result, both nationalities have frequent cause for making allowances for the other's "poor stewardship" (missionaries) or "lack of business sense" (others).

There is evidence that adjustment is more difficult for a value which is held strongly in one's own culture but held weakly in the host culture. Spradley and Phillips (1972:526) found that a sample of 83 American Peace Corps veterans considered adjustment in the areas of punctuality, personal cleanliness, and privacy to be much more stressful than adjustments to differences in family closeness and parental obligations to children. A sample of Chinese students in America gave the opposite ranking. In American culture punctuality, personal cleanliness and privacy are strongly-held values. Chinese see family closeness and parental obligations to children as much more important. "...it would appear that difficulties in cultural readjustment often arise from the feeling that individuals in the new culture are violating norms [values] learned in one's native land."

3. *Frustration*

A great deal of *frustration* arises from dealing with the people of the new culture over and above the actual process of adapting to their culture. Life in a village can be very trying for an outsider. He arrives with various goals in mind, such as language learning, academic research, literacy, evangelism, improved hygiene, economic development, and Bible translation. But he soon finds that interruptions are normal and misunderstandings frequent. Cultural differences, the demands of the people, and the lack of the usual amenities cause a thousand little frustrating hindrances to his work. His goals for his hosts and their own goals may be utterly different. The process of discovering the underlying value differences by trial and error brings frequent conflict and frustration.

Besides being a basic component of culture stress, all of this frustration builds negative attitudes toward the new culture, and increases inner resistance to acculturation. This uncomfortable situations sets into motion the mind's automatic censoring system which attempts to shield the conscious mind from unpleasant thoughts or actions through fairly predictable defense mechanisms or reactions.

4. *Temperament Differences*

Individual *differences* in *temperament* and personality cause each individual to be affected differently by the same cross-cultural situation. In general, the more differences there are between the field workers's own temperament and the "modal personality" (Honigmann, 1967:118-122) of the host community, the more difficult adjustment will be. For instance, shy, reserved people find it hard to adjust to the boisterous and affectionate New Guinea Highlanders. Decisive government officers are often frustrated by the indirectness and traditional orientation of many peasant peoples.

In a few months' visit, people who thrive on variety adjust to a new culture better than those who depend on regular habits and customs for their emotional stability. But the long term situation may be quite the opposite. One American couple found the "dull gray sameness" of village life, where nothing new or different seemed to happen, to be the most difficult adjustment of all.

Factors Which Decrease Stress

1. *Acceptance*

Acceptance of the host culture as a valid way of life decreases stress. Conversely, if a missionary cannot see how the host culture can become a valid vehicle for Christianity, he cannot adjust to it.

Acceptance has both an intellectual and a non-intellectual, component. The intellectual component is the extent to which one accepts other customs and values as being equally "right" as one's own, and how much one understands the host culture. This understanding can be taught (Brewster, 1972:31). The non-intellectual component is a product of moral and value training in childhood and individual character. This is much more difficult to change.

It is easier intellectually to consider a custom to be valid for others than to become so convinced of its worth that one can live comfortably with those who follow it. It is still more difficult to make a formerly repugnant custom one's own.

In rural Papua New Guinea a measure of accommodation is all that most Westerners aim for. They never really come to prefer local customs for themselves. For this reason acceptance is much more difficult when one's children live in the village. A mother may be able to accommodate herself to a new culture, but when she sees her children genuinely adapting to it, she feels threatened. She fears they will lose their own cultural heritage, and that they will not fit into their home country after growing up in the village. One linguist and his wife forbade their children to learn any more words of the new language that they were picking up so readily.

In this cross-cultural environment a mother is torn between two natural desires. She wants to have her children with her in the village, but that means they will absorb much of the new culture. She wants them to grow up in her own Western culture and fit into it as adults, but that often necessitates their living away from her in a European enclave or in the homeland.

2. Communication

Communication reduces stress in several ways. Most people inherently need to communicate and interact with others. Loneliness and a sense of isolation from one's own kind is very difficult. Many people, in talking about culture stress, have focused on the difficulty of isolation. But further questioning nearly always shows that they are not isolated from all people. Usually they are in daily contact with dozens of people. They are isolated from others with whom they can relax and be themselves, that is, from people with whom they share common language, viewpoints, and interests that allow them to really communicate.

One expatriate in Papua New Guinea said to a visitor, "You are most welcome, as you are the first human being I've talked to in months." At that time he was living within a mile of 10 other Westerners and taught dozens of individuals each day in school. But none had exactly the same culture and religious background.

A Westerner living in rural parts of an underdeveloped country often lives on an isolated government or mission station rather than within a local community, partly so that he can maintain his own cultural heritage. Learning the local language may seem too difficult and time consuming, and the local culture may offend him. As a result he cannot really communicate with anyone and the sense of isolation is almost unbearable.

At one small government station, a day's travel from the nearest other expatriates, at least five people have had to leave in the last decade because of aberrant emotional behavior. Many others showed signs of stress after their term of service. The stress of isolation is so severe that the government allows its officers only six months non-renewable tours of duty there. Hundreds of nationals live near this post but the cross-cultural situation is such that communication is minimal.

Communication also builds mutual understanding with one's hosts and so aids acceptance and minimizes frustration, anxiety and resentment.

Communication also helps to bring value differences into conscious focus so that one can adjust one's behavior to cope. When one of my friends in the village capsized my motor canoe after not following instructions, I insisted that he pay for someone else's axe lost in the accident. Only after the village leader complained to me of my unfair attitude did I learn that in Bahinemo culture borrowed items are used at the lender's risk, not the borrower's. Now, what used to be seen as irresponsibility can be recognized as a different rule for behavior, and I have adjusted my own behavior accordingly.

3. *Emotional Security*

Emotional security is an important factor because acculturation inherently involves a change in one's personality. Our culture is the part of ourselves that we hang on to most strongly. When we change our customs we are changing part of our very selves. While one's conscious mind is keeping to the task of learning the new culture, the inner self that has been shaped by all our previous childhood experiences is resisting acculturation.

Dr. Kenneth Pike suggests that learning a language can also threaten the self:

Our language is a system of cast iron units, patterns, rules. So precisely is the language of, say, Timbuktu. The clash between them draws psychological sparks when I try to shift from one set of whirling gears to another...It hurts (Pike, 1967:109).

Because acculturation often appears as an attack on the self, it will cause more stress on those with inferiority feelings or who are unsure of themselves. For them, change becomes a greater threat to the self. For this reason, the kind of acculturative changes which damages one's self-image are more difficult to make than those which are neutral.

For example, it has long been recognized that culture shock often affects Western wives more than their husbands (Oberg, 1960:180). A man's self-image is largely derived from his success in his occupation. His surroundings do not affect his psychological well-being very much. A wife's principal work is the maintenance of a home, making it a worthwhile place to be. The kind of food she serves, the standard of cleanliness, and the general quality of the home are what affect her image of herself. Because her own domestic standards are difficult to maintain in a cross-cultural situation, a woman is often unable to do her work effectively enough to feel successful. Consequently, difficult living conditions are not only uncomfortable, but they attack her sense of self-esteem.

In contrast, difficult living conditions are not as often a threat to her husband. Adjusting to the host culture can ultimately produce satisfaction for him because it helps his work. But if the wife becomes like the local people, she is thereby failing to maintain the standard trained into her by her home country.

On the other hand, a missionary wife's personal goals may enable her to have more "success" in the long run than her husband. Because maintaining the home and caring for and sometimes educating the child take so much time, she may limit herself to such additional tasks as sewing classes, dispensary or local public health programs, and small scale literacy instruction. These are much more likely to be accomplished successfully than her husband's goals of making converts, developing an indigenous church, or training effective Christian leaders, which are more subject to factors outside his control.

4. *Inner Spiritual Resources*

One's *inner spiritual resources*, including the power of Christ and His Spirit, constitute an important factor in reducing stress (II Peter 1:3,4, Philem. 4:13). But, however available these are by faith, they don't really help until the benefits and power of these resources become a reality in the life of that individual. This may require spiritual renewal.

It is recognized that this analysis is tentative. There may be *unknown factors* that have not been mentioned that could be most important of all in producing or reducing culture stress.

Other Stresses Add to Culture Stress

There are other kinds of stress present in a village situation which add to the stress of acculturation. Oberg (1960:179) mentioned some of these. The most important in the first year or so is *culture confusion*, the disorientation from loss of cultural cues mentioned above. Adjustments to tropical heat, new health hazards and danger from animals are stressful, especially to parents of small children. Such things as using pressure lamps instead of unlimited electric lighting, having woven or mud walls instead of painted ones, shortages of water, and the presence of cockroaches, scorpions, rats or snakes in the house can cause stress. New roles, loneliness, a new work load and new responsibilities, problems in travel, and supply difficulties are all stressful.

Children's health is the most frequently expressed fear of a Western mother. Child molesting is another great fear.

Single women linguists in an isolated village find role conflicts a special problem. In the first place, they must be very self-reliant, often doing tasks such as plumbing, carpentry, and generator repairs that would be a man's job in the home country. Women liberationists might like this, but most women are not prepared for it.

Much more serious is the conflict between the requirements of their work and the role of a woman in village cultures. In Papua New Guinea, women are expected to keep busy gardening and raising pigs and are under the authority of their brothers or husbands. They do not teach men, supervise their work, talk as equals with community leaders, or know religious secrets. Only bad girls remain single and talk frequently with men. But the linguist's work requires them to teach literacy to men, to do desk work instead of gardening, and to be somewhat independent of community leaders. The language helpers they employ usually must be men, for women are too busy with gardening for consistent employment and too low in prestige to introduce translated Scripture effectively.

The only solution seems to be to avoid fitting completely into a woman's role in the host culture. Instead, a woman must establish a new role which, in terms of local role expectations, is neutral or even somewhat masculine. This facilitates the work, but may result in internal conflicts in the single woman.

Added to the cultural and environmental stresses might be any of the normal life stresses which are experienced by people anywhere, such as emotional problems from childhood frustrations, marriage, problem children, and living and working with colleagues from different backgrounds and with different personalities. It has been demonstrated that any change, even a beneficial one, causes its measure of stress (Time, March 1, 1971:43).

Since the emotional loading of culture stress is essentially no different from any other kind of stress, all of these add together to produce the resulting load on the individual. A formula for this might be:

$$\begin{array}{ccccc} \text{Culture} & + & \text{Culture} & + & \text{Other} & = & \text{Total} \\ \text{Stress} & & \text{Confusion} & & \text{Stresses} & & \text{Stress} \end{array}$$

An individual can easily cope with a certain amount of stress. In fact, some psychologists hold that man needs a moderate amount of tension to work productively (Spradley and Phillips, 1972:520). But as stress increases, more and more creative energy must be used to handle it.

Most long-term workers in foreign countries have been screened by some sending organization and are able to cope with a large amount of stress. Nevertheless, culture stress remains a significant problem. Of over two hundred Westerners we have known who have lived in Papua New Guinea villages for long periods of time, about 10% have suffered reactions from stress which have seriously hindered their work and even the work of some of their co-workers. In most instances cultural stress seems to have been the main cause. These reactions included incapacitating fatigue, physical illness, emotional symptoms, and work and living habits which prevented them working with reasonable productivity. Another 15% were seriously hindered by these same symptoms, but the extent to which stress was a precipitating factor is uncertain. Another 70% seem to have experienced varying degrees of stress, but have found solutions without extensive hindrance to their work. The remaining 5% do not appear to have been affected by culture stress.

These variations underscore the fact that individual reactions to stress vary widely. Individuals vary in temperament and emotional security and in patterns of operation of psychological defense mechanisms. If one perceives difficulties as a personal threat, his reaction will be more severe than if he perceives them merely as obstacles to be overcome (Lehner and Kube, 1955:102, 104).

When stress overloads the individual's psychological defense system, he can go into a state of emotional shock or even breakdown. (This process is explained in S. Dye, 1974.) The state of emotional shock resulting from culture stress could logically be called "culture shock," except that "culture shock" is widely used as a cover term for all of "the difficulties and frustrations of living in a foreign culture" (Spradley and Phillips, 1972:520). Confusion between these two senses of the term is one reason that very few people ever admit to experiencing culture shock.

Ways to Decrease Culture Stress

The following suggestions, based on factors in the formula, are not necessarily new, but provide ways for an individual to decrease stress in a contact situation.

1. *Recognize the Culture Stress*

Recognize that culture stress is inevitable in cross-cultural contact. Everyone experiences it to some degree depending upon the intensity of the contact. When stress occurs, it must be recognized for what it is--ordinary stress. If one's father just died, his wife is in the hospital, and he is left with the four children, and on that day he has a minor collision, he should not be surprised at being a bit irritable and overly tired and unable to work at full efficiency. Under these conditions one has been taught to say, "That's understandable. I'm under stress. I'll have to make allowances for myself for a while." All his friends recognize his situation and make allowances for him, too.

But when one is suffering from culture stress, he may simply push on as if nothing happened, leaving his mind's censoring system to make all the adjustments. The consequence is a psychological chain reaction which eventually results in culture fatigue, illness, or emotional symptoms. Most of this chain reaction can be avoided by conscious recognition of the fact that one is facing stress.

To look for stress one might ask himself questions like these: Have a lot of irritating things happened lately? Have the local people been doing unusualy inexplicable things? Does the work load seem mountainous? Have I become indignant more frequently? Are there more problems than usual? Have certain colleagues become especially unpleasant or unfair? Would a vacation really be nice, though out of the question with my work load? Do I seem nervous? Is it unusually hard to sleep? Have headaches or backaches or indigestion been more frequent? Each person must recognize his or her own characteristic stress symptoms and look for the cause.

This is usually more difficult for men in Western culture than for women. A man is trained to ignore difficulties and never to complain about stress, even to himself. It is acceptable for a woman to admit discomfort and difficulty, so women are more often aware of stress and can do something about it. Men suffer also, but bottle it up to react in more indirect ways.

2. *Escape*

Since involvement is a key factor in culture stress, temporary escape is an effective remedy. One can escape from an alien culture and a difficult living situation at the same time. Temporary escape in light reading, music, or sports is not a new idea. We and our colleagues have often proven its effectiveness.

During our first two years in a village, my wife and I never seemed to complete enough work during a week to "justify" taking time off on Saturdays. The work was burdensome and progress was poor. Finally we decided to take hikes in the forest every Saturday "for the children's sake," even though our week's work was not complete. We soon found that significantly more work was getting done in five days than we had been doing in six.

More complete escape is also important. One should be disciplined to take vacations and make them as much a relaxing escape as possible. Time and money spent on getting completely away from our normal surroundings, or even from the host culture, and in doing something really enjoyable is actually a far-sighted investment in the work.

Many people feel guilty about rest times, but a pattern of life that includes daily, weekly, and annual relaxation usually results in diminished stress and, therefore, much greater effectiveness during work periods. This is particularly true with missionaries for whom success is more a result of love and joy manifested to one's neighbors than it is to getting a certain amount of work done.

3. *Decrease Frustration*

The frustration factor can be decreased by increasing one's sense of accomplishment. The most effective way to do this is to set realistic goals that can be achieved. Missionaries and academic researchers in particular frequently come to the field with great ideals and ambitious goals. Goals must be based upon the real situation or the continuous frustration of these unattainable goals will greatly increase the emotional conflict. Since success will decrease stress, one should divide the work into short-term (weekly and monthly) goals that are realistic and can be achieved, as well as keeping reasonable yearly goals and flexible long-term goals. Accomplishing these goals will increase the satisfaction in the work and decrease the sense of frustration and failure.

When one organization began encouraging its translators to count Bible verses completed instead of books, many of them were much encouraged. A printed chart was distributed which showed exactly how many verses are in each New Testament book and that book's percentage of the whole. Formerly, only a few people took the trouble to measure their progress toward a translated New Testament. Now everyone's progress is measurable, realistic goals can be set and achieved, and the New Testament no longer seems like a lifetime job.

One must also be aware of how often the "interruptions" are more important to long-term goals than "the work." This is often the case when a teacher is approached by a student while preparing a lecture, or when a government officer is visited by a village leader, or when an agriculturalist is interrupted to explain about a crop which he is not planning to introduce. Missionaries especially need to be sensitive to the opportunities presented by such "interruptions."

4. Build Acceptance

One must recognize that most of his own cultural values are not absolute. A missionary must, in addition, carefully identify which of his long-held "Christian" values are really just values of his own culture; as a Christian, he can only justify holding tightly to those values that are specifically commanded in the Bible. Since the tremendous variety of peoples and cultures around the world are all equally a part of God's creation, one must learn to accept and appreciate another people's set of values as valid for their lives, just as my American values are largely valid for my life in the United States. Learning as much as possible about the host culture builds understanding and appreciation of the reasons for their customs. Reading about many other cultures in books or magazines can help condition one to accept the specific culture where one is a guest.

5. Improve Communication

Larson and Smalley have shown (1971:43) how the ability to communicate meaningfully with one's hosts decreases stress. For this reason, it may be less stressful in the long run to plunge in and learn the language, even though language learning itself causes stress. In a recent survey (Spradley and Phillips, 1972:524), 83 Peace Corps veterans rated language difference as almost twice as serious as any other cause of culture stress.

Language learning is only a part of communication, however. As is true in one's own culture, one can know the language perfectly, but be unable to communicate genuinely with others. This is related to attitudes of respect and eagerness to listen to others. It requires learning the host culture's system of gestures and facial expressions, their rules of conduct and etiquette, and what all kinds of life experiences mean to them (Hesselgrave, 1972:9).

6. *Strengthen Emotional Security*

Emotional security requires self-acceptance and self-forgiveness. But both of these must begin with self-awareness, because one's unconscious mind is constantly reacting to one's limitations and past failures (Smalley, 1963:55). Genuine self-acceptance recognizes and finds a way to live with these limitations. Self-forgiveness deliberately quits accusing or punishing oneself for these failures. For Christians this can be achieved by a deep awareness of God's forgiveness. Participating in sharing groups with these purposes and confession have both helped many people become emotionally secure.

One can also be strengthened by encouragement and other supportive measures from one's colleagues. Receiving understanding and love are especially valuable when one's inner self seems to be under attack, as it does during adjustment to a new culture.

Several excellent books on this topic have appeared recently. I found *I'm O.K. You're O.K.* (Harris, 1967) and *The Art of Understanding Yourself* (Osborne, 1967) especially helpful.

For many anthropologists the process of learning the new culture builds up their self-confidence, instead of threatening their emotional security. The same is true of linguists who make good progress in learning and analyzing the language of the host culture. This seems to happen unconsciously. For anthropologists this is a result not only of their achieving specific research goals, but also of their growth in "objectivity" and cross-cultural understanding.

But one can do this consciously by realizing that he is really a kind of bi-cultural or multi-cultural person, capable of operating within more than one cultural milieu and playing more than one role. When in the home country he is able to live as its citizens live. When in a village of the host culture, he can live like the people in that village and play the appropriate role while in that environment. When among colleagues in the city or on a mission compound, he can change roles again and live like those in that community.

For example, when in the village, my wife is accepted as a equal with the women. She dresses similarly to them and is called by the appropriate name, though she is respected for her teaching and her Western medical knowledge. They relate to her in this role. But in the European town where our children attend school, she is a mother and refers all medical problems to the medical doctor. She is one of the Bible translators. All her daily routines, living style and relationships are different. When in the home country on furlough, she has yet another role *vis-a-vis* our home constituency. Each of these roles is a part of her personality, but not one of them is the total.

You may be a missionary, a parent, a husband, a teacher and an employer. You do not have a split personality. You can shift from one role to another without difficulty because each is a part of you.

As acculturation is faced in these ways, one can become such a versatile person that he can adjust to any of the two or more cultures he has learned to live in. So the sum of his personality is more than any one of these alone. Instead of becoming a less proper American (or Englishman or whatever), he is actually becoming a kind of world citizen, a more capable human being. If he is a missionary, he can say, "So I become all things to all men, that I may save some by any means possible" (I Cor. 9:22 TEV).

References

Brewster, E. (1972). Involvement as a means of second culture learning. *Practical Anthropology, 19*, 27-44.

Dye, S. (1974). Decreasing fatigue and illness in field-work. *Missiology, 2*, 79-109.

Harris, T. (1967). *I'm O.K. You're O.K.* New York: Harper & Row.

Hesselgrave, D. (1972). Dimensions of cross-cultural community. *Practical Anthropology, 19*, 1-12.

Honigmann, J. (1967). *Personality in culture.* New York: Harper & Row Publishers.

Larson, D. & Smalley, W. (1972). *Becoming bilingual: A guide to language learning.* Ann Arbor: Cushing-Malloy, Inc.

Lehner, G. & Kube, E. (1955). *The dynamics of personal adjustment.* Englewood Cliffs: Prentice-Hall.

Oberg, K. (1960). Cultural shock: Adjustment to new cultural environments. *Practical Anthropology, 7*, 177-182.

Osborne, K. (1967). *The art of understanding yourself.* Grand Rapids: Zondervan.

Pike, K. (1967). *Stir, change, create.* Grand Rapids: Eerdmans.

Smalley, W. (1963). Culture shock, language shock, and the shock of self-discovery. *Practical Anthropology, 10,* 49-56.

Spradley, J. & Phillips, M. (1972). Culture and stress: A quantitative analysis. *American Anthropologist, 74,* 518-529.

Taber, C. (1971). The missionary ghetto. *Practical Anthropology, 18,* 193-196.

34

Sally Folger Dye

Decreasing Fatigue and Illness in Field-Work

Fatigue and illness often hinder the productive field-work of missionaries, linguists, anthropologists, government workers and others who attempt to live in foreign cultures. Many well-trained workers are forced to leave their fields before achieving their goals. They often feel a deep sense of frustration and a vague sense of guilt for years afterwards. This article attempts to bring research and experience together to create a fresh understanding of common human reactions in a cross-cultural environment. It then suggests specific ways of recognizing and controlling these reactions to prevent fatigue and physical, as well as emotional, illness.

Many field organizations today have found that actually living among indigenous peoples in their own setting is the most effective and, in the long run, the most satisfying way of communicating any message: educational, spiritual, or political. But a clash of culture values and ways of living occurs whenever people from two cultures attempt to live together, no matter how desirous they are of making it work. It puts strain upon the individuals involved. Field-workers must take upon themselves most of the strain of adjustment. Their goals often include a loving, helpful relationship, but they find themselves falling short of these goals in rather similar and predictable patterns. These patterns are the focus of this article.

Wayne Dye has presented the basic sources of pressure and frustration that a field-worker is likely to experience in the cross-cultural situation (1974). A person who is placed in unusually frustrating and unpredictable circumstances where his goals are not easily met, will experience anxiety, fear and hostility. These often lead to feelings of failure and inferiority if the frustration persists. But all these emotions are hard to accept and admit when one sees himself as a good person. They conflict with the image he has of what he is like. For example, a missionary nurse may see herself as lovingly devoted to helping people. She cannot readily accept or express angry thoughts toward an indigenous patient, even when he tears the fresh bandage off his deep wound and smears on a mud plaster.

The Mind's Normal Defense Against Stress

The following are unconscious adjustment mechanisms used by normal people everywhere to deal with unpleasant or unacceptable emotions and painful experiences. However, the illustrations given are of people in cross-cultural situations.

1. Through the mechanisms of *denial* one is able to ignore the existence of unpleasant circumstances or feelings. A field-worker may find himself telling jokes and stories emphasizing weaknesses and failures of nationals, but he is consciously unaware of, and quickly denies, any hostility toward them. One missionary who faced many frustrating experiences and worked long hours said, "The doctor says my illness is caused by strain, but I've never been under strain..." Most field-workers deny ever experiencing culture shock.

Denial offers temporar relief, but it removes "the opportunity to understand and conquer his problem" (Lehner & Kube, 1955:114).

2. By conscious *suppression*, most people try to put objectionable thoughts and memories of unpleasant experiences out of their minds. "But nothing is ever put out of mind. Unacceptable feelings about which we feel guilty are simply rejected and pushed down deep into the unconscious mind..." (Osborne, 1967:86). The unconscious process is called *repression*. There these emotions interfere with adjustment, because even after the original incident has been "forgotten", the emotions associated with it remain stored until the energy and guilt related to them can be released in more acceptable ways.

3. In *reaction-formation* one's actions are the opposite to one's repressed feelings. For instance, when a person feels inferior among people of another culture, he may react by being domineering and proud.

A foreigner who has repressed hostile feelings toward his hosts in a country may speak to them with excessive sweetness. He may say emphatically, "My people are wonderful. I love them and enjoy living among them." But the hosts generally sense this hidden hostility through actions and expressions of which the foreigner is unaware. Some missionaries have been told years later, "You didn't want us in your house," or even, "You were always angry with us." The missionary had never been aware of his feelings.

4. Through the *displacement* mechanism, the tension from a repressed emotion can be discharged through an unrelated, trivial act. "Feelings can be attached to things, groups, parts of the body, activities and many other objects in our environment" (Brown & Fowler, 1955:42). A linguist found himself kicking toads on the path. Sometimes a campaign against pigs, polygamy or betel nut displaces hostility originally felt toward the nationals themselves. Oberg speaks of concern over germs expressed in "excessive washing of hands; excessive concern over drinking water, food, dishes and bedding" (1960:178).

Such substitutions permit the individual to maintain satsifactory relationships with his fellows, and even more important, to preserve a good opinion of himself. Displacement provides an outlet for emotion and minimizes the possibility of outward conflict. But it creates substitute areas of conflict and maladjustment within, thereby making discovery and resolution of the real problem even more difficult (Lehner & Kube, 1955:114).

5. Through the *projection* mechanism an individual attributes to others the qualities and emotions that he cannot accept in himself.

The person who is quick to condemn and find fault is usually projecting. The inordinately suspicious individual is really telling us of his own inner struggle with the thing he suspects in others (Osborne, 1967:124).

For example, a Bible translator who repressed urges to quit was always suspecting others of this intention.

Smalley says that the rejection frequently observed in culture shock is a form of projection. One may project unacceptable "hostility arising out of culture shock against the symbols of authority over him" (1963:51-52). He may feel that his mission board or field executive committee are hostile to him, when in fact the hostility is his own, arising from the frustrations in his work. Another may project his hostility onto the host country and its people with endless complaining that they are unfair to him.

Parents frequently but unintentionally project their own emotions upon one or more of their children, imagining the child as disobedient or failing, making it difficult for them to love and support him as they would like. This puts the child under a strain too, and hinders him from realizing his potential, physically or emotionally. It also creates anguish for everyone else involved, and may even force the parents away from pursuing their family goals later on.

After a person has transferred unacceptable or undesirable emotions or attitudes to another person or group, he is free to launch an attack, to direct suspicion toward the other person or group by innuendo, gossip, or slander (Lehner & Kube, 1955:123, 124).

Many field-workers find themselves attacking their field organization in this way after leaving the field.

6. Nearly every reaction must be supported by a logical-sounding reason called *rationalization*. These plausible and acceptable reasons come to mind frequently when an individual's self-esteem is disturbed or threatened. They originate in a person's unconscious and may wholly or partially true, but not his real motivations. These logical "reasons" help him to avoid acknowledging his real reasons which are unacceptable to him.

The "folklore" of overseas workers is replete with "reasons" to avoid involvement with their hosts. "If you do anything for them, they'll take advantage of you." "We wouldn't want to make 'rice Christians'." "They don't want to eat with us." "They prefer their tiny quarters in the back yard." That this is rationalization becomes obvious when some foreigner *does* eat their food, invite them to dinner as equals, or shows genuine respect. They talk about it to everyone. And once the field-worker establishes a "family" relationship, they seldom take advantage of him.

"Rationalization is important psychologically because it helps us to maintain our self-respect and self-confidence..." and provides "protection against anxiety and failure." But rational reasons can be harmful. "If we refuse to accept responsibility for our failures, we shall never be able to overcome them...Rationalizations may in time shade into delusions" (Lehner & Kube, 1955:119).

7. One may unconsciously seek *compensation* for a sense of failure when work goals are not easily fulfilled. Since language learning and other research projects are often tedious, with many kinds of obstacles that hinder the fulfillment of goals, one may find himself devoting more and more of his time to a hobby which he considers necessary and useful, and which provides him with the sense of success which he needs. But such a hobby saps creative energies that are needed to accomplish the main goals.

One sometimes finds oneself competing with colleagues in order to compensate for feelings of failure.

A person who is adapting to another culture may try to compensate for the loss of his cultural self by clinging more tenaciously to parts of his own culture. Constructing a house like the ones at home, and an elaborate celebration of the home country's holidays are examples of this kind of compensation.

8. The *withdrawal* mechanism often shows itself in excessive reading, sleeping, listening to music or daydreaming. Too much time spent at the desk for study or letter writing, housework, staying in the house, and unnecessarily frequent trips for supplies are all ways of avoiding the more unpleasant involvement of language learning or personal interaction. All these activities are healthy when consciously planned in moderation, but they can become hindrances when controlled by the unconscious mechanism. One's hosts often recognize that these are merely ways to avoid being with them.

A colleague told me that when he first began to live in the village, a bookcase divided the guest area from the personal living area. "You know," he said, "I realize now that my way of escaping was to sit down with a book and become completely absorbed, forgetting the people who were there to talk with me."

Another man picked up a book whenever he sat down to do his field-work. Justifying himself by the need to keep informed, he read for long periods, sometimes hours, before he was aware that the time had passed. When he tried to stop the reading habit, he found it took years to overcome the compulsion.

Alcohol and tranquilizers are commonly used for escape by those who accept these means.

Prolonged strain may result in an intense compulsion to get away. Then one's unconscious mind searches for a rational reason to justify this withdrawal to himself, his colleagues, and his sponsoring agency. This kind of reaction becomes a particular problem for someone attempting to complete a long-term project, such as a thesis or the translation of the New Testament. As soon as a convincing reason is found, he may exit as quickly as acceptable, saying, "I know this is God's will for me because..." (Lehner & Kube, 1955:118).

A growing desire to go home--which is contrary to the original goals--for further specialized training, to care for parents, for a child's sake, or even prolonged illness can at times be justification for getting away from an intensely stressful situation.

9. Through the *insulation* mechanism, one avoids activities where interaction with nationals is necessary. People in cross-cultural situations often insulate themselves from their hosts by joining enclaves of like-minded people, as in clubs or on missionary compounds. But even field-workers actually living in a village may build an insulating wall around themselves. One way to build a wall is to teach some local people to be more like Westerners. These more "cultured" individuals may then act as go-betweens serving as a buffer for the field-worker.

The frequent imposition of certain Western customs upon national churches can originate as insulation for the missionary. He insists that the new parishioners be "democratic", and they follow western time schedules, worship styles and music systems. He can give many reasons why they should do it his way. Thus, he unconsciously insulates himself from their jarring indigenous patterns.

The insulation mechanism can prevent a field-worker "from interacting with others or anything more than a superficial level (Brown-Fowler, 1955:49), thus preventing him from communicating his real message and from knowing whether or not that message was understood.

10. In the *regression* reaction, past situations become more important, even glorified. Preoccupation with the home country, dependence on fellow expatriates, and childish behavior (Oberg, 1960:177), give temporary relief but later increase the guilt and sense of failure.

One anthropologist found living in a New Guinea village extremely painful. She constantly consulted the nearby linguists for help and reassurance. She went into tantrums, crying to get what she wanted from the villagers. Her previous life in a ghetto of a large American city began to seem wonderful to her. Anxiety and guilt over her behavior led her to fear she was going to "break".

Overloading the Mind's Defense System

A majority of people in everyday situations will use these defense mechanisms and make the adjustments necessary without overloading their automatic defense systems. But in a stress-filled environment, such as a cross-cultural living situation where one may be constantly frustrated in achieving his goal, or where the environment may become more and more objectionable or unpredictable for long periods of time, adjustment is difficult. His mind begins to overuse the defense mechanisms in order to avoid the threatening situation and to preserve an acceptable image of himself.

The way defense mechanisms become overused can be seen in the following example: A young mother working with her husband among isolated Papua New Guineans found living in a village and learning an unwritten language extremely frustrating. When she found language learning difficult, she postponed it and instead worked long hours on a linguistic paper that would simplify initial phonemic analysis (compensation). When the paper was not accepted and her husband's language skill exceeded hers, she became unable to work on language learning at all. Instead, she took up several hobbies and occupied herself with the children and elaborate cooking (compensation). As frustration built up in the cross-cultural situation, she aggressively killed the many insects, took up the villagers' habit of kicking the village dogs, and yelled at the children, building up conflicts with one child in particular (displacement). She began criticizing the training program, her colleagues, and her husband, giving elaborate reasons for her complaints (displacement, projection, rationalization). After the birth of her fourth child, she sought frequent periods of refuge in the bedroom to read and sleep for long periods (withdrawal, regression). She began to suffer more frequent headaches and backpain, depression and crying spells (tension release and physical illness). Fatigue set in for increasing periods (fatigue). Her anxiety increased with feelings of guilt and fears of rejection from childhood (emotional conflict, guilt). She had thoughts of suicide, feared insanity, felt a failure, and wanted to go home. After several years, most of her activities centered around avoiding excessive anxiety. Only a strong desire to accomplish her goal, and her husband's commitment, kept them from leaving the field-work. Eventually, her husband was able to assist her in sorting out many of these conflicts. She sought spiritual renewal and began to practice forgiveness. Relief came, and within a year most of the symptoms disappeared. She could again work productively to learn the language, though it took several years to resolve and prevent ensuing conflicts. She began to enjoy her work, her family and the villagers.

Different individuals react to overload in different ways. Individual training, temperament, physical make-up and past experiences will determine the defense mechanisms an individual will use, what kind of tension-releasing reactions he will experience, and whether or not his reactions to moderate overload will be predominately physical in nature or predominately emotional.

The following kinds of reactions result from overuse of the defense mechanisms.

1. *Emotional Conflict*

Rationalizations come to mind to justify denial, insulation, compensation, regression and withdrawal reactions. Reaction-formation, projection, and displacement occur to release repressed emotions. Then repression, denial, insulation, withdrawal, projection, rationalization, etc., occur again to cover emotions related to the previous reactions.

One mechanism works to cover another, continuing on until inner conflicts result. The real emotions that caused the conflicting unconsciousness transactions are stored away in the brain, safely hidden from consciousness by the tangled multiple reactions.

2. *Changed Goals*

A person who is over using the defense mechanisms often finds himself doing things he never wanted to do. If he takes time to compare his past and present goals, he realizes they have changed. He may no longer be in a good position to accomplish his real goals.

One translator believes that identification with the people by living in the village was essential to his goal of preparing a clear translation of the Bible that people would read and follow. However, once he had visited the village, he found several good reasons why his family would be better off on a hill between several villages. But the people never really accepted him; they cheated him and stole from him. They took no interest in his literacy classes or Bible reading. After a while, he began to pursue practical hobbies as compensation. As these took more time, he found little creative energy left for his original goal. After years of deep frustration, he built a new house in the village. Immediately, he was accepted into the clan; the people began to cooperate and his hobbies were taken up as community development projects.

Some people find out too late that defense mechanisms have driven them to quit and return to their home country. They may live the rest of their lives disappointed because they never achieved their original goal.

3. *Guilt Feelings*

In spite of all the attempts of the mind to cover up, hidden emotions produce a sense of guilt. Osborne points out that many different feelings lead to a vague sense of guilt: "shame, inferiority, feelings of rejection and worthlessness, together with thoughts, desires and impulses which we feel are 'bad'." No matter how much one tries to repress guilt...

...the inexorable inner self knows the truth. From this inner tribunal there is no escape. It demands repentance and forgiveness, or punishment; it is judging constantly....In some subtle way condemns us to mask our true selves from the gaze of others....We become persons who cannot afford to be open lest we reveal the dishonesty within (Osborne, 1967:100, 104).

This unconscious inner refusal to face up to the kind of person one really is, and the fear of revelation of this truth to others, hinders "self discovery." Attempts at introspection to find reasons for the fatigue, illness, tension or changed goals may reveal some sources of conflict. But the more severe and unacceptable the hidden emotions are to the self-image, the more intense the anxiety and pain upon its revelation.

As Smalley has pointed out (1963:55), it often comes as a painful shock when a missionary discovers that he is not as loving as he expected to be, that he is not the selfless person that the people at home feel he is. His spiritual goals become impossible to fulfill because the deceptive nature of the mechanisms hinders an open relationship to Christ--the source of spiritual power. He may find himself calling out like Paul, "I don't do the good that I want to do, instead, I do the evil that I do not want to do....What an unhappy man I am! Who will rescue me from this body that is taking me to death?" (Rom. 7:19, 24 TEV).

4. *Tension*

The energy from repressed emotions and the guilt that is related to them generates inner tension that builds up and must be released. The mind seeks to release tension in socially acceptable ways to avoid guilt and anxiety. Mechanisms like compensation, reaction-formation, displacement and projection can accomplish this. However, community service that is an unconscious cover-up for hostility or a way to compensate for inferiority feelings creates, at best, a superficial sweetness and shallow helplessness that does not form a good basis for relationships. The familiar martyr complex that can result from inner resentment projected onto others makes life unnecessarily difficult for the one who is suffering, and causes bitterness in everyone around him, especially his children. Even the harmless smashing of a tennis ball is not satisfying, when the energy arises from personal hostility toward someone and the inner self registers a sense of guilt.

Phobias or compulsions are also ways to release tension. For instance, a fear of mice or cats may be an innocuous enough front to justify a woman's screaming and releasing pent-up emotions (Lehner & Kube, 1955:146) without revealing the real emotions her mind is hiding from herself.

Some people release tension by burst of anger, crying or laughing in certain contexts. However, their minds quickly find rational reasons for these outbursts to protect themselves from experiencing more anxiety, guilt or fear. This explains how a normally calm carpenter may find himself becoming unreasonably angry when a national trainee makes a simple mistake in judgment. The pent-up energy from repression is released in what would seem to an onlooker to be an unjustified outburst.

Many expatriates gather together to discuss the inexplicable behavior of their hosts, colleagues, or leaders in a joking manner, laughing boisterously. This serves as a catharsis and releases tension. Likewise, after a long period in the village, women may find themselves crying over little things. Two mature women co-workers commented: "After a couple of years we knew we were getting over culture shock when we went one whole day without either of us crying."

Some people feel more free to express tension by emotional release as long as it is not irrational. Others are trained never to show emotion from childhood, therefore, their self-image will not tolerate emotional expression. Women accept emotional expression more readily than do men; Pentecostals accept it more than Baptists or Anglicans, black Americans more than white Americans. Thus, a white middle-class American Baptist male will find himself particularly intolerant of emotional release or emotional symptoms in any form. He may hold a great volume of tension inside, but show no signs of it to others. This inner tension will have to be released in some way. It may exert pressure on some organ system of the body causing real damage to it, or to its function.

If one cannot accept emotional expression, but senses an inner buildup of emotional tension, he may take refuge in his objectivity and fear of losing face before others. He often goes to great lengths to avoid any risk of emotional gatherings and emotional experiences such as inspirational speeches, "singspirations," evangelistic meetings, sharing groups, weddings and funerals, fearing that all the emotion might be released at one of those times.

5. *Fatigue*

Some mechanisms channel energy into substitute efforts, some direct creative energies into running away from the main goal, others waste creative energy by producing and then resolving other conflicts. Some authorities believe that most people use more than half their psychic energy just to keep repressed memories below the level of consciousness. If that psychic energy could be freed for creative living, it would change our destinies (Osborne, 1967:37). All this diffusion of psychic energy leaves little physical energy left to accomplish the main goal.

Paul Tournier says, "Fatigue is the characteristic sign of nervous prostration." He states that over-exertion is *seldom* the cause of prolonged physical fatigue (1963:101-107).

Recently, E.T. and E.S. Brewster warned new missionaries of "culture fatigue." The symptoms "linger, gnawing and sapping one's strength" (1972:40, 41). This sense of fatigue can be mild, transient, or in extreme reactions, completely incapacitating. Exhaustion itself can become the body's defense in a difficult situation. For example, a missionary took frequent trips to the town where he felt well and worked at capacity. But as soon as he drove into the village, an overwhelming fatigue settled over him for the duration of the time he ministered to the people there. He wondered if it wasn't some kind of Satanic oppression. However, when he moved to the town to work permanently, the fatigue became constant there.

A conscientious man working with his family in a very remote area became completely incapacitated by illness and overwhelming fatigue. Doctors found no physical cause. He recovered slowly at home, but each time he prepared to return to the field, all the symptoms came back.

One group doing field-work in Papua New Guinea found that, after struggling with the difficulties of cross-cultural contact, over 25% of their field-workers were unable to meet the normal work requirements of the organization because of fatigue and illness.

One couple never expressed unacceptable emotion during long periods of living among villagers. They were always loving and positive and never defended themselves nor expressed any negative emotion toward anyone for many years, even though some questioned their methods and abused them. That the hurts were felt deeply was mentioned only in private conversations with friends. Fatigue and one illness after another forced them out of their field-work. Severe physical damage resulted, requiring surgery and extensive rest.

Tournier presents some aspects of the quandary a physician is in when treating this fatigue. Since "patients demand of their physicians devices and recipes for resolving through chemistry the problems of their lives" (1964:54), it is a real temptation to simply give them the drugs they demand. Dr. Sarradon explains how physicians balance between stimulants to decrease fatigue and depressants, tranquilizers and sedatives to prevent anxiety.

The medicines we serve give us a good conscience. But having done this, to a certain degree we avoid considering the patient in his somatic and psychic totality, in his environment, his situation, his past, his hopes, and his problems of life. We deal with an illness separately in the history of the patient instead of attacking the deep, lasting causes at the base of his troubles (*ibid.* 55).

Few physicians today have time to counsel all of their patients. The patient continues to live on stimulants and sedatives while the illness "persists or breaks out in some other form because the real problem that has caused the illness is still there" (Osborne, 1967:56).

6. *Physical Illness*

Since the central nervous system controls all physical and emotional actions, these are very closely intertwined. Doctors assume that physical impairment is a more common reaction to stress than are severe emotional symptoms. Osborne has summed up their views:

Man is body, mind, and spirit, and what affects one affects all. If there are inner conflicts and tensions, anxiety and guilt at some point in his life, the individual will tend to manifest this spiritual disease by some physical symptom...(*ibid.* 47).

Physicians no longer doubt that emotions produce stress in the body.

This stress creates a chemical imbalance resulting in malfunction of glands and other organs. The body then becomes unable to provide resistance to germs which are otherwise held in check.

Since the mind tends to hand its pain, guilt, and grief over to the body by an unconscious process, we find it easier to incur physical illness than mental anguish. For one thing, we receive sympathy, which is a form of love, when we are physically ill; but the person suffering from mental anguish or depression is likely to be told to 'snap out of it' or to 'pull yourself together' (Osborne, 1967:198).

Anxiety and emotion seldom bring sympathy, but a physical problem with real symptoms is the acceptable kind of sickness in our society. One's unconscious mind is amazingly sensitive to this fact because it has been programmed into us by those around us from childhood. When one's mind, therefore, becomes desperate to relieve its anxiety, it channels the stress into the body, allowing illness to develop. Disease, in turn, relieves the anxiety, because the body is unconsciously bearing it. To a person in this situation, even having a serious disease can be more satisfactory than being well, because one's anxiety is relieved and excess tension can be attributed to the illness. Instead of criticizing him, people around him give sympathy and loving concern, helping him in many concrete ways. Everyone can see that the problem is real and not just "in his head."

Dr. McMillen gives more details on how stress results in physical illness and presents the spectrum of physical diseases that result from it.

The emotional center produces these widespread (physical) changes by means of three principal mechanisms: by changing the amount of blood flowing to an organ; by affecting the secretions of certain glands; and by changing the tension of muscles...

The influence of emotional stress on the human body can be demonstrated by a partial listing of diseases it causes or aggravates. Of course, it could not be assumed that the emotional factor is the sole cause of these diseases (McMillen, 1963:59).

He puts ulcers, diarrhea and constipation on his list of digestive disorders. High blood pressure, arteriosclerosis, coronary thrombosis, rheumatic fever and strokes are some diseases of the circulatory system that are often caused by stress. Painful menstruation, frigidity and impotency, on his list of diseases, as well as nephritis, are some of the disorders of the genito-urinary system. Among others in his list are hyperthyroidism, diabetes, obesity, hives, hay fever and asthma, backaches, rheumatoid arthritis, mononucleosis, polio, and many infections, and several kinds of dermatitis (*ibid*. 61, 62).

He does not deny that many of these diseases also have other contributing causes, such as bacteria, viruses, or chemicals. But a person who is physically and emotionally healthy can resist them, while one who is debilitated by inner conflict is susceptible.

Heredity and individual weakness, along with "successful" past illnesses, determine which organs or organ systems will bear the stress in each individual. The physical symptoms may disappear when one realizes what caused them, but then the anxiety returns unless one has come to grips with its source.

Some physicians tell me that they prefer not to suggest the truth to such patients because they are better prepared to treat physical illness than severe anxiety.

The damage done to an individual's organic system by stress is destructive and often irreparable. He may need extensive care and even surgery. In many ways a stress-originated illness is more difficult to treat than any other kind of illness. Physical illness that is not based on emotional conflicts will usually respond readily to treatment without further complications, but illness originating from stress continues on until the real source of stress is removed.

The individual with inner conflict needs more skilled medical care, more adequate psychological help, more loving support from his family and friends than one without emotional conflict. Given his particular personal history, there is nothing he could have done to change his immediate situation. Criticism and rejection only make his situation worse. Skilled medical care and unconditional love, acceptance, and support by everyone are essential for his recovery.

7. *Nervous Breakdowns*

Nervous breakdowns occur when the emotional conflict and strain exceeds the individual's tolerance in controlling his physical and emotional reactions. Chicago psychiatrist, David Busby, regularly treats furloughed missionaries, as well as pastors and other Christian workers. Dr. Busby refers to two general kinds of breakdowns: "cumulative and coincidental."

Cumulative is each factor in sequence added to another--like the proverbial straw which breaks the camel's back. You don't solve the problem by simply identifying and/or removing the last straw which triggered the breakdown. One must find and remove where possible all straws. The coincidental method is that wherein several force-factors occur in a person simultaneously (rather than consecutively) analogous to the rays of the sun coming together on one spot (Hafely, 1967:115).

The "coincidental" reaction is the one that people in a foreign country instinctively think of as "culture shock." I know of at least eight tourists who suffered this kind of reaction after a short visit to a New Guinea village. Several were hospitalized for a short time.

Most well-trained field-workers experience the cumulative type of breakdown when overload occurs. They experience varying amounts of strain from different sources, both past and present, until they reach their individual tolerance. At times they will exceed their tolerance, since it is more than they can handle; then take a rest until they can function normally again. But then, during a time of unusual strain, they will push beyond their bodies' ability to cope with the reaction and lose control of their emotions. Norbert Weiner has suggested that this breakdown is caused by an overload of the neurological channels in the brain from excessive unconscious mental activity (1966:33).

When overload occurs the individual may cry or laugh uncontrollably or begin talking inappropriately or in some other way lose touch with reality. Normally, rest and removal from the stressful situation allows the symptoms to subside. The person regains control until he pushes himself again beyond his limitations. This kind of transient stress reaction should not be confused with psychoses or other chronic mental illnesses which result from more long-term factors (Lehner & Kube, 1955:141, 142, 159).

On one isolated government station in Papua New Guinea, at least six men have been hospitalized with breakdowns in the last 8 years as a result of the contact situation.

Field-workers seldom identify this cumulative reaction as relating to the cross-cultural situation. Oberg's and Smalley's classic articles on culture shock have been read by most missionary candidates, but they do not identify their problems as like these. Attempts at differentiating culture stress from other kinds of stress are fruitless. The overload results from the accumulation of many factors: childhood trauma (Missildine, 1963:13, 19, 20, 32); adolescent frustrations, marriage strains, parental difficulties and all the emotions that have resulted from adjustment to living in the cross-cultural situation (Dye, 1974). All of the memories and the emotional energies from them remain stored up in the mind unless they are specifically erased in some way. The total stress is what is exerted on the individual. Finally, one more difficult experience becomes "the last straw."

The tendency to experience emotional reactions during normal life stresses while in the cross-cultural situation forces many field organizations to put restrictions on field-workers after marriage, childbirth, or death in the family. For instance, only an occasional woman has a nervous breakdown after childbirth. But if she is also adjusting to a new climate, a cross-cultural situation, and using fewer amenities than she is accustomed to, she may well exceed her threshold for handling emotions.

When a physician sees the patient, he has a choice of diagnosis. He could diagnose the woman as having post-partum psychoses, culture shock, inability to adjust to tropical climate, or even relate the diagnosis to some childhood frustration that she tells him about. The physician will give the patient a diagnosis he feels most helpful to the treatment. It can either be designed to help her face the source of her illness, or it can be another rationalization that helps her to rest for a while, if he feels she is not yet ready to face the real reasons.

In one group of 200 field-workers surveyed, 3% had breakdowns, but they faced their illness and within a few years all recovered, continuing in their work. On the other hand, 10% had long-term debilitating illnesses, predominantly fatigue and glandular dysfunction, which continued on for years with little improvement. Many have remained on the field, working at half productivity or less. Others have left, showing some improvement upon return to the home country, with recurring symptoms during periods of stress at home. Some suffered permanent physical damage which doctors have diagnosed as due to stress. The few who accepted emotional causation as the original source of their physical illness have been able to face their weakness and have recovered. Others, whose self-image cannot accept stress as a causal factor, continue to search for a physician who will give them a "medical reason" for their illness.

Dealing with Stress and Conflict

In the past, the best hope in dealing with emotional conflict among field-workers was in the home country. Persistent emotional or physical symptoms forced field-workers to return home earlier than they had intended simply because of hidden sources of stress in their environment. They did not know what they were fighting, so there was no hope of overcoming it. Now that we have begun to identify some major causes of emotional conflict, we can prevent its occurrence in many instances and even hope to unravel the conflicts when they have already occurred.

Prevention is always best. After emotional conflict occurs any admission of reality is difficult. It implies that one has failed in some way. Any suggestion that there is hidden resentment or a spiritual problem, or emotionally caused illness, makes one feel threatened, anxious and insecure.

If one tries to analyze his thoughts and sees anything counter to his image of himself, he is tempted to blame and even reject himself. Direct introspection is painful and generally ineffective. It can even be harmful. If anyone else implies that his motives are not right, he finds himself rejecting, criticizing and deprecating that person. Therefore, it is best to approach the problem as objectively as possible.

1. *Learn to Recognize the Signs of Strain*

Strain is inevitable in a cross-cultural situation. Everyone has to deal with it. Since the main function of the adjustment mechanisms is to conceal painful experiences from us, one can be under much strain without even knowing it. Anyone going into a stressful environment must recognize this important syndrome and try to prevent its overuse in his life.

One can detect early symptoms of stress if he is aware of the kinds of behavior to watch for in himself. He may feel more tired than normal or be unable to sleep. He may overeat or lose his appetite. He may become irritable, accident prone, or worry more than usual, lose his temper more quickly, laugh less or much more than usual, and cry more easily or never express any emotion at all. He may experience fear and anxiety more frequently and dream more than usual. He may become more talkative, rambling on, or feel his thoughts interrupted, speak hesitatingly, inappropriately, or stutter.

He may desire to be with people all the time or he may develop a fear of being with people. He may find himself complaining more about the actions of people around him, feel rejected by them and even become preoccupied with the actions of certain people against him. He may become untidy, depressed, constantly discouraged and lose his drive to work, or he may work constantly, never taking time to stop and rest or think about anything serious. He may experience more frequent headaches, back or stomach aches or pain, itching, or other functional disorders. He may suffer prolonged complications and major infections after minor colds, or even lose his normal resistance to infection and suffer from one infection after another, becoming ill most of the time.

Some individuals will experience only one or two of these symptoms. Others will experience more. When one is in a cross-cultural situation, any changes in attitudes, relationships, and/or physical changes might be an indication that the strain has become excessive and overuse of the defense mechanisms has begun.

One must learn to recognize his own characteristic responses to stress, and notice the particular times these occur. Then steps can be taken to alleviate it. Women may find they handle stress less easily at certain times in their monthly cycle.

2. *Decrease Stressful Stimuli*

When symptoms of strain occur, one must remove as many sources of strain as possible. Decreasing one's workload and responsibilities, at least temporarily, may be necessary. Leaders must learn to be sensitive to the workload of those working under them. Tournier considers leadership a significant source of pressure in modern society (1964).

McMillen gives this advice:

Diversify the stressful agents. It is important to remember that man cannot take long or continued exposure to any one stress factor....Take the proper attitude of mind....Our attitude is a most important factor in determining whether we shall suffer from exposure to life's daily stresses. Chronic brooding over sorrows and insults indicate faulty adaptation...[also] self-pity....We hold the keys and can decide whether stress is going to work for us or against us. Our attitude decides whether stress makes us 'better or bitter.'...Avoid...long and continued exposure to severe stress agents, without resting. There is a limit to the stress that any person can endure, and every physician sees men and women who pay dearly in body and mind for their excessive application to work without proper rest periods. Many people could be alive today if they had heeded the admonition of Jesus to His laboring disciples: "Come ye apart into a desert place, and rest awhile" (1963:107-111).

Conscious withdrawal can work for one when used at the right times in regulated amounts before the desire for unconscious escape becomes too insistent. One should plan short daily and weekly breaks while in a cross-cultural situation. Picnics, hobbies, music, reading, parties and exercise provide escape and release tensions. One also needs holidays where one can get completely away from the source of strain before he or his partner feels he needs it.

Withdrawing into a sanctuary of the home culture for short periods may be essential for field-workers to regain equilibrium if the sense of self is threatened by the new culture. But not every expatriate enclave or missionary compound is a sanctuary. These may contain Westerners from many national backgrounds. One expects the small cultural cues and basic values to be the same among all English-speaking groups, but they are sometimes disconcertingly different. The value of a sanctuary varies with the individual, the amount of conflict he is struggling with and the nature of his interaction (Taber, 1971).

Consciously controlled compensation is also healthy when one knows visible success will not be possible for several years. Planned hobbies can give a sense of accomplishment as long as they do not rob time and energy from the main goal. Even one's own cultural luxuries can give security if one does not allow guilt about these luxuries to rob him of the benefit for which they are intended, if they do not become a wall between him and his poorer neighbors. Breaking the task into smaller sub-goals helps prevent frustration and brings a sense of accomplishment.

3. *Build Physical and Emotional Resources*

Physical resistance to disease can be built up by a more healthy diet, physical exercise, vitamins and other good health measures. When a field-worker contracts flu or colds or other symptoms, he should overcome the temptation to push himself to work harder and make up for lost time. He needs to take a day off for rest and meditation, taking care of any emotion that might create conflict and weaken his physical resources before emotional conflict builds up. Otherwise, his body will not be ready to fight off germs or counteract glandular or other dysfunction. He should seek medical help if symptoms persist, even if he feels that they might be caused by strain. If the body exhausts its resources to repair itself, there can be permanent damage.

As each field-worker learns to face his symptoms he will become more and more aware of his individual reactions to strain. Then he can use these symptoms as flags to let him know it is time to deal with his emotions. For example, my own headaches and heartburn tell me I must deal with my attitudes immediately. When the emotions have been dealt with, the pain always stops within a day and a sense of peace returns. This is not so simple, however, after emotional conflict has built up.

Routine quiet periods for meditation, Scripture reading and memorization build up one's ability to recognize and deal with emotion. For Christians, communion was meant to include a time of self-examination in order to prevent sickness, weakness and even death (I Cor. 11:30-32).

4. *Consciously Accept Emotions*

Frustration, hostility, failure, fear, guilt and anxiety are sure to occur within anyone in stress-filled situations. One must learn how to deal with them straightforwardly. When any emotion is experienced there are three choices of action: (a) allow its expression; (b) repress and allow the mind to change it to something more acceptable; or (c) acknowledge and deal with it.

Everyone has experienced direct expression of emotion as a child. Some psychiatrists are teaching immediate expression for adults as the best way to prevent the emotional conflict that normally results from repression. But most adults reject this way of handling emotion as unsatisfactory and dangerous. Field-workers who express their hostility bring guilt upon themselves; they may also trigger hostile reactions in their hosts

Most field-workers attempt to control their emotions by holding themselves in check and only allowing acceptable emotions to be expressed.

Once thoughts come to mind they cannot be simply rejected or case off. They are already a part of the unconscious thoughts that must be dealt with or they will be handled in the uncontrolled and frequently undesirable way through the defense system. Osborne paraphrases Proverbs 4:23 this way: "Watch very carefully what you put into your unconscious mind, for it will determine your very destiny" (1967:161).

We have already seen the kinds of unconscious reactions and conflicts that result from denial and repression of inferiority feelings, the kind of "acceptable" actions that result.

Repression produces a more shallow quality of behavior than most field-workers want. Repressed emotions can never produce genuine love desired by the self-image. When one acknowledges all his thoughts and emotions there is no reason why they have to ever go into the unconscious mind. If emotions are never rejected and repressed, they will not trigger the defense mechanisms which only work on objectionable emotions. One short-cuts the whole defense system.

All of the mechanisms work against facing one's self, but facing one's self is the main road to healing. When one accepts his threatening emotions, it is possible to act on these emotions constructively, and completely eliminate them through a simple process involving *confession* and *forgiveness.*

Accepting the emotions requires acknowledgement that these can exist within oneself. Missionaries may find this acknowledgement more difficult than other field-workers because of the pedestal their friends at home put them on--one of spiritual superiority. This becomes a part of his self-image and keeps him from obtaining the genuine love he needs.

5. *Forgiveness*

A daily preventive technique and cure is available to anyone who wants to practice it. If used it is adequate to completely eradicate unacceptable emotions, guilt and emotional conflict. It is found in a prayer that is repeated often: "Forgive us the wrongs that we have done, as we forgive the wrongs that others have done to us." Jesus' warning immediately following that prayer was, "For if you forgive others the wrongs they have done you, your Father in heaven will forgive you. But if you do not forgive the wrongs of others, your Father will not forgive the wrongs you have done" (Mt. 6:12, 14, 15 TEV).

He gave another warning later that year to His disciples, when they asked Him how often to forgive. In His story, the lord of the unforgiving servant "delivered him to the tormentors....So likewise shall my heavenly Father do also unto you, if ye...forgive not every one of his brothers their trespasses" (Mt. 18:34, 35 KJV). Two kinds of forgiveness are presented here: forgiving others, and asking forgiveness for the wrongs one has done himself.

(a) *Forgiving Others:* Forgiving others is essential before anyone can receive forgiveness. The Greek word for "forgive" in these passages does not necessarily imply pardoning or condoning another's behavior as the English word often does. Rather, it means "to let go," "forsake" or "yield up." This yielding up does not even imply that an offense is essential before one can forgive, nor does it imply that someone has to accept the guilt before the forgiving process is completed. It does mean that if I feel I have been hurt or poorly treated, or I am upset that someone else has been wronged, I must forgive him. If I justify my resentment I cannot be freed of whole layers of projected and displaced emotions.

Thoughts about times others have hurt me come to mind much more frequently in stressful situations. These offenses may be real, they may be imagined, or they may be due to the work of the defense mechanisms. This complicates my forgiving others. For example, if I have repressed my own resentment and displaced or projected it upon someone else, I will feel that he resents me, whether or not he really does. Because I feel wronged, it is real to me. I must forgive him in order to deal with my own problem. In the same way, I may even have to forgive God if I feel He has been unfair to me.

Forgiving another person frees me to love him whether or not he is guilty. It also frees me to obtain forgiveness if I am the one who is actually guilty. Forgiving another is usually best done in secret without going to him. Jesus' instructions for reconciliation with a "brother" only apply when "your brother has something against you" or actually "sins against you" (Mt. 5:23, 18:15 TGV). Confession and forgiveness should not be more public than the original accusation. This avoids a lot of embarrassment and confusion. If it is my own projection, I find my colleague bewildered and wondering what he ever did that needs forgiving. Or he may feel that I am actually accusing him of doing something by insisting, "I forgive you." It is also easy to unconsciously force him to take the blame.

Generally, after forgiving a person upon whom I have projected my guilt, I am better able to face my own guilt without emotional trauma. Afterwards, I may find it even more difficult to forgive myself for not being the person I thought I was. Forgiving one's self and others is very important, for it helps to unravel the deception of the defense mechanisms without the pain of introspection.

By daily forgiving others one can actually prevent conflict in a cross-cultural situation. He can forgive anyone he finds himself misunderstanding, thinking of with a twinge of pain or complaining about. He can routinely forgive those in authority over him, his colleagues, the nationals, his spouse, his children and himself. He may need to forgive his neighbors, his teachers, his child's teachers or those who come to his home to serve him. Parents, brothers and sisters, or others causing childhood trauma or earlier stress are also "straws" that contribute to the present overload. Forgiving the people of one's childhood experiences is very helpful before going into a stressful situation.

Thankfulness is also an extremely effective tool, to go one step further than forgiveness. One can not only "let go" of an offense to him by some person, but he can "accept" the situation by being thankful for it. One cannot change his past, but a changed attitude toward the past can make it seem very different and have a different effect upon him. If one actually thanks God for a painful experience in the past, something happens to the memory of that experience. Thankful acceptance of past experiences frees a person to forgive and love the people involved in that experience. An illustration of the power of this kind of thankfulness to change attitudes and help people is described by Chaplain Carothers in his books *Prison to Praise* and *Power in Praise* (1970, 1972).

One can change the present also by learning to specifically praise God for insects, germs, dirt, dogs, and unlovely (to him) parts of the national culture, anything causing frustration or strain or that might be an object of displacement. Daily forgiveness and praise considerably reduces the strain in the cross-cultural experience.

(b) *Obtaining Forgiveness and Cleansing*: If a person is willing to equate the Biblical concept of sin with the guilt and emotional conflict that results from hidden emotions and reactions to unpleasant experiences, then he can deal with it. The Bible defines sin this way: "For the man who does not do the good he knows he should do is guilty of sin" (Jas. 4:17 TEV). Since the mechanisms only hide the things one feels he shouldn't do, then most of the emotions hidden by the mechanisms would fit this definition of sin.

One who accepts the Bible's answer to the problem does not need to be afraid of admitting sin, for God offers cleansing from all sin and failure as soon as it is confessed to Him (I John 1:8, 9). He also offers power to do what one feels he should do (Jas. 4:7). Sin will have no power over a Christian if he deals with it daily as Jesus suggested. But it does regain control over him again if he represses it, putting it in the darkness of the unconscious mind.

When a person under stress begins to see that God forgives and accepts him as he really is, and he accepts himself, dealing with his emotional conflict by forgiveness and confession, he begins to experience whole cycles of forgiving others, confessing sin, being forgiven, remembering new resentments, forgiving, etc. This untangles conflicts, freeing him from guilt and unacceptable emotions. Then genuine peace fills his mind. One can judge his own mind by whether or not he has inward peace (Col. 3:15). Peace disappears when conflict builds up again, letting one know it is time to deal with unacceptable emotion.

6. *Helping Each Other*

One seldom experiences emotional conflict without other people being involved. Fear, inferiority and projection lead to criticism, a common problem among many groups of field-workers. Criticism sets people against each other when they need each other most. It triggers everyone's defense system, increasing conflict for all.

However, as one faces his own emotions and feels the weight of his burden of conflict, he is better prepared to bear the burdens of others and help them become free of their guilt without judging them. As he understands and accepts himself with his failures, he can begin to accept others and their failures, and they in turn can begin to accept themselves. As each acknowledges and deals with his emotions, attitudes toward emotional symptoms and stress-related physical illness can change. When field-workers can live in harmony, loving and encouraging one another, they are more likely to get well.

Family doctors and religious groups all over the world are writing about the amazing results from small sharing groups. "Healing came when the sick person dealt with the underlying causes: guilt, fear, hostility, inferiority resulting in self-rejection, jealousy, envy, or whatever they were" (Osborne, 1967:198).

Harris reports that the new transactional analysis method of group therapy "is enabling persons to change, to establish self-control and self-direction" (1967).

Sharing groups are distinct from other kinds of Bible study groups, in that people come with a common sense of need, expressing feelings freely and honestly, each seeking to change himself rather than others. When a group shows openness, and unconditional and confidential love, this provides the non-judgmental acceptance needed for true communication and resolution of conflicts. Some persons are unable to experience the forgiveness of God except as it is mediated through such a group (Osborne, 1967:178, 179, 193, 200).

In addition, Toffler suggests that group orientation sessions are valuable for preparing people even before they go into stressful situations.

By bringing together people who are sharing, or are about to share, a common adaptive experience, we help equip them to cope with it....If we bring him together with others who are moving through the same experience, people he can identify with and respect, we strengthen him. The members of the group come to share, even if briefly, some sense of identity. They see their problems more objectively. They trade useful ideas and insights. Most important, they suggest future alternatives for one another (1971:347).

Training programs can be designed to provide this kind of grouping.

Something also is needed after two or more years of cross-cultural living, when emotional conflict often reaches a peak. For example, after a group discussion on culture stress, one veteran missionary remarked, "I'm so glad I'm normal. I could never tell anyone my problems before for fear they would think I was unspiritual." She was able to adjust much better after that group experience. Without these kinds of group discussions, people often have no way of seeing how normal they really are.

Some field-workers, however, would prefer a counselor to a sharing group. Professional counselors are not usually available in a foreign country, though some pastors have left churches in the home country to minister to missionaries. One of these has helped missionaries in several countries to overcome fatigue and inner conflicts. He has recognized that aberrant behavior is the result of chains of reactions to stress, sometimes from events many years earlier. After a short counseling session to determine symptoms, he asks God to forgive and heal whole sets of repressed memories that caused the symptoms. After this prayer for deep forgiveness, the emotionally charged feelings usually disappeared and the motives could be seen in retrospect without the guilt and shame of introspection. At times, relief of the symptoms is dramatic and permanent after one session. With other people deeper conflicts surface and need to be dealt with in more sessions.

Many field-workers are now using praise and prayer for forgiveness and healing of past experiences in cross-cultural situations. The results have been helpful both individually and in small supportive sharing groups. Co-workers who have experienced culture stress have proven helpful and effective in helping other field-workers to resolve conflicts. The main qualification is the ability to listen with genuine love and acceptance, giving hope and reassurance. Such a lay counselor can be a catalyst to help the individual obtain the assurance of forgiveness that is so important to obtaining the clear conscience and clean unconscious mind--the essential prerequisite for loving behavior (I Tim. 1:5 TEV).

A lay counselor must remember that the individual with emotional conflicts seldom needs to be told that he has conflicts or what caused them. All of the past experiences that have created the conflict are actually recorded in his unconscious mind, along with his feelings about these experiences (Harris, 1967). "For who could really understand a man's inmost thoughts except the spirit of the man himself" (I Cor. 2:11, Phillips). Condemnation by the counselor triggers the defense mechanisms of the one being counseled and makes him unable to face his own difficulties.

Conclusion

In conclusion, stress is normal in an alien environment. The most encouraging result of this study is that stress and fatigue can be decreased. The high incidence of prolonged illness in field-work can be reduced. Breakdowns can be understood and some can be prevented. It is possible to overcome guilt, unacceptable emotions, and undesirable actions in field-work.

Westerners can learn to live happily in a foreign culture without undue strain. As co-workers learn how to support and strengthen each other, they will overcome their inner reactions, bear each other's burdens and be able to work together effectively with genuine love even while under strain (Col. 3:11-17). As these techniques are applied there is hope that field-workers can more effectively reach out in friendship to people of other backgrounds, building love and understanding with people of other cultures without being sabotaged by their own inner defenses.

References

Brewster, E. (1972). Involvement as a means of second culture learning. *Practical Anthropology*, *19*, 27-44.

Brown, M. & Fowler, G. (1955). *Psychodynamic nursing.* Philadelphia: W.B. Saunders.

Carothers, M. (1970). *Prison to praise.* Plainfield: Logos Institute.

Carothers, M. (1972). *Power and praise.* Plainfield: Logos Institute.

Dye, T. (1974). Stress-producing factors in cultural adjustment. *Missiology*, *2*, 61-77.

Harris, T. (1967). *I'm O.K. --You're O.K.* New York: Harper & Row.

Hefley, J. (1967). *Adventures with God.* Grand Rapids: Zondervan.

Lehner, G. & Kube, E. (1955). *The dynamics of personal adjustment.* Englewood Cliffs: Prentice-Hall.

McMillen, S. (1963). *None of these diseases.* Old Tappan: Revell.

Missildine, W. (1963). *Your inner child of the past.* New York: Simon & Schuster.

Oberg, K. (1960). Cultural shock: Adjustment to new cultural environments. *Practical Anthropology, 7,* 177-182.

Osborne, C. (1967). *The art of understanding yourself.* Grand Rapids: Zondervan.

Smalley, W. (1963). Cultural shock: Language shock and the shock of self-discovery. *Practical Anthropology, 10,* 49-56.

Taber, C. (1971). The missionary ghetto. *Practical Anthropology, 18,* 193-196.

Toffler, A. (1971). *Future shock.* New York: Random House.

Tournier, P. (1963). *The strong and the weak.* London: S.C.M. Press.

Tournier, P. (Ed.) (1964). *Fatigue in modern society.* Richmond: John Knox Press.

Weiner, N. (1966). Cybernetics. In *Communication and Culture,* A. Smith (Ed.). New York: Rinehart & Winston.

35

Dorothy Gish

Sources of Missionary Stress

The present investigation sought to determine some common sources of stress for missionaries working abroad. A 65-item rating scale was given to 547 missionaries on the field. The problem of confronting others when necessary and the difficulty of communication across language and cultural barriers caused considerable or greater stress for over half the population. Approximately half the population were stressed by the time and effort required to maintain relationships with donors, too much work, and decisions about work priorities.

Stress is a non-specific response of the body to any demand made upon it. A natural by-product of all our activities, stress is thus a normal part of everyday life (Selye, 1976). Just as a violin with strings too loose will moan, so too little stress results in boredom. But a too tightly strung violin will screech, and, if the pressure continues to increase, will snap. On the human level, too much stress results in eventual breakdown.

Around the beginning of this century, a Johns Hopkins psychiatrist was impressed with the fact that many of his patients became ill shortly after major changes in their lives. By 1965, Holmes and Rahe (1967) had evolved the now widely known Social Readjustment Rating Scale which measures the stressfulness of one's life on the basis of the change-causing events one has recently encountered. The more readjustment points accumulated

---

during a given period, the greater the likelihood of becoming ill in the not-too-distant future.

However, Kobasa (1979), using the Holmes and Rahe Schedule of Recent Life Events, identified two groups of middle and upper level executives who had had high degrees of stress in the three previous years. One group reported becoming ill after their encounter with stressful life events. However, the other group had not fallen ill. Data collected on the two groups showed that the high-stress, low-illness executives possessed more hardiness (i.e., stronger commitment to self, an attitude of vigorousness toward the environment, a sense of meaningfulness and an internal locus of control) than their high-stress, high-illness counterparts. A number of studies focusing on the desirability/undesirability of change found that undesirability measures were more highly correlated with psychological disturbances or distress than were total change measures (Dohrenwend, 1973; Gersten, Langner, Eisenberg, & Ozrek, 1974; Vinokur & Selzer, 1975; Mueller, Edwards, & Yarvis, 1973; Ross & Mirowsky, 1979).

These data support psychological stress theory which claims that cognition, emotions, and coping processes mediate the outcomes of the social functioning, psychological morale, and physical health of the person. Thus, stress depends at least in part on whether the individual appraises a given situation as benign, neutral, or stressful. Even appraising a situation as stressful does not necessarily result in distress for those who view that stress as a challenge. However, if the person sees harm, loss, or threat in the stress, the result is very different. Assuming that stress depends on one's personal appraisal of any given situation or factor, and that the response to that appraisal may be influenced by mediating variables, does not mean that we should not attempt to identify variables which generally produce stress in a given situation or for a particular population.

Organizational stress research by French and Caplan (1972) at the University of Michigan's Institute for Social Research has identified eight occupational stressors: Role ambiguity, role conflict, qualitative role overload, having to cross organizational boundaries (e.g., being an administrator in a scientific setting), responsibility for people, poor relations with others, and participation in the organization's decision-making processes.

In their extensive review of literature on burn-out and the pastorate, Daniel and Rogers (1981) refer to the ministry as a vocation under stress. The stressors they cite include having to be "all things to all people":

There is never any time when they are free from their duties; their duties are often not clearly defined and criteria for knowing when they have done their duty are often ambiguous. The responsibility for people's souls seems to takes its toll. (p. 244)

Attempting to identify "stressors...perceived by the minister and the minister's spouse", Gleason (1977) studied 21 clergy and 11 spouses attending a workshop on "stress in the clergy." Based on a 5-point rating scale (1, "no strain," to 5, "extremely upsetting"), the top stressors for clergy were activities ($M=$ 2.9), perfectionism ($M=$ 2.8), and no time for study, role conflicts, and unwelcome surprise (all rated $M=$ 2.7). For spouses, unwelcome surprise ($M=$ 3.0) and anger ($M=$ 2.6) topped the list, and no tangible results of work, perfectionism, proliferation of activities, and self-image (all rating $M=$ 2.5) closely followed.

Stress in missionary service was the focus of a study by Ediger (Note 1). Based on interviews with 20 missionaries about their stress in missionary service, her study provided anecdotal data relative to 24 areas, but gives no quantitative data. Moorehead (1981) studied 87 missionaries in Japan. Her questionnaire, focusing on 25 areas of missionary life, identified those areas rated most stressful by respondents as being language (57%), separation from children (33%), children's education (25%), and change of work/status (20%).

The extant body of non-empirical Christian literature on stress is relatively limited. Collins (1977), in one of the few Christian books on stress, devotes three pages to "Stress and the Work of Missions." He identifies nine stresses common to missionaries: Loneliness, pressures of adjusting to a foreign culture, constant demands on one's time, lack of adequate medical facilities, overwhelming work load and difficult working conditions, pressure to be a constant, positive "witness" to the nationals, confusion over one's role within the local church, frequent lack of privacy, and inability to get away for recreation and vacation.

The purpose of this study was to attempt to identify specific stressors for a wide range of missionaries in active service.

Method

Instrumentation

Empirical and theoretical literature, while limited, does suggest that there are stressors common to Christian missionaries. However, no instrument exists to measure such sources of stress.

The author, therefore, developed a Likert scale questionnaire identifying specific stressors from extensive review of the literature, extended discussions with missionary society executives, exploratory conversations with missionaries, extrapolations from the experiences of a psychologist working with missionaries, and an examination of the author's personal recollections of missionary life. For an item to be included, it had to meet two criteria: (a) Having been identified from one of the previous sources as a stressor, and (b) proving equally applicable to all missionaries regardless of age, sex, or marital status. For example, a number of sources identified problems related to children's education as a stressor; however, such an item would likely be applicable only to those with dependent children. Thus no item relating specifically to children's education was included. However, an item on extended family concerns was included.

After being pretested on missionaries and critiqued by missionary psychologists and mission executives, a number of revisions were made. The final version used for this study contained 65 items to be rated on a 0-5 scale, with 0 representing "does not apply," 1 representing "no stress," and 5 representing "great stress."

Independent Variables

Eight mediating variables were hypothesized as having an effect on degree of stress reported: Place of service, age, sex, marital status, nationality, length of service on the field, type of service, and average number of hours a week on the job. The anonymous questionnaires were distributed from August through December, 1981, and were collected by the author during a site visit. The responses to each of the 65 source items were analyzed relative to each of the eight independent variables. If the analysis of variance indicated a significant difference, the Scheffee posteriori contrast test (Nie, Hull, Jenkins, Steinbrenner, & Bent, 1975) was then used to locate the difference.

Subjects

The sample for this study of missionary stress was missionaries serving in various fields (i.e., Australia, Canada, Hong Kong, Japan, New Guinea, Philippines, and Zambia) and with various mission boards (i.e., Summer Institute of Linguistics, Brethren in Christ, Mennonite Central Committee, and several Christian academies). The total number of questionnaires sent out was 970. Five hundred fifty-six were returned. Three were incomplete and thus had to be discarded and four were received too late (therefore, *n*=549). The return rate varied from 48% (210/438) for the largest group (SIL:Papua New Guinea) to 100% (11/11) for the smallest group (Brethren in Christ: Montreal Lake, Children's Home, Saskatchewan, Canada).

Results

A rating of 3-5 was interpreted as indicating considerable to great stress, and 4-5 indicating great stress. Nineteen items were indicated as causing considerable to great stress for 30% or more of the subjects. Table 1 lists those items and also indicates what percentage of the respondents indicated that they were sources of great stress. It will be noted that "confronting others" and "communication difficulties" caused undesirable or greater stress to over half the sample with more than a quarter of the sample indicating great stress. One-fourth of the missionaries studied also found "too much work" a source of great stress (rating it 4 or 5), with nearly half giving "too much work" a rating of 3 or higher (i.e., considerable or greater stress).

Place of Service
Significant (*p* <.05) site differences emerged on sixteen items. Some of them had to do with the physical environment. Health hazards including physical dangers caused significantly more stress in the Philippines than in Australia. Climate was rated as a significantly greater source of stress in Australia, the Philippines, and Taiwan than in Papua New Guinea or Zambia. Some other significant differences had to do with issues that are current branch concerns. Missionaries in Papua New Guinea and Hong Kong experienced significantly more stress from co-workers' paternalism towards nationals than did missionaries in Australia. Those working in the Philippines found significantly more stress relative to their relationship with nationals than did those working in either Australia or Taiwan.

A number of other significant differences were found for specific groups relative to items dealing with superiors, top-level administration, and teamwork.

Sex
Of the eleven significant (*p* <.05) sex differences revealed, women (*n*=341) indicated all but one of them significantly more stressful than did men (*n*=205): Co-workers attitudes toward their job, extended family concerns, loneliness and isolation,

Table 1
Items Identified as Sources of Stress by 30% or More
of the Respondents (*n*=549)

	% Rating Considerable to Great Stress	%Rating Great Stress
Confronting Others When Necessary	54	27
Communicating Across Language-Cultural Barrier	53	26
Time and Effort Maintaining Donor Relationships	50	22
Amount of Work	48	25
Work Priorities	47	18
Time for Personal Study of the Word and Prayer	37	14
Progress on my Work	36	14
Need for Pastoral Care	35	15
Making Decisions Affecting Others' Lives	35	15
Need for Confidant	34	19
Self-Acceptance Including Self-Forgiveness	34	14
Conflicts Between My Values and Host Culture's	34	13
"Gold-Fish Bowl" Existence	33	13
Certainty About My Future	33	13
Freedom to Take Time for Myself	32	12
Extended Family Concerns	31	12
Frequent Moving	31	18
Task Orientation vs. "Servant Attitude"	31	11
Recreation and Exercise	30	09

self-acceptance (including self-forgiveness), confronting others when necessary, communicating across the cultural and language barriers, lack of pastoral care, inadequate rest, climate, and travel difficulties. Maintaining public relations caused significantly more stress for men than for women.

Age

For purposes of analyzing the data, ages were divided into five-year segments, from 20 to 64. There were few under 25 (*n*=11) or over 60 (*n*=17). For the "under 25," the "40-49," and the "over 55" age groups, there were no significant differences in their ratings of sources of stress. The 25-39 year-olds (*n*=290) experienced significantly ($p<.05$) more stress than the 50-54 year-olds (*n*=52) over loneliness and isolation, lack of pastoral care, inadequate rest, and housing policies. The 30-34 year-olds (*n*=104) also had significantly more stress over inadequate rest and the "fish bowl" existence than did the 50-54 year-olds. Travel difficulties caused more stress to the 25-29 (*n*=79) and 35-39 year-olds (*n*=107) than it did to the 50-54 year-olds.

Marital Status

Married people (*n*=168) found relationship with spouse (or partner) and insufficient finances to be significantly ($p<.05$) more stressful than did singles (*n*=168). Singles, on the other hand, experienced significantly more stress over loneliness and isolation, and self-acceptance.

Nationality

Americans, Australians, British, and Canadians were well represented in the study. Seven other nationalities (Dutch, Finish, German, Japanese, New Zealanders, Swiss, Paraguayan) each had an *n* of 6 or fewer. While the statistics used took into account the varying sample sizes, the data did not indicate any significant national differences in source of stress ratings on the items measured.

Years of Service

Since the first 18 months on the field is regarded as a time of adjustment, it was used as a category by itself. In coding the data, six months or more was converted to the next highest year. The categories were: Less than 18 months, 18 months to 4 years, 5 to 9 years, 10 to 14 years, 15 to 19 years, and 20 years or more. Those who had served 20 or more years found the demands of nationals with whom they worked significantly ($p<.05$) more stressful than did those who had been there less than 18 months. However, newcomers were more stressed by inadequate diet, lack of pastoral care, type of housing, living conditions, travel difficulties, and the "fish bowl" existence were more stressful to those who had been there 18 months to 4 years than for those who had been there for more than 20. Moving, with its associated problems, was a significantly greater cause of stress for the 18 months-to-4-year people than for those who had been there for less than 18 months. Those who had served 15 to 19 years on the field were more stressed over political stability of the host country than those who had been there less than 5 years, and had greater concern about their future than those who had served 20 years or more. Relationships with spouse (or partner) and with local and government officials caused significantly more stress for those who had served from 15 to 19 years than for those who had been there less than 5 years.

Type of Service

Type of service was classified into six different categories: Tribal (including literacy and translation personnel; n=171), support (n=236), education (n=95), church planting (n=8), language study (n=8), and medicine (n=16).

The things which caused significantly (p<.05) more stress for the tribal personnel than for support personnel were lack of tangible, visible results, having a different temperament from that values by the host culture, loneliness and isolation, and self-acceptance. Tribal personnel found significantly more stress from six other items than did either support or education people: Insufficient progress on work, demands of natonal co-workers, conflicts between personnel values and those of the host country, maintaining public relations with local and government officials, relationship with spouse (or partner), and relationship with nationals.

On the other hand, both support and education personnel found significantly more stress from the feeling that some co-workers devalued their job. For educators, swings in policy, dissatisfaction with top level administration, lack of unity and teamwork among top level administration, and disagreement with principles and practices of the organization provided significantly more stress than they did for the tribal personnel.

Amount of Time on Job

Five categories were used to analyze the data on the basis of time per week spent on the job: Half-time or less (2-20 hours; n=91), full-time (21-40 hours; n=186), slight overtime (41-50 hours; n=150), overtime (51-60 hours; n=44), excessive overtime (more than 61 hours; n=43). The latter group includes those whose response to number of hours worked per week was "all the time" or a similar response. The half-time group consists largely of missionary wives. The higher stress ratings came from those who spend more than 50 hours a week on the job. The excessive overtime group may well include those who define their job so broadly as to include nearly all they do. However, it is interesting to note that they found inadequte rest a significantly greater source of stress than any other group.

Discussion

The five major sources of stress identified by this study are: Confrontation, cross-cultural communication, support maintenance, work overload, and establishing work priorities.

Confronting others when necessary is a source of high stress for a majority of the missionaries. While neither sex finds it easy to confront others, it is not surprising to find that women who are traditionally socialized to be "nice" and not to "rock the boat" find confrontation significantly more stressful than do males. Living in a restricted environment (i.e., limited as to amount and kind of contacts with those "like them") would likely increase both the need for and the difficulty of confrontation.

Cross-cultural communication provided the second major source of stress, with over half finding it stressful, and slightly more than a quarter finding it very stressful. Those working directly with the people (tribal, educators, church plantrs, medical people, and those in language study) found significantly more stress relative to cross-cultural communication than did support personnel.

The third largest cause of stress was "time and effort required to maintain relationship with donors." Half of the missionaries found this a source of considerable stress, with not quite a quarter of them finding great stress from it. In subsequent analysis, the data was divided into three groups: (a) Interdenominational faith groups (68% of the sample), (b) Christian schools (20%), and (c) denominational groups (13%). Those in the interdenominational group are responsible to raise their own support as are many, but not all, in the Christian schools. Support for the denominational group is provided by the denomination. The interdenominational group found this source significantly more stressful than did the denominational group. Thus, it appears that being responsible to raise and maintain one's support is stressful.

The fourth major source of stress was "too much work." Three other items of the organizational skills/management type were the source of considerable to great stress for over a third of the people: Decisions about work priorities (47%), insufficient progress on work (36%), having too many decisions that affect the lives of others (35%). For tribal personnel, insufficient progress proved a significantly greater source of stress than it did for support or educating personnel.

The most striking thing about these results is that those sources identified as producing the greatest amount of stress are all causes which can be to some degree alleviated by training. Many missionary organizations have orientation programs of some type. This study would suggest that conflict resolution and basic management skills should be included in such programs (or better yet, be part of missionaries' basic training). However, it seems likely that preservice training is not enough. Administrators at a large mission station reported that the orientation for new missionaries arriving on the field had been considerably reduced because of a negative reaction from "throwing all that stuff at them when all they wanted to do was to get to work."

What seems to be called for is some on-site, inservice training. For example, learning about confrontation and conflict resolution is fine, but how much better to have an on-site workshop where one has to practice those skills with the same fellow-workers with whom one has conflicts. Even though one has acquired basic management skills an on-site, inservice workshop could help with specific applications. Many professionals in mental health, management, higher education, et cetera are able to take extended leaves. Among these are certainly a number of "former missionaries" and/or others with cross-cultural experiences who could help provide inservice training.

References

Collins, G. (1977). *You can profit from stress.* Santa Ana, CA: Vision House.

Daniel, S. & Rogers, M. L. (1981). Burn-out and the pastorate: A critical review with implications for pastors. *Journal of Psychology and Theology, 9* (3), 232-249.

Dohrenwend, B. S. (1973). Life events as stressors: A methodological inquiry. *Journal of Health and Social Behavior, 14,* 167-175.

French, J. R. P., & Caplan, R. D. (1972). Organizational stress and individual strain. In A. J. Marrow (Ed.), *The failure of success.* New York: AMACOM.

Gersten, C., Langner, T. S., Eisenberg, J. G., & Orzek, L. (1974). Child behavior and life events: Undesirable change or change per se? In B. S. Dohrenwand & B. P. Dohrenwend (Eds.), *Stressful life events: Their nature and effects.* New York: Wiley.

Gleason, J. (1977). Perception of stress among clergy and their spouses. *The Journal of Pastoral Care, 31,* 248-251.

Holmes, T. H., & Rahe, R. H. (1967). The Social Readjustment Rating Scale. *Journal of Psychosomatic Research, 11*, 213-218.

Kobasa, S. C. (1979). Stressful life events, personality, and health: An inquiry into hardiness. *Journal of Personality and Social Psychology, 37*, 1-11.

Moorehead, T. (1981). *The missionary family.* The Christian Family in Japan. Major papers from the 22nd Hayama Men's Missionary Seminars, January 5-7, 1981, Anogi Sanso, Japan.

Mueller, D., Edwards, D. W., & Yarvis, R. M. (1977). Stressful life events and psychiatric symptomatology: Change or undesirability. *Journal of Health and Social Behavior, 18*, 307-316.

Nie, W. H., Hull, G. H., Jenkins, J. G., Steinbrenner, K., & Bent, D. H. (1975). *Statistical Package for the Social Sciences* (2nd ed.). McGraw Hill: New York.

Ross, C. E., & Mirowsky, J., II (1979). A comparison of life event weighting schemes: Change, undesirability, and effect proportional indices. *Journal of Health and Social Behavior, 20*, 166-177.

Selye, H. (1976). *The stress of life* (rev. ed.). New York: McGraw-Hill.

Thoits, P. A. (1981). Undesirable life events and psychophysiological stress: A problem of operational confounding. *American Sociological Review, 46*, 97-109.

Vinokur, A., & Selzer, M. L. (1975). Desirable versus undesirable life events: Their relationship to stress and mental distress. *Journal of Personality and Social Psychology, 33*, 329-337.

Weller, L. (1963). The effects of anxiety on cohesiveness and rejection. *Human Behavior, 16*, 184-197.

36

Kenneth L. Williams

Worksheet on Balanced Living

This worksheet is designed to help you deal with tensions in relationships between your work and your other life priorities. It covers several specific areas. Concentrate first on those areas which you find particularly difficult in your present situation. If possible, discuss your responses with a loved-one or friend.

A. Assessing the Amount of Work (Eccl. 3:12,13)

1. Rate your work load in terms of: Completely impossible, Overwhelming, More than I can do consistently, A little too much, Just right, Not enough work.

2. In the past year, has your work load increased, decreased, or stayed the same? If it has changed, why?

B. Overwork Symptoms (Luke 10:41,42)

1. *Physical Symptoms.* Common ones include chronic fatigue, gastrointestinal malfunctions, cardiovascular disturbances and neuromuscular complaints. What physical symptoms are you experiencing now that might be from overwork?

Based on a paper presented at the Fourth Annual Conference on Mental Health and Missions held at Angola, Indiana in November 1983. Reprinted by permission of the author.

2. *Spiritual-Emotional Symptoms.* Common ones are prayerlessness, disinterest in God's Word, false guilt, low self-esteem, sleep disturbances, difficulty concentrating, confusion, depression, anxiety, apathy, irritability and temper outbursts. What symptoms are you experiencing now that might be from overwork?

3. *Distresses*. These differ from symptoms in that they are painful emotions which relate consciously and directly to overwork. For example, overwork can cause one to feel angry, afraid, sad, disgusted, inadequate, guilty, anxious, frustrated, manipulated, helpless or hopeless. These responses are not usually damaging if dealt with effectively. What distresses are you experiencing now that you link to overwork?

C. Effects of Your Work on Relatioinships (Luke 5:15,16)

1. Describe how your work load may be affecting your relationships with the persons below. Use words such as *helping, strengthening, harming, destroying,* or *having no effect.*

The Lord

Your spouse

Your children

Your partner, if single

Your friends

2. You might ask your spouse, children, partner, or others close to you how they see the work affecting your relationship with them.

D. Renewing the Spirit, Mind, and Body (Mark 6:31, Matt. 11:28-30)

1. *Spiritual Renewal.* What activities and relationships are you involved in regularly which bring spiritual renewal? (Bible study, ministering to others, time alone, etc.)

What would you like to be different in this area?

2. *Mental Renewal.* What activities and relationships are you involved in regularly which bring intellectual and emotional renewal? (hobbies, games, stimulating friendships, etc.

What would you like to be different in this area?

3. *Physical Renewal.* What activities and relationships are you involved in regularly which bring physical renewal? (vacations, jogging, rest, tennis with a friend, etc.)

What would you like to be different in this area?

E. Strategy for Handling Actual Work Load

1. *Clarify Your Values.* To get a perspective on what you value in life, list on a separate sheet every concept, person, activity, and object you consider truly important to you. Examples might include relationship to Christ, health, spouse, partner, work, ministry to others, children, etc. Keep these values in mind as you work through the rest of the strategy. Answer the following 3 questions:

a. In light of your life values, are you unhappy with the amount of time you spend at work?

b. Does your work load and its pressures have a negative effect on you emotionally, so that it is difficult to "let go" of it when you leave work?

c. Are you sometimes frustrated over not having time to work on important tasks?

If your answer to any of the 3 is "Yes," work through the following steps. If all answers are "No," you may want to skip this section and go on to Section F.

2. *Prioritize Your Tasks.* List on a separate sheet every task you do which takes more than half an hour per week. Note how much time you average weekly at each task. Then place a priority on each task, using this designation: "A" for tasks which are absolutely necessary, "B" for ones which seem very important, but not absolutely necessary, "C" for those which are good, but could be dropped with no serious consequences.

3. *Consider and Apply Options.* If your supervisor should be involved, show him your list of prioritized tasks. Tell him you cannot get all the work done, and that this is how you see your priorities. Ask for his feedback on priorities and work through the following steps with him:

a. Can any "A" or "B" tasks be delegated to someone else? If so, try delegating them.

b. Which "C" tasks can you drop completely? Weigh the positive and negative consequences of dropping each one. Decide which ones can be dropped and drop them.

c. Of those "C" tasks which remain, decide which ones can be put into a category where they would only be done if all "A" and "B" tasks were under control. (Possibly all "C" tasks would fit this category.) Then decide not to work on these tasks until all other tasks are done. These comprise a guilt-free area of your work. You need not feel guilty over not working on these tasks. They can be considered at any time, to be dropped altogether, delegated, moved up in priority, or left the same.

d. If you still have more work to do than can be done, look over the rest of the tasks on the list (with your supervisor, if appropriate) and determine if any of them can be delegated. If so, decide to whom they will be delegated, who will delegate, and when.

e. Look at the remaining tasks and ask yourself, "In what ways can I do this task more efficiently? Must this task be done as completely or as perfectly as I'm now doing it? (Not every task worth doing is worth doing well!) Is there someone I can ask to help me with this task? Are there other resources I can call on? Is there an expert who can give me ideas on doing it in less time and/or better?" Write out any conclusions and decisions you make on any task. Try them and note the results.

F. Strategy for Handling Emotional Responses to Your Work

The work load or inherent stresses in the work may be causing you some negative emotional reactions which are difficult to deal with. If so, try the following steps in dealing with them.

1. Handling Distresses. Look at your answer in B.3.

   a. List here the distresses which are most painful for you.

   b. Try to identify specifically what factors in the work cause each distress. Write them here.

   c. Look at each factor and ask what options you have in reducing its stress. On a separate sheet, write out each option. If possible, discuss these with your supervisor or someone else. Decide which options you will put into practice. Note your decisions on the sheet.

   d. Express your feelings to the Lord, aloud if possible. Leave them with Him, and thank Him for His joy and peace.

2. *Handling Guilt.* Guilt over work left undone or not done as well as it might have been is a major problem for Christian workers.

   a. If you experience guilt over the work, note specifically what is causing it.

   b. Try to determine if this is *true* or *false* guilt. Do you believe God is condemning you? (See Rom. 8:1.) If not, it is probably false guilt. You can *feel* guilty and not *be* guilty! If in doubt whether it's true or false, ask someone you trust what their judgment is. If you decide it's true guilt, confess it and decide what you can do to change your behavior. If false guilt, acknowledge that to yourself and God, thank Him that He is not condemning you, and claim His promises that you are not condemned by Him. For further help in this, see *Freedom From Guilt* and *The Workaholic and His Family,* especially chapter 7.

3. *Leaving Work at Work.* For a balanced life, you may need clear time and space barriers between work and the rest of your life. If you have difficulty with this, try the following steps. Use a separate sheet for your responses.

   a. Working in the home.

   1) If you actually work in the home, why do you?
   2) How does this affect you, your wife, your children or partner?
   3) Note what options you have for getting all or part of

your work out of the home. List positive and negative effects or any options which may be viable.
4) If you choose an option, write what you will do and when.

b. Bringing work home.

1) Do you bring extra work home to do?
2) How often?
3) Are you satisfied that this is right for you and your family or partner?
4) Note positive and negative effects of doing it.
5) Ask your family or partner how they see it.
6) Decide what you want to do about it, e.g. continue as is, set limits on how much work you will bring home, stop altogether. Write down your decision. Try it for a month and reevaluate.

4. *Becoming Mentally Free from the Work.*
a. Do you at times "take the work home" mentally and emotionally, or are you able to go home and be free from thinking about it and feeling anxious over it? Write how you see yourself in this area.

b. If you have difficulty in this area, describe specifically what you think and/or worry about, e.g. too much work, too difficult, interpersonal conflicts, unresolved decisions.

c. Then try the following technique for 2 weeks: Before leaving work each day, get alone with the Lord. Specifically describe to Him (write down if needed) what is bothering you. Verbally give it to Him to hold until you return to work again (Psalm 55:22, I Peter 5:7). It may help to visualize stuffing it into a garbage bag, tying it tight so the fumes can't get out, and dumping it into His hands. If you take it back, just do it again, and keep doing it until you can let go. This process takes practice, so keep at it.

d. If you're in the habit of discussing work problems at home, especially at the dinner table, ask yourself if this is uplifting and helpful. Does it fit the criteria in Phil. 4:8? If not, agree as a family (or partners) that you will no longer discuss work problems at that time. You might set aside another time if you're convinced that it is necessary and helpful. Morning may be a better time for this.

G. Strategy for Building Relationships

If the work has been harmful to your relationships as determined under C.1, decide which relationships you want to work on first.

Discuss this with the person(s) involved, and decide together what you will begin doing differently and when. Be specific in your goals, e.g. "We will begin tomorrow to set aside 15 minutes after breakfast to pray together about our concerns and give thanks for what God is doing." Write down your decisions and goals. See *The Secret of Staying in Love* for other ideas.

H. Strategy for Renewing Spirit, Mind, and Body

Look at Section D to review what you would like to do in each of the three areas. Choose one goal in each area, and write them under the points below.

1. *Spiritual renewal.* For example: "I will begin tomorrow to take 10 minutes during lunch hour each day to memorize Scripture, beginning with Psalm 103."

2. *Mental renewal.* For example: "I will begin taking one evening a week for reading in areas which stimulate me intellectually."

3. *Physical renewal.* For example: "I will begin this week to walk with my wife for at least 20 minutes 5 evenings per week (assuming she wants to)."

Conclusion

You will grow best if you don't become overwhelmed by trying to work on too many areas at once. Look over your worksheet and prioritize your goals and decisions for change. Choose 2 or 3 to begin working on. When these are under control, you can go back and choose one or two more. New habits often take 3 to 6 months to settle in.

Suggested Reading

Grossman, P. *The work/test balance.* Dallas: Wycliffe Bible Translators.

Minirth, F., et al. (1981). *The workaholic and his family.* Grand Rapids: Baker.

Narramore, B., & Counts, B. (1974). *Freedom from guilt.* Irvine, CA: Harvest House.

Powell, J. (1974). *The secret of staying in love.* Niles, IL: Argus Communications.

Williams, K. *Biblical strategies for handling stress.* Dallas: Wycliffe Bible Translators.

Williams, K. *Handling negative emotions.* Dallas: Wycliffe Bible Translators.

Questionaire for Discussion of Work/Rest/Living Balance

This questionnaire is confidential. Answer each question as honestly as you can. Rate yourself using the numbering system described below. Also rate your spouse or partner as you perceive him/her.

Almost always	Most of the time	Less than half of the time	Seldom
4	3	2	1

1. I am able to keep up with my work load.
2. I finish my work day with a sense of satisfaction rather than frustration.
3. When there is more work than I can handle, I can leave it, not only physically but mentally, so that it does not bother me after work.
4. I am free from guilt feelings for work not accomplished as well as it might have been, and for work left undone.
5. I am satisfied with the amount and quality of our holiday and recreation times.
6. I am free from symptoms of overwork, such as fatigue, irritability, sleep disturbances, depression and difficulty concentrating.
7. My work load is free from harmful effects on my relationship

with my spouse/partner.

8. My work load is free from harmful effects on my relationship with the Lord.

(For people with children):

9. My work load is free from harmful effects on my relationship with my children.

10. I am able to give adequate time for planned or regular family activities with the work load I now carry.

TOTAL SCORES: Self   Spouse/Partner

37

Marjory Foyle

Missionary Relationships: Powderkeg or Powerhouse?

Problems People Have with Administrators

Difficult relations between a mission's personnel and its adminstration are among the problems that introduce stress into the lives of missionaries. As I have studied these conflicts, I have often found poor administrative patterns that lead to profound staff insecurity. The following areas contribute to these tensions:

An inadequate constitution. Some missions do not realize they need to modernize their administrative structures. Their constitutions are dated and reflect conditions that existed many years ago. As such, they undermine confidence, with the result that missionary personnel are insecure, and administrative committees are bogged down in minor details. A major administrative committee may, for instance, waste time making individual decisions about personnel matters that ought to have been covered by personnel policies, which then creates insecurity and frustration for the people who are waiting for decisions to be made. These same people are also sometimes uneasy because they fear decisions about them may be made on the basis of some vague feeling that committee members might have instead of on objective realities.

Poor channels of communication and decision making. "No one listens to me" and "No one tells me anything" are two common complaints that often arise because of poor communications between administrators and personnel. Administrators often have similar complaints--things are happening that they should know about, but no one tells them--and both situations arouse anger and anxiety. They lead to a breakdown of basic trust between administration and personnel, and tension results.

One mission that recently needed to make an important policy decision communicated the problem to their personnel and asked them to discuss it at their regional conference. The findings were reported and collated, and the decision was then communicated back to personnel. Though there were some individuals who did not agree with the verdict, they were willing to accept it because they had been consulted.

Simple principles of management such as this are too easily overlooked. Leaders either do not ask for opinions--or they do not consider those opinions carefully. As a result, people feel undervalued, and relationships become strained. If a decision is not communicated to personnel, they may feel left out, or up in the air, because they do not know what was decided. In the extreme, splits can occur when one group pits itself against another.

Problems Administrators Have with Personnel

The administrator's task is often thankless, and a leader may become the target of people's anger. The anger may be justified if an administration is incompetent and unwilling to change. But administrators also must be willing to be the target of displaced anger--from people who are really angry about something else (perhaps their own inadequacies) but who may "handle" it by displacing it onto the administration. (We should, of course, check to see if there is a real problem; anger is not always displaced.)

Few administrators understand that being a displacement object is necessary to their job. Yet our Lord was himself the displacement object for all our sins and infirmities, and he accepted that as part of his redemptive and creative ministry.

Administrators also must sometimes make decisions their personnel do not like, and this too can occasionally lead to a breakdown in communications. A missionary involved in such a decision may feel undervalued, anxious, depressed, or angry, and their reactions are usually related to the length of time the administrator has known and had dialogue with the missionary (though sometimes a reaction may be totally unexpected).

Mission adminstrators must surely pray daily, "Lord, send me adaptable, willing people."

Addressing Administration/Personnel Conflicts

The problems described may be addressed in the following ways:

1. Constitutions and personnel policies should be clearly written and reviewed often. All members of a mission should possess a copy of these documents, and preferably in their own language.

2. Rules should leave room for individual decisions. While the nature of their service and ministry often means that missionaries have many decisions made for them, it is dangerous to deny them all decision-making rights; to do so may perpetuate immaturity or lower people's self-esteem. Personnel policies should be written in such a way that workable alternatives are evident and people's preferences are respected.

3. Communication channels between administration and personnel should be carefully designed and implemented to allow for free flow in both directions. This is especially important in countries that are politically unstable, or when there are staff changes. Missionaries must know what to do in emergency situations, and they surely need to know the names of new staff members.

4. Personnel should love, cherish, and respect their administrator--which implies that he or she is fit for the job. If that is not the case, the administrator needs to be replaced. Missionaries should remember that their administrators are human beings like them. They too can get amoebic dysentery, and their health should be safeguarded.

Some missions limit the term of office for their leaders, which can be helpful if it is possible to re-elect someone who has done an excellent job.

5. Administrators should have training in management. I have found that new missionaries, who are used to trained management, are increasingly unwilling to be led by administrators who have had no training. Tailor-made courses need to be made available to mission administrators--though unfortunately, these are extremely difficult to find.

Cultural Differences

Because many of our personal life patterns are based on what we learned in childhood, problems can arise when these patterns differ; we think our own way is the right one. Differences in dress, in manners, in cultural customs, and in religious practices can all cause strained relationships simply because they are different.

I once worked in a hospital whose staff came from nine different countries. One Good Friday, I was horrified to discover that all the men on the hospital building site had come to work. The missionary in charge, in working clothes, was busily getting them organized. I was incensed and became very critical, because in my own background, Good Friday had always been a very special day that Christians spent in a long church service, or in prayer or meditation at home. I thought to myself, "He can't be much of a Christian." Later, God taught me that not only was he a much better person than I, but that in his country Good Friday was not observed in any way.

An incident such as this explains why numerous problems develop between nationals of different countries: We often misunderstand simply because we do not take the trouble to ask.

Expatriate Relationships

Problems of interpersonal relationship can arise between expatriates from different countries, or between expatriates and the nationals of the countries in which they are serving. Here are some typical areas of conflict:

Language. English is frequently the language missionaries use to learn the vernacular and to communicate with one another. A person for whom English is not the mother tongue may use words incorrectly and offend someone for whom it is. A Scandinavian nurse once told me that a ward into which I had put a great deal of effort was "revolting." I began to bristle--until God reminded me to ask her what she meant. I discovered she was only trying to say it was a bit dilapidated and needed white-washing!

Furthermore, people who do speak English do not all speak the same kind. What does a "rain check" mean to a Briton, or "the shops" to an American? Always ask people what they mean instead of trying to guess.

Working patterns. I once worked in a hospital where temperatures were taken in Fahrenheit. Then some Scandinavian nurses joined us, and they took temperatures in centigrade. Consequently, someone had to change. I became all senior doctorish, insisting on Fahrenheit, and the new staff were thoroughly confused. (Later on I learned about a chart in which the figure could be entered in both measures.) Problems like this often do arise, and it is important to find a workable compromise.

Social and cultural customs. It is easy to hurt colleagues from other countries by neglecting their important festival days. Take

Christmas: in some countries the big celebration is on Christmas Eve, while in others it is on Christmas Day. Festivals also take on greater importance away from home, and failure to recognize them may be very stressful.

Financial disparity. Not all expatriates have the same allowances, and most national friends believe that missionaries are all at the rich end of the scale. This can be painful, especially if children are involved, for missionaries with less money cannot provide the same things for their children as those who have a greater abundance. Though many young people understand and accept this, a group of missionary kids recently admitted to me that despite their understanding and acceptance, they had real problems in being poor, and they felt demeaned by handouts.

Expatriate-National Relationships

Our national friends are not often willing to discuss this subject openly, but the following areas have been mentioned to me. Undoubtedly there are others of equal or greater importance:

Manners and customs. Usually through ignorance, missionaries may behave in a way that is offensive to nationals. For example, what you do with your feet is very important in parts of Asia. In India, one should never use the foot to indicate something, even if the object is on the floor, and in some areas you should not show the sole of your foot when you are seated in public. Christian nationals often understand that the missionary simply does not know, but others may become upset at what appears to be rudeness or insensitivity. For instance, it is acceptable in some rural areas of India to blow your nose politely with your fingers--but it is a terrible thing to use a handkerchief.

Working concepts. Expatriates do not always understand the pressures that nationals' families put on them. In countries where women do little by themselves, a child with a toothache must be taken to the dentist by the father. Whatever his work responsibilities, the father takes casual leave for the day; it is a culturally accepted pattern that the needs of the family take priority over those of the work. Westerners with a rigidly work-oriented outlook may develop real resentments.

Also, both national and expatriate single people sometimes feel that married couples with children are unreliable workers. One very experienced Indian nurse told me that single workers in her hospital often feel aggrieved because they could not plead children's needs in order to go off duty. While the personal lives of the single people were frequently subordinated to the needs of the hospital, this rarely happened to married nurses. At the same time, married workers were frequently under great pressure as they worked at balancing the demands of home, work, and church.

Integration. Most missionaries long to integrate closely with the nationals they have come to serve. To this end, some make external adaptations in language, dress, and food. Though these things are valuable, they are not all there is to true integration. Nationals know whether missionaries sincerely know them. That is of greater value to them than external adaptations, which they regard as matters of common politeness and cultural suitability.

Resolving Relationship Problems

Here is some practical advice to help solve some of these areas of problem relationships:

1. If you do not understand something, ask. Never act precipitately; first make quite sure that what is understood is what was meant.

2. Discover the meaning of your colleagues' degrees and the patterns of their educational backgrounds. Training patterns vary from country to country, but is usually possible to place people in identifiable categories. Others can easily feel that we minimize them if we have not troubled to understand their training.

3. In expatriate-to-expatriate working conflicts, ask the advice of nationals, then follow the custom of the country.

4. Do not make jokes about one another's accents, dress, or behavior. This may be acceptable once you know each other well, but early on, such teasing may be interpreted as a cultural slur.

5. Try to avoid national stereotypes. Be prepared to accept people as *people,* and not as citizens of a particular country.

6. Live humbly and genuinely. When you do, national colleagues feel free to relate to missionaries as human beings and to help them in their integration.

The Perils of Missionary Subcultures

Missionary subcultures are dangerous, but they are rarely discussed. By "subculture" I mean the kind of group behavior and thinking that develops when missionaries live in a small group that is separated from the larger outside group. The living arrangement is not important in itself, but the degree of detachment from, or integration with, the larger outside community is an indication of whether a subculture has developed.

A subculture may provide considerable support; however, it is often more dangerous than beneficial for the following reasons:

1. The subculture becomes increasingly inward directed and loses interest in the outside world. I know of a subculture that remained remarkably uninterested in a serious political crisis in the country in which the people were working. They neither read the paper, heard the local radio, nor discussed what was happening.

2. An overpreoccupation with group concerns develops. When this happens, a group will concentrate almost entirely on its own relationships, spiritual desires, and personal problems. When that happens, common preoccupations emerge--such as demonology, eschatology, or spiritual gifts--to the exclusion of other topics.

3. Subcultural behavior and thought patterns are imposed on new members as the norm. Those who accept these are "suitable"; those who do not are considered "unsuitable" or "unspiritual."

4. Unhealthy emotions may spread. Depression, inferiority, fear of other people's opinions, or anxiety can sweep through a group. Any who may have remained on the fringe are not usually infected, and they are often puzzled by what is happening.

Countering the Subculture Mentality

The growth of missionary subcultures can be oppsoed by taking some practical steps:

1. Maintain a healthy balance between the outside world and the missionary or Christian community, and mix with both worlds within the boundaries of a healthy Christian conscience. Remember, the outside world needs you. I once worked in a remote mission hospital in the early days of Christian enterprise in that area. The wise American doctor in charge taught us a great deal about mixing with the outer world in a healthy manner: we enjoyed the local music group and shared our talents in a most enjoyable way.

2. Maintain the integrity of your own person. You are body, mind, and spirit, and you need to care for each aspect.

Take great care of your body. We are expendable in God's service, but we should not be stupid about looking after our bodies.

Read as much as you can--books, magazines, papers, when you can obtain them.

Have an interesting (and cheap!) hobby. Birdwatching, for example, is great: once you have bought binoculars and a bird book you do not need to spend any more money.

Move in local society, see how people live, and share their lives wherever it is possible. Keep your mind alert by making notes of what you observe. Who knows, an anthropologist may someday bless you for them!

Be careful to take holidays, combining spiritual refreshment with total relaxation from your job.

Beware of unhealthy overpreoccupations. By this I do not mean the continual preoccupations of the missionary but constant brooding on a particular topic. Periods of intense God-given spiritual preoccupation are usually succeeded by a balanced pattern of thought and life. If that balance does not return, you need to take a break from your work--and possibly have a chat with your doctor.

38

Frances J. White
Elaine M. Nesbit

Separation: Balancing the Gains and Losses

With mixed feelings of joy and sadness, the missionary family looked through the windows of the Boeing 747 as it slowly began to taxi toward the runway. They were hoping to get a last glimpse of relatives and friends inside the terminal building.

Their furlough in the United States was over. Soon their plane would be flying over a broad, silent ocean on its way to the Orient, returning them once again to the mission field. A variety of emotions began to surface.

The mother was happy and excited that their oldest son had been accepted at a prestigious Midwestern college. Yet she was saddened at leaving him behind. Would he be all right on his own? What if a problem arose and they were unavailable to help him sort through it?

The father had feelings of frustration. The year's furlough had gone by too quickly. Many of the things he had planned to do never got done. He felt uncomfortable and inadequate, ill-prepared to return to his work on the mission field.

At the same time, their daughter was excited about the prospect of rejoining her friends in the Orient. But even so, a tear came to her eye as she waved good-bye to her grandparents.

The aging grandparents were filled with genuine joy that their daughter and son-in-law were serving the Lord overseas. Yet their health had been deteriorating lately and they wondered if they would be alive to see them again when they returned home in four years.

Happiness, frustration, and sadness were only a few of the intermingled emotions flooding everyone's minds. There was also an uneasy anxiety about returning to a country they had been away from for a full year. They knew the political climate had changed. What new restrictions and challenges awaited them? Would they find the same satisfaction in their work as they had in the past?

As the plane flew toward its destination on the other side of the world, the missionary family was lulled to sleep by the calming drone of the plane's engines. Theirs was a common sleep of sadness, contentment, and anxiety.

Handling conflicting emotions is a difficult task. Yet it is something we all face at one time or another. As we progress through life we inevitably encounter change, separation, and loss. In fact, the three words can be used almost interchangeably. Change is separation from the past, loss occurs as a result of separation.

Two Basic Types of Separation

There are two basic types of change/separation/loss. The first type is *developmental*, or that which occurs naturally and predictably. These are the physical and mental changes shared in common by most of mankind as we progress from infancy to old age. For example, going through puberty, getting married and raising a family, and encountering old age.

All of these changes involve gains and losses. An adolescent, for example, gives up the security of depending primarily upon parents in order to consolidate his or her own identity. Parents separate from the satisfactions--and frustrations--of raising children to eventually regain some of the pleasures through their grandchildren.

The second type is more *traumatic*, for example, accidents, natural disasters, and unexpected deaths of friends or relatives. An unexpected missionary evacuation often results in separation from meaningful nationals, loss of personal belongings left behind, possibly changing languages, and facing new schedules and pressures.

Missionaries and their families seem to be vulnerable to an inordinate amount of intense and complex change/separation/loss. They separate from friends, families, homeland, cultural values, language, eating habits, and even recreational habits. Their children go to and return from boarding school, or perhaps enter a national school with different educational methods and philosophy. The process reverses itself each time the missionary returns to his or her home country.

Interestingly, humans experience common feelings and reactions as a result of separations. Understanding the process permits us to view our responses for what they are--a part of our humanness, the way God created us. What, then, can we expect in the face of change/separation/loss? And when will we know when we are reacting in an unhealthy manner?

Four Stages of Anxiety

The all-inclusive term for change/separation/loss reactions is "anxiety." Anxiety tends to express itself in four stages.

The distinctive behavior of the first stage is *denial*, or a way of minimizing losses. Often denial occurs in subtle forms. For example, a missionary who is leaving behind family and friends may make unrealistic promises and plans, such as, "We'll write several times a week," or "I'll be home for the big event." If a missionary were to try to carry out all of these well-intentioned promises, little time would be left for the task. Nonetheless, they help cushion the pain of leaving loved ones.

Another form of denial is reflected in missionary responses to a new culture. They may at first spend a great deal of time admiring the scenery, or ambitiously taking photographs of the landscape and people, almost as though they were in a vacation spot rather than a new residence. A feeling of permanence usually sets in, gradually allowing the missionary time to adjust to the tremendous changes.

The second stage of anxiety is characterized by *anger*. Like denial, anger protects us from the intense pangs of loss. Often, individuals do not connect their particular way of expressing anger--impatience, gruffness, silence, foot-dragging, criticalness--with the changes taking place. For example, as a missionary passes through the initial phase of being tantalized with a new culture, he or she may become irritated with some of the culture's nuances, such as material inconveniences or personality differences.

Often, a missionary will act irritably to those with whom he or she has the most meaningful relationships, even before leaving the home country. As a missionary experiences increased tension with family members or mission board personnel, leaving the country becomes easier. A familiar thought is, "It's good we're (they're) leaving next week." Both parties may feel that the separation is timely indeed.

Sometimes, instead of feeling actual anger or frustration, individuals simply distance themselves from others before and after a difficult change or separation. One illustration is the husband who leaves his wife for awhile to go on a project for the mission. When they reunite the husband may be ready for a cozy, romantic evening, but is surprised to find his wife cool and unresponsive. Her behavior is caused by having had to "gird up the loins" of her emotions in order to handle family responsibilities during his absence. In many instances, time is needed to regain closeness after separation.

The third phase of anxiety is *sadness*, or a feeling of being "down." This feeling often surfaces when a person begins to come to grips with the reality and significance of a loss. The length of time that the sadness lasts is different for each person and situation. Usually if the loss is significant, feelings of sadness will linger, occurring occasionally long after the person has recovered from the loss.

Resolution is the final stage of anxiety. Resolution involves acceptance and a growing ability to adjust to the new culture or situation positively. Accepting the loss is what allows people to integrate the new situation into their lives and to live in the present.

Resolution frees people to make new commitments. However, acceptance of the present does not mean that what has been left behind is forgotten. Rather, resolution involves taking a part of what was formerly appreciated and incorporating its traits into the new situation. Therefore, those who undergo change/separation/loss become richer individuals because they now have more to offer to others.

Reactions to change/separation/loss tend to vary according to the situation and the individual. Neither can it be assumed that the stages follow a neat, sequential pattern for all individuals. Indications that the anxiety syndrome is being resolved include a diminishing of the intensity of feelings, increased response to the feelings of others, reactions that are more widely spaced, and a sense of comfort with the new.

However, the intensity of the reaction will increase in direct proportion to the significance or importance of what was left behind. In addition, extreme dissimilarity between the old and new usually causes a more pronounced reaction. When there are many similarities, reaction may be delayed. For example, missionaries who serve in a country whose language and dress are similar to their home country, may experience a delayed response to the change because the deeper cultural differences are masked and become visible only after some time. Finally, the more sudden the change, the more marked will be the response to it.

Unhealthy Reactions

The common feelings that have just been described are both normal and healthy reactions to change/separation/loss. What then constitutes a negative or unhealthy reaction?

One unhealthy reaction is *suppressing emotions.* This can lead to relationships that develop slowly or develop only at a superficial level. These friendships lack the openness and honesty that results when feelings are shared. By ignoring or pushing away strong feelings we can also become expressionless and aloof. Parents must be particularly careful, because these suppressed emotions can easily affect the emotional growth of their children.

Remaining "stuck" in some phase of the process is also an unhealthy response. To continue to deny feelings or to hold anger for prolonged periods of time are typical examples of being "stuck." Perhaps a missionary is stil afraid to leave the house, although he or she has been on the field for over a year. There is not set amount of time for recovering from separation or loss. However, if a response continues to interfere with a ministry or lifestyle, perhaps professional counseling should be considered.

An inability to form new and deep relationships, or a hesitancy to make commitments, can also be a signal that a change or loss has not been resolved. This may appear as an attitude of aloofness in a new situation. A missionary may be working in a foreign country, yet mentally still be living at home.

It is evident that the way we respond to change affects our lives and our ministry. Depriving ourselves of new and meaningful relationships deprives us of all that the Lord intends us to be and interferes with the task he has set before us. Unhealthy reactions are also witnessed by children, who are themselves struggling to reattach to new people and a new environment.

How to Promote Healthy Attitudes

How then do we promote a healthy attitude toward change/separation/loss? Here are a few practical suggestions that may be helpful during those trying times of change or loss:

1. Take time to be aware of your particular reactions to change. Take a few moments from your schedule to analyze your emotions and feelings.

2. Talk about your feelings with others. This may be difficult at first, but it is probably the most valuable and effective way of dealing with anxiety.

3. Listen carefully to family members. Be especially alert to your children. Try to read behind their words. They may express their anxiety in behavior rather than words. Common signs are increased clingingness, irritability, combativeness, defiance, or even a return to more infantile behavior such as bed-wetting. Letting them know you understand what they are going through assures them that they have been heard and understood.

4. Make allowances for one another to experience the various stages at different times and in a different order. Reactions are not entirely predictable, nor are they the same for everyone.

5. Hold gatherings such as farewell or welcome parties. They can be very helpful during transition periods because they tend to give a feeling of reality to the change. They also help to emphasize the positive aspects. In addition, they provide a time to appropriately express the sadness that people feel.

6. Allow yourself and others to be happy in the new situation or environment. Don't be afraid to form new attachments and make new commitments.

7. Allow time to "defrost" after a separation or loss has occurred. Avoid initially overwhelming one another with affection. Sometimes we need to warm up gradually. When children return from school be careful about smothering them with hugs and kisses before they're ready for it.

8. When returning for furlough, take your time in coming back. Avoid the sudden change of foreign country to home church and family. If possible, take a detour to permit a more gradual adjustment to the change.

9. Create as much sameness and predictability as possible within the family as it adapts to the new. This is a time when family togetherness is particularly important. It is a time when single missionaries should find or create an opportunity to fellowship with others in a close, personal way.

10. Should your children be returning home, don't panic if they don't immediately like the schools, or feel they don't fit in. Allow them time to express negative feelings. Again, show understanding by restating what they say in their own words, verbalizing the feelings they seem to be experiencing.

11. Remember, change of any kind always involves some form of change/separation/loss. As we recognize this we can more fully accept the normal emotions that we encounter in our day-to-day living. As missionaries begin to better understand the changes they undergo, they will learn to live richer and fuller lives that are more meaningful not only to themselves, but to those they come in contact with.

39

Marjory Foyle

Overcoming Stress In Singleness

The term "single" has changed remarkably over the past 20 years. It once meant an unmarried person, and it implied virginity. Today, to be "single" means "being alone." It not only describes people who have never been married, but also the divorced and bereaved. No longer does it imply virginity, merely the absence of a current sexual partner.

For the purpose of this article, "single" means those who have never married and who for God's sake live celibate lives. Virginity may have been lost, but for religious reasons further sexual activity outside legal marriage is denied.

In the passage on eunuchs in Matthew 19, it would seem clear that the Lord is speaking of people who live celibate lives for a variety of reasons:

1. *Those who are eunuchs from birth.* These are people who cannot marry due to some physical, mental, or social defect that has been present from birth. We recognize these as people who are seriously handicapped, physically or mentally, and certain cases of sexual or personality deviation.

2. *Those who have been made eunuchs.* There are people born normally who became eunuchs through some accident or illness. Historically, such individuals would include boys castrated to preserve their singing voices, while today, radiation victims may fit this category.

---

3. *Those who have made themselves eunuchs for the kingdom of heaven's sake.* Included here are men and women who have taken a vow of celibacy, such as religious monks, clergy, and nuns. Many Protestant missionaries whose response to the call of God includes an involuntary celibacy also fall into this category. Often no vow is involved, but to go overseas as a missionary is to markedly reduce one's marriage opportunities.

The full implications of singleness are often difficult to understand in a missionary's home country. Too often, a future missionary pays little or no attention to the potential of a single life overseas. Only after arrival does singleness become a practical reality--and an issue to be faced.

I recently asked a new group of single missionaries what had been the hardest part of their experience so far. They responded with one voice: "Being single." Not only had they no husband and so no children, they also felt deprived of normal male companionship in their social circle, and isolated in their struggles with singleness.

Is it any surprise, then, that the Lord ended this passage with the words, "Let anyone who can, accept my statement"?

Stages in the Acceptance of Singleness

Single adults do not always accept their situation immediately. Many progress by stages. These stages have been effectively discussed in a booklet by Fowke and Long, who have permitted me to use their material and translate it into missionary terms.

Hope. Many single missionaries hope to marry when they go overseas. Language schools, in fact, have the reputation of being matchmaking institutions. It is at language school, however, that the truth often sinks in. The fact is that there are very few single men missionaries--and large numbers of single women. Logically, not all can hope to marry.

Doubt. Single male missionaries usually marry. When they do, many other women are left out. One who has been passed over may entertain real personal doubts about her own attractiveness and value. It is not always easy to resolve these doubts, and personal stock taking may prove painful.

But doubts of this kind can be helpful. A missionary who pays inadequate attention to herself often remains a dreary person, while a somewhat dull individual can become the kind of person others like to be with through attention to dress (even within a limited budget), cultivation of graciousness and concern for others, and a widening of interests. Negative misery can be useful when it becomes an active force in personal growth.

Acceptance of reality. Too often people fail to understand what God is asking them to accept. What they need to perceive is that now--at this moment--they are single in God's best will. Accepting that reality does not involve an unknown future other than in general terms of commitment to the will of God.

I know two women who for many years made regular acts of acceptance of singleness. To their great surprise, both were married soon after retirement from active missionary service. Few single missionaries should make acts of acceptance of their singleness for the whole of their lives; rarely is the will of God revealed so far into the future.

An added difficulty arises when the hope of children begins to fade at the time of menopause. I have had several single missionaries tell me they wept quietly when they reached forty. Often, at this time, a new act of acceptance is required.

Maturity. Maturity involves accepting singleness in the present as God's first-best will--not a form of punishment handed out by an inscrutable heavenly Father. It means accepting the truth that God has no favorites. It also means understanding that marriage per se is not a bed of roses, and that married missionaries have multiple problems. While they have the companionship of a spouse, and the joy of children, they face many problems that never touch the single missionary.

There are some single missionaries who may never go through these stages, or pass over them quickly. But there are others who experience the agonies of each stage to the full. I personally believe this difference in individual responses is because God has different things for each individual to learn. He alone understands what we need to know to reach maturity so that we may be of maximum service.

Practical Problems

Social invitations. Generally speaking, the mission groups in which most missionaries live are couple oriented. Single people, especially women, often have special problems where this is the case. When social invitations are based on professional roles, the difficulties can become formidable.

For example, as a physician in India I am often asked to attend medical dinners. The other doctors are usually all men, and in typical Indian style they gather in one corner, and their wives in another. It is not appropriate for me to join the men--in whose group I belong professionally--so I gravitate toward the women. But then another problem emerges, for the women speak little English. They are offended if I speak in the vernacular, for that implies that I must think they are not educated. Their English is soon exhausted, and my presence puts a damper on their own conversation.

One solution is to take a female hospital staff member to the party, who acts as a bridge between the other women and myself. They are usually quite happy to talk to her in the vernacular, for they think she does not speak English. So we end up all chatting together happily.

Difficulty in obtaining housing. Some missions have a long tradition of subordinating the needs of single people to those of married couples. This only encourages a feeling of second-class citizenship on the part of the single people.

Recently I visited a very remote mission work where there was one single woman and several married couples. The single woman had to wait nine months for housing, while the single men and married couples who came after her were accommodated immediately. Housing was provided only after the mission pastoral staff intervened. The missionary's health and work efficiency improved immediately.

Permanent accommodation with a married couple. Only a few missions still permit this arrangement. In my experience, it is a potential disaster course. The privacy that both married and single people need is nonexistent, and there are obvious dangers in such a situation. Close relationships have been known to develop between the husband and the single girl, or between the wife and a single man. Missionary marriages have enough strains upon them without the introduction of another potential stress area. When such an arrangement is unavoidable, it should only rarely become permanent.

Living with strangers. Married people have at least said "yes," but single missionaries cannot always choose their living companions and often have to move into any place there is a vacancy. Constant readjustments often must be made because companions are always changing due to leave or transfers. One person recently told me she had had 16 living companions in 18 years. She could not even learn their names--let alone their family backgrounds.

Furlough accommodation. Some missions do not understand that single people on leave need their own place to stay as much as do married couples. Single missionaries used to return automatically to the family home, but in our modern society this practice may raise many problems and create unhelpful tensions.

Single missionaries often have held positions of great responsibility at a comparatively young age. They have become mature adults, while the family has adjusted to the loss of their missionary child and developed new patterns. Despite all the good will in the world, role problems may develop as the adult missionary strives to behave suitably as an ex-child. Trying to live at two levels of maturity and in two roles can be devastating. At the same time, the family has a new life pattern and does not know how to cope with the returned child.

Many mission boards understand this problem and offer the single missionary a choice of furlough accommodation. The operative word is choice: it should always be offered and nothing should be taken for granted.

Practical Advice

Single people living with an uncongenial companion should not feel compelled to continue for too long. Paul could not get on with John Mark, and they finally split up. There is no sin in this, and it may be sound common sense. Give the situation a good try, but if it is really not working out, ask for a change. Paul and John Mark got on very well together after a break from each other.

While trying to make a relationship work, allow plenty of talking time. One missionary told me she and her companion talked for 18 hours (not all at once) before they came to understand each other.

Some time each week should be set aside for prayer, even if it may not be possible daily.

Remember that all reasonably mature people have their own habits of life. Take preparation of the humble boiled egg, for example. Punjabis eat them hard-boiled, Chinese drop them raw into hot soup, and the British eat them soft-boiled (*exactly* 3-1/2 minutes). Americans never use egg cups, the British always do. Some people bang the top of the egg, and take the shell off with a spoon; others cut the shell nearly at the top. It sometimes seems there are more critical comments over a boiled egg than anything else--which only illustrates the importance of remembering that we humans are all different. Rather than get annoyed about differences, we can learn to enjoy them.

Those whose personality it suits should try living alone. It is important, however, not to become a recluse; entertaining keeps a person sane. It is also important to determine whether living alone is understood by the local culture, and if it is reasonably safe.

Sex Problems

There are some single missionaries who believe that all sexual feelings will magically vanish if they obey God's call to serve him overseas as a missionary. When this does not happen, they worry that something is wrong with their commitment. But the only persons with no sexual feelings are the very old, the very ill--or the very dead! Problems arise when we confuse "biological" sexuality with "creative" sexuality and try to handle both aspects in the same way.

Biological sexuality. This is the urge, the instinct, the innate drive to mate and to reproduce. Many Christians believe the sex drive has a deeper significance than other drives--such as hunger--and this may be true. Nevertheless, it is a basic bodily drive that we can never expect to lose.

Here single missionaries make a mistake. Because they remain seuxal beings they think their dedication is inadequate. Some ask God to remove sexual feelings if they are not going to marry. This, of course, God will not do, for it would make them less than human. It is also futile to attempt to feel totally fulfilled. Single people can never be fulfilled biologically. They have usually not mated or had children, to use my original definition of singleness. In dealing with biological urges, it is important simply to accept them as indications of normality. Continued trust in God's overall plan for the life, together with a wise life pattern, helps the single missionary maintain celibacy for as long as God wishes. But it is important to use common sense. Single missionaries need to be wise in avoiding situations that may make chastity difficult to maintain.

Creative sexuality. This aspect of the sex drive is utilized in many different ways: care of children, service, maintenance of good personal relationships, work, and many other things; all are empowered by creative sexuality.

Creative energy is reduced when single persons use a lot of energy in resenting their singleness. In reality, this energy holds abundant possibilities for personal fulfillment. A profitable habit single persons might adopt is to thank God at the end of each day for the volume of creative sexuality expended during the day's ministry.

Being Alone

Handling domestic matters. Single people must learn to cope, and they should not depend on others for help. Skills needed for their location should be learned--from opening a complex fuse box to repairing the oil lamp or even trimming the candle wick.

Discussing personal matters. Single missionaries who have no permanent confidant need to learn how to be a unit of one instead of a family group. Lacking someone with whom one can share regularly can lead to overcompensation. Some want to share everything with their living companion, using that relationship as an equivalent of marital companionship. But that kind of sharing may develop an unhealthy compulsive quality: one or the other may feel guilt if not everything is shared. We must always remember that people have an inner core of privacy. Few husbands and wives, if they are wise, share *everything.* They understand that being "of one flesh" does not mean one person, but two persons in harmonious unity.

Belonging to someone. It is rare for the relationships between single persons to carry the same sense of belonging to one another that happily married people experience. But we can remember that the pain of this experience was fully shared by our Lord, who also was single. Though he had many good friends, he lacked the close tie of marriage.

There is also a danger of functioning on the principle of "If only." "If only I had married I would have a companion." "If only I had children, then such and such would not have happened." When we say,"If only," we indicate that we believe God has favorites, and some of them have an easier time than others.

Other Considerations

Never sink back resentfully into the classical spinster or bachelor image. Take singleness from God's hand alone, and use it to the full.

Make a personal decision about how to handle both the biological urges and the need to belong to someone. The most important decisions concern homosexual and extramarital relationships-- neither pathway, in my opinion, is suitable for Christian single people.

There is great danger in the area of stress-related homosexuality. People who have never before engaged in homosexual relationships may do so if they come under an unusual amount of stress (such as the early days of missionary adjustment). I have found that an initial decision made about homosexuality acts as an anchor in times of pressure. Missionary candidates should study possible adult sexual patterns both academically and biblically, and should give these patterns the most careful consideration. A well-informed deliberate decision to abstain from homosexuality, or heterosexual relations apart from marriage, can be the greatest help later on. Missionaries often think, "It can't happen to me." It can! Language teachers are attractive; single girls are lonely; temptations are great. Single men often have to handle an upsurge of sexual feelings resulting from the move to another country and culture. While prior acts of decision and dedication will not always prevent problems, they are a great help.

Masturbation, another problem area, is, in my view, often no more than a pressure cooker blowing off steam. Missionary life should be as balanced as possible, but some missionaries are so spiritually intense that they never read a book or newspaper, or enter the daily lives of the people they serve. Such an imbalance can produce tension, and then the pressure cooker blows: in anger, in masturbation, or in other ways. We should not forget that our Lord often went out to dinner, and he appeared to enjoy himself at a wedding.

There are some, however, who develop a compulsive habit of masturbation. This may indicate an underlying illess, and if a sensible rebalancing of the life does not help, professional advice should be sought.

Remember that God uses different channels through which single people can experience love. A marital relationship with its love is not the only one. Love between nationals and missionaries, between missionaries, among friends from many countries, and the love of our families all stem from the love of God. Our Lord, who was single, had wonderful, loving relationships with both men and women. He both gave and received love. When we accept our singleness from the hand of God alone, we single missionaries can have a rich experience of the love that Jesus knew and gave to others during his own ministry.

ATTRITION

40

Frank Allen

Why Do They Leave?
Reflections on Attrition

"Is is true that the main reason missionaries leave the field is because of poor interrelationships?"

This question has been put to me twice in recent months. The first came from a young man writing an article saying that the answer was Yes. The second came from a young couple, Bible school graduates.

Their question reflected a popular assumption. I have never seen any studies to substantiate it. But my observations cause me to doubt is validity.

During much of my nearly 29 years in the Philippines, I was either a college administrator or the field director. Until I left in 1981, I knew all but one of our missionaries who had served there since 1947. I also knew why those who had left had done so.

Of course, some left for natural reasons: marriage, health, retirement, and death, to name the most common ones. But as I have reviewed our field's history, I would say that poor interpersonal relationships were only one of a number of reasons why our people left, and certainly not the paramount one. There are many other reasons that must be given at least as much credence. These I am going to discuss below: lack of gifts, culture shock, unfulfilled expectations, morals, family problems, disagreements with the mission, and difficulties with the language.

I am also going to suggest that in many cases deeper problems lie behind so-called poor interpersonal relationships.

Lack of gifts. How many missionaries have tried a field ministry without the requisite gifts? We can only guess, but I have been shocked looking over candidate papers of potential evangelists and church planters. When asked about their evangelistic experiences, most could only say that they had led a junior Sunday school boy to Christ, or an "eight-year-old girl at camp." Few could tell about any experiences with adults on a regular basis.

Yet here they were, wishing to minister to adults in another culture, in a strange language, to establish churches. They had never done anything like this in their own culture and tongue. Their subsequent work revealed their lack of gifts and many gave up and went home.

Culture shock. Luzbetak defines culture shock as "a breakdown, an attack, a stroke, or exhaustion resulting from improper adjustment to cultural frustrations and jolts" (*The Church and Cultures*, p.98). He explains that the victim of culture shock "either clings blindly and immovably to his original ways, or he blindly and indiscriminately renounces his former ways and values in favor of the ways and values that are responsible for the culture shock" (p. 97).

Although it is not popular to admit, culture shock is responsible for a significant number of missionary dropouts. It may be seen as a refusal to accept any changes at all. Those going through cultural shock constantly talk about how great the United States is, even though they may be very critical of the U.S. when at home. They look at everything that's different as being wrong.

Perhaps its ultimate expression is reflected in this comment by a missionary: "I have not yet met a national I can respect." This was said in a country where national church leaders can genuinely be described as outstanding.

Obviously, this feeling is closely linked to ethnocentricity. It is, no doubt, easier to say that one's fellow missionaries are "impossible" to live with than it is to admit one's inability or unwillingness to overcome culture shock.

There is, perhaps, a more subtle form of culture shock to which many missionaries succumb. A colleague once referred to this as "culture fatigue," where, although they have adapted well, they may eventually be worn down by the constant adjustments to different ways of doing, thinking, and speaking.

Unfulfilled expectations. Years ago when things did not always turn out right for new candidates, someone would remind us that there was "many a slip 'tween the lip and the ship." There still is.

Sometimes years can elapse between the time a person is contacted by a mission and the time he or she arrives on the field. By then, the position for which he or she was recruited has been filled--many times by a qualified national--and another role is called for.

Some missionaries can make the switch, but others can't and they are devastated. That means another missionary casualty, another volunteer returning home with deep disappointment.

Morals. Given the circumstances, it's cause for praise that missionaries do not more often fall into sexual immorality. After all, the missionary community is a microcosm of U.S. churches where, tragically, such cases are on the increase. Some missionary husbands neglect their wives, and vice versa. When this happens and either one is thrown into close, continuous contact with another man or woman (including nationals), there's grave potential for an affair. Single missionaries, too, face unique temptations and sometimes they are overpowered in trying to meet their needs. But on the whole, from what I've seen in many missions over many years, relatively few missionaries are sent home for sexual immorality.

Family problems. Here is a major reason for missionary attrition, with several contributing factors. For one, parents may be overly permissive and feel that any kind of limits, guidelines, or discipline for their children are old-fashioned. Their children grow up with all kinds of problems and insecurities, which in the end demand departure from the field. Of course, overly strict parents can produce similar problems by removing all choices from their children and turning them into automatons.

A second factor is disagreement among parents over the nurture and discipline of their children. Problems between spouses cause tensions that ultimately tear up the children emotionally.

Third, parents, especially husbands, may be too busy doing "the Lord's work" to give sufficient attention to their families. Samuel Rowen of Missionary Internship asks, "Does God ever lead people to neglect their God-given responsibilities in order to serve him elsewhere?" (*Evangeliscal Missions Quarterly,* July, 1985).

I once knew a father who, after traveling hundreds of miles to visit the school where his children lived, to pay their fees, would leave before school was out without seeing them. He said he had much work to do in that city. Imagine what this communicated to his children.

Disagreements with the mission. Disagreements fall into two categories: those with mission policies and practices (including finances), and those with field leaders. Probably one of the keenest disappointments that new missionaries face is that everyday life on the field is a far cry from what was told them by the agency's recruiter. The romantic days eventually end.

The candidate selection process should include a question-and-answer session on mission policies, practices, and doctrines. Such matters are far too important to take for granted, especially the sensitive issue of finances.

Regarding friction between field leaders and missionaries, the characteristic North American individualism does not make for either good teamwork, or for the recognition of duly delegated authority (especially among peers).

Ralph Winter once remarked that the words, "The Lord is leading me," are probably one of the greatest obstacles to effective missionary work. Individual "leading" can wreak havoc with the carefully laid plans and strategies of mission leaders.

When missionaries talk about poor interpersonal relationships, they usually mean friction between themselves and their leaders. If the mission director disagrees with the "leading of the Lord" in someone's life, he may be suspected of unspirituality or even heresy.

Language. Much missionary work, especially in evangelism and church planting, demands a mastery of another language. To accomplish this requires rigorous discipline and self-effacement. Missionaries must be willing to be embarrassed, to be laughed at, and at times to be humiliated.

Willingness to subject oneself to this discipline does not come easily, and some are either unable or unwilling to do so. At times a ministry in English can be found for the language dropout, but for others there is no alternative but to return home.

Experience and observation tell me that the above circumstances account for more missionary casualties than do poor interpersonal relationships. As a field director, I did encounter problems between missionaries, but I can't recall a single case where someone had to leave the field for that reason. Therefore, when I hear that reason given, questions are raised in my mind: Are the poor relationships between missionaries and their field leaders? Are the missionaries unwilling to submit to authority? Or, do the missionaries have deeper problems?

Poor relationships do exist, but I am not convinced that they are the major cause of missionary attrition. My theory that poor relationships indicate deeper problems needs to be tested. Mission agencies must do more research on missionary attrition. Mission agencies also can assist dropouts to leave the field with dignity and encourage their home churches to accept them with genuine understanding. If headquarters can accomplish this, ex-missionaries will then feel free to disclose the real reasons why they left the field.

(*We have asked four agencies to summarize their studies of missionary attrition. Their responses follow.--The editors of Evangelical Missions Quarterly*).

The Evangelical Alliance Mission

Michael Pocock

Looking at attrition--other than retirement and associates ending their regular time of service--34 missionaries separated from The Evangelical Alliance Mission (TEAM) in 1984-85. The reasons given for termination are as follows: health, 7; changed to another mission, 4; married outside the mission, 2; unilaterial personal decision, 13; dismissed, 8.

Total attrition for the above two years was 143. Thirty-one were retirees. Exact associate turnover is not listed, but must have been about 78. The true make-up of the total terminating for reasons other than retirement, associate turnover, or those listed above is somewhat uncertain. Periodically, the records are purged of those who have been detained at home for considerable periods with little likelihood that they will reactivate.

A number who are eventually lost to the mission simply "fade out." They remain in good graces with the mission and they seem for the most part to think highly of the mission, but they do not continue in active service.

The purpose of any attrition study is to find out if a significant turnover problem exists, and if there are ways to prevent otherwise avoidable dropouts. At TEAM, the total annual attrition is about 8 percent, but when retirees and associates are discounted, presumably avoidable attrition is 1.6 percent. The mission needs to concern itself for every individual, but 1.6 percent is a low figure in an organization of TEAM's size.

It is hard to quantify the exact reasons for other than normal attrition. Combinations of reasons are frequently given, but here are some reasons for staying home that are increasingly voiced. They grow not necessarily from mission-related conditions, but from society-wide trends.

1. *A desire to help children over the hurdle between high school and college.* Behind this is a sense of having been separated from children a lot during schooling and a desire to make up for it by being together for a few years in the homeland. Failure of children to adjust to a schooling situation on the field, or inability of a

mission school to provide special education where needed, also figure in family movement from field to home. The "home school" movement does exert some influence in schooling for MKs. This approach is very wary of any out-of-home influence on children. Any situation at home or abroad that would interfere with home school is viewed with distrust.

2. *Caring for elderly parents.* Sometimes active missionaries are the only family members who can care for aging parents, but sometimes it is because the children who are missionaries are the only ones willng to care for their folks.

3. *Chronic overextension.* Insufficient support (sometimes relief was impossible) accounts for others making a decision to step out of active service.

4. *Underproductivity, misconduct and friction with coworkers.* Each of these accounts for a few terminations initiated either by the mission or the worker.

In the cases of avoidable attrition, what do the trends say to the mission?

1. Continued provision of good schooling as close as possible to parents, openness to various educational alternatives, and care for the slower student is needed. Both in the public schools of some countries (Europe and Japan) and in missionary children's schools almost everywhere, education is in the "fast lane." This is not generally a problem because the children are usually well-motivated, have well-educated, supportive parents, and present few discipline problems. But anyone less than a good student may have trouble maintaining the pace, and the facilities are often not available to help these children.

2. With the North American population growing older on the average and family sizes decreasing, we can expect that there will be less family members to care for older parents. This means the lot will more likely fall on the children who are missionaries. Possibly assignment to homeland ministries directed to ethnic minorities similar to those the missionary served overseas would enable missionaries to care for elderly parents while continuing active service. The secret is to require that such missionaries live where the ethnic pockets live in North America. This they (or their parents) are sometimes unwilling to do.

3. Loving confrontation of inappropriate behavior or underproductivity is a definite need that is sometimes lacking. Missionaries are each others' friends, part of the family, and it's hard to "yank the chain" on those you love. The answer? Tough love and commitment to be counseled, no matter what the missionary's age and experience.

4. More support, change of high pressure assignments, and careful monitoring of staff who may be in difficulty. Direct, genuine, verbal and nonverbal encouragement of productive missionaries and reinforcement of their achievements will go miles towards keeping the whole work force moving along.

Some positive moves to conserve valuable workers in TEAM have been: (1) the appointment of a full-time supervisor of pastoral care and counseling; (2) training conferences for field administrators on alternating years, covering both their pastoral and administrative roles; (3) more flexible furlough and rest schedules for some high pressure situations, and (4) placement of workers needing extended time home in "bridging ministries" for two-year periods (usually on loan to another organization).

The Christian and Missionary Alliance

Tim Ratzloff

The Christian and Missionary Alliance study on attrition included all missionaries (633) who dropped out for any reason--death, retiral, sickness, completion of contract, transfer to North American ministry, personal and family problems, moral failure, doctrinal deviation, etc.--during the 11-year period from 1973 to 1983. The C&MA report recognizes the difficulty of analyzing subjective data obtained in studying personnel files. Still, its observations provide meaningful and necessary information as missions study attrition.

The active missionary staff of the C&MA increased 14.6 percent from 865 in 1973 to 991 in 1983--an annual average increase of 1.4 percent. While the average annual increase for "regular missionaries" was only .08 percent, "missionary associates" increased at an average annual rate of 7.8 percent.

During that period the attrition rate for regular missionaries was 5.37 percent. The rate was stable from year to year--except for the year 1975 when three fields were closed in Southeast Asia. That year the attrition rate was 8.26 percent.

Missionary associates experienced a much higher attrition rate--14.6 percent. The report says most missionary associates serve on a contract basis and do not anticipate a career ministry. Those not renewing a contract are included in the attrition rate, thus skewing the overall rate.

The report categorizes the reasons for attrition into two groups--acceptable and unacceptable. Among the unacceptable reasons, personal, family or emotional problems ranked first. Other reasons included moral and marital problems, unsatisfactory service, and incompatability with leadership. Acceptable reasons include death, retirement, marriage, health, home service, leave of absence, completed contract, and transfer to another mission or a different position within the C&MA.

When overall attrition (6.2 percent per year) of the total active missionary staff is divided into these categories, the acceptable attrition rate is 4.9 percent. The unacceptable attrition rate is 1.3 percent of the active missionary staff. In other words, if there were 1,000 missionaries, 13 would withdraw for unacceptable reasons during the year. Another 49 would withdraw for acceptable reasons.

The actual attrition total from 1973-1983 was 633 missionaries. Of those, the greatest number (105, or 16.6 percent) dropped out of the work force after completing their contract. Retirement caused 97 missionaries (15.3 percent) to withdraw. Next in line came personal, family or emotional problems--a factor regarded as unacceptable by the C&MA. A total of 89 missionaries (14.1 percent) were attributed to this category.

Sixty-two (9.8 percent) transferred to a ministry in North America. Health caused 42 missionaries (6.6 percent) to withdraw. Forty missionaries (6.3 percent) asked for a leave of absence and are counted in attrition statistics.

Fourteen other reasons were cited, each ranging from 29 people (4.6 percent) to two people (.3 percent). Other unacceptable reasons cited were moral or marital problems (23 people), unsatisfactory work (nine people), incompatibility with leadership (eight people), doctrinal differences (five people), and lack of language facility (five people).

Greatest attrition took place during or at the end of the first term when 237 missionaries (38.1 percent) withdrew. The report recognizes the increase in those serving on contract, as well as the "short-term psychology prevalent today." However, it also says that insufficient attention has been given to the peculiar needs of first-termers.

The report says that the Department of Overseas Ministries should assess its share of responsibility in missionary attrition in order to prevent similar problems in the future. It also encourages evangelical missions to work together as research continues. "With clearly defined parameters such a study would benefit all," it said.

The Conservative Baptist Foreign Mission Society

Dave Camburn

Why do missionaries resign? Nearly 50 percent do so for personal concerns. Number one on the list was a breakdown of physical or emotional health. These results were compiled from a study done by the Conservative Baptist Foreign Mission Society (CBFMS), Wheaton, Ill. Respondents included resignees, field chairmen, and missions staff.

The next most frequently cited reason for leaving missionary service was family problems, particularly concern for children. "This is especially critical once they are of college age and studying in the USA," a field chairman observed. "Before I had a child in college, I had no idea it would be such a trying time....it would not take much to pack our bags and be on our way home."

A resignee wrote, "I came to the conclusion that for the good of my whole family, this was the direction to go."

Slightly more than 20 percent left missionary service for reasons based on the nature of the work. Nearly half of this group cited interpersonal conflicts as the major reason they resigned. One missionary thought that "his ideas were ignored," or that "decisions were made which affected my future" without him being consulted.

Another 20 percent resigned for reasons related to administration, citing such things as poor field structures, an unresponsive mission staff, or disagreement with the mission. Several missionaries mentioned that there should be less emphasis on lifetime service. One coupled indicated that they went to the mission field with the intention of staying "until God should change our direction."

Other reasons resigning missionaries gave included personal unhappiness, doctrinal differences, or simply that they felt their work was completed.

What can the missions staff do to forestall future resignations? One field chairman suggested "more counsel when the missionary is on furlough regarding job satisfaction and even possible change of field...Ask key questions such as 'What are the problems you as a missionary are facing?' 'Are you really happy in the work?' 'What tension do you have with the fellow missionaries?'"

Another field chairman observed, "The mission board seems to favor creativity. Often the field structure can jump up and strangle the creativity. Might the emphasis in field structure be on efficiency and fulfillment, rather than on restrictions and confinements?"

Of those that responded to a question regarding personal fulfillment, nearly 80 percent indicated they had the same or a greater sense of fulfillment now than when they were missionaries. Nearly 75 percent were involved directly in Christian ministry; 32 percent were pastors.

Several missionaries indicated that the supporting churches didn't understand and were less than sympathetic when they resigned. Most resignees, however, generally felt their reasons for leaving were understood, although they felt their former missionary colleagues were the most understanding.

For the most part, relationships with resignees and CBFMS remain good. One missionary wrote, "We believe that God raised up this organization and that He continues to bless it. We thank God for every minute we spent with CBFMS."

The World Gospel Mission

Burnis H. Bushong

Perhaps the most significant statistic is that of the 577 missionaries in our survey, 174 were lost to WGM (other than by death or retirement), or 30.1 percent. A previous study of the 25-year period, 1946 through 1971, showed a 32 percent dropout rate. Our survey dealt with those who served with WGM from 1954 until March, 1984. We got a 78 percent response to our questionnaire from those who had left the mission.

On the positive side, none of our people left because they felt their living allowance was too small. None left because they lost their financial support. No one left because of doctrinal differences.

The primary reason for leaving the field was the need to care for the health of family members. Other significant reasons for leaving were a desire to work with another mission and unsatisfactory educational opportunities for children on the field.

Basically, we learned that if present trends continue, we will lose three out of 10 of our missionaries, half of them during or at the end of their first term. We learned that the care of family members, the education of children, and physical and psychological illnesses are major problems that we have to face.

We also found out what these people felt were important good things about our mission: prayer backing, our commitment to holiness, our family spirit, good leadership, and our spiritual emphasis. We learned that we have a tremendous amount of good will among our former missionaries. We need to find out how to use this reservoir of good will. Sadly, some of our ex-missionaries still feel guilty about having left the mission.

We are asking each field to study negative characteristics cited by respondents, to see if there are particular weaknesses in their areas. Headquarters is doing the same. We are making a special study of first-term dropouts, to find out their unique frustrations and problems. We need to know more specifically where we are failing our first-term missionaries.

41

Laura Mae Gardner

Proactive Care of Missionary Personnel

The author studied terminations from the Wycliffe Bible Translators, using the case method. The purpose of the study was to permit a new look at internal structures and procedures and to make recommendations for missionary care in a rapidly changing world. This article looks at those structures and procedures and suggests some refinements that will result in better care of Wycliffe members.

The author of this study has taken an investigative look at the matter of personnel terminations from the Wycliffe Bible Translators. It was a proactive appraisal because the organizations rate of personel loss is low and healthy (see note 1). It was proactive in that the mission is looking to a future when major internal and external changes will take place. Large numbers of experienced personnel will have to be redeployed as the translation program is completed in major areas of the world. There will be an increasing number of retirement-aged personnel. New members are being added to the mission at an unprecedented rate and the average age of the working missionary force is lowering. An external change that must be considered is the increasing politicization of the world in which Wycliffe members carry on their linguistic and translation task. These factors suggest that existing procedures and structures within the organization be examined for their future validity and efficiency, so that appropriate adjustments may be made in advance of pressing need.

One way to accomplish such an unbiased examination was to take a backward view of stuctures and procedures in areas of intake, processing, training, assignment and field service, as well as considering what actually happened to specific people during the exiting process. This backward look was taken from the stance of 16 units (individuals if single, couples if married) who terminated with difficulties which might have been addressed much earlier--at intake, processing, training, or during their field service.

The case method was the instrument of choice with which to conduct this study because there are dynamics involved within the person and externally in relationships and environment which cannot be measured by statistical methods or predictive instruments.

The examples chosen for case studies are not typical of all terminations from the Wycliffe Bible Translators since the purpose was not to give a statistical display of reasons why people leave mission agencies. In order to carry out the purposes listed below, the author chose those terminations which seemed most fruitful of information relating to these purposes.

Purposes of the Study

1. To examine existing procedures in the mission's candidate department;

2. To validate or challenge existing candidate precedures;

3. To bring to light additional factors that should be considered or changed in orientation, administration and counseling areas;

4. To look for dynamics in relationship and environment through the case study method that cannot be pinpointed by statistical methods;

5. To demonstrate the mission's concern for individuals that extends beyond their productivity in and for the organization; and

6. To establish a positive focus for career shift within the mission or from the mission to another ministry or occupation.

While the recommendations resulting from this study are directed specifically at the Wycliffe Bible Translators, there are factors pertaining to intake procedures, inner-mission training programs, assignment ot a task or to an area, and exiting from a mission which are applicable to most, if not all, Protestant missionary sending agencies, especially those staffed by North Americans.

Missionary terminations cost all concerned. The agencey loses time and money. Personnel exiting from the mission pay a high price in time and emotional terms. The staff remaining on the field looking at the unfinished task feel an emotional and spiritual loss. Financing supporters pay a dollar price. Because of the inadequacy of psychological testing instruments to predict accurately which factors will ensure success on the mission field, this author has chosen to approach the matter from a different point in time and a different point of view, committed to profit from the benefit of hindsight.

How many missionaries quit? How many leave the Wycliffe Bible Translators? What is the rate of terminations from other mission agencies? The answers to these questions are somewhat difficult to find. Mission leaders are often reluctant to report their loss rate. However, enough records are available on the quantity of terminations to establish general parameters.

Statistics on Missionary Termination

Lindquist (1982) hints at a 50% rate of return from the field: "Experts in this field report that up to 50 percent of first termers return early, or do not return after the first term" (p. 22). Southern Baptist missionaries and a return rate of 23.5% in 1965 (Lindquist, 1982). More recent statistics from the Southern Baptists show a return or loss rate of 4% in the late 1970s, and a downward trend since then. Bridges (1982) reported that 114 Southern Baptist missionaries resigned in 1981 (about 3.7%).

In a survey of missionary candidate selection criteria, Ferguson, Kliewer, Lindquist, Williams, and Heinrich (1983) sent a survey instrument to 78 Evangelical Foreign Missions Association (EFMA) member agencies. This association represents a broad base of evangelical mission sending agencies. Questionnaires were returned by 39 agencies. There were an average of 116 persons on the field per agency at the time of this study. The data on discontinuation of service among long-term members indicated that, on the average, 32 persons terminated their service for each agency during each 5-year period. Averaged out, we find that 6.4 persons annually left each mission agency, representing a 5.5% rate of loss for the 39 sending agencies.

In contrast, Wycliffe's loss rate is less than 2%. E. R. Rowland (1983), Vice President for Personnel, reported a loss of 56 members from a career membership of 4,320 for 1983, giving a loss rate for that year of 1.3%.

This data might be compared with the return rate experienced by secular businesses with personnel serving overseas. Tucker (1982) reports that 33% of all overseas employees (non-mission) return within the first year.

These figures provided the quantitative basis for the study.

Assumptions of the Study

The following assumptions were observed as the study was carried out:

1. A "terminee" is not a casualty or a drop-out. These terms are perjorative and inaccurate.

2. Longevity is not success on the mission field; leaving the mission is not necessarily failure.

3. A zero personnel loss rate is not necessarily ideal.

4. Statistics do not tell the whole story.

5. Success or failure, longevity and productivity on the mission field are not matters that can be accurately, statistically predicted. There are factors involved, such as motivation, commitment, dynamics in relationship and environment, and idiosyncratic elements (temperamental or constitutional differences or personality peculiarities) which prohibit firm predictions.

6. Much missionary stress comes form value dissonance and a lack of coping strategies or devices.

7. A transformational shift (Nelson & Surns, in press) is necessary to keep abreast of the cultural and occupational demands that frequently fall heavily on a missionary--that is, unless workers can adjust their values, presuppositions and coping devices, they become candidates for burnout. Unless this attitudinal, volitional, conscious shift can be made, missionaries will find their energies being depleted by merely trying to cope with the dissonance. They have little energy left over to give to production.

8. Responsibility to stay or go does not fall on the worker alone. All departments of the mission have a responsibility to the individual. The candidate department is responsible to screen out people who have significant problems or combinations of difficulties which weigh heavily against their becoming long-term, productive workers. The pre-field training programs are responsible to continue the screening process as well as carry on programs of information and orientation. The assignments staff have a critical responsibility to place workers individually and carefully after considering the personality of the field and the personality, skills and weaknesses of the worker as well as aiming

for a good "mesh" of field needs and abilities of the worker. Field administration must monitor the worker's production, coping strategies and prioritizations. The counseling department must be staffed by trained professionals equipped to meet personal, spiritual, emotional or relational needs of the membership.

Resulting Observations

The following observations are made on the 16 case studies. These observations should be examined further with more extensive data to determine their validity.

1. The stated reason to terminate was seldom the actual reason (see Bridges, 1982). In only one or two cases did the stated reason mesh with observed factors. Further, there was very seldom a single reason behind the decision to leave the mission. Many times the reasons were so long-standing and complex that they seemed unresolvable to the member, who did not ask for help or take advantage of help when it was offered.

2. The area (task) of assignment calls for specialized personality traits as well as specialized skills. An administrator, a finance officer, a pilot, a language worker, a consultant, a counselor--each of these needs not only the technical skills prerequisite to the job, but also the specific personality traits that make the difference between success and failure in the job.

3. There was recurrent evidence of lack of Bible knowledge that expressed itself in not utilizing spiritual resources, and in unawareness of the scriptural principles for making decisions, resolving conflicts, responding to correction and authority, and for meeting one's own emotional and spiritual needs.

4, Other recurrent themes included a defensive attitude toward correction and a restive spirit under authority (see Britt, 1980). Low self-esteem and lack of education also were frequently observed elements as was concern for money and possessions.

5. Overwork or job frustration were seldom mentioned as reasons for terminating missionary service. Yet it was observed that the struggle to do all that was apparently expected by the various groups to whom the worker felt responsible--the host country and field, the mission leaders, the home constituency, and internal family needs and pressures--seemed to be too great. There was too much to do, too many demands on the worker.

6. Stress appeared to be part of the decision to terminate but was not specifically mentioned. Attention is called to Gish's (1983) study on missionary stress and to the unpublished material by Sally Folger Dye (1979) on missionary stress levels. Chester's (1983) conclusion that missionaries often do not accurately

perceive their own stress levels, and frequently do not take proper steps to alleviate their stress must be noted.

7. This study showed no particular pattern or similarity as to the time of exiting from the mission. While it may well be true that leaving the organization was part of a midlife crisis, such a conclusion cannot be borne out by this study.

The above observations are general, because it was never intended that statistical conclusions would be drawn from this study. Rather the study suggests further attention to certain areas as recommended at the end of this presentation.

Two cautions must be considered:

1. Oftentimes the problem which results in a member leaving the organization appears as a highly spiritualized deviation from the norm. For example, unreasonable risks can look like "faith ventures." A domineering husband and overly submissive wife can look like "God's chain of command at work." What appears to be high level of spirituality can, in fact, border on pathology.

2. A risk-free system of recruitement is not possible. A mission must be willing to take risks. No one is free from problems. Applicants' personal awareness of their problem(s), movement in the direction of growth, experiencing the confidence of supervisors, the provision of such in-house services as field-experienced and professionally trained counselors--these things make a mission's risk a reasonable one.

Recommendations

1. More attention should be given to the applicant's attitude toward authority and his or her openness to direction. Response to authority has been found to be significant variable (Britt, 1980).

2. When body weight is a matter of concern at intake the candidate department personnel must look carefully at areas of marital adjustment and happiness, self-discipline in other areas, compensating skills, and general health.

3. It is suggested that there be a stronger emphasis on communication skills. Communication problems appeared at all levels in the study on terminations--between marriage partners, among family members, between the family and field colleagues, between the worker and the administration, and between the worker and his home constituency.

Money management and money matters along with attitudes toward possessions have been recurring notes in these terminations. Living contentedly on a missionary salary requires a high degree of self-discipline. Maintaining income in a faith mission depends heavily on one's ability to communicate orally and in written form with one's constituency. Ability to communicate should be pointed out as a necessary missionary skill.

4. Attention should be given to the call and motivation of both partners of a couple who apply for missionary service. If both are not committed to the task of serving God in a missionary endeavor, it will be easy for the one who feels pulled along to sabotage the whole enterprise. In many missions this is the wife, because she feels unimportant, even unnecessary (Maines, 1983).

5. Candidate procedures and screening standards must not be lowered but ways should be sought to streamline procedures by eliminating those areas which do not yield significant information. An average of 25 hours of staff time goes into the processing of each applicant. With approximately 350 new members being received annually into Wycliffe, this is a great investment of time. However, the cost of lowering the standard is still higher--the cost to the candidates themselves, the dollar cost to his financing contstituency, and the cost in terms of consultant and administrative time when high-risk people are admitted.

6. Thorough training must be given to candidate screening people, to aid them in gathering and sorting of information, to teach them to interview with skill and insight, and to alert them to potential problem areas.

7. A trained counselor should look at the complete files of all high-risk candidates and/or sit on each decision-making committee.

8. In the screening process, negative comments or trends noted give the most fruitful information--that is, they are more predictive of failure in missionary work than positive comments are predictive of success (Williams, 1973).

9. The degree of rigidity in the candidate must be noted. Inflexibility, dogmatism, and unyieldingness in doctrine, behavioral standards, roles of husband and wife, and priorities are signals of lack of adaptability. A high degree of flexibility has been found to be almost essential on the mission field (Britt, 1980), although there are obvious limits to which one's doctrinal stand can be stretched.

10. Once received into membership, the candidate should not expect to be free from the evaluating process, nor the mission's membership free from a continuing responsibility to help and stimulate this new member to greater growth. I Thess. 5:11-15 and II Tim. 4:2 and other passages indicate that mutual care is a basic Christian responsibility one to another.

11. During the assignment process, care must be taken to mesh not only primary skills of the worker and field needs, but

personalities of both field and worker, family needs of the worker, and the potential and desire for growth of both husband and wife (in the case of a couple) (Bowers, 1984).

12. Attention must be given to the individual skills, energies, and work patterns of a married couple seeking specific field assignment. If the husband and wife on the new team seem highly competitive, or if the wife has skills superior to those of her husband, care should be taken in their field assignment, lest they be placed in a situation potentially or actually destructive to either or both of them.

13. Careful attention should be given to the specific work assignment after the worker arrives on the field. Administrators cannot assume that the worker's desire for a particular group of indigenous people or a geographic location is necessarily the best place for him or her.

14. Conditional assignments should receive formal or informal input from an experienced mission counselor if possible.

15. As much as possible, field administrators should honor the job for which the new member applied and was trained. Job descriptions should be clear and complete.

16. Official performance evaluations should be conducted annually in the case of seemingly healthy, productive teams and semi-anually in the case of probational, conditional, or potentially high-risk teams. This will let members know they have not been forgotten and are consideed important. If things are not going well, they will have a stated time to express needs and ask for help. Such evaluation will insure that an unproductive team cannot continue indefinately within the mission.

17. Field administrators should quickly encourage or require counseling in the case of nonproductive workers or unhappy people when other means of help (goal-setting, supervision, confrontation, discipline, etc.) have been tried. (In instances of moral lapse or insubordination, discipline is more appropriate than counseling. Counselor resources must be guarded for those members who sincerely want to change.)

18. Mission administrators should look for and develop a therapeutic community that can skillfully serve their member's varied needs. Specifically an administrator should have access to a referral list of experienced counselors who can help their members with specific difficulties.

19. If counseling has been required, the member's problems must be very serious indeed, and the choice of a counselor should not be left to the member. A counselor who is also an experienced

missionary, preferably one within the organization, is likely to give better understanding help to the troubled member.

20. After a team has gone through serious trauma on the field-- accidents involving death or high-risk, a kidnapping guerrilla activity--administrators should encourage the members involved to discuss these matters with a trained counselor.

21. Administrators should give heed to those individuals who are chronically ill. In addition to physical causes, chronic illness can be caused by stress overload, by psychological or emotioal factors, or may be an expression of unbearable frustration, or of loyalty to a spouse who is not coping adequately.

22. Mission leaders and workers alike should learn timing and techniques of appropriate confrontation. Gish's (1983) studies on sources of missionary stress assigned the greatest amount of stress to confronting others when necessary. An administrator is often tempted to avoid a problem, or transfer the troublesome member to another department, or pass it on to his successor, rather than confront. A member's reluctance to confront when necessary may result in manipulative behavior, gossip, and other unproductive ways of coping with problems.

23. Substantial attention must be given throughout a mission to the practice of encouraging on another. Affirmation is an essential prerequisite to the practice of confrontation. Only when a relationship of mutual respect and care has been established can an administrator assume that a troubled member can receive corrective feedback.

All too frequently missionary work is done without either explicit or implicit reward; encouragement from colleagues or administrators may be their only tangible reward (Doering, 1983).

24. Legislation should not be used to solve personnel problems. Using restrictive legislation instead of appropriate confrontation to resolve personnel or inter-departmental problems should be utilized only when the problem is widespread and touches many people. Administrators should understand the distinction between restrictive and enabling legislation. Making creative ways for people to be effective is enabling legislation. Legislation telling people what they cannot do is restrictive and de-motivating (although there is a place for this--note the Ten Commandments!).

25. Both administrators and counselors should be aware of the symptoms of heavy stress loads and burnout in others and in themselves (Maslach, 1982).

26. Exiting from the organization should be made more structured and as positive as possible. Members going on furlough should be debriefed; members going on leave of absence should be talked with at length to be sure both they and the mission leadership understand the reasons.

27. Though all terminations cannot be prevented, they should be neutralized as much as possible so the leaving process does not damage the mission, the departing member, or the member's colleagues through bitterness and unresolved conflict, nor does it leave the terminee with feelings of failure and inadequacy.

28. There must be a prevailing attitude of commitment to growth, to maturity, and to excellence throughout the mission. This would be expressed intellectually, spiritually, socially, and technically by encouraging the reading of specific books, by attendance at retreats and seminars, by in-service training, by guidance and counseling, and by regular vacations. Such a commitment, modeled and verbalized by mission leaders, would move an entire mission into a proactive sphere where people/members become important as individuals and not just producers.

29. Vocational guidance personnel and offices should be part of the mission's administrative structure. Attention must be given to those personnel most affected by close-down of field programs and redeployment--experienced senior members. Ways must be found to utilize this pool of experience and potential leaders.

30. A commitment to the status quo is unhealthy. These times are characterized by change more than any single factor. It is unrealistic to expect that change can be excluded from missionary strategy. Change is best handled when anticipated and absorbed, with appropriate structures and procedures established in advance. This is proactive thinking, proactive management, and proactive care of personnel.

Note

1. proactive. Oriented to the future, anticipatory, committed to values, as opposed to reactive, which is past-oriented, focusing on problems and struggling for survival. A business term describing a mind-set out of which flows specific leadership behaviors and practices.

References

Bowers, J. (1984). Roles of married women missionaries: A case study. *International Bulletin of Missionary Research, 8,* 4-7.

Bridges, E. (1982, February 26). Missionary resignations down, but reasons still complex. *Foreign Mission News*, p. 1.

Britt, W. G., III. (1980). The prediction of missionary success overseas using pretraining variables. *Dissertations Abstracts International, 42*, 1162B.

Chester, R. M. (1983). Stress on missionary families living in "other culture" situations. *Journal of Psychology and Christianity, 2*, 30-37.

Doering, J. (1983). *The power of encouragement*. Chicago: Moody.

Dye, S. F. (1979). To put down or build up. (Available from Sally Dye, 7500 W. Camp Wisdom Rd., Dallas, TX 75236)

Ferguson, L. N. Kliewer, D., Lindquist, S. E., Williams D. E., & Heinrich, R. P. (1983). Candidate selection criteria: A survey. *Journal of Psychology and Theology, 11*, 243-250.

Gish, D. (1983). Sources of missionary stress. *Journal of Psychology and Theology, 11*, 236-242.

Lindquist, S. E. (1982). Prediction of success in overseas adjustment. *Journal of Psychology and Christianity, 1*, 22-25.

Maines, C. (1983). Missionary wives: Underused asset. *Evangelical Missions Quarterly, 19*, 290-295.

Maslach, C. (1982). *Burnout--The cost of caring*. New York: Prentice Hall.

Nelson, L., & Burns, F. (in press). High performance programming. In J. D. Adams (Ed.), *Transforming work*. Alexandria: Miles River Press.

Rowland, E. R. (1983). *Personnel report to the board*. Dallas: Wycliffe Bible Translators.

Tucker, M. (1982). *Cross-cultural adjustment and effectiveness*. Paper presented at the meeting of the Society for International Education, Training and Rsearch, Long Beach, CA.

Williams, K. L. (1973). Characteristics of the more successful and less successful missionaries. *Dissertations Abstracts International, 34,* 1786B. (University Microfilms No. 73-22, 697).

PART FOUR

SPECIAL ISSUES

PART FOUR
SPECIAL ISSUES

The final part of this compendium examines some current topics in missions which have a bearing on the mental health of mission personnel. Four general topics are addressed: the structure and function of mission agencies, the role of women in missions, the reentry experience, and counseling others from different cultures.

The first section examines the *use and development of mental health services by mission agencies*. Johnston's introductory article is intended as a bridge to link mental health professionals with mission agencies. The author suggests ways for dealing with the differing needs of mission executives, personnel directors, and missionaries. The research by Johnson and Penner examines the different types of psychological evaluation, counseling, and in-service training reported by a wide range of mission agencies which these individuals surveyed. The article also includes a rank ordering of missionary problems and a listing of the educational backgrounds of mental health service providers. A suggested ethical code for the provision of psychological services in mission settings is presented by O'Donnell in the last article. Intended as an interim document, the proposed code offers guidelines for working through some of the common ethical issues occurring in the mission context.

Women's roles in missions is explored in the next section. Bowers' article begins with a sensitive discussion of the place of "feminism" in world missions. She describes the typical roles for women on the field and advocates the greater utilization of the

447

talents and gifts which women have. De Vries focuses on the importance of childbearing responsibilities, yet like Bowers, encourages the possibility of dual roles as mother-mission worker. Some suggestions for personnel directors are made to encourage the development and use of women in missions. While the article by Marshall on "Current Issues of Women and Therapy" is not written for missionaries per se, it is nonetheless highly relevant to the growth struggles experienced by many North American female missionaries. Biblical perspectives are discussed pertaining to the psychology of women, along with current concerns of self-esteem, vocation, achievement, and intimacy.

The third section presents two articles on missionary adjustment during the *repatriation process*. In the first article, Austin describes some of the common reactions of missionaries returning to their homeland. Patterns of reentry responses are identified, together with some practical steps for making it through this transitional period. The second article by Pollock deals with the experiences of adolescent missionary children during reentry. Three approaches to reentry care are described. Some ways to provide follow-up care after reentry are also noted.

The last section of Part Four is oriented towards mental health specialists and mission personnel who engage in *cross-cultural counseling*. This section contains an article by Hesselgrave which introduces several of the complex issues comprising this specialized area of counseling. The author highlights some of the ways which non-Western cultures characterize and treat human problems. Ethical and successful counseling, he argues, necessitates an appreciation of culturally conditioned interpretations of behavior, an understanding of the role of change agents in the different culture, and the use of modified, eclectic counseling methods. Two respondents then discuss Hesselgrave's assertions, followed by his own response to their comments.

The variety of subjects explored in the nine articles of Part Four comprise but a minor portion of the many topics important to mental health and missions today. Other areas which deserve the cooperative attention of mental health professionals and mission specialists include the recruitment of potential candidates, training strategies for missionary counselors, missionary marital adjustment, treatment approaches with missionary clients, and retirement preparation for career missionaries, to name a few.

42

LeRoy N. Johnston, Jr.

Building Relationships Between Mental Health Specialists and Mission Agencies

There is a new openness today between the mission agency and those working in the area of mental health. Although the crack in the door might not be as open as some mental health specialists would like, there is still plenty of room for exchange between these groups as well as room to carry on some very important work.

The opening in the door came approximately 30 years ago when psychological assessment was initiated in the screening process with missionary candidates. Although it took a few years for this psychological screening to be accepted, virtually every major mission board now utilizes some form of psychological screening, including psychological tests, in the process of selection.

With the growth of counseling courses offered at the seminary campus and the availability of trained pastors and Christian psychologists, mission leaders have recognized the value of the mental health professional. Mission boards have indicated their willingness to use appropriately trained mental health specialists to counsel missionaries who are experiencing some form of emotional stress, psychological depression, psychotic episode, etc.

The use of psychological services with the treatment of missionaries has increased in the past decade, but there still remains an underlying suspicion, if not fear, of the "shrink." In

Based on a paper presented at the Fourth Annual Conference on Mental Health and Missions held at Angola, Indiana in November, 1983. Reprinted by permission of the author.

almost every case where a mental health professional is used by a mission board, the person possesses "secondary" credentials which make him acceptable. Thus we see persons who have been pastors, missionaries, administrators, etc. trained in some area of therapy and counseling returning to work with their own colleagues. This continues to underscore the underlying hesitation and fear that most "shrinks" who are not part of "the mission group" or "church group" are so steeped in Freud that they themselves are too messed up to do any good for anyone else.

Mission executives and those who are working directly with the candidate process are asking good questions, seeking specific direction from those in the mental health areas. Mission agencies want missionaries who will be effective cross-cultural workers and not hinder the work of the mission due to some type of personality or emotional upset. There is a recognized need on the part of the mission agency for help, although there is a question as to what can actually be provided by those who are not closely involved or associated with missions, and especially cross-cultural living.

To understand what mission executives, personnel directors, and missionaries are expressing in terms of their felt work needs, I would like to share with you the findings detected in some studies.

Recently, I assisted a group of mission executives from various locations and groups in North America to generate what they considered to be the major concerns facing the mission agencies today. This was given from the perspective of the mission executives who plan, coordinate, and implement the mission programs. From this, one can gain insight into the struggles from the mission executive point of view and they rank ordered felt needs. The following list was developed:

Mission Executives
(North American-Based) Major Concerns:

1. Church-mission relationship; fusion-parallelism-dichotomy.
2. Dealing with totalitarian governments; visa concerns; closing countries.
3. Nominalism of second or third generation Christians; renewal of church.
4. Having correct personnel in ministry locations.
5. Untrained mission field leadership.
6. Education of MKs--mobility concern.
7. New methods of doing church planting--models.

8. Redeployment/responsiveness.
9. Training national leaders/T.E.E.
10. Finances: inflation, missionary support.
11. Polarization of urban vs. rural work.
12. Unreached people groups--new areas.
13. Tentmakers and alternatives to transitional missions.

Secondly, I would like to share with you what personnel directors have stated to be their felt needs in terms of work-related responsibilities. Ninety-five personnel directors from approximately 45 missions associated with IFMA/EFMA generated and then rank ordered the following needs. This is an indicator of where they felt deficient and requested help in order to be more effective in their work. It forms the basis for some of the comments and suggestions that I would like to make later in this paper.

Felt Needs of Personnel Directors--IFMA/EFMA:

1. Interviewing factors, procedures, and skills.
2. Administering and understanding diagnostic testing.
3. Establishing criteria for predicting success on the field.
4. Recruitment skills and procedures.
5. Developing on-field training programs.
6. Developing means for missionary placement.
7. Enhancing interpersonal relationship skills.
8. Leadership development for missionaries.
9. Developments in personnel research.
10. The missionary family.
11. The role of the local church--developing implementation strategies and procedures.
12. Field evaluation of missionaries.
13. Study of missionary losses and causes for drop-outs.
14. Evaluation and counseling to facilitate personal development for veteran missionaries.
15. Continuing spiritual/psychological care of missionaries.
16. Candidate school/orientation/
17. Personnel records systems, data keeping.
18. Personnel department staffing.
19. Short-term utilization.
20. Developing closer relationships with on-campus (groups) colleges and seminaries.
21. The personnel director: his role, ministry, and personal development.

Finally, we come to what would be the felt needs of missionaries who are serving in overseas cross-cultural, church-planting situations. Two hundred eighty-seven missionaries were surveyed and asked to list what they considered to be the major needs and pressing issues which confronted them on a daily basis. These needs were gathered, rank ordered, and the following list was developed. I am sure the rank order of these particular items would vary according to the mission agency. Research has shown that smaller mission groups would rate some of these issues more prominent than larger denominational mission groups. Obvious areas were in financial support, the educational systems for children, the type of deputational ministry required, etc. But overall this list is probably quite characteristics of the kinds of pressures, stresses, and concerns that confront the missionary doing church-planting work in a cross-cultural situation.

Missionary Needs Assessment Priority of Needs

Scale: 1   2   3   4   5
         No need at all   A major need

Issue	% indicating 4 or 5	% indicating 1 or 2
1. Spiritual renewal (3.76)	60%	8%
2. Personal devotional time (3.26)	46%	23%
3. Family time (3.12)	36%	29%
4. Ministry skill training (3.08)	36%	28%
5. Continuing language training (3.03)	42%	38%
6. Time management (3.03)	38%	37%
7. Interpersonal relationships among missionaries (2.94)	33%	35%
8. Continuing education/vocational training (2.91)	35%	39%
9. MK adjustment when returning to North American (2.91)	31%	39%
10. Field organization (2.91)	31%	38%
11. Personnel needs (2.84)	29%	39%
12. Too heavy workload (2.84)	30%	39%
13. Knowing where I fit in with missions purpose (2.75)	28%	48%
14. Finances (2.65)	26%	47%

Missionary Needs Assessment (continued)
15. Formal evaluation of ministry (2.63)	25%	45%
16. A job description (2.62)	27%	51%
17. MK adjustment at boarding school (2.60)	23%	48%
18. Relationship with nationals (2.57)	21%	52%
19. Adjustment to new responsibilities (2.53)	20%	55%
20. Improvement in communications with D.O.M. (2.52)	20%	52%
21. Career assessment (2.48)	19%	49%
22. Immediate family relationships (2.45)	19%	57%
23. Greater accountability for work (2.40)	18%	56%
24. Family privacy (2.31)	17%	57%
25. Marriage relationships (2.27)	14%	62%
26. Depression/discouragement (2.24)	16%	64%
27. Extended family relationships (2.18)	12%	66%
28. Career guidance (1.94)	11%	72%
29. Living conditions/housing (1.87)	8%	71%

Areas Where Mission Agencies Need the Support of Mental Health Personnel

I would like to suggest five particular areas where mental health professionals could be of benefit to the missionary and mission agency. Some specialists may want to focus attention in one of the areas and others may find it profitable to be involved in all five areas:

1. *Preparation*

There needs to be very specific involvement in the education and training of missionaries. The effect would be profound as courses and seminars would be offered to those who are involved in overseas work.

The three areas where the greatest impact would be of most benefit would be: (1) in the college and seminary training; (2) during orientation programs; and (3) at furlough seminars. These three distinct settings usually provide the greatest degree of opportunity for input and change.

2. *Assessment and Selection*

There needs to be the continued development and utilization of instruments and methodology that will help identify the persons who would most likely succeed in cross-cultural ministry. No tests or instruments have been developed to be specifically utilized in the assessment of missionary candidates. Simulation games and other types of training methods have been adapted from the business world. But specific assessment techniques still need to be a major focus of those who are involved in psychological services.

3. *Counseling and Therapy Opportunities*

There needs to be a provision for individual, group, and family services that are preventive as well as remedial. Whether these services be short-term or long-term is not the issue. But each family or individual, being unique, needs to have readily available the type of therapeutic experience that would care for any important psychological health need. These services would be available for those in preparation, but especially valuable when provided on-location overseas.

4. *Equipping Mission Executives/Leaders*

Field and national leadership should be able to do limited assessment and provide recommendations regarding missionaries already on the field. Every mission board has a number of field representatives who travel extensively and work with missionaries on location. Field directors should be able to recognize positive and negative signs of mental, emotional, and spiritual health found in missionaries. Many mission agencies are not sure who could teach and what would be taught to these administrative leaders.

5. *Research and Consulting Services*

Empirical study of the unique dimensions of cross-cultural living with specific recommendations provided to administrators would prove to enhance the work of missions. Recently, attention has been given to family life, the issue of singleness, the question of separation and relationship to schooling of children, etc. But much more research needs to be done so that the recommendations and advice upon which executives act has some basis. In the past, the laws of pragmatism and tradition directed most approaches to decision-making. Sound research provides the data so effective consulting can be done with various mission agencies.

Thus I would see these as five areas in which mental health specialists could use their expertise to enhance mission agencies and the work of missionaries.

Some Concepts for Mental Health Specialists to Explore in Providing Care

There are some approaches and ideas that I think persons in mental health might find useful in building a relationship with any mission organization.

1. *Know and Be Known.*
I would encourage those who desire to work with missions or missionaries to initiate meetings with mission leaders, especially the leaders of your own denomination. Become acquainted with their felt needs as well as their job-related needs. Earlier I included what a group of mission executives listed as their job-related major concerns. To be aware of the areas in which they are struggling is important. Already they are afraid you are trying to "psych them out." They are waiting for you to tell them that they are workaholics, overstressed, developing an ulcer, and providing very poor role models for junior missionaries. This may be true, but they are not ready to hear you. But if you can meet them on "their turf," and talk about their needs, you will gain an acceptance and a hearing.

I would encourage you to subscribe to one or two of the more prominent periodicals. Good reading materials are available to inform you on missions and the struggles going on in the work of missions today. You would find it profitable to attend the meetings of the IFMA or EFMA or your own denominational mission-planning sessions. Once again, this indicates your willingness to come part way and understand the world of the mission executive.

2. *Specialize in One Area or Section of the World.*
It appears that many persons who are involved in helping mission agencies have become "globe trotters." Every so often they find themselves in a different part of the world on a short-term junket trying to put out the fires of emotional disturbance found in missionaries. I am sure there is some value in this "hit and miss" situation. But I question the long-term results. I would suggest that you get to know mission personnel in one or two countries at the most. Try and provide some type of continual mental health services for these missionaries. It may not be necessary to make a visit every year, but if you continue to go back to the same place

year after year or over a period of time, relationships will be constructed. These people would be willing to accept tapes, printed material, or data that would help them. With an established relationship, the missionary may be able to settle near you during furlough so that extended contact would be possible. Not only is it good stewardship to select one country, you will probably be able to work with a number of mission boards in that one country, thus providing a lot of service with a minimum amount of travel on your part. Needless to say, it is not as glamorous and you will not use as much film. But in terms of helpfulness, it might prove to be the most beneficial way.

3. Develop a Network of Services in North America.

The networking of mental health services is important because of missionary mobility during furlough and the multiplicity of problems facing the missionary family. Mission boards usually are aware of one or two persons in the area of mental health and, when missionaries reside near those persons, the mission recommends them. But furloughing missionaries of most agencies scatter all over the country. The mission agencies are not aware of the locations of people in mental health services who are capable of working with missionaries.

It might be helpful if there was a central contact point to disperse information about types of services available and their location. Mission boards could be apprised of who is available, their speciality, and their location.

4. *Creation of Team Ministries for Overseas.*

The mental health specialist could be part of a team approach which includes a pastor, career counselor, educators in cross-cultural studies, etc. In some cases, the missionary does face a unique psychological crisis that needs the competencies of a skilled therapist. But quite often it is multi-faceted. The individual could use some skill training, career assessment, family counseling, etc. The team approach might offer a more diverse method of meeting a group of missionaries who come together for a week-long seminar. It would also soften the concept that "the problem is mental." In other words, the mental health specialist is not the highlight of the occasion, but one member in a unified team to help meet the needs of the missionary.

5. *Sharing and Comparing Experiences.*

Persons interested in related aspects of missionary care should meet to benefit from dialogue and exchange of insights. One of the reasons most of us have gathered at this conference is because of this particular concept. The mental health care of the missionary and the missionary family is a unique concern because of the unusual ingredients that go into overseas living. Concerns of cross-cultural living, location of ministry, need for family separation, etc. create dimensions of living that are idiosyncratic to missionary life. Thus the exchange of ideas with persons directly involved in providing mental health services to missionaries should prove to be extremely valuable.

Conclusion

As a clinical psychologist, I have had the opportunity of working with missionaries while they are on furlough. It has been my privilege to travel overseas a number of times to be involved in counseling and conduct seminars on the field with missionaries. While serving as a missionary, I have observed the unique needs faced by my peers. As a mission executive, I have been able to contact a number of mental health specialists asking them to work with missionaries who are on furlough and candidates in the preparation process. I have seen the networking of mental health specialists prove to be very valuable in the process of restoration of the mental health of missionaries. Thus the impact of the mental health specialist continues to be felt in the area of missions.

I believe as counselors, therapists, and educators become more aware and concerned about providing services related to the specific needs of cross-cultural workers, we will see a greater degree of acceptance on the part of the mission agencies. But at this time I would encourage those in the mental health services to maintain a positive attitude, to remain professional in their approach, yet helpful in their conversation. Keep the utlization of your professional jargon to a minimum. Get to know your mission leaders, their concerns, and demonstrate a willingness to understand them. Keep your comments practical but, above all, make sure they are biblical. Intrapersonal and interpersonal relationships still continue to be the major concern for effective and productive cross-cultural ministry. The best book written on the subject is the Bible, although there are other texts that provide good supplemental information. Keep a balanced focus.

43

Cedric B. Johnson
David R. Penner

The Current Status of the Provision of Psychological Services in Missionary Agencies in North America

A survey of the use of psychological services by missionary agencies is reported. Despite the widespread use of these services in candidate selection and counseling for career missionaries, there is a need for the development of uniform and validated procedures by most of these agencies.

Two fundamental issues confront missionary agencies as they contemplate the use of psychological services for their personnel. First, what procedures (e.g. tests, methods of counseling) are relevant to the selection of candidates for field placement? Second, how does one identify and intervene when career missionaries manifest problems of a psychological nature?

The issue of prediction of an employee's performance has been addressed in the field of industrial organizations (Ghiselli, 1971). Tests, interviews, references, and assessment centers are providing valid predictions of career success in business and industry. Missionary agencies are seeking to refine their candidate selection procedures. Their goals are to prevent missionaries from dropping out of their careers and insuring successful accomplishment of the missionary task (Williams, 1978). The present article surveys the role of psychological services in the evaluation of candidates for suitability for missionary service.

Counseling services for career missionaries represent another concern of this paper. Agencies such as the Link Care Foundation in Fresno, California serve as psychological consultants to mission agencies. Many missions send their personnel who encounter emotional problems to individual practitioners. The present survey evaluates issues such as types of problems encountered by career missionaries, the qualifications of the providers of these psychological services, and the types of services provided.

Method

The population of missionaries was identified with reference to *Mission Handbook: North American Protestant Ministries Overseas,* 11th Ed. (E. D. Dayton, Editor, MARC, 1976). This directory listed 620 agencies. Mission agencies with over 100 missionaries outside of the United States and Canada were selected for the survey. The top ten agencies accounted for 13,016 people or 35% of the total missionary force. In December 1980 questionnaires were mailed to 75 mission agencies.

The questionnaire contained 11 items. Two items dealt with candidate selection. The percentage of potential missionary candidates undergoing psychological evaluation and the nature of this procedure (tests, interviews, references) were described. Four items dealt with the type of problems encountered by career missionaries. Also surveyed were the average number of therapy sessions and the location of such psychological services (e.g., at home or on the field). The qualifications, types of services, relationship to the mission, and areas of specialization of the providers of these services were examined. Final items included additional comments and a statement of reservation/no reservation about the use of the name of the mission in the article.

Of the 75 questionnaires mailed, 55 were returned. This return rate of 73% was unusually high in comparison to surveys published in journals such as *The American Psychologist* (e.g., Demarest, 1980).

Results

Survey Respondents

The survey was completed by individuals holding a variety of positions within the mission agencies. The greatest number of surveys were completed by the personnel director (36%), followed in order of frequency by the director of the mission agency (22%), an associate director or vice president (14%), with the remainder completed by persons in a variety of other positions. Three surveys were completed by psychologists and two by physicians.

Mission Service Criteria

Of the 55 completed surveys, 76% reported that all of their permanent missionary candidates undergo psychological evaluation. Several agencies distinguished between short-term and permanent missionary candidates, with the permanent candidates undergoing more extensive evaluation. The mission agencies were asked what criteria they used for determining suitability for mission service. Psychological testing is used by the vast majority of agencies, with 80% reporting the use of one or more psychological tests. A total of 25 different tests were listed as being used for this purpose. Of these, the Taylor-Johnson Temperament Analysis was the most common, with 20 agencies reporting its use. The Minnesota Multiphasic Personality Inventory was also frequently used, with 19 agencies reporting its use. Other tests repeatedly mentioned included the 16 Personality Factor Questionnaire (5), Sentence Completion (5), unspecified vocational tests (4), the Edwards Personal Preference Schedule (3), and a wide variety of other tests mentioned by one or two respondents. Of the agencies who use psychological tests, ten used one test only, nine used two tests, five used three tests, four used four tests, and four used five tests. Other respondents stated that the nature and number of tests used depended on the specific situation, with no general test battery specified.

The most common criteria used for determining suitability for mission service included an evaluation of the applicant's background (93%). Closely following was an evaluation of the applicant's autobiography or statement of purpose (89%). Psychological interviews were used by 75% of the mission agencies. A linguistic aptitude evaluation was used by 31%. The survey did not include a category for the use of references in determining applicant suitability; nevertheless, ten agencies reported this as a criterion in an "other" category, suggesting that this is a prevalent criterion for determining mission service suitability. A unique method of determining mission service suitability used by one mission includes having the candidate spend a week-end in self-assessment with a psychologist.

Counseling Missionaries

The most commonly reported time for counseling missonaries was during orientation or training sessions, with 95% of the agencies reporting some form of counseling during this phase of preparation for field service. Counseling of missionaries occurring during furlough was reported by 87% of the agencies, and 53% of the agencies reported that counseling missionaries occurs while on the field. The majority of respondents, 51%, stated that counseling of their missionaries occurs during all three phases: Orientation or training on the field, and during furlough.

The mean number of counseling sessions for those agencies who specifically specified this information is 3.09. The modal number of sessions was three. The interpretation of these averages should be cautious, since many agencies (M =14) stated that the average number of counseling sessions varies considerably according to the individual situation.

Respondents were asked to rank in order the most frequent problems of missionaries which require psychological counseling--the lower the number, the greater the frequency of the problem. Relationships with other missionaries was the most frequently cited problem and finding God's will was the least frequent. Table 1 summarizes these data.

Table 1
Rank Order of the Most Frequent Problems of Missionaries Requiring Psychological Counseling

Problem	Mean Ranking
Relationships with other missionaries	1.99
Cultural adjustment	3.26
Stress	3.45
Children	3.66
Marriage difficulties	4.15
Financial pressures	4.96
Loneliness	5.12
Individual problems not elsewhere listed	5.36
Finding God's will	6.26

Note--The lower the mean ranking, the greater the frequency of the problem.

Consultation

One question on the survey asked the respondents to specify the topics of workshops offered for their missionaries. As one might expect, a great diversity of workshop topics was reported. The most frequently reported workshop topics focused on some aspect of family living, such as "the family in missions" or "marriage enrichment." In addition to workshops, 23 agencies provided some type of leadership development and 14 agencies provided some other form of staff training. Ten agencies provided seminars, leadership development and staff training. Thirteen agencies provided a combination of two out of the three consultation activities, and 17 agencies provide one of these activities. It should be cautioned that the ambiguous wording of this item on the survey may make any clear differentiation between these services somewhat difficult.

Psychological Service Providers

The educational backgrounds of persons performing psychological services to mission agencies varied considerably. Table 2 shows the number of persons from each discipline. Psychology was the most common educational background.

Table 2
Educational Background of Psychological Service Providers

Educational Field of Study	N	Percentage of Total
Psychology	40	28.17
Theology	30	21.13
Marriage & Family Counseling	27	19.02
Psychiatry	15	10.56
General Medicine	15	10.56
Educational Psychology	10	7.04
Other	5	3.52
Total	142	100.00

The highest degree held by the individual performing psychological services was tallied. A Ph.D. or Psy.D. was held by 44% of the individuals. An M.A. or M.S. was held by 16.6%, M.D. by 14%, M.Div. by 11.6%, D.Min. by 5.8%, B.A. by 3.5%, and unspecified degrees accounted for 2.5%.

The persons performing psychological services were listed as permanent full-time employees of the mission agencies in 34% of the reported cases. A consultant hired on an as-needed basis composed 60% of the individuals. Permanent part-time employees accounted for the remaining 6% of the psychological service providers.

General Discussion

The willingness of mission agencies to respond to the survey was appreciated. Many expressed an interest in the topic and seemed to be open to new possibilities of approaching the task of missionary candidate selection in particular, and in effective utilization of other psychological resources in general. There were, however, some notable exceptions. One respondent stated,

We, frankly, have had very little problem over the last 15 years in this area. We have had 250 missionaries, and we have had three situations in which psychological counseling was suggested. In only one was there a follow-through, and in the other two cases the people went their own way, leaving the Mission. One related to marital difficulty, a second to homosexual tendency, and a third to stress revolving primarily around learning of language.

By contrast, another agency reported,

Psychological testing has proven very valuable in determining strengths and weaknesses of prospective candidates. It provides insights into further personality development needed (e.g., maturing emotionally and in marriage relationships). We believe it may be saving some from potential "casualty" or unfulfilled goals and ministry.

The responses to the survey have revealed widespread use of psychological services by Protestant foreign mission agencies. Although the nature of such services vary, there is a definite utilization by most mission agencies of some form of psychological sservices. Psychological testing for determining suitability for mission service is one clear use of psychological services.

In light of the most frequently reported problem area, relationships with other missionaries, there is the need for a psychologcal test that identifies interpersonal rather than intrapersonal problems. Most of the tests utilized by mission agencies identify primarily intrapersonal issues. Other tests that measure the degree of adaptability to a new culture, analyze spiritual giftedness, and evaluate rigidity in relation to cultural values need to be constructed. Such instruments would enhance the efficiency of candidate selection procedures.

The data from this survey do not indicate how widespread psychological problems facing missionaries are, but only the relative frequency of these problems in relation to each othe. We trust that our survey can provide information useful to the preparation of missionaries for the most likely problems which they will encounter. Thus, workshops on interpesonal relationships, cultural adjustment, and coping with stress would assume a high priority. Future research is needed to assess the efficacy of such training programs on later psychological adjustment.

There is also a need for psychological consultants to visit the various fields that can identify emotional problems in their personnel. Personal and group counseling, conflict management, and a ministry of general encouragement could prevent a relatively high casualty rate. Another area of concern is for missionaries who encounter reentry problems. One agency wrote,

...missionaries no longer go overseas with the expectancy of life-time service but serve at the invitation of our overseas partners for varying peiods of time. Many are involved with training oveseas nationals to assume roles formerly held by foreign missionaries so that when a missionary has worked out of a job, an uncertain future must be faced.

The major limitation of the survey is that many responses given by the agencies were based chiefly on the respondent's general impressions rather than on objective data. Thus, the responses to some questions, such as the item which asked for a rank ordering of the most frequent problems of missionaries requiring psychological counseling, were subjectively determined by the respondent before reporting results on the survey. It would be interesting to compare how different individuals within the same mission agency respond to the same question. Perhaps administrators in home offices view things differently than field administrators or the direct service missionaries themselves.

References

Dayton, E. (1976). *Mission handbook; North American Protestant ministries overseas*. Morovia, CA: MARC.

Demarest, J. (1980). The current status of comparative psychology in the American Psychological Association. *American Psychologist, 35,* 980-990.

Ghiselli, E. (1971). *Explorations in managerial talent.* Pacific Palisades, CA: California Goodyear Publishing Co.

Williams, K. (1973). *Characteristics of the more successful and least successful missionaries.* Unpublished doctoral dissertation, United States International University (University Microfilms No. 73-22, 697).

44

Kelly S. O'Donnell

Some Suggested Ethical Guidelines for the Delivery of Mental Health Services in Mission Settings

This article provides some ethical guidelines in codified form for mental health specialists who work in a missions context. Several professional codes of ethics are drawn upon in formulating these guidelines, the primary one being the American Psychological Association's "Ethical Principles of Psychologists" (1981). Seven general areas are addressed, including responsibility, competence, values and legal standards, confidentiality, welfare to the consumer, professional relationships, and assessment. Suggestions for the possible uses of these guidelines are also given. The article concludes with an appendix summarizing some of the common ethical issues involved in mental health and missions.

Mental health professionals (MHPs) who provide services to missionaries and mission agencies inevitably deal with various ethical issues during the course of their work. Typical examples include identifying the limits of confidentiality in counseling, evaluating the appropriateness of psychological tests administered to individuals from different cultural backgrounds, knowing the legal regulations which relate to the services one provides while in a foreign country, and maintaining professional objectivity while also being a member of the missionary organization. In seeking to work together, it is critical for both mental health

---

Based on an article presented at the Eighth Annual Conference on Mental Health and Missions held at Angola, Indiana in November, 1987. Reprinted by permission of the author.

professionals and mission administrators to carefully consider the ethical and legal complexities involved in organizing and providing mental health services.

This article presents several ethical principles in a codified format which relate to the practice of psychology in mission settings. These principles are intended as common guidelines which can be referred to by various types of MHPs working in missions. Examples would be part-time consultants who provide on-site services at overseas locations and expatriate professionals who engage in full-time practice in missions. The present specialty code may also be of particular use to mission personnel who perform some type of mental health service, yet are not formally involved in a discipline or organization which has a governing code of ethics (e.g., field directors, personnel directors).

The ethical provision of psychological services is discussed under seven different headings: responsibility, professional competence, personal values and legal standards, confidentiality, client welfare, relationships with other professionals, and psychological assessment. Each of these sections focuses, to varying degrees, on the basic services usually provided by MHPs, namely, psychological assessment with missionary candidates and missionaries; counseling with individuals, couples, and families; in-service training; research; and organizational development.

Several of the ethical principles suggested in this article are based on the American Psychological Association's (APA) document, "Ethical Principles of Psychologists" (1981). This document was chosen for its broad treatment of the ethical issues which arise in the practice of psychology as well as for its widespread acceptance among professionals. Six additional sources have been consulted: (a) the ethical principles established by the American Association of Marriage and Family Therapy (1985); (b) the code of ethics of the American Association of Pastoral Counselors (1986); (c) the ethical guidelines formulated by the National Association of Social Workers (1980); (d) the code which was proposed for the Christian Association for Psychological Studies (see King, 1986); (e) the APA's "Standards for Educational and Psychological Tests" (1974); and (f) the "Specialty Guidelines for the Delivery of Services" (1981) for clinical, counseling, industrial/organizational, and school psychologists published by the APA. Many of the principles found in the application sections are paraphrased from each of the above ethical codes. Interested individuals would do well to read these documents for a fuller appreciation of the ethics involved in mental health work.

Responsibility

MHPs working in mission settings remain accountable to the highest professional and Christian ethical standards. They acknowledge responsibility for their actions and make reasonable efforts to ensure the appropriate use of their services.

Application
a. MHPs accurately represent their backgrounds, skills, and experience with cross-cultural issues to mission organizations who use their services. Mission agencies may need to be oriented as to how and which mental health services may be useful to them.

b. MHPs carry a heavy social responsibility because of their potentially influential positions and recommendations. They avoid any situations and resist pressures thay may lead to a misuse of their influence.

c. MHPs providing professional services clarify the parameters of ethical practice within their specialization and the particular mission setting in which they work. They abide by the commitments which they make to the employing mission agency.

d. MHPs recognize that interventions which serve one person's best interests will also affect others. They thus attempt to anticipate and clarify the impact of the decisions and changes which may result when doing marital, family, small group, and organizational interventions. In addition, they respect the right of clients to make their own decisions.

e. MHPs are responsible for planning, directing, and reviewing the services which they provide. An evaluation of services is done at least annually and includes an assessment of service effectiveness, efficiency, and availability. MHPs advocate policies and practices which promote human health and competence.

f. MHPs participate in the overall planning, development, and improvement of mental health services within the mission organization whenver appropriate. Services are to be designed so as to be responsive to the needs of mission personnel. When important services are either inadequate or not available, MHPs inform responsible individuals of the lack of these needed services.

g. MHPs who oversee the provision of mental health services are responsible to provide a written description of the objectives, scope, and organization of the services, and the lines of responsibility and accountability for each MHP providing service.

h. MHPs seek to use preventive interventions as a means to decrease the incidence and duration of problems among mission personnel. Prevention is thus an essential component to include in the planning and delivery of mental health services.

i. MHPs encourage the appropriate use of psychological findings from research and testing by the mission agency. It may be necessary to educate agency staff as to the nature and limits of research and testing.

Professional Competence

MHPs are dedicated to high standards of competence in the interest of the individuals and mission agencies which they serve. They recognize the limits of their training, experience, and skills, and endeavor to maintain and develop professional competencies. MHPs keep abreast with current professional information and scientific research related to their work in mission settings.

Application

a. MHPs may desire or be asked to provide services in which they have minimal or no skills. MHPs, however, only practice within their current sphere of expertise. One's professional skills, rather than organizational needs, determine what services can be provided. Further, MHPs recognize that competence in one type of organizational or cultural setting is not necessarily generalizable to other settings.

b. MHPs take precautions when working in this relatively new area of mental health, especially when they are minimally familiar with the mission organization and/or cultural setting. Experience and study in cross-cultural psychology, missiology, and ethnic mental health are usually standard.

c. MHPs stay updated on the current research and techniques with regards to the services they provide. This requires continuing education and regular contact with other professionals working in the area of missions. Training and supervised experience in working with different ethnic groups, age groups, modalities, techniques, and problems are needed. MHPs, as Christians, also pursue spiritual growth to aid their effectiveness in working with those in need.

d. MHPs who present psychological information through seminars and teaching make sure that it is accurate, current, and scholarly.

e. MHPs who make or influence decisions about missionaries based on tests should have a background in this area. Tests should be administered and interpreted by trained professionals.

f. MHPs may, from time to time, experience personal problems which interfere with professional effectiveness. They thus avoid professional activities where personal problems influence the quality of service. Finding a counselor or confidant is especially important for those who primarily work in counseling missionaries.

Personal Values and Legal Standards

MHPs are aware of the values and standards held by both the mission organization and the community in which they practice. While their own values are a matter of personal preference, they are sensitive as to how these might impact the agencies and individuals with whom they work. Legal regulations regarding the provision of mental health services in the particular country or state where one works are understood and followed.

Application
a. MHPs recognize that what is identified as healthy or unhealthy behavior may vary between individuals, between mission organizations, and between cultures. They are aware of their own values and are sensitive to individual, organizational, and cultural differences with regards to healthy, appropriate functioning.

b. MHPs who teach acknowledge that their personal values affect the selection and treatment of topics. Different values and positions should be presented. A high level of professional judgment must be exercised when giving specific advice to individuals at training lectures and seminars.

c. MHPs make their values explicit as much as possible in seeking organizational change and, whenever appropriate, in conducting therapy and teaching in mission settings. An accurate representation of one's theological values and doctrinal beliefs is provided when required by the mission agency.

d. MHPs clarify with mission organizations the bases of their professional recommendations for employment, promotion, or termination. Factors such as race, national origin, denominational affiliation, theological orientation, gender, handicap, age, political beliefs, and marital status must be discussed so as to prevent discriminatory practices. This may often involve some delicate issues such as an organization's desire to maintain doctrinal cohesiveness among personnel or the organization's view on the roles which men and women can assume.

e. MHPs work towards changing practices and policies that are not beneficial to organization members and the public interest.

f. MHPs are familiar and comply with the national and local laws requiring the delivery of mental health services for the country in which they work.

g. MHPs remain accountable to the standards of their respective disciplines during the course of their professional work in missions. MHPs, paraprofessionals, and trainees who do not formally belong to a professional group are encouraged to familiarize and commit themselves to an appropriate professional code of ethics.

Confidentiality

MHPs respect the confidence of clients who share information with them during the course of their professional work. Ownership of and accessibility to records must be clarified in advance between MHPs, mission agencies, and individual missionary clients. MHPs also advise their clients on the legal limits and the organization's policy on confidentiality.

Application
a. MHPs inform their missionary clients prior to rendering services as to who will have current and future access to the information they share. MHPs also help to develop appropriate organizational policies on confidentiality, accessibility to records, and client rights when such policies are inadequate or nonexistent.
b. MHPs inform missionary clients in advance about the conditions in which confidentiality must be breached. This would involve a clear risk of suicide, danger to others, child abuse, and possibly "moral failure" that would jeopardize the credibility and functioning of the organization (e.g., embezzlement of funds or sexual immorality). Otherwise, confidential information is not released without the written consent of clients or their client's legal representative.
c. MHPs who provide psychological evaluations discuss their findings only with those concerned with the case and avoid undue reporting of private areas unrelated to the evaluation.
d. MHPs acknowledge that missionary clients have the right to obtain information from their records. Records, though, are the property of the MHP and/or the mission organization. In providing clients with access to records, MHPs protect the confidence of others who have provided information which is contained in the record.
e. MHPs disguise any cases they discuss during presentations. It is generally preferable to use cases from outside of the mission organization in which one works when teaching or conducting seminars.
f. MHPs make sure that client records are kept secure and remain intact for at least three years after the completion of

planned services. After three years, the records may be summarized and kept for at least another twelve years, after which time they may be destroyed.

g. MHPs clarify confidentiality issues when conducting marital, family, and group therapy. The therapist clearly establishes a policy as to how material shared in confidence is to be dealt with by the other client(s) and the therapist.

Client Welfare

MHPs respect the dignity, worth, and integrity of missionary clients. Further, they seek to promote the welfare of both the individuals and mission organizations that they serve. Should a conflict of interest occur between the missionary client and the missionary organization, MHPs clarify the nature of the conflict as well as their own position and commitments with all parties involved. They also provide information to missionary clients and mission organizations concerning the nature and purpose of the evaluation, counseling, research, and other procedures they perform. Clients are always given the freedom to choose or discontinue services provided by the MHP.

Application
a. MHPs are aware of their own needs and the position of influence that they hold. Professional relationships are not used to advance one's own interests. Dependency is minimized and the development of personal competencies is pursued for clients.

b. MHPs avoid dual relationships with mission personnel and clients that decrease objectivity, impair judgment, or lead to exploitation. Professional relationships and friendships are not necessarily incompatible, yet must be clarified. MHPs carefully consider what roles to assume when working in a mission agency as well as the pros and cons of functioning as an outside consultant versus an in-house consultant. Both objectivity and familiarity with the organizational system need to be maintained.

c. MHPs only provide services within the context of a professional relationship.

d. MHPs clarify in advance the nature of the relationship with all parties when a third party (e.g., a personnel officer) requests services for a missionary.

e. MHPs make financial arrangements in advance with all clients and/or third parties. Fees are to be fair and commensurate with the services provided.

f. MHPs who provide counseling and therapy begin treatment only after receiving the "informed consent" of missionary clients.

Clients are apprised of the procedures that will be used, the role and qualifications of the therapist, any discomfort and risks involved, the benefits that may reasonably be expected, costs, and alternatives to treatment.

g. MHPs who are counselors or therapists terminate services if the client is clearly not benefiting from their services. Six months is usually considered to be the maximum time frame for determining whether or not the service is beneficial.

h. MHPs providing short-term services such as seminars and counseling are aware of the limitations of these approaches and the potential issues which may surface and require additional and/or longer-term intervention.

i. MHPs obtain appropriate authorization to conduct research within the mission organization. Informed consent, confidentiality, and an analysis of the study's ethical acceptability by other MHPs are required. When actual subjects are used, care must be taken to minimize any discomfort, to allow them to withdraw from the study at any time, and to debrief them at the end of the research.

Relationships with Other Professionals

MHPs stay informed of the services provided by colleagues in different mental health disciplines. They also establish relationships and cooperate with other professionals working in this specialized area and, where appropriate, with professionals working in the local community.

Application
a. MHPs consult with other professionals from similar or different disciplines when needed.

b. MHPs are responsible to be informed about and to secure complimentary or alternative services needed by their clients. When such services are not readily available due to language and cultural differences, geographic location, and/or insufficient funds, MHPs apprise their clients and responsible mission personnel of the lack of available services. MHPs continue to advocate for the needed client services.

c. MHPs proceed with caution when contacted by someone who is already receiving mental health services. An example would be a missionary who is being counseled by a pastor or another professional, who desires to switch counselors.

d. MHPs who provide supervision should offer opportunities for professional development, timely evaluations, adequate working conditions, and a caseload which reflects the skill level of their supervisees. Paraprofessional workers and trainees should receive ongoing and regular supervision, preferably by MHPs who are located at the same mission setting.

e. MHPs attempt to informally resolve any minor ethical violations committed by other mental health workers. Major violations are brought to the attention of the governing professional body to which the other individual belongs and the organization in which he or she works.

f. MHPs contribute to the knowledge base of mental health and missions by sharing research and practice information with colleagues.

Psychological Assessment

MHPs who provide assessment services such as testing and clinical interviews do so with a view towards the health and welfare of the missionary client. They take precautions to prevent the inappropriate use of assessment results. MHPs endorse the client's right to receive feedback on the results and to know the bases for arriving at any recommendations and decisions. They also endeavor to safeguard the tests and assessment tools which they utilize.

Application

a. MHPs inform missionary clients about the nature and purpose of assessment techniques unless an explicit waiving of this right has been agreed upon in advance.

b. MHPs establish procedures for ensuring the adequacy of explanations when assessment results are explained by others.

c. MHPs include reservations concerning the validity, reliability, and norms of tests used for a person tested in their reports. This is especially needed when testing members of different subgroups or ethnic groups.

d. MHPs who are competent in testing can provide evidence of validity for the procedures used in arriving at their interpretations. In many cases norms for the group being tested will have to be established.

e. MHPs do not encourage the use of psychological assessment techniques by unqualified persons.

f. MHPs encourage the use of test results in conjunction with other information on the client (e.g., references or other tests). A particular test is rarely the sole basis for making important decisions. Test interpretations and assessment reports also emphasize individual strengths and not just deficits or problem areas. Alternative explanations for results are also concerned.

g. MHPs formulate clear goals and hypotheses which determine the choice of tests or test batteries which they or the mission organization will use.

Discussion

The foregoing principles have been largely derived from standards which are common to most professional codes of ethics. While the principles themselves are not new, their contextualization within the mission setting is. Mission agencies may want to further contextualize these principles by using them as a point of departure to establish their own organizational code of ethics for mental health services.

Due to the different types of mission agencies and settings, it would also be useful to arrive at an interorganizational consensus as to what constitutes ethical mental health practice in missions. Envisioned is a committee comprised of MHPs from different agencies and disciplines which would develop general ethical guidelines which could then be expanded and enforced by the individual mission agency. The inclusion of people from different agencies and disciples would likely increase the comprehensiveness and acceptability of the resulting general guidelines.

Many of the issues brought up in this article will need to be addressed in light of each mission agency's unique setting and ministries. For example, defining different organizational policies on confidentiality may be needed when screening mission candidates back home, as opposed to counseling missionaries on the field. Another area of special concern, requiring extensive review, involves the validity and use of assessment procedures for evaluating and promoting missionary personnel, as well as predicting their overseas performance. In addition, clarifying the value of both psychological and theological perspectives may be important when treating aberrant behavior in therapy--for instance, seeing some forms of acting out responses as both sin and as a defensive, inappropriate solution to an inner conflict.

Still another area for discussion may be the need to carry malpractice insurance by the mission agency and/or the MHPs themselves. It is possible that in many settings, legal liablity for the services rendered will be clearly different from the ethical responsibility for one's professional practice. For example, legal action could conceivably be taken by a missionary client when confidentiality is breeched for reasons of "moral failure". In this case, breaking confidentiality may be required by the mission agency, yet is mandated neither by law nor professional ethics codes in the United States. These and other issues will have to be explored by both mental health specialists and mission leaders as they seek to work together to promote healthy and ethical mental health policies and practices.

Notes

1.The author wishes to thank William F. Hunter, Ph.D. (Rosemead School of Psychology) and Brent Lindquist, Ph.D. (Link Care Center) for their helpful reviews of this article.

2. The intervention categories of *support, re-education*, and *reconstruction* in the Appendix are taken from Wolberg, L. (1977), *Technique of psychotherapy*, New York: Grune & Stratton.

References

American Association of Marriage and Family Therapy (1985). A*AMFT code of ethical principles for marriage and family therapists.* Washington, D.C.: Author.

American Association of Pastoral Counselors (1986). *Code of ethics.* Fairfax, VA: Author.

American Psychological Association (1974). *Standards for educational and psychological tests.* Washington, D.C.: Author.

American Psychological Association (1981). Ethical principles of psychologists. *American Psychologist, 36,* 633-638.

American Psychological Association (1981). Specialty guidelines for the delivery of services. *American Psychologist, 36,* 639-681.

King, R. (1986). Developing a code of ethics for the Christian association for psychological studies. *Journal of Psychology and Christianity, 5,* 85-90.

National Association of Social Workers (1980). *Code of ethics.* Silver Springs, MD: Author.

Appendix
A Summary of Important Ethical Concerns
for MHPs in Missions

Responsibility
1. To whom am I accountable spiritually, professionally, and organizationally?
2. In what ways am I involved in the planning, directing, and reviewing of the services that are provided to the mission agency?
3. Does the mission agency need to be oriented as to the type and use of mental health services which I can provide?
4. Steps to take in evaluating ethical practice:
   a. Identify the ethical issues that are involved.
   b. Clarify the various options available.
   c. Describe the bases for your decisions.
   d. Explore the possible consequnces for your choices.

Professional Competence

Levels of Intervention	Types of Intevention		
	Support	Re-education	Reconstruction
Individual			
Couple			
Family			
Team			
Base			
Agency			

Examples of intervention:
1. Support--crisis intervention, psychogical assessment
2. Re-education--growth counseling, in-service seminars
3. Reconstruction--psychotherapy, agency reorganization.

Important issues to explore:
1. In which areas of the above competency chart can I function?
2. Which specific types of problems (e.g., personality disorders, communication bottlenecks in the agency), groups of people (e.g., ethnic groups, children), and techniques (e.g., gestalt therapy, vocational assessment) can I work with competently?
3. How will intervention or treatment in one area affect other areas?--e.g., the impact of marital therapy on family life and team functioning.

4. What types of intervention at which levels are needed for my client(s)?--e.g., supportive group counseling for couples on different teams acccompanied by re-educative intervention for a few of the spouses to improve their parenting skills.
5. What training and experiences are necessary to provide additional services beyond my present level of competency?

Personal Values and Legal Standards

Relevant Standards	Service Location	
	Own Country	Host Country
Legal Regulations		
Judicial Decisions		
Professional Ethics		
Christian Values		
Organizational Policies		

Important issues to explore:
1. Which standards in the above chart do I need to consider when providing mental health services in different countries?
2. In what ways do the various standards overlap, harmonize, and/or conflict?
3. What potential professional issues may occur as a result of giving heed to one standard at the expense of another?

Confidentiality
1. Who owns and has access to client records?--i.e. the organization, the MHP, and/or the client.
2. What are the conditions for breaking confidentiality?--e.g., suicide and homicide threat, child or elder abuse, serious moral failure.
3. What confidentiality procedures are used for the information shared during work with couples, families, and teams/departments?
4. How much and what types of information should be provided to the mission administration when doing candidate evaluations, therapy with voluntary missionary clients, and restorative counseling required by the mission agency?

Welfare to the Consumer
1. Under what conditions am I willing to provide services to individuals with whom I have previously had a nonprofessional relationship?--e.g., providing short-term counseling to the

daughter of a mission administrator with whom you served on a committee.

2. To what extent do current "dual relationships" with clients (if any) affect my objectivity, professional judgment, and service effectiveness?

3. How will potential conflicts of interest between missionary clients and missionary agencies be handled?

4. What potential longer-term issues may arise for individuals when conducting seminars and providing brief counseling?

Relationships with other Professionals

Levels of Intervention	Type of Intervention		
	Support	Re-education	Reconstruction
Individual			
Couple			
Family			
Team			
Base			
Agency			

Important issues to explore:

1. What resources are available within the organization, the local community, and the host country to meet the various mental health needs represented in the above chart?

2. What are some of the special needs of the missionaries in the agency?--e.g., geographic location, language, culture, actual problems.

3. With whom can I consult professionally when needed?

4. Who can serve as confidants to support me in my own growth?

5. What procedures are established to deal with ethical violations?

Psychological Assessment

1. What evidence is there for the psychometric adequacy (construct validity) of the tests and test batteries that are used?

2. How will the tests and assessment information be used?--i.e. what decisions will be made and what will be the potential consequences of such decisions in terms of acceptance, promotion, remediation, job change, or termination.

3. What norms are available when testing individuals from different cultures?

4. What are the minimum qualifications needed to provide assessment and testing services?

WOMEN IN MISSIONS

45

Joyce M. Bowers

Women's Roles in Mission:
Where Are We Now?

The most recent major movement for women's rights, often referred to as "women's lib," began in 1963 with the publication of Betty Friedan's, *The Feminine Mystique*. As a controversial issue in public debate, the movement gathered momentum during the 1960s and was at its peak in the late '60s and early '70s. This phase is remembered for angry rhetoric, refusal to wear bras, and other features that were distasteful to conservative Christians. In a parallel fashion, the biblical feminist movement had its birth in 1974 with the publication of Letha Scanzoni and Nancy Hardesty's *All We're Meant To Be*. This book raised controversy among evangelical Christians as Friedan's book had in society at large.

As the '70s progressed, women's lib lost some of its extremely radical nature. In part, leaders of the movement increasingly used socially accepted means of pursuing their goals; and in part, issues of equal opportunity, equal pay for equal work, etc., were more widely recognized as legitimate issues. Women not only returned to wearing bras, but the "dress for success" business suit became a dominant image of the modern career woman.

Also during the 1970s there was a tremendous amount of energy spent in Christian circles examining the role of women in the church, in the home, and in society, especially in light of

Scripture. The evangelical feminist movement, while perhaps rather small, became organized and visible; the Evangelical Women's Caucus was one expression of this movement. At the time, innumerable books, seminars, and magazine articles promoted a hierarchical view of women as being properly under male authority both in the home and in the church. One of the most widespread and visible examples of this sort of teaching was Bill Gothard's Institute in Basic Youth Conflicts.

Open debate regarding women's issues in U.S. Christendeom may have peaked around the late 1970s, although it certainly has not disappeared. In a number of denominations, ordination of women is increasingly acceptable and no longer a matter of dispute. There has been a virtual explosion of highly respectable feminist research in history, anthropology, theology and biblical studies. But in the opinion of some, the yeasty ferment of the 1970s has been replaced by a polarization and hardening of views, so that evangelistic feminist perspectives are farther and farther removed from recently restated and reinforced hierarchical or authoritarian viewpoints, with less and less true debate between camps, and more mud-slinging from afar on both sides.

One author who has refused to choose sides is Kari Torjesen Malcolm. I strongly recommend her *Women at the Crossroads: A Path Beyond Feminism and Traditionalism* (1982), Inter-Varsity Press). She gives a cross-cultural perspective.

Feminism and World Mission: Is There a Connection?

What does all of this have to do with world mission? Those who feel called to overseas work in the spread of the gospel usually see their call as coming directly from God, and their response and commitment as a matter of personal obedience to that call. They rarely see themselves in the context of the kingdom of God as a whole, let alone in the context of what is happening in society. Foreign missions as a grand scheme does not like to see itself as deeply affected by what happens in secular society; it sees itself as actor or initiator rather than reactor or follower. Yet we serve a God who has always acted in history and has used unbelievers to effect change within his household. One cannot understand the dynamics of the early history of the modern missionary movement, for example, without considering what was happening in the Western world of the 18th and 19th centuries--politically, socially, and technologically.

Similarly, a close look at the history of women's involvement in foreign mission reveals changing patterns within sending agencies that are results of or reactions against changes in Western society.

R. Pierce Beaver's classic study, *American Protestant Women in World Mission* (1980, Eerdman's) details the rise of women's missionary societies in the late 1800s as "the first feminist movement in North America." At that time, American women had few outlets for their evangelical zeal in the church at home, but were able to pour their time, money, and prayers into sending and supporting women overseas.

Since around 1910 and 1920, women's overall influence and involvement in world mission has declined drastically, for many reasons outside the scope of this article. For several decades now, women have largely been taken for granted or ignored. The beginning recognition that there are significant contemporary women's issues in world mission organization has been one of the more recent spinoffs of a movement (modern feminism) which was for a long time unknown or repudiated in mission circles. In the last few years there has been a growing realization that there are legitimate, pressing issues which demand attention and action.

Women overseas have always been more "liberated" than their Stateside sisters, in the sense that they have taken roles as missionaries that they would not have considered, or which were denied them in their home country. A woman who could not even take up the offering in her home congregation, and for whom ordination was unthinkable, might evangelize, plant churches, and train men to lead them in desperately needy areas of the Third World. However, women doing magnificent jobs in remote villages have rarely been rewarded by adequate recognition, except by the now-defunct women's missionary societies. Examples abound of married women who have served faithfully and effectively for 25 years but whose folders in the home office file are empty except for candidate information. One ripple effect of the feminist movement is for women to realize and make known their basic human need for well deserved respect, recognition, and affirmation in their work.

In virtually all mission situations, a husband's work assignment takes priority over his wife's, and single women are sometimes at the bottom of the totem pole in terms of status, recognition, and having one's unique needs and gifts taken seriously. Often, stated mission policy gives men and women equal status in that both are commissioned and sent as full missionaries, but in many subtle ways women are given the message that they are subordinate or even inferior members of the mission team--but that to complain about their "place" would be unspiritual.

Roles of Married Women Missionaries

An umbrella issue that encompasses many specific concerns is that of role, particularly for married women missionaries. For single women and married men, the work assignment is the primary focus of attention throughout the missionary career. In contrast, the missionary wife's role goes through drastic changes in focus as children are born, grow up, go to boarding school, and eventually leave the family. The role of the missionary wife needs frequent reevaluation, redefinition and restructuring. Much better use could be made of the gifts of women if role considerations and career guidance were built into long-term planning for missionary wives. Wives need to be encouraged strongly to develop their abilities, as they often see themselves primarily as supporters and nurturers.

The following are excerpts from the final report of the Consulting Committee on the Married Woman Missionary of the Division for World Mission and Ecumenism, Lutheran Church in America. The report was completed in July, 1981, and reflected this writer's study as well as many other contributions.

God calls men and women to himself in Jesus Christ. The primary vocation of each of us is, then, to be Christian...We rejoice in the diverse ways in which Christians fulfill their individual callings, each contributing to the workings of the body of Christ, and therefore acknowledge no hierarchy of vocations or persons. We believe that wherever stereotypes and culturally defined roles deny or limit any individual's possibilities for participation and personal growth, the working of the body of Christ is diminished and Christian freedom thwarted...

A role is a cluster of behavior patterns that carries with it expectations on the part of the person filling the role, and also expectations on the part of others who are related to a person in the performance of the role. In the case of the missionary there are exceptions on the part of the family, the sending agency, supporting congregations, the missionary community, the national church, and the local culture. The missionary role is a representative role--the missionary represents the Christian faith, the sending church, and his or her home country to the people of the host country. Generally speaking, the more representative a role is, the more pressure there is to fulfill role expectations.

The role of the married woman missionary has usually been a derived role in that her role was largely defined by her husband's assignment.

Within this framework, several role patterns, or "wifestyles," have emerged, depending on individual situations and preferences. They may be categorized as follows:

1. *Homemaker.* She is primarily a full-time wife and mother. Her main focus is on the home and the support and nurture of her family. She is an enabler to her husband in his work. She may have very young children and/or may teach her own school-age children.

2. *Background Supporter.* She actively supports her husband and his work. She is moderately involved in outside activities, many of which relate to her husband's assignment. Her main focus may be on ministry that can be carried out within the home, such as entertaining, listening/counseling, Bible classes, or language classes.

3. *Teamworker.* Her main focus is on a team ministry with her husband, and both work full-time. She feels free to choose a variety of activities, some of which relate directly to her husband's work. She may have part-time paid employment, but it does not detract from her sense of teamwork with her husband.

In addition to these role patterns, another pattern has emerged in recent years:

4. *Parallel Worker.* She sees her missionary role as distinct from her husband's role. She may work within the same organizational structure as her husband's assignment, which may be in a church-related setting or a nonchurch-related setting.

In the last category, a sense of teamwork expresses itself in mutual support as persons, even though the work assignments may be functionally unrelated. Both husband and wife are involved in creating a nurturing home environment, and ideally both are enabled to find fulfillment in the stewardship of their abilities and gifts.

All four of the foregoing role patterns are valid for married women missionaries. However, not all options are viable in every location. Individual wives may not fit clearly into one category or another, because of the diversity of situations.

The diversity of roles, individual differences, and conflicting expectations may pose a dilemma for the married woman missionary when: (a) there is a lack of role definition; (b) there is a lack of job description; (c) there is a lack of role recognition and acknowledgement; (d) there is a change from one role pattern to another without corresponding changes in the expectations of others.

The key issue in the above categorization is not what the wife *does*, but *how she sees herself*, and secondarily how she is seen by her husband. One very live issue is whether or not both marital partners agree on the wife's role, or have (perhaps unrecognized) differences of perception or opinion.

The following diagrams may be used to illustrate the four "wifestyles" described above:

1. Homemaker

2. Background
   Supporter

3. Teamworker

4. Parallel Worker

The circle in each case answers the question, Who is the missionary? For the homemaker, the husband is clearly the missionary and she is not (even though her mission board may say that she is). Experience has shown that women with this perspective have a much harder time enduring the vicissitudes of missionary life, as loyalty to one's husband and his call can wear thin rather quickly. The background supporter also sees her husband as the primary missionary, but sees herself as a missionary assistant. Women in categories 1 and 2 usually have heavy family responsibilities.

The teamworker and her husband are a single missionary unit-- a true team, with what has been called a "two-person single career." The teamworker sees her role as a missionary as fully equivalent to and inseparable from that of her husband. The parallel worker sees her missionary role separately, much like the role of the professional working woman--not primarily in relation to her husband's work. In real life situations, few women fit exactly into any one category, and there are many combinations and variations.

In the past few decades the dominant patterns in evangelical missions have been #2 and #3. The typical wife would be a background supporter while children were small and then gradually move into a teamworker pattern as she gained experience and confidence and was relieved of child care responsibilities. In recent years there have been increasing numbers of women, particularly those with specific professional training, who see their own ministries as separate from those of their husbands.

Another even more recent trend is the opposite of the above, and reflects the polarization of views regarding women mentioned earlier. That is, many mission personnel who are involved in the candidate process report a growing (and alarming) number of young couples who want the wife to be a homemaker and nothing more. This role pattern is seen by the young couples to be an ideal and not only a response to necessity when children are very young. Such views can be so extreme as to approach "family idolatry."

Concerns about role, recognition, etc., do not occupy the missionary wife's daily attention. Much more immediate and pressing problems demand her attention--coping with primitive living conditions, adapting to a different culture, child rearing, etc. Issues discussed here are often ignored because they are less obvious and relate to underlying assumptions and tensions. However, failure to recognize and deal with them often leads to low self-image and long-term, low-grade depression which in turn contributes to health problems, marital and family stress, and a tragic misuse and waste of precious human resources.

Women in Positions of Leadership

One area in which little has been resolved is that of leadership by women within mission structures. Attitudes and expectations on all sides are greatly influenced by theology and by cultural traditions that have become so entwined with theology that it is difficult to tell which it is. Though they comprise as much as two-thirds of the missionary roster, women in evangelical missions generally do not expect or seek leadership positions within the mission. In contrast, many women exercise gifts of administration and leadership in running schools, clinics, and other projects as part of their mission assignments. The presence of numerous gifted, experienced women who are natural leaders combined with an almost complete lack of recognized, legitimized channels for female leadership results in manipulative and often disruptive methods of influencing decision making--which, in turn, reinforces male fears of female leadership. Some wives of men in administrative positions have de facto recognition and are channels of communication in both directions between male hierarchies and female constituents; while this can be a saving grace, it is surely not ideal. Single women are given little or no opportunity for leadership or sanctioned influence and may feel like second-class citizens.

While many issues relating to women in mission have come to be recognized and are being openly discussed and wrestled with, leadership issues are still in the earlier stages of consciousness-raising and token responses. Why are there fewer women in administrative positions in mission in the 1980s than there were in the 1920s? Women's unique perspective on all mission issues (not just relational or home-and-family ones) is lost because neither women nor men recognize the value of women's potential contributions. The goal is not for women to take over doing what men have done, but for the entire mission enterprise to be enriched and refined by reflecting God's full image in humanity, male and female.

Responses of Sending Agencies

How are women's issues being dealt with in mission agencies? Ideally, awareness of and attention to these issues should be a thread running through all of the personnel practices of the organization, from recruitment and candidate selection on through the missionary's career, including consideration of post-field re-entry into U.S. society. Critically important are the attitudes, awareness, and sensitivity of the men in top administrative positions who are able to recognize and encourage the development of women's gifts.

Sessions that focus on women's roles and responsibilities may be a part of candidate orientation, for both men and women. Other important times for special attention are field council meetings, on-field supervisory visits by area secretaries, annual retreats, and mid-furlough debriefing sessions (not only for the just-got-off-the-plane sessions with physically and emotionally exhausted missionaries). At these times it is very helpful for all missionaries, but especially missionary wives, to set goals for themselves, both short-range and long-range, and to evaluate previously set goals to see where changes need to be made. If women are not encouraged to give their work adequate recognition and to strive for the best of which they are capable (not just the greatest quantity of work), much of their potential may be lost.

Specific nitty-gritty issues that need discussion vary widely from place to place and from time to time, and must be handled as they arise. Many agencies have had study commissions and/or surveys to determine what the pressure points were and to make recommendations. Even though the perfect answer is rarely found, sensitivity, flexibility, and open discussion go a long way toward reducing tension, frustration, and guilt feelings that arise around issues of role, responsibility, recognition, and decision making. There is always a tension between being responsive to the needs of individuals and, at the same time, being responsible to the larger group and to its mandate.

The purpose of consideration, discussion, and action relating to male/female issues is not to keep women and their issues in the focus of attention--but rather to relieve the pressure points so that men and women may serve God and His kingdom in full partnership, with greater liberty, effectiveness and joy, to God's greater glory.

Note

Much of the material in the second section of this article was published in the *International Bulletin of Missionary Research* in January, 1984, under the title, "Roles of Married Women Missionaries: A Case Study", by the same author.

46

Susan B. De Vries

Wives: Homemakers or Mission Employees?

Picture the field leader of your mission in Outer Mosquitoland, tearing his hair in frustration over his "Catch 22" predicament: The directive from the home office says, "Discover the gifts of the women on your field and give them more opportunities for development, place them in position with real authority, and encourage them in their career development. P.S. We're sending out some recruits and these women expect full integration with the men on your teams. See that they get it."

But listening to his field workers, he hears the scrape of dragging feet from the men on his field council, the skeptical sighs of burned-out single women workers, and the fearful door-slamming of young mothers who already have their hands full. The older married women respond, "What's all the fuss? We've been doing mission work for years anyway, usually without credit or under the signature of our husbands." And the younger, more educated women charge, "Tokenism!"

What's a field leader to do?

There are many obstacles to fuller integration of women in mission work. Some of these obstacles, such as younger children in the family, cannot be eliminated. Other deterrents can; these include the attitudes of both women and men, the lack of accountability or rewards for women, low educational standards of acceptance for wives, and lack of long-range career planning for wives.

Many mission boards place heavy expectations for mission work on the wives; other missions are coming from an opposite position. In my own mission, Overseas Crusades, family is a stated priority. Our 1981 policy handbook states, "A missionary wife, although appointed as a missionary with her husband, is encouraged to make her first ministry her home. Well cared for children, hospitality, and the support she gives her husband in his work are in themselves a powerful statement of the power of the gospel. Beyond this, however, she may undertake outside ministries as God gives her ability and opportunity."

We appreciated this freedom of choice for the wife's level of involvement, and it was one of the reasons we chose OC.

Children: A Valid Hindrance

A married woman in a missionary role is particularly unsettled because her life is constantly in change--patterns dictated by the arrival and special demands of her children. Men and single women do not experience these same primary responsibilities, so their job defines their role in a more consistent manner. Children, wonderful and indispensable as they are, make up one of the major roadblocks for the full utilization of married women in missions.

Missionary wives carry a double job description: they want to be a supermom and a super missionary at the same time.

An example of conflicting interests brought about by this dual role is found in the situation of one of my friends. Her mission's stated policy and actual expectation is that mission work comes before family. Parents are forbidden to teach their children in the home or send them to local schools because the mother's time available for ministry would be curtailed. "I've always considered myself a working mother," Sandi told me. She copes with full-time job, four children, a traveling husband, and cross-cultural stress.

Examine the guidelines suggested by Joy Turner Tuggy in her handbook, *The Missionary Wife and Her Work.* In chapter two, the missionary wife is exhorted to take on the following responsibilities: run the household, prepare nutritious meals, keep the family's clothes in good order, assume the greater part of the burden of letter-writing, and share actively in many ways the ministry to which they have given themselves, "keeping always in the background."

To this the author adds the time-consuming ministry of hospitality and the wife's primary responsibility for the children's daily discipline and emotional well-being. Can you not empathize, then, with the door slammed in the face of the field director who comes offering the missionary wife a fulfilling career as field council secretary?

An ancient but still lively belief is the assumption that if the missionary couple puts the Lord's work first in every case, they will find God obligated to keep their children from all harm. This belief guided Hudson Taylor, Jonathan Goforth, and many other missionary "greats." Yet sometimes this well-meaning philosophy had tragic and hidden results in bitter, broken-hearted children who rejected both God and his servants, their parents. No survey has been successful in counting the number of children of missionaries on whose hearts is written in indelible ink, "You are less important than the Work." Mission boards that insist on moms working full-time in ministry foster family tensions which often result in damaged kids.

Resistance by Men

Another roadblock to the full utilization of women and their gifts in mission is men. R. Pierce Beaver points out in his book, *American Protestant Women in World Mission*, that objections usually do not come from the home office, but from the men in the field councils. This may take the form of a subtle, unconscious by-passing of women rather than outright discrimination.

Says Grace Frizen, editor of the IFMA News, "The kind of men who feel very threatened by women in mission leadership are usually the men who have a very domineering wife, or whose wives are more capable than they, or else men who are generally incompetent." She feels that most women have just accepted the fact that they will be by-passed for positions of leadership or teaching and have learned not to hope for any change in the status quo.

Sometimes the local culture will limit the degree of freedom that a woman may have to minister. But often a foreign woman is tolerated in an unusual role because she is already expected to be different. It is more likely to be the missionary men who resist her full participation.

While most women under evangelical mission agencies are appointed regular missionaries, the wives frequently do not receive a definite work assignment, nor do they turn in monthly reports. Women are usually forbidden to work outside the mission for additional income, yet the same rule is not applied to a pastor or a stateside mission administrator. We seem to have a double standard.

However equally the wife may contribute toward achieving mission goals, she is not likely to be given the opportunity of forming those goals. "There are a few women on our field council, generally the more passive, quiet type and always they are the singles," one wife told me.

This situation is not atypical. In the chapter updating the newest edition of *American Protestant Women*, R. Pierce Beaver states: "The governance of the nondenominational societies and the evangelical denominational boards, except for the few founded by women, is strictly male, and in some instances male domination has strengthened [since the 60's]" (p. 213). "Out of 620 sending, supporting, and specialized agencies, only five of the older and larger ones had a woman president or chairwoman for at least part of the decade [of the 70's]. Women have seldom been admitted to major administrative posts in the nondenominational societies and evangelical denominational boards..." (p. 214).

In 1984, only 44.5 percent of the Interdenominational Foreign Mission Association member missions' total workforce were male; yet I estimate that 95 percent of their personnel supervision, counseling, and arbitration of disputes is done by men. Experienced women could well serve in supervisory and counseling roles. This probably would prove less threatening to the newer men on the field and more comfortable for the women.

Resistance by the Women Themselves to Accountability

What about job accountability? Do women really want this? Of course, single women have had accountability (monthly reports, job descriptions, and their own separate salary) for many years now. But seldom the missionary wives. Why not? Sometimes the reason given is that the wives were not required to devote their full time to ministry. When the children are young, this is often true.

I informally polled a group of 10 women, asking if any of the eight mission boards represented really didn't expect any mission work from them. Al- were 35 or older and all responded that they were indeed full-time mission workers. Apart from a few mainline denominational mission boards, we couldn't think of one board that did not require or expect the missionary wives to work at least half-time.

Most of my missionary wife friends, however, seem happy with this status quo. They want to work quietly alongside their husbands. They feel equally called and commissioned to be missionaries in their own right. They don't really want to be invited to field council meetings, nor to be made field chairman. (Well, maybe a few would. Some wives do have gifts in strategy planning and administration, and the ambition to use those gifts.)

Most women knew when they joined that they could expect a life with many demands in mission-related work, without separate salaries. But when I pin them down, they acknowledge that they don't have much say in mission policy making. There are few women in positions of leadership, in personnel departments, or even in authority over women.

Perhaps equally wasteful of our resources is the fact that the women's work is not always coordinated or integrated with the men's overall field strategy. Even single women missionaries have long complained that they do not have any say in policy decisions affecting their own ministry or personnel placements.

Lack of Rewards of Recognition

Married (and single) women have found greater freedom to tackle non-traditional tasks and take initiative in mission work overseas than in their home sending countries, particularly in earlier years when Victorian society limited women's roles severely. But what has been their reward? Primarily, the gratitude of their husbands and the sense of having pleased the Lord. Tangible rewards are rare. Few missionary wives even receive separate social security payments, much less their own paycheck.

We need the encouragement of recognition. The contributions of working missionary wives could be enhanced by things like office space, job titles with corresponding authority, the responsibility to help form and achieve team goals, and commendations when specific projects are completed.

The salary question will naturally raise righteous hackles. Admittedly, most mission boards do not consider the salaries of missionaries as equivalent payment for services rendered. Most men would be earning far more in a profession in the States utilizing their seven or eight years of post-secondary school education. These uniform salaries are more realistically called "living allowances." Both sending church and mission board assume that the couple who commit themselves to mission work overseas are virtually making a vow of poverty. (Whether this is right is another question.)

These "facts of missionary life" often come as a rude awakening to men recruits, especially those accustomed to a two-income lifestyle as well-educated professionals.

But the inevitable question arises: How on earth could we afford to compensate the working missionary wife? In faith missions, where the couple is responsible to raise the required support quota, the current allowance could be divided proportionately between husband and wife, depending on the amount of time they are each giving to mission work. Most families would likely pool both husband's and wife's income; the difference would be that both partners could feel equally responsible and compensated.

For denominational boards, providing salaries for the wives who choose to work would increase the cost of personnel. But then, it is possible that mission boards have been receiving two workers for the cost of one for many years now.

The Lutheran Chuch in America is experimenting with changes in "wifestyles." Depending on individual preferences and life situations, their missionary families are free to choose among four levels of involvement and are compensated proportionately. Joyce M. Bowers reports on this new policy for the LCA in the *International Bulletin of Missionary Research* (January 1984).

Standards of Acceptance

If wives are going to be full co-workers and held more strictly accountable--and this is the trend in missions today--their qualifications must be more nearly equal to the men.

Many mission boards require only two years of college (which must include 30 hours of Bible courses) for a married woman applicant, whereas a single woman often is required to have a college degree plus professional training of some sort. For men, the minimum requirement in many boards is a college degree, a seminary degree, and ordination. This discrepancy is too large.

For highly educated men to accept as peers women with only a high school diploma or a year or two of college is difficult. It is short-sighted to accept women without any special training; their productive years with the mission after the children begin school and/or leave home are often double the number of years when they will focus on just their house and children. Though few may appreciate the delay in getting to the field, most women will be thankful later on.

We should also increase their access to furlough or on-field study programs (Azusa Pacific College and Trinity Evangelical Divinity School offer extension courses convenient to some, for example), as well as motivate them to participate. There are still too many roadblocks.

When our girls had all started school, my husband felt it would be a good time for me to pursue graduate studies on our furlough, to increase my proficiency for future ministry. Several missionary wives have whispered to me, "My husband would never dream of devoting a furlough to my schooling." When we reported the hefty expenses of tuition on our income tax report, however, our accountant informed us that it was not a legitimate educational deduction, since I am not officially employed by the mission.

Variety of Viewpoints and Wifestyles
I wish to make my assumption very clear: namely, that each family should be free to choose it own role for the wife, just as they are free to choose the number of children they will have. Full missionary careers will never be mandatory nor desirable for every missionary wife. In this transition period there will be much variance; we need tolerance for a plurality of viewpoints and lifestyles.

Special care needs to be taken that everyone on a particular station is informed of the limits of each wife's commitment. One of the ripest areas for resentment and discord on a station is the disparity between contributions of work time made by the various women.

Suggestions for Mission Personnel Directors
1. Begin at the very start of the family's association with the mission to make long-range plans for both partners' development as mature missionary workers. Set target dates that can be adapted to family needs. This would give women a sense of direction, of self-worth, and perhaps motivate them to more dligent language learning and occasional educational coursework.

Discuss career options for all women within the mission, both older women and incoming recruits. This would have to include possible accommodation to a very male-dominated culture where the family is working, particularly when the wife would have national men as co-workers.

2. Make it very clear to all that the mission regards homemaking and child-care as high priorities; thus, it will be the norm (with very few exceptions) for a wife with preschool-age children not to be involved in any formal mission activity. If we are serious about our witness as strong family role models, we need to allocate our manpower (mothers!) to full involvement when the nurturing of children is most crucial. This means that younger mothers should not be assigned mission work while they have any children at home under six years of age, or while they are teaching their children at home. Work that can be done in the home, such as hospitality, correspondence, home Bible studies, or work for her husband might be allowed as her time and health permit.

3. After the children begin school and require less time, it should be time for a discussion between the husband, the wife, and the field director as to just how much of her time she is able to

give to mission work. The couple should be allowed several options, from part-time to full-time separate ministry for the wife. At that time, the wife should be supervised, evaluated, and given opportunity for monthly reporting, involvement in decision and policy making, and advancement to positions of administration or leadership if she has those abilities.

It would also be helpful to divide their paycheck and issue the amounts in their two separate names. Remember, a job without accountability and reward is only a volunteer position.

4. To increase communication and lessen friction between the men, the married women, and the singles in every mission, we need more frequent discussion concerning women's changing roles. We need to schedule group discussions on women's roles in annual field conferences and in leadership training with national co-workers as well.

5. Another help to the administrator in understanding how to be a better leader to all his missionaries, both male and female, would be the use of the Myers-Briggs personality indicator. This tool could help the field leader know when and how to use motivational techniques. For example, some of us respond best to structured roles, commendation, and check lists; others are self-starters who need freedom and just occasional guidance. While not all women are alike, there are some typical patterns of male and female interactions which any administrator needs to know.

Conclusion

I have explored several obstacles to women's full involvement in missions: some, such as children, can't be changed. Their nurture is too crucial to make it secondary to a woman's ministry. Other obstacles can be changed. These include an attitude of superiority or disdain on the part of men, resistance to accountability on the part of women, the lack of recognition and reward for women's work, and ignorance of what a woman could and would like to do with her skills and gifts.

Long-range career planning for wives, higher standards of acceptance, and promotion of qualified women to positions of leadership should be the pattern for missions in the next decade.

47

Diane Marshall

Current Issues of Women and Therapy

This paper explores some of the current issues affecting therapists in working with women in individual, marital, and family settings. It touches on concerns of self-esteem, vocation, achievement, and intimacy. It seeks to reflect a Christian understanding of contemporary developments in the psychology of women.

I would like to approach the topic of "Current Issues of Women and Therapy" from a few perspectives: First, a brief history of Women and Psychology; second, a look at what Scripture teaches about our calling in Christ; and third, some comments on the meaning of "Adulthood" and the effects of broad social change, as embodied in the women's movement. I would like to look at what I see as five major obstacles to our growth as women and make some concluding remarks.

Throughout this paper I want to make clear that the comments I make about where I see women as being, do not in any way imply an anti-male or anti-family stance. I believe in reconciliation and in interdependence, but I'm also aware that these concepts have been used against women. In fact, in the history of psychology in this century alone, they have been used to deny women full personhood. For centuries we have labelled anger in women as being "unfeminine," and so women have not been encouraged to seek justice for themselves, and instead, models of marriage and family and society have depended on women being passive and dependent, psychologically as well as economically.

Thus, as a Christian feminist and therapist, the key issue that I see we need to address is the creational given that women are made in the image of God. This may seem an unnecessary commonplace, but I would like to posit for our consideration that for *many* women, Christian and otherwise, the Good News of creation and redemption is not seen as applying to them. The consequences in terms of these women's self-esteem, in terms of emotional and mental health, in terms of structures of marriage, family, work place and church, are horrendous.

History of Women and Psychology

It is an interesting historical phenomenon that sex role specialization has developed in sedentary societies, vs. hunter-gatherer societies where everyone is a "Jack/Jill of all trades." The extreme extension of this historical development is seen in North American women at home with children in suburbia, cut off from peers, where there is a loss of sense of community in work, and an experience of being *isolated*.

Learning psychologists have described the cognitive styles of women as contextual, whereas men are described as more specific and analytic (Van Leeuwen, 1984). This contextual style has been profoundly affected in North American culture by the isolation of women and by women's low self-esteem, and both have contributed to the following developments in the history of the psychology of women:

1. *Sigmund Freud* said "Anatomy is destiny" and asked "What do women want?" He invented theories such as "penis envy" to describe ambitious women. His theories delineate mental health as basically being masculine in nature: there are few positive aspects to female psychology. Women are seen as deterministic, "feminine nature" being determined by anatomy and physiology. Christian writer Tim Lahay echoes this Freudian determinism when he writes: "Woman by nature is a submissive creature."

2. *Carl Jung* described the "feminine principle" as feeling-oriented, intuitive; and the "masculine principle" as Logos, rational. The problem lies in equating "masculine" with females, although Jung himself argued for androgyny.

3. *Alfred Adler* talked about things like the "will to power," striving for superiority, family birth order, early recollections and life scripts, and seemed to have a broader understanding that a psyche, male or female, is formed in the context of a society.

Adlerians have made some significant progress in non-sexist views of male and female.

4. *Karen Horney* did some major work in the psychology of women, as a neo-Freudian, but working with a much more holistic approach.

5. *Naomi Weisstein*, the first feminist psychologist, writing in the late 1960s, dismissed psychoanalysis as being ideologically motivated and supporting the status quo of the "woman's place." She wrote, in her article "Psychology Constructs the Female" (1968) that "a woman has an identity if she is attractive enough to obtain a man...and her true nature is that of a happy servant." Weisstein saw women and men largely as products of immediate social expectations, "a function of what people around expect him/her to be," and therefore she denied any *innate* sex differences: "Woman is made, not born," and all behavior is learned. Thus, she represented a behaviorist approach, with confidence in the changeability of human behavior as a function of immediate environmental reinforcers.

6. *Carol Gilligan*, in her recent book, *In a Different Voice* (1982), discusses her research in women's moral development. Gilligan challenges Kohlberg's so called "mature" Stage 6, impersonal universal principles: women in his model usually only achieve Stage 3 development of "helping and pleasing others." Gilligan says that Kohlberg's research takes male experience, rooted in separation and autonomy, as being normative; and dismisses equally valid women's experiences, rooted in *connectedness.* Thus she avoids questions about the origins of sex differences and looks at the strengths and advantages of both ways of being. *In a Different Voice* speaks of the "different voice," a voice often silenced, of women and women's ethical concerns and behavior. She postulates that, rather than a hierarchical model of moral development which slots people into levels, we have two different developmental patterns of moral reasoning: the male pattern concerned with a morality of abstract individual rights; and the female pattern concerned with a morality of conflicting human relationship, where women strive to preserve *all* relationships through dialogue. Therefore women's moral development centers around the understanding of responsibility and relationships rather than rights and rules.

The "shadow side" of women's striving to preserve a network of relationships is that women often evade adult responsibility for their decisions, "someone else made me do it," but when pushed beyond this undifferentiated altruism, women do finally develop a sense of vocation: adult work tasks. On the other hand, men have the advantage of a stronger sense of both individual purpose and individual moral responsibility, but are ambivalent about intimacy. Gilligan sees men as being more legalistic and often indifferent to the relational context. In fact, she recounts research which shows that the men who serve as models of adult development have a *diminished* capacity for relationships and are constricted in their emotional expression.

So Gilligan argues that male and female "voices" typically speak of the importance of different truths: men of the role of separation as it defines and empowers the self, i.e., integrity, and women of the ongoing process of attachments that create and sustain human community, i.e., caring. So there appears to be a conflict between self-expression and self-sacrifice, between integrity and intimacy. Gilligan argues that the key to the convergence of intimacy and truth, others and self, lies in making a necessary connection between integrity and care; therefore establishing *interdependence*; not an either/or, but a both/and.

Thus, for women, the constraints of choice sometimes involves the reality that there is no way not to hurt, but the key to maturity is a woman claiming the right to include herself among the people for whom she considers it moral not to hurt!

7. *Ann Wilson Schaef*, in *Women's Reality* (1981), resonates with Gilligan in describing what she calls the "Female System," a way of being, of existing within the dominant culture of the "White Male System." She defines several aspects of the "Female System," including *Time,* which for women is perceived as a process, a series of passages and interlocking series and rhythms, not as *Clock Time; Relationships,* which among women are peer-oriented, not dominant-submissive; *Center of Focus,* which for women is centered in relationships, not in self and work as with men; *Intimacy,* which for women is verbally approached, not physically approached as with men; *Love,* which for women is a flow of energy, not rituals as with men; and *Friendship,* which for women is open sharing and closeness, not an experience of being "teammates" in work or sports as with men. All these dimensions of "women's reality" Schaef sees as creating a tension for women who have to adapt themselves to a dominant white male culture.

8. *Jean Baker Miller*, in *Towards a New Psychology of Women* (1976), also looks at women as a subordinate group in a male dominant society. She examines female psychology from the perspective of women being socialized to be dependent, always seeking male approval, because subordinates always need the approval of dominants to gain self-esteem, and as struggling with intense conflict between intimacy and achievement needs. Baker

Miller has an excellent understanding of women's depression as being connected to women's inability (because deemed "unfeminine" to express anger.

Baker Miller makes a pertinent insight in her analysis of women's sense of *self.* In commenting on prevailing psychoanalytic theories about women's weaker ego or super-ego, she points out that:

Women do not come into this picture the way men do. They do not have the right or the requirement to become full-fledged representatives of the culture. Nor have they been granted the right to act and to judge their own actions in terms of the direct benefit to themselves. *Both of these rights seem essential to the development of ego and super-ego.* This does not mean that women do not have organizing principles or relate to "a reality" in a particular way. But women's reality is rooted in the encouragement to "form" themselves into the person who will be of benefit to others. Thus they see their own actions only as these actions are mediated through others. This experience begins at birth and continues through life. Out of it, women develop a psychic structuring for which the term "ego," as ordinarily used, may not apply. (p. 72)

Baker Miller goes on to argue that women's selfhood is derived not directly from reality but by mediating through the other person's purposes in that reality. This selfhood thus hinges ultimately on the other person's perceptions and evaluations, rather than one's own. She is describing what I call a "fused" identity.

In looking at these various perspectives on the "nature of women," I have decided to limit the vast subject of "Who is woman, that Thou art mindful of her?" to a few basic issues which continually seem to appear in my own clinical practice, and in dialogue with other women therapists. To begin, let us take a look at our Christian calling.

Our Christian Calling

Our mandate as Christians, in the words of Ephesians 4, is to "grow up into the stature of the fullness of Jesus Christ," and through the indwelling of God's Holy Spirit to bear fruit of love, joy, peace (not a false peace or accommodation), patience, goodness, kindness, faithfulness, gentleness (not passivity), and self-control. I realize that the danger of using Scripture is that we have filters of our experience--e.g., social filters, and so we need to redefine these terms. We are admonished to "let *love* be our aim," and in the words of Galatians 5: "For you were called to freedom, sisters and brothers: only do not use your freedom as an opportunity for the flesh, but through love be servants of one another. For the whole law is fulfilled in one word, 'You shall love your neighbor as yourself. For against the fruit of the Spirit there is no law.'" (vs. 13-15, NEB)

Again, in Ephesians 3, we are promised that Christ "will grant us to be strengthened with might through the Spirit in the inner being" and that "Christ...will dwell in our hearts through faith; that we, being rooted and grounded in love, may have power to comprehend with all the saints what is the breadth and length and height and depth, and to know the love of Christ which surpasses knowledge, that we may be filled with all the fullness of God." (vs. 17-20, NEB)

Our concern is to seek, in part, to reconcile the powerful promises of Scripture that are held out to us as members of the Body of Christ, created in the image of Jesus Christ, and redeemed, through Jesus Christ, with the stark and painful reality that as women--as Christian women--we are so frequently full of that spirit of fear, so lacking in self-love, and so unable to grasp fully the fruit of the Spirit and to live out the gifts of the Spirit. We must ask ourselves these questions: Why are so few Christian women unable to be "good and faithful stewards" of the gifts that God has given us? Why do we fail to grow into *maturity* in Christ, and remain so long awkward adolescents? What are some of the bonds we must seek to unshackle, personally and corporately, in the Church with one another's help, in order to find that full freedom promised to us?

Adulthood and Change

"Adulthood" can perhaps be described as the period in life when we have learned to value both ourselves and others; when we are able to make a conscious consent to intimacy and to interdependence in family, marriage, friendship; and when we have a clear sense of self and of vocation. There are various stages of adult life and various tasks we are called to. I operate always from the premise that the deepest human need is for meaning.

Gail Sheehy, in her book *Passages* (1976), describes women's life passages as revolving around the struggle between being a "caregiver" and an "achiever." She describes five adult stages of development: (1) *pulling up roots*, and making the break from our parents' home and often from their values in order to find our own world view; (2) *the trying twenties*, a taking hold in the adult world; to shape a dream, to prepare for a life work, to find a mentor, to form the capacity for intimacy; (3) *the catch thirties,* which may begin when feeling narrow and restricted and needing to expand, often causing disruption to roots already put down, e.g. marriages, and which may include a deeper rooting and extending, buying houses, focusing on raising children, or a crossroads, a time of danger and opportunity and rethinking of the narrow identity of the first half of life; women usually sense this mid-life transition earlier than men; (4) *the mid-forties on,* when new stability is achieved, either a staleness calcifying into resignation or a renewal of purpose and meaning; and (5) *growing into old* age: making peace with our pasts.

Another contemporary woman writer, Ellen Goodman, in her book *Turning Points* (1979), which examines how people have been affected by the great social change of our time and the evolving roles of women and men, sees that a great social change like the Women's Movement cuts across the life cycle as described by Sheehy. She understands change as "often being an effort to conserve meaning." In her epilogue to *Turning Points*, Goodman speaks of our traditional sex roles as confessing to that need for meaning:

[North] Americans have always valued individual rights on the one hand and a sense of community on the other. We believe in the independence of family members and the importance of the family unit. We value both self-realization and self-sacrifice: the quest for personal growth and the virtue of doing for others....We need tradition and roots on the one hand, and excitement, risk, and exploration on the other.... *traditionally* these conflicting values were dealth with through sex role assignments. Men were encouraged toward self-realization while women were allotted self-sacrifice. Men were keepers of the adventurous spirit, while women were the ones who made and kept homes, families, roots. Men worked in the material world, while women were in charge of the spiritual values. (pp. 287-288)

Today men are questioning this role and not feeling self-realized. So, both men and women together are faced with changing these traditional roles; engaged in a new search for meaning.

Obstacles to Women's Growth

In addition to looking at what these women commentators, along with several women psychologists, have had to say in writing about women's lives today, I will suggest five major obstacles to our growth into maturity as Christian women, which I will deal with under broad headings.

1. Caregiving and Guilt

Firstly, I would like to make mention of what may seem to be a contradiction and that is: women in our society, and as taught by the Church, are expected to be "caregivers," the ones who nurture and take care of others in society; children, the sick, the helpless, the handicapped, the aged, and also men! At first glance this would seem to be a primary Christian virtue but I list it here as a potential obstacle to growth because of what I and others consistently observe this role does to women. It seems, as Carol Gilligan says, that we have been so conditioned to need to be needed and so conditioned to define ourselves *in relation to others,* and especially others who need us to care for them, that we often fail to grow and mature as whole persons. We remain reactive, adjusting and adapting to conditions set for us by others. If we have gifts which do not fit this mold, we suppress them, feel guilty, feel "selfish" when we do not use them, are often labelled as such, and in general do not feel good about ourselves unless we are giving to others. Because of this expectation of us we actually see ourselves as being responsible for whether or not our spouse, children, friends, family, co-workers or whoever, are happy! A surefire recipe for *guilt!* We can become godlike in our self-appointed role of making people happy; and by doing so we unwittingly rob our spouses and children of taking responsibility for their own emotional growth and well-being.

The risk of defining ourselves as separate persons, and not with a "fused" identity; and as having our own needs, frightening to women. We are so conditioned to endure and adapt that we fear creating conflict if we pull out of the supporting roles. I see many women in my practice, Christian women, who are driven by this fear, and as women we need to face squarely what II Timothy 1:7 means for us, where St. Paul writes: "For God has not given us a spirit of fear, but of power, and of love, and of a sound mind." (NEB) Sometimes growth involves conflict, and we must not be ruled by a spirit of fear but by the deep faith that the God of peace will be with us and bring healing where there is disruption.

I would like to give an example here of a friend of mine, a gifted artist, in her mid-forties. Her three children are grown and have left home. She wanted to go to Art College to pursue her gifts of creativity, which she believe are a gift from God, but her husband was very threatened and actually forbade her to go, saying he needed her at home. Her conflict was between her life-long pattern of adjusting to others' needs and wishes in the task of being a "caregiver," and developing the gifts God had given her. She felt she could do the latter without destroying the marriage, but was aware that her husband would have to make some changes. My friend is deeply aware of Christ's teachings to be "good and faithful stewards" of the gifts God has given; thus her dilemma: should she capitulate to her husband's demands in order to "keep peace at any price?" In this case she would have paid the price, as she had done before, in the form of depression. Or should she quietly yet determinedly choose to study art, trusting that God would teach her husband that "love is not possessive?" That was her conflict, and whichever way she had chosen there would have been risk and pain involved. I am glad to report that she graduated with honors at the end of May 1984, and her marriage, though stressed, is still intact!

Another example is of a young woman whom I met through my work with single, sole-support mothers in an inner city mission in Toronto. This young woman has one child and is on welfare. She is unmarried. She wants to go to a government retraining class in order to gain some "marketable" skills to support herself and her child. Some of the members of her church frown upon her doing this because she would have to put her son into day care. They tell her that it is her job to stay home and bring him up even if it means living below the poverty line in a rough public housing complex. Her conflict is in risking the displeasure of her church support group, her Christian friends, in order to get out of the terrible situation of poverty and dependency. Does going back to school and work mean she is being a "poor mother?" Yet this is the accusation made against her when she talks of *not* being a "full-time caregiver."

2. *Powerlessness and Victimization*

This brings me to my second point concerning obstacles to growth. The II Timothy passage speaks of God giving us, through His Spirit, "power, love and a sound mind." Acts 1:8 says: "You shall receive power when the Holy Spirit comes upon you." Why is it that so many women, including Christian women, feel powerless, and often feel that they are *victims,* feel worthless and lacking in self-respect? I'd like to agree with Jean Baker Miller (1976) that where women are concerned, historically we have been placed in a subordinate role, while men are in the dominant role, and as such we have not been free to choose servanthood but rather it has been imposed upon us. Even in seeking therapy, women have been placed in subordinate roles, and the therapeutic relationship has frequently failed to model mutuality. Women's real experiences as victims, of sexual abuse, incest, rape, spousal assault, economic powerlessness, to name but a few, have often not been taken seriously by male therapists, and labelled neurotic or hysterical.

But there is no place in Christian therapy for preeminence, for "lording it over others." Jesus taught his disciples to serve, not to dominate, and indeed use His power to become powerless. Yet Christ was not a victim. He said, "No one takes my life from me. I have power to lay my life down." This is our model of true servanthood and I differentiate this from *servility*. The definition of "servile" in the Oxford English Dictionary: "That which behaves like a slave, cringing, fawning; subject to despotic, oppressive government or domination." The God we worship asks us to worship in freedom and in truth--to *love* God. This is not an attitude of one who is oppressed. Thus as women we need to look again at our understanding of servanthood in light of being empowered by God's Holy Spirit. I suggest that our chronic feeling of powerlessness, of behaving like a subordinate group, not as equal persons, needs to be examined critically. I am convinced that certain clinical conditions, such as depression, eating disorders, and alcohol and drug abuse in Christian women are directly linked to feeling worthless, powerless, as though "I don't count." To experience the empowerment of God's Spirit is not a quest after power and position, it is to be *in-spired*, in the true sense, to actualize the talents and gifts God has given us. To have self-respect *does not mean we are selfish.*

First, however, we must reclaim the creation mandate: that we as women are "made in the image of God" and are called to be partners with men, as stewards of creation. Thus we must seek to redress that dominant/subordinate status in which we so often find ourselves in relation to the men in our lives, and so help them also to be obedient to God in being co-partners. For men are wounded, I am convinced, in their power to love, when they are always in control and always in the dominant role. Our goal as members of the Body of Christ is *mutuality* and *interdependence*, sharing, being "mutually accountable to one another in Christ Jesus," as Ephesians 5:21 teaches us. For, "in Christ there is neither Jew nor Greek, slave nor free, male nor female. All are one in Christ." (Gal.3:27)

3. *Fear and Dependency*

Thirdly, and connected to the first two points, is the psychological phenomenon of women being described as "children."

I am not referring here to Christ's admonition to "become as a child" in order to enter the Kingdom of Heaven, but of what psychologists see as a failure to grow into adulthood. I personally see this as again linked to a "spirit of fear." We are notoriously anxious. We fear independence. We are afraid to take a stand on important social and justice issues. We fear being alienated and, as a result, we often choose to remain dependent, passive, dominated and angry; the very struggle the young woman on welfare is going through. Our churches play into this with their very powerful male hierarchy. All the role models we have are of Christian men, and women are just "helpers." Our daughters do not prophesy because our churches have silenced women, kept them subordinate, and labelled them as "uppity women" or "castrating females" when a woman knows her convictions and displays that very trait of II Timothy: a "sound mind." Yet the book of Acts tells us that Philip had "four daughters who prophesied!" We are taught to think it is "cute" when women are flustered, hysterical or incompetent, and we are threatened when our sisters display qualities of strength, determination, articulateness, and leadership.

A very critical issue that I see regularly is the lack of support given to women who do take the unusual path, or who do stand up to injustice, and use their anger to fight against broken personal and social relationships. We forget that Jesus used anger to heal (Mark 3). Often women become defensive, seem hardened and "tough," when underneath they are longing for love and encouragement. Why is it that women so seldom nurture each other? Are we threatened by and jealous of anyone who breaks the status quo? Do we compete, and are we jealous because we are secretly afraid of ourselves losing the approval of the dominant group in our society, namely, male, if we seem to support liberation for women? Sixty years ago, Nellie McLung, a deeply committed Christian, wrote about her experience of risking the censure of her sisters in Christ when she so articulately fought for the vote of women in Canada.

The gifts of the Spirit spoken of in II Corinthians, Romans and Ephesians *are not sex linked.* The early church had women leaders: bishops (e.g. Theodora), elders, and deacons (Priscilla). Jesus numbered women among his followers, and gave his supreme revelation, of his resurrected self, first to Mary, who was a woman, and a healed woman at that, freed from demons! Jesus treated women as *adults*, not *children*; as his sisters and friends, not as his servants. He blessed, healed, and taught women, unheard of in rabbinical Jewish circles, and liberated women from the drastic sexual taboos of his day, e.g. when the woman with the menstrual flow touched his garment, Jesus did not go through three days ritual purification rights as was customary.

Our age is calling women to stand up and be counted; to challenge the myth of male supremacy; to exercise freely and in obedience to our Lord the gifts that God has given us; and to grow into *maturity* in Christ, not remaining as children but answering the call to become adults. We need support and encouragement in this process--to stay connected, in a liberating way, and not become isolated or cut off from the Body of Christ.

4. *Sex Role Stereotyping*

My fourth point, pertaining to obstacles in the path of our growth, relates to what is popularly called "sex role stereotyping." Our churches have played right into this slotting of people into roles based on sex, and thereby failed to encourage women to have a full understanding of stewardship and ministry. We have met the roles and demands which the dominant male culture has imposed on us, and for many women this has been a fulfilling and meaningful challenge. But let us not forget countless sisters who have married young, not knowing who they were as persons; had babies they didn't know how to nurture properly; often dying young, like my great-grandmother who died at 42 after giving birth to 16 children; struggled with "emotional problems" of which they did not know the origin, the "disease that has no name," as Betty Friedan called it in *The Feminine Mystique* (1963); felt deserted and empty when at mid-life these children left home and there was no longer the same role to fulfill.

My concern here is *not* to negate the task of being a homemaker, mother and wife. I also share in this, but my concern is that women need to have a choice of how they are going to spend their energies and that this choice needs to be rooted in what Romans 3 calls "a sane estimation of your own abilities." Not all women are gifted to be nurturant mothers; some may be called to be engineers or lawyers or artists or musicians, or secretaries, or union workers, or clergy/priests. Not all women can be expected to be "full-time" parents; *fathers* also need to share the responsibility and the calling of being a parent to growing children. Not all women are gifted with the ability to be household managers or good hostesses or good cooks. As a matter of fact, some women get caught up in competing with each other in terms of decorating houses, being a gourmet cook, or in entertaining, and fail to fulfill Christ's command to feed the hungry, visit the prisoner, and clothe the naked. Some women's gifts may lie in writing a poem or visiting the sick or working with prisoners, or lobbying for environmental laws and pollution control; or in gardening and tending to God's beauty in creation. What I am trying to say is that if little girls are slotted into roles of being dependent, of being emotional caregivers, and not allowed to explore and develop the world around them, even by the toys we give them, and if little boys are taught to be aggressive and independent and in control of their environment, we end up with people programmed into roles based on their six, and are not encouraged or taught to grow fully into the "fullness of Christ" as whole persons.

Many *men* today are complaining that they have never been taught to express their feelings. "That's women's work." So they do not know how to be warm, tender, loving, sensitive, joyful. They have developed the fruit of self-control to an extreme; they know the meaning of a sound mind and of being empowered, but they do not know the fruit of humility, gentleness, and kindness. Where we as women are afraid to be strong, they as men are afraid to be vulnerable. They call it "weak." Yet Scripture teaches us that "it is in our weakness that we are made strong." Christ wept; He expressed a broad range of emotions. In today's stereotyping would He be labelled as "weak?" Men I see in my practice are saying that they feel emotionally impoverished and that women have the upper edge where feelings are concerned.

5. *View of God*

This brings me to my fifth point in obstacles to our personal growth. Our view of God profoundly affects even what we expect of ourselves. Do we see God as loving, caring, compassionate, and forgiving, often referred to as the "feminine" attributes of God, or as a punitive male, judgmental and unforgiving? So often as Christians we "labor and are heavy laden" with burdens of guilt because we do not feel that we are perfect, because we are sinners, because we are never good enough to pull ourselves up the ladder to heaven. Yet is that not what the Gospel is all about: that we are freed from compulsive guilt and are set free by Christ's death and resurrection to serve God gladly with our whole lives, knowing that we are forgiven and that redemption is an ongoing process?

Thus Christian growth and maturity is profoundly related to our personal relationship with God. We are affected by our images of God and therefore also by our images of ourselves. How often our relationship with God is restricted and stifled by the roles we play and the expectations of us that people around us have. That is why it is essential for us to challenge our churches, in a spirit of gentleness, to teach and to provide opportunities, for men and women alike, for stewardship and ministry in all areas of life. We need female role models; and women need *training in making choices.* As women we need to be empowered by God's spirit to overcome the obstacles which have crippled us and too often caused us to live by a spirit of fear. We need to learn to trust our own perceptions; to turn the obstacle of *dependency* into interdependency; to turn the obstacle of *fear of conflict* into creative confrontation, in which we learn "to speak the truth in love;" to turn obstacles of our inner making, *bitterness, guilt, depression*, into acceptance and self-love; to turn *suffering* into healing love; to turn *mid-life crisis* into new beginnings for ministry.

The Road to Freedom

We need to take a new look at the ways we have traditionally defined some of the "fruit of the Spirit." For example, "gentleness," "peace," and "forgiveness." These are not *passive* qualities. True gentleness is the fruit of working through anger in a healthy way, not denying or suppressing it. True peace-makers are those who enter into a conflict and work for peace, not those who avoid and withdraw! *Peace* is the fruit of facing conflicts, differences and injustice squarely in the face, and "speaking the truth in love."

We need to find ways of channeling anger into justice: seeking; justice for women, and for men, and for ourselves; and not to succumb to depression and self-hate.

Rosemary Reuther describes six stages in coming to terms with anger, which is an essential prerequisite for anyone seeking justice. Genuine forgiveness she sees as stage 5, *after* acknowledging and working through feelings of anger. Premature forgiveness is often hollow, without depth, yet how often we have beentold to "forgive and forget" as befitting of a "Christian woman!"

We need to strive to claim the "promise of restoration" that we are made in God's image, and so learn to care in the right way for ourselves, to respect and to love ourselves, because God first loved us!

We need to work at new understandings of "power" and being "empowered." Women have a lot to offer here because they do not need to assume a will to power, which implies being dominant or controlling. So often "controlling women" are women who have not had legitimate ways of exercising their talents, especially leadership gifts. So we need to work together to understand "power" as power to exercise gifts, with the result being true servanthood and not servility.

Our faith has given us the rich heritage of prayer, of fellowship, of the promise of "Christ in us, the hope of glory." Women have a rich heritage as caregivers, which we perhaps need to give to one another for the time being. Let us draw on the support we can give each other as sisters and friends, as daughters and mothers, as grandmothers and aunts, and as *members of a community*. We need each other to enable us to meet new challenges, to repent of our sinfulness in often failing to live obediently, and exercise the various gifts God has given us. We need *encouragement to turn away from fear* and allow God's Spirit to equip us with self-esteem, power, love, and a sound mind. With repentance comes forgiveness and the freedom to begin again. No matter what our age, it is never too late for a new beginning to serve God in the task of bringing healing, seeking justice, and loving our neighbor and ourselves.

References

Baker, M. (1976). *Towards a new psychology of women*. Boston: Beacon.

Friedan, B. (1963). The feminine mystique. New York: Dell.

Gilligan, C. (1981). *In a different voice*. Cambridge: Harvard.

Goodman, E. (1979). *Turning points*. New York: Fawcett.

Lahay, T. (1970). *The Christian family*. Minneapolis: Bethany.

McLung, N. (1972). *In times like these.* Toronto: Toronto.

Reuther, R. (1973). Sexism and the theology of liberation. *The Christian Century*, December 12, 1973.

Schaef, A. Wilson (1981). *Women's reality*. Minneapolis: Winston.

Sheehy, G. (1976). *Passages*. New York: Bantam.

Van Leeuwen, M. (1984). *The female reconstructs* psychology. *Radix,* January, 1984.

Weisstein, N. (1968). Psychology constructs the female. *Psychology, Sociology and Religion.*

Appendix

Stages of Liberation

Speaking at a recent conferences in North Carolina, noted theologian Rosemary Reuther outlined six stages of the liberation process as they relate to coming to terms with anger:

Stage 1. Fear of anger not being ladylike. Women, especially white, middle-class women, find it difficult to experience rage. We are socialized not to get angry. To deny anger is to deny evil; it is to escape.

Stage 2. The breakthrough of anger. Reuther compared it to a breakthrough of grace. It is overcoming the cultural barriers to feel the anger that is under the surface.

Stage 3. In this stage the rage deepens. Women often read a lot of women's histories and get into women's issues.

Stage 4. "Going mad." The floodgates are open. Women are innocent victims and men belong to an alien species. Men are seen as evil by nature, not just by socialization. Women who spend their time with men are said to be selling out. Reuther says this is not a good place to stay. Those of us who have lived at this stage for very long would agree with her that one finds oneself personally living in an untenable situation, believing that half the human race is essentially evil (female counterpart of Tertullian's "woman is gateway to hell--the Temptress").

Stage 5. Regaining balance, forgiving men and oneself. There is a sorting out of the respective socialization groups and a new understanding of inherited sin. Although men do not feel they have personally initiated sexism, they have inherited it. By forgiving, we do not regret or diminish the clarity or consciousness about the issues.

Stage 6. Not getting burned out. Reuther suggests that we cannot be vulnerable on all fronts at the same time. One has a right to seek a place to relax and be supported.

48

Clyde Austin

Reentry Stress: The Pain of Coming Home

A substantial number of missionaries find the homecoming process to be more difficult than the initial adjustment to the field. Some ask, "Can we go home again?" or "What are the hazards of home shock?" A readjustment period of six to twelve months is normal. Reentry *can* be a "growth" process (Adler, 1981). Meintel (1971) sees reentry potential as "exhilarating," with opportunities for personal and intellectual growth. Indeed, traumatic experiences during reentry sometimes help to strengthen returnees.

The formidable challenge confronting the missionary and the sending organization is to keep our missionaries whole throughout the international cycle. Key elements of the cycle--recruitment, training, adjustment to the new assignment, continuing rigors of service, and reentry--are best established in the framework of man's developmental process. The missionary needs a definite understanding of missionary service as it continues through young adulthood, middle age, and old age. Clague (1980) accurately says, "Expatriation and repatriation should be examined as parts of an integrated whole--not as unrelated events in a person's life" (p. 11).

Conspicuous characters in the many-sided drama of reentry are missionary parents, their children, and individuals in the receiving society (e.g. church leaders, relatives, and friends). The drama intensifies as the homecoming date draws near. Parents often agonize. "Should we have reared our children overseas?" "Where do we fit in the USA church scene?" "Can I endure the shock of rediscovering self in a changed setting?" "How do I deal with the affluence of 'rivers of energy?'"

Self-concept

On the eve of reentry the question "Who am I?" may perplex a missionary. Meintel (1971) argues, "The most significant 'shock' potential in strangerhood is that of self-discovery" (p. 47). In any major transition in life, to question self intensively is appropriate. Reentry is no exception. With a more accurate knowledge of oneself comes a relaxed acceptance of self (Smalley, 1963, p. 56).

A new identity emerges from the sojourn experience. One group of Peace Corps volunteers (Haan, 1974) underwent substantial change in self-definition. The women became more competent and assertive and the men more tender and emotional. For many teenagers, the Vietnam War drastically interrupted the processes of identity formation. The impact of the Vietnam War on the psychological identity of the teenage veteran was drastic. Likewise, the major problem for the missionary teenager seems to be the management of social identity (Downie, 1976; Gleason, 1969; Herrmann, 1977; Shepard, 1976; and Werkman, 1980). Just as the American people did not comprehend and give a responsive welcome to the Vietnam veteran, many stateside Christians do not grasp the importance of a homecoming celebration and orientation for the returning missionary family.

Werkman (1980) reported, "The self-concepts of overseas teenagers appear to be less positive, and they seem to show less of a feeling of security and optimism about life in general" (p. 243). He points out that these results do not indicate that overseas-experienced adolescents are "less psychologically healthy," but rather that the sojourn does have an important effect on their values and attitudes. Useem (1981) adds the further word of caution that many overseas children are so protected that they experience "a very late adolescence." Whereas the normal period of adolescence is 14-18, overseas children may experience an adolescence which ranges from 18-28. Therefore, one might expect a later period of adolescent rebellion.

Value Change and Choice

Clashes in inner values may occur between homecomers and "receivers" in bewildering arenas: material possessions, family life, racial prejudice, national priorities in areas of ecology and politics, and Christian community conflicts. Sensitivity must prevail on both sides of what might be a considerable chasm in values if a "common pool of hurt" (Morrow, 1981, p. 19) is to be avoided.

Interviews with returning missionaries as well as formal studies (Bwatwa, Ringenberg, Wolde, & Mishler, 1972; Moore, 1981) indicate that missionaries experience the USA as possessing "an embarrassment of riches." One missionary mother returning from the Far East said:

Everybody looks rich to us. We stayed with good friends in a Western state who complained about the high cost of living. Yet, they were overweight; lived like royalty. Many people talk about inflation and how they are cutting corners...but most are wasteful and keep on buying. Why is air conditioning kept so low? We freeze everywhere we go.

Perhaps few value conflicts hurt so much as those in the religious area. Far too many missionaries are tempted to assume a "holier-than-thou" attitude. Stateside Christians are characterized as "being more tolerant of sin" and "not as diligent in their service to God."

Expectations

When missionaries enter the mission field, they *expect* to have difficulty with language, religions of the host culture, attitudes of national Christians, nostalgia for the USA, and maintaining their own spiritual adjustment. Who would *ever* expect to feel like a stranger in his own country? Yet, overidealized expectations about "home" are a puzzling paradox.

The groundwork for this obstacle is often laid during the initial phases of culture shock. When difficulties with culture shock arise, expatriates tend to "glorify" institutions and traditions of their home country. However, when missionaries return, they do not *experience* the USA as they had remembered it. Sapir (1979) states, "It is often precisely the familiar that a wider perspective reveals as the curiously exceptional" (p. 1). The psychological discomfort resulting from this conflict can be harsh.

One major expectation of must returnees is that people will be interested in their experiences. An unusually capable missionary from Oceania relates:

We were invited to a large family reunion shortly after our return. We discovered that most people were not interested in hearing the stories

516 Special Issues

we were most anxious to tell. Oh, they listened about five minutes!
Then they continued to talk about the Dallas Cowboys.

Another reports:

One lady interrupted me to tell about their bus program. People want to
know a *little* about the Philippines....not a lot. I must remember that.
Answer questions briefly.

A returned missionary wife from South America laments:

I wish that people had assumed less about us and helped us more. I went
through this first year alone and I'm just now making some friends. It
would have been nice to have someone to talk to about these things;
someone you felt you could ask dumb questions like, "Is this a good
price?" or "How do I change an air conditioning filter?"

In the area of personal grooming, a wife who has served many
years in the Middle East observes:

How I looked was a problem to me. Some women at church said, "Your
hair is too short," some "too long." Someone said, "Everyone goes to a
beauty shop." I didn't want to be pushed into a mold. Finally I said, "I'll
do what I want."

A final therapeutic observation seems to be in order. This author
is aware of a number of cases where the readjustment symptoms
of severely troubled teenagers were relieved substantially by a
return trip to the country of prior service. During the trip, these
teenagers were guided lovingly through a reexamination of their
overidealized images of that country. Upon reentering the USA
after this "journey of clarification," parents, therapists, and the
children have more realistically addressed the mental health
problems confronting the family. Church officials might object to
the high cost of this procedure. However, if many other
therapeutic approaches have been attempted unsuccessfully, such
a trip might be the "missing piece" in the therapeutic "puzzle."
More thought and prayer need to be given to this particular
intervention.

A Sense of Loss

Another prevailing motif of reentry is a sense of loss. Moore
(1981) discovered, in a study of 288 returned missionaries, that
the second most diffcult problem listed was "nostalgia and

homesickness" for the mission field. Jansson (1975) graphically sketched what she calls a "sense of powerlessness" (p. 139). Useem (1981) affirmed, "The loss of an elite status is very difficult for parents." Zimmerman (1970) mourned, "What is most disturbing is a sense of loss. Where is the America I left four years ago? What has happened to Washington? The changes are so terrifying that it is hard to accept reality as real" (p. 38).

The sense of loss is pictured in an expressive manner by several representative missionaries:

I am still not comfortable shopping here. It's not so much the variety, which some returned missionaries find daunting, but the lack of what I want. I can't stand canned things. I like to buy just fresh fruits and vegetables.

I wish we could walk more. It's no wonder everyone has trouble with their weight here. So many of the streets don't even have sidewalks. Why is this such a motorized society?

I'd forget to sweep the floor. It never occurred to me. I'd not cleaned house in the Middle East for eight years. It almost felt degrading to clean my home. I looked for a maid--couldn't find one.

I miss taking time for people.

In the summer of 1968, my father was involved in an automobile accident on his way home from a tent campaign in the northern hill country of Antonio. Unfortunately, the accident accelerated his kidney disease. We returned to the USA. Leaving that country was a traumatic experience for a 13-year-old boy who was not fluent in English and was leaving everything he loved. By the age of 10, the only thing that distinguished me from a citizen of Antonio was my blue eyes and blonde hair. Adjusting to the American scene was extremely difficult; it was as if I had completely missed seven years of my life.

Other perplexing loss problems for the missionary parents are: (1) the big-fish-in-a-little-pond syndrome (one generally becomes a medium-sized fish in a bigger pond); (2) an underutilization of the skills and experience gained on the field; (3) the loss of some degree of independence; and (4) a feeling of being in the old "rat race" again.

The Value of the Family

Prayerful preparation in all stages of transition helps to cushion the impact. A renewed commitment to Christ and the maintenance of a wholesome home atmosphere form the bedrock of a fruitful homecoming. In a dissertation of much practical importance, Sensenig (1980) stresses the invaluable role of the missionary father. Too often the father is a "phantom." Herrmann (1979) further underscores the importance of the role of the family.

"MKs who have experienced these three elements of a basic sense of identity--belonging, worth, and competence--within their family, indicate having an easier time with identity formation in late adolescence and early adulthood. They are ready to adapt to new situations as they arise" (p. 5).

Predeparture Preparation

When mother and father are at the helm of an adequate family communication process, several further steps are suggested as they contemplate reentry.

1. Begin preparation at least six to twelve months in advance.
2. Review reentry materials as a family.
3. Make a list of one's use of time overseas and then examine what needs to be changed or maintained on returning.
4. Develop a tentative USA family budget based on information from various stateside sources.
5. Examine possible difficulties you might encounter in family and friendships, as well as professional relationships in the areas of verbal and nonverbal behavior.
6. Use correspondence with friends, relatives, schools, and employers to communicate your future needs and learn what to expect.
7. Read USA magazines, journals, and newspapers. Talk to recent on-the-field arrivals from the USA about current events. Ask for a "refresher course" on slang.
8. Be aware that you may experience depression, loneliness, fatigue, and illness as reentry symptoms of stress. You can be stressed either by happy or sad events. It will be normal for your family to go through a grief process.
9. Be alert to your own expectations and the expectations of others. Value conflicts are inevitable.
10. Be sensitive to a new discovery of self. Seek hobbies and community/church activities that fit new interests.

11. Reevaluate parenting procedures. Do not retreat from problems or other people. Monitor television offerings carefully. Our family didn't have a TV set overseas. When we returned, in a family vote, TV lost, 6-0. Bring back special belongings of children.

12. Begin an adequate vocational information program for the children. Many nations do not permit children to work. Acquaint them now with the world of work in the States--part-time and full-time jobs. One of the missionaries in your team might become a vocational resource person for all of the missionary "cousins" in your group.

13. If possible, allow time for a gradual "decompression period" of two to four weeks on the homeward trip in order to relax and make adequate mental preparation for reentry.

14. Remember that reintegration will take time, possibly a year. Be resilient and keep a positive outlook.

15. Search for ways to meet others' needs (Philippians 2).

Patterns of Reentry Response

Asuncion-Lande (1980) suggests four "distinctive patterns of response" to reentry shock: excitement, re-establishment/ frustration, sense of control, and re-adaptation (p. 4). The *initial phase* involves the joy of greeting relatives, friends, and former colleagues. Proud mothers and grandmothers prepare your favorite delicacies. In the *reestablishment phase*, you attempt to develop neighborhood friendship "roots," become reacquainted at church, and assist your children in adapting to school. Inevitably, there will be conflict and frustration. The "honeymoon" is over. The family members may then strive to *control* friends or fellow workers in various conscious or unconscious ways to eliminate dissonant feelings they are experiencing. A sense of control lowers stress levels. The homecomer may question his decision to return. Finally, returnees look for ways to cope or *adapt*. Intercultural communication, verbal and nonverbal, plays an important role in readjustment.

Coping Strategies

Since there are "no absolute, universal consequences" of reentry (Segal, 1981, p. 13), returnees need a repertoire of coping strategies to meet different demands. Useem (1981) differentiates between "adjusting" and "coping." She says that although learning how to cope with American life is important, a child may not adjust. In some cases individuals may not be psychologically "at home" in the USA.

A refrain of reemphasis and caution is appropriate. Reentry stress *is* normal. However, reentrants *do* form a minority. As with other minority groups in our culture, certain prejudices or stereotypes are exhibited toward returning missionaries. Jansson (1975) has suggested that reentrants may acquire a "deviant identity." Returning teenagers are most susceptible to a heightened sense of not deviating from social norms. Werkman (1977) has stressed the principle that high school culture places a premium on excluding "unusual" people. Since established students are locked into groups or cliques, some returning children may be tempted by those teenagers living on the fringe of moral existence. According to Opubor (1974), "In both the host and home cultures, the individual will be something of a deviant. The most edifying choice for the individual, and the goal of all constructive strategy, is how to make the individual a responsible deviant" (p.29).

A support group can serve as a forum for exchange of information and expression of feelings (Jansson, 1975; Werkman, 1980). Returned missionaries claim that the following individuals, groups, and/or activities were most helpful to them upon reentry, in descending order: spouse, friends, relatives, former missionaries, church members, college missions department personnel, reading materials, personal counseling, church leaders, debriefing with overseeing church personnel, psychological testing and evaluation, reorientation program, and family counseling (Moore, 1981, p. 45). It is important, but sad to note, that few churches sponsoring these missionaries provided personal and/or family counseling, psychological evaluation, or debriefing and reorientation programs. One missionary wrote the author after a program on reentry:

Your presentation last year was very timely in our lives. We were just returning from 16 years of mission work in Latin America. We were on a very bad guilt trip. We felt we were abnormal. We consulted a professional. You helped us put our lives in perspective.

After a counseling session, a young single lady declared:

After reflecting on what we discussed, I realized that you shed a lot of light on my confusion and you encouraged me. I guess I just wanted to hear you say I was "normal" for feeling such things.

A Heritage of Tradition

One Christian professor (McMillon, 1982) has characterized the importance of tradition as follows:

Tradition is important to the life of a family because it reinforces and sustains ideas, values, and practices that are valuable and meaningful to them....Paul encouraged the Thessalonians (2 Thess. 2:15), and Corinthians (I Cor. 11:2), to maintain the "traditions" delivered to them....Every family needs its own traditions. They become a subtle reinforcement to the cohesiveness of the family as a unit (p. 18).

The benefits flowing from the traditions described by McMillon could be of inestimable value to the readjustment of a returning family in terms of: identity, roots, security, continuity, and celebration.

What about the Future ?

To the best of the author's knowledge, no longitudinal study (before, during, after) has been conducted on missionary families. Further, there seems to be no comprehensive, in-depth study of serious mental illness among former missionary adults or children. Why do some families return with relatively few problems? Assumptions can be made, but no definitive research has been conducted. One missionary has wisely observed that a study should be made of families returned longer than a decade. He is convinced that only after a lengthy period of time can a family determine objectively what transpired in the first few years after reentry. Brislin (1981, p. 295) confirms the importance of later measures which show delayed effects. Special attention also needs to be given to the homecoming of singles. Loneliness has often been their unrelenting foe.

The home church or other sponsoring organization must be engaged in a continuous process of care, prayer, and inquiry on behalf of missionary families. The missionary family *must* be kept whole.

Bibliography

Adler, N. (1981). Re-entry: Managing cross-cultural transitions. *Group & Organizational Studies,* September 1981, 341-356.

Asunction-Lande, N. (1980). On re-entering one's culture. *NAFSA Newsletter 31,* 142-143. (National Association for Foreign Student Affairs, Washington, D.C.)

Brislin, R. (1981). *Cross-cultural encounters: Face-to-face interaction.* New York: Pergamon Press.

Bwatwa, J., Ringenberg, R., Wolde, N., and Mishler, J. (1972). A *study of the adjustment of missions and service personnel returning from overseas assignments.* Course Paper, Goshen College.

Clague, L., & Krupp, N. (Spring, 1980). The repatriation problem. *The Bridge, 37, 11-13.* Reprinted from The Personnel Administrator, April, 1978.

Cleveland, E. (1979).*A program of orientation for missionary kids enrolled at Samford University.* Doctoral dissertation, Southern Baptist Theological Seminary.

Downie, R. (1976). *Re-entry experiences and identity formation of third culture experienced dependent American youth: An exploratory study.* Doctoral dissertation, Michigan State University.

Gleason, T. P. (1970). *Social adjustment patterns and manifestations of worldmindedness of overseas-experienced American youth.* Doctoral dissertation, Michigan State University.

Haan, N. (1974). Changes in young adults after Peace Corps experiences: Political-social views, moral reasoning and perceptions of self and parents. *Journal of Youth and Adolescence, 3,* 177-194.

Herrmann, C. (1977). *Foundational factors of trust and autonomy influencing the identity-formation of the multicultural life-styled MK.* Doctoral dissertation, Northwestern University.

Herrmann, C. (1979). MKs and their parents. *Emissary, 10.*

Jansson, D. (1975). Return to society: Problematic features of the re-entry process. *Perspectives in Psychiatric Care, 13,* 136-142.

McMillon, L. (December, 1982). Traditions: A way to enrich your family life. *The Christian Chronicle, 18.*

Meintel, D. (1971). Strangers, homecomers and ordinary men. *Anthropological Quarterly, 46,* 47-58.

Moore, L. (1981). *A study of reverse culture shock in North American Church of Christ missionaries.* Master's thesis, Abilene Christian University.

Morrow, L. (1981). The forgotten warriors. *Time,* July 13, 1981, 18-25.

Opubor, A. (1974). *Intercultural adaptation: Resocialization versus reacculturation?* Paper presented at the First National Conference on Transition Programming.

Sapir, E. (1979). *In American Field Service, Program Development Department.* The AFS student study guide. New York: AFS International/Intercultural Programs.

Segal, J., In Schaar, K. (1981). Hostage crisis in review: Psychology's continuing role. *APA Monitor,* March, 1981.

Sensenig, J. (1980). *Perceptions of family and vocational responsibilities of missionary fathers: Educational implications.* Doctoral dissertation, Michigan State University.

Shepard, F. (1976). *An analysis of variables of self-perception and personal ambition in overseas-experienced American teenagers: Implication for curricular planning.* Doctoral dissertation, Michigan State University.

Smalley, W. (1963). Culture shock, language shock and the shock of self-discovery. *Practical Anthropology, 10,* 49-56.

Useem, R. (1981). *Personal communication.* November 9, 1981.

Werkman, S. L. (1977). *Bringing up children overseas.* New York: Basic Books.

Werkman, S. (1980). Coming home: Adjustment of Americans to the United States after living abroad. In Coelho, G. V., and Ahmed, P. I. (Eds.), *Uprooting and development: Dilemmas of coping with modernization.* New York: Plenum Press.

Zimmerman, C. (1970). Washington is home. *Foreign Service Journal, 47,* 38-39; 45.

49

David C. Pollock

Welcome Home! Easing the Pain of MK Reentry

For many missionary kids (MKs), the reentry experience is really more entry than reentry. Having spent a significant number of their developmental years in a culture other than their own, MKs have a sense of relationship to both host and home cultures. But they lack a sense of full membership in either.

However, whether the experience of moving from host to home culture is reentry or entry, a major adjustment must be made.

The need for this adjustment is strong, and the human organism, being what it is, will adjust--either for good or bad. What an MK brings into this transition will contribute largely to the result. However, immediate factors during the course of the experience will also affect attitudes that in turn determine behavior and relationships.

There are a number of views concerning reentry shock. Some have viewed it as a type of temporary mental disorder characterized by anxiety, disorientation, paranoia, and depression. Others see the reentry experience as a prelude to adjustment during which the person tends to be bewildered, confused, lonely, and defensive.

An emerging view is that the process of reentry is an intensified and accelerated form of the learning-growing-development process. In this view, the cycle of adjustment consists of an

---

experience followed by a reaction, then reflection, and finally conceptualization.

The Chaos of Transition

At the core of the process of reentry is the transition experience itself. Like the small end of a funnel, it is a process through which one may quickly pass--or become stuck. The heart of transition is characterized by a sense of chaos. Structure is lost, problems are exaggerated, and the ability to understand and respond appropriately may be greatly impaired.

Typical transition experiences include a loss of status, a sense of grief, emotional instability, an exaggerated sense of "special" knowledge, and feelings of isolation, anxiety, and self-centeredness.

It is during this reentry transition that the cross-cultural sojourner may require special care to insure proper adjustment. The reentry facilitator must learn to play the role of midwife. The facilitator is not the cause of "birth," nor is he or she fully responsible for its ultimate outcome. The facilitator simply supports the person through the trauma of transition, hopefully with positive results.

Admittedly, reentry care is limited in its total impact. In the short period of time during which the transition takes place, one cannot undo the affects of the past, nor guarantee the future. However, much can be done to enable the sojourner to maintain equilibrium learn the basic data necessary for preservation, and develop a plan for the future.

Reentry for MKs

Types and kinds of reentry vary from pre-departure workshops, reentry seminars, and the "total immersion" model. However, the best reentry care seeks to understand and address all the varied aspects of the reentry process. Finances, time, and personnel may dictate less than this. But a coordinated effort among those involved with MKs on the field, during transition, and through the early months of adjustment can produce an effective program.

In a special sense, the development of pre-departure ties are important. Prior to leaving for the host country and during furloughs, parents of MKs should try to establish relationships with relatives and friends to whom the MK can return. The home church can also help to provide a place and people the MK can look forward to seeing again.

MK schools play a key role in laying groundwork for reentry. School personnel and resource people can provide up-to-date information on college life, current lifestyle trends, popular fashions, etc.

Some help must come from on-field services. It is extremely important to encourage and assist MKs in drawing healthy conclusions about the overseas experience. Resolution of conflicts with friends, teachers, and family are an important part of this process. Broken relationships and unfinished business can hamper reentry adjustment.

Adequate farewells are also important in pre-departure preparation. Opportunity to do never-before-experienced things as well as saying good-by to people and places helps to create a smooth and pleasant conclusion.

Another area of pre-departure care is the development of proper expectations. These expectations should be both realistic and positive. The MK must recognize there will be areas of conflict and distress; yet he or she must have a sense of anticipation of successful adjustment.

Pre-departure preparation is sometimes limited, however, by the fact that because of their inexperience MKs do not always ask the right questions. Nevertheless, proper instruction and information still provide a solid base for decision-making during reentry.

Reentry Seminars for MKs

The disorienting experience of reentry creates attitudes--both good and bad--that will profoundly affect early adjustment and behavior. At or near the time of reentry, special programs can play an important part in the transition process. There is some debate as to the optimum time for such programs. However, positive results may be gained at seminars held either before or after the MK has been immersed in the new culture.

The value of the later seminar is that by the time it is held, the MK usually has many questions and is eager for help. The weakness of a late seminar is that early needs have not been met and some key choices may already have been made that can adversely affect the MK's future.

The early seminar is able to help MKs adjust their expectations so that they are both realistic and positive, thus preventing possible future stress. They can learn key strategies to help them understand the new and strange. In company with other MKs from around the world, the individual MK will feel that he or she is part of a fraternity. They discover that others also have the same feelings of anxiety, confusion, and uncertainty.

The reentry seminar may be structured in one or two ways. The "psychological model" emphasizes psychological needs and leans heavily toward testing, evaluation, and personal counseling. The cross-cultural model emphasizes cultural variation and the process of cross-cultural learning and adjustment. Simulation games, role-playing, and discussion sessions all dominate in this model.

An effective reentry seminar should incorporate both methods. Evaluation and testing become the catalyst to healthy counseling by qualified staff members. Psychological as well as sociological needs must be addressed. Cross-cultural stresses should be explained and appropriate coping solutions given. The approach is not an issue of either one or the other, but both.

Building Confidence in God

Development of a proper overall perspective is essential to reentry adjustment. Most importantly, however, an MK needs a healthy perspective on the God who controls his or her life. Joseph was unique because he never seemed to lose his equilibrium. He had an unshakable confidence in God's person, purpose, promise, and process. The MK needs this same type of perspective.

After attending a reentry seminar and then starting college, one girl wrote, "Yes, I do get lonely, and making friends is not as easy as it would be in a group of MKs. But God is definitely the same here as he is anywhere else in the world.

A proper perspective of God is a solid foundation for building and reinforcing the healthy self-view so critical to making a good adjustment. And there is a base for evaluating the experience of transition, including culture shock, being an MK, and changing values.

The reentry seminar should also address specific problem areas and the development of practical living skills. Issues such as dating, establishing status, learning how to learn in a new environment, and dealing with grief and depression, must be confronted. Confidence-building skills such as opening and managing a checking account, how to shop for various items, and how to manage your time, should not be neglected.

After Reentry, Then What?

Post reentry care is also important if ongoing development and full release of potential are to be realized. Dave Early of Wycliffe Bible Translators has pointed out that no true cross-cultural adjustment occurs unless a person is fully immersed in the culture. In the immersion stage questions are clearly defined, needs cease to be vague anxieties, and specific concerns surface.

MKs begin to ask questions like: How do I use a library? Why do other students seem so shallow? Where can I go for the holidays? Is anyone really concerned about missions, or even international affairs? Why do I feel out of it? How do I get a driver's license? A network of care can provide answers to these questions and help to meet needs.

A caring community on a Christian college campus can help by forming an MK or International Club where common backgrounds and interests meet intellectual, sociological, and psychological needs. A big brother/sister program involving MKs who are upperclassmen helps to establish contact between people with similar backgrounds. The hospitality of local churches and an alert college administration that provides services and programs to meet the needs of MKs are also an essential part of a caring network.

It is important that qualified counselors be identified and made available to MKs. Counseling care begun in a reentry seminar should be followed up by counselors qualified to work with MKs.

Church Ministry to MKs

The church or churches that financially support the missionary family have an opportunity for a special "hands on" ministry by helping with the reentry transition. The church can provide a home away from home and a family away from family. An MK may not always need the caring support of the church, but just in case, it's great to know it's there. The initiative to open the way for the MK must be taken by the home church, the mission board, and church families who may be interested.

Other MK needs can be met through a caring network of doctors, lawyers, counselors, and home hosts who make themselves available for at least the first two years an MK is back in the home country. A communications network must be put in place in order to facilitate this. This caring Christian community should have the resources necessary to meet the specialized needs of reentering MKs as they encounter various problems, difficulties, and frustrations.

Good reentry adjustment is not an event. It is a process that continues throughout the entire life of the cross-cultural sojourner. Help from family members, school staff, and the Christian community is crucial for successful adjustment. Pre-departure contacts and input help the MK to cope with conflicts from the past and create positive expectations for entry. The reentry seminar meets the sojourner at the point of crisis and helps to maintain perspective and equilibrium through the period of early adjustment. The ongoing care of a variety of agencies and individuals insure that the MK will continue to make progress toward security.

Those who are already active in the lives of MKs can encourage others to become involved at other needed points of intervention. If care is to be made available to all MKs, parents must take the initiative in preparing the way for adjustment and in encouraging their children to take advantage of available services.

Not long ago, while I was speaking at a retreat, a 40-year-old MK told me through a veil of tears, "I have struggled all my life with issues I didn't understand about myself. Where were the people like this to help us 25 years ago?"

Today, we have a team of dedicated people around the world to help develop and release the potential of MKs. We have the ability to construct a network to care for the missionary family in the belief that MKs can make a marked impact on the world for our Lord and his kingdom. God willing, 25 years from now, no one will need to ask, "Where were the people when I needed them?"

50

David J. Hesselgrave

Culture-Sensitive Counseling and the Christian Mission

Peoples of non-Western cultures have their problems and difficulties--many of them very similar to our own. But very likely they will characterize and categorize those problems differently. And they will go about solving them in culturally appropriate ways. "Culture is a great storehouse of ready-made solutions to problems which human animals are wont to encounter."[1]

The assumptions that underlie the present discussion are as follows. First, the very nature of the missionary task has always required that missionary personnel engage in counseling people of other cultures (in the broad sense of advising and helping people in solving problems and directing change, not necessarily in the technical sense of administering therapy where a pathology is present). Second, given the increasing prominence accorded to training in psychology and counseling in our theological schools, particularly in North America, more and more missionaries and foreign nationals are availing themselves of that training and are attempting to apply what they learn in non-North American contexts. Third, a viable counseling theory and an effective counseling practice are inevitably and inextricably interrelated with culture--the feelings, beliefs, and behavioral patterns of any given people. And, fourth, a sensitivity to the etiological, therapeutic, and counseling orientations of the second culture constitute a kind of sine qua non for developing counseling principles and practices for that culture.

We have long analyzed the problems of people in other cultures from a biblical perspective and (with much less validity) from the vantage point afforded by research and experience within Western culture. What I would like to encourage here is a long look at human problem-solving as it appears *within* certain cultures that are alien to us as North Americans, not with the purpose of passing judgment but, rather, with a view to sensitizing ourselves as to the kind of rethinking and adjustments that are called for when counseling cross-culturally.

We shall proceed by looking at some culturally defined problem areas in the non-Western world, some typical helper and adviser roles, and common approaches taken to resolve these problems. Then we shall examine in more detail some typical therapeutic and counseling approaches, focusing on Japan. Finally, we shall summarize some of the lessons to be learned from the foregoing materials by missionaries and foreign nationals who are trained in Western counseling theory.

Indigenous Orientations

As an indication of the differences in ways of viewing causative factors of human problems around the world, one need only refer to a classic study that plots primitive theories of disease causation. A generation ago, Forrest Clements plotted these theories by means of an extensive survey of ethnographic literature. Ultimately, he focused on five types of causes most frequently found among non-Western peoples: soul loss, breach of taboo, disease sorcery, object intrusion (which we shall not be dealing with here), and spirit intrusion.[2] A more recent case study of the indigenous people of St. Lawrence Island, Alaska, underscores the pervasiveness of these casual types.[3]

Soul Loss: St. Lawrence Island Eskimo informants explained the local belief that when a person sleeps or sneezes or is frightened, especially at night, the soul wanders away from the body. At these times the soul may be captured by evil spirits that abound in the universe. Until the soul is found and returned to the body, the person remains ill.

Breach of Taboo: Such acts as incest, sexual perversion, and masturbation are widely considered to be taboo among St. Lawrence Islanders. To break such taboos is to invite disease and perhaps insanity. In fact, the consequences may be visited not only upon the offender, but also upon the family, the community, and even progeny to the seventh generation. Taboo-breaking is therefore a community concern. This being the case, offenses of this kind that involve other people and are more or less public, such as sexual perversion or violation of the hunting code (e.g., killing a whale first sighted by someone else), are of greatest import.

Disease Sorcery: A clear distinction is made between the sorcerer who utilizes black magic and the shaman who employs "healing magic." Traditionally, St. Lawrence Island Eskimos have believed that a sorcerer (or witch) has the power to effect all kinds of illness. This evil power is exercised through a variety of formulas, prayers, rituals, and mechanisms. For example, the sorcerer might persuade someone to secure some hair or a nail paring or a piece of clothing of the intended victim. Only by employing the aid of a shaman who is able to identify the sorcerer, discover the kind of black magic that has been used, and resort to the right kind of counter-magic can the effects be nullified.

Spirit Intrusion: Finally, St. Lawrence Islanders have long believed that a foreign spirit can invade a person's body. In many primitive cultures this belief has two aspects. First, in some cultures (including Eskimo cultures), it is thought that the spirit must be identified before exorcism can be employed. More common and well developed in St. Lawrence culture, however, is a second aspect of spirit intrusion. Namely, the ghost of a recently deceased relative might hover about and cause the sickness of a living relative, especially when the living relative my be linked with the person's death by having broken a taboo. The ghost of the deceased is especially powerful during the period of mourning. Subsequently, the power gradually wanes. One way of counter-acting this sort of spiritual intrusion is to name a newborn child after the deceased. This is tantamount to reincarnation and means that the deceased is once again a member of the human community.

Though the foregoing orientation focuses primarily on one culture and worldview, it reflects a much wider incidence and significance. Christian workers will encounter similar beliefs and practices among primitive peoples around the world--and vestiges of such beliefs and practices among many peoples with more developed cultures.

Helper, Healer, and Adviser Roles in the Non-Western World
In the context dealt with above, the resort to shamans was almost universal. In the wider context of cultures and problems with which cross-cultural workers must concern themselves, help

may be forthcoming through a wide variety of agents. Wise men, tribal elders, clan heads, religious leaders, family heads, governmental authorities, entrepreneurs, innovators--numerous leader-types and agents of change are involved in resolving human ills and charting the future course of societies and their members.

"Non-Specialist" Helpers: Problem-solving activities and roles tend to be less specialized and discreet in the non-Western world than they are in the Western world. In his informative study, *A History of the Cure of Souls*, J. T. McNeill notes that the separation of healing functions from their religious and philosophical roots and their conversion into scientific activities are comparatively recent Western developments.[4] (He notes also that theological and other disputations in Western churches have obscured the fact that their fundamental task is the "curing of souls.") Individuals and families in difficulty are less likely to seek out a "professional counselor" as Westerners use that designation. In many if not most cultures, it is unlikely that such an individual could be found. The notion that formal education rather than broad experience qualifies one to be a counselor seems to be a largely Western notion. But even where professionals might be available, to seek one out may entail a degree of shame.

"Lay people," especially heads of nuclear and extended families, play a much larger helping and guiding role in non-Western churches as compared to Western cultures. Patriarchs, matriarches, grandparents, parents--all are concerned that younger members fit into the family and larger society in a positive and productive manner. With that end in view, the family is organized vertically and hierarchically rather than horizontally and in an egalitarian fashion. Decisions are usually made by the group rather than by the individual. In the Philippines, for example, even the civil code says that grandparents shall be consulted by all members of the family on all important questions.

Furthermore, one would be correct in inferring from the foregoing that group counseling and decision-making plays a much larger role in non-Western cultures than has usually been the case in Western cultures and especially the United States. The recent interest in group support systems in the United States has long been reflected in non-Western societies.

Specialist" Helpers: All societies have specialists who have the socially sanctioned role of healers. Because of the religious orientation of these healers, McNeill refers to them as a "spiritual elite."[5] Because they "stand between" persons and powers, P. Meadows refers to them as "mediatorial elite."[6] Since these specialists constitute the non-Western counterparts to Christian psychiatrists, counselors, and pastors in the West, we shall largely concentrate on them and their techniques in the remainder of this paper.

Anthropologists distinguish two polar types of spiritual "helper leaders": shamans and priests. They often work side by side in a complementary relationship. At other times they are in competition. Shamans are characteristically charismatic leaders who claim to have been in contact with the supernatural. By virtue of that contact they have the power to perform supernatural feats. They can also deliver messages from the gods and ancestors in prophetic fashion. Priests derive their authority from institutionalized religion rather than from their own charisma or personal contact with supernatural beings. They learn and pass on traditional beliefs and rituals. Standing between the deities and the people, priests speak to the gods and spirits on behalf of the people and represent and lead them in appropriate rituals and rites.

In and between these two polar types are to be found a variety of healers and helpers such as the *bomoh* in Malaysia, the *babylan* in the Philippines, the *dang-ki* in Taiwan, among others. When Western physicians are also present, the local people are often presented with quite an array of specialists to whom they may resort when confronted by psychological and other problems. A realization of this fact forcefully alerts us to the fact that the Christian worker who ministers interculturally must be prepared for a wide variety of perceptions as to his or her role and function. Like it or not, at least in the initial stages of any relationship, that role and function will in a significant sense be prescribed by the receptor society. On the positive side, this realization may jolt Christian workers out of some preconceptions stemming from Western culture and force them into a more biblical worldview wherein the spirit world is more immediate and powerful. On the negative side, Christian workers may well be frustrated in attempts to overcome local expectations as to their role and purpose.

Counseling and Therapeutic Approaches in the Non-Western World

Various scholars have attempted comparisons of counseling and therapeutic approaches employed in the West with those utilized in the non-Western world. Not surprisingly, they come to somewhat different conclusions.

E. Fuller Torrey believes that psychiatrists perform basically the same functions in their respective cultures and that they get similar results in about the same ways. He says that the essence of psychotherapy is communication that depends not only upon a shared language but also upon a shared worldview. For Torrey there are four components common to all psychotherapy: (1) a worldview that is common to healer and sufferer; (2) the personal qualities of the therapist, which allow for a close, personal relationship between therapist and sufferer; (3) an expectation on the part of patients that they will be helped; and (4) therapeutic techniques. Torrey insists that techniques are essentially the same the world around, whether they be physical (drugs, electro-shock, etc.), psychosocial (confession, suggestion, hypnosis, psychoanalytic techniques, conditioning), or group and milieu therapies. He does concede, however, that a number of techniques used in the non-Western world are not much used in the West; that the same technique may be used, but for different reasons; and that the goals of therapy vary with the culture.[7]

Most researchers do not go as far as Torrey in emphasizing cross-cultural commonalities. After making a thorough study of a schizophrenic girl and her treatment by a local shaman in the Philippines, George Guthrie and David Szanton take exception. They note that three of Torrey's four components were operative in the case but that there was little that distinguished the shaman's personality when it came to genuineness, empathy, or warmth.[8]

Again, in his examination of the literature on psychotherapeutic procedures used around the world, Raymond Prince examines the widespread use of indigenous mechanisms such as sleep, social isolation, and altered states of consciousness (dreams, mystic states, dissociation states) in psychotherapy.[9] However, as he moves in his considerations from America to Africa to Asia, it is apparent that he believes that the ways in which these mechanisms are introduced and employed constitute major differences between cultures.

Finally, Wen-Shing Tseng of the department of neuro-psychiatry in the School of Medicine at the National Taiwan University Hospital in Taipei emphasizes both commonalities *and* differences. At the same time, Tseng offers advice that underscores cultural differences. He writes:

It is very important to study further how people handle their problems in ways which are provided for and channeled by their culture. From this point of view, the study of folk psychotherapy will certainly help us learn more about how the problems of life have been traditionally perceived and interpreted by the local people and what coping strategies have been specified by the culture. Thus, we can learn how to modify modern psychotherapy in culture-relevant ways, so that treatment will be more effective.[10]

We seem justified in concluding that universal characteristics in cross-cultural counseling and therapy tend to be rather general in nature. When it comes to specifics, one must be prepared for a wide variety of understandings and approaches. These differences will not always be as apparent as some of those we have described. They may be very subtle. But they will be no less significant for their subtlety. And to illustrate this we turn next to one of the most developed nations in the non-Western world--Japan.

Naikan Therapy

In spite of the tightly knit family structure and communal orientation that are so pervasive in Japanese society, statistics and experience make it clear that the pressures associated with coping and competing in modern Japan have occasioned an unusually high incidence of stress and frustration, psychological and spiritual disorientation, nervous breakdowns, and even suicides. With a population about half that of the United States, Japan has twice as many psychiatric patients in its hospitals.[11] There are various reasons for this besides the obvious one. Since the Japanese attach a stigma to emotional and mental disorders, those who need help are less reticent to undergo treatment in a hospital than in their local community. Also, National Health Insurance offers little assistance to those who are not hospitalized. Nevertheless, because of the high incidence of psychological breakdowns, the persistence of cultural ways and values, and the familiarity with Western ways of approaching these problems, Japan provides us with some examples of therapy approaches that prove to be especially instructive in the present context. Some of them--such as Morita therapy[12]--reflect a debt to Western theory. Others--such as Naikan therapy[13] and Rissho Koseikai Hoza[14]--reveal a profound dependence upon traditional Japanese thinking and values. That being the case, we shall briefly examine one of them (Naikan therapy) in order to highlight the contrast between Western and a distinctly Japanese approach to counseling therapy.

Naikan therapy is a form of guided introspection directed toward attitude and personality change. Developed in the 1940s by Inobu Yoshimoto, it is clearly related in philosophy and worldview to the Jodo-Shin sect of Buddhism, one of Japan's most popular Buddhist groups. The therapy is based on the premise that people are basically selfish and guilty, yet are all the while favored with unmeasured benevolence from others. By focusing on all the kindness one has received and one's own reactions toward those who bestowed it, patients come to grips with their own guilt and selfishness, and are then encouraged to adopt new patterns of behavior toward others. (Note that the emphasis on guilt seems to be somewhat out of keeping with the "shame orientation" that generally characterizes Japan. But we may be dealing with a semantic problem only.)

The actual therapy consists of seven consecutive days of concentrated reflection, from 5:30 a.m. to 9:00 p.m. each day. The volunteer patient sits in a quiet, isolated corner, alone and free from distractions. The patient is guided and supervised by the Naikan counselor for about five minutes every one and one-half hours. The counselor makes certain that the patient is following the prescribed course of reflection and is thinking about the assigned topics. The patient is expected to examine himself or herself with respect to others along these lines: (1) to recollect and examine memories of the care and benevolence received from a particular person (usually beginning with a parent) at a particular time in life; (2) to recollect and examine memories of response to one's benefactor; and, (3) to recollect and examine the troubles and worries one has caused that benefactor. This cycle of self-examination is repeated again and again for different relationships and at different depths throughout the therapy period.

The role of the counselor in Naikan therapy is to direct the counselee toward meaningful self-examination. The counselor instructs the counselee in the procedure and lays down and enforces the ground rules by directives and persuasion. The brief interactions every hour and a half are designed to ensure that the patient has followed the introspection cycle; to keep the patient from making excuses or rationalizations or from beginning aggressive toward others; and to lead the patient to vigorous and severe self-examination. The counselor is more concerned with procedure than with the content of the interactions or with the counselor-patient relationship. Direct contact with the patient is authoritarian, intensive, and highly directive. The therapy does not rely on warm and personal empathy between counselor and patient. The counselor's goal is not to understand the patient, but to direct the patient into self-understanding.

Since the Naikan environment is both physically and emotionally difficult, some obstacles must be overcome. Many patients do not find it easy to concentrate, while others react negatively to the physical isolation and confinement. It usually takes two or three days to adjust to the new situation. Resistance against the past and against personal guilt (shame?) is often in evidence. But as the process goes on, introspection becomes more and more meaningful. Insights into personal faults and the love for others emerge abruptly or gradually, leading the patient to self-criticism and repentance.

The most common outcome of successful Naikan therapy is the improvement of the patient's interpersonal relationships as the person rekindles gratitude for others, increases in sympathetic and empathetic regard for others, and realizes one's own personal responsibility for social roles. The patient's personal identity is further established, and security, confidence, and self-disclosure are achieved. Yet these feelings and resolves sometimes fade after therapy is concluded and the patient returns to the old environment.

Joe Yamamoto is indubitably correct (especially in the case of Naikan therapy) when he says: "Both Morita and Naikan therapy are rooted in the Japanese culture. They share several common features: (1) introspection, (2) directions about what to think about, (3) expectations of behavior to suit the Japanese values, and (4) the objective of a person who fits into the Japanese way of life including having filial piety, and achievement orientation, and a strong sense of obligation and responsibility."[15]

Without an understanding of Japanese culture, then, a practicing counselor in Japan would be at a severe disadvantage and might indeed exacerbate the presenting problem. In fact, without that understanding, a counselor would likely find it difficult to appreciate fully the nuances of the therapies and approaches reviewed above, and even those of Yamamoto's conclusion.

Lessons for the Contextualization of Counseling Principles and Practice

Our inquiry into four areas intimately related to counseling in other cultures has led us unerringly to at least two fundamental conclusions. First, differences between cultures in the major aspects of counseling and curing are of a magnitude great enough to require major adjustments in the practitioner's approach as he or she moves from one culture to another. Second, an examination of indigenous ways of advising and helping people in problem-solving and directing change will yield important lessons for the contextualization of counseling principles and practice. (In using the word "contextualization" here, I simply mean "to make culturally relevant and meaningful.)

As concerns the first conclusion, I merely add reports from three church-related institutions in Asia to reinforce the thrust of our previous discussion.

After spending a year as clinical director of the Churches' Counseling Service in Singapore, Charles A. Raher indicated that the "Rogers-with-a-dash-of-Freud" approach simply did not work because of too little experience in "caring" in that society, insufficient motivation on the part of counselees, and the influence of the authoritarian orientation of Asian societies. Interestingly enough, he thinks that another American model--that of Howard Clinebell--might be more useful in Singapore.[16]

A seminary professor in Thailand notes that a course in pastoral psychology and counseling does not merit a place in theological training in Thailand because of a variety of factors. First, the Thai have a very different concept of human nature and community. Second, the traditional way of facing problems in Thai society is to withdraw and find an "inner core of peace." Third, since the Buddhist priest is not related to people in the way that pastors are related to their congregations in the West, the expectations of Thai congregations are quite different from those of their counterparts in the Western world. Because of these and other factors, it is difficult in Thailand to sustain the kind of pastoral education that makes a significant place for counseling.[17]

Even in Australia--geographically Asian but culturally Western in large measure--difficulties growing out of the "stiff upper lip" philosophy and other cultural factors have resulted in a shortage of pastoral theologians.[18]

As concerns the second conclusion, I would like to make explicit some of the lessons that would seem to be implicit in the materials of the previous pages.

1. When counseling cross-culturally, it is imperative that the counselor ascertain and attend to the counselee's culturally conditioned interpretation of the presenting problem. A careful reading of relevant literature reveals that one of the most common mistakes of Western missionaries (and Western-trained national counselors) is their failure to take indigenous etiologies and remedies seriously. That a hysteria neurosis has been induced by breaking a taboo such as hearing one's wife sing the marriage song may be as difficult for the counselor to consider seriously as would be the explanation that an American fell and broke a leg because of walking under a ladder. Both explanations may be airily dismissed as superstitions. But to do so--particularly in the case of the hysteria neurosis--may be to disqualify oneself as an agent of healing and change in the culture in question. Counselors who

insensitively dismiss local understandings of such etiologies as hexes, black magic, and the influence of offended spirits have certainly disqualified themselves.

A missionary friend of mine recently aided an African national with a bad machete wound. From an African perspective the "real cause" of the wound was not the misdirected machete, but a hex put on the "victim" by a "hateful" bystander. Both of the principals and their families are professing Christians. But long after the physical wound has healed, my missionary friend (and the local pastor) are counseling all concerned in an effort to heal the "bad blood" that is poisoning them and the whole Christian community!

2. Foreign-bred and foreign-trained counselors should take careful note of the presence and roles of the varied agents of change within the culture in which they minister. By so doing they can make important determinations as to the way in which they themselves will be perceived, the change agents with whom they may or may not ally themselves, and the approaches appropriate to their own status. Some of the early missionaries in Korea took advantage of the advising/counseling role modeled by Buddhist priests in order to minister Christ to the people. Bruce Olson temporarily allied himself with a Motilone shaman in order to demonstrate the power of Christ to heal and save.[19] Taking another look at African culture, Walter Trobisch questioned the way in which he had played his counseling role in a well-known case of disagreement over bride-price.[20]

3. Western advising and therapy approaches certainly have their applications in the non-Western world, but one must be prepared to use them eclectically, to modify them, and to augment them in accord with local practice. One Western-trained Indian psychiatrist reports that it took him five years after returning to India to unlearn what he had learned in the West.[21] This may be an extreme case, but it speaks eloquently against the other extreme of uncritically exporting Western understandings. Review again the approaches of Morita and Naikan therapies in Japan. It is difficult to imagine how such approaches could be utilized successfully in the United States without significant modification, if they could be used at all. Why, then, would anyone suppose that Rogers' client-centered approach, Berne's transactional analysis, or Glasser's reality therapy--or Adam's nouthetic counseling, Solomon's spirituo-therapy, and Clinebell's growth counseling, for that matter--would be capable of unaltered application cross-culturally?

4. Finally, we conclude on a very positive note by pointing to the tremendous potential of the counseling method for varied aspects

of cross-cultural Christian ministry from evangelism to church discipline to just plain "people-helping." One can hardly stand on the fourth or fifth balcony of the Rissho-Koseikai temple in Tokyo and gaze upon the "counseling circles" that are all around below without commenting, "Why didn't we think of that?" Of course, there are Christian efforts, which, though they tend more toward Western models, are pioneering in this area. The Breakthrough Counseling Centre in Hong Kong has expanded, since its founding in 1975, until in 1981 it had three administrators, six professional counselors, fifty volunteers in para-professional training, and preventive as well as therapeutic counseling programs.[22] The Amani Counseling Center in Nairobi employs the service of both counselors and medical people in its various programs, and in 1983 has offered seminars on alcoholism, marital and sexual problems, traditional healing, family planning, and mental illness.[23] Much else is being done. Much more could be done.

Conclusion

Additional research remains to be done with regard to Christian counseling programs and approaches in the non-Western world. In the process it will not be to the credit of Christian scholars and practitioners if they are less sensitive to considerations of culture than are their secular counterparts.

Notes

1. Clyde K. Kluckhohn and Henry A. Murray, eds., *Personality in Nature, Society, and Culture.* (New York: Knopf, 1948) (p. 54).
2. Forrest E. Clements, Primitive Concepts of Disease. University of California Publications in American Archeology and Ethnology, *32*, no. 2 (1932): 185-252; quoted in Jane Murphy, "Psychotherapeutic Aspects of Shamanism on St. Lawrence Island, Alaska, in *Magic, Faith, and Healing: Studies in Primitive Psychiatry Today,* ed. Ari Kiev (New York: Free Press, 1964), p. 61.
3. See Murphy, *"Psychotherapeutic Aspects,"* pp. 61-69.
4. J. T. McNeill, A History of the Cure of Souls (New York: Harper & Row, 1965); quoted in Julian Wohl, "Intercultural Psychotherapy: Issues, Questions, and Reflections," in *Counseling across Cultures,* rev. and expanded ed., edited by Paul P. Pedersen, Juris G. Draguns, Walter J. Lonner, and Joseph E. Trimble (Honolulu: Univ. Press of Hawaii for the East-West Center, 1981), pp. 140-41.
5. McNeill, *A History of the Cure of Souls,* p. 330.
6. P. Meadows, "The Cure of Souls and the Winds of Change," *Psychoanalytic Review, 55* (1968): 497.

7. E. Fuller Torrey, *The Mind Game: Witch Doctors and Psychiatrists* (New York: Emerson Hall Publishers, 1972).

8. George M. Guthrie and David L. Szanton, "Folk Diagnosis and Treatment of Schizophrenia: Bargaining with the Spirits in the Philippines," in *Culture-Bound Syndromes, Ethnopsychiatry, and Alternate Therapies*, ed. William P. Lebra. Mental Health Research in Asia and the Pacific series, vol. 4. (Honolulu: Univ. Press of Hawaii for the East-West Center, 1976), pp. 161-62.

9. Raymond Prince, "Variations in Psychotherapeutic Procedures," in *Handbook of Cross-Cultural Psychology*, vol. 6, ed. Harry C. Triandis and Juris G. Draguns (Boston: Allyn & Bacon, 1980), pp. 291-349.

10. Wen-Shing Tseng, "Folk Psychotherapy in Taiwan," in Lebra, *Culture-Bound Syndromes*, p. 165.

11. Joe Yamamoto, "An Asian View of the Future of Cultural Psychiatry," in *Current Perspectives in Cultural Psychiatry*, ed. Edward Foulks, Ronald M. Wintrob, Joseph Westermeyer, Armando R. Favozza (New York: Spectrum Publications, 1977), pp. 210-11.

12. Abstracted from Kyoichi Kondo, "The Origin of Morita Therapy," in Lebra, *Culture-Bound Syndromes*, pp. 240-48.

13. Abstracted from Takao Murase, "Naikan Therapy," in Lebra, *Culture-bound Syndromes*, pp. 259-69.

14. Cf. Kenneth J. Dale, *Circle of Harmony: A Case Study in Popular Japanese Buddhism* (South Pasadena, Calif: William Carey Library, 1975).

15. Yamamoto, "*An Asian View*," p. 213.

16. Graeme M. Griffin, "Pastoral Theology and Pastoral Care Overseas," in *The New Shape of Pastoral Theology: Essays in Honor of Seward Hiltner*, ed. William B. Oglesby (Nashville: Abingdon Press, 1969), p. 56.

17. Ibid.

18. Ibid., p. 56-57.

19. Bruce Olson, *For This Cross I'll Kill You* (Carol Stream, Ill.; Creation House, 1973), pp. 142-48.

20. Walter Trobisch, *I Loved a Girl: Young Africans Speak* (New York: Harper & Row, 1965), p. 105.

21. Norman D. Sundberg, "Research and Research Hypotheses about Effectiveness in Intercultural Counseling," in Pedersen, et al., eds., *Counseling Across Cultures*, p. 331.

22. "Counseling Centre in Hong Kong," *Asian Theological News 7*, no. 1 (January-March 1981): 18.

23. Joe S. Udoukpong, Bethani Fellowship Resources, letter to Timothy M. Warner, July 29, 1983.

Response by John E. Hincle, Jr.

"Culture-Sensitive Counseling and the Christian Mission" intends to raise the consciousness of Western missionaries about some of the significant cultural dimensions that arise in attempting to apply pastoral care and counseling modalities in non-Western cultures. Hesselgrave dips into relevant literature to provide a basic framework for the discussion. Materials from Kluckhohn, Clements, Torrey, and Sundberg are central. Additionally, the author brings forward case materials from a variety of cultures to illustrate his points. The Western reader who is just beginning to explore possibilities for doing counseling as a missionary in another culture, or who is training for such work, will find leads into further materials of a more technical nature and will be able to begin developing a conceptual framework for use in thinking about the cross-cultural counseling enterprise being discussed. The author is to be commended for tackling such a multifaceted problem in such a short piece.

This particular respondent would fault the paper for failing to do a thoroughgoing cultural analysis of the paper's own starting point. The ethnocentric approach that is embedded in the entire Western counseling and psychotherapeutic enterprise is not adequately addressed by the author. For example, the writer starts with the "typically Western" assumption that *life is a series of problems to be solved*: this view of daily functioning penetrates the de-facto worldview of the dominant-majority culture of Americans from the United States. The view seems so natural that it is scarcely noticed or questioned. An illustration that this is a natural Western assumption is to be found on the first page of Scott Peck's popular book, *The Road Less Traveled*. On page one of the text Peck says, "Life is a series of problems to be solved." While, on reflection, few would agree with this narrow definition of the meaning of life as adequate, and certainly Hesselgrave would not, given his announced commitment to biblical perspectives, this view in nevertheless an assumption made by Hesselgrave about the function of pastoral care and counseling that runs through the entire piece. Translating such an assumption into another cultural context so unaware is highly problematic from the point of view of this respondent.

This "problem-solving" view of the function of pastoral care and counseling is problematic in that it is embedded in the task-orientation values (in contrast to person orientation) that are in many ways endemic to Caucasian culture in the United States.

Here then is an example of the kind of thoroughgoing ethnocentrism that is manifested in the presentation of pastoral care/counseling as methods of problem-solving without a proper cultural analysis of the assumptions, content, and procedures that these activities involve. The cultural analysis must begin with an analysis of Western ethnocentric assumptions embedded in the very fabric of pastoral care/counseling theory and practice, as a first step. Only then would it be appropriate to ask the question, may such assumptions be appropriately made about pastoral functioning in another culture?

Ethnocentric bias in the theory and practice of pastoral care/counseling and pastoral counseling/psychotherapy is sufficiently deep-rooted in both the literature about and the training for such activities received in those disciplines in seminaries across the United States that a counseling model for ministry in other cultures appears, to the writer of this response, to be quite cumbersome in many instances and highly questionable in others. Attempts to translate the Western care/counseling model into other cultural settings is, as Hesselgrave points out, fraught with difficulties. In some cultures there may be no genuine "fit" at all (as Hesselgrace notes in quoting the Thai professor). It seems rather remarkable that Hesselgrave then goes on to say that pastoral care/counseling "certainly" applies in cross-cultural settings. It seems to this respondent that one cannot have it both ways.

A second major point of difficulty in the essay is that the author does not adequately distinguish between pastoral care/counseling and pastoral counseling/psychotherapy. Instead the discussion moves across the entire spectrum from pastoral care to psychotherapy in a somewhat indiscriminate manner. This respondent is introducing the notions of "pastoral care/counseling" and "pastoral counseling/psychotherapy" in this response as a way of pointing to two qualitatively and methodologically different levels of pastoral functioning. Such a distinction becomes important relative to the article under review in that pastoral-care practices in the United States are often directed at problem-solving, as is counseling and advising. Pastoral counseling/psychotherapy is much less typically involved with immediate problem-solving.

Finally, this respondent would agree with the author's indication that local therapy practices would provide a good starting point for the analogy of what may or may not work with a client from another culture. Additionally, this respondent agrees with the main point of the paper, namely, that cultural sensitivity is essential to effective cross-cultural work of any kind in which the "culture-crossing" person is working with other persons (rather than tasks) as a focus. However, as noted above, unless the missionary crossing cultural boundaries is transparent regarding the ethnocentric bias in his or her training in pastoral care/counseling, and has taken these biases into full account, there is little likelihood of effectiveness in any event. For example, in discussing "specialist" helpers, the author makes an invidious comparison between utilizing social-science theory in other cultures inappropriately and utilizing biblical understandings appropriately. In the opinion of this reviewer, what the author really should be saying is that it is our *Western understanding of the biblical understandings* that we are utilizing when we approach another (a third) culture rather than to say, "*the* biblical understanding." This respondent, for one, is not as convinced that counseling and psychotherapy approaches are useful in cross-cultural settings as the author of the article in view. Clearly, the usefulness of such approaches could be enhanced if the user first becomes transparent about his or her own ethnocentric bias, and whatever cultural bias exists in terms of *both* theory and practice, before moving to the point of engaging in what David Hesselgrave is pointing to as a thoroughgoing analysis of the cultural setting in which these activities are to be carried out.

When it comes to cross-cultural counseling, the first word to those who would engage in it should be, "Become transparent about your own ethnocentric bias and the ethnocentric bias of the theories and practices of counseling that you are seeking to utilize." The second priority would be, "Be very sensitive to the implications of seeking to apply those counseling procedures and methodologies" in any non-Western culture. The third priority would be, "Persons are more important than problems. The counselor should remain focused on persons as a first priority and problems only insofar as they are important to the persons receiving ministry."

Response by David Augsburger

The "culture-sensitive counseling" concept is a major step forward from the present widespread practice of psychological imperialism. The pastoral-counseling movement is indebted to David Hesselgrave for initiating one of the first serious encounters among missiology, anthropology, and pastoral psychology in his recent book on the subject.

Perhaps it is because he is writing of pastoral counseling and psychotherapy from outside the disciplines that he handles the agenda in ways that parallel cross-cultural communication or cross-cultural church-building. But the need for pastoral counselors is to move even beyond cultural sensitivity to cultural embeddedness in theory and practice. Personality and culture are part-processes of human systems that are jointly encountered in counseling and therapy. Thus my response to Hesselgrave's article is less a disagreement with what is said than a concern for what is unsaid about the essential depths of persons, relationships, groups, and systems. The basic assumptions that Hesselgrave expresses at the outset are cases in point.

First, the distinction between counseling and psychotherapy in the difference between problem-solving or directing change versus administering therapy to alter pathology cannot be neatly maintained. People on cultural boundaries become involved with persons in deep pain where more than problem-solving techniques are required. Since pathology is culturally defined, it is experienced as internal dysfunction in individualistic cultures and as sociofamilial dysfunction in more sociocentric cultures. Missionaries have often dealt with intensely therapeutic issues when they saw themselves as directing change or helping people to solve problems, but their individualistic theology and psychology blinded them to what was occurring.

Second, the problem of imported values has deeper and longer-term roots than the use of psychology and counseling methods learned in Western seminaries. The individualism of fundamental, evangelical, mainstream Protestant or Catholic theologies alike has been a secularizing, fragmenting, and Westernizing force, the impact of which becomes particularly visible as persons attempt to apply Western counseling remedies to individuals in a corporate context. Pastoral counseling must confront theological as well as psychological and sociological imperialism.

Third, every culture contains health and unhealth, healing and transformation. Counseling and therapy help to free the power within persons, families, and communities for healing to occur. Thus effective therapy is an extension of the cultural depths of person, family, community.

Fourth, the counseling principles and practices must arise from within the culture, although all cultures may be enriched by cross-fertilization with a second culture, and any therapy may be deepened by gifts from another community. No therapy is culturally, politically, or morally neutral. Each theory and theology of therapy is shaped by the context in which it is articulated and is powerful to the extent that it taps the depths of the culture's inner realities.

Soul loss, breach of taboo, sorcery, and spirit intrusion are key elements in cultures where they are metaphors for deeper visions of the human condition. The pastoral counselor must come to prize and respect these cultural depths, and honor and follow them carefully in the process of healing.

Naikan therapy is an example of a healing process that is fundamentally different from Western processes because it is congruent with the characterological and developmental personality structures of Japanese families and persons. Hesselgrave selects it is an appropriate case study of culturally grounded therapy.

The four conclusions that Hesselgrave draws in ending his article are helpful, hopeful, and heuristic steps toward an authentically transcultural vision. To them I would add: (1) the counselor must be capable not only of attending to the culturally conditioned interpretations but of experiencing what I call "interpathic listening, intuiting, and understanding," which goes beyond empathy to perceive from an alternate epistemology; (2) roles and models of helping in the culture in question must be honored as well as the deeper contents of group, family, and personality of all parties in any therapeutic transaction; (3) Western approaches need more than eclectic selection or enlightened modification; they must be owned, transformed, and grounded in the host culture; (4) learning methods from other cultures, religions, and traditions will be a great source of enrichment for us. We shall gain much by interpathic listening and learning.

Hesselgrave deserves careful reading by all counselors who work along cultural boundaries. One hopes that they will use his insights as incentives to move more deeply into dialogue on the nature of pastoral counseling and psychotherapy in different worlds of tradition, vision, and values.

David J. Hesselgrave Replies

I would like to thank my respondents sincerely. A large part of my purpose in writing my book *Counseling Cross-Culturally* and, indeed, this particular article, was to expedite just this sort of dialogue. That two such eminent colleagues would take the time to respond so thoughtfully is a source of great encouragement.

It hardly seems necessary to point out that the article before us represents a decidedly limited effort to contribute to what I hope will be an expanding literature on an important area of inquiry.

On the one hand, viewpoints within the field of psychology and counseling are so numerous and diverse as to discourage branching out into cross-cultural concerns. On the other hand, the stakes are so high that we dare not procrastinate any longer. That I could not address all of the questions with which my respondents would like to have me deal is a source of frustration to me as well as to them.

Drs. Hinkle and Augsburger have their own distinctive perspectives while agreeing with each other (and also with me) at certain important points. Allow me to address several more or less unique criticisms first; and then to emphasize a point or two at which their remarks tend to converge.

Hinkle takes exception to my starting point and, indeed, to the starting point of the larger inquiry. He says that the problem-solving approach is ethnocentric and that we would do well to begin cultural analysis by developing an awareness of our Western worldview with its cultural biases.

It may be that Kluckhohn and Murray reflect a Western bias when, from an anthropological perspective, they define culture as a storehouse of ready-made solutions to human problems. However, in view of the other ways in which they define culture, I suspect that they have a very encompassing understanding of "problems" in mind rather than the more narrow implications involved when a counselor speaks of the "presenting problem." All cross-culturalists are familiar with the gulf that exists between such cultural differences as task orientation and relationship orientation and individualistic-independency cultures and collectivistic-dependency cultures. By coupling problem-solving with effecting change and emphases on sociological groups, I would have hoped that the purview of my article would not be perceived as limited to the more narrow meaning common to the problem-solving approach to counseling. Evidently I did not succeed and Hinkle's criticism is therefore well taken.

The larger question of where to begin the study of cross-cultural counseling is an interesting one. To Western logic it does seem that we should begin by unmasking our ethnocentrism. However, experience seems to indicate that from a practical point of view this does not really work. It is extremely difficult to recognize and analyze one's own culture without external points of reference. With that in mind, I have tried to contrast relevant and salient features of other cultures as they relate to counseling in order to heighten sensitivities in this area.

As I read Augsburger's response, one of his main points is that we must move beyond cultural sensitivity to cultural embeddedness. He says that effective therapy is an extension of the cultural depths of a person, family, and community. He insists the counseling principles and practice must arise from within the culture, though cross-fertilization is helpful. In all of this I could not agree more. Once again we are dealing with what may be thought of as a truism espoused by all cross-culturalists. (To draw upon an analogous contemporary discussion, all serious advocates of contextualization agree that contextualization ultimately must be done from within a culture.) Very few individuals are sufficiently knowledgeable and bicultural to be able to do "cultural embedded" counseling in a second culture, however. If we are to counter the "psychological imperialism" that both Augsburger and I deplore, we must begin somewhere. Cultural sensitivity would seem to be as good a place as any.

Both of my respondents speak to the relationship between what may be termed care/counseling and counseling/psychotherapy. Hinkle criticizes me for not making a clear distinction between them. Augsburger says that they cannot be neatly divided. After surveying much relevant literature, I am confident that each could make a good case for his position. Personally, I find it helpful to place the various approaches on a continuum, while urging practitioners to stay within the bounds of their expertise. I doubt that very much dogmatism is warranted in any case. It seems to me that there are few areas of inquiry where there is more radical disagreement than in the area of psychology/counseling, unless perchance it would be missiology!

Finally, both respondents speak to the theological question. Hinkle admonished me to use the phrase "our Western understanding of the biblical understanding." Augsburger warns against theological imperialism in pastoral counseling. It may well be that extended discussion would reveal both a common concern and deep differences at this point. My own perspective is based on a commitment to the unity and authority of Scripture. I believe that it is not only allowable but essential to talk about *the* biblical teaching and understanding so that we point in the right direction. At the same time, it is freely admitted that all of us must strive to overcome cultural and other predilections that militate against full apprehension of the biblical understanding.

Wherever we might agree or disagree, I am indebted to Drs. Hinkle and Augsburger. When I review my own cross-cultural experience, the relevant literature, and the counseling books and programs that we have exported to other parts of the world, I become anxious. I am hopeful, then, that this kind of dialogue will further the kingdom cause, and I look forward to the stimulation that these and other colleagues continue to provide.

APPENDIX

Bibliography of Readings in Mental Health and Missions

The following bibliography lists approximately 175 important articles and dissertations during the last 25 years which have been written in the area of mental health and missions. Most of these works come from seven sources: *Evangelical Missions Quarterly, Missiology, International Bulletin of Missionary Research, Journal of Psychology and Theology, Journal of Psychology and Christianity*, Proceedings of the Mental Health and Missions Conferences[1] held in Angola, Indiana, and doctoral dissertations. Presentations from the International Conference on Missionary Kids[2] held in 1984 and 1987, as well as other conferences, masters' theses and magazine articles, are not included.

Selecting the readings for this bibliography was quite a challenge due to the quantity and diverse content of the works done in this area. In general, readings were chosen based on their usefulness for missionaries, mission agencies, and mental health professionals working in missions.

A second challenge involved how to best organize the works that were chosen. Three basic types of categories were considered: (a) the types of services provided by mental health professionals, for example, psychological assessment, therapy with missionaries, and interventions in the mission agency; (b) the stages which missionaries go through in their ministry, such as candidate preparation, cross-cultural adjustment, and retirement; and (c) general topics of import for missionary adjustment, for instance, stress management, education of missionary children, and cross-cultural counseling.

As no one organizational scheme seemed adequate for the purposes of this bibliography, elements from all three approaches were actually combined to form nine general categories. These are: psychological assessment and screening issues; preparation; missionary children and families; stress and adjustment challenges; helping missionaries; mission agencies and organizational development; cross-cultural issues; women in missions; and reentry issues. Each reading is categorized according to its main area of emphasis, although several could easily fit into two or more categories. Note that each listing which is preceded by an asterisk (*) also appears in this compendium.

Psychological Assessment and Screening Issues

Arndt, J., & Lindquist, S. (1976). Twenty to fifty percent fail to make it: Why? *Evangelical Missions Quarterly, 12,* 141-148.

Bates, G. (1977). Who is qualified to be called as a missionary? *Evangelical Missions Quarterly, 13,* 213-218.

*Britt, W. (1983). Pretraining variables in the prediction of missionary success overseas. *Journal of Psychology and Theology, 11,* 203-212.

*Cureton, C. (1983). Missionary fit: A criterion-related model. *Journal of Psychology and Theology, 11,* 196-202.

Cureton, C., & Kliewer, D. (1983). Service effectiveness at home and abroad: An annotated bibliography. *Journal of Psychology and Christianity, 2,* 45-51.

Dillon, D. (1983). Personality characteristics of evangelical missionaries as measured by the MMPI. *Journal of Psychology and Theology, 11,* 213-217.

Ferguson, L. (1983). Issues in missionary assessment. *Journal of Psychology and Christianity, 2,* 25-29.

*Ferguson, L., Kliewer, D., Lindquist, S., Williams, D., & Heinrich, R. (1983). Candidate selection criteria: A survey. *Journal of Psychology and Theology, 11,* 243-250.

*Foyle, M. (1986). How to choose the right missionary. *Evangelical Missions Quarterly, 22*, 196-204.

*Graham, T. (1987). How to select the best church planters. *Evangelical Missions Quarterly, 23*, 70-81.

Hanscome, C. (1979). Predicting missionary drop-out. *Evangelical Missions Quarterly, 15*, 152-155.

Howard, E. (1985). Personality strengths and temperament traits: Factors in continued and discontinued missionaries (Doctoral dissertation, University of Alabama, 1984). *Dissertation Abstracts International, 45*, 3533A.

Iwasko, R. (1986). *Danger in the parsonage: Why missionaries and ministers fail.* Proceedings of the Seventh Annual Conference on Mental Health and Missions, Angola, Indiana.

*Johnston, L. (1983). Should I be a missionary? *Journal of Psychology and Christianity, 2*, 5-9.

Kennedy, P., & Dreger, R. (1974). Development of criterion measured of overseas missionary performance. *Journal of Applied Psychology, 59*, 69-73.

*Lindquist, B. (1983). Misuses of psychological assessment with missionaries. *Journal of Psychology and Christianity, 2*, 15-17.

Lindquist, S. (1982). Prediction of success in overseas adjustment. *Journal of Psychology and Christianity, 1*, 22-25.

*Lindquist, S. (1983). A rationale for psychological assessment with missionaries. *Journal of Psychology and Christianity, 2*, 10-14.

Lindquist, S. (1983). Is the psychological test worth it? *Evangelical Missions Quarterly, 19*, 114-119.

*Link Care. (1981). *The use of psychological assessment in the evaluation of missionary candidates: A handbook.* Fresno, CA: Author.

Olson, V. (1978). Five fundamentals in evaluating missionaries. *Evangelical Missions Quarterly, 14,* 163-167.

*Parshall, P. (1987). How spiritual are missionaries? *Evangelical Missions Quarterly, 23,* 8-19.

Pollock, W. (1986). A theoretical consideration of selection for training for ministry. *Journal of Psychology and Theology, 14,* 125-134.

Reapsome, J. (1983). Recruiting: The right way and the wrong way. *Evangelical Missions Quarterly, 19,* 132-149.

Skarsten, S., & Morehouse, M. (1981). *Critical factors in missionary assessment and placement.* Proceedings of the Second Annual Conference on Mental Health and Missionaries, Angola, Indiana.

Williams, D. (1983). Assessment of cross-cultural adjustability in missionary candidates: Theoretical, biblical and practical perspectives. *Journal of Psychology and Christianity, 2,* 18-24.

Williams, K. (1973). Characteristics of the more successful and less successful missionaries (Doctoral dissertation, United States International University, 1973). *Dissertation Abstracts International, 34,* 1786B-1787B.

Preparation

Brewster, T., & Brewster, E. (1982). Language learning is communication--Is ministry! *International Bulletin of Missionary Research, 6,* 160-164.

Cummings, D. (1987). Programmed for failure--mission candidates at risk. Evangelical Missions Quarterly, 23, 240-246.

*Dyer, K. (1985). Crucial factors in building good teams. *Evangelical Missions Quarterly, 21,* 254-258.

*Elkins, P. (1981). Preparation: Pay the price! In R. Winter & S. Hawthorne (Eds.). *Perspectives on the world Christian movement: A reader* (pp. 800-807). Pasadena, CA: William Carey Library.

Escobar, S. (1987). Recruitment of students for missions. *Missiology, 15,* 529-545.

Greenway, R. (1983). Don't be an urban missionary unless.... *Evangelical Missions Quarterly, 19,* 86-94.

Hubble, D. (1969). In-service preparation: Language study and orientation. *Evangelical Missions Quarterly, 5,* 219-233.

Kornfield, D. (1979). What it costs to prepare. *Evangelical Missions Quarterly, 15,* 223-229.

Landis, D. (Ed.). (1986). Special issue on theories and methods in cross-cultural orientation. *International Journal of Intercultural Relations, 10,* 1-164.

Larson, D. (1977). Missionary preparation: Confronting the presuppositional barrier. *Missiology, 5,* 73-82.

Mayers, M. (1985). Training missionaries for the 21st century. *Evangelical Missions Quarterly, 21,* 306-319.

Missions Advanced Research and Communications Center. (1981). You can get there from here. In R. Winter and S. Hawthorne (Eds.), *Perspectives on the world Christian movement: A reader* (pp. 782-787). Pasadena, CA: William Carey Library.

Mulholland, K. (1985). Keys to effective graduate training. *Evangelical Missions Quarterly, 21,* 402-406.

*O'Donnell, K. (1987). *A preliminary study on psychologists in missions.* Proceedings of the Eighth Annual Conference on Mental Health and Missions, Angola, Indiana.

Piepgrass, C. (1972). A suggested program for field orientation of first termers. *Evangelical Missions Quarterly, 8,* 93-97.

Pocock, M. (1985). A recruiter's view of missionary training. *Evangelical Missions Quarterly, 21,* 409-412.

Scott, W. (1971). Teams and teamwork. *Evangelical Missions Quarterly, 7,* 111-121.

Ward, T. (1987). Educational preparation of missionaries--A look ahead. *Evangelical Missions Quarterly, 23,* 398-404.

*Warner, T. (1986). Teaching power encounter. *Evangelical Missions Quarterly, 22,* 66-70.

Missionary Children and Families[3]

Bowers, J. (1986). *Young adults/young children: Coping with competing needs and demands.* Proceedings of the Seventh Annual Conference on Mental Health and Missions, Angola, Indiana.

Boyce, E. (1981). How good are schools for missionaries' children? *Evangelical Missions Quarterly, 17,* 149-152.

Campbell, J. (1985). *Re-entry adjustment and the third culture kid.* Proceedings of the Fifth Annual Conference on Mental Health and Missions, Angola, Indiana.

*Chester, R. (1983). Stress on missionary families living in "other culture" situations. *Journal of Psychology and Christianity, 2,* 30-37.

*Chester, R. (1984). To send or not to send? Missionary parents ask. *Evangelical Missions Quarterly, 20,* 252-263.

Danielson, E. (1981). *The effects of foreign residence in personality development of children of American evangelical ministers.* Unpublished doctoral dissertation, University of Santo Tomas, Manila.

Downs, R. (1976). A look at the third culture child. *Japan Christian Quarterly, 42,* 66-71.

Empson, P. (1974). The care of missionary children--What priority? *Evangelical Missions Quarterly, 10,* 138-144.

Far Eastern Gospel Crusade (1974). Survey shows how MKs feel. *Evangelical Missions Quarterly, 10,* 161-166.

*Foyle, M. (1987). Stress factors in missionary marriages. *Evangelical Missions Quarterly, 23,* 20-31.

Foyle, M. (1987). Adolescents, stress, and the missionary family. *Evangelical Missions Quarterly, 23,* 144-150.

Foyle, M. (1987). Burnout or brownout? *Evangelical Missions Quarterly, 21,* 262-270.

Gleason, T. (1970). Social adjustment patterns and manifestations of world-mindedness of overseas-experienced American youth (Doctoral dissertation, Michigan State University, 1970). *Dissertation Abstracts International, 31,* 2494A.

Hager, J. (1979). The schooling of third culture children: The case of the American school in the Hague (Doctoral dissertation, Michigan State University, 1978). *Dissertation Abstracts International, 39,* 6050A.

Herrmann, C. (1978). Foundational factors of trust and autonomy influencing the identity formation of the multicultural lifestyled MK (Doctoral dissertation, Northwestern University, 1977). *Dissertation Abstracts International, 38,* 5373A-5374A.

*Hill, B. (1986). The educational needs of children of expatriates: Parental perceptions. *Missiology, 14,* 325-346.

Hogben, M. & Sherlock, C. (1978). Effects of separating school-age children from their parents: A statistical survey. *Social Psychiatry, 13* (4), 187-192.

*Holzmann, J. (1986, April). What about the kids? MK education symposium. *Mission Frontiers, 8,* 18-22.

Hsieh, T. (1976). Missionary family behavior, dissonance, and children's career decision. *Journal of Psychology and Theology, 4,* 221-226.

Kenny, B. (1980). What it takes to have good relations with your children. *Evangelical Missions Quarterly, 16,* 97-102.

Kladensky, G. (1974). The advantages of going to national schools. *Evangelical Missions Quarterly, 10,* 154-159.

Krajewski, F. (1970). *A study of the relationship of an overseas experienced population based on sponsorship of parent and subsequent academic adjustment to college in the United States.* Unpublished doctoral dissertation, Michigan State University.

O'Brien, D. (1983). A needs assessment of third culture children and the administrative implications for an orientation program (Doctoral dissertation, Virginia Polytechnic Institute and State University, 1983). *Dissertation Abstracts International, 44,* 1999A.

*O'Donnell, K. (1987). Developmental tasks in the life cycle of mission families. *Journal of Psychology and Theology, 15,* 281-290.

Peters, D. (1987). *A model for measuring socio-cultural age in the re-entry MK.* Proceedings of the Eighth Annual Conference on Mental Health and Missions, Angola, Indiana.

Schipper, D. (1977). Self-concept differences between early, late, and non-boarding school missionary children (Doctoral dissertation, Rosemead School of Psychology, 1977). *Dissertation Abstracts International, 38,* 1905B.

Schulz, D. (1986). *The study of third culture experience in relation to the psychosocial adjustment of returned Church of Christ missionary families.* Unpublished doctoral dissertation, University of Nebraska--Lincoln.

Sensenig, J. (1981). The missionary father's perception of family and vocational responsibilities (Doctoral dissertation, Michigan State University, 1980). *Dissertation Abstracts International, 41, 3867A.*

*Sharp, L. (1985). Toward a greater understanding of the real MK: A review of recent research. *Journal of Psychology and Christianity, 4,* 73-78.

Shepard, F. (1977). An analysis of variables of self-perception and personal ambition in overseas-experienced American teenagers: Implications for curricular planning (Doctoral dissertation, Michigan State University, 1976). *Dissertation Abstracts International, 37,* 5735A.

*Taylor, M. (1976, Spring). Personality development in the children of missionary parents. *Japan Christian Quarterly, 42,* 72-78.

Troutman, C. (1974). Family security--Wherever home is. *Evangelical Missions Quarterly, 10,* 146-152.

Wager, R. (1980). Advantages of home instruction. *Evangelical Missions Quarterly, 16,* 23-28.

Werkman, S. (1972). Hazards of rearing children in foreign countries. *American Journal of Psychiatry, 128,* 992-997.

*White, F. (1983). *Characteristics of a healthy mission system.* Proceedings of the Fourth Annual Conference on Mental Health and Missions, Angola, Indiana.

White, F. (1983). Some reflections on the separation phenomenon idiosyncratic to the experiences of missionaries and their children. *Journal of Psychology and Theology, 11,* 181-188.

*Wickstrom, D., & Fleck, J. (1983). Missionary children: Correlates of self-esteem and dependency. *Journal of Psychology and Theology, 11,* 226-235.

Stress and Adjustment Challenges[4]

*Allen, F. (1986). Why do they leave? Reflections on attrition. *Evangelical Missions Quarterly, 22,* 118-129.

Banks, D. (1976). Causes of friction between missionaries and nationals. *Evangelical Missions Quarterly, 12,* 149-156.

Bates, G. (1977). Missions and cross-cultural conflict. *Missiology, 5,* 195-202.

*Bolyanatz, A. (1985). How we reduced those early cultural surprises. *Evangelical Missions Quarterly, 21,* 266-273.

*Brewster, T., & Brewster, B. (1981). Bonding and the missionary task. In R. Winter and S. Hawthorne (Eds.), *Perspectives on the world Christian movement: A reader* (pp. 452-464). Pasadena, CA: William Carey Library.

Coots, D. (1973). What to do about those new missionary frustrations. *Evangelical Missions Quarterly, 9,* 205-209.

Davis, J. (1983). *A personal constructs measure of cultural threat.* Unpublished doctoral dissertation, Rosemead School of Psychology.

*Dye, W. (1974). Stress-producing factors in cultural adjustment. *Missiology, 2,* 67-77.

*Eagle, R. (1984). Positive possibilities of mid-life transitions. *Evangelical Missions Quarterly, 20,* 38-47.

Ensworth, G. (1983). *Ecclesiogenic illness of the missionary.* Proceedings of the Fourth Annual Conference on Mental Health and Missions, Angola, Indiana.

Foyle, M. (1984). Missionary stress and what to do about it. *Evangelical Missions Quarterly, 21,* 32-43.

*Foyle, M. (1984). Overcoming stress in singleness. *Evangelical Missions Quarterly, 21,* 134-145.

Foyle, M. (1985). Why it's tough to get along with one another. *Evangelical Missions Quarterly, 21,* 240-247.

*Foyle, M. (1985). Missionary relationships: Powderkeg or powerhouse? *Evangelical Missions Quarterly, 21,* 342-351.

Foyle, M. (1986). Gorillas get along: Why can't we? *Evangelical Missions Quarterly, 22,* 14-19.

Gardner, L. (1987). A practical approach to transitions in missionary living. *Journal of Psychology and Theology, 15,* 342-349.

*Gibbs, T. (1980). Finding a sense of belonging in your new place. *Evangelical Missions Quarterly, 16,* 159-167.

*Gish, D. (1983). Sources of missionary stress. *Journal of Psychology and Theology, 11,* 238-242.

Herndon, H. (1980). How many "dropouts" really are "pushouts"? *Evangelical Missions Quarterly, 16*, 13-16.

Newbrander, V. (1981). *Mid-life crisis*. Proceedings of the Second Annual Conference on Mental Health and Missions, Angola, Indiana.

Quarles, C. (1987). Kidnapped! A 'successful hostage' will emerge alive. *Evangelical Missions Quarterly, 23*, 342-350.

Reyburn, W. (1966). Perspective on missionary loss. *Evangelical Missions Quarterly, 2*, 84-90.

Satterwhite, J. (1966). Learn to cope with stress. *Evangelical Missions Quarterly, 2*, 91-95.

Smalley, W. (1966). Emotional storm signals: The shocks of culture, language, and self-discovery. *Evangelical Missions Quarterly, 3*, 146-156.

Stringham, J. (1970). Likely causes of emotional difficulties among missionaries. *Evangelical Missions Quarterly, 6*, 193-203.

Stringham, J. (1970). The missionary's mental health. *Evangelical Missions Quarterly, 7*, 1-9.Taylor, B., & Malony, N. (1983). Preferred means of hostility expression among missionaries: An exploratory study. *Journal of Psychology and Theology, 11*, 218-225.

Thompson, J. (1983). Factors related to retention of teaching and missionary personnel in overseas work environments (Doctoral dissertation, University of Houston, 1982). *Dissertation Abstracts International, 43*, 2300A.

Troutman, C. (1983). Steps to mature servanthood overseas. *Evangelical Missions Quarterly, 19*, 26-30.

*White, F., & Nesbit, E. (1986). Separation: Balancing the gains and losses. *Evangelical Missions Quarterly, 19*, 22, 392-401.

Williams, K. (1982). *Biblical strategies for handling stress.* Proceedings of the Third Annual Conference on Mental Health and Missions, Angola, Indiana.

*Williams, K. (1983). *Worksheet for balanced living.* Proceedings of the Fourth Annual Conference on Mental Health and Missions, Angola, Indiana.

Helping Missionaries

Beck, J. (1987). Elective mutism in a missionary family: A case study. *Journal of Psychology and Theology, 15,* 291-299.

Coote, R. (1983). Ministry to missionaries on furlough: The overseas ministries study center, 1922-1983. *International Bulletin of Missionary Research, 7,* 53-57.

*Dye, S. (1974). Decreasing fatigue and illness in field work. *Missiology, 2,* 79-109.

Fife, H. (1970). The pastoral care of missionaries. *Evangelical Missions Quarterly, 7,* 10-18.

Fleck, J., McThomas, A., Nielsen, L., & Schumaker, D. (1973). Self-concept change in ministers and missionaries. *Journal of Psychology and Theology, 1,* 28-34.

Gardner, L. (1987). *An administrative response to crisis in the missions community.* Proceedings of the Eighth Annual Conference on Mental Health and Missions.

Gardner, R. (1987). *Morality: Which way is up?* Proceedings of the Eighth Annual Conference on Mental Helath and Missions.

Harder, K. (1985). *In-service training: Who is responsible?* Proceedings of the Sixth Annual Conference on Mental Health and Missions, Angola, Indiana.

Hesselgrave, D. (1987). Can psychology aid us in the fulfillment of the great commission? A missiologist speaks to Christian psychologists. *Journal of Psychology and Theology, 15,* 274-280.

*Kruckeberg, J. & Stafford, A. (1981). The missionary's need for family life training. *Evangelical Missions Quarterly*, *17*, 163-172.

Lindquist, S. (1979). The service and repair of overseas units. *Evangelical Missions Quarterly*, *15*, 25-28.

Lindquist, S., & Lindquist, B. (1982). *Missionary family restoration for early returnees.* Proceedings of the Third Annual Conference on Mental Health and Missions, Angola, Indiana.

*O'Donnell, K. (1987). *Some suggested ethical guidelines for the delivery of mental health services in mission settings.* Proceedings of the Eighth Annual Conference on Mental Health and Missions, Angola, Indiana.

United States Catholic Mission Association. (1985). Crisis management in the event of arrest, disappearance, or death of mission personnel. *International Bulletin of Missionary Research*, *9*, 115-116.

Viser, W. (1978). *A psychological profile of missionary children in college and the relationship of intense group therapy to weekly group therapy in the treatment of personality problems reflected by the MMPI.* Unpublished doctoral dissertation, Southwestern Baptist Theological Seminary.

*Williams, K. (1985). *Conflict resolution: A seminar format.* Proceedings of the Sixth Annual Conference on Mental Health and Missions, Angola, Indiana.

Mission Agencies and Organizational Development

*Gardner, L. (1987). Proactive care of missionary personnel. *Journal of Psychology and Theology*, *15*, 308-314.

*Hunter, W., & Mayers, M. (1987). Psychology and missions: Reflections on status and need. *Journal of Psychology and Theology*, *15*, 269-273.

*Johnson, C., & Penner, D. (1981). The current status of the provision of psychological services in missionary agencies in North America. *Bulletin of the Christian Association for Psychological Studies, 7*, (4), 25-27.

*Johnston, L. (1983). *Building relationships between mental health specialists and mission agencies.* Proceedings of the Fourth Annual Conference on Mental Health and Missions, Angola, Indiana.

Kliewer, D. (1983). Missionary program evaluation: An assessment strategy. *Journal of Psychology and Christianity, 2*, 38-44.

Pocock, M. (1987). Gaining long-term mileage from short-term programs. *Evangelical Missions Quarterly, 23*, 154-160.

Reapsome, J. (1983). Missions under attack: Risking hard questions about our empires. *Evangelical Missions Quarterly, 19*, 316-319.

*Wilson, D. (1981). *Therapeutic impact on an organization.* Proceedings of the Second Annual Conference on Mental Health and Missions, Angola, Indiana.

Cross-Cultural Issues

Deuck, A. (1983). American psychology in cross-cultural context. *Journal of Psychology and Theology, 11*, 172-180.

Hesselgrave, D. (1985). Christian cross-cultural counseling: A suggested framework for theory and development. *Missiology, 13*, 203-217.

*Hesselgrave, D. (1986). Culture-sensitive counseling and the Christian mission. *International Bulletin of Missionary Research, 10*, 109-116.

Hiebert, P. (1981). Culture and cross-cultural differences. In R. Winter & S. Hawthorne (Eds.). *Perspectives on the world Christian movement: A reader* (pp. 367-379). Pasadena, CA: William Carey Library.

Jennings, G. (1987). Psychocultural study in missiology: Middle astern insecurity. *Missiology, 15,* 91-110.

Kelly, D. (1978). Cross-cultural communication and ethics. *Missiology, 6,* 311-322.

Nida, E. (1981). Why are foreigners so queer? A socioanthropological approach to cultural pluralism. *International Bulletin of Missionary Research, 5,* 102-106.

O'Donnell, K. (1986). Community psychology and unreached peoples: Applications to needs and resource assessment. *Journal of Psychology and Theology, 14,* 213-223.

O'Donnell, K. (1984). Community psychology in missiological context: Applications to service delivery and service providers (Doctoral dissertation, Rosemead School of Psychology, 1984). *Dissertation Abstracts International, 45.*

Ridley, C. (1986). Cross-cultural counseling in theological context. *Journal of Psychology and Theology, 14,* 288-297.

Whiteman, D. (1981). Some relevant anthropological concepts for effective cross-cultural ministry. *Missiology, 9,* 223-239.

Women in Missions

Adeney, M. (1987). Esther across cultures: Indigenous leadership roles for women. *Missiology, 15,* 323-337.

Beck, J. (1986). Women in missions: A pilot study. *Journal of Psychology and Theology, 14,* 224-232.

Bowers, J. (1984). Roles of married women missionaries: A case study. *International Bulletin of Missionary Research, 8,* 4-8.

*Bowers, J. (1985). Women's roles in missions: Where are we now? *Evangelical Missions Quarterly, 21,* 352-362.

*DeVries, S. (1986). Wives: Homemakers or mission employees? *Evangelical Missions Quarterly, 22,* 402-410.

Hesselgrave, D. (1987). Women missionaries speak out on issues from their perspectives. *Evangelical Missions Quarterly, 23,* 82-89.

Hunt, C. (1977). Women missionaries: Making more of their potential. *Evangelical Missions Quarterly, 13,* 149-154.

Jackson, E. (1980). Women's role in missions: Issues and expectations. *Evangelical Missions Quarterly, 16,* 197-206.

Liefield, W. (1987). Women and evangelism in the early church. *Missiology, 15,* 291-298.

Maines, C. (1983). Missionary wives: Underused asset. *Evangelical Missions Quarterly, 19,* 290-297.

*Marshall, D. (1985). Current issues of women and therapy. *Journal of Psychology and Christianity, 4,* 62-72.

Skelton, M. (1986). Gap in women's needs addressed. *Evangelical Missions Quarterly, 22,* 411-419.

Sullivan, M. (1979). Career counseling for single women missionaries. *Evangelical Missions Quarterly, 15,* 29-34.

Turner, R. (1981). *Singleness on the mission field.* Proceedings of the Second Annual Conference on Mental Health and Missions, Angola, Indiana.

Van Leeuwen, M. (1984). The female reconstruct psychology. *Journal of Psychology and Christianity, 3,* 20-31.

Reentry Issues

Alford, T. (1987). *Project Reentry: A reentry program for returning Free Church MKs.* Unpublished doctoral dissertation, Trinity Evangelical Divinity School.

*Austin, C. (1983). Reentry stress: The pain of coming home. *Evangelical Missions Quarterly, 19,* 278-287.

Austin, C. (1986). *Overview of reentry*. Proceedings of the Seventh Annual Conference on Mental Health and Missions, Angola, Indiana.

Austin, C., & Beyer, J. (1984). Missionary repatriation: An introduction to the literature. *International Bulletin of Missionary Research, 8*, 68-69.

Austin, C., & Van Jones, B. (1987). Reentry among missionary children: An overview of reentry research from 1934-1986. *Journal of Psychology and Theology, 15* ,315-325.

Downie, R. (1976). Reentry experiences and identity formation for third-culture experienced dependent American youth (Doctoral dissertation, Michigan State University, 1976). *Dissertation Abstracts International, 37*, 3493A.

Frisbey, N (1987). Retirement of evangelical missionaries: Elements of satisfaction and morale. *Journal of Psychology and Theology, 15* , 326-335.

Jordan, K. (1982). The adaptation of third culture dependent youth as they re-enter the United States and enter college: An exploratory study (Doctoral dissertation, Michigan State University, 1981). *Dissertation Abstracts International, 42*, 3545A.

Moore, L., Van Jones, B., & Austin, C. (1987). Predictors of reverse culture shock among North American Church of Christ missionaries. *Journal of Psychology and Theology, 15* , 336-341.

Odman, R. (1964). Ten tips for the missionary on furlough. *Evangelical Missions Quarterly, 1*, 35-42.

*Pollock, D. (1987). Welcome home! Easing the pain of MK reentry. *Evangelical Missions Quarterly, 23*, 278-283.

Schulz, T. (1985). *A study to determine the basic needs of MKs upon reentry to the United States and to define and describe a reentry program designed to meet the needs*. Unpublished doctoral dissertation, University of Nebraska--Lincoln.

Notes

1. Additional information on the annual Mental Health and Missions Conference held at Angola, Indiana may be obtained by writing to Dr. John Powell, Olin Center, Michigan State University, East Lansing, Michigan 48823.

2. The ICMK conferences have served as the primary means of bringing together individuals and mission organizations in their concern for the well-being of missionary children. A compendium of readings based on the presentations at the Manila conference can be ordered through Missionary Internship, P.O. Box 457, Farmington, Michigan 48024. The presentations from the Quito conference are currently being organized into a second compendium. Tapes of the Quito presentations are available through Kingdom Tapes, Department A, P.O. Box 506, Mansfield, Pennsylvania 16933.

3. A complete and updated bibliography on MKs can be purchased through the Billy Graham Center Library, Wheaton College, Wheaton, Illinois 60187. This library has also established an MK section containing most of the readings listed in their extensive bibliography.

4. A six-part video series dealing with mission stress and adjustment is available through Wycliffe Bible Translators. It was developed by Dr. Kenneth L. Williams and may be ordered through Wycliffe Bible Translators, Photo Department, Huntington Beach, California 92647.